TONY BENN
THE END OF AN ERA
DIARIES 1980–90

Tony Benn has been the Labour Member of
Parliament for Chesterfield since March
1984, and was MP for Bristol South-East
from 1950 to 1983. He was elected to the
National Executive Committee of the
Labour Party in 1959, and was Chairman of
the Party in 1971/72. He has been a Cabinet
Minister in every Labour Government since
1964, holding the positions of Postmaster
General, Minister of Technology, Minister
of Power, Secretary of State for Energy, and
one-time President for the Council of
Energy Ministers of the European
Community. He contested the leadership of
the Labour Party in 1976 and 1988.

He is the author of thirteen previous books,
including *Arguments for Democracy* and
Fighting Back. He is married to Caroline,
and they have four children and seven
grandchildren.

D0907541

TONY BENN

The End of An Era

DIARIES 1980–90

Edited by Ruth Winstone

ARROW

Published by Arrow Books in 1994

1 3 5 7 9 10 8 6 4 2

© Tony Benn 1994

First published in the United Kingdom
by Hutchinson, 1992
20 Vauxhall Bridge Road, London SW1V 2SA

Arrow Books Limited
20 Vauxhall Bridge Road, London, SW1V 2SA

Random House Australia (Pty) Limited
20 Alfred Street, Milsons Point, Sydney,
New South Wales 2061, Australia

Random House New Zealand Limited
18 Poland Road, Glenfield
Auckland 10, New Zealand

Random House South Africa (Pty) Limited
PO Box 337, Bergvlei, South Africa

Random House UK Limited Reg. No. 954009

A CIP catalogue record for this book is available from the
British Library

ISBN 0 09 997110 0

Printed and bound in Great Britain by
The Guernsey Press Co. Ltd, Guernsey, Channel Islands

Contents

This book is dedicated with love to our grandchildren:
Michael, James, William, Jonathan, Caroline, Emily and Daniel.

Acknowledgements

The immense task of researching, editing and preparing this book for publication has been undertaken by Ruth Winstone, the editor for all five volumes of the Diaries: without her political understanding, combined with formidable research skills, this series could not have been published.

Kate Mosse, former Editorial Director at Random House, has overseen the publication of all five volumes and has given unfailing encouragement from the outset. Her shrewd judgement and editorial wisdom have been exercised at every stage.

My grateful thanks also to Linden Stafford, whose meticulous attention to style and detail has been invaluable.

Sheila Hubacher has transcribed from tape more of the Diaries than any other person, with good humour, constructive criticism – and sometimes exasperation – throughout. I also had constant help and courtesy from Karen Holden and Neil Bradford of Hutchinson.

I would like finally to thank all those at Random House who have supported the Diaries project from first to last, in particular the Publicity Director, Bridget Sleddon, whose enthusiasm and commitment to the project have been much appreciated.

Illustration Acknowledgements

Hutchinson would like to thank the following for their kind permission to use various illustrations in this volume:

PHOTOGRAPHS
Popperfoto; Universal Pictorial Press; Times Newspapers; *Independent*; Chris Mullin; John Harris; Benn Archives.

CARTOONS
Nicholas Garland © *Daily Telegraph* plc (pp. 47 and 610); Nicholas Garland © *Sunday Telegraph* Ltd (p. 79); Franklin © *Sun* (p. 30); Cummings © *Daily Express, Sunday Express* (pp. 338 and 475); Colin Wheeler © *Independent* (p. 521); Tony © *Labour Herald* (p. 415).

Whilst every effort has been made to clear copyright, in some cases this has not been possible. The publishers would like to apologise in advance for any inconvenience this might cause.

Editor's Note

When I agreed to undertake the task of editing the Benn diaries for publication my overriding concern was that the balance and integrity of the original typescript were preserved and that the 'Hansard rules' of editing were followed. This volume, encompassing as it does a full decade of political life, has presented a greater challenge than any of the previous volumes which covered the years 1963–80.

The original transcript for 1980–90 is three and a half million words long; to reduce it to 325,000 words for publication has meant that the requirement of continuity has been exceptionally difficult to meet. Some areas of political activity and individual episodes regrettably have ended up on the cutting room floor. For example, the Labour Party's obsession with internal disciplinary matters, though described fully, has not been accorded the proportion it occupied in the original diaries; many of the proceedings against individuals have had to be omitted altogether.

The End of an Era also inevitably deals in greater detail with the early Eighties, when changes to the Labour Party's structure and leadership were crucial in the Party's history. The latter half of the book is more diverse in nature, reflecting Tony Benn's interests outside the confines of Party and Parliament.

I have added detailed chapter notes and linking passages where, in my view, amplification has been required; but this is not a history text book and some other contemporary references which we take for granted may for future readers require some explanation.

Throughout I have tried to interweave the serious, the significant, the light-hearted and even the trivial to give the flavour of the full work. These have been my own editorial judgements, for which I take full responsibility: the uncut diaries are available to those wishing to study the complete text in depth.

Ruth Winstone
July 1992

Foreword

The years covered by this volume of my diaries were marked by enormous political changes both here and abroad, and we are still much too close to those events to be able to assess their full significance.

Certainly the Eighties saw a major swing to the right in all industrial countries; the crumbling of the communist regimes; the first falterings in the boom years in the capitalist west; the consolidation of the European Community into a tighter bloc; the slow collapse of apartheid; and many other events of comparable importance.

Throughout this decade my diaries are necessarily concerned mainly with political life in Britain, dominated as it was by the Conservatives, a decade ending with the abrupt overthrow of Margaret Thatcher and with the Labour leadership believing that the Party was poised for an imminent triumphant victory.

Neil Kinnock, elected Leader in 1983, had tried to transform the policies of the Party and to restructure its organisation; and in doing so, he enjoyed the support of the overwhelming majority of the Shadow Cabinet, the National Executive and the trade union leaders. This plan was endorsed by the political commentators, in the hope that it would eliminate socialism as a force in British politics – and they set out to persuade the Party that it was the only way to make it electable. The Party leadership carefully distanced itself from many of the important grassroots campaigns that were mounted against Government policy, especially the campaign by the miners against pit closures, the campaign by the print unions against unfair dismissal and the hugely successful campaign against the Poll Tax which led to its repeal. The Policy Reviews were used to secure the abandonment of unilateralism and to commit Labour to retain nuclear weapons and high levels of defence expenditure; to adopt a bi-partisan policy on Northern Ireland; to embrace a fully federal European union; to give up Labour's opposition to many of the Conservative's anti-trade union laws; and to offer full support to the Americans in the horrific Gulf War. The NEC also embarked upon an internal disciplinary programme, expelling a number of good socialists and imposing election candidates on constituencies and suspending local parties that took an independent view.

From 1980 to 1982 the left in the Party had campaigned for

democractic constitutional reforms to make the leadership more accountable to the membership; but after 1983 power in the party became more and more centralised, a process which downgraded the role of both the Party Conference and the NEC and led to the introduction of new rules, after the 1988 leadership election challenge, designed to exclude left-wing MPs from being. nominated for the leadership in the future. The Party gave up any genuine political education and analysis; concentrated its attacks on individual Conservative ministers; reduced public expectations by narrowing the vision of the Party to the single, simple objective of installing Labour ministers in office; and adopted high-powered American advertising techniques to secure victory.

In short, the Party was following the pattern set by most Western European Social Democratic parties and the Democrats in America.

Meanwhile the Conservative government was adopting highly radical policies that were designed explicitly to strengthen the power of capital, and weaken the power of labour. The strikes that did take place were dealt with ruthlessly, and the Government was ready to place all the resources of the state at the disposal of employers in their conflicts with labour, using high unemployment, repressive legislation and a sustained public campaign against the trade unions, local democracy and the public sector to achieve their aims.

The price was – and still is – industrial decline, lengthening dole queues, rising homelessness, and the stifling of dissent.

The leadership of the labour movement unhappily came to accept many of these conservative arguments in the name of 'New Realism', embracing a new political consensus that almost converted Britain into a one-party state. This shift in the Labour Party from a commitment to social transformation towards a new and more modest role as an alternative management team was summed up in the notion 'there is no alternative'.

The advent of Gorbachev in the Soviet Union with his promise of perestroika and glasnost, and the overthrow of the Eastern European regimes – symbolised by the fall of the Berlin Wall – were seen as evidence of the final collapse of socialism everywhere. Francis Fukuyama went so far as to describe these events as marking 'the end of history' and President Bush, after the Gulf war, proclaimed a New World Order in which the USA was to be dominant.

But this right wing triumphalism ignores the inescapable fact that the gap between the rich and poor in Britain is wider than it was a hundred years ago; that every year millions of lives are lost worldwide, quite unnecessarily, through starvation, poverty and preventable disease; and that a massive environmental crisis threatens the globe. It ignores the reality that slump in the capitalist world, and disintegration of the communist governments, have given rise to disillusionment and despair on a huge scale and this is fanning the flames of nationalism, racism and fundamentalism.

British socialism, rooted in Christian ethics, enriched by the lessons of collective action and committed to democracy – illuminated by the analysis of socialists as diverse as Robert Owen, Karl Marx, Keir Hardie and Nye Bevan – points us towards a totally different society, based upon clear concepts of public morality, democratic control and international solidarity.

Although this is a political and not a personal diary I must record again the enormous debt which I owe to Caroline, my life-long partner and closest friend, over the last forty-four years. During those years she has published a great deal of original work on various aspects of socialism and education, and because we have talked over everything together, I have had the immeasurable advantage of her knowledge and judgment, as well as her unfailing personal encouragement and support.

Tony Benn
Chesterfield
May Day 1992

1
The Soul of the Party
June–December 1980

Tuesday 3 June
The *Daily Mail* had the headline, 'Centre Party To Be Formed on Monday', claiming that Roy Jenkins was going to resign as President of the European Commission within a month and return to British politics. I think it is unlikely, but it is part of an extraordinary political saga.

Thursday 5 June
Today Moss Evans said something about supporting Jim Callaghan's leadership, and the word is beginning to get out that Moss and Clive Jenkins just don't want Denis Healey to be Leader, nor do they want a leadership decision before the Party Conference – until they have the electoral college sorted out.

Friday 6 June
Had a cup of tea at the House with Joan Lestor and Neil Carmichael [Labour MP for Glasgow, Kelvingrove], and Joan asked, 'How are we going to get you as Leader of the Party when the press hates you so much? People think you would lose us the next Election if you were Leader.'

I said, 'I think the real issue is this: that if the press is to choose our Leader it will also choose our policy, and, once you accept that, then you are saying there can't be a Labour Party.'

Caught the shuttle to Edinburgh for the Scottish Miners' Gala tomorrow. At dinner I sat next to Ruth Fisher, the wife of Alan Fisher, General Secretary of NUPE. She is a former Young Communist, a very nice woman. On my other side was Mick McGahey, the President of the Scottish miners, who is exactly my age, a very principled guy. He was talking about the need to have a broader alliance to fight the right, which is very much the old popular front idea; but it has got to be an ecumenical movement and not a monolith, and I think the old popular front idea is out of date. He was sympathetic about Militant, which I found interesting. He thought they were good socialists and the real question was why they had not gone into the Communist Party.

Mick's father was a miner and founder member of the Communist

Party and had not worked from the General Strike of 1926 to the Second World War: a tremendously scholarly man who when he retired read Gibbon's *Decline and Fall of the Roman Empire* and Churchill's history of the Second World War. Mick is also highly knowledgeable. He had read E.P. Thompson's biography of William Morris. He said he had read *Arguments for Socialism* and, though he didn't agree with everything I had said, at least I was getting back to fundamentals. He couldn't have been nicer.

Saturday 7 June

I marched between Arthur Scargill and Mick McGahey at the Gala.

Arthur told me that the President, Joe Gormley, would have to go at the end of next year. Under the rules of the NUM Mick McGahey can't stand for national office because he is over the age of fifty-five, which is why Joe Gormley has stayed on. It is a ridiculous rule but Mick has accepted it uncomplainingly and so he is now campaigning for Arthur Scargill for the presidency of the NUM.

We got to the park and even the Edinburgh evening paper tonight said there were 10,000 people present. Later we had lunch in the marquee. I sat between Mick and his wife who were absolutely delighted by their seven-month-old grandchild – they had brought her along and Mick's face was creased with smiles. I thought, if only the press could see him as a father, and grandfather, the image would be so different.

Sunday 8 June

Bill Rodgers, Shirley Williams and David Owen have issued a statement saying they could not remain in the Party if it decided to support withdrawal from the Common Market. Clive Jenkins on the radio said that they couldn't blackmail the Party in that way, and 'We don't want to lose you but if you feel you ought to go . . .', and so on. Peter Shore said much the same, that the Party couldn't cater for people who transferred their allegiance from Britain to the European Community.

Wednesday 11 June

Watched Robin Cook and Mary Kaldor, the Labour Party's adviser on defence, talking about nuclear weapons on a marvellous party political broadcast. It was principled, serious, straight, with no rhetoric; I felt it was tremendously effective.

Thursday 12 June

A journalist came to interview me about bias in the media and before we started I said, 'I don't want to be interviewed just for you to edit and cut it, because that is one of my objections to the media, so tell me how long you want.' So he said, 'Five minutes, but I may have to cut it a *bit*.' I said, 'No, if you want four minutes, give me the general areas and I will give you the right amount of time.' I did give him four minutes and zero seconds, absolutely to the dot.

Heard Bill Rodgers attacking Robin Cook on *The World at One*.

Went into the House to meet a deputation of shop stewards from Ferranti presenting their case against the sale of Ferranti shares to the public. It was in September 1974 that I arranged for the National Enterprise Board to buy Ferranti, and now they are being sold off to the highest bidder. I said a few words about it – and some of the people who were present were working at Ferranti in 1974 – very nice men.

At the PLP Phillip Whitehead [Labour MP for Derby North] asked what the position was on the draft manifesto and whether there had been proper consultation about Wednesday's party political broadcast.

Jim Callaghan replied, 'The draft manifesto does not commit the PLP, and there would have to be a constitutional change for it to do so. The foreword has been changed to make this clear.' On the defence broadcast he said, 'Robin Cook did his best. The NEC has a greater say, but I am not prepared to let them have the whole say in party politicals.'

Following its defeat in the 1979 General Election by a radical right-wing Conservative Government, the Labour Party by June 1980 was deeply involved in an intense debate concerning its future organisation and philosophy.

The left wing of the Party had come to see that radical policies adopted at Conference were ineffective if these policies could be vetoed by the Party Leader when the manifesto was drawn up, and if they could be ignored by a Labour Cabinet and Parliamentary Labour Party, some of whose members were hostile to the manifesto anyway.

In an attempt to resolve this rising discontent within the Party, a Commission of Inquiry had been established in 1979 comprising the trade union leaders and members of the NEC and Parliamentary Party. By June 1980, with James Callaghan still Party Leader, it was just finishing its deliberations with a view to producing recommendations, but most trade union leaders had used the Commission to forestall radical changes. In retrospect it can be seen as an expensive and prolonged procedure which ended up recommending comparatively little of substance.

The main emphasis in the campaign to reform the Party was to urge fundamental constitutional changes to the Party's structure and conduct intended to produce greater democracy and accountability. There were three major objectives, and some other minor ones, in this effort.

The first was that the Leader and Deputy Leader of the Labour Party should no longer be chosen by the Parliamentary Party alone, but by an 'electoral college' which comprised the local constituency parties and affiliated socialist societies, the trade unions, and all MPs, and which would be held at Conference. The principle of this having been agreed in 1980, much of the debate within the labour movement, before and after, concerned the proportions which each element should have.

The second proposal related to the traditional means of selecting and reselecting Labour candidates and MPs. The existing system in 1980 allowed a sitting MP to remain in that seat for life, unless a motion asking him or her to retire was passed by the general management committee of the local party – as in the celebrated case of Reg Prentice.

The proposed reform – that MPs be subjected to a regular selection or reselection procedure – was designed to make Labour MPs more accountable to their local parties and more sensitive to their views. It was never intended to start a vendetta against certain Members of Parliament, as was widely claimed.

The third proposal related to the drafting of the programme or manifesto itself, which the reformers believed should be entrusted to the National Executive, instead of to a joint meeting of the NEC and the Cabinet or Shadow Cabinet which the Party Leaders invariably controlled. Both Harold Wilson and James Callaghan had claimed that they had a personal veto over elements of the manifesto.

These were fundamental changes, not unnecessary 'constitutional wrangles'. I saw them as essential if democracy was to be the agency for social change brought about through parliamentary activity, and I worked hard with others to achieve them. After the Election defeat of 1979, I had decided not to stand for Shadow Cabinet election, and devoted my energies to the campaign for greater Party democracy.

This campaign was seen to pose a real danger and threat to the established power of the PLP and future Labour Governments and to the dominance of the parliamentarians over their parties and constituents, and indeed the electorate. James Callaghan and his successor Michael Foot both favoured the status quo, and fought to retain the right of the PLP to elect the Leader of the Party.

To the reader not familiar with the labyrinthine nature of the Labour left at the beginning of the 1980s, the groups which were committed to achieving these reforms may appear confusing.* However, in this diary, at the forefront there were essentially three organisations, many of whose members moved between the groups according to their different purposes and activities. The Campaign for Labour Party Democracy had been established in 1973 by Labour Party members committed to public ownership and the trade union links, disillusioned with Harold Wilson's leadership and interested in advancing the role of the constituency parties in policy through having greater accountability of MPs to their local parties. An integral part of their programme was mandatory reselection.

The Labour Co-ordinating Committee, founded in 1978, was from the start a London-based group and included MPs or parliamentary candidates such as Michael Meacher, Audrey Wise, Stuart Holland and Tony Banks among its members. It was particularly interested in industrial policy and, initially, withdrawal from the Common Market.

In May 1980 the CLPD, the LCC and other groupings were brought together in

* *The Battle for the Labour Party* by D. Kogan and M. Kogan (Kogan Page, 1982) is a valuable guide to the developments in the Party at this time.

a formidable alliance called the Rank and File Mobilising Committee, co-ordinating support for three demands: an electoral college, mandatory reselection and the drafting of the manifesto by the NEC.

These groups need to be understood if readers of this diary are to see how profound the argument in the Party was and how much it affected everyone from top to bottom in the Labour Party at that period of the Party's history. These changes almost more than any other led to the breakaway by the Social Democratic Party, whose members were only prepared to remain within the Labour Party if they could control it, and had no intention of allowing the constituency members of the Labour Party, with whom they were out of step on policy, to have any real say once they themselves were sitting on the green benches in the House of Commons.

What to the casual reader may be recalled as a squabble inside a defeated Labour Party can be seen as having great importance for the political life of Britain as a whole.

In the event, two of those changes were achieved: the establishment of an electoral college for the election of the Party Leader and Deputy Leader at Conference; and the new arrangements for the selection and reselection of MPs. The proposed change in the method of deciding the manifesto was defeated.

These differences have never been properly reconciled, and many Labour MPs felt personally threatened by reselection, or strongly opposed to it on principle. The electoral college was in place for the election of Neil Kinnock, and has, paradoxically, increased the power of the Party Leader, who can today claim to represent the whole Party and not just the PLP. It remains to be seen how this authority will be used by a Labour Prime Minister.

Friday 13 June

Set off with Caroline and Hilary for Whitehall College, the ASTMS country club, which is a most beautiful place, built at the turn of the century for the Gilbey gin firm. It has now got a swimming pool and sauna, and beautiful lawns. Hilary told me that Clive had actually bought some goldfish for the water garden especially for this weekend. In each room there were drinks, and in our room a kettle and two ASTMS mugs – and two penknives with ASTMS inscriptions!

The whole of the Commission of Inquiry was gathered for its final discussions over the weekend: David Basnett, Eric Heffer, Michael Foot, Jim Callaghan, Terry Duffy, Moss Evans, Bill Keys, Norman Atkinson, Frank Allaun, Joan Lestor, Jo Richardson and myself.

The first session was about the Party's finance and organisation: the need for a senior financial administrator; a five-year plan; reformulation of the annual accounts; a national appeal day, and so on.

Several suggestions were made, but it was clear that David Basnett, who was in the chair, didn't want a vote on anything. The thought began to cross my mind that he might not want *any* decisions reached, that this year's Party Conference would not get a recommendation from the Commission, then the whole thing would peter out and by next year they would hope to have changed the composition of the Commission. Since we wouldn't have settled, for example, how the Leader should be elected, Denis Healey would simply succeed under the old scheme of election by the PLP in October.

I went and had a swim and took some marvellous movie pictures of Jim Callaghan swimming in the pool.

When we resumed, we agreed to raise the CLP minimum affiliation fee to £5, which is a tremendous leap from £3. The only other thing we agreed was to drop the idea of legislation to control companies' political donations, on the grounds that it would trigger off a Tory attack on trade union money. I raised the whole vexed question of whether the state funding paid to the PLP to finance the work of the opposition should be given to Labour Party headquarters direct, as I believe it should; it was agreed that that was not a matter for the Commission.

To bed at midnight. I feel that the weekend is going to be inconclusive and that's the worse thing that could possibly happen. Clearly nobody wants to alienate the trade union leaders, particularly not the left, because we should be in alliance with them. So what I thought was going to be a momentous weekend has begun most unmomentously, indecisively, and generally speaking the situation is very uncertain.

Saturday 14 June
I had a troubled night; I worried that we were going to waste all our time on the preliminaries and never get to the main decisions. I woke at 6.30 and got up and went through all my papers again looking out of the window on a tremendously rainy day, unlike yesterday's beautiful sunshine. Four policemen were walking in the gardens, and I must say the whole thing is rather absurd.

After the afternoon session we were summoned up to Jim Callaghan's room for a party to which Clive had contributed some bottles of champagne. It was very jolly. I had a quiet word with Moss, Clive and Bill Keys. I think they have tried to get a compromise which they think will get them through, but they are not prepared to say what it is.

Back into the Commission after 8, and reselection of MPs was the key question. Eric Heffer moved, straight away, that the Commission adopt last year's Conference decision on mandatory reselection; Frank Allaun seconded Eric, David Basnett in the chair accepted it, and the debate began.

Michael Foot was opposed to it. Clive Jenkins said, 'Reselection should be mandatory unless 60 per cent don't want it.' This was very complicated, and Jim argued that if you went for mandatory reselection it would encourage factions such as the anti-abortion lobby, and it would work against the unions in that those who got seats would be slick media people.

I said I had been a Member for thirty years and, if my local Party wanted to get rid of me, they could just nominate somebody else and choose them. 'I don't believe for a moment that the trade unions will be disadvantaged. Indeed, I think they would benefit, because it is the media men that they want to get rid of and replace with good, solid local people. It will affect very few people, but it will mean that MPs listen to their GMCs.' Jim Callaghan got angry at this.

Moss Evans said, 'The Transport and General Workers' Union is firmly committed to mandatory reselection and so am I, but I am not mandated here. Therefore, I favour what Clive says, that if 40 per cent of a party wanted it there would be mandatory reselection.'

Moss continued, 'Jim has shown that the evidence in favour of mandatory reselection is not strong and therefore I would like to build a bridge by laying down criteria that *60 per cent* of a party would positively have to want a reselection conference before it was agreed.'

Clive said, 'No, there should be an obligation on all constituency parties to hold reselections unless 60 per cent *don't* want it.'

It became a great muddle, and Bill Keys suggested we adjourn for five minutes. When we returned, David put the main question, ie that we supported last year's Conference resolution, and that was carried by 7 votes to 6.

So David Basnett said, 'Well, we've disposed of that', but Jim added, 'Ah no, we've got the question of *who* is going to reselect – a lot of people think it should be done by *all* the members of a local party, not just the GMC.'

He went on, 'I can only tell you you have got a fight on your hands. The PLP will never accept this. I can't recommend this to the PLP.' And he picked up his papers and walked out; it was a tense moment, the Leader of the Party and a former Prime Minister picking up his bag and leaving a committee.

David Basnett said, 'We'll adjourn until tomorrow.'

Eric Heffer said, 'I am not accepting an adjournment.'

People began moving about, David Basnett picked up his stuff, and gradually the left were the only ones who remained; it was very dramatic and people thought Jim would go back to London. We began discussing among ourselves what we would do and it was clear that there can't be any reversal of the vote. But we will vote for the GMCs to reselect because it's the only way it can be done.

I went down to have a drink and it was most dispiriting. Clive was sitting there absolutely depressed, and he said, 'You've wrecked it now,' which Bill Keys repeated: 'You've wrecked it.'

'What have we wrecked?' I asked.

'You've wrecked the arrangement we had that the electoral college and the manifesto would be part of a compromise on reselection.'

I said, 'Well, look, if you intended that this was going to be a deal, you might have mentioned it to us so that we could have thought about it. I could have given you a better arrangement.'

They were really angry, and the truth is that the trade union leaders and Jim had tried to get this one through and Moss had let them down, because he wouldn't be able to face his Executive Council if he voted against mandatory reselection. I did wonder whether Jim had stormed out because he couldn't face the PLP.

Sunday 15 June

The Commission met at 9 with Eric Heffer in the chair. He said, 'As far as reselection is concerned, the question of the participation of all members of the Party in the process doesn't arise because we agreed we would adopt the reselection policy voted on at last year's Conference, which was that the GMCs would decide.' So that was that. 'Now we come to the Leader.'

Basnett said, 'I want wider consideration to be given to the whole question of the election of the Leader.' Of course he was referring to his own concept of the electoral college.

Michael Foot moved the status quo. 'We have had two Conference decisions in favour of it, the PLP want it to stay as it is, and I therefore move election by the PLP.' Terry Duffy seconded it.

Jo Richardson seconded the proposal that we adopt the principle of an electoral college.

Basnett said that he favoured a National Council of Labour which would deal with the manifesto, and the rolling manifesto, and approve the Leader. 'We should be uniting round a Council of Labour.'

Eric Heffer asked, 'Anyone second that?' Nobody did, so David Basnett's National Council of Labour died.

Then Terry Duffy said, 'There's no need for a change. We are satisfied with the PLP and we are satisfied with their choices in the past – Gaitskell, Wilson and Callaghan were all good lads.'

In a funny way, my respect for Terry Duffy has increased; he is a straightforward, right-wing, honest guy.

Moss Evans said, 'It is the electoral college which is under discussion. The T&G favour a college and the unions and the CLPs agree. Let's discuss the principle. As to the manifesto, if we have a college and mandatory reselection, we don't need to change the way it is produced.'

Jim argued, 'This is not an issue of principle. There are problems – we have got to consider the psychological impact of change. If MPs are reselected and the Leader is elected by a college and the power over the manifesto is taken away, it will damage the Party. If, for example, the PLP get a Leader *they* haven't chosen, they might not accept him. The system in the SPD in Germany works well but it might not work here. And there are two practical problems. One, who does the Queen send for? She might send for someone else if the PLP don't accept the Leader imposed by the electoral college. Secondly, if a Prime Minister resigns or dies, can an *electoral college* advise the Queen?'

Here was Callaghan using the monarchy to limit the democracy of the Labour Party. It really was significant because it shows how the elected monarch lives by the approval of the real monarch. I think that's an absolutely sensational comment. My reaction is to take away the prerogative of the Queen to appoint the PM.

Jim went on, 'If the trade unions had 50 per cent of an electoral college, the country wouldn't accept it; it would give the impression the trade unions were running the country.' He favoured the present system and added, 'This is the last chance to unite the Party.'

Bill Keys said, 'The problems of an electoral college are not insurmountable. We wouldn't wish 50 per cent trade union represent-ation, but the PLP are not the be-all and end-all, they are not the Labour Party.'

Later Jim remarked, 'I cannot recommend to the PLP things with which I do not agree. Let's try for a consensus. These proposals fragment the central authority of the Party; MPs will be more responsive to their GMCs and this will threaten Labour Governments, indeed Labour Governments will break up. How do you prevent *two* Leaders from being elected, because the PLP may well elect their own Leader. Then if you abolish the House of Lords, you'll have an elected Senate with more power. If you make these changes, you will have a break with the PLP, there will be a wave of national resistance, we shan't win the next Election.'

Joan Lestor thought the newer MPs accepted the need for change.

'I want to comment on what we are discussing and why,' Eric Heffer said. 'But this has come about because of what happened at the last leadership election. Jim was a good Leader, I've no complaint about Jim. But the PLP vote was derisory against an electoral college, and next time round we could have a Leader, if we weren't careful, who was hated in the country or by the Party.'

Michael Foot disagreed. 'The PLP views against any proposal for an electoral college are strong. The trade unions don't want to elect the Party Leader, and the Commission would be daft to come out for an electoral college on the basis of 50 per cent trade union vote, 50 per cent the rest. The relations with the trade unions are the best in the world. Be careful, because Mrs Thatcher will win the next Election if we go on like this. If we have mandatory reselection and a college and the NEC running the manifesto, there will be real trouble with the PLP.'

At 10.30 someone suggested a withdrawal and there was caucusing for some time. When we resumed, Eric said we had wasted an hour and a half and we would now proceed.

Foot proposed the status quo – which he lost, with 3 for and 9 against.

Moss and Clive then moved their new proposal of a 50–25–25 split: 50 per cent to the PLP and 25 per cent each to the unions and constituency parties. This caused heated argument. 'Can't we keep our voices down a bit,' pleaded David Basnett.

As people adjourned for lunch, I found myself left with Michael Foot. I forget how it began but I made a comment and he turned on me over something I had said about pay policy. 'There you are, always going on. You've got a bee in your bonnet. You supported the pay policy. Why should you complain now and suggest that the Party didn't support the pay policy?'

I said, 'Michael, I put in a paper to the Cabinet on pay policy in October 1978 and Jim wouldn't circulate it.'

Unknown to me, Jim had come into the room to pick up his bag, and I had my back to him so I didn't see him. I said, 'Now look, Michael' – the first time I have ever shouted at him – 'for the last ten years if I have come to see you and said I want to discuss policy, you have said, "Don't rock the boat!" For the last ten years your only answer to any question is "Don't rock the boat, you'll bring in Thatcher, lose power . . ." You haven't thought about anything for ten years, that's what's wrong with you.'

Jim then asked, 'What's this about?'

'I am talking about the question of your Cabinet's pay policy.'

Jim looked very embarrassed and walked out.

At 2.30 we resumed.

To cut a long story short, when Eric Heffer put the final proposals to the vote, ours was lost 6–7, and Moss's was carried 7–6, and at least we established the principle that the electoral college would choose the leadership.

I had a word with Moss and Clive and tried to be friendly.

Drove home and slowly unpacked.

Looking back on the weekend, Eric, Jo, Norman, Frank, Joan and I stuck together. Clive Jenkins and Bill Keys are just fixers. Moss Evans is absolutely unaffected by the mandate of his trade union. David Basnett is devious and cynical but hasn't got real strength; you can beat Basnett. Duffy is much tougher and honest and straightforward. Jim is angry and cross, on his way out. Michael Foot is hopeless. Anyone who reads this will think what an awful man to say those things about his colleagues but I'm getting it off my chest.

Whitehall College itself is like an executive mansion for the chiefs of multinational companies to relax in. Eric Heffer said on the phone how corrupt it was, and this is the form the corruption takes. The saunas, the swimming baths and champagne, everything laid on, is corrupting and you can't produce reform unless you withdraw from that, challenge it. But when you do, and are serious, you are up against bitter opposition.

Monday 16 June
I wrote and dispatched a memorandum to the Select Committee on Energy before which I am appearing on Wednesday to give evidence on the Government's nuclear power programme. I included the background note prepared by the Department of Energy in 1978 and I called for the publication of all the documents by both the last Labour Government and the present Government. I said in my memo that, as the years went by, I had become more and more sceptical about the claim that nuclea power could solve all our problems.

I rang the Friends of the Earth to talk to them.

This is the moment, under severe parliamentary questioning, when I shall disclose exactly what I feel about the problems of nuclear power. I am looking forward to it. It is an important hearing.

Wednesday 18 June
Went into the House and briefed myself for the Select Committee on Energy. They have allocated an hour for me. There was a huge crowd of people – from the Department of Energy, the Atomic Energy Authority, General Electric, Parsons, Friends of the Earth, etc. I was called in at 10.55 and I was in the event kept there for two and a half hours. Not having thought about these matters for a year, I found that when I read my briefs, and particularly when I was questioned, all the relevant figures and the events came back. It does show your mind is a filing system and all the information is stored there. A tremendous argument developed. The members of the committee were unsympathetic; they were all pro-nuclear.

Thursday 19 June
Listened to the 10 o'clock news and there was an interview with Robert Worcester, chairman of MORI, about a poll today which shows me as the most popular choice for Labour Leader among Labour voters: 22 per cent want me and 13 per cent want Denis. (But my negative vote is 34 per cent.) However you look at it, it is significant. I have risen enormously in the last three months.

Saturday 21 June
Spent the day working. I have decided to go for the CLPD prescription for the election of the Leader: 50 per cent of the votes for the trade unions, and 25 per cent each for the local parties and the PLP. I've got to try and persuade Eric Heffer, Joan Lestor and Jo Richardson to go along with me. I think it has the best chance of success: the TGWU are committed to it, so are all the constituency parties and some other unions. I don't want to launch an alternative scheme which will muddy the waters, make it harder to win, confuse people and set the Executive against the campaigners for Party democracy. The more I think about

it, the more I think we are inevitably discussing the power structure in the Party, and if we were to go for the one-third, one-third, one-third solution for the election of Leader, it would be bound to be applied in other votes at Conference, and elsewhere. It might even spread to the NEC, and we are not a tripartite party in which parliamentarians have an equal right with the trade unions and the constituency parties.

Sunday 22 June

Caroline and I went to join the big Labour Party demonstration on the South Bank against Polaris and nuclear weapons. The weather was awful, with bucketing rain and tremendous thunderclaps. So it was a tribute to the Party that 25,000 people turned up. We joined in the front of the procession with Labour MPs – Michael Foot and Stan Orme, Eric Heffer, Dennis Skinner, Joan Maynard, Jo Richardson, Frank Allaun, Norman Atkinson. Clive Jenkins was marching with us, which was very nice, and it was a jolly day really. We got to Hyde Park and gathered round the Reformers' Tree. It pelted down with rain and it was difficult to hear or speak. There was a little speech by David Lestor, Joan's boy, aged ten, and Mary Kaldor and the actress Susannah York spoke. I went on the platform at the end. Bruce Kent made a marvellous speech. Michael emphasised that it was about *multi*lateral disarmament, but still there you are.

We had a lovely family tea party and watched *The Magnificent Seven*.

Tuesday 24 June

In the evening I went to address a meeting of Labour First, a gathering of thirty-five members of a new centre group set up by people who are dissatisfied with the Manifesto Group which is right-wing and pro-Common Market, and with the Tribune Group which they think of as dangerously left-wing. Quite a few turned up from both wings, like Labour MPs Jim Wellbeloved (Manifesto), Roy Hughes (Tribune), Joan Lestor, David Young, Frank Hooley, Gerald Kaufman, Peter Archer, David Clark, Arthur Davidson, John Grant, David Stoddart and others.

I had a lot of questions which were all from a right-wing point of view.

Wednesday 25 June

Today was the official opening of the Labour Party's new headquarters at Walworth Road, after the NEC this morning.

When we came to the resolution from Home Policy instigated by the Young Socialists, severely criticising the treatment of prisoners in Northern Ireland prisons, particularly the H-Blocks of Long Kesh prison,[1] Michael and Jim tried to get it referred back – Jim said it was the 'marching season' in Northern Ireland, and he had heard on good authority that the resumption of violence was under consideration, and so on. But the resolution was passed by 11 to 8.

Came back to the House and talked to a few people about reselection; it is probably unwise to go on about it because it really worries Members that they might lose their seats. I was arguing the case, saying I was against 'sacking anyone', and so on, and Robert Kilroy-Silk [Labour MP for Ormskirk] commented, 'Your financial position is different, you're all right whatever happens to you.' I said, 'I don't think that's a fair argument.'

'That's the way people see it,' he told me.

I suppose like everyone else in Britain today they are worried about their jobs and I must take that very seriously, and we ought to do more for MPs on the pensions side.

Voted against the Sunday Trading Law Amendment Bill introduced by Clement Freud, Liberal MP for Ely.

Friday 27 June
Sat in the Tea Room and had a talk about Bill Rodgers, who is threatening yet again to leave the Party. I said he was like a chap on a skyscraper who kept threatening to jump. Norman Atkinson said, 'Yes, and the crowd is beginning to disperse!'

Saturday 28 June
Caroline went to the Socialist Educational Association Conference; I went with Dawn Primarolo to the Bristol City Farm which is apparently the biggest and best in the country. It was lovely. There are geese, goats, rabbits, ponies, a barn, a workshop for mothers and children, and it is run by a heavily tattooed man of about twenty-five who had six ribs shot away and his liver damaged while serving in the army in Belfast.

Sunday 29 June
The *Western Daily Press* rang to ask me if I was related to the actress Margaret Rutherford.[2]

I said, 'Yes.'

He asked, 'You knew her?'

'Yes, I've got a picture of her sitting on the beach with me in 1938, and I saw her just before she died. I saw her regularly, a very nice old lady.'

So that proves to me that Debrett's Ancestry Research are publishing a story tracing my ancestry back and linking me with Margaret Rutherford.

Monday 30 June
Up at 7 and sure enough on the Radio 4 news there was a reference to

the Margaret Rutherford story. The *Guardian* had a piece on its front page and other papers had references. Debrett's were trying to suggest that, just as Margaret Rutherford was the daughter of a murderer and ended up as a quaint and eccentric woman, so I was quaint and eccentric. They were quoted as saying 'If Tony Benn had been an actor, he would have been as universally loved as Margaret Rutherford.' It was a bit of character assassination and this was presented as a great discovery, whereas if anybody had asked any of the family we would have boasted of our relationship with her.

To Düsseldorf for the Confederation of EEC Socialist Parties meeting. In the conference there were tables with the flags of the member states of the Community and simultaneous translation equipment on every desk. It was well organised. There is this whole new European political culture and I must say I think it's a good thing. What I can't stand are the European political institutions which restrict our freedom.

The chairman, Joop den Uyl, former Prime Minister of Holland, spoke and said that the visit of Chancellor Helmut Schmidt to Moscow was of great significance in the context of east-west relations. He criticised the EEC Council of Ministers who at their Venice summit on the international situation had said practically nothing, argued that the Third World had been ignored, that there was no initiative on energy, and we needed action on South Africa.

I said I welcomed this debate; it was a critical moment for us, the Bureau of the Confederation should give a lead on events and not just respond to European leaders, and we should respond as socialists, not just as inhabitants of European institutions. Our belief, in Britain, was that peace, jobs and freedom were the three great aspirations of people. On peace, there was a direct threat to our survival as a result of the arms race, which wasted resources that should go on the Third World. I said I thought it was a deliberate political strategy. We wanted a wider European response to defence, and we should recognise the fears of the Soviet Union. Energy, environment and transport under the UN Economic Commission for Europe would be helpful. On security, Europe should move towards being a nuclear-free zone, with no Cruise missiles.

On jobs, I said, 'Unemployment is an instrument of political policy and it isn't just an oversight by political leaders; they are using it to weaken the powers of the trade unions. Monetarism is simply a theological cover for the policies they believe in anyway.

'Socialists and trade-unionists should work together. Our problem is not that we cannot persuade the right wing, who are in a majority, to do our policy; the problem is that the left is in a minority, because we have been in retreat. Let's make it something of a crusade, talk about right and wrong and not just confine ourselves to economic language. We should appeal to the people of Europe.'

Barbara Castle reported on behalf of the Socialist Group at Strasbourg. She talked about reform of the Common Agricultural Policy. 'We shall produce proposals because the CAP is bankrupting the Common Market', and she said she would like to set objectives for ending food surpluses and protecting the consumer.

The Leader of the Irish Labour Party, Frank Cluskey, said, 'We should listen to Tony Benn and direct our message to the people and not just to the leaders because our people need a moral boost.

'On the CAP, we are in favour of reviewing it but we don't want a new statement on it coming from this conference because it is a vital interest of Ireland and we don't want to exploit the primary producers.

'On the Middle East, I am against the PLO recognition, not because I am anti-Palestinian but because the annihilation of Israel is the PLO objective, and they are associated with terrorism. But I am also against Israeli colonisation of the West Bank.'

I was quite content with the summing up, but I said I hoped that in our declaration we would be seen as European socialists looking at the world and not just as socialists looking at Europe; otherwise we would be guilty of the very offence for which we criticised the EEC summit at Venice.

Barbara asked, 'Could we make a reference to the release of Nelson Mandela?'

I picked up the views of the various parties there, and the conference wasn't absolutely obsessed about what we did with the Treaty of Rome; the Commission was only mentioned in passing.

Went back to the hotel and made myself a cup of tea.

At dinner I sat next to Tony Brown of the Irish Labour Party. He told me that Charles Haughey, the new Irish Prime Minister, and Mrs Thatcher were both monetarists and nationalists and they hoped something would emerge on Ireland.

I said I was strongly in favour of the objective of independence and unity; he wasn't very enthusiastic about this. I don't think the Irish Government want to be landed with this problem, but it is time the British said something clear. There is no will in Britain to fight to keep Ulster as a part of the UK.

Tuesday 1 July
I talked to Jenny Little, Secretary of the International Committee of the Labour Party.

Jenny launched into a long discussion about security, and how, when she had been to the Foreign Office, they had carried out a tremendous vetting on her because she had previously been with the MoD. She couldn't have got into that job unless the vetting had been 100 per cent successful. She said, 'You know, there are people who think I might be an FO plant in the Labour Party.' I said nothing.

Caroline was at home, absolutely delighted because the press today reported on the many millions of public money put into the private education sector annually, something which Caroline has been working to expose for years.

Went into the House and voted. I heard a few interesting things in the Tea Room. Joan Lestor and Eric Heffer had been to the Northern Ireland Study Group where an enraged group of former Ministers –Roy Mason, Merlyn Rees, Stan Orme, Don Concannon and so on – had denounced the Executive for passing the resolution last week severely criticising conditions of prisoners in the H-Blocks at Long Kesh prison.

Wednesday 2 July

David Butler came to lunch. I haven't seen him for a while and he's been slimming, which has made him look old. I have known him for forty years.

He doesn't understand at all what is happening in the Labour Party and takes the view that democracy cannot survive if there is too much of a choice, and that there can't be fundamental choices; there has to be basic agreement in society, and then marginal arguments between one party and another.

David works at Nuffield College which is stuffed with academics who either appear on the media or – like Professor Hugh Clegg and Bill McCarthy (Lord McCarthy) – act for the Government on various industrial-relations inquiries, or work on contract for business. The students mainly go into business – as David Butler said, they go into the Bank of England, the City, and so on.

I have resolved as I get older to devote more and more time to explanation and analysis. Indeed, I said to Caroline last night that, when I retire from politics, I shall write a book that will deal with everything from the influence of the monarchy through to the Civil Service, a sort of testament.

The more I think about it, the less wanting to be Leader of the Labour Party is relevant.

Went into the House and we had the final meeting of the Commission of Inquiry. There was a bit of paper before us from the Drafting Committee saying that the Commission, having carefully considered all the evidence on the constitutional issues and having discussed them at length, in the absence of a consensus makes no recommendation! So that is the end of that particular story.

Jim Callaghan said, 'The whole Party democracy issue was a false issue from the start, the manifesto and reselection of MPs were all constitutional hares.' Bill Keys added, 'We've achieved a lot, but I am sick to death of all this argument about Party democracy. Let's kill the argument and close ranks.' Anyway, it was agreed we would present the report to Conference.

Friday 4 July

To Bristol, where I was met by a student nurse, who took me to a Royal College of Nursing meeting held at the Bristol Royal Infirmary. I had some interesting talks. The Professor of Child Welfare, Neville Butler, who was obviously a Labour man, said that the disparity between the health of people in the north and areas of high unemployment and that of people in the south and south-east was as wide now as before the war.

The same nurse dropped me back at the hotel and said, 'I was so frightened of meeting you!' I must remember that the press does succeed in alarming people about me.

Sunday 6 July

The papers reported Callaghan's big speech yesterday in which he has made it absolutely clear that he wants all the constitutional changes defeated at Conference. Television last night showed him getting a standing ovation.

Monday 7 July

To the Organisation Committee of the NEC. We came to the crucial vote on the format for the election of the Leader of the Party. To cut a long story short, Joan Maynard put forward the CLPD resolution that the trade unions have 50 per cent of the vote and the constituency parties and the PLP have 25 per cent each.

John Golding and Alan Hadden moved the retention of the status quo, and that was defeated by 5 votes to 2. Joan Lestor, seconded by Eric Heffer, moved the Tribune Group motion, ie one-third to the PLP, one-third to the constituencies, one-third to the trade unions. That was defeated by 7 votes to 2. Joan Maynard's motion was carried by 6 votes to 2. So that is the resolution which will go forward to the Executive.

Then Home Policy Committee to discuss the fifty-page document on private schools. Neil Kinnock was totally accommodating and was prepared to accept almost any amendment that was suggested.

Tuesday 8 July

To the International Committee of the NEC, held at the House.

We have had 140 resolutions on defence and disarmament submitted for this year's Annual Conference and I wouldn't be surprised if the Labour Party committed itself to unilateralism at this Conference. There will be the most frightful bust-up, but I am fed up with the right-wing leaders of the PLP: they don't agree with the Party on defence, on economic policy, on the Common Market, on Cruise missiles, on wages, and it can't go on for much longer.

We discussed one or two other items and I suggested that we pass a resolution complimenting the Pope on what he had said in Brazil. So I was given permission to draft something. 'The NEC welcomes the statements made by the Pope in Brazil in defence of human rights, in asserting the rights of peasants to have access to land and in calling for the recognition of the rights of trade unions and greater social justice.' That was carried unanimously, with Eric Heffer seconding.

Wednesday 9 July
The PLP met to discuss Northern Ireland in view of the Government's discussion document on a devolved government for Northern Ireland. There were only thirty people present at the most.

Tam Dalyell attacked the appointment of Maurice Oldfield, former MI6 Director, as security co-ordinator in Northern Ireland as provocative. He said it was also a great mistake to send the 5th Inniskilling Dragoon Guards, which has one-third Irish make-up, into Northern Ireland. A third of his constituents in West Lothian were Irish, both Protestant and Catholic, and there was a strong feeling that the British Army was counter-productive; he would like to see the withdrawal of the army.

John Fraser [MP for Norwood] believed that reunification was the only objective but the Protestants didn't want integration.

Alex Lyon [MP for York] thought that our civil liberties in Britain were at risk because of the Irish situation and that our approach to law and order was being undermined. 'Terrorism is seen by the people in Northern Ireland as being an act you would expect from freedom fighters.'

Clive Soley [MP for Hammersmith North] said he had always been for a united Ireland, there must be reunification, and he reiterated Alex's point about it affecting our civil liberties.

I said that what had interested me was that everybody who had spoken wanted reunification, with Ireland put back on the agenda. The PLP view was important, partly because Labour MPs had a lot of experience of the impact of Irish policy on their own constituencies, particularly in Glasgow or Liverpool, but also because there were Ministers who had had valuable experience. In the long term there had to be a British Labour view and the National Executive was also looking at it, but there was the problem of trade unions who had members in the North and South of Ireland and didn't want the issue of whether the Labour Party should extend membership to Northern Ireland to be raised. We had never discussed it at Conference in the past because we were told it would 'cost life', but the time had come when we had to discuss it. I hoped they would have another meeting before the end of the summer so the PLP view could be fed into the inquiry.

Brynmor John, our Northern Ireland spokesman, wound up, saying, 'Labour must face the fact, of course, of sixty years of partition, of what we said sixty years ago, and how you deal with it. There is a real fear of a boycott of a Labour Secretary of State if it were thought we would press for reunification.'

He went on to say the NEC resolution calling for reunification had been unhelpful, there had been dismay in Northern Ireland and the Republic at the resolution.

In the end it was all left in the air again. The PLP is a dead loss. It does nothing; it doesn't assert itself.

Thursday 10 July

Had a call from Chris Mullin, who said the *News of the World* had financed the genealogical research in Debrett's, and they had apparently traced the Benn family back to the sixteen great-great-grandparents, to 1720. The Benns were a German immigrant Protestant family. It is fascinating, and I felt quite excited by it. I almost forgave the *News of the World* for their malice.

Tuesday 15 July

I left for Birkbeck College for the debate with Eric Hobsbawm, the famous Marxist theoretician, which *Marxism Today* is going to publish in its September issue. He had sent me his line of questioning but I didn't prepare myself in any great detail for it, as I thought it would be better to be more informal. Eric Hobsbawm is Professor of Economic and Social History at Birkbeck, a very charming man of about sixty-three, a real intellectual with a pinched face and flowing hair. He looked like a thinner version of Jimmy Maxton. Bernard Crick, Professor of Politics at Birkbeck, and his wife were present. The meeting was packed out with research students and other people. I was then subjected to this most penetrating cross-examination. He was fair but pressing, and I'm not sure my answers were all that good. There were questions and answers from the floor which I enjoyed.

Tuesday 22 July

Went to the Commons and heard the unemployment figures – nearly 1,900,000, a jump of 250,000, I think, in a month. James Prior was not convincing and when Mrs Thatcher got up people shouted 'Resign' and 'Out'. Jim said there would be a motion of censure.

I had a telephone call from Paul Boateng, the solicitor representing blacks in Bristol, and a call from the Labour Action Committee on Race. I phoned the Attorney-General's Office to convey their view that it would be a great mistake to prosecute eighteen blacks in Bristol for riotous assembly[3] because it would simply reopen the whole business. I have never approached the Attorney-General before about a possible prosecution but I am glad I did in this case.

There was a division in which I voted in favour of an amendment to the Criminal Justice Bill bringing the rights of homosexuals in Scotland in line with those in England, that is to say consenting adults over the age of twenty-one could have sexual relations without breaking the law.

Wednesday 23 July
National Executive at 10, a really tense one, and I was tired and anxious when I arrived.

There is to be an anti-Cruise missile march on 26 October organised by CND, and Shirley Williams said we shouldn't have anything to do with CND. Jim supported her and said we were a major world party and we shouldn't do things like this, or something. The vote was 15 to 9 to attend the march and Jim said, 'I will never agree to unilateralism, whatever the Party says.'

Then Joan Maynard's motion which had been carried at the Organisation Committee – calling for the election of the Leader by an electoral college on a 50–25–25 division – came up. Shirley Williams wanted to refer it back to Organisation. Michael Foot seconded her and said, 'The Commission of Inquiry could not agree on this, and the PLP has got the right to elect the Leader.'

Callaghan said that the Conference had already voted on this twice – in 1978 and 1979. So Joan Maynard declared, 'When Gaitskell was defeated on unilateralism he said, "I will fight and fight again", and so will we.'

After some discussion Kinnock said, 'The weakness is that there are no alternatives, and we do want a broader electorate for Leader. It's better to have a varied choice, and we are in a cul-de-sac, though I am against this particular solution. The trade union votes can be moved with great dexterity.' He preferred one-third for each section, rather than fifty per cent for the trade unions.

Shirley moved that the draft amendment be referred back, but she was defeated by 14 to 11. So the division of a college into 50–25–25 was accepted by the NEC.

Tonight Sir Michael Havers, the Attorney-General, came up to me in the Lobby after my phone conversation about not prosecuting the people in Bristol. He told me they were ringleaders and had been identified for this and that. I said, 'Even so, if you triggered off the last riots by going to a café to arrest people because of cannabis, then charging people with riotous assembly will create a hell of a problem.' So I registered my point, and he said, 'Please don't say we've had a talk.' I don't mind that, but it was interesting that the Tories take a much broader view of what is wise and what is unwise in prosecutions. I know if I had spoken to our Attorney-General, Sam Silkin, about it, he would have refused to discuss it.

Thursday 24 July
Worked at home all day. I've had an invitation from Bruce Kent to

speak in Trafalgar Square at the 26 October rally. He put at the bottom of the letter in his own handwriting, 'You *must* come', and I certainly will, particularly as Jim Callaghan has now launched this great campaign against the NEC for its unilateralism.

Rang the manager of BBC Television News, who had asked for details of recent criticisms I have made of the media so that he could answer them. I told him I had two complaints. 'One is that you don't feel under any obligation to balance the reporting of capital versus labour. You put out what has happened to the pound sterling every day but you don't publish pay slips. You are not interested in the problems of labour. Secondly, you have a labelling system – "The well-known left-wing member" and so forth – which is a BBC health warning. When you have a right-wing person on he has "great ministerial experience".'

The Social Democratic Alliance* announced today that they are going to put up candidates against Labour MPs, including against me, in the General Election.

Caroline came into the House in the evening and I left her talking to Clare Short while I voted. Clare used to be a civil servant working with Alex Lyon, and when I came back from the Division Lobby she started on at me. Why do you only talk about the constitution? Why don't we attack the Tories? Why don't we forge closer links with the unions? Why is the left alienating the unions?

She is a very radical woman, more so than Alex Lyon, who, she said, was an old right-winger with good ideas. 'What is our policy for full employment? You make beautiful speeches but what is our policy?' she asked. So I really turned on her. 'The media have persuaded you there is no policy. There are masses of policy statements published, and discussion documents.' I admire her actually. She's a tough cookie. She resigned from the Home Office when Alex was sacked. She asked me to speak for the Labour Committee for Ireland at the Annual Conference and added, 'But if I were your political adviser, I would advise you not to.' I said, 'Well, thanks very much, but I will do it.'

Came home, and this evening, to commemorate the death of Peter Sellers, television showed the film *Doctor Strangelove*, a fantasy which alerts people to the dangers of nuclear war and the madness of the military mind.

Tuesday 29 July
Went into the House to hear Prime Minister's Questions and the censure debate.

Jim Callaghan was heavy, concerned, sincere, and said it was wrong to spend money on the Trident missiles when the public services were

---

* The Social Democratic Alliance was an extra-parliamentary group on the right of the Labour Party, predominantly London-based.

being starved (even though it is widely alleged that he spent £1000 million on Chevaline without consulting the Cabinet; also, it is alleged in American reports that he was strongly in favour of the Trident). Next he called for import controls in a way that sent my mind back to the 1976 IMF discussions. But otherwise his remedies were trifling. They were just intended to edge the present Government back to the policy he had pursued – which hadn't been all that successful.

Thatcher got up and she just romped home. She quoted what Healey and Callaghan had both said in office. She demonstrated that there was no difference in analysis between herself and them but that, whereas they were weak, she wasn't. The Government were determined, they wouldn't do a U-turn, the public supported her, and so on. It was a parliamentary triumph really.

Wednesday 30 July

The Labour Party's Media Study Group made up of MPs and others met at 6 to discuss a draft consultative document on the media. There was a useful discussion about monitoring. James Curran of Central London Poly, Chris Mullin, Paul Walton from the Glasgow University Media Group, Eric Heffer and some trade-unionists were present, and Frank Allaun was in the chair.

Afterwards I had a drink with Paul Walton and James Curran and they said they would like to organise a batch of academics to advise me on my speeches. I find that an attractive offer because I do need help and I think I could get quite a useful band of people together. I promised to let them have a list of all my speaking engagements so they would know what research would be needed.

Thursday 31 July

The Post Office Engineering Union published their report on telephone tapping today, and when I was in the House later John Golding of the POEU told me that individual union members were approached and recruited into the tapping service, and were paid £250 a week. They were all right-wing members of the union and they disappeared from sight into the phone-tapping building, and therefore the union knew nothing more about them.

It was clear this was going on on a big scale. The man who wrote the pamphlet is Merlyn Rees's former political adviser, so the whole credibility of Merlyn Rees and all Home Secretaries who talk about warrants and so on has been completely destroyed.

Tonight Caroline and I went to dinner with Lisa Appignanesi of the Writers and Readers Co-operative, publishers of the biography of me by Robert Jenkins. Among the guests were Tariq Ali and his friend Susan Watkins. I had only met Tariq Ali casually once or twice before but he has great charm and is a good listener. He obviously had a lot of connections, because he was able to give me the text of the open letter from David Owen, Bill Rodgers and Shirley Williams to the Labour Party, which is being published tomorrow morning in the *Guardian*. He also told me that Michael Foot had had lunch with the *Guardian* recently and had made it clear that Jim Callaghan would retire as Party Leader after the next Conference which Michael said 'we would win'. Somebody at the lunch asked, 'What do you mean by "we"?' So Michael, identifying himself entirely with the right, said that Denis Healey would make a very good Leader of the Party. That's a pretty fair confirmation, I think, of the whole position.

We talked about what the eighties might be like. Tariq Ali was depressed that we might sink into a right-wing period.

Friday 1 August

The *Guardian* and the *Daily Mirror* both printed the full text of the open letter from Owen, Rodgers and Williams which was disgraceful because, apart from attacking the 'far left' and accusing it of being hostile to representative democracy, it also went on to attack the idea that welfare capitalism wasn't working and said that some Labour leaders were flirting with the extreme left. It then went on to identify four issues that really mattered in addition to the maintenance of representative democracy: membership of the Common Market; membership of NATO; the mixed economy; and a permanent incomes policy.

Sunday 3 August

Mass coverage in the Sunday papers in support of Owen, Rodgers and Williams as you would expect, with a cartoon in the *Sunday Express* showing me as the gravedigger of democratic socialism wearing a top hat with a hammer and sickle on it.

In the evening we went out to dinner with Stuart Holland [Labour MP for Vauxhall], his wife Jenny and their very precocious three-year-old daughter Becky. Richard and Patricia Moberly were also there – Richard is an Anglican vicar who has been driven out of his parish altogether, having offered, I think, to take part in a team ministry. He is now going to be an industrial chaplain with the South London Industrial Mission. Patricia Moberly is an agnostic, having been converted to agnosticism by the scandalous racist attitude of the whites in the Anglican Church in Zambia, where they lived in the sixties. A very interesting woman. Chris Mullin was also there with a Chilean actress, the daughter of an admiral. She was arrested at the time of the Allende overthrow. She was kept in a cell in darkness, totally incommunicado, and tortured, including by electric shock treatment, and she described how she had been deafened in one ear – it was horrifying. She was finally released, no doubt because her father was an admiral, and escaped and worked in the Chilean resistance.

At the end of the evening we had a talk about the Labour leadership election and how we would run a campaign.

Thursday 14 August

Jimmy Carter has secured the nomination at the Democratic Convention in America. It has been a strange and unsatisfying period in American politics. Of course, after Nixon and Ford, who was a bungling nobody of an American President, Carter came along as the decent guy who would clean up American's corruption and reintroduce decent values. But ever since he arrived he has given the impression that he has not been in charge at all. He has the glazed-eyed look of somebody who is out of his depth and is being controlled by other forces.

Edward Kennedy, whom I have never liked, being a sort of American aristocratic clan leader, put up a considerable fight, no doubt with a lot of money behind him. He has tried to recall to the Democratic Party its New Deal tradition of being pro-labour, pro-jobs and pro-welfare, and to that extent Kennedy is a symbol of the re-radicalisation of the old Democratic Party. The Democrats had gone the way of the Labour Party, ie ended up with somebody who is really a nothing, an old uncle. Jimmy Carter is an old uncle like Jim Callaghan. On the other hand, Kennedy has always seemed to me a centre-party figure in British terms, a sort of Roy Jenkins/Shirley Williams type, and this makes him unattractive.

Anyway Kennedy made a great speech on the Democratic platform yesterday which earned him enormous applause. Carter came along today and in a wooden speech with a fixed smile got the nomination, but with no enthusiasm.

Friday 15 August

Tony Banks telephoned to say he thought it would be useful if he, Chris Mullin, Michael Meacher and I had a meeting soon to plan a strategy on the leadership. I think that is right. Chris Mullin will deal with the left, Tony will deal with the union side, at which he is very good, Michael Meacher will deal with the parliamentary side, and we'll bring others in later.

Sunday 24 August

Stansgate. Clive and Moira Jenkins and their teenage children came for the day. After lunch, sitting out on the grass, I had a talk with Clive about trade union politics. He said Moss Evans and Ray Buckton [General Secretary of ASLEF] were having lunch with him tomorrow at the ASTMS Whitehall College and he had had the swimming pool cleaned and warmed up.

Clive is basically a bouncy, Welsh radical who has got immense imagination and who has arrived and is now busy organising and fixing everything. I don't think he has an awful lot of influence but he did tell me some interesting things. For example, he had been to have dinner with Jim Prior and Peter Carrington and others, and they were all wildly disloyal about Mrs Thatcher; Clive thought she would go and probably be replaced by Lord Carrington. He also told me he had dined with Geoffrey Howe at Number 11 with others – not only trade union people I think – and they had told Howe that the economic policy was a disaster: Geoffrey Howe had been quite shaken by this. Then he said that he had invited Ted Heath to lunch and gained the impression, though he hadn't asked him explicitly, that Ted Heath would agree to serve under Carrington.

I told him that when the time came for the election of the Labour Leader I would campaign, but I was not allowing it to influence me in the short run. He was very uneasy. He protested his support for me as first choice and John Silkin as second, but I don't know that he will have any influence.

Sunday 31 August
There was an attack by 'Cross Bencher' in the *Sunday Express* today saying that I was finished – historically such comments have always preceded a tremendous advance of one kind or another!

Monday 1 September
Travelled to Brighton for the TUC Conference and at lunchtime went to the Market Wine Bar, which Clive Jenkins had taken over for the ASTMS delegation. Tony Banks was there with his wife Sally, a lovely woman. We had fun talking and planning.

Caroline arrived from London and we went and had tea. I had a long argument with Dick Clements about *Tribune*'s line and how it had got to fight now. But he said, 'This is the moment for retrenchment', and so on. The old left has nothing to offer at the moment; it just nestles in the embrace of the right, while being called the legitimate left.

We went over to a meeting organised by the Rank and File Mobilising Committee in the Royal Albion Hotel, with Tony Banks in the chair; 300 people were turned away. There were four television cameras set up. John Bloxam from Socialist Campaign for a Labour Victory, Ron Todd of the TGWU and I were speaking. The temperature must have been 100°F I would think.

Tuesday 2 September
Big coverage of the TUC in the papers. 'Shirley Savages Benn' in the *Mail*, 'Shirl Biffs Benn' in the *Sun*, 'Benn Disloyal' in the *Telegraph* – because Shirley, Bill Rodgers, David Owen and Terry Duffy had at their own fringe meeting launched into a personal attack on me. Well, that suits me fine; I couldn't be more pleased.

When you go into the TUC Congress they have people who search you – but they don't search you for bombs, they search you for leaflets! I must say that is in its own way a classic little example of how the TUC excludes political ideas. Indeed, I heard from a number of people today that the general secretaries resent there being so many 'politicians' at Brighton.

The Congress adjourned at 12.30 and Tony Banks picked me up. He has been magnificent. He has organised all the parties, brings people up to see me, organises the media, gets taxis, and so on – he has been a marvellous help. He knows the trade union movement better than anybody else. We went across the road and sat in two deckchairs and had a talk.

At 2.15 I went back into the Conference Centre and heard Jim speak. I had heard him in that very same spot two years ago when he had left the TUC guessing about the Election date. Here he was, young and vigorous, arguing his case with great charm, saying, 'We must all unite against the Government', how the Labour Party mustn't divide itself, etc., and he then went on in effect to develop the old pay policy argument. You have to give him credit; he believes that's the only way to do it, and they trust Jim because of his trade union origins and his long experience. It was a good speech in the sense that it will appeal to all the right-wing trade union leaders and all the cautious delegates who are frightened about the future and who will say, 'Well, Jim's Government wasn't so bad.' I didn't get the impression that it was the speech of a man about to retire: I don't think he is.

Wednesday 3 September
Every trade union leader attacked Mrs Thatcher and the Government today, but not one of them had anything constructive to offer except that the TUC should meet the Government. Len Murray indicated the TUC was prepared to talk about anything with any Government, and said full employment could be restored if only the Government would change course.

I had lunch at the Market Wine Bar again with Clive Jenkins. He is always surrounded by television people. There was a television crew watching us having lunch with Arthur Scargill; we were eating avocado and lobster or something, and it will all be presented as tremendously luxurious. I was slightly anxious, but Tony Banks thought it would be helpful to be there.

To the Fire Brigades Union party in the evening. I saw Jack Jones and tried to persuade him to write his memoirs.

The delegates are all very friendly to me. But the TUC leadership and the parliamentary leadership are suffering from post-operative shock and finding it hard to recover from the fact that the corridors of power are closed to them. Because of that, the confidence of the rank and file is growing.

Tony Banks took me to the station. I came home having had three of the busiest days ever at the TUC, and it was all Tony's doing.

Monday 8 September

Roger Fox, the National Organiser of the Social Democratic Alliance, was interviewed on Radio 4 this morning in advance of today's Organisation Committee of the NEC. He referred to 'those who adopt policies akin to revolutionary violence, that is to say the Trotskyites within the Party', and he said that I had encouraged Trotskyite groups to join the Party. I rang Eric Heffer and he rang the BBC up about it.

The announcement today that two rods of plutonium have disappeared at the atomic power station, Dounreay, has led to a tremendous amount of comment and I have been asked for my view. I decided in the end to write a letter to the Energy Secretary, David Howell, which I released to the Press Association. It simply said:

> Dear David,
>
> Plutonium incident.
> Can you please let me know:
>   1.   When was the loss of plutonium rods first reported (a) to the Director at Dounreay, (b) to the Nuclear Inspectorate, (c) to the Chairman of the AEA, (d) to the Department of Energy, (e) to Ministers, and who were they?
>   2.   When – precisely – was it reported to you?
> I would value an urgent reply.
>
> Yours,
>
> Tony Benn

I think that to interrogate is the right thing to do. It is the dishonesty of the AEA, rather than the fact that a bit of plutonium is lost, that really matters.

At the Organisation Committee we came to the question of the Social Democratic Alliance and, in the end, the National Agent recommended that the SDA be effectively a proscribed organisation. I was against this because it would mean an inquisition of individuals and so on, and Frank Allaun moved that we write to them and, if they refused to undertake not to stand as candidates against Labour Party candidates in elections, we would expel them. Frank's motion was finally carried by 9–4.

Monday 22 September

To the new Labour Party headquarters, Walworth Road, at 10.20, and there was Denis Healey standing outside. I said, 'I really liked your book of photographs. I had no idea what a good photographer you were.'

'Ah, you see, I'm not as daft as I look,' he replied.

'I always thought you were much *more* cunning than you appeared, but anyway they were really good pictures.'

So then he said, 'I enjoyed listening to your mother on the radio.' It was all very matey.

Then we went in for the TUC-Labour Party Liaison Committee meeting.

Denis opened with an attack on the Government's economic policy. He said the policy was in a shambles, there was accelerating decline, output was falling faster than forecast, and retail sales, trade exports and investment were falling sharply. 'We have to consider how to exploit the discontent of the Tory wets, how to get the CBI to speak out more frankly. Eric Varley, Peter Shore and I dined with the CBI the other night and pressed them to speak out on the Minimum Lending Rate, which they did.'

I said, 'From Mrs Thatcher's point of view, her policy has been a triumphant success because it has weakened the unions, and she is very unlikely to change her policy as a result of representations made by them. Even if she did, it wouldn't help very much, as a U-turn would not be sufficient to resolve this crisis. I doubt whether the trade union co-operation is worth it. It is entirely a matter for the trade unions to decide but I think it is highly questionable. But I do think that we ought to launch into a tremendous public campaign to explain to people what is really happening. If Labour won, what would we actually do that would help? Because, in my opinion, emergency policies will be needed. We will have to start work now and we must be prepared to think beyond economic management, because it has got quite beyond that stage.'

David Basnett asked, 'What do you mean by withdrawing trade union co-operation? Do you mean taking Clive Jenkins off BNOC or withdrawing from the NEB or ACAS? It would be against our members' interests to withdraw, and our members are not all Labour Party activists.'

I had to leave at this stage. The trade union leaders have got an interest in working with the Government of the day and I can understand that. Therefore, the political leadership does fall to us, and they must accept that that is our function.

Tuesday 23 September

I had intended to spend today at home, but the *Bristol Evening Post* rang up at 9 am to say that the management of St Anne's Boardmills were about to announce the closure of the whole mill – 800 jobs. Some redundancies were made in 1979. The mill has been in Bristol since 1913. So I caught the 2.20 train to Bristol. I had a tough interview with the local radio and BBC television. At Bristol Transport House I met some of the shop stewards, who said, 'Be careful, Tony, we are probably going to get three or four times the Government minimum redundancy, and we don't want anything you say to affect us getting that money.'

I have a terrible cough and cold, I haven't been smoking for a week. The cough and cold and sore tongue really frightened me, and I have a pain in my leg which makes me think I have got circulation trouble.

Labour Party Conference, Blackpool
Friday 26 September
The Imperial Hotel was more run down than ever. They have redecorated downstairs, but the rooms upstairs are really crummy.

There was a thundering disco going on all evening and the whole hotel vibrated with the noise until 2 am.

In yesterday's *Listener*, Barbara Castle's diaries were reviewed by Michael Foot, who was violent against diarists. Enoch Powell in *Now!* magazine was also strongly against them. It is interesting because Powell and Foot, who were thought of as tribunes of the people, want to keep the mystique of the state in order to make it easier to govern the people.

Watched *Newsnight*, which included a profile of me that Adam Raphael had put together. It lasted about sixteen minutes; I thought it really was an assassination job, done with considerable skill. Barbara Castle was quoted to my disadvantage and then David Owen, who said I was phoney and bogus for being 'ashamed of my middle-class background' and that the PLP didn't like phoney, bogus people. Sir Antony Part, my former Permanent Secretary at Industry, thought my problem was that I was a radical Minister in a non-radical Government (which was quite fair). Then an awful interview with Joe Ashton, who said, 'The trouble with Tony is that he idealises the working class and there are as many shits in the working class as there are in the middle class – I know because I am in the working class.' There was no reference to the fact that my father had been a Labour MP.

Saturday 27 September
This evening I went to Jo Richardson's hotel room with Joan Maynard, Judith Hart, Neil Kinnock, Tony Saunois, Joan Lestor, Eric Heffer and Dennis Skinner, and we planned how we would handle the leadership question.

Sunday 28 September
Shirley Williams on *Weekend World* said she would leave the Party if the Conference voted to come out of the Common Market.

'And now the moment you've all been waiting for . . .'

Monday 29 September

Michael Foot opened the economy debate with a speech entirely without content, just rhetoric.

On behalf of the NEC, I made a competent, 'prime ministerial'-type speech, putting forward the possibility of a Labour Government creating a thousand peers to abolish the Lords and hence their power to delay our legislation on public ownership and industrial democracy.

Caroline attended the education debate as she has contributed to Party policy. Apparently Neil Kinnock got a standing ovation – for the second year – and he got it partly for saying that Government cuts would have to be more than restored. Actually he has been saying elsewhere that he couldn't guarantee to restore them at all.

Shirley Williams delivered a violent personal attack on my speech, and this has been in all the news bulletins, indeed it took pride of place over the Conference itself on the 10 o'clock news. As I left the hotel earlier tonight, Peter Sissons said to me, 'You can have five minutes on *News at One* tomorrow', as if he was offering me a great gift.

Tuesday 30 September

Woke up early. Papers are pretty hysterical about my contribution yesterday – 'Smash and Grab' and all that.

Jim made his speech – a farewell speech is the only way you could describe it – and I felt affectionately disposed towards the old man. He was amusing, cheerful, covered the issues he cared about, and was himself. He got a warm ovation at the end; I think a leadership election will probably be announced in three or four weeks.

In the debate on health and poverty Lena Jeger, who is chairing the Conference, called Hilary [Benn] to introduce a composite resolution – good and clear.

Stephen got 323,000 votes in the election for the Conference Arrangements Committee. Stephen and Hilary are their CLP delegates. It was really formidable, and I am very proud of my family today.

At lunch I went to the Lobster Pot to speak at the Glasgow University Media Group's fringe meeting. It was thrilling because all the media people were there – Julian Haviland, Fred Emery, George Clark. There was a super guy, Greg Philo, of the GUMG, who described the language the media used for discussing wage rates and average earnings and so on.

Wednesday 1 October

The Common Market motion was moved brilliantly by Clive Jenkins, talking about food mountains. He said, 'We have had a marvellous barley harvest. Next year we're having harvest festival in a hangar at Heathrow.' It was hilarious.

I went up to Ron Hayward and asked when Peter Shore was going to be called, and he said, 'I don't know whether Lena Jeger will call him.' I argued that he should; after all, he was the parliamentary spokesman. As a result the whole debate was given another ten minutes and Peter got in with a Churchillian-type speech. By 5 million to 2 million, we voted to withdraw from the Common Market. That is sensational, a fantastic victory.

In the afternoon we had three great debates on the constitutional changes.

The first was on mandatory reselection of Labour MPs. Joe Ashton made a notable speech against it. Joe is an old friend – he was my PPS – but he said something disgraceful.

'When you were sacked, Tony, from your seat by the House of Lords in a very unfair way, you fought and fought again, and you have never stopped fighting the House of Lords since . . . MPs who think they have been unfairly sacked will tend to react in the same way. Because if an MP gets the sack and walks away into the sunset, and says nothing, he does not get a penny redundancy. [But] if he stands and fights he can pick up nearly 13,000 quid.' This was a reference to MPs who, if they are defeated in an Election, get a lump-sum payment. He said it was letting a Trojan horse into the Party. 'If Roy Jenkins wanted to form a party of twenty-five sacked MPs now in this Parliament, they would be in business in six months', because, historically, sacked MPs won their seats when they stood as independents.

His speech did the PLP no good at all.

At the end Sam McCluskie delivered the most devastating argument in favour of mandatory reselection and it was carried: the Conference nearly went berserk.

Next was the manifesto. The NEC amendment was moved formally, and its effect would be to remove the Shadow Cabinet's joint control over the manifesto and to provide only *consultation with* the Leader. Very little was said during the debate. David Warburton of the GMWU, one of these well-dressed, right-wing, clever young trade union leaders, who are very pro-EEC, attacked the National Executive.

I was called to reply, and I described what had happened, why the manifesto was important, why in the past it was secretly killed, and then I dealt with Warburton and said all the measures Trade Unionists for a Labour Victory had wanted had been ruled out in the manifesto last year. I must say it was the best speech I have ever made at Conference, probably the best speech I have ever made in my life at a public meeting. It was followed by tumultuous applause from the CLPs and a standing ovation, while the trade union delegations sat looking very uncomfortable. By a narrow majority – 100,000 or so – it was defeated, but I had heard that they had expected it to be lost by more.

Then we went on to the manner of election of the leadership, which Eric Heffer introduced in a halting way. He outlined the procedure the Conference had to follow which was extremely complicated, and there was an absolute uproar when the Conference voted by a pretty narrow majority – 98,000 – to support the principle of an electoral college for electing the Leader and Deputy Leader. This was not what had been expected. Indeed, the *Express* said this morning that the left would be defeated on all three issues.

It was a most thrilling day.

Caroline and I went to the *Tribune* meeting and 1900 people were in the Pavilion Theatre. Neil Kinnock was extremely amusing during the annual collection – exceptionally talented and funny. After I spoke, the general consensus was that I went on too long.

Then Michael Foot, now the old lion, wound up and got a cheer although he hasn't been a figure of the left for a decade. His usual line is to warn that we face the greatest crisis since Hannibal's march on Rome and that we must do nothing whatever that might interfere with total mental inactivity and 100 per cent loyalty to the Leader, whoever he may be – but particularly Callaghan, followed by Healey, followed, if all goes wrong, by Roy Mason and Eric Varley in about that order!

At 11 pm Vladimir Derer, Tony Saunois, Joan Maynard, Margaret Beckett and others met in Jo Richardson's room. The general feeling was that at tomorrow morning's NEC we should propose a new constitutional amendment based on a division of 40 per cent to the PLP and 30 per cent each to the unions and constituencies, because that was thought the one most likely to get through. Tony Saunois, the YS representative on the NEC, emerged in the discussions as the most formidable, principled and serious politician, at the age of twenty-five.

However, just as I was going to bed, the phone rang and it was Frances Morrell, and a few minutes later, with Caroline and Melissa in bed, she plonked herself down in the same room and said this had been a terrible sell-out, the left never knew when it had won, we should *not* give the MPs 40 per cent but should insist on the unions getting 40 per cent because *anything* we put forward would be accepted tomorrow. Pressed and somewhat overpowered by Frances, who was in her full battle-gear while I was in my underpants, I conceded that this seemed logical at 1.45 am and so she retired.

Thursday 2 October

When I went downstairs I found Stephen sitting in the hotel lobby with a typewriter, having worked all night on an emergency resolution about Chile.

'Benn's a Liar', 'Labour in Chaos', 'Anarchy Here', 'Callaghan Denounces Benn', and so on, the papers all said. I heard that Callaghan had denounced me at the miners' dinner, which did cause great offence to the miners because I had been a good Energy Minister.

The National Executive met at 8, and it was clear that Frances, Vladimir, Jon Lansman, Peter Willsman, Victor Schonfield and Francis Prideaux had bullied members of the Executive into agreeing to the new CLPD alternative – 40 per cent for the unions and 30 per cent each for the MPs and constituencies. We kicked this around for a bit, and eventually it was carried by 13 votes to 7 which was excellent.

Out of the blue, Jim announced that if this was implemented he would withdraw what he had said about Labour unity, he would open up a campaign and he would recommend to the PLP that they elect their own Leader. Neil Kinnock said this was all rather regrettable.

I said, 'Jim has made a very important statement and I think we should consider it. If he tries to get the PLP to vote for a Leader in this way, for which there is no provision in the constitution, either he would fail (and I think he will because most Labour MPs are good loyal members of the Party), or he will succeed and set up a centre party. Either way it would be very bad for us. All these threats do no good.'

So Jim announced, 'Well, I tell you that the Parliamentary Party will never accept a Leader foisted upon them', and added, 'I'll tell you something else, they will never have Tony Benn foisted upon them.'

I said, 'Jim, you speak for yourself and nobody else.'

So, on that happy note, we went into the Conference. The morning debate was on defence, and passed two unilateralist resolutions overwhelmingly.

Then to the NEC statement agreed this morning on the election of the Leader, and Eric introduced the debate. To cut a long story short, there was a bitter debate, with Tom Jackson of the Post Office Workers accusing the Executive of being a conjuror producing white rabbits out of a top-hat, Andrew Faulds [MP for Warley East] attacking 'the Right Honourable Anthony Wedgwood Benn' (inaudibly, since the mike was switched off), and Martin Flannery saying what he thought of Terry Duffy. In the end all the options for the electoral college were defeated, leaving only the principle agreed. Then David Basnett, who had spoken against the NEC constitutional amendment, moved an emergency resolution that we hold a Special Conference in January to resolve the method of electing the Leader of the Party, and that was agreed. So we are back where we started.

Friday 3 October

It has been a watershed of a Conference, of that there is no doubt, and, unlike any other Conference, it will continue to cast its influence over the PLP, over the leadership and over the future of British politics.

Sunday 5 October

The *Telegraph*, the *Sunday Times* and the *Observer* all presented the week entirely from a right-wing point of view – 'Representative Democracy Threatened', 'The Left Tyrannicals', and so on.

That it was the culmination of years of work to get a democratic Party in which the leadership was more responsive to the rank and file never surfaced at all. The *Sunday Express* raised the question whether the Queen could ask someone who had been made Leader by the Party outside Parliament to form a Government.

Caroline has a bad cold. Got on with a bit of work but, having stopped smoking, I am putting on weight.

Monday 6 October

Jim Callaghan has let it be known that in nine days' time he will tell the Shadow Cabinet what he intends to do, and my guess is he will decide to go.

Wednesday 8 October

The *Times* front page was 'Benn Spectre Haunts Tory Conference', and my name has been mentioned more times at Brighton than you would have thought possible.

The fact is that last week at Blackpool we really pulverised the Tories by the strength and force of our alternative policy. Nobody is going to tell me that Mrs Thatcher is frightened of Shirley Williams or Bill Rodgers or Jim Callaghan, of Denis Healey or Peter Shore. But they are transfixed by the thought that there might be a radical Labour Government.

Though Labour Party Conference had agreed to establish an electoral college for the election of the Party Leader and Deputy Leader, the details concerning the composition of the college were to be worked out at a Special Conference in January 1981. In the meantime, Jim Callaghan indicated that he would resign, and would prefer Michael Foot as his successor. This posed a dilemma to the left within the Party – whether to fight a leadership contest under the existing PLP rules, whereby only the Parliamentary Party voted, a course which would upset those who still saw Foot as representing the left; or to wait until the electoral college was in place and contest the leadership at some point after that.

Sunday 12 October

We had guests at 8 – Norman Atkinson, Geoff Bish, Chris Mullin, Frances Morrell, Vladimir Derer, Tony Banks, Audrey Wise, Martin Flannery, Jo Richardson, Reg Race, Ken Coates, Stuart Holland and Julie Clements. There was some discussion as to whether we might have witnessed a real split in the Party. Sixty MPs have demanded that the PLP maintain the right to elect its own Leader, and it looked as if they were calling for Callaghan to go.

Jo Richardson then proposed that if Michael Foot stood no one else should. Stuart Holland agreed.

Chris Mullin turned to me and asked, 'Tony, are you going to stand? You shouldn't. You have nothing to gain from standing, and everything to gain by abstaining.'

At some stage I was asked to speak. I said, 'First of all, this is a political and not a personal question. I have consulted my GMC and have made no commitment. Leaving aside the split question, we must see this in the wider context.' I thought the correct strategy was for us to challenge the leadership, the deputy leadership and the Shadow Cabinet appointments. I went on, 'The Party needs a strong Leader now, and if the left abstains there will be continued personal conflict with the left leader-in-waiting, and the incumbent will win in the electoral college. I don't think I could fight and win the college if I abstained now.'

But the unanimous view was that I shouldn't stand yet. After the discussion, I drafted a couple of resolutions, one for the NEC and one for the PLP.

'The NEC, having taken into account the decision of Conference that the Leader and Deputy Leader of the Party should be elected on a wider franchise, calls upon the PLP to suspend its standing orders so that the elections for the following session are deferred and that the officers and Parliamentary Committee for the 1979–80 session continue until the Conference decision has been carried out.'

That was agreed, and I then drafted the second resolution, asking the PLP to suspend its standing orders 'so as to permit the officers and Parliamentary Committee to continue until the Leader and Deputy Leader of the Party are elected under the wider franchise as agreed by Party Conference.'

Just to sum up the evening. First of all, it was a meeting of the left in strength, and very formidable they are, but they were unanimous that I shouldn't stand and I am bound to take that seriously. I am in no hurry, and I have lots of meetings in which I can talk about the issues. But they were strong and firm, and clearly the view that Frances Morrell, Victor Schonfield, Dennis Skinner and others put forward earlier was right, so I simply bowed to the will of the majority.

Monday 13 October

The press covered an open letter from these sixty right-wing MPs saying they wouldn't accept an electoral college. Letters are pouring in to me, the overwhelming majority friendly and touching, and some of course saying 'Go to Russia.'

Wednesday 15 October

To Coventry for a union meeting, and at the station I heard the news that Jim Callaghan had resigned. The media had all got in their taxis and cars and arrived at the station. Caroline had advised me simply to say, 'Although I have had many personal differences with Jim Callaghan, I feel that in the hearts of many people will be a desire to say thank you for his personal contribution; as to the future, nothing must be done that divides the Parliamentary Party from the Party in the country.' I said that several times.

Got home at 6, and on the news it was announced that Michael Foot had decided not to stand. I had a word with Eric Heffer, who said, 'Now look, I have consulted Doris' (very important, because Eric takes a lot of notice of his wife, quite properly) 'and if Michael Foot is not going to stand, and if there are no candidates other than Silkin and Healey, you and I should stand for the leadership and deputy leadership.'

Thursday 16 October

I had fifteen phone calls, one of which was from *TV Eye* which is made by Thames Television, who rang to tell me that they had telephoned 250 constituency Labour Party chairmen, and that just under 40 per cent said it was acceptable for the PLP to hold a leadership election, and 61.6 per cent said it was wrong. As to the possible leadership candidates, 38.4 per cent favoured Tony Benn, 28 per cent Denis Healey, 15 per cent Shore, 11 per cent Foot and 4.8 per cent Silkin.

I have two things to say about that. First of all, the lead I had over Denis Healey wasn't quite as commanding as I thought, but I think the Shore, Foot and Silkin votes would come my way, which would probably mean that I would end up with a majority of about three-quarters. But my other thought is of the incredible expenditure involved in getting the names and addresses of CLP chairmen and phoning them. They told me they had six people working on it for forty-eight hours – which reinforces my view that the media are running the Labour Party leadership election.

Saturday 18 October

To Bristol to the Corn Exchange, where CND was under-way with a festival of actors, poets and music, including the actress Julie Christie. She was the first speaker from the platform; she read her piece, which was very carefully written, and was listened to intently and got huge applause at the end. After her, Bruce Page, editor of *New Statesman* read his speech, which was boring, but he did draw attention to the point that we have to have a non-nuclear defence strategy. Joan Ruddock, Labour candidate for Newbury in 1979, made a good speech.

I developed the idea of a non-nuclear defence policy and told a few stories about my time in the Home Guard during the war.

I came back on the train with Julie Christie, whom I have never met before, but who lives close by, in Linden Gardens in Notting Hill Gate. She is making a film of a book by Doris Lessing and when she is not working she lives in Wales with several friends in a community, I think. She likes farm life and is a dedicated sort of socialist. We talked about Vanessa Redgrave and Jane Fonda, and whether they suffered for their views.

Sunday 19 October

The papers are beginning to hint that Michael Foot might stand, and it would be a sensation if he did. I watched Brian Walden's show, *Weekend World*, which is a party political broadcast on behalf of the right-wing of the Labour Party.

A lot of people arrived at home in the evening for a left gathering. I mentioned Alex Lyon's initiative that all candidates for the leadership should be asked to indicate that they were only standing as caretakers pending the decision on the electoral college next January. Eric and I had agreed that we would stand for the 'real' election, and might possibly consider putting our names in the ballot this time. Audrey Wise feared Alex's initiative because there would be division over tactics.

Victor Schonfield said, 'We should start straight away on the real

Benn-Heffer campaign for next year. Don't ask the PLP to elect a caretaker or to support Party Conference policy because that is a diversion. We should make the vote derisory by boycotting any leadership election.'

'I am opposed to Tony standing in any circumstances at the moment', said Chris Mullin, 'because the principle is wrong and tactically he will do badly. Tony is the real election candidate of the left and should declare that, and then interrogate the candidates in the forthcoming PLP ballot.'

Reg Race agreed. 'Tony should not stand now, whatever happens.'

Frances Morrell said, 'If we believe there should not be an election now, we cannot ride two horses by asking the candidates their views. How will MPs be rung up for their support for suspension of the procedure? We need organisation. If the PLP goes ahead with the election, the NEC should interrogate the candidates. Secondly, Tony should not start the campaign for the real leadership election until we know what the PLP will do. Thirdly, we had better consider the electoral college itself.'

'I agree with Frances. We cannot do contradictory things,' Audrey Wise said. 'We must lay the groundwork for the real campaign. It will help to focus attention on the real election if we talk about it. There are two dangers: we will be attacked for wanting a leaderless Party, and our CLP supporters may accept that there has to be a Leader and go for the best one. I favour Tony talking about the real election.'

Norman Atkinson argued that I must stand, while Martin Flannery said I should not stand in any circumstances.

Geoff Bish said, 'A boycott means a statement should be made about why they are not standing and a manifesto issued for the real election. If Foot stands, we vote for him; if not, we boycott.'

I said, 'I think we should certainly wait for the National Executive meeting on Wednesday before we do anything, and then Eric and I could announce that we won't stand for the PLP election.'

Ken Coates wanted to put up a candidate now. 'I am not convinced by the idea of a boycott. Don't let's go for a confrontation with the PLP.' He thought Healey would win, and asked, 'Is it better to let him get it without a proper left candidate?'

The discussion went to and fro for some time. In the end the question was put to everyone around the room: 'Should Tony stand for the PLP election?' It was agreed that I should not.

I said, 'Well, in that case, because I accept your judgement, let me start with the real election campaign as soon as I can.'

Monday 20 October
At the TUC-Labour Party Liaison Committee at Congress House, I asked Denis how his book of photography was going and he told me

they had sold 10,000 copies in a week, which I must say is amazing.

In the meeting he was flushed; you can always tell by his colour when Denis is embarrassed. Michael Foot looked uncomfortable, obviously because he *is* about to stand. Peter Shore was being brave. John Silkin looked shifty and silly. David Owen sat writing silently and guiltily, no doubt because he didn't think (quite rightly) that his recent speeches had pleased the trade union leaders. Hattersley looked pompous and angry.

At 5 Michael Foot declared. Then a couple of hours later we heard that Peter Shore was going to stand, so we have now got Healey, Foot, Shore and Silkin. Silkin will do badly. Michael gave the extraordinary reason that he had decided to stand because of the pressure of advice and because his wife would divorce him if he didn't. I think Foot has a good chance of beating Healey. So the whole thing looks shabby and calculating.

Tuesday 21 October

There was a lot of criticism in the press of the Labour Co-ordinating Committee's suggestion in a letter to the CLPs that parties ask their local MP to bring the ballot papers to the CLP, discuss the election with members and vote in their presence.

At 8.30 am a car collected me for a talk I was giving to the American Embassy staff. After I spoke I had fifty minutes of questions. I was asked about the Labour Party, nationalisation, economic policy and defence. They were obviously worried about the Conference decision on the use or the threatened use of nuclear weapons. I explained it as best I could. I must admit that the detailed decision about defence and how our non-nuclear strategy would fit in with NATO was something that hadn't been worked out. But I said at the end, 'Whatever you think, don't imagine I am coming along and saying we are not serious, because we *are* serious. I have played it rather hard today because I think it is important that you should hear me saying the same thing to you as I say at the Labour Conferences or the National Executive, and not put a soft touch on it for you. I say this out of respect and friendship.' I did get a lot of applause at the end.

I heard later at home that Denis Healey had launched into a violent attack on the Labour Co-ordinating Committee letter which in every broadcast is described as being issued by 'friends of Mr Benn'.

Masses of photographers were outside the house. Caroline sent them all away, saying I wouldn't be out until tomorrow, so I suppose they will photograph me in the morning on the way to the National Executive. They are a lot of vultures.

Had a thumping headache all evening.

Wednesday 22 October

The NEC, and we came to the motion to ask the PLP to suspend the leadership election procedure. Michael Foot said the Parliamentary Committee had considered it, and it was feasible to suspend standing orders, but we didn't want to have a conflict. Eric Heffer moved the motion. John Golding was against it.

Neil Kinnock spoke in support of the motion and it was carried by 16 votes to 7, a tremendous victory. Only one in four of the National Executive want the elections to go ahead. So that will now go before the PLP.

The NEC adjourned at 2.30, and as I walked out with Norman Atkinson I got a battering from newsmen, television cameras, journalists and interviewers. They asked if I would comment on what had been decided at the Executive. I said, 'No.'

Then they asked, 'Did you know about the Labour Co-ordinating Committee letter to constituency parties?'

I said, 'That didn't arise and it wasn't discussed.'

'Did you agree with that letter?'

I said, 'Well, it didn't arise.'

They went on and on, so in the end I said, 'Would you please allow me to go ahead and get in the car.' I could hardly contain my anger.

I was upset, and I came home and talked it through with Caroline.

Sunday 26 October
The clocks went back so we had an extra hour in bed.

Caroline, Hilary and I went to Hyde Park for the CND march and rally. It was a fantastic day. I am not a descriptive writer but everything about it was thrilling. There were fourteen columns – the national column first, then Scotland and Wales, then East Anglia, and so on, right the way through. There was a huge balloon in the sky shaped like a hydrogen bomb with a mushroom cloud, and there was a children's puppet theatre. It had this element of gaiety and festivity about it, and there were tens of thousands of young people. I would think there were 100,000 in total.

Caroline didn't want to come on to the plinth but I clambered up. I talked to Susannah York, and to a Sister Provincial of the Order of St Joseph for Peace who is the elected head of the English Order, a very nice woman in plain clothes, not wearing her habit. I chatted to Bruce Kent, whom I dearly like. In the front of the plinth was Phil Noel-Baker in a bath chair, covered in an overcoat and scarf, ninety-two years old, and a Nobel Peace Prize winner.

Fenner Brockway, another old peace campaigner, spoke with amazing strength – he's ninety-three. I gave him a hug, I was so proud of him. The speakers were introduced by Lord Jenkins [former Labour MP for Putney], Bruce Kent and Neil Kinnock. Sister Mary Byrne, the nun, upset the crowd by mentioning abortion.

Later, ITN news showed two Communist Party banners and me, and that was all. It didn't quote the speeches at all.

It has been a really exciting day. The old CND is back, stronger, more determined, more united, with the Labour Party altering its view on nuclear disarmament. But I daresay when I get to the House of Commons I will find that there is great bitterness among some MPs at what is happening.

Monday 27 October

While I was in the House of Commons Library, Mr Griffiths Jones, the librarian in the Research Room, came up to me and said in a bantering way, 'I see you had a big meeting in Trafalgar Square yesterday.'

'Yes, it was marvellous,' I replied, 'there were nearly 100,000 people. I've never seen such a demonstration in my life!'

He got a bit closer and said, 'And I was one of them.'

I couldn't have been more surprised. He's about my age. I got to know him in 1960–1 when he was a junior library clerk and he had a little room high up in the Commons where we did all the research on the peerage case. I record that because it gave me a tremendous kick.

Tuesday 28 October

Saw Harold Wilson in the House for the first time since he had an operation. He looked terribly thin but really not too bad and he walked up the stairs, so he has obviously got some strength.

At 11 in Room 14 we had the special PLP meeting to consider the election of the Leader. Fred Willey was in the chair, and the meeting began with a tribute to Jim by Michael Foot.

'I saw at first hand Jim's sense of dedication to the Party, to the movement and to the country. His premiership has not been properly recorded and I might even do it myself, though not immediately, but history will record it. I wish him luck for himself and Audrey.'

Frank Hooley [MP for Sheffield Heeley] seconded it and said, 'There will be other occasions when we can comment on this, but Jim's career has been one of outstanding contribution to the labour movement, using Parliament to fight oppression. I see him in the tradition of Ernie Bevin, Herbert Morrison and Nye Bevan. He has never shirked the responsibility of power. He led the Government without a majority and his campaign for the Special Drawing Rights was perhaps the most significant contribution he made to the sorting out of the world financial system. I was once a guest with my wife at Number 10 and it was most relaxed and pleasant.'

Jim replied, looking cheerful and not at all tearful. He said he was grateful for the speed of the tributes, which was in the best tradition of Clem Attlee! It reminded him of the trade union secretary who was taken ill and a motion wishing him a rapid recovery had been passed by 6 votes to 5.

He said he greatly valued the thanks of the parliamentary Party moved by Michael and Frank. 'I have never been ashamed of being a Party man, despite the media, because in my generation we owed a great debt to the Party. When education was a privilege and not a right, the movement was our education. We joined it out of our experience. We didn't express that in class terms, we joined the Party because of inequality – the theory came later. The Workers' Educational Association, the TUC and the National Council of Labour Colleges opened my eyes to Harold Laski, to G.D.H. Cole, to the Webbs, to Tawney, to Shaw, to Wells and to Brailsford. We had our gaps: we looked at the Communist Manifesto and found parts of it interesting. This is the reason for our indebtedness, and I know I could not have done or been anything without the Party. The need for unity arises from indebtedness. We can achieve what has to be done if there is mutual trust; of course the Party must change and move, and each new generation will want to make its changes, and I hope the questions will be posed in the Party's own way. I know I have lost my temper and was unfair on occasions and, when I was, I knew it as soon as I had done it.

'We must accept that there is a naïve sense of idealism in the Party and that we have to remove the crass materialism from a capitalist society. I shan't be silent on the back benches, I hope to speak, and I want the Party to be a vehicle for social change.'

It was a very good speech actually. I felt quite sentimental about the old man, though I haven't written to him yet because I will wait until the election is over before I decide what I really want to say. He got a standing ovation from the meeting and then he left.

Then we came to the NEC motion moved by Eric Heffer, to suspend standing orders until the Leader and Deputy Leader had been elected under an electoral college. Eric read it out and added, 'Our motion has the support of fifty-nine MPs and they repeat its sentiments. The NEC do not regard the proposals for the election as illegitimate or illegal. The PLP is perfectly entitled to have the election, but we do say it would be ill advised because it could cause problems for the Party and its unity relating to Conference decisions. We should suspend the standing orders to avoid a clash. I am not arguing who should be Leader of the Party' (at which there was some laughter). 'I will support whoever it is. If it's Denis Healey I will support him. The Party in the country is watching because it wants unity, and I ask the PLP to listen.'

John Morris [MP for Aberavon] spoke. 'Nobody has any authority to take away this power without the consent of the PLP. If legitimacy is to be conveyed to the new system, then it is obligatory for those who want a new system to carry the support of the PLP. The only person with the right to become Prime Minister is the person with the confidence of the House of Commons, and no other outside body, whether it be Conference or an electoral college, has any power over Labour MPs.'

Mike Cocks wound up briefly, 'I thank Eric for the way he moved his motion. The January Conference may not resolve the problem. We are here to do a job, we need a Leader to fight the Tories, and I ask for your support against the resolution.'

The vote was 66 for suspension of standing orders, 119 against, with 72 people abstaining.

Wednesday 29 October

Went into the Tea Room after a joint meeting of the NEC and Shadow Cabinet. I sat down next to Jim Wellbeloved who was talking to Joan Lestor, and I heard him say, 'There'll be a split.'

I said, 'I don't think there will be a split.'

All of a sudden, the atmosphere turned nasty, and Jim Wellbeloved rounded on me. 'Well, I can tell you that these four issues at Conference – the Common Market, unilateralism, the House of Lords, and nationalisation by statutory instrument – will not be acceptable, we won't have it, we won't have it.'

I said, 'Well, you'll have to campaign.'

He snapped back, 'We're going to campaign.'

I said, 'The trouble is that now *you* are in a minority; I have been in a minority most of my political life.'

'I doubt that,' he retorted. 'Indeed, we're doing research on your background. You stayed in the Government.'

So we had the whole argument about the efficacy of resignation from the Labour Government. I said, 'Well, I put in Cabinet papers and argued as strongly as I could, but I believe I was absolutely right to stay in the Government. Why should I have resigned when I supported Party policy?'

By this time, people had started to gather round. There was David Stoddart, white with anger about mandatory reselection, saying two members of his general management committee had been members of the Workers' Revolutionary Party. Reg Freeson [MP for Brent East] shouted at me that he was more left-wing than I. Mike Cocks complained about something. There was Joan Lestor who was rather making a thing about the fact that she had resigned from the Government when I hadn't.

The point was, they were having a collective nervous breakdown. They are in a state of panic, and the hatred was so strong that I became absolutely persuaded that this was not a Party I would ever be invited to lead, and nor could I lead it.

Thursday 30 October

I voted last night for Michael Foot as Leader of the Party.

Friday 31 October
To Bristol to the Wills tobacco factory to meet the shop stewards. The President of the Tobacco Workers' Union was also present. Their joint complaint was that I had approved a resolution calling for the banning of cigarette advertising and they were angry with me, but it was really that they were terrified that the cigarette industry was running down, that Imperial Tobacco might be pulling out of Bristol. We calculated that there were about 35,000 people in Bristol who individually or in families derive their income from cigarette manufacture.

Sunday 2 November
We had a small meeting of the left in the evening – Stuart Holland, Chris Mullin, Hilary and Stephen, Victor Schonfield, Tony Banks. Tony inclined to the view that if Michael Foot won the leadership he would hang on to it, and I would not do very well in an electoral college. I tend to agree; I could always take the deputy leadership. But others took a very different view – that it was absolutely essential that the flag be hoisted.

Tuesday 4 November
At the PLP we had the result of the first ballot for the leadership, which was as follows: Denis Healey 112, Michael Foot 83, John Silkin 38 and Peter Shore 32. My own opinion is that Michael Foot will be the Leader, and that will be a tremendous event.

It looks as if Reagan has beaten Carter in the American presidential election, and it is a dark day for the western world. With Thatcher and Reagan in power, the polarisation, and the choice for British electors, will be clearer.

Wednesday 5 November
I stayed at home all day. I must admit that, just at the moment, I feel such an outcast from the PLP that it is hard to face going into the House. I don't go there unless I have to, and I've got a pair all week.

Reagan had a landslide victory, and the Republicans captured the Senate, which is even more stunning. A lot of things have happened in America. The old liberal Democrat idea, which had hardly survived in Carter, has been killed stone dead, just as the social democratic wing in the Labour Party has been killed. It does rather show that if the British Labour Party had modelled itself on the Democratic Party it would have done just as badly.

Thursday 6 November
Melissa came and had breakfast with us.

Got to the House, and voted for Michael Foot in the second ballot for the leadership.

The Russian Embassy's annual party to celebrate the Revolution took place tonight, and I heard that Ambassador Nicolai Lunkov was leaving, so I went to say goodbye. Lunkov told me that he had been given lunch today by some members of the Cabinet. I wandered round, had a talk to Jack Dunn of the Kent mineworkers and to Arkady Maslennikov, London correspondent of *Pravda*. Clive Jenkins told me that the TULV was of the opinion that we must make a success of the electoral college conference in January but he wanted to defer the election of Leader until October 1981. Well, that may be right.

Heard on the news that Heseltine and the Cabinet have announced a 6 per cent pay norm for the public service workers, which means that they are to be kept on wage increases 10 per cent below the rate of inflation. This will drive the economy into deeper and deeper slump. The whole situation is now quite absurd. Apparently Ted Heath, in an interview with Milton Friedman on the radio yesterday, was violently opposed to monetarism and looked back with happiness to the period when he was Prime Minister. This has infuriated the Tory establishment because the splits in the Party are now becoming acute. Industrialists, of course, support Ted Heath, and I think Thatcher will be driven at some stage to change her policy.

Friday 7 November

Peter Shore asked me the other day, 'I wonder if you have done more meetings than John Wesley?' I can't believe he can have done as many as I have, because transport is better, but I looked him up in the *Encyclopaedia Britannica* and it estimated that he had delivered 40,000 to 50,000 sermons in his life, beginning at the age of thirty-five. Well, as I have done 200 meetings a year for perhaps ten years, that is 2000, and that's maybe on the high side. He must have counted every little stop where he addressed one person as a sermon.

Up at 7 and went by train to Nottingham to the funeral of Ken Coates's daughter Natalie. It was cold and raining, and it was a tragic occasion. Natalie was only nineteen. She had married in April; he was standing there looking absolutely shattered. They had both been at the Trafalgar Square CND rally last Sunday week. On the Tuesday she had suffered from asthma and had a double lung collapse, with severe brain damage. It has been the most appalling experience for Ken and Tamara, and, having lost Rosalind last year, I knew how he felt. The coffin lay covered in flowers. Someone stood up and said, 'I am Tali's uncle and I want to tell you about her.' He described her life, how she had developed into a mature and full person. Somebody else talked about her, then Ken himself stood and described his own daughter, how she had become a comrade, and how her last public act was to attend a big demonstration for life.

It was so sad, and I cried unashamedly. Ken is one of my dearest friends and it was a terrible stroke of ill fortune for his family.

Monday 10 November
At 6 I went into the PLP meeting to hear the result of the second ballot. Michael was as white as a sheet, Denis was red in the face and smiling, and I concluded that Denis had won – that was what the rumours were. But when the results were announced Michael Foot had won 139 to 129 for Denis. So it was a convincing majority against all the odds. Michael stood up, said he had prepared two speeches, but he was grateful, it had been a very clean election, he had talked to Denis beforehand and that was the way they had wanted it, and he was determined we should lead the Party forward to unity. He quoted Nye Bevan's remark: 'Never underestimate the passion for unity in the Labour Party.'

Then Denis said *he* had prepared two speeches and fortunately he would be delivering the shorter one; and the points he wished to make were that he was grateful for the way the election had been conducted despite the external pressure (which was a reference to the Labour Co-ordinating Committee letter), that the Party had to recover its electoral strength, because it had lost votes consistently over the last thirty years – and those votes had not gone to extreme left-wing parties. It was odious, but he got a lot of cheering, particularly when he said he would serve as Deputy Leader.

Then Jim Callaghan stood up and said a few words, and that was it. People were staggered, and members of the left were cheering, while those on the right were discomfited. As I left the room, with the press crowded outside, Chris Moncrieff of the Press Association said to me, 'Have you anything to say?'

'I am very pleased,' I said, and left it at that.

To a TULV dinner at St Ermine's Hotel. When Michael Foot came in, everybody rose and cheered, and he said, 'I want a double whisky and another double whisky. What I want to say is that I have got to go and record a programme, so do forgive me. But we will beat the Tories, we'll fight them on jobs and on nuclear weapons.'

He looked cheerful, and anyone who becomes Labour Leader becomes a little bit different. They step outside the mainstream, and now Jim Callaghan has dropped back into normality, as Harold Wilson has. Of course, an ex-Leader still has a certain something, but they lose that magic power. With a new suit and a haircut, Michael already looked a bit different.

Tuesday 11 November
I heard tonight that the new electoral boundaries in Bristol will produce only four constituencies – North, East, South and West – and that means I will have to fight either Mike Cocks for the Bristol South

'Never underestimate the passion for unity in the party and don't forget it is the decent instinct of people who want to do something.'

(Aneurin Bevan to Michael Foot)

nomination or Arthur Palmer, who will probably go for Bristol East. I must confess I am very uncertain about it, but clearly one seat will be winnable; I think probably East and South will be Labour, and North and West, Tory. I'll have to mend some fences with the Bristol Labour leaders, otherwise there will be pressure to see I don't get it. I just won't worry about it.

Thursday 13 November
Had a friendly letter from Michael Foot today.

> Dear Tony,
>
> My apologies for the slight delay in replying to your letter which I can assure you I greatly appreciated. I would love to have a talk and I suggest we might do it early next week if that seems okay for you. I will give you a ring on Monday morning and fix the time; however, if that is not suitable to you, you can let me know and we can fix something else. I am sure we can help each other and the Party.
>
> Best wishes,
>
> Michael

Caroline went off to Stansgate and I went into the House for the end of the parliamentary session.

After we had debated picketing and the closed shop in the Employment Act, somebody got hold of the fact that Heseltine had announced in a written answer an increase in council house rents of between £2.50 and £3 a week, and there was an explosion of genuine anger in the House. The Speaker, George Thomas, would not accept our objections, and said, 'We are waiting for Black Rod.'

He refused points of order, appealing to us to 'Make way for Black Rod!'

Well, Members got incensed, and a body of really tough Labour MPs like Eric Heffer, Russell Kerr, Stan Newens and others stood so that Black Rod couldn't get through the Chamber, and the Speaker suspended the session twice. Michael Foot was good and demanded that the document be withdrawn until the new session, and in the end Heseltine capitulated. But it was shocking that the Speaker should have come out with the doctrine that the Commons could not delay Black Rod, because the whole principle is that the Commons does delay a message from the Crown. After all, we close the door to Black Rod at the opening of Parliament, we debate the Outlawry Bill before we come to the Queen's Speech, and there was Speaker Thomas saying the opposite. Anyway, it was a great success because the Government withdrew.

Sitting on the bench in the House, Dale Campbell-Savours, the MP for Workington, told me he had come into the House in 1979 as a supporter of mine, but that I was so dogmatic and bitter, and all this reselection business was so worrying, that he couldn't support me any more. So I did turn on him, because I had actually had enough. I don't see why all these MPs should sit about in the Tea Room, read the newspapers and believe every word. I rather lectured him.

Friday 14 November
At the Bristol GMC this evening I was asked to say a few words about the present parliamentary position. So I said, 'It was agreed that I shouldn't stand if Michael Foot stood, which he did, and we got him elected even though we would have preferred to defer the elections altogether. My present inclination is to stand for the Shadow Cabinet and to try to get our views through on the Front Bench, but not to stand against Michael Foot in a forthcoming leadership election.'

Saturday 15 November
David Owen and Bill Rodgers attacked the MPs involved in the demonstration over the Tory rent increases on Thursday night and it was all over the papers, so clearly the right are going to attack Michael Foot – which will make them terribly unpopular. Roy Hattersley was involved in the demonstration, so he is angry with Owen and Rodgers. They have gone over the top, and I think they are on their way out, though Michael appealed to them today to stay.

Monday 17 November
I rang Cardinal Hume's office at Westminster Cathedral to convey a message that a number of MPs felt it might be a good idea if he went to see the Prime Minister about the hunger strike in the H-Blocks.

Tuesday 18 November
At 4 I went to see Michael Foot as arranged, and as I entered I said, 'Well', and he said, 'Well', expecting me to say something. So I continued: 'I won't waste your time. I have made a few notes, but first of all I would like to congratulate you because you have given everybody a lot of heart, and as a man who has been in the wilderness since the Referendum it's very nice for me too. We've had our differences over the years, but I have been thinking about how we can win the Election, and I think there are two main areas.

'One, we have got to get confidence restored in the Party, in the constituencies, in the unions, at Conference, in the NEC and the PLP. That raises some issues about the electoral college, about reforms in the PLP, about the Shadow Cabinet balance and about relations between the Shadow Cabinet and the Executive, particularly relating to the manifesto. Second, the Party must have a much wider appeal. We have thought of the Party a bit narrowly, in terms of economic and industrial policy, as if every problem could be solved by setting up a quango. We have got to think of the appeal to women, to blacks, to the wider peace movement, the ecological movement and the regions. We have got to think out the whole devolution argument. I think the manifesto should be discussed more regularly so that we have policy worked out in advance of elections.

'On the other matters, I have been lashed by your nephew Paul Foot, I have been shouted at by immigrants and roasted by women. But, after thirty years of disappointment, they now feel it is worth taking an interest in us again.'

'Well,' said Michael, 'I think that is very interesting.'

I concluded, 'You and I come from old-fashioned radical liberal families, and libertarianism is what it is about.'

We went on to discuss the electoral college, and Michael declared, 'I want the PLP to have the biggest percentage possible.'

I said, 'I understand that, but you have got to remember that this is not just about you – you will be absolutely safe, nobody doubts you will be re-elected as Leader – but it is also about future leaders, the question of this being the future pattern for the Party. I think one-third, one-third, one-third is just about right.'

So he said, 'I'll live with that. I accept that the NEC are honestly trying to help.' On the PLP reforms, he commented, 'I would go for an elected Cabinet.'

'What about raising the number of Shadow Cabinet members from twelve to fifteen?' I suggested.

He said, 'I am in favour of that but I don't know how we could do it this time round.'

On the point about wider Party appeal he was keen. I had mentioned affiliation, for example, of the Indian Workers' Association. He said, 'We'd have to think about that. I think it's a very imaginative and interesting idea.'

Then he raised the forthcoming Shadow Cabinet elections.* 'What are you personally going to do?' he asked.

'I have consulted widely, including my local party, and I have got an absolutely free hand – so I would like to stand.'

He said, 'I hope you will be elected. Moreover, after the elections, when we know whether you are on or not, I will not allocate portfolios until I have had a word with you.' That was a very generous offer because he was asking me to tell him what I wanted, and I want the Home Office.

Tom McCaffrey, Jim's chief Press Secretary, who has become Chief Assistant to Michael, came in and said, 'The Lobby is bubbling with the news that this meeting is taking place.'

So I told Tom, 'Well, it's not from me. I have not told one soul, and I deliberately didn't tell them it was today in case it had to be cancelled.'

Michael said, 'It doesn't matter.'

I asked Michael what David Owen and Bill Rodgers were going to do and he didn't know. 'They are going to let me know later in the week.'

A very full and important day. I think I can have good working relations with Michael. I like him. We don't have to have those awful rows about incomes policy and I think it will be a creative relationship. If I am the Shadow Home Secretary with Peter Shore as the Shadow Chancellor and Denis as the Shadow Foreign Secretary, it will be a formidable team.

Wednesday 19 November
I was just about to go to bed when Eric Heffer rang, and he said this evening's Shadow Cabinet was bloody awful. There was Denis Healey banging the table and shouting at Michael Foot. It was Denis trying to bully Michael; obviously Denis still thinks he is Chancellor of the Exchequer in the Cabinet and Michael is just the Leader of the House, but Michael is not having it.

Thursday 20 November
The BBC had been putting out stories that if I wasn't elected to the Shadow Cabinet I would stand next year against Michael Foot, which is pure black propaganda.

* Elections to the Parliamentary Committee, from which the Shadow Cabinet is drawn, are held every session, usually in November, while the Labour Party is in Opposition. The Leader was and is not obliged to keep members of the Parliamentary Committee in Cabinet once the Party assumes Government.

Went into the House for the opening of Parliament. Michael couldn't go into the Lords because of an injury to his foot, so I went and sat in the row behind and talked to him over the bench. 'By the way, these stories that I am standing against you if I am not elected to the Shadow Cabinet are rubbish.' He said, 'Well, I guessed that.' I added, 'I indicated on Tuesday when I saw you that I was going to give you support.'

To the Speaker's party. I had a word with John Biffen and his wife and with Dean Carpenter, who took me over to see Runcie, the Archbishop of Canterbury.

I told him, 'I saw you on television last night criticising the aid programme and I also saw you on television when you were appointed, saying we were at Oxford together.'

He said, 'Yes, I boxed the compass politically. I was in the left-wing Socialist Labour Club in 1941 with Kingsley Amis and that crowd, and when I came back from the war I joined the Conservative Association. That's how I met the Prime Minister, Margaret Thatcher, when she was Margaret Roberts.'

I must say I find him a bit flabby.

'I have got a question for you,' I said. 'All over the world, religion is really alive again – the Pope is travelling, there is the Ayatollah in Iran, liberation theologians in Latin America, the born-again Christians – what about here?'

He replied, 'It is not clear what my position is. Am I simply a titular head of the church trying to keep the show on the road or am I supposed to be the leader of a religious movement? I don't want to get involved in politics.'

The very fact that he thought of it in those terms indicated that he had no idea that his role was to be a teacher – a role in which you could combine titular authority with active social campaigning as the Pope and the Ayatollah do.

Michael Foot made a most Gladstonian reply to the Queen's Speech today. I say Gladstonian because it was broad and political and not concerned with the details of statistics; to that extent it was acceptable and it struck Mrs Thatcher where she least expected it. She responded by rattling off a prepared text denouncing Michael Foot's past, but it wasn't very credible. I thought the Tories were a bit uneasy.

Friday 21 November

Tonight I heard that David Owen will not be standing for the Shadow Cabinet. He has made a great mistake. The thing David will learn is that if you have no grass-roots support – and he has none – going on to the back benches means you simply sink into insignificance. Although the press will use him as long as they can, and no doubt he thinks it's a matter of principle, he will disappear completely into the woodwork.

Saturday 22 November
Caught the train to Newcastle for a book-signing of the Penguin paperback of *Arguments for Socialism*. A man came up at the station, produced a little plastic ID card and told me he was a police inspector. He said they had had a threat that I was going to be killed today when I visited a particular bookshop so wherever I went I would find plainclothes policemen and policewomen.

Wednesday 26 November
The hunger strike in Northern Ireland is beginning to loom over the horizon.

At today's NEC, Michael was welcomed as Leader and we had a letter from Jim Callaghan thanking us for the help we had given him while Leader of the Party. It was just a line or two, absolutely amazing! It was the sort of letter you'd write to somebody who had picked up your umbrella at Victoria Station and returned it to you.

Thursday 27 November
At 4 I met Andreas Papandreou, the Leader of PASOK, the Greek Socialist Party. I have been in touch with him indirectly for a long time – he has sent lots of people to see me. We talked about his prospects next year in the elections in Greece. He said, 'The Government really has no economic policy and has complete control of the media.'

Papandreou opposes the Common Market and thought the Americans might try to undermine a PASOK government, either by a flight of capital or by a military coup, but he thought the latter unlikely because the army was now pretty loyal to Greece and it was more likely the Americans might encourage a Turkish attack on Greek islands. This was his real fear, as he told me at tea – that there might be US support for a Turkish attack and this would be a serious danger for the Greek Government. He said, 'We must explain to the United States and hope they will be mature enough to understand.'

He and I struck up a rapport immediately. I suppose he is a bit older than me, about sixty. He is married to an American woman, speaks perfect English and was in America during the Colonels' control of Greece.

Papandreou thought his party's links with the Labour Party were very important, and I asked, 'How could we help you to win?'

He replied, 'I would welcome a Labour Party delegation to Greece. The Party is respected in Greece and it has a clear dynamism and virility. We would like to discuss NATO, the Common Market, defence, disarmament and détente.'

Sunday 30 November
Caroline and I travelled to Bristol for a party to celebrate my thirtieth

anniversary as MP. We talked to as many people as we could. Robert Glendinning, the constituency chairman, presented me with two beautiful gifts including a hand-crafted leather briefcase which had been made by Arnold Smith, who had retired from the army about four years ago and had taken up the crafting of leather. It had taken him fifty-two hours to make. On the front it said, 'Tony Benn, Bristol South East for thirty years'; on the back was the famous Walter Crane illustration 'Solidarity of Labour', with Big Ben, a broken coronet and a CND badge, a mug of tea, a pipe and other illustrations. The nicest gift I have ever had. I was overcome. Then three men sang folk-songs and, specially for me, 'The Ballad of Joe Hill'.

We left Bristol at 12 and drove back to London with the engine knocking like anything and the clutch sticking.

Wednesday 3 December

Voted at 10 and went to see Michael Foot by arrangement earlier today.

Michael said, 'Well now, look, I understand you want the Home Office, but if Merlyn Rees is elected to the Shadow Cabinet it will be very difficult to shift him.'

I remarked, 'Well, you have got to have a balanced Shadow Cabinet, you know, at the top.'

He said, 'Well, I understand that, but would you consider Environment?'

'I'll have to think about about it and let you know as soon as I possibly can. I'll ring you tomorrow when I get to Washington, to find out the Shadow Cabinet results.'

'What happens if you don't get on to the Shadow Cabinet?' he asked.

'I think in those circumstances I shall probably take the hint and stay on the back benches and give support as best I can.' I don't believe in patronage anyway. I added, 'The Home Office or Leader of the House or some special policy appointment linking up with the NEC, that would all be very useful.'

Michael said, 'Thanks very much. Give me a ring tomorrow.'

Thursday 4 December

Up earlyish and caught the tube to Heathrow for the conference in Washington on 'Eurosocialism and America' arranged by the Democratic Socialist Organising Committee.

I was met at Dulles airport by the Ambassador and driven to the Capitol Hilton Hotel. As soon as I got in, I rang the Whips' Office and heard the result of the Shadow Cabinet elections.

Denis Healey's place was filled by Neil Kinnock and David Owen's by Gerald Kaufman. Neil Kinnock was lowest with 90 votes and I was the runner-up with 88, so I didn't get on. In a way, I am quite pleased because I think it would be wrong to be on at this moment. I certainly shan't accept a Front Bench job from Michael Foot because, if the PLP prefer Bill Rodgers and Roy Hattersley and Eric Varley to me, that's for them.

I rang Caroline. Then the phone in my hotel room went continuously – the *Daily Mirror*, the *Western Daily Press*, the *Daily Mail*, the *Daily Telegraph*. I simply said, 'No comment.'

Friday 5 December
At the International Inn I met Ron Dellums, a black guy, the only socialist in Congress, and Bill (Wimpi) Winpisinger. We went down to the auditorium, where 1500 people were crowded in. On the platform were Willy Brandt, Michael Harrington (the president of the conference), Joop den Uyl and Olof Palme, former Prime Minister of Sweden, whom I have known for thirty years. Ron Dellums made a terrific radical speech. I found it quite thrilling. After me came Wimpi, then a Swedish woman who talked about the women's movement, then Gloria Steinem, an attractive American, editor of *Ms* magazine, who made a marvellous speech about the women's battle, about patriarchy, the right of women to control their bodies, and the need to humanise life and to redefine work.

Saturday 6 December
The plenary session was today and I sat on the platform between Stuart Holland and a Swedish economist. Except for a few trade union leaders, who do make a difference, the conference is made up mainly of parliamentary élites. But, even when the trade unions are involved, they are still only the trade union élites.

After lunch, Joop den Uyl gave a lecture that lasted for about one hour. He talked about democratising the social services, about the welfare state, and so on. Dull and predictable. He's a nice, grand-fatherly figure but basically a monetarist.

We went to the Bagatelle restaurant for dinner. Sitting round the table were Michael Harrington, Olof Palme, Jerry Wurf, Clive Jenkins, Nancy Lieber (the conference director), François Mitterrand, Ron Dellums, Senator George McGovern, Willy Brandt, Bill Winpisinger, Ruth Jordan, Felipe Gonzales (the Leader of the Spanish Socialists), Horst Emke (an aide to Willy Brandt), Joop den Uyl and others.

I talked to George McGovern, and asked him what he was going to do now he has been defeated for the Senate; he said he planned to set up a new public service organisation to develop alternative policies for the next generation of Democratic politicians. He said he wouldn't run again for the Senate. He is only fifty-eight. I had often wondered about him, and admired his campaign in 1972 when he was beaten by Nixon, but truthfully I found him vacuous; he had nothing of any substance to say.

We had just sat down to dinner when Senator Edward Kennedy arrived. He walked round the table and shook hands with everyone, and said to me, 'Glad to see you again', but in fact I have never seen him before. I suppose he felt it was on the safe side. I watched him carefully, – he's getting fat, self-important, very much the world statesman, and immediately he opened his mouth I thought of Roy Jenkins.

During dinner there was a lively discussion and I scribbled notes as best I could on cards.

Edward Kennedy said it would be a great mistake to interpret the American election results as a swing to the right. American citizens cared about the economic order and competence, and what was required was creativity, imagination and leadership. 'We have got to bring the banks, the Government and the unions together, and we have to deal with this problem of people feeling that they are running against the Government. What the American people want is leadership.'

Well, I thought that was crap. It was personalised crap, implying that, had his leadership been available, he would have been able to win the election. Without criticising President Carter explicitly, he said he had not been able to secure a satisfactory economic order and that, although he was well-meaning, his policies had not worked out.

Horst Emke and Olof Palme made contributions, and I said, 'Far be it from me to comment on the post-mortem in the United States on the defeat of the Democrats, but in Britain we are eighteen months into our post-mortem and, the more I think about it, the more I think that what happened was not that we were beaten but that we capitulated.' It did seem to me that the welfare state as it had begun under Roosevelt in America or under the 1945 Labour Government had got centralised and bureaucratic and authoritarian and in effect we had come to the end of the road; anyway, the IMF four years ago had told the Cabinet that, unless it cut public expenditure, the pound would be destroyed. That was really an indication that you couldn't even sustain the welfare state without looking at the effect that strong trade unions and public expenditure had upon market forces.

Willy Brandt thought that too much of what had been done had been imposed from above, that some of the radicals now were rather like the old Catholics who believed in self-help: people take direct responsibility for their own affairs. He thought co-determination had helped, and said we had to humanise our work and recover our liberal heritage.

I must say I didn't find that very encouraging either.

François Mitterrand spoke next in French, and Nancy Lieber translated. He said, 'I hear, senator, what you have said. The Socialists in France have got strong leadership over the Communists. Most Communist Party voters are now drawn to the Common Programme and away from the leadership of the French Communist Party. We don't have much of an anti-Government vote; indeed, if anything, there is a fear among the French electorate about the unknown. The French left really needs to fight on popular issues, to have a sort of liberation theme and to indicate a real change. We must radicalise the struggles, and that means workers' control and changes in the fiscal laws. France is in penury now. The Communist Party demagoguery will not work and the best response is an ideology to give hope and enthusiasm. Frankly, if you concentrate on wages and social security and security against terrorism, that's not enough. The French will reverse the swing to the right, and I will be President of France next year, probably.' Everybody laughed.

Kennedy left about then. He had apparently dithered no end about whether he would come because he feared it might be unpopular to attend a socialist dinner, but the Democratic Socialist Organising Committee see Kennedy as their best hope. This again I find very discouraging, because the rhetoric of Mike Harrington and the rest is quite radical but they are attaching themselves to a man who is on the extreme right of the Labour Party, if not a Liberal. He came round and shook hands with us all, and everyone treated him with enormous respect, but I can't say that there is much leadership possible under Kennedy.

But Jerry Wurf, to whom I confided this view, said, 'Ah well, in American terms, he is the extreme left.' I think that really is the truth, because the United States is so right-wing.

Afterwards I moved round and sat next to Mitterrand and congratulated him. 'Yours was the only speech that was any good. Why don't you come and speak at the Glasgow rally in February? We might be able to help you.' He and I have a certain sort of rapport.

Ron Dellums spoke next and was excellent. 'I want to put a different view to the one that has been expressed. In my opinion, the 1980 US election subverted the integrity of the electoral and political processes because it was all about personalities and not about issues. The media made it about personalities. Quite frankly, Cabinet Ministers came to the Democratic convention and intimidated decent delegates who wanted to raise important matters. The President was autocratic and dictatorial, and there was no competing analysis. The right wing has dominated US politics for years, and Democrats have capitulated. The left is in disarray and the Democratic Party is bankrupted. The trouble with Washington is that it has no ideology at all, and in my opinion it will be a ten-year struggle.'

Felipe Gonzales, of whom I have long been suspicious, particularly because of his dramatic gesture in resigning the leadership of the Spanish Socialist Party when it wanted to keep Marxism in its policy, said he wanted to add a few points.

Frankly I found what he said real liberal crap again, and it confirms my own view that the leadership of the social democratic parties in Europe pays lip-service to radicalism.

Olof Palme added that he had recently been in Iran, where he had seen people literally flagellating themselves at a religious festival until the blood ran down their backs. He said. 'We mustn't go in for that masochism. Why should it take ten years? It's terrible; why wait? Let's get "them" out quick.' (That was a reference to Thatcher, and the Tories in Sweden.)

Willy Brandt said, 'Well we have been fifteen years in Government and there is no lack of values, you know. We may not be close enough to the demands of the day because the old answers are not sufficient, and we need a new dialogue with North America and Europe about the next dimension beyond industrial and social democracy.'

I walked back with Joop and Olof and I said, 'You are in a fortunate position. You have been Prime Ministers, you are therefore beyond ambition and yet you are free to reflect.' They said it wasn't at all a fortunate position, and obviously they both want to get back as Prime Ministers – possibly they will one day.

To sum up the evening, it did confirm me in my view that there was nobody there except perhaps Ron Dellums and Bill Winpisinger who are serious socialists. For the rest, it was just a matter of grasping for office, indicating that they would be better managers when they got there because they would think up some new ideas. This is the great weakness. Whether I am correct to write off the leaders of the left-wing movements is a matter which history will settle for me. But then why, when you are at the top, should you feel that anything needs to be changed? You're treated with great respect everywhere, you make speeches, you sit on the platforms.

Got back to the hotel and brought my diary up to date.

Sunday 7 December

Woke at 6 and turned on the television, and for one hour I listened to a man called Pat Robertson, who runs a right-wing born-again Christian evangelical movement. It was such a hair-raising programme that it undid all the optimism that I had begun to feel when I came to this conference. This guy Pat Robertson, who looked like a business executive of about forty-five with one of those slow, charming American smiles, was standing there with a big tall black man beside him, his side-kick, and he talked continuously about the Reagan administration, about the defeat of the liberals, about Reagan's commitment to the evangelical movement. He had a blackboard showing what in the nineteenth century 'liberal' meant. He then wiped that from the blackboard and said that today the liberals are Marxists, fascists, leftists and socialists.

Then he showed an extract of Reagan saying, 'We want to keep big government out of our homes, and out of our schools, and out of our family life.' He went on and on for an hour like this. At the end, he said,

'Let us pray', and, his face contorted with fake piety, pleaded with Jesus to protect America, 'our country'.

I couldn't switch it off. It was so frightening, the feeling that we are now entering a holy war between that type of reactionary Christianity and communism. It is a thoroughly wicked and evil interpretation of Christianity.

Went down to breakfast. Nancy Lieber came and sat by me and said to me, 'You must not leak to the American press that Senator Kennedy was there last night. Kennedy would be in serious danger if it was known that he had had dinner with us.' Well, I must say, for the great champion of the alleged left in the American Democratic Party to be frightened of being seen with the Democratic Socialist Organising Committee, particularly when the dinner included Willy Brandt and Joop den Uyl and Olof Palme and Mitterrand, let alone myself for that matter, was incredible.

Then she told me that Horst Emke had organised it all, and he had persuaded Kennedy to come. She also said that Emke was in fact the head of Military Intelligence in Germany. When I look at that man, I am suspicious of him.

It all fits together really because Willy Brandt (whom I much admire), once he ceased to be Chancellor, became in effect the world figure of the social democratic movement. I think there is no doubt whatever that the influence of the German Social Democratic Party played a large part in defeating the Portuguese revolution, and I think they have been supporting the Greek Socialist Party, PASOK. I think they have been influential all over the world in trying to establish a German dominance of the Socialist International. Of course, in the special relationship between Germany and the United States, which has always been very strong and is building and building, Reagan will be working closely with Schmidt, and Willy Brandt will be fitting into that. The German Marshall fund, which Willy Brandt himself set up allegedly to thank the Americans for the support in the Marshall Plan, would be a way the Germans could finance and to some extent shape what is happening.

When I spoke to Emke last night, he said to me, 'Somebody told me that Tony Benn is a demagogue.'

So I replied, 'Well, a demagogue and a populist is the charge made by those who find that they don't have an audience of somebody else who does have one.'

Bill Winpisinger heard me and said, 'I'll remember that!'

Nancy Lieber's comment made a lot of things fit together, and I think the Democratic Socialist Organising Committee is really advocating a right-wing social democracy of the kind that flourished in western Europe during Tony Crosland and Hugh Gaitskell's time, when the

Intelligence Services' penetration of the democratic labour movements was going on apace.

I checked out from the hotel and went into the Conference to hear François Mitterrand give the keynote speech. I have heard him on a number of occasions and I find him rather boring and platitudinous, but today he was excellent. He made a most sensitive speech about the development of socialism, beginning in a very human way by showing a picture of the fist holding the rose and describing how it had developed. He went on to talk about economic and political democracy and traced the ideas of democracy through to the rights of man, together with the principles of the French Revolution, liberty, equality and fraternity. It went down extremely well.

After lunch Willy Brandt gave the closing speech and talked about the three challenges: new technology, the Cold War and the north–south divide. He went through it in his thoughtful way, as he always does, and he got a warm reception. I must say, my feelings did change a little. I felt more warmly disposed to them because they may sound pretty conservative in Europe, but when you hear them in America they are beacons of light in a dark continent.

Looking back on the conference, it was a significant event, although the media didn't cover it at all in America as far as I can make out.

Afterwards I went to the Aeronautical Space Agency museum with Edith Cresson, a French socialist deputy in the European Parliament, and together we touched the piece of moonstone that was there – it was exciting to see and feel it.

Friday 12 December

The Prime Minister yesterday was in South Wales, where there was a big demonstration, with 1200 police on duty and fifty-five arrests. And an egg hit her car. Then there were pictures on television of her speaking at a CBI dinner in Cardiff saying demonstrations don't help to get jobs – that it gives Wales a bad name for investors, and all the rest of it. Here is a woman entirely without any human sympathy whatever, applying rigidly capitalist criteria at a time of great hardship and deliberately widening the gap between rich and poor. The country is ready now for major unrest.

Went to Bristol, and on the way back I missed the train by ten seconds, so I had to wait for an hour. I talked to a couple of ASLEF drivers who were full of anti-working-class stories about scroungers on the welfare state, Pakistanis queuing up for supplementary benefit, etc. The press do a brilliant job. Here were two old trade-unionists who had been on the railways for forty-odd years, near to retirement, pumping out what they had read in the *Mirror* and the *Sun* and the *Mail* and the *Express*. I appreciated, yet again, what a huge uphill job it will be to shift opinion. Indeed, how can we shift opinion, given the continual propaganda from the media, who are the main supporters of the capitalist system?

It's been a tremendously busy week. I'm longing for Christmas. I've got no fight left in me at the moment and yet I know I must go on. There is an inherent fraud in telling Labour activists and Labour voters that if they vote Labour something real will be done to change society, when I don't believe that that is really the case.

Monday 15 December

The TUC–Labour Party Liaison Committee met at 10.30 and we discussed the TUC Economic Review. I thought it was the best TUC review yet because it was written in popular language for the wider audience and not just for economists. I said it needed a broader international section. We had to get across the fact that it was an international slump but there were different interests internationally between labour and capital and we could not use the international instruments.

'The main problem is the lack of demand,' Denis Healey said. There were also international issues but it was absolutely wrong to suggest that there was an opposition of interest between capital and labour internationally, and capital and labour must work together. Here we were seeing Denis the non-socialist emerging clearly.

I questioned the poor productivity figures which we are always being given. For example, we were told that the British iron and steel industry produced 100 tons of steel per man compared to 200 tons in Germany, but the ISTC had shown that this was not a comparison of like with like, and that in fact British steelworkers produced 192 tons of steel per man against 200 in Germany, at about half the wages – and we produce coal at half the cost in Europe.

Kaufman said, 'Socialism depends on getting high productivity. Investment does not guarantee high productivity.' We had poured billions into Leyland with lamentable results, and capital investment did not itself produce high productivity.

So Gerald Kaufman, the new grey man and rising star of the PLP, was repeating 100 per cent Tory arguments.

This line of argument is an attack upon the role of trade unions. Saying that it is trade unions that are responsible for our problems – that it is the working people of Britain who are to blame – has been the standard establishment answer for years. I made this point and added, 'We don't want to begin each day's work in factories with a hymn of praise to the owner, to Weinstock, like the Japanese.' I said we had to recognise that we were being conned by this argument.

The new list of Front Bench spokesmen has been published, and I think I am right in saying that not a single person who advocated the reforms in the Party was given a job.

Wednesday 17 December

Stephen was adopted yesterday as the GLC candidate for Chelsea. It's a hopeless seat but he'll campaign well and hard. Also Joshua had a call today from Keni St George, his Nigerian friend, who runs a studio and wants Josh to do the piano track for a record.

Thursday 18 December

John Palmer, the *Guardian*'s Brussels correspondent, came to see me. He is a former member of the International Socialists, a genuinely dedicated socialist. He said some important things: first of all, that the Labour Party must think internationally, that withdrawal from the Common Market is not going to solve the problem as such without there being an alternative. He thought that Hans-Dietrich Genscher, of the Free Democratic Party, and the German Liberals would break with Schmidt and form a coalition with Kohl, the Christian Democratic Leader, leaving Strauss out in the cold. This would be a new dimension in European politics of a formidable kind.

Sunday 21 December

There was a shrewd article by Peregrine Worsthorne in the *Sunday Telegraph* called 'Gentlemen, Relax': he argued that in the event that I became Prime Minister the only option open to my Government would be to go along with the middle-class, or to alienate them and be removed as Allende was in Chile.

The polls this morning show a 24 per cent Labour lead but you can never be sure. Also the polls said that 50 per cent of the British public want us to get out of Northern Ireland. It looks to me as if by her talks in Dublin and the negotiated end of the prison hunger strike Mrs Thatcher is probably making a move in Northern Ireland that a Labour Government would find much more difficult. So that does mean that the reunification of Ireland has got to be put on the agenda by the Labour Party.

Monday 22 December

To the Friends of the Earth Christmas Party. What became clear from chatting to people there was that they were mostly pre-socialist in their thinking. One felt that all this concern was the middle class expressing its dislike of the horrors of industrialisation – keeping Hampstead free from the whiff of diesel smoke, sort of thing. It was also a bit of a warning that local Labour Parties could become full of people like this, like the Liberal Party with no solid working-class and trade union experience behind it.

Wednesday 24 December
Traditionally Mark and Val Arnold-Forster come over for a drink on Christmas Eve, but Mark has been very ill and they didn't come. I rang Mark and had a word with him. He had read my piece in the *Guardian* about the security services and he said, 'They are very simple people really', which I am sure is true. 'MI6 take no interest in domestic British politics. There was one occasion when there was to have been a peace conference in Sheffield, which was really just a cover for support for the North Koreans, and Clem Attlee ordered it to be stopped. So it was transferred to Warsaw. On that occasion, MI6 had arranged to bug every single telephone within half a mile of the conference centre in Sheffield and had set up recording devices.' Then he added, 'Wasn't Clem Attlee a marvellous Prime Minister?'

Friday 26 December
Late lie-in. Collected Melissa and she and I walked across the park. It was a fantastic year for press hysteria and violence; a few days free of that at the moment is welcome.

In 1981 there will be the Special Conference and I think some form of electoral college will be established. Michael Foot will certainly be re-elected unopposed. My intention at the moment is to stand against Denis Healey for the deputy leadership in order to pinpoint the real issues for the Party, but I don't expect to succeed.

I think the possibility is that there might be some minor breakaway from the Labour Party encouraged by Roy Jenkins and supported by Shirley Williams; if Mrs Thatcher gets into serious trouble, they may try to bring together a sort of national reconstruction Government with a Federal European shift, a statutory pay policy and proportional representation. I have a feeling that the political fight that lies ahead will be a bitter one.

I must do more work in the House of Commons because it is there that the biggest reforms are needed if the next Labour Government is to be any use at all, and there will be a long hard struggle because many Labour MPs are furious at the criticism there has been of their conduct.

NOTES
Chapter One

1. (p. 12) The latter half of 1980 and most of 1981 witnessed bitter and ultimately fatal protests by Republican prisoners in the so-called H-blocks of the Maze Prison, Northern Ireland. Hundreds of prisoners had, since 1976, refused intermittently to cooperate with the prison authorities, arguing for reinstatement of 'political prisoner' status. As a result of their protests 'privileges' afforded prisoners had been progressively withdrawn – such as books, papers and writing materials – and the protests took the form of the

prisoners making their cells uninhabitable with filth and refusal to wear prison clothes (hence their nick-name 'blanket men').

In October 1980, seven prisoners began a hunger strike – six members of the Provisional IRA and one of the Irish National Liberation Army. Several women in Armagh prison joined the strike, which was ended on 19 December following a statement by the British Government, but resumed in March 1981 when the prisoners announced that they had been 'morally blackmailed' by false promises to end the fast. One of the hunger strikers was Bobby Sands who, in April 1981, stood as an 'Anti-H Block/Armagh, Political Prisoner' candidate in a by-election in Fermanagh and South Tyrone, and was elected MP. Sands died a month later, from starvation. Between May and August 1981 nine others died; the hunger strike was called off by the Provisional IRA in October 1981.

2. (p. 13) The actress Margaret Rutherford was my first cousin once removed. Her father, William Rutherford Benn, suffered from mental illness, and struck and killed his own father (Margaret's grandfather), the Reverend Julius Benn, in a fit of insanity in 1883.

3. (p. 19) In April 1980, riots had broken out in the St Paul's district of Bristol (which was not within my constituency of Bristol South East), during which large numbers of police and young people clashed and vehicles and shops were burned and looted. The immediate cause was a police raid on a club, but similar episodes in 1981 in Southall (West London), Toxteth (Liverpool) and Brixton (South London) all had common underlying factors – high unemployment, poor housing and tense relations between the police and young people, both black and white.

In the case of the St Paul's riots, by April 1981 all of the defendants had been acquitted of any charges. An enquiry was set up under Lord Scarman to investigate the causes of inner city disturbances, and, in an ominous move, the Government sanctioned the use of CS gas and plastic bullets in riotous situations.

2
The Deputy Leadership Battle
January–October 1981

Tuesday 6 January 1981
I went down to Bristol to present a clock to Bill Isaac, who has retired as secretary of St George East Ward after twenty-five years. I rang him up and got his life story: he moved from Wales in 1914, joined the General Workers' Union in 1917, devoted much of his life to the trade union movement, became vice-president of his branch, has been active in the Labour Party since 1920, and so on.

I arrived at the party headquarters at 7.15, and there were about twenty-five people gathered. I repeated this history, and Bill kept interrupting and correcting me while I was telling his story. Then he replied and said, 'Thanks for the clock. My house is full of them – that one will do for the lavatory.' Then when I presented his wife with a bouquet of flowers, he said, 'Freda, put those in my bedroom.' He talked about councillors in the old days and how marvellous they were, 'unlike the ones we have today', indicating one of the YS Militant group.

Herbert Rogers, who is eighty-four, made a little speech, and to round it all off I said, 'Well, Bill, here you are, at eighty. Your job is to encourage younger people like Fenner Brockway and Phil Noel-Baker!'

He then chipped in and said, 'My advice to you, Tony, is to pipe down. People don't know what you're saying. They say you are a communist and a Marxist and they don't know what you're up to. What are you up to anyway?'

Well, since I had come all the way down to Bristol just for his presentation, I must say I was kind of fed up. So I said, 'Well, Herbert has been a Marxist all his life, Herbert Morrison was a Marxist, Stafford Cripps was a Marxist', and I left it at that.

Monday 12 January
Parliament reassembles. Norman St John Stevas was sacked earlier this week.

Just before the Organisation Sub-committee started, I asked Tom Bradley, 'Is there going to be a split?' He said, 'I am afraid so, and thinking about it is making me ill.' He's a decent chap, Tom Bradley. He's a close friend of Roy Jenkins and he is clearly finding it all very worrying.

Wednesday 14 January

To Glasgow for the Labour Co-ordinating Committee's meeting. There was a strike of firemen at Glasgow airport, so we were flown to Edinburgh and collected from there. It was snowing and icy cold in Glasgow.

There were 780 people in the hall – it was an excellent meeting. Like most Scottish audiences, it was quiet and attentive. People had come from all over Scotland.

Afterwards Greg Philo of the Glasgow University Media Group took me back to his flat and we talked about their study of the coverage of the Foot/Healey contest just before Christmas. It is most scholarly, and it reveals that the BBC and ITN take on board an analysis of the right and build all their news bulletins around that, and give four times as much coverage to right-wing criticisms of the left as to left-wing cricitisms of the right. This study, together with a summary of their books *Bad News* and *More Bad News*, is going to be published as *Really Bad News* by the Writers and Readers publishing co-operative. So all the elements of the left alliance are coming together now – the Campaign for Press and Broadcasting Freedom, the Glasgow University Media Group, the Labour Co-ordinating Committee, the publishing co-operative, and so on.

I caught the sleeper back to London.

Thursday 15 January

Last night Roy Jenkins said he was available for what he calls a 'radical initiative' in British politics, and this is being trumpeted by Fleet Street. Roy has made a terrible mistake in returning from Brussels.

I went into the Chamber and heard Mrs Thatcher. I must say, I give her full marks, she certainly fights her corner and gets across her propaganda every Tuesday and Thursday: she attacks Labour MPs visiting Afghanistan, or the latest strike, or whatever. Michael Foot does his best.

Peter Shore opened the debate on the Government's monetarisim – his first speech as Shadow Chancellor of the Exchequer. It was full of statistics, painstaking and analytical: very Fabian. He was followed by Geoffrey Howe, who is a lawyer: he was slightly better than last time.

I was called next. I spoke without a note because, although I had prepared a speech, I wanted to be free to respond as necessary. In effect, I argued that the Chancellor was not credible because the Government's policy was to push up unemployment, to discipline workers in order to lower wages; there were some grunts of approval from the Tory benches. I analysed what was wrong with that strategy – it was authoritarian and it had failed in successive Governments since the war. I said we were driven to more radical solutions and I encouraged trade unions to refrain from helping the Government and to start planning, in their own areas, how to tackle the problem.

I popped in and out to hear other speakers. Eric Heffer, Michael Meacher and Stan Thorne [MP for Preston South] spoke, so the Party view was clearly expressed. The right wing of the Labour Party has disintegrated.

Went back into the Chamber and heard the wind-up. Eric Varley gave his usual line: a few statistics followed by intense and violent, but harmless, abuse of Tory Ministers he could see – not a word of future policy. Then Prior differentiated between me and Peter Shore, and he turned to attack me for having encouraged the Leyland car workers against the chairman of BL, Michael Edwardes, just before the ballot of employees on a new corporate plan.

So I intervened. 'The Right Honourable Gentleman is guilty of odious hypocrisy in supporting free trade unionism in Poland while denouncing it in this country.'

Prior replied to the effect that, 'Well, you don't understand the British working man: he would eat you for breakfast and, if you are interested in Poland, why don't you go there?'

It was a low intellectual level of debate but it was worth speaking.

Sunday 18 January
I watched a bit of David Owen on Brian Walden's programme. It is staggering what the media are doing – they are 100 per cent in favour of a centre party. Every programme gives it enormous coverage. David Owen made it clear that he would leave the Labour Party if there was an electoral college.

As soon as the Conference is over, we will plan my contest for the deputy leadership, campaigning in every local constituency and through the PLP. I don't think it matters who wins as long as the manifesto is agreed. While the left is quiet, the right is doing itself great damage with the solid members of the Party, and those people who leave the Party will disappear from public life. Those who leave the Labour Party and go with David Steel would not expect to win a majority in the Election, but they might win forty or fifty seats and they would then have a choice: to put a Labour Government in power – in which case why had they resigned simply to put Labour in power again? – or to put the Tories in power. So actually the Members who leave us are on their way to becoming backbench Tory supporters, and some of them maybe to becoming Ministers in a right-wing coalition Government.

Monday 19 January
Peter Hain telephoned me today and asked if I would address a Labour Co-ordinating Committee rally of trade-unionists. So that's fixed for 20 June.

Tuesday 20 January

The hostages were released from Iran thirty-three minutes after President Carter had seen his successor President Ronald Reagan sworn in. A bitter pill for Carter, a deliberate punishment by Khomeini, and a dark day with the inauguration of such a right-wing president.

Wednesday 21 January

Got to London Airport just before 8, and caught the flight to Copenhagen, where I was to address a conference at the Technical University.

I was collected by the international secretary of the SDP, and he took me to meet the Prime Minister, Anker Joergensen, in the Palace where the Parliament and the Supreme Court meet. Joergensen, whom I have not met before, is a short man with a little goatee beard, looks very like the captain of a Danish ship, if you know what I mean, cunning and clever, cautious and right-wing. He was accompanied by Ivor Norgaard, who is Minister of Finance, I think, and also a nice woman who is the Vice-Chairman of the Party.

I asked Joergensen how he had managed to hold back the swing to the right. He said, 'We persuaded people that we were fairer than anybody else. We have ten parties in the Folketing, and that makes it difficult for our Government to be displaced, as we have sixty-eight seats and the next largest party has twenty-two, so we keep them at odds with each other. We told people that even in economic decline we have managed to reduce living standards in a fair way.'

I saw in him no perspective, no hope, no vision, nothing. I don't feel there is any inspiration of any sort. When I put to him that you had to have some sort of a vision, he didn't quite know what I was talking about. I may have been influenced by the fact that he was very pro-Common Market.

I found it a bit depressing but, as someone said at lunch, 'We have discovered that dull is beautiful', and that's the basis on which the Social Democrats in Denmark survive. It may be right but it's not very attractive.

Thursday 22 January

Got up at 6 and had breakfast in my room. I went downstairs and was taken to the Technical University to the conference on the Democratic Control of Science and Technology, which I was to address. There were about 500 people there and I spoke for 55 minutes. It is an amazing thing really that Danish engineers can understand English so well.

I was driven to the airport, flew back to London, and was actually at Notting Hill Gate Underground station one hour later.

Saturday 24 January
Caroline and I set off at 8.15, and drove in a great hurry to the Wembley
Conference Centre for the Special Conference.

The news had said that USDAW had withdrawn their amendment,
which proposed 40 per cent for the unions and 30 per cent each for the
PLP and constituency parties. If this were true it would destroy the
entire strategy of the CLPD; but in the event it turned out not to be true.
Also there was a bit of coverage on television last night about the Rank
and File Mobilising Committee showing Eric Heffer talking about
'saboteurs' and me saying that we would go on until we won.

After attending an NEC meeting with the Conference Arrangements
Committee, I went on to the platform for the Conference, due to begin
at 10.

The Conference had first to vote in an elimination ballot on the
options open for choosing the Leader: an electoral college held at
Conference, a postal electoral college, a college held separately from
Conference, a ballot of individual members ('one member one vote').

Eric Heffer moved the principle of the electoral college, and Frank
Chapple of the EETPU then proposed the ballot of individual
members. Moss Evans spoke for the college at Conference. David
Owen said he stood by the principle of 'one member one vote', and
talked about communists and conservatives.

There was a marvellous speech from the floor in favour of the
electoral college at Conference, arguing that we want active and not
passive democracy and that there was no complaint about the block
trade union vote when it favoured the right.

John Morris said the priority was to get Thatcher out and a Labour
Government in, and he attacked a speech I had made last night about
how we should go on until we win; and said that the Prime Minister
must have majority support in the Commons.

To this Joe Gormley said, 'We must decide today, and the minority
must accept the majority decision; we mustn't make a mess of it.'

The vote was about 6.2 million in favour of an electoral college held
at Conference, so that was overwhelming.

Then the conference began debating the various amendments which
would decide the percentage divisions: Eric moved a revised NEC
amendment proposing one-third, one-third, one-third, and so on.

At lunchtime I went to the Severn Suite, which was pretty crowded
with CLPD supporters, and in effect in my speech I said, 'Vote for
USDAW.'

*After some behind-the-scenes negotiation, the final choices laid before the delegates
were: (i) the USDAW proposal, for the trade unions to have 40 per cent of the votes
and the PLP and constituency parties 30 per cent each (ii) the NEC preference, for*

each section to have a third, and (iii) a proposal for the PLP to have 50 per cent and the other two sections 25 per cent each.

The proceedings were complex, but in the end, as a result of a misjudgement on the part of the AUEW and the General Secretary of USDAW (who was not in favour of his own union's amendment) the USDAW 40–30–30 proposal went through.

In the final card vote it was 5 million for USDAW and 1.8 million against, so it was an absolutely astonishing result.

No praise is high enough for the enormous skill of the CLPD, who worked tirelessly to get constituencies and smaller unions to vote for the 40–30–30 option.

I wandered round between the votes and talked to people. A man from *Weekend World* was livid about my attack upon public opinion polls like the one done by Brian Walden with David Owen last week, really angry. Elinor Goodman, political correspondent of the *Financial Times*, asked me if I would be standing for the deputy leadership and I said, 'If I am nominated I shall certainly consider it.' I refused all television and radio interviews – except one for the Soviet labour magazine, *Trud*.

So that was the end of a historic day – the product of ten years of work. I think the Campaign for Labour Party Democracy was really triggered off by the votes of certain Labour MPs in 1971 against a three-line whip, to give Heath the majority needed to take us into the Common Market. I was Chairman of the Party that year and I identified Party democracy as the crucial question, and that same year, in a Fabian lecture, I raised the question of the Leader being elected in a different way. We have lost the manifesto fight, but we have won the battles over the leadership election and mandatory reselection and this has been a historic, an enormous change, because the PLP, which has been the great centre of power in British politics, has had to yield to the movement that put the Members there. I don't know what the outcome will be. Bill Rodgers, Shirley Williams and David Owen have been talking to the press all day, and there are rumours that something is going to happen. Something will have to happen or their credibility will be destroyed.

Chris Mullin told me one very funny story. At the end of the Conference, he went up to David Owen and said, 'Well, what do you think?' David Owen replied, 'It is what I expected.' So Chris Mullin asked what he meant, and David Owen said, 'Well, I always expected it would end up with 40 per cent for the PLP.' So Chris said, 'But it didn't.' David Owen asked, 'What do you mean?' So Chris told him, 'It was 40 per cent for the trade unions.' David Owen's face fell a mile and he turned to Bill Rodgers and said, 'Bill, did you know that it was 40 per cent for the unions?', and Bill said, 'Yes, of course I did.' It confirmed what Julie Clements, my secretary, had told me. She was sitting near

David Owen and she said he wasn't listening to the debate at all but was talking to the press all day.

It was an important day. It will never be reversed, and nothing will be the same again.

Sunday 25 January
From 11 until 2, I had a group of people here to discuss the next stage – Tony Banks, Ken Coates, Vladimir Derer, Stuart Holland, Frances Morrell, Julie, Michael Meacher, Chris Mullin, Jo Richardson, Reg Race, Victor Schonfield, Audrey Wise, her daughter Valerie Wise and Stephen and Hilary. I made careful notes. We put Jo Richardson in the chair until she left, and then Michael Meacher.

I outlined the priorities, ie PLP democracy, local government democracy, trade union democracy, a collective leadership programme and a campaign to deal with the media.

We spent a long time just laughing and joking about what had happened yesterday – it was a victorious group that met. Then we began the discussion as to what to do.

Tony Banks said, 'The nomination for the deputy leadership is the key.'

Michael Meacher thought we should let the dust settle, then go for the restructuring of votes at Conference and the reselection of general secretaries.

Reg Race said, 'It was a flukey victory and we must shore up our trade union base; and Tony must join the Tribune Group.'

Frances Morrell said, 'Once the dust settles we launch the re-selections, that's the next step. The LCC is drawing up a list of candidates. The Gang of Three are suggesting that Labour councillors may leave the Party now, and we must concentrate on the GLC campaign.'

Audrey Wise believed we couldn't afford to let the dust settle. 'There is a surge of energy – nothing succeeds like success. We must now forge links with local government. We must encourage local enterprise by the GLC, as in Sheffield. The people locally need our help.'

Chris Mullin agreed with Audrey about going ahead quickly. 'We must link the issues, go for the deputy leadership, and Tony should make a statement now.'

Tony Banks said, 'We should allow one week for the Gang of Three to respond. The unions and the Party should not press for an early electoral college, but build up the demand for a deputy-leadership contest.'

'The framework for our campaign is the deputy leadership and we need a person and a programme. We should link it all to Tony,' Victor Schonfield argued. 'There's a danger of missing the bus. We must focus on the MPs and do this via the constituency parties.'

The secretary of the CLPD, Vladimir Derer, said, 'We should start with the deputy leadership at once and use the CLPD machinery to get it going. We must activate the new college at once. The issues should be both national and local ones.'

Frances Morrell wanted to concentrate on the deputy leadership. 'We must be careful not to seem destructive and cause conflict. Obviously Tony Benn, Peter Shore and John Silkin will stand. Shouldn't we consider a slate for the Shadow Cabinet and run Tony for the deputy leadership plus a Tribune list?'

Ken Coates was less certain about the deputy leadership. He thought a new campaign on jobs should begin now, before the deputy leadership campaign, and he offered help from the Institute for Workers' Control. He was afraid of likely defections by Labour councillors who would leave after they had been elected in May and who would therefore have a power base: we should make councillors sign an undated letter of resignation.

Reg Race said, 'We can't reform the unions from the outside. The deputy leadership contest will be in October and the campaign should be on jobs, living standards, wages and public spending. Jobs must be central and we must point out that real wages will drop this year. We need a strategy for MPs concentrating on the Tribune Group and Tony must join the Tribune Group.'

Then Chris Mullin read out a draft resolution which he thought we could send to local parties and trade unions to adopt: 'that this local party/branch calls on Tony Benn to accept nomination for the deputy leadership to implement the socialist programme agreed at Conference: to restore full employment, to achieve nuclear disarmament, to expand the public services and to carry through Party policy.'

Broadly, it was agreed at the end that this should be sent out to CLPs and trade unions.

Audrey took up the Tribune point. 'Tony must join Tribune because it *is* the left in the PLP. The Tribune Group think Tony should join them, and they are the only forum in the PLP. We won't get the votes of MPs if Tony doesn't join.'

But Stuart Holland warned, 'There is a lot of anti-Benn feeling in the Tribune Group. Jeff Rooker, for example, is for Peter Shore as Deputy Leader. Kilroy-Silk is against Tony. John Garrett has said he is against planning.'

Then the question of the role of the Mobilising Committee arose, and Ken Coates thought it should cease.

Victor Schonfield thought the Tribune Group had no cohesion and we needed a new body in the PLP.

The Tribune discussion went on and on, so I asked for a straw poll. By 10 to 2, they voted that I should join the Tribune Group, with only Ken Coates and Stuart Holland against.

Frances Morrell said, 'The Labour Party is now considered beyond the pale: after what happened yesterday, the whole Party will be under huge attack from the media. We must now campaign on full employment, peace and public spending, and the PLP must fight for it.'

But Stuart Holland went back to Tribune. 'The Tribune Group may nominate somebody else for the deputy leadership and then it would be difficult if Tony had joined.'

Frances Morrell added, 'This campaign is the last push because after that people will want unity and we mustn't be insensitive to Labour MPs in the centre. We must be broadly based.'

I spoke at some stage and said I would be ready to stand, there had to be a deputy leadership election, we would have to discuss the manifesto and we would have to have a campaign strategy. 'I would have thought the right thing to do would be to start by ringing up individuals. Arthur Scargill said I should stand but we have got problems with others – what about Ron Todd? Bob Wright of the AUEW? Jack Dromey of the TGWU? And what about local parties? Somebody has got to suggest it, and when I am asked I shall say, "Yes, I shall stand if I am nominated."'

We broke up and agreed to meet next Sunday. I must say the discipline of that group is good for me. Afterwards, Frances Morrell rang and talked for over an hour about how I had upset people in the media, which I am afraid is certainly true. One journalist was very upset because I had refused to be interviewed by him and had insisted instead on a radical journalist like Jonathan Dimbleby, and Vincent Hanna was annoyed because I had attacked *Newsnight*. Frances, who is close to the media, said I must control that.

Ken Coates rang with a few points, but he was particularly concerned that you shouldn't put new wine into old bottles with the Tribune Group, and I don't think I will join. I think what I will do is to build support round the campaigning meetings at the House of Commons.

Roy Jenkins, Shirley Williams, David Owen and Bill Rodgers have issued a call for a Council for Social Democracy, and Shirley said on the news that it was likely she was on her way out of the Labour Party. But her intention in delaying the break until after the May elections is to get right-wing Labour councillors in and then have them leave the Party – that would be dangerous, and we agreed tonight we would do something about that.

Monday 26 January
Roy Jenkins, Shirley Williams, David Owen and Bill Rodgers were splashed all over the front pages with their 'Limehouse Declaration', so called because it was made from David Owen's home there in East London. It is a turning point in a way because from now on the Labour

Party is going to be treated as if it is illegitimate, and resentment is growing strongly in the Party about this.

The big news tonight is that thirteen MPs are supporting the Council for Social Democracy, and the media are giving it massive coverage. If there is going to be a new political party, which the Gang of Four claim, that is important news. But the left are holding their hand and I think that is right. I don't think it's sensible for us to attack the Social Democrats at the moment; let them come out with their own policies and then we shall raise the question whether Tom Bradley and Shirley Williams on the NEC, and Bill Rodgers in the Shadow Cabinet, can be allowed to plan a new political party while remaining in the upper leadership of the Party. It is absolutely wrong.

Tuesday 27 January

A really dramatic day. Papers still full of the Council for Social Democracy, and banner headlines in a number of papers about the 'loyalty oath' which I am allegedly moving tomorrow at the NEC.

At the PLP about fifty-five Members turned up to discuss the working party report on the election of the Cabinet and Shadow Cabinet. Eric Heffer and I had submitted proposals for the PLP to elect the Cabinet yearly.

Dick Douglas [MP for Dunfermline] said it was difficult to talk about these problems at the present time. 'There is the danger of goodwill being eroded. Nye Bevan said power lay in Parliament. We are free men and women not tied to the manifesto, and MPs have to make up their own minds.' He complained that I had never come to the PLP to explain my philosophy.

I welcomed the report, though it was a bit late; our amendments were about a fully elected Cabinet, open government, recorded votes. They were really an attempt to bring about greater collective leadership of the PLP, which would improve our prospects of victory, because of the credibility problem. MPs at the moment had no knowledge of what was going to be in the manifesto, because they were never shown it. I said it would strengthen the PLP in government, because at the moment the patronage was unacceptable, it was not desirable (I may have said corrupting in character). 'You can't say that electing the Cabinet would turn it into a popularity poll, when we can elect the Shadow Cabinet. General Elections could be dismissed as popularity polls. The problem is that there is no role for backbenchers in government. For example, my advisers, Frances Morrell and Francis Cripps, were very good –'

At this people shouted out, 'They weren't elected!'

I said, 'That's my point. They were useful because they could see Cabinet papers, whereas Brian Sedgemore, my PPS, was not allowed to. For my part, I would rather see whole committees of MPs going to departments to take them over when Labour is in power.' I didn't agree with those who said real power lay in Parliament. Parliament was the place where state power was controlled, and that was not adequate for dealing with the problems of our society.

During my speech I was interrupted many times. There was a really nasty atmosphere.

Ioan Evans [MP for Aberdare] then said that the PLP was a shambles. 'A Labour Government will have to carry the PLP, and the PLP must be democratic. We have borrowed the Tory view of government.'

Giles Radice [MP for Chester-le-Street] thought there was a case for electing the Cabinet, and he wanted more power for Labour MPs, but 'Tony wants to gag and bind us. The NEC has a contempt for Labour MPs and we don't want to be puppets as in eastern Europe.'

Jeremy Bray [MP for Motherwell and Wishaw] said we needed a job specification for the PLP in opposition and in government: the old role of Cabinet Ministers was being challenged, and he preferred the appointment of Ministers to the election of the Cabinet.

Eric said he wanted to comment on what Dick Douglas and Giles Radice had said. 'Their fears should not be dismissed. We are free men and women, and we do not want to shift from Roman Catholicism to Calvinism, from Savonarola to John Knox. But our amendments do not do this.'

Michael Foot wound up. 'I share Eric's view. We don't want to jump out of the frying pan into the fire. I do have memories of the disciplines of the past, and Labour MPs are free men and not delegates. We are all individuals and we don't want discipline from the NEC or the PLP. I disagree with Tony. I don't want a permanent democracy. Votes have nothing to do with democracy. We must give leaders rights to do things. We don't want votes at the PLP every week. Nye argued that the House was the place where an MP could speak when the PLP wouldn't listen to him, and the House of Commons has protected the rights of voices that the Party would have silenced.'

There were tremendous cheers for all these comments by Michael.

He went on, 'We can solve the problem on the manifesto. Last year's Conference agreed to retain the status quo on the manifesto, and there are a lot of myths about the previous manifestos. It is quite untrue to say there was no consultation in 1979 and I don't want the Party manifesto drawn up at every Conference. This meeting should reaffirm that we are free men, and MPs have every power to do what they like. Our appeal comes from our diversity, and this Party is tolerant; we will win the Election, and it will be all right', or something.

It was interpreted afterwards as a tremendous attack on me – 'Foot Flays Benn' said one bulletin later. The right wing stamped and cheered and banged the table.

As I went through the Members' Lobby at about 4.45, someone said to me, 'I see Bill Rodgers has resigned from the Shadow Cabinet, so you're on it.'

I went to ask Bryan Davies, Secretary of the PLP, but he hadn't heard. So I came back to my office, and the 5 o'clock news reported his resignation and stated that I would take his place, since I was runner-up in the contest last November.

I had a long talk to Alf Dubs, the MP for Battersea South, and Jack Straw, who were anxious and wanted to put a number of points to me. I have lost a lot of support in the PLP by what I have done over the last eighteen months and I think I had better be more patient.

Went to the meeting of the left group on the NEC. We discussed the resolution for tomorrow's NEC, and I agreed I would amend my resolution, the so-called 'loyalty oath', to say 'that this committee pledges itself . . . to work together for the return of a Labour Government at the next Election'. I tried to persuade Tony Saunois not to proceed with his much harsher condemnation of the Social Democrats.

At 9.30 I went to see Michael Foot, and it turned into the most sensational interview.

He mentioned the Executive tomorrow, and said, 'I don't see why we should pass this resolution of Party loyalty. Why do we need it?'

I explained, 'Because the Social Democrats are saying they are going to leave.'

He said, 'It's quite unnecessary.'

So I replied, 'Well, it's quite straightforward: if you don't like it, vote against it.'

He was angry and red-faced.

I said something like, 'You're certainly very soft on the right, buttering up Bill Rodgers all the time, but I notice you chose this morning to attack me violently in the PLP meeting. You have really been all over the shop to try and keep the right in the Party, and you don't feel quite the same about the left. Why didn't you attack Bill Rodgers for the "myths" *he* is spreading?'

He was angry about that. So then I said, 'I have come from the left group on the NEC who asked me to request a meeting with you.'

He snapped, 'Oh, so you meet before the NECs, do you?'

I said, 'Yes, we do.'

He said, 'Well, that's very disruptive of committees if people meet and discuss them in advance.'

'I don't know about that,' I remarked. 'You went round and saw people to try to get 50 per cent for the PLP at the Wembley Conference.'

'I did not,' he said.

'I heard you had, but if I'm wrong . . .'

He repeated, 'It's very disruptive, a caucus of that kind.'

Well, since the husbands' and wives' weekly dinners met at his house throughout the whole of the Labour Government, to do exactly the same, I couldn't understand his anger.

Then he asked, 'You try to fix votes in advance, don't you?'

I said, 'No, I try to reach a sort of general agreement about things.'

'You're a bloody liar,' he said.

So I just walked out, and that was my first meeting with my Leader as a member of his Shadow Cabinet. I am not being called a liar by anybody. I was pretty steamed up. So I went back to the left group of Eric Heffer, Tony Saunois, Eric Clarke, Norman Atkinson, Frank Allaun, Joan Maynard and Jo Richardson, and I told them what had happened. They said, 'Keep cool.' I said, 'I'm as cool as a cucumber.'

Later, while I was sitting in the Division Lobby waiting to vote, I talked to Peter Shore and told him that, in some ways, I admired David Owen because he was saying what he believed. I didn't agree with him, but at least he was arguing his case.

Peter said, 'If you admire that, you'll have a lot of admiring to do in the next year.'

'What do you mean?' I asked.

He said, 'Well, there's a lot of fighting going on and I shall be in on it.'

We went through the Lobby together and as we walked along the corridor I sensed an absolute reservoir of anger against me. Peter said I was obstructive; I think my relations with him are temporarily ruptured. As he is a very old friend, I am extremely sorry about that.

Wednesday 28 January

George Brown has joined the Council for Social Democracy.

I got to the NEC and there was this huge gathering of the media. I just walked through them – I have learned that that is the one way of dealing with them. They are very frightening: a mass of people with flashing cameras and microphones which are stuck in your face. I dehumanise them in order to keep my own humanity.

After business, the main item was the motion, which had been drafted by Geoff Bish, referring to the need for the Labour Government to be re-elected and pledging the support of the Executive to the 'programme, principles and policies of the Party'. It then went on to deal with unemployment.

Shirley moved two amendments, one with Tom Bradley seconding. The first was something about the principles of social democracy as far as I remember, and the other was to leave out 'programme, principles and policies of the Party'. This led to a furious argument in which I took part.

I said this was not a matter of Shirley's opinions, I had never wanted anybody to leave the Party for their opinions, but I greatly resented the charge of left-wing fascism that had been made, and I did think it was fundamentally immoral for anybody to stay within the Party, and in its higher echelons, seeing all the documents, while planning a new party. That was a question of personal morality and should be seen in that way.

Michael Foot came in and said it was one thing to disagree but another thing to plan to form a new party, and he, too, severely attacked those who were planning that.

So Shirley read a long statement which she had in front of her and said she was not prepared to answer any points until the Party dealt with the question of the Militant Tendency.

At about that stage, Tom Bradley said he was prepared to accept the phrase 'programme, principles and policies' because it had been redrafted to bring it in line with what we all endorse when we join the Labour Party.

At one point Joan Lestor said, 'Shirley hasn't got a clue whether she is going to stay in the Party or not.'

To cut a long story short, and leaving out some of the anger which was so strongly expressed around the table, the motion was carried and Shirley abstained, so she did identify herself as being unable to continue to support the Party.

That was about it, and I came downstairs quite drained of energy. I don't usually lose my temper but I really did on that occasion.

Shadow Cabinet at 5. Michael Foot gave Kinnock's apologies and said that, as Bill Rodgers had resigned, I was now in the Shadow Cabinet. We went through next week's business, with Peter wanting to speak on the economic situation instead of Denis, and that was agreed.

When we came to PLP affairs and the political situation, Michael reported on the NEC and on the Wembley Conference. He said a general statement had been made at the NEC, other motions had been withdrawn, and Shirley had abstained. On the Wembley decision on the electoral college, Michael asked what we should do about the 40–30–30 decision. He said, 'We have a motion before us from Merlyn Rees and Roy Hattersley "that the PLP notes the decision and recognises that this is now part of the constitution but offers inadequate representation for the PLP and welcomes proposals for change at the 1981 Annual Conference." '

Michael went on, 'The Wembley decision will not be allowed to stand, and proposals to alter it will come forward. That does not mean we should defy the Conference. The likelihood is that a leadership or deputy leadership election will take place under those rules, but proposals to revise the decision will come forward and there is a strong case for altering them. The PLP is right to recommend a change and there will be an opportunity to discuss it.'

I had to leave at that stage.

Thursday 29 January

Julian Haviland of ITN came to see me. He's such a smoothy. Clearly he wants to establish a link with me now because, if ITN is completely out of touch with what the Labour majority is thinking, it puts him in a difficulty. I told him what I thought was happening. I said this personality obsession was simply blanking out the real news. He argued that there was no time to deal with issues, and individuals were what people were interested in.

I said, 'I think you are quite wrong. For example, when the leadership election comes up, you will find it is going to go on all year. It will spread outside Westminster into the trade union conferences and the constituencies.'

It had never occurred to him that that would happen. But he was trying to apologise for individual injustices that he had to admit had been done to me.

I said, 'I get angry occasionally but it's nothing to do with me personally.'

I don't think he believed it. But I stressed that I thought the media were the main enemy of democracy and socialism in Britain at the moment. I think that did register. But if he wants to talk to me I am happy to do so.

At 2.45 I went into the House for Questions. I walked to the Front Bench and sat next to Michael. There was a lot of sort of suppressed laughter on the Tory benches. Jack Dormand, the Chairman of the Party, sat next to me, and then John Silkin arrived and I was squeezing Michael. Then Michael Cocks arrived and there was a lot more squeezing, by which time there was a lot of laughter on the Tory benches. Then Denis Healey came up and there was no room for him, so he stood there until somebody moved and he sat down, at which there was a lot of cheering and laughter. I simply sat there solidly until after 3.30 and then left. But it was a way of saying, 'To hell with you all, I have been put in the Shadow Cabinet and I intend to stay here', and so I do. The Wembley decision isn't the key question; the key question is how we can get a Labour Party leadership that is prepared in the House to support the Party.

Friday 30 January

Last night Frances Morrell, David Owen, David Steel and Peter Walker were on Robin Day's *Question Time*, and it was just another party political for David Owen and David Steel. Frances was good. She said, 'The problem is that these people agree that there is nothing you can do about full employment, but what we want is full employment to be restored in the lifetime of another Parliament.' She kept her cool.

I had a word with Michael Foot's office and let it be known, as I had to Bryan Davies yesterday, that I would be very happy to do the

'The cartoonist presents a fair and unbiased comment for once.'

regional unemployment brief, which was the one he offered to Bill Rodgers. I would have thought it was quite sensible to offer it to me, but Michael wants to see me on Monday.

Sunday 1 February
The three heavy Sunday papers were full of the Social Democrats, an amazing coverage really.

I went off to the Labour Party Young Socialists Conference. As I left, there was a BBC unit trying to get me to comment on the fact that Sid Weighell, the General Secretary of the NUR, had said yesterday that he would like to spit in my eye if he was asked to sign a loyalty oath as he had been in the Party since birth, 'unlike people who had come in with a silver spoon in their mouth', which was typical Sid Weighell talk – high in class consciousness and low in ideological content. Denis Healey had also attacked me and I just declined to respond to Healey or Weighell. I simply said, 'I've made a speech. You've had a camera in there. Cover the speech.' The reporter said, 'Well, we want to give you a chance to answer Sid Weighell.'

So I looked straight into the lens and said, 'Can I appeal to you, as news editor, not to censor my speech? I have talked about full employment, the restoration of public services, withdrawal from the Common Market, and the withdrawal of Cruise missiles. May I appeal to you?'

So the guy asked me again, and I repeated my answer, looking straight into the camera. This may be a way of getting through to news editors.

Worked at home in the afternoon. In the evening, the left arrived – Tony Banks, Ken Coates, Stuart Holland, Frances Morrell, Jo Richardson, Reg Race, Victor Schonfield, Audrey and Valerie Wise, Stephen and Hilary and Julie Clements.

Except for Ken Coates, who would agree to anything he thought I wanted, and Stuart Holland, who has got rather mixed feelings about it, they pressed me for the second week to join the Tribune Group.

I thought I should join the Tribune Group *after* I had announced that I was standing for the deputy leadership. But everyone said, 'No, no, no.'

On the deputy leadership question, Tony Banks said, 'We mustn't lose our nerve. We must proceed at once to contest the deputy leadership. The media will have to cover the candidates, and this will fix the workings of the college.'

Audrey Wise said, 'I agree, but not this week. Let's stick to the formula "If nominated, I will consider". The USDAW broad left want Tony Benn, and the unions will be radicalised by this discussion.'

'There is a problem of timing,' I pointed out, 'because the Shadow Cabinet meet on Wednesday and they may press me to accept collective responsibility if there is a reversal of the Wembley decision.'

Stuart Holland warned, 'We have got a problem. If there is no candidate, people can't respond, but on the other hand, if you stand now, it will be held to be the cause of the split with the Social Democrats. Where are the demands to stand to come from? We must fix who will mobilise the demand.'

I argued that we wanted to trigger the campaign and hasten the departure of the Social Democrats, and that there would be no groundswell *until* a candidature was announced; and we would need to raise a flag to mobilise the campaign against Michael's attempt to reverse Wembley. 'My instinct tells me to go now, and then the thing would gather support.'

But Stuart Holland said, 'Don't. The PLP is vitriolic about you. Just say, "I'll stand if nominated." '

Both Victor and Reg thought the 'loyalty oath' was an error. 'You have got to restrain yourself,' said Victor, 'and give them rope to hang themselves.'

Stephen said, 'You must separate the announcement of a candidature from the statement in defence of Wembley. This is a bad week; therefore don't go on television. The Social Democrats didn't realise they would be pushed so quickly. Let's get them out early, but don't get mixed up in it. The press are precipitating the departure of the CSD.'

Tony Banks summed up the discussion and we agreed we wouldn't meet for a few weeks.

Monday 2 February

Went into the House and saw Michael Foot at 2.30. I said, 'Let's just forget last week completely. We were all under strain and I know you have got a great problem on your plate.' So that made things seem all right. I asked if the Gang of Four would go.

'It looks as if they will. I am seeing them this afternoon.'

I said, 'I don't want them to go, but at the same time I don't think we ought to offer them anything to keep them in.'

He replied, 'Well, I won't. On your job, I can't really do a reshuffle of the Shadow Cabinet at the moment.'

I said, 'I understand that. Do whatever you need, but I would like Regional Affairs.'

I went to the Library and wrote out a brief which I dropped in for him to look at.

At 4.15, having paid my cheque for £50, I went to the Tribune Group meeting. I hadn't told anybody I was going to join so people came in and looked at me slightly strangely. Ian Mikardo welcomed me briefly and it was decided to discuss Wembley.

Bob Cryer, the MP for Keighley, was quite tough. 'We should reaffirm our belief in the democratic process. Wembley must be defended, and Michael is wrong. We should reaffirm the decision.'

Stan Orme was harsh, strident, angry and red-faced. He said, 'Wembley was wrong. It is not progressive. The PLP and Michael Foot were defeated, and it is right to try and change it.'

Jo Richardson was very cool. 'Everyone has the right to change it, but I hope we won't waste time on the fight – if the PLP urge a fresh campaign, it will produce doom, gloom and disaster.'

On the Council for Social Democracy, Robin Cook pointed out that, despite the media interest, Jim Sillars' breakaway Scottish Labour Party had collapsed. This was not an issue for high-profile attention from us. He added, 'Tribune can't regard Wembley as a victory because Tribune wanted one-third, one-third, one-third, and the constituency parties don't like the trade union predominance. We should keep cool, get on with attacking unemployment, and hope no unity is sought in support of Wembley.' Robin was clear.

John Silkin was very harsh. He thought the electoral college was good news but he was angry at the Wembley outcome. He said it was a conspiracy.

Jack Straw spoke; he is right-wing and ambitious. In response to Reg Race, who talked of 'parliamentary paranoia', he said, 'It is a Soviet tactic to accuse people of paranoia. I am against accusing our enemies of psychological disorders. There are *real* anxieties in the PLP. There is not a full majority for the Wembley decision and the left will lose if we push too far. The unions are swinging to the right.'

Oonagh McDonald [MP for Thurrock] said, 'The NEC loyalty oath about seeking support for the manifesto was authoritarian in its approach and we should dissociate ourselves from authoritarianism. We should support Michael. I voted for John Silkin on the first ballot, then for Michael Foot, and it is damaging to Michael if he doesn't get the support of the Tribune Group. We must focus on unemployment and support Michael's leadership.'

Mik said, 'Silence after Wembley would be best. Wembley was a cock-up because of USDAW, the AUEW and the GMWU.'

I emphasised, 'We should separate the Social Democrats from the Wembley question and remember that they are really the first Brussels party – they are financed by Brussels and the merchant bankers, and they are the Common Market Party.'

So it was agreed not to have a statement, but just to say that sixteen people had spoken in a debate that had gone on for an hour and a quarter. I rather enjoyed it.

A demonstration had been laid on by Ted Knight, leader of Lambeth Council, and the Lambeth trade unions to protest against Government public expenditure cuts. I went to lend support, and there were a couple of thousand marchers, with the disabled in wheelchairs, nurses from the Brixton college and lots of photographers. I spoke for about ten minutes and I heard that the teachers in Lambeth who were supporting this strike had been suspended by the NUT President Fred Jarvis. I promised I'd try to do something about that, though God knows what.

Dashed to the Fabian Society's Executive Committee, of which Shirley Williams is chairman, and it turned out to be an interesting meeting. It began with Shirley Williams announcing that she had sent a letter to the general secretary, Dianne Hayter, about her own position and that of John Roper, the treasurer of the society, as members of the Council for Social Democracy. They had both agreed in the letter that if :' ey left the Labour Party they would 'put their offices at the disposal of the society's officers'.

David Lipsey raised a *Guardian* story that the Fabian Society might disaffiliate from the Labour Party.

Larry Whitty, for the GMWU, commented, 'A large chunk of the labour movement have got doubts now about the Fabian Society. The trade union movement fears that the Fabians may be moving away, and a clear public statement reasserting its affiliation to the Labour Party is now necessary.'

'We should write to the *Guardian*,' Brian Abel-Smith said.

Phillip Whitehead disagreed. 'A statement from the Fabian Society executive would draw attention to the wider differences.'

So it was left.

Thursday 5 February
Today a list of 100 Council for Social Democracy supporters was

published. It included ex-Labour Ministers like George Brown and Jack Diamond, and Lord Donaldson, Michael Zander, Brian Flowers and the actress Janet Suzman. It was the middle class coming out in support of a break from the Labour Party. The BBC gave it tremendous coverage – the BBC is now the voice of Shirley Williams and Roy Jenkins.

I had an interesting phone call from Tony Saunois, saying that every member of the NUR executive except one had signed a letter condemning their General Secretary Sid Weighell for his recent statement that he would 'spit in Tony Benn's eye'.

Voted at 10, and in the Division Lobby an extraordinary incident occurred. Earlier I had watched Denis Healey on *Nationwide*, pleading with the dissidents not to leave the Party. Stuart Holland was standing behind me in the lobby and he asked, 'Did you see Denis Healey on TV?'

I said, 'Yes.'

He went on, 'Did you notice that he talked about Dunkirk as if somehow *we* were Hitler?'

I said, 'Well, the Labour Party is now led by two groups of people: those who want to leave the Party in order to fight it and those who want to stay in the Party in order to fight it.'

At this stage, Leo Abse, the MP for Pontypool, turned on me and announced, 'You are destroying the Labour Party.'

I said, 'Not at all, I agree with the Labour Party.'

He repeated, 'You are destroying the Party.'

I said, 'Look, Leo, you are in a minority. I support the Labour Party. Anyway, I don't know whether *you* are going to stay or go.'

'Nothing will get me out of the Labour Party except death or expulsion.' His voice was raised so loud that everybody crowded round: the clerks in the Lobby heard every word of it, and I came home feeling slightly distressed about the bitterness in the Parliamentary Party.

Friday 6 February

I went off to the Commons to support Frank Hooley's Private Member's Bill on Freedom of Information, but the Government had laid on 172 MPs to vote against the closure of the debate, so in effect they killed the bill.

Saturday 7 February

On the train back from Bristol I read R.H. Tawney's book, *The Attack*, which is a series of pieces written over the course of his life, including one about the Labour Government of 1931, and another on Christian socialism. Reading it, I realised that the right wing of the Labour Party, that is to say the Croslands and the Hattersleys, have really stolen Tawney and made him their apostle, whereas when you actually read what he has written you find he was an intensely radical man. I have been asked to write a preface for the new issue, and I intend to try to get him reinstated as the spokesman for the mainstream, democratic, Christian socialist left. This will be part of the battle for the intellectual and spiritual reconquest of the Party through the ideas which it was set up to serve. It sounds a bit cynical to suggest that dead people and great writers and philosophers and sociologists like Tawney are there to be stolen by one group or another, but it is a fact that you can lose a great contributor to a debate if the other side decide to grab him and use him against you. The more I read Tawney, the more I become convinced that his words would be helpful and comforting to us now and would assist in preventing the so-called Social Democrats from breaking away from the Labour Party.

I went to the front of the train as we drew into Paddington, and a short, thin man of about sixty peered across and said in a Scottish accent, 'Are you Mr Benn?' I said, 'Yes.' He told me, 'Well, I was a fitter with your brother Michael in North Africa in 1943.' It gave me such pleasure to talk to someone who had known Michael, and he said, 'He was a nice man. Did he survive the war?' I told him he had been killed in 1944 at RAF Tangmere. At that point a big man with a trilby hat and moustache who was standing next to us said, 'RAF Tangmere? I was the station commander there. I was a wing commander in 1943.'

So at that moment, quite unexpectedly, on a Saturday night on a train from the West Country to Paddington, I tumbled back nearly forty years, and it gave me enormous pleasure.

Monday 9 February

The *Guardian* had some marvellous letters attacking Shirley Williams and indicating that support in the Party for what we are saying is overwhelming. There was also an article about Lord Salmon, who has recently retired as a judge. He had told the reporter that he feared there might be a totalitarian government in Britain in 1984, and remarked that I was 'very dangerous'. Somehow, when a judge says that about you, you really do feel that you are becoming an outlaw.

I heard a rumour from a journalist that Shirley Williams had resigned from the NEC. It was later confirmed, and Ron Hayward let me read her letter, in which she said that the Party she had joined no longer existed. Such an arrogant statement, and designed to do damage to us.

Tuesday 10 February

In the evening I went with Caroline to St George's House in Windsor Castle to address a 'Senior Church Leaders' course. We were greeted by Professor Charles Handy, the warden of St George's House, and Mrs Phyl Carswell, the bursar. The meeting was held in the library, the site of the first performance of *The Merry Wives of Windsor* in the presence of Shakespeare and Elizabeth I. We were shown the place where the head of Charles I was sewn back on his body before he was buried, so that the body was complete for resurrection.

The Dean of Windsor, the Right Reverend Michael Mann, is a former Bishop of Nigeria. He told me that as dean he was the personal vicar of members of the royal family: personal problems would go to him but constitutional questions would go to the Archbishop of Canterbury. He said, 'For example, the Duke of Kent's son has failed his A levels – that would come to me; whereas Princess Margaret's relationship with Peter Townsend would have gone to the Archbishop of Canterbury!'

I asked if he had watched *Edward and Mrs Simpson* on television.

'Yes,' he replied. 'I think it was a great pity they depicted the Queen Mother during her lifetime.'

So I pointed out, 'They also depicted the Duchess of Windsor.'

He said, 'Oh yes, but she didn't really know what was going on. I go and see her regularly. But doesn't it show the public interest in the monarchy?'

I said, 'Yes', and added, 'and there was that other programme about Edward VII and Lillie Langtry.'

He remarked, 'Of course, that was different; but today the monarchy is in the hands of a queen whose morality is impeccable.'

It really was the old, paternalistic Church of England establishment. This place trains bishops, and one had the feeling that it was not the Tory Party at prayer but the multinationals at prayer. They had got Lord Harris of High Cross, the Director of the Institute of Economic Affairs, to speak this morning on the authority of the market, and Sir Kenneth Newman, the Commandant of the Police Staff College, speaking this afternoon about police authority. It was just a top management course for bishops.

The people attending were interesting – Friedrich Huebner from the Evangelical Church of Germany, the Chaplain to the Fleet, someone from the Salvation Army, the Convener of the Church of Scotland General Assembly and the Chairman of the Birmingham Methodists.

At dinner Huebner was describing how young people are virtually stopping nuclear power in his area. I respected the old boy; he was ordained as a pastor in 1935 when Hitler was in power, and he must have had a pretty rough time. The dean was just full of 'royal this' and 'royal that'.

Afterwards I asked to visit the staff in the kitchen, and discovered that one girl, called Sally, had brought *Arguments for Socialism* with her and wanted me to sign it.

I asked them if the oil and smoke in the kitchen really went through the stove hood, because it looked as if it was blocked. One of the chefs, a woman of about twenty-five, said, 'No, we've often complained about it.'

'What you need is a trade union to deal with matters like that,' I told them.

The dean looked horrified. 'Oh, we don't need trade unions here. We look after everybody very carefully.'

As I walked out, I could hear a gale of laughter.

I do feel that the Church of England and its upper echelons (ex-public-school bishops), the Civil Service and its upper echelons (ex-public-school Permanent Secretaries), the military and its upper echelons (ex-public-school generals) and the BBC and its upper echelons (ex-public-school broadcasters) are totally out of touch with what is happening. I was so glad Caroline came, and I think she will probably be asked back to talk about voluntary schools.

Wednesday 11 February

I attended the first meeting of a new body called the Policy Co-ordinating Committee – ten members of the NEC and ten from the Shadow Cabinet – which has been set up with a view to getting early agreement on the policy for the next General Election. There were apologies from a number of people, including Tom Bradley, who is now expected to leave the National Executive.

Alex Kitson was in the chair. The first issue raised was the need for the absolute confidentiality of our proceedings, and Mike Cocks said, 'I hope we will agree on this, particularly in view of Tony Benn's attack at the 1980 Conference on the Clause 5 manifesto drafting meeting.'

Well, as my 'attack' was a retrospective comment on how the 1979 manifesto came to be written, it was nothing to do with secrecy at all. But I did not rise to the bait, although, once it was said, I realised the atmosphere of the meeting was going to be hostile.

Peter Shore said, 'The real problem is – and colleagues must face it – that there are some people here who believe in openness as a matter of principle.' He looked at me and I took no notice of him. He went on, 'And it is impossible to have confidentiality while there are people who believe in openness as a principle.'

Others chipped in, and he concluded, 'I want to bring these matters to a head. I want anyone sitting round this table who cannot accept confidentiality to say so now.'

So Alex Kitson said, 'You're asking for a loyalty oath.'

Michael Foot stressed that secrecy was the key, and we went on to the Election campaign document which we agreed we wanted in advance of the next Election – a sort of rolling manifesto timed for January 1982.

'We have a dilemma,' said Peter Shore. 'In 1973 we had a document ready, and published it before the oil price increase and before the miners' strike. I am afraid there is danger of our being premature again. What do we do if there is a crisis?'

Joan Maynard answered, 'Well, that's a case against our making any commitments at all.'

I said, 'I think what Peter is arguing for is a doctor's mandate, which keeps the Party in the dark and keeps the public in the dark, and you can't win on that basis. Of course you will have to put the policy in an envelope reflecting the current situation. But my own view is that we will inherit a broken-backed economy which will need a radical policy. Anyway, socialist measures don't always cost money. If you bring all the private hospitals into the health service or bring all the private schools into the maintained system and then use them, that doesn't cost any money.'

Hattersley warned, 'We must be careful that we don't promise too much and when we get into power have to tell people, "It's a bit more difficult than we thought", because this would cause disillusionment. We do not want to raise expectations we cannot fulfil. As far as Tony's comment on education is concerned, *of course* it will cost money to go for comprehensive education, and for a health service as well.'

Norman Atkinson said, 'Look, we are talking about a fundamental reconstruction. Is Hattersley really trying to get us to run a social-democratic ticket? You' – turning to Hattersley – 'can't deliver three million new jobs without a fundamental transformation of our economy. And there is no hope if the Treasury is in charge. We have got to think it through.'

Denis Healey said, 'I agree with Norman Atkinson that we must think it through, and we shall all watch with interest while he attempts that task himself.'

So Atkinson retorted, very angrily, 'We shall watch your demise too.'

Hattersley asked, 'What the hell does that mean?'

'Well, what the hell did Denis mean when he said he would watch me thinking?'

I hope I have given an idea of the hostility and the gap there still is between the right-wing former Cabinet Ministers and the sentiments of the Executive. It was a most unpleasant meeting, and whether they will get any better I don't know.

Came home and had Arthur Scargill to lunch. Today Derek Ezra, Chairman of the Coal Board, announced the closure of about fifty pits with 25,000 miners' jobs going. This is what Arthur has been predicting for some time, having been bitterly attacked as a troublemaker by the right-wing members of the NUM. He was tremendously bouncy and cheerful.

'If you can pick up the same votes in the NUM for the deputy leadership that I am hoping to pick up for the presidency, that will withdraw a quarter of a million NUM votes from Healey and that would do the trick.' I began to think that he was probably right.

Went to see Michael Foot as arranged at 4.45. I'd assumed he was going to offer me responsibility for the regions, but he said, 'I put it to one or two people and they were concerned and thought it wouldn't be acceptable.'

So I asked, 'Well, what *have* you got to offer?'

'Nothing.'

'Well, I'll carry on campaigning in the country and continue my work on the National Executive, and in liaison with the Executive, and leave it at that, but I must make it clear, and you must make it clear, that you have offered me nothing and I've refused nothing.'

He said, 'All right.'

Then I remarked, 'I've got an issue to raise with you. I am fed up with the charge that is continually made that I leak information. I do not leak. I am a diarist, I am the Hansard of the Party, but I don't do all the gossiping and I don't leak to the lobby. You had better tell Peter that his continual references to the philosophy of open government, if directed at me, are very offensive. I don't respond because I don't want to.'

He looked very uncomfortable. 'Well, I know you don't.'

Thursday 12 February

Went into the Tea Room at 6.30 and I stayed there until the vote at 10, talking to MPs, including Dale Campbell-Savours, who turned on me on the question of reselection.

'Take John Sever, for example,' he said (the MP for Brian Walden's old seat, Birmingham Ladywood). 'He's a good man, votes on the left, a decent guy, and he's in danger of being deselected.'

Alex Lyon, who was sitting with us, said, 'Half a minute. When Brian Walden sat in that seat he wouldn't let people join the Party. The selection conference which selected John Sever was made up of twelve people: seven were old ladies and five were from the Asian community and it was a rotten party; indeed, the agent there was a former member of the National Front.'

The discussion got wider and hotter. Alex said he had been a good right-wing Jenkinsite until he went to the Home Office and realised that Roy Jenkins wasn't remotely interested in socialism but only in himself, and that in the first six months of the Labour Government of 1974 Roy and John Harris, a Home Office Minister, had been discussing a split in the Labour Party because they didn't think they would win the October 1974 Election.

Chris Price, the Member for Lewisham West, came and joined us. 'Look, what really happened to the Party was that when Gaitskell became Leader in 1955 there was a plot to put in an elite of Oxbridge right-wingers to take the Party over. They were pro-American, pro-European and anti-communist, and they got all the jobs in later

Governments. I never had a chance.' He was really bitter, absolutely right, and he threw a new perspective on the Party.

Friday 13 February

Went to Bristol for my surgery, an absolute mass of tragedies. Dawn picked me up and took me to the constituency's Annual General Meeting. She had written a marvellous report on the Bristol South East Party. At the end, we had a discussion on my reselection and Cyril Langham said, 'Why bother with a selection conference?' I said, 'That's the whole point; we must do it properly.'

Then there was a series of speeches on the deputy leadership and the meeting was unanimous, with one abstention, that I should stand, so in reply I said, 'I think if we are going to use the reselection procedure for choosing the MP here, we must use the electoral college to fight the deputy leadership. This is not a personal but a political fight and defeat doesn't matter; if we let the media pick the Leader, they'll soon pick the policy.'

Monday 16 February

The *Guardian* had a story that Michael Foot was about to or already had put forward to Mrs Thatcher the names of future Labour peers to strengthen Labour representation in the House of Lords. It made it absolutely clear that patronage was available again to the Leader of the Opposition. As far as I know there was no consultation with the Shadow Cabinet, and any such action contravenes the NEC resolution two years ago asking the Leader not to appoint further Labour peers, an agreement which Callaghan abided by.

At 2.30 in the House I wrote a letter to Michael Foot, having discussed the matter with Eric, and asked to see him about the *Guardian* story. In the afternoon, Elinor Goodman of the *Financial Times* came up and asked if I was going to do anything about it, so I said, 'I only saw it this morning, and I don't know what to make of it.'

'It's quite true,' she told me. 'Before Christmas, Michael Foot appealed for peers to be made to help the Labour Party in the House of Lords.'

I got an immediate response to my letter, suggesting I meet Michael tomorrow at 10.

Tuesday 17 February

Eric and I went to see Michael Foot about the nomination of Labour peerages. I thanked him for seeing us, said we were very concerned, drew attention to the NEC resolution and pointed out that Jim Callaghan had followed it. I said we hadn't known anything about Michael's decision, and that it would cause dismay and would mean the use of patronage again. There were 150 Labour peers in the Lords, and, if you had to have them there, surely the right thing was to get existing Labour peers to work harder. I hoped he wouldn't do it because it would look as if none of the things we had been saying was making any impact on the Party leadership. Eric said it would be a grave mistake.

Michael was red-faced and embarrassed and said, 'I have to make a judgement on this, and the NEC didn't consult the leadership when they passed their resolution, didn't consult the House of Lords, and the Lords have got a job of work to do.'

Eric asked, 'What job of work?'

Michael replied, 'They know what their work is, and you don't. Everyone who went there would know what Party policy was on the abolition of the House of Lords, and it would be absolutely clear that they were only there to do a job.'

Anyway, to cut a long story short, Michael said, 'Well, it isn't settled, but, if it's done, when it's announced I hope that you won't say anything that would make things difficult for the Party.'

We left on that note.

Today, Duncan Campbell, a writer on the *New Statesman*, rang to tell me that two years ago he had heard from an intelligence agent that Airey Neave had planned to have me assassinated if a Labour Government was elected, Jim Callaghan resigned and there was any risk that I might become Leader. Then Neave was murdered, and now this agent was ready to give his name and the *New Statesman* was going to carry the story. He asked what I thought.

I said, 'I've never heard it before. I can't comment anyway; it would sound paranoid if I did. I get threatening letters of a similar kind.'

It doesn't ring true in a way; it sounds like the dirty tricks department trying to frighten me by implying that a serious assassination attempt was being planned. No one will believe for a moment that Airey Neave would have done such a thing.

Stephen came over and we went for a meal at the House, and Mrs Thatcher came in to the dining-room with Denis Thatcher and Ian Gow, her PPS. Last Saturday Mrs Thatcher had said that the only difference between Shirley Williams and me was that she was the slow-acting poison and I was the instant one. So later, as I left, I said to Ian, 'I hope the Prime Minister is taking the quick-acting poison. I wouldn't want anything to go wrong.' He laughed.

Voted at 11 and came home.

Wednesday 18 February

Talked to Caroline about the Duncan Campbell story, and her view was that this was the dirty tricks department at work.

I rang Duncan Campbell and put this to him. But he said, 'This man is a cynical, right-wing intelligence man who has given me accurate information in the past; he gave me this story two years ago, when I discussed it with Bruce Page, but we sat on it.'

I said, 'It's probably come back because, whereas two years ago the likelihood that Labour would make me Leader was very remote, today, now that Callaghan has gone and we have got an electoral college, the possibility that I will be elected Leader when Michael Foot goes is obviously more real. Therefore this is more relevant now.'

Of course Bruce Page would be delighted at the publicity that would attach to the *New Statesman* though it would involve sinking to the *News of the World*'s level of coverage. Then if I was polished off, the *New Statesman* could say, 'Ah well, our man predicted it.'

Spoke to Frances Morrell, and she said I should write to the *New Statesman*, which I did, and later in the day they confirmed that they were going to publish my letter.

Shadow Cabinet, and the question (postponed from last week) of the Wembley decision on the electoral college arose. Peter Shore had a motion down, calling for a rethink of the electoral college and adoption of the 50–25–25 proportions, ie fifty per cent for the PLP. I had submitted my own, endorsing the Wembley decision.

I moved mine first, and didn't say very much. 'I have given my reasons before. One is that I think we should support the Conference. Otherwise it looks as if the parliamentary leadership of the Party is divided into those who are leaving to fight the Party and those who are staying in to fight the Party.'

Roy Hattersley said, 'Not the Party.'

'Well, to fight Conference, to fight our policy on nuclear weapons, to fight our policy on leaving the Common Market, to fight the alternative economic strategy; and somebody must support the Party.'

Merlyn, Denis and Roy Hattersley argued against the Wembley decision, Denis wanting to go back to the election of Leader by the PLP. At the end of the discussion, I asked if there was a seconder for my motion and there wasn't, so it fell.

Then Peter moved his resolution. He said there was no true majority at Wembley for this, there had been a mad-cap rush to get it through, and that the PLP should have 50 per cent because the PLP must have confidence in the Leader. Hattersley seconded it.

Stan Orme had put down an amendment, supported by Silkin, Albert Booth and Neil Kinnock, which was to provide 40 per cent for the PLP, and 30 each for the unions and constituencies. He was sorry that one-third, one-third, one-third had been defeated but thought 40 per cent for the PLP would be acceptable. Neil Kinnock seconded. Albert Booth said that it was only the fluke of the USDAW vote which had led to this result and it had produced the worst of all worlds, that there was no support for the USDAW vote and the trade unions were now embarrassed by their 40 per cent share.

Kaufman argued, '50 per cent for the PLP is a compromise. We wanted 100 per cent, and, if 50 per cent is a compromise, why should we accept 40 per cent? When is this salami process going to stop?'

Michael Foot announced, 'The amendment falls', because only Orme, Kinnock and Booth supported, Silkin being absent. 'Therefore Peter's will go forward to the PLP. We can't have different Members moving different things at the PLP – we can't all vote the way we like, so I shall therefore propose Peter's motion on behalf of the Parliamentary Committee. We'll minimise the quarrel, and the PLP can put the matter to Conference.'

Thursday 19 February
I went to a dinner for Jim Callaghan at Locket's restaurant, which I dreaded. There was a huge crowd of media people all asking why Bill Rodgers, Shirley Williams and David Owen had been excluded.

I went in and nodded at Jim, who just gave me a smile, and I was put just where I hoped to be – with Stan Orme on one side, Joel Barnett [former Chief Secretary to the Treasury] on the other, and opposite Albert Booth, Elwyn Jones [former Lord Chancellor] and Pat Llewelyn-Davies [former Chief Whip in the Lords] were nearby so I was in an agreeable little group and we had a lot of fun over dinner.

After dinner Michael made a speech devoting an enormous amount of time to the problems Jim had faced, and how he had been right to postpone the General Election because we weren't defeatist, and we would have been defeated in an Election in autumn 1978.

Denis followed and said how clever Jim had been as Leader, how he had suffered all these pyrrhic defeats, because he would go to the Cabinet pretending he didn't want something that he really wanted and, when the Cabinet overturned him, he accepted it in a gruff way. Denis had his camera and took lots of pictures but I didn't take mine. I just didn't feel popular enough to get away with it.

Jim then got up and said he had enjoyed dinner, and what a struggle government had been; it was the old Jim, jolly and friendly externally. He went on to say he had been abroad during the Wembley Conference, which he had heard about in Australia, and did people realise what an influence Britain had abroad, and what a tragedy had happened to the Party. People didn't understand what was happening and thought the things the Party was saying now were irrelevant to the real crisis. We had done the best we could within the conditions laid down by the capitalist system. He had visited Singapore, and he praised the brilliant achievements of Harry Lee (he's an absolute dictator) in closing textile mills, and going upmarket; we had to go upmarket now, Jim wanted consensus politics, and so on. It was nothing to do with socialism.

Michael Foot called Harold Lever [former Chancellor of the Duchy of Lancaster], who regretted that the Gang of Four had not been invited to dinner; he said it without rancour and hoped to welcome them back. Someone had suggested that his links with socialism were tenuous but in fact he thought about socialism every day and had refined it precisely; nobody could have been more committed to socialism than that.

I write this with some bitterness because, oddly enough, it could have been quite a good evening.

Friday 20 February
Melissa's twenty-fourth birthday.

Bought all the papers, and there was not one word about the *New Statesman* story – which was amazing, because if it is true it is the most sensational story for years.

To Bristol, and who should I see but Keith Joseph, the Secretary of State for Industry, so we got into an empty first-class compartment and talked all the way back to London. It was great fun.

I said, 'At least we agree on this, Keith, that the last thirty-five years have been a disaster!'

We talked about the centre party, and he asked what I made of it.

'Well, I have no time for them at all. Roy Jenkins is not very interested; Shirley is pessimistic; Bill Rodgers is an organiser; David Owen was jumped up as Foreign Secretary above his ability, and they all agree with David Steel and Ted Heath. I think now we have got to reorganise politics on the basis of three parties representing monetarism, corporatism and democratic socialism.'

Keith didn't disagree with the analyis. He talked about crippled capitalism, and I talked about the log-jam in a market economy – we got on famously!

I told him, 'I respect Mrs Thatcher, but I think your way will lead to a breakdown of the social fabric and that actually in ten years' time our view will prevail. But we will see.'

He was saying the usual things about trade unions not representing their members properly, that they shouldn't be political, and talked about overmanning. I told him, 'You sound like Denis Healey.' He said I was a romantic about the shop-stewards, and I said he was a romantic about market forces.

Keith talked about the possibility of the 'embourgeoisement' of the working class, and I answered, 'Capitalism can't afford to embourgeois people any more; it's got to return to unemployment. When will we get back to full employment?'

He said, 'I don't know.' He didn't care about lack of investment because he thought there was overmanning, and he didn't care about unemployment because he thought it was the way to reduce overmanning.

I didn't ask him anything embarrassing about the miners or anything else; but he was interested in industrial democracy, who would take the decisions in cooperatives and so on.

It was great fun. I haven't had a discussion like that with him for ages. We talked about Russia and about defence and he said, 'Do you think the Russians would invade?'

'I doubt it. They are just a big power who want a cordon sanitaire.' I mentioned Switzerland and said that I would rather be neutral like the Swiss – better than wasting so much money on defence. Then I asked, 'Why don't you make *everything* commercial – commercial defence, commercial universities and the coronation financed by Benson & Hedges?'

He laughed actually; I think the idea of further inroads into society by market forces appeals to him.

Then he said, 'You know, Enoch was right in the sense that we shouldn't have had immigration without consulting the people.'

I said, 'If you are believer in the free movement of capital, why not the free movement of labour?' I repeated what Amir Hoveyda, the executed Prime Minister of Iran, had said to me in 1976: 'Money, like people, should have a passport to move about.'

He hadn't thought of that. 'The free movement of labour interferes with the whole cohesion of a society,' he argued.

So I asked, 'Well, what do you think the international movement of capital does? If firms or investors can move their money out of Britain and destroy the economy of this country, that's just as important and serious as bringing in a lot of people.'

'Why do you think you frighten people so much with your speeches?' he asked.

I said, 'Well, I don't. When I make speeches people ask me why I don't make more and I tell them I do.'

'Well, your language in the House of Commons is a bit extreme. It frightens people.'

'I don't believe I frighten people, but I do speak strongly in the House because I think there is a dangerous gap now between the feeling in the country and what is said in the House, and it is important that clear things are said in the House. So I rather deliberately pitch it hard there.'

Then he reverted to Russia, and I said, 'It just doesn't attract anybody any more. Soviet communism is most unattractive.'

What satisfied me, apart from there being a friendly and non-provocative talk between us – and I have known Keith Joseph for thirty-five years – was that I was able to give the impression of confidence and show him how much I enjoyed life.

When we arrived at Paddington, blow me down, he said, 'I'll take you home.' He told me his Government driver was waiting for him and he could drop me at Notting Hill Gate. As we walked off the train together, the engine driver leaned across and called out, 'I wish I could get a picture of you two buggers for the newspapers!'

On the midnight news were details of the first resignations of MPs from the Party. I recorded it because it is a historic event.

'Three Labour MPs, all of them supporters of the Council for Social Democracy, have announced that they are resigning from the Party. They are Mr Ian Wrigglesworth, Member for Teeside Thornaby, Mr Tom Ellis, the Member for Wrexham, and Mr Richard Crawshaw, Member for Liverpool Toxteth . . . All three say they plan to continue as MPs but Mr Crawshaw is giving up his post as a Deputy Speaker of the Commons. Another MP, Mr Tom Bradley, a former Labour Party Chairman and a member of the National Executive, told his constituency tonight that he no longer wished to be considered as a Labour candidate at the next Election . . . Mr Wrigglesworth said he was not convinced that the Labour Party could reform itself adequately . . .

'Mr Bradley said nothing tonight about his future as a member of Labour's National Executive Committee but he looks set to resign: he said that the NEC and the Party's Annual Conference had knocked the living daylights out of decent, well-established Party practices. He would be morally compelled to join a new Party if the Council is formed into one, and that is expected to happen towards the end of next month. Tonight, the Shadow Chancellor, Mr Shore, attacked those planning to leave the Party and the NEC itself . . . He blamed the left-wing majority on the Executive and others for trying to put Labour MPs under closer control. It was a fallacy to believe that Labour's problems and the country's difficulties were to be solved by tampering with internal constitutional arrangements: effective policies were needed.'

Sunday 21 February

The *Morning Star* reported the *New Statesman* story, but no other daily papers did, and that somewhat rouses my suspicions that it may have been true. I noticed *Newsline*, the paper of the Workers' Revolutionary Party, reported it today and suggested there had been a D-notice on it in Fleet Street.

Sunday 22 February

Ken Coates rang to say he thought there should be a Parliamentary Question to get an inquiry or the Privilege Committee to look at the assassination story, and Dave [Benn] had a rather similar idea. But my feeling is we should just wait and see. I think it's psychological warfare of a strange kind, and I don't feel interested in getting involved.

Dick Crossman's *Backbench Diaries* for 1951–63 have been published, and they recalled so much of the period 1960–3 when I was out of Parliament. You see the left, Michael Foot in particular, getting excited at the election of Wilson as Leader, and of course everyone knows how it all finished. Wilson had a reputation for being at least as left-wing as Michael Foot, though in neither case was it really justified.

Monday 23 February
At the TUC-Labour Party Liaison Committee at Congress House, the first paper in front of us was 'Industrial Trends' by the Director-General of Neddy (the NEDC), and it showed a catastrophic future for British industry. Len Murray introduced it in a very gloomy way. Clive Jenkins said, 'We have met the Government and have argued with them, and they are beginning to think a bit more positively about finance for industry and an investment bank.'

Later the Tribune Group was extremely interesting. We were told there might be a Commons nuclear debate on 3 March, and discussed whether the Tribune Group should table an amendment of its own; if so, it would be the first real test of Party policy in the Commons.

I had copied on to videotape a *Panorama* programme on the security services. I know a lot had been cut, but even so it was clear that the security services were completely out of control. Lee Tracey, the intelligence man who was named in the *New Statesman* story about me, was in the programme, and I was watching my potential assassin. It was a very strange feeling. David Owen was on looking pompous, and Merlyn Rees was talking about how he had complete control of the security services when he was Home Secretary. There was news of a plan to assassinate Nasser. I must say I am pleased that I did get in early in 1978 with my paper on the security services for the NEC, and no wonder the security services were worried.

I also read today that Howard Smith had been sacked as the head of MI5.

The news today was that paramilitary police – the Civil Guard – surrounding the Spanish Parliament in Madrid have moved in and taken hostages, including Santiago Carrillo, the Communist Leader, Felipe Gonzales, the Socialist Leader, and Adolfo Suarez, the former Prime Minister; a general has seized Valencia and it looks as if there is an attempt to reimpose a fascist government in Spain.

I have a feeling – and I said this to Ken Coates – that everything has turned nasty, with the overthrow of left-wing governments in Europe and Latin America, and with Reagan, a very unpleasant right-wing President, in the White House. I think we've got to step back a bit now and see if we should be worrying so much about 40–30–30. The whole political atmosphere has changed imperceptibly since the beginning of the year, and the struggle within the Labour Party is a part of this; but we also have to see the movement broadly too. A new and very unpleasant situation is developing.

Wednesday 25 February

Shadow Cabinet at 5, and predictably there was the usual unpleasant exchange. Michael Foot began by mentioning the fact that leaks from the previous meeting had occurred. So Eric Varley said, 'I would like to say that it is very inhibiting having Tony Benn writing down everything we say.'

Michael replied, 'Well, people keep diaries. I'm not much in favour of them, but people do and can keep them.'

'I notice that in a letter to the *Guardian* recently Tony said that he had kept a note of a Cabinet discussion in 1974 – about who had spoken and so on,' remarked Eric.

I kept my mouth shut while this was going on. I thought: why be drawn into a row with Eric Varley?

Denis Healey suggested, 'Let's ban all diaries.'

Michael tried to defuse it. 'Well, people have funny habits.'

I let it go by, but it was just nasty.

On the nuclear weapons debate on Tuesday, we were told that the Government motion, which was originally drafted in terms of the Trident missile, which the Labour Party has agreed to oppose, has now been amended to include the endorsement of Cruise missiles. The object, obviously, is to embarrass the Opposition, and by doing so the Cabinet has been very clever. Many members of the Shadow Cabinet are in favour of Cruise missiles – Denis Healey, Roy Hattersley, Roy Mason, Eric Varley, etc. A number of MPs including myself will vote against the main Government motion. I am not prepared to sit in the Shadow Cabinet and vote in a way contrary to Party policy, and I can see there is going to be trouble ahead about that. It was deferred until we have seen the words of the Government motion.

Before I went to bed, I read the *Bristol Evening Post*, in which there was a letter from Pastor Shackford, 'Pastor Warns on Benn Remarks'. This pastor, of the Pentecostal Holiness Church in Bristol, wrote 'I warn believers of Jesus Christ to beware of Mr Benn's remarks . . . for part of that insidious teaching (Marxism) is to make "friends" with the religious and then to eventually exterminate them. Such is happening all around the world wherever there is Communist Government in control.'

So I rang up Pastor Shackford and had a long argument with him over the phone. I was extremely angry. I said, 'There's not a word of truth in what you say. I am not a Marxist, not a communist, and it isn't even true that in communist countries the church is exterminated. Look at Poland.'

'I have a very different political view from you, Mr Benn,' he replied.

'Maybe you do; that's your business. I am not complaining about that. I may have a different theological view from you, but you shouldn't lie.'

'I didn't lie. I wasn't getting at you.'

'Of course you were,' I said, and read him the passage. I went on, 'I was invited to Windsor Castle recently to talk to several bishops, Methodists and the Salvation Army. I have been invited to the Baptist College in Bristol, and to give sermons in Oxford and Cambridge, and I have been asked to do BBC's "Thought for the Day". You have absolutely no right to say that, and you should apologise.'

He said, 'I wasn't meaning to be—'

I said, 'You were. It's a sin against the Holy Ghost.'

'That's not what a sin against the Holy Ghost is.'

I said, 'Oh yes it is. It is telling a lie about someone who is part of the family of man.'

He was a real American-type born-again Christian.

In the end I said, 'May God forgive you, Pastor Shackford', and I rang off. I was cross with myself for having lost my temper, but I was glad in the end – he won't do it again, even though he probably won't write a letter of apology.

Thursday 26 February

Following my difference with Michael Foot over peers, I dug out several items on the House of Lords, including the Conference resolution to abolish it, which was proposed by Jack Jones when he was General Secretary of the TGWU and carried by about 6 million votes to 91,000: and the resolution of the NEC which appealed to the Labour Party Leader not to make more peers and to Labour people not to accept peerages.

Having done so, I went off to BBC's *Newsnight* who had asked me on to discuss it. I went upstairs and sat in the studio next to Peter Snow, whom I do dislike.

The Lords item reported that Michael Foot was under pressure to appoint peers, that this had created trouble in the Party, and that Mikardo had seen him. Then they showed Jack Jones moving the resolution at the 1977 Conference, the whole Conference cheering. It looked marvellous. When they came to me, Peter Snow's whole object was to create a division between me and Michael Foot. I said there were three ways of dealing with the problem – to try to get more peers to turn up to the Lords (because most of them don't); to create new peers, which would cause dismay; or to disengage, which a lot of people thought we should now do.

At the end, Peter Snow said, 'You've only been in the Shadow Cabinet a few weeks, and yet you are at odds with your Leader, you're at odds with them over the Wembley Conference.'

'I thought we were going to talk about the House of Lords,' I replied. 'What do you think goes on in Cabinets and Shadow Cabinets? Mrs Thatcher sat in Cabinet under Ted Heath and disagreed with everything. Dick Crossman's diaries and Barbara Castle's diaries describe Party disagreements. Maybe even you here disagree among yourselves – there might even be people in *Newsnight* who support the blacks in South Africa, or strikers in Britain.'

'Well, don't you think this has led to disenchantment with the Party? Aren't you responsible for splitting the Party?'

'Not at all. And I think the BBC has been running a campaign against the Labour Party for years, particularly *Newsnight*.'

Then he said, 'We've only got thirty seconds left . . .'

So I concluded, 'Well, I thought you would cut me off when I got to the real point, which is that there is documented evidence of bias in the BBC. The Glasgow University Media Group has interesting findings, which you will never discuss on television – that is what it is about.'

I looked cheerful, and on the way out a couple of people wished me luck, so I came away feeling better than when I had gone in.

Friday 27 February

Had a long telephone conversation with Frances Morrell, who is extremely depressed because the left is in a state of disarray at the moment. Also she wonders whether she is going to get into Parliament, and I can understand the anxiety.

In the evening I went to a reception organised by the TGWU from the area round Bridgewater, Taunton and Wiveliscombe. A woman had been paid to sing and dance and I felt sorry for her because Somerset people are very taciturn and they didn't exactly enter into the spirit of it, but she managed to get four men to put funny hats on and play tambourines.

Saturday 28 February

Travelled to Bristol and was met by Dawn, who told me I wasn't doing enough in the constituency; I tended to appear like Lord Bountiful, and I should pop into ward meetings for a bit and listen to what members were saying. I wasn't appearing at local events, wasn't involved in the Labour Group, and so on. She was nice about it, but it was a serious criticism and I have sensed in a way that, with all the meetings I do around the country, I don't do enough in Bristol.

Monday 2 March

The day twelve Social Democrats resigned the Labour whip.

Worked at home all morning and had a mass of telephone calls fixing appointments.

To ITN for an interview on the Social Democrats for ATV in the Midlands. I made it clear and straightforward: they were a Common Market party; we were going to get out of the Common Market; this was how we were going to do so; we were against Cruise, Trident and

Polaris; we wanted full employment, and so on. I declined to talk about individuals and just talked about policy. I was pleased with it.

In the evening I watched the second part of the *Panorama* programme on the security services – all about tapping and bugging. The former Yorkshire Chief Constable said he was not responsible in any way to political chiefs and that matters of security were the concern of the law – by which he meant himself.

The resignation of the Social Democrat MPs was the big news, and it is an important moment in British political history; but I don't think you can invent a political party in Parliament and I don't believe there will be the long-term support they expect.

Tuesday 3 March

I have a great sense of relief at the resignation of the twelve Labour MPs and, I think, nine Labour peers – among them, Alf Robens, Hartley Shawcross, Dick Marsh, George Brown, Ray Gunter, Roy Jenkins, Herbert Bowden, David Owen, Shirley Williams, Bill Rodgers, Edmund Dell and Jack Diamond.

Worked at home in the morning, then went to a meeting organised by the Middle East Sub-Committee of the Labour Party. Nick Butler, who is a member of the Fabian Society, introduced it with a paper on oil and foreign policy; he was extremely good. He told me before the meeting that there would be an attempt to keep Shirley Williams in the Fabian Society as a full member and use her on Fabian platforms. If that's the case, there will be a hell of a row and the Labour Party will disaffiliate the Fabian Society.

Nick talked about the old structure of power in the Middle East, about the changes, and the key strategic interests, the exchange of arms for oil.

Had a bite to eat, then went to the Library to read the *Baptist Times* and the *Universe* covering my talk at Windsor Castle. The *Baptist Times* was disgraceful – 'Wedgie Lashes the Churchmen'. I feel let down and I have had a couple of angry letters from Baptist ministers.

The Home Affairs Committee of the PLP met to discuss the Government's desire to extend the Prevention of Terrorism Act for a further year. Alex Lyon was in the chair and he gave us the figures: some 5000 people had been arrested under the Prevention of Terrorism Act, but only 280 had been sentenced, I think, and a number had been deported from Britain to Northern Ireland. The police originally didn't favour the Act, and it was passed at the time of the Birmingham bombings, though the bill had been drafted before the bombings – which I think is very significant. The third provision of the Act, I might add, is to proscribe the IRA in Britain.

Shirley Summerskill said, 'I think it would be unwise to criticise that part of the Act which proscribes the IRA.'

Clive Soley thought the Act just helped recruit for the IRA and they loved it.

Andrew Bennett said the Act had been a temporary measure, and the Party should take it up and get it phased out instead of leaving activity to backbenchers. 'It is used to harass the Irish,' he said.

Kilroy-Silk agreed, 'We should phase it out.'

'Should the Party reverse the line it took in government? We can't stand on our head,' George Cunningham said.

Alex pointed out that of the three provisions – the proscription of the IRA, the exclusion of people, and arrest for a week without trial – arrest had to go to the courts, and it was there that the police were unable to produce evidence.

The purpose of the Act was not to prevent terrorism, Joan Maynard believed, but to collect information, and it infringed civil liberties. 'We should admit we were wrong in government.'

Martin Flannery stressed the point that the IRA liked the Act. It terrorised the Irish and even left-wing MPs were terrorised because they didn't want to vote against it.

'The exclusion clause, of course, breaks the unity of the United Kingdom, which is why Enoch Powell is against it,' said George Cunningham.

Roy Hattersley was sitting there, so I turned to him. 'I don't know whether you were in the Cabinet at the time the Act was passed' (knowing he didn't get into the Cabinet until six months or a year later) 'but it was a panic response to the Birmingham bombings. They were emergency powers, really, and we could quite easily now say that they suffer from serious defects. There are constitutional objections to restriction or internal banishment. The powers are arbitrary because they don't apply to everybody in respect of exclusion, and the balance is wrong between civil liberties and safety; and anyway they were meant to be temporary.'

Roy Hattersley remarked, 'Well, we've got to consider those in the Shadow Cabinet who have responsibilities for Northern Ireland. We could change our line, though better to stand on principle and say we are against banishment and the rest. But on proscription it is a political matter. Perhaps we could put a reasoned amendment down.' Roy's was quite a good response actually.

After more contributions, Alex said, 'Can I sum up and indicate that our view is that we should oppose continuation of the Act? The Northern Ireland Group of the PLP is opposed, so that will help.'

Had a meal in the Tea Room, and talked to a few people. Then there was a straight vote against the independent nuclear deterrent by the Party led by Michael Foot – marvellous! Came home, and I feel the tension is easing a bit.

Wednesday 4 March

Worked at home and signed a mass of letters.

Vincent Hanna rang, and suggested I should meet the NUJ chapel at BBC TV. He told me some interesting things. When the recent *Panorama* programmes on the Security Services were being made, the Director-General, Ian Trethowan, had taken away the script and had asked for a video of both programmes to be sent to him – an unusual procedure – instead of watching it in the viewing room. He took then away for a fortnight and when the script came back it had been corrected in two hands, his and another, and he called for cuts in the video. He wrote a minute stating that some Labour MPs were in the hands of the KGB. Secondly, he wrote that none of the producers were to make any contact with past members of the security services. Thirdly, he said the BBC was not in the business of examining the security services, and he tried to cut out an interview with Gordon Winter (an ex-security services man) in which Winter said, 'Our boys are in every left-wing organisation that is bigger than a football team in Britain, either as chairmen or vice-chairmen, and, if we need to, we can pull out individuals in the key positions and put our people in.' Now that's a quote from memory of what Vincent Hanna said, and it is a very interesting piece of information.

Got to the PLP meeting a bit late, and the debate was in full swing over the motion from the Shadow Cabinet regretting Wembley and proposing that the PLP should have at least 50 per cent of the vote in the electoral college. Michael Foot had opened the debate and Eric Heffer and Bob Cryer had spoken. (Bob had proposed the amendment maintaining the Wembley decision.)

Alex Lyon was on his feet, and he said, 'Look, the worst that could happen would be for Tony Benn to be Prime Minister, and Eric Heffer Chancellor of the Exchequer, and, whatever you may say about that, it would not be undemocratic because there is no one in the Party, no one at all, who wants an eastern European-type state. We only give credence to our enemies if we talk as if there were. I have absolute confidence in the democratic bona fides of all the members of the Party in Parliament. What we want is a policy, and we want to know what the policy is. What is our policy on nuclear weapons? I am not a unilateralist, but if the Party's policy is unilateralist I'll accept it, just as the others had to accept it when it wasn't. What is our policy on Europe? What is our policy on full employment? The trouble is that reselection is eating into our hearts at the moment. We're not talking about nuclear policy or Europe or full employment in the Tea Room, all we are talking about is reselection, and in a year's time, when we have all been safely reselected, I hope things will be better.' An excellent speech.

Then Joan Lestor said, 'I agree with Alex that reselection is the main fear. It is a neurosis, and what we need is to get on to policy. I favoured one-third, one-third, one-third, but we should accept that it is 40–30–30. We must get back to policy this year.'

Then John Morris spoke. 'We've gone down the wrong road with this college. The PLP role is a very important one, and, the smaller the PLP part in it, the greater the conflict. If the Leader is not accepted by the PLP when elected by the college, it will be a disaster. Constitutionally, the Prime Minister, when appointed, has to carry the House of Commons.'

He went on, 'Tony Benn, in a speech on the eve of the Wembley Conference, was reported as saying, "We will go on until we win", and therefore it is hypocrisy for him to sign Bob Cryer's amendment, which says that if you reopen this issue it will "exacerbate the divisions within the party and detract from the fight against the Tories".' John Morris was loudly cheered.

Went to the Shadow Cabinet at 5, and Mike Cocks formally reported the resignation of the twelve Social Democrat MPs.

Then we came to the Prevention of Terrorism Act. Roy Hattersley reported on the Home Affairs Group and concluded, 'I don't think we really can support this bill in its eighth year, but I will be guided by what my colleagues think.'

Merlyn Rees declared that the terror attacks were still going on, that the IRA was Marxist, the Provisional IRA were the main murderers, there was a revolutionary socialist party, there was the UDA and the UVF. His son had been under threat and he had sent him away to Canada. What an agony it was to have a police guard all the time! Public life was hardly worthwhile, and so he went on.

Of course I have some sympathy for him.

Don Concannon said that his family too had been under perpetual threat while he was Minister of State for Northern Ireland, that the police and the Intelligence Services wanted this Act to be maintained.

Gerald Kaufman had been against the Act but, having heard the discussion, he now thought we should maintain it, and perhaps Privy Councillors should look at the working of the Act.

I supported Roy Hattersley. 'Nobody doubts the mood of the Cabinet after the Birmingham bombings, but that shouldn't determine the policy seven years later. The Intelligence Services want it, of course; they always want intelligence and information.' I pointed out what the former Chief Constable of West Yorkshire had said on *Panorama* – that 'anyone who thinks there shouldn't be a file on him probably should have a file on him'.

I continued, 'There are the personal dangers to our colleagues who have done this difficult job but the Prevention of Terrorism Act doesn't prevent terrorism. I don't think the Act is justified on those grounds. It was temporary but, above all, it is a defective Act. For example, it does not exclude Irish born here, and arrest can become a form of harassment. I think we should put down a motion of some sort in the Commons because it would be a mistake to allow it to go through without expressing our reasons for opposition, and then force the Government to do do something about it. You mustn't think that public opinion would necessarily be against the repeal; there is a great deal of anxiety about civil liberties, there have been these two *Panorama* programmes.'

Peter Shore was for keeping it. Neil Kinnock said somebody should speak to Whitelaw but he didn't want us to propose a motion of any kind.

In the end, it was left that Roy Hattersley would go and see Whitelaw, and the whole thing is back safely in consensus politics, Michael Foot not wishing to make any move. I did support Roy Hattersley as best I could, and he was courageous – I give him full marks for that.

At the underground station coming home I bought a bar of chocolate and two women said, 'You'll raise your blood sugar level!' So I sat beside them and chatted. One was the Chief Nursing Officer of the Fleet, the equivalent of a brigadier in rank. The other was a naval captain, the Deputy Matron-in-Chief of the Fleet. They had been to a party and were a bit tight: we had a lovely jolly talk.

Melissa and I watched the news and it was fascinating. Mrs Thatcher was giving a speech in a church about Christian values and monetarism, and some young people got up and shouted, 'Jobs not bombs!' They were Young Communists, and of course that was all she needed. She said in her most pious way, 'Now you know what I am fighting against.' It will have given the Communist Party a tremendous boost. They were very courageous, well-scrubbed, decent kids.

Then President Reagan was interviewed. He said Mrs Thatcher had admitted to him that she should have made more cuts sooner, but of course she had terrible problems because the Labour Party was split and the left-wing was now dominant. As if that had in any way affected her position!

Thursday 5 March

Melissa stayed until 1 am, so I didn't get to bed until late and I overslept. Came down to my office at 10 – absolutely disgraceful, might have been a Sunday.

Went to the House, where I had a meeting with David Holmes, who was a BBC lobby correspondent and is now chief assistant to the Director-General. I said I hoped he took seriously the left's criticism of the BBC.

'We don't know what to make of it.'

I said, 'At least the bias is all confirmed now because people in the

BBC regularly send us the minutes of your News and Current Affairs meetings.'

He asked, 'Is that how they got in *Labour Weekly*?'

'Yes. We've got lots of friends in the BBC now. You have been getting hold of Labour Party minutes and NEC papers and publishing them, so now we are doing the same to you because you are the biggest political force in Britain. Moreover, there is an MI5 man at Broadcasting House.'

He said, 'That's not true.'

'I think it is true,' I told him. 'Don't forget, I have been a security Minister. What about Ian Trethowan taking away the *Panorama* transcripts for a fortnight and showing them to MI5 and MI6?'

He said, 'That's quite untrue.'

I continued, 'When the scripts came back, they had been corrected in two different hands, and cuts had been made. Trethowan even wrote a minute in which he said that there were Labour MPs under the control of the KGB and nobody was to be interviewed who was or had been in the security services.' I repeated what I had been told in private about BBC policy on investigating the security services. It's all come out now.

He went absolutely white. 'We have to handle this on the question of news value.'

'Let me give you an example of news value. Why did you not comment on the story in the *New Statesman* that Lee Tracey was going to kill me?'

'Well, it was so fantastic, it was unbelievable.'

'Well, imagine if it had been the other way round – that I had been thought to be planning Airey Neave's assassination. Do you imagine *that* wouldn't have been reported? If the guy's story was so fantastic, why did you use him on *Panorama* the following week and the week after?'

Frankly, I felt I was taking pennies from a blind man's tin. He didn't know what to do or say. So I told him, 'It's nothing personal, of course.'

'I wish you would come to the News and Current Affairs meetings,' he said.

'I'd like to very much.'

Sunday 8 March

Went to bed at 12.40 with a pain in my leg, which had gone very cold. I began to think I had overdone it.

Friday 13 March

Caught the train to Bristol for the NALGO meeting – a one-day strike of social workers against the cuts in social work in Avon has been called. I think they are sacking 210 people.

Then to a meeting with unemployed workers who are on job

experience schemes under the Manpower Services Commission. It was one of the most depressing meetings I have ever been to. When I looked round, there were these kids of sixteen and seventeen, utterly hopeless and demoralised – punk rockers, a black boy with purple hair, guys in sort of Hell's Angels outfits with holes in their trousers.

One young guy with hair all over the place interrupted me all the time. The first thing he said was, 'What is the difference between nuclear weapons and machine-guns? You're still killing people.' He went on and on about that. He might have been an anarchist or nihilist.

They asked all sorts of questions – 'You're a millionaire anyway, aren't you? 'There are millionaires in council houses, aren't there?' 'I've heard of one in Radstock.' 'Of course, you've got a bomb-proof shelter to go to, haven't you?' Then they expressed their hatred for the royal family – not the Queen, but all the hangers-on. 'Why should we pay for Prince Charles's wedding?' and all that. Then they said there was nothing they could do. 'You just come in here for our vote.' 'How much do you earn?'

It was a combination of the hopelessness, defeatism and bitterness bred in our education system and encouraged by unemployment. But at the same time a really bitter critique, and at least they were arguing, which showed some confidence. But, by God, I could see them joining the National Front, and I thought the only people who might possibly make something of this crowd would be the Militant Tendency with their philosophy and their analysis and their socialist explanations. I felt for the first time the collective guilt of anyone who has held Cabinet office over the last fifteen years and who has allowed unemployment to rise, and allowed education to remain as it was, and allow these people to be thrown into despair and apathy and hatred and confusion.

Monday 16 March

Laurie Flynn of Granada's *World in Action* came to talk about a programme on pressure on the BBC and media bias. He is looking for evidence for it. He thought there was ministerial pressure on the BBC Governors on matters of political content: and pressure of cash limits on the BBC by the Government through the control of the licence fee, which could force broadcasters into commercial channels. And there was the Trethowan story of enormous pressure on the *Panorama* team, who felt terribly harrassed. I added to that the Social Democratic bias of many of the people who ran the programmes, like *Newsnight*, and listed some of the ways in which the bias was expressed.

To the Tribune Group meeting. They agreed they would try to increase the number of people voting against renewal of the Prevention of Terrorism Act. I shall be in Lisbon, so I won't actually be voting, and if I did vote against there would be a hell of a row in the Shadow Cabinet.

Went back to the House. I had heard that in the Budget debate Christopher Brocklebank-Fowler, Tory MP for Norfolk, said he couldn't vote for the Government and would vote against, and that he was going to join the Council for Social Democracy, and he walked across the House and was greeted by Neville Sandelson and David Owen and co. It's all very sensational and insubstantial.

We had six votes on the Budget, and the smallest majority the Government had was 16, instead of 60, because a lot of Tory MPs wouldn't accept the 20p increase in the petrol tax. So it has given Mrs Thatcher a bit of a jolt.

I saw Mik and asked him about the deputy leadership, and he said, 'Funnily enough, Robin Cook and I were talking about it at lunch and we took different views, though we both have your interests at heart. I think you should stand to establish a claim, and Robin thinks you shouldn't because it would damage your cause. You wouldn't win.'

'I know that, but I wouldn't be standing for those reasons. I would be standing on a policy.'

He said, 'I think that is right, really.'

Wednesday 18 March

Up at 6, and a BBC car took Caroline and me to London Airport to catch the flight to Lisbon, where I am to deliver the BBC-Gulbenkian Foundation lecture. On the plane I read the briefs the BBC had provided on the various personalities in Portuguese politics I would meet, and I had photocopied the *Encyclopaedia Britannica* account of Portuguese history, which was all about the kings and their marriages and the civil wars and so on.

At 6.45 Caroline and I were taken to the Socialist Party's head-quarters, where we had a meeting with the leader Mario Soares and his International Secretary, Rui Mateus. Soares spoke for fifty minutes. He explained that the present Government was led by the most moderate of the Social Democrats who would not last much beyond early next year; the economic situation was such that he might be able to form a new Government in alliance with the Social Democrats. His main concern was the Communists; when he had been Prime Minister he managed to prevent a Communist takeover which was being organised by Alvaro Cunhal, Leader of the Portuguese Communist Party, who was once Soares's tutor. I read Cunhal's biographical note on the plane – he had suffered the most appalling torture in prison in the 1930s and 1940s and was seen as a hard-line Communist. He is clearly a remarkable man. Much of what Soares said was against Cunhal and the Communists.

He said he had been to see Felipe Gonzales, the Spanish Socialist Leader, and Mitterrand and Schmidt, I think. He felt there was a general withdrawal on the part of the European socialists, so I said,

'What do you mean, withdrawal?' In effect, he meant a withdrawal from their socialist position, and he thought the situation in Poland was such that the European socialists felt they needed the American umbrella.

Looking back on it, one gained the impression that the role of the socialists was to save capitalism whenever it was threatened, to shelter under the umbrella of America and to fight the communists both at home and abroad. Soares was *very* charming and courteous and gave me an hour and ten minutes of his time, but I can't say I found him different from what I had expected – a vain man who had no real perception of the historical events in which he was taking part.

It was a very enjoyable day; the BBC have done us proud. It is nice to get away for a few days, to see another country, and to see one's own country through the eyes of others. I am not regarded as a bogeyman and a dangerous red, as I am in Britain. The Portuguese are interested in the development of ideas and argument in the British Labour Party, which is a famous and distinguished party in the world socialist movement.

Thursday 19 March

I was taken to the Presidential Palace, while Caroline went round Lisbon. I was shown into Antonio Eanes's office and stayed for an hour and a half. He is in his middle forties, quiet, modest, neat, military – a general in rank – thoughtful and serious, not charismatic in any way. But I found it a most interesting discussion.

I asked him about the Portuguese constitution, in which there is a conflict over the powers of the President and Prime Minister, and the likely fate of the military body, the Council of Revolution, formed in 1974 during the Portuguese Revolution.

Eanes explained that everybody agreed that the Council should go, and constitutional change would have to be made with a two-thirds majority in Parliament. I thought it would be interesting to ask him, 'Why have a change in the constitution at all? Does it matter very much?'

He said, 'I don't know that it does matter very much, though everybody thinks we should have a new constitution. If we fail and things go wrong, it will be blamed on the constitution. The right wing attack the constitution because the Council of the Revolution represents the military commitment to a return to democracy. It is said to be a Marxist constitution and to be hostile to the interests of Portugal, and the media attack it.' But I got the impression he was quite relaxed about it, I really did.

We discussed the question of bringing Communists back into the mainstream of pluralistic politics. Eanes is reported to have defeated the Communists in 1975 and yet he received their support for his presidential candidature in 1980. I said it seemed to me that the Communist Party had grown in opposition to fascism and that in Britain, where we had no fascism, and where there was a common front in the unions and a single political party representing this interest in Parliament, it would be sensible to try to find a way of domesticating the Communists by bringing them in. Our electoral system had played a dominant part in forcing a coalition before instead of after an Election, and that had brought the left together and created a more stable political situation.

After lunch I was taken to see the Prime Minister, Dr Pinto Balsemao, in the house where the old dictator Salazar lived. I spent an hour and a half with Dr Balsemao, who spoke fluent English, was relaxed and very Americanised. He said he thought things were going well – they had reduced inflation, the Socialists were in disarray, but they needed more foreign investment, they wanted competition to challenge the nationalised banks, and they had had a problem of productivity. He spoke of the need for wage restraint and the need to modernise agriculture. It was the Roy Jenkins approach. He had all the smooth talk of an editor and very little understanding of the day-to-day problems of the people. But I found it useful.

Then to the Gulbenkian auditorium for the lecture itself. I was introduced by an old socialist pioneer who had been a former Ombudsman of Portugal, and I gave my lecture on 'Europe – A New Perspective'. The occasion was well attended: every political party was there, including a representative of the Communist Party, who came up afterwards and said they would like relations with the British Labour Party; the Cardinal Archbishop of Lisbon had sent his representative; and the Indian Ambassador was there.

Saturday 21 March
Home. So many things have become clear in the last few days. In Portugal you see the Portuguese Socialists as an absolute fabrication by right-wing social democrats, financed by the Americans, to keep the Portuguese Communist Party out, though it was the only party that fought the fascists. Secondly, you have the feeling that this is happening in Britain too, that the right-wing of the Labour Party is American-financed for that purpose. There is an article in this week's *Leveller* about the links between the CIA and the Gang of Four, and Gaitskell, Crosland, Melvyn Lasky, Stephen Haseler and so on.

R.H. Tawney, whose book *The Attack* is just being republished and for which I am writing a foreword, says that when fascism comes to Britain it will be very gentlemanly and will be called 'true democracy'. The left knows the score, the polytechnic graduates do really know the score now: to that extent at least the labour movement won't be taken unawares.

Then I thought about Northern Ireland and how, when I said the security forces were using Northern Ireland as a test-bed for Britain in the event of 4 million unemployed, I was violently attacked; which meant in effect that I had struck a sensitive note.

Michael Foot has come out in a violent attack upon Militant and named Bristol as one of the centres in which it operates, along with London and Liverpool. Denis Healey has called for Militant to be expelled, so the right within the Party are making a last stand. I don't think you could get rid of the YS with their Militant influence now because people would not allow it to happen, but it is an indication that Michael Foot is a leader of the right and it means that I am going to be driven into this campaign for the deputy leadership. In this way we might rally the forces of the mainstream labour movement.

Sunday 22 March

Geoffrey Goodman rang to say that he and Mike Molloy were the only two key people in the *Daily Mirror* who were still pretty loyal to the Labour Party, though Paul Foot, who writes a most successful column in the *Mirror* was beginning to look a bit more sympathetically at what was happening in the Labour Party. Geoffrey said the Social Democrats included Marjorie Proops, and the wobblies were Joe Haines and Terence Lancaster.

Monday 23 March

I had a phone call from Michael Foot saying he wants to see me tomorrow.

To the BBC studios at Lime Grove at about 6.45 for the meeting of the NUJ chapel. Vincent Hanna is father of the chapel, and there were a lot of other people there including MPs John Forrester and Tony Banks, and Sally Banks. All the current affairs programmes were represented.

My opening statement was soft and quiet, I related coverage to the development of politics in Britain. I was cross-examined on my attack on television, particularly on *Newsnight*. I was asked for examples, so I gave a couple, in connection with Michael Cockerell, in Bristol in 1974, and Vincent, over the coverage of the Southend by-election in 1980. I was sharply criticised for disengaging from the BBC for six months, but I explained I had done it because I didn't want to be drawn into what the news editor decided was the big story, ie the split in the Labour Party. It was worthwhile, with some good questions and discussion.

Tuesday 24 March

Went in to see Michael, who said, 'I asked you to come and see me about the deputy leadership, to find out if you are going to stand, because I think it would lacerate the Party if you did, would be deeply divisive, would ruin the annual Conference and would make it much harder for us to be elected in the next Election.'

I replied, 'Thanks for asking me. I have thought about it, and a number of people have pressed me to stand. I haven't finally made up my mind, but I think there is some support for a contest, and I will certainly take account of what you say. But, Michael, you fought Denis Healey only three months ago. I don't know why it should be right for you to do it and not for me.'

He said, 'That was quite different.'

'Well, I don't know that it was. I didn't think there should be an election at all, I thought you should have succeeded, as Deputy Leader, but given the fact that you were elected I think you have got a lot of support. You can tell that from the Party meetings.'

So then he said, 'Oh well, there would be a bitter conflict all summer; if it would help, I am quite happy for you to say that I have asked you not to stand and you have responded to my appeal.'

'I don't think that is the issue, quite honestly. I don't regard elections as being divisive, I regard them as being quite unifying, and it means that the winner gets support even from those who supported his opponent because they have had a chance to vote. Anyway, Denis Healey has been going round making the most violent attacks upon the NEC on Party policy. I went to a meeting in Perth recently and heard Roy Hattersley attacking the LCC and the CLPD and the Rank and File Mobilising Committee, quite apart from Militant, which Denis wants to expel. And Peter Shore is now well to the right of Jim Callaghan.'

'Well, that just proves you are going to attack them.'

I said, 'I am not; I have never attacked anybody.'

'You are very clever in how you deal with your attacks, but all these speeches were only in response to ones you have made.'

'I don't really think so. I don't mind people trying to change Conference policy – that's one thing – but at least you have to accept that until it is changed it is the policy of the Party.'

Michael said, 'You've got to make accommodations.'

'Accommodation is one thing, but it's another thing for the Deputy Leader to go around attacking Party policy. I believe there is a letter coming before the NEC tomorrow which I have signed, just simply regretting the fact that the Deputy Leader of the Party, while giving the fraternal greetings of the National Executive, should have chosen to attack the NEC.'

'There you are,' he said. 'Every meeting will be like this, and it will be like this all summer. It will ruin the Conference.'

'Well, for a start,' I replied, 'the electoral college will meet on the first Sunday, so, by the time the Conference starts, the election of Deputy Leader will be out of the way. But, even if I do stand, I don't think I would win, as I'm sure the trade unions would like to keep Denis.'

Michael said, 'I'm not so sure. You might easily win or come in very close anyway.'

'Well, how do we know John Silkin isn't going to stand? Or Peter Shore, or Eric Heffer, or Roy Hattersley?'

He said, 'I never thought of that. I shall have to ask them and say the same to them.'

'How do you know Denis Healey isn't going to stand against you?'

He said, 'I know he won't.'

He got himself into a typical Michael Foot state where everything you want to do will always lose us the next Election. Well, as we followed his advice rigorously for the last five years of the last Labour Government and we did lose the Election in May 1979, I can't say I found it very credible.

But it must have been clear that I did intend to stand, and I said, 'If I do, I promise I'll let you know in advance. The real problem is that the people who have left the Party to attack it are now being matched by those *within* the Party who attack it, and somebody has got to get up and say we agree with Party policy and the electoral college decision at Wembley.'

'Well, I think we may change the decision to get one-third, one-third, one-third at the Conference this year,' he said.

'You may or may not; I am not particularly hyped on percentages. But that's not the point. The point is that the election will take place on the existing system.'

Michael said, 'Well, it will be very much to your credit if you decide not to stand.'

'I am sure I will be clobbered if I stand, but I don't think that is really the issue. Denis wasn't elected by anybody, he was just allowed in unopposed, and so there is a genuine vacancy for the deputy leadership.'

That was how we more or less left it, but he was white and angry, as he always is.

Wednesday 25 March

To the NEC. Michael Foot reiterated his fear that month after month there would be mutual attacks in the Party, and said he had told the Shadow Cabinet this and he hoped there would be a speedy end to the discussion. The Party would be appalled at what was happening, and he still thought there would be no Social Democratic MPs in the next Parliament.

Neil Kinnock said that Michael Foot had appealed to the Shadow Cabinet for a truce last week and that we now needed unity.

Friday 27 March

Did a lot of phoning round and inviting people on Sunday to plan the deputy leadership campaign.

Saturday 28 March

A perfect spring day. The horrible winter seems to be behind us and the spring is coming; by God we need it.

The launch of the Social Democratic Party took place last Thursday and it was exactly as everybody predicted – a major media festival. It is unreal and potentially dangerous. It reminds me of what Tawney said. The attack on the two-party system, the attack on the democratic process, the attack on choice, the attack on debate, the attack on policy – all these have within them the ingredients of fascism. Of course, as British politics returns to the nineteenth century, it is appropriate that there should be two bourgeois parties – the Conservatives and the Social Democrats. In my heart, I don't believe it can capture support, though it is going to be a huge long struggle to get through to the British people and to create conditions under which they can really govern themselves.

Sunday 29 March

The group arrived – Tony Banks, Ken Coates, Vladimir Derer, Jenny and Stuart Holland, Frances Morrell, Stephen, Chris Mullin, Reg Race, Victor Schonfield, Audrey Wise and Valerie Wise. We had three hours' intense discussion. First of all there was absolutely no doubt that I should stand as a candidate: it was unanimous. It was agreed that I should issue a statement announcing why I was accepting the candidature, and it was agreed that the issue should not be raised at the Tribune Group on the grounds that it had nothing to do with them.

It was also agreed that an attempt would be made to get people to sign a simple statement saying, 'I support the candidature of Tony Benn for the deputy leadership of the Labour Party', and these signatures would come to me by Wednesday. I would put out on 2 April a statement giving my reasons, a draft of which we went through very carefully. A lot of amendments were made.

Chris Mullin stayed, and we went through four chapters of the new book, *Arguments for Democracy*. I drove him home and then went to see Mother, who is a bit better, but I'll have to keep an eye on her, what with her arthritis, her heart trouble, her hernia, her eyesight, her migraine, her new knee and her bad hip. She needs watching, but her mind is as clear as a bell.

A very useful day and a historic decision taken collectively.

Monday 30 March

Tribune Group meeting. Frank Allaun had originally said he would like to think about supporting me, then sent me a note saying he would support me, then came up to say he wanted to withdraw his name. I believe Eric Heffer is very cross about the whole thing, because he wants to stand.

Before the meeting Stan Orme said to me, 'What's this I hear about you standing for the deputy leadership? It would be a disaster. We had better have a talk about it. I want to warn you about the consequences.'

I said I'd be happy to have a talk.

Wednesday 1 April

Went to the Shadow Cabinet, where very little occurred; the real problem is that the Shadow Cabinet feel under no obligation to promote Party policy, and the Party senses that. Ernie Roberts pointed out in the Tea Room tonight that this is one of the reasons there is such a lot of activity at the local level – parties feel they have no control at the national level, whereas locally they do have some control.

We had a report from Pat Llewelyn-Davies, the Labour Chief Whip in the Lords, about defecting peers: thirteen Labour peers and six cross-benchers have joined the SDP, plus one Tory today.

Afterwards I asked Michael, 'Could I have a quick word with you, following up our talk last week?' I said I had considered it very carefully but I had decided to stand, and I gave my reasons – to campaign on Europe, defence, unemployment and so on.

'I think that is most inadvisable,' said Michael.

'I don't want to mislead you in any way. I have decided.'

Michael said, 'Well, I must ask you to postpone the announcement for a week.'

'Well, I have decided, and it is all set.'

He asked, 'Why, why can't you postpone it?'

I said, 'It may leak, because a lot of people know about it.'

'Well, I ask you not to do it today.'

I answered, 'I did take account of everything you said last week, and I have talked to Mik and others, and they think it is right.'

He said, 'If you go ahead, I shall let it be known that I asked you not to.'

'That's of course a matter for you, but it would be entirely unprecedented for the Leader of the Labour Party to interfere in a candidature. Never, to the best of my knowledge, has a leader of the Labour Party ever commented upon candidatures for Parliament, for the Executive, for the Shadow Cabinet, for the treasurership, or anything.'

I think it took him aback a bit and I added, 'You must do what you think is right, but it would be unprecedented, and a very dangerous precedent.'

He went on and on about how divisive it would be. I said, 'Michael, to be honest, you'll be spending the summer trying to get Wembley reversed, the Solidarity campaign* is going on all the time, and a

* Solidarity was formed by Labour MPs, councillors and others in 1981 after the breakup of Campaign for Labour Victory and the emergence of the SDP.

perfectly straightforward candidature, when there is a vacancy, is not divisive compared to that.' He really got quite cross and difficult.

We talked for three-quarters of an hour.

Had to stay all night for a three-line whip.

I went into the Tea Room and Joe Ashton approached me. 'Can I speak to you on a private matter?'

I said, 'Yes.'

'You know there is a Tribune meeting going on downstairs. They know about your announcement tomorrow and the press conference with all cameras laid on, and everything.'

I said, 'Joe, there is no press conference laid on, no cameras. I was just putting out a statement.'

He went on, 'Well, anyway, they know about it and they are having a special meeting. They are going to write to you asking you not to go ahead, and requesting that the Tribune Group discuss it on Monday.'

I said, 'It isn't really very much to do with the Tribune Group, you know. I would not have raised it at the Tribune Group because it would have looked as if I was trying to get their support, which I'm not.'

'Well, Jack Straw and one or two others are very worried about what's going on. They think you will do yourself damage. They are not hostile to you. But there is a big swing to the right. Unions are losing membership, they can't get branch officials, active members of the unions are weak. The whole thing is moving that way.'

I answered, 'You may be right, Joe. I am not doing it for myself anyway, you know me well enough to know that. I am not worrying about what is going to happen to me but I think somebody has got to advocate Party policy in Parliament.'

Afterwards I had a quick word with Reg Race and Dennis Skinner. Dennis thought it would be damaging if the Tribunites put out a statement against me.

But Reg Race said, 'Let them do it. It will show things up.'

I said, 'I want to be absolutely clear – as far as I am concerned, I am going ahead with it.' So I went into the Library, sealed up all the letters and got them off to the MPs, and sent the press statement over to the Press Gallery, though at 3 am there would be nobody there. Once I had done it, I felt greatly relieved.

Thursday 2 April

When I got to the House there was a lot of fuss, and Bob Hughes, the Labour MP for Aberdeen North, said that a number of people in the Tribune Group had opposed my candidature. I asked who they were and he said, 'Frank Field, Robert Kilroy-Silk, Oonagh McDonald, Robin Cook and so on.' Anyway, Martin Flannery, Reg Race, Jo Richardson and Stan Thorne were totally behind me.

The 7 o'clock news contained the first announcement, and the coverage was very interesting.

'Mr Tony Benn has declared he is to stand for the deputy leadership of the Labour Party. In an announcement at Westminster in the early hours of this morning, he issued his challenge to the present Deputy, Mr Denis Healey. The election will take place on the eve of the Party's Conference in October, but already Mr Benn's decision has aroused considerable anger among fellow Labour MPs. From Westminster, here is our political correspondent, Peter Hill.

' "Mr Benn dropped his bombshell at half past three this morning. His statement said he has the support of his constituency party, and sixteen MPs, nearly all on the far left of the Party, have nominated him. He says he has accepted nomination to give the Party an opportunity to discuss policy and he intends to run on a five-point programme containing such proposals as withdrawal from the EEC, a non-nuclear defence strategy, an end to the House of Lords, expanded public services and restoration of full employment." '

I was asked to go on various news programmes, so I borrowed Robin Cook's razor and sat with him in his room. While I was there he told me I was becoming isolated with the far left and out of touch with parliamentary opinion. I think the truth is that parliamentary opinion is out of touch with what is happening in the Party, but I get on very well with Robin and I like him, and I listened carefully to what he said.

Julian Haviland interviewed me for ITN, and I did a much shorter interview with Brian Curtois for BBC1. He was savage, and only wanted to examine the question of MPs being angry. There was a strong anti-democratic emphasis to all the questions – that an election was in itself bad – and you realise that the BBC are really against democracy, as are the media generally and the right of the Party.

At 2.30 we had the last votes and by then I was quite punch-drunk with tiredness.

The media reaction has been exactly as I expected; tomorrow it will be completely hysterical, just as at the time of the Common Market Referendum – but this time it is a six month campaign which will blow itself out. What it has done, of course, is to force people to make choices. That's what's called polarisation, divisiveness and all the rest, but it's true. You can't go on for ever and ever pretending you're a socialist party when you're not, pretending you'll do something when you won't, confining yourself to attacks on the Tories when that's not enough. People want to know what the Labour Party will do and I think this process is long overdue; the Labour Party are having a Turkish bath, and the sweat and the heat and the discomfort are very unpleasant. I am sure Denis will win – I will put that on the record now – because the Party never sacks anybody, and why should it sack its Deputy Leader, particularly when many people think he should have been the Leader? But I think there will be a sizeable body of opinion which can't be entirely ignored or neglected.

Friday 3 April
The press today is hysterical, or, put the other way, just reflects the Tory view and the view of the right-wing of the Labour Party.

Saturday 4 April
Today the papers printed an open letter from Alex Kitson in his capacity as Deputy General Secretary of the TGWU, asking me not to stand. I decided that this really had to be replied to. Also, in the *Mirror*, Geoffrey Goodman said there had been a secret arrangement between Michael Foot and the senior trade union leaders after Blackpool that, if they did have an electoral college, it would not be used. Geoffrey Goodman said that I knew about this agreement, and therefore why was I standing? It could only be to wreck things. I suspected there was an agreement, but I had no specific knowledge of it and, even if I had, it wouldn't have made the slightest bit of difference because elections are not about fixing things.

Sunday 5 April
A few MPs have been in touch with me since the announcement. Joan Maynard rang last night to say 'Stay firm', Bob Cryer and Martin Flannery came out today in favour of the contest, and David Winnick wrote to support me.

Monday 6 April
Paul Johnson had a piece in the *Sun* saying the trouble was that Foot was no good, and an article in the *FT* also stated that this really revealed what a weak man Foot was. The *Daily Mail* and the *Sun* had a tremendous attack on me by Terry Duffy.

At 4.15 I went to the Tribune Group meeting. At the beginning Stan Orme said he wanted to raise the deputy leadership, and it was agreed that it would be discussed next week.

Looking back on the day, I do feel that the worst is over, and it is a good thing that the Tribune Group have delayed the discussion on the deputy leadership, because in a week's time it will all look much more secure and on Friday I will have been formally nominated by Bristol South East.

Fenner Brockway, much to my disappointment, wrote and said I shouldn't stand, and so did Stan Newens, the Member for Harlow; the wobblies include very good people who just don't want trouble and think we should fight Mrs Thatcher. But the toughies are the ones who see what it is about and want to keep Denis Healey as Deputy Leader, who not only manifestly does not support Party policy but is violently opposed to it.

Tuesday 7 April

I was told today that Neil Kinnock had been trying to get a round robin signed by the staff at Transport House, urging that I be persuaded not to stand.

I must be clear that no one in the Shadow Cabinet supports my candidature. However, some more Labour MPs – Ray Fletcher, David Marshall, Andrew McMahon, Stan Thorne, and Mick Welsh – have come out in support. I think there are a lot of left MPs who are doubtful about it, partly because of the ambition involved in it, but partly because they think it might put at risk socialist policies. I can see that a solid block of what one would call responsible opinion thinks it is unwise but is not unsympathetic to me. On the other hand, I don't see any other way of getting these clear policy commitments projected at the top, and it may be that there will be a great sacrifice and I will be humiliatingly defeated.

Wednesday 8 April

I left at 12.30 and went to Tower Hill for the march against unemployment organised by London print union branches. It was led by Jack Dromey and Jimmy Knapp, the Chairman of the South-East TUC. Dennis Skinner was speaking when I arrived, and I spoke for a few minutes. Then Dennis and I headed off and walked with 1300 people all the way through Fleet Street to the Embankment, where we dispersed.

I am doing far too many meetings at the moment and I am getting stale. The summer campaign will be exhausting. Jack Dromey said, 'We're going to win the T&G. It will be all right.' If I do win the T&G and the miners, which I might, that will be a formidable base for the advance towards the Conference. I have the feeling that parliamentary anxieties and opposition are beginning to subside a bit, so it may not be a humiliating defeat, but actually I don't really care because it is only the beginning and it may be necessary to fight this battle year after year.

Thursday 9 April

Had a word with Bob Mellish, the MP for Bermondsey, who was telling me about all the 'awful young left-wingers' who were joining the Bermondsey Party. He gave me a long lecture about standing down in the campaign, and said I would be the Leader of the Party one day, and would succeed Michael Foot if only I would work with Michael now, and so on.

The Rank and File Mobilising Committee have issued a statement calling for support for free elections in the Labour Party and welcoming my candidature. They have got a lot of resources, what with the IWC, the CLPD and the LCC, so the machine at work in the Labour Party is going to be formidable; since the press don't know much about it they may be surprised at the amount of support that can be drummed up. In that connection, yesterday and today Reg Race released the names of seven other MPs who have asked to be put on the list of sponsors for my candidature, and no newspaper had published any of the lists – which sort of indicates that they are moving from hysteria to silence.

Sunday 12 April

An interview I did with Hugo Young appeared in the *Sunday Times* today: 'Benn at 56, a sage rather than a demon', which is a new line – an old and experienced political leader who, from his own experience, has come to certain conclusions. I must say Hugo Young had played it quite squarely; he had taken a lot of trouble, had let me check the quotes, and his own assessment wasn't really obtrusive and a lot of the argument got across.

I left at about 9 to drive to Hastings for a meeting, avoiding Brixton, where there was a tremendous riot last night, triggered off probably by the desperation of the black community at police harassment.

Monday 13 April

Had lunch with Clive Jenkins, and we had a fancy meal – he really is a big business executive.

In the course of the meal he said something like 'You're not serious about it, are you?'

I replied, 'Of course I am serious about it.' And I realised immediately that the purpose of the lunch was to persuade me not to stand for the deputy leadership. I said, 'Clive, the policies may have been agreed at the Conference, but the argument has not been accepted by the Shadow Cabinet or by the TUC General Council.'

'Oh yes it has,' he declared. 'They are all for the alternative economic strategy.'

I said, 'Clive, they are not; you know very well they are not. It's all very well people like Len Murray appearing on the television saying they are fed up with the Government, but it cuts no ice at all.'

'Oh yes, we're all in favour of it, but this is the worst time to stand.'

'Well, candidly, this is what it was all about. We have had the campaign for the wider franchise and now we use it.'

Then Clive admitted that there had been an agreement between all the general secretaries and the TULV that there would be no contest for the leadership, that all of them had agreed it and had told the Shadow Cabinet when they met them, probably just before Christmas – before I was on the Shadow Cabinet. So the story Geoffrey Goodman had printed in the *Mirror* was true. I had suspected that there had been a general understanding but I had not realised exactly what had been agreed. It is scandalous that at the Conference in Wembley, when they were all arguing for a new franchise, they should have secretly agreed that the franchise would not be used, and now they are acutely embarrassed by what has happened.

He asked, 'Would you meet some general secretaries?' I said I would and he added, 'With an open mind?'

I said, 'If you mean by that, would I withdraw, no, under no circumstances would I withdraw.'

Then he sort of gave up and had nothing else to say, but we had a friendly lunch. However, when I mentioned I was going to the ASTMS Conference to speak at a fringe meeting, he told me he would regard that as an unfriendly act. I said, 'Well, why not. It's a CND fringe meeting.'

At the end of the lunch he asked if I would like a cup of tea, and on a tray in came the most beautiful loving-cup – a large china cup with two handles and a gold rim – and inscribed on the front in black letters was:

Elections can be poisoned chalices, Tony

and on the back:

Don't do it, Tony

I suppose he had thought this would be a consolation if I had agreed not to stand. Later today, I wrote and thanked him for lunch and added, 'I might need the cup again next year.'

Went to the Commons. Had a word with Mik in the Library before the Tribune Group meeting today and he told me, 'There will not be a vote on your decision to stand, not while I am in the chair.'

There were forty-nine or fifty Tribune Group members present, and Mik said, 'After this meeting there is going to be the largest press conference we have ever held, and I hope we shall have a comradely spirit here and in what anyone says to the press lobby.'

Then Stan Orme opened. 'We face a very serious situation; there is unemployment, there are racial problems, and the Party and the left must maintain unity because we must secure the return of a Labour Government. We should support Michael as Prime Minister, and consolidate the policies on nuclear weapons, on the EEC and on public ownership. Tony's statement was a manifesto and it delighted our opponents. Some of us have supported these policies all our lives, and we have now got Foot as Leader and therefore we have got the policies. This action can only divide the left. We shall have a very unpleasant weekend. The deputy leadership has been elevated to an importance it does not deserve; this will elevate the electoral college above the Conference, because if Healey wins he will cite the college as proof that he has support. We will have six months of campaigning, and the trade union conferences will be dominated by it.'

The next speaker was David Winnick, who said, 'I don't want to weaken the Tribune Group but I don't accept that the Party is weak and demoralised. I would not support a campaign for the leadership but this is for the deputy leadership, because Healey does not support Party policy.'

Robin Cook urged me not to waste the next six months. When Martin Flannery spoke, he said it was inevitable in this situation that colleagues would differ and we shouldn't cry about that. 'There has been a two-year witch-hunt, much bigger than the witch-hunt against Nye Bevan, and Tony has borne the brunt of it. Don't fuel the media in its witch-hunt against Tony Benn, don't lend our voices to the media, or the unity of this group will be weakened.'

Jeff Rooker believed I should not stand.

John Prescott said, 'Tony should back down or we should disown him. I hope very much Tony speaks today. I can't understand why there was no discussion when he joined the Group. Tony has sought to pre-empt our decision.'

At the very beginning of the meeting, Mik had said he hoped I would speak if I wanted to, and I had made my notes, but I didn't indicate I wanted to speak until John Prescott said this. After him, I got up and said, 'These are difficult decisions but I didn't take them alone. My GMC discussed the matter four times before they nominated me, twenty-three MPs support me, and there are others, like the Yorkshire miners. I have made my statement, and everybody knows what the policy is about. I have had plenty of opportunity for hearing the arguments against: John Silkin said on television that the challenge was asinine, I have had open letters through the press from Alex Kitson and Judith Hart, public speeches by Denis Healey, and so on. As to no consultation, it is not true, I did consult Mik as the chairman of the Group and Jo Richardson, and I consulted a lot of trade union leaders and others who are around this table, some of whom I knew were hostile. I didn't consult the Tribune Group because I thought it wouldn't be right to ask the Group to support me so soon after I had joined the Group.'

Eric Heffer indicated that he wished to speak. 'If Tony is defeated, his campaign for the deputy leadership will set back our policies and strengthen the right wing. Healey is thrilled at the idea of an election. He thinks he has defeated us. But there should be no vote today, please, and I recognise that it won't stop Tony from standing.'

I know that Eric has been trying to get people to nominate him for some time.

Mik said, 'I want to speak as a member of the Group, not as chairman. The growing power of the left dates from Nye's decision to challenge Gaitskell for the treasurership year after year and to compel the trade unions and the CLPs to discuss policy and choose. Nye was defeated for years, but he politicised the movement and the unions on a left-right basis, and the argument that occurred in the movement over the treasurership began the advance of the left. Today is a rerun of the Bevan-Gaitskell arguments. If I thought elections divided the Party, then I would be adopting the Russian view. As to the behaviour of the Tribune Group, this is the first time the Group has ever decided to carpet a member. When we had the leadership election last November, John Silkin challenged Denis Healey and we all applauded, and then we persuaded Michael Foot to stand – so that was two Tribunites fighting one another.'

At this stage, Jim Marshall, the MP for Leicester South, whispered to me, 'You know what this is about, don't you? It is really about who is to be the leader of the left, and they don't want to concede it to you.'

There were nineteen speakers – nine for and ten against. If you include me, it was evenly balanced.

It was then nearly 7 pm and I went back to my room.

On to the Rank and File Mobilising Committee, which had been summoned to discuss the campaign. Reg Race was in the chair and he gave a report on the Tribune Group meeting. Then the Labour Action for Peace resolution was reported to us; they had voted unanimously that they wanted a Deputy Leader who will support the 1981 Conference resolutions on unilateralism.

Nigel Stanley, the secretary of the LCC, declared that Independent Labour Publications would support me.

It was agreed to get £50 from each organisation.

Wednesday 15 April

Shadow Cabinet, and I raised the question of Bobby Sands, the hunger striker from the H-Blocks who has just been elected as the new MP for Fermanagh and South Tyrone. I said perhaps we could be told something about it.

Michael said, 'We took soundings after the Election, and Pym made contact with Roy Hattersley and John Silkin, and we agreed we wouldn't press that he should be unseated.'

I remarked, 'Well, I think he should take his seat.' People looked absolutely shocked. 'Well, he has been elected, and that would seem the normal thing to do.'

Roy Mason said, 'He is a convicted terrorist.'

John Silkin declared 'It would be impossible.'

Denis Healey attacked the idea, and I answered, 'The conversion of a terrorist to a statesman by a process of election is normal. Look what happened to Robert Mugabe in Southern Rhodesia; and after all, when Ian Smith was in revolt against the Crown for fifteen years, nothing happened to him. There was an amnesty passed by Parliament that allowed him to get out of all the penalities.'

Peter Shore and Merlyn Rees were horrified.

Neil Kinnock banged the table and said, 'I am absolutely against violence, which destroys democracy.'

He is such a pompous constitutionalist now, so I whispered across to him, 'Maybe you would feel differently if Wales was partitioned.' He said, 'Well, we have bombers in Wales and we are absolutely against violence.'

Friday 17 April

Spent the whole day answering letters of support about the deputy leadership – I wrote 320 replies by hand! Stephen, June, Hilary and Melissa wrote the envelopes out, and I was really grateful.

Wednesday 22 April

Yesterday there was an article in the *Guardian* by Peter Jenkins saying the Benn bandwagon would have to be stopped by the trade union leaders and, if I got more than 40 per cent of the votes, thirty or forty more Labour MPs would join the SDP. The whole thing is being built up as a tremendous scare. But the fact is that the excitement about the candidature has subsided and it is accepted that there will be a ballot.

Saturday 25 April

I had a phone call from Jon Lansman, who reported that things were going well on the deputy leadership campaign and he is going to take up the defection of the Wales Labour Co-ordinating Committee, who have written asking me not to stand. Frances Morrell rang and said I should never appear on a platform without another MP. The campaign is progressing well, and I just feel there is a groundswell at the moment.

Monday 27 April

The Tribune Group had a discussion about the hunger strike, which was raised by Ernie Roberts, the MP for Hackney North.

Bobby Sands is very near to death. Ernie Roberts said that the line dividing the hunger strikers from the Government was very thin, that it revolved around the wearing of civilian clothes and exemption from certain types of prison work, and we should appeal to the Government to save his life.

Stan Orme argued, 'Sands is committing suicide. He is a convicted prisoner, and the prisoners at Long Kesh have used violence for political ends.'

I repeated my view that Bobby Sands should take his seat as an elected Member of Parliament.

Bob Hughes said, 'His election as an MP is irrelevant because he wouldn't take his seat anyway. Sands is determined to die, and Tribune should say nothing, because none of us have an answer.'

Mik summed up the discussion. 'There is no real agreement, unless we were to say we are in favour of the peaceful reunification of Ireland', but Stan Orme objected to that. So nothing is to be done by Tribune.

Wednesday 29 April
Canvassing for Stephen in the GLC elections, I went to a block of flats, and people were terrified of coming to the door. They just called through the letterbox, 'What do you want?' The state of the stairways was awful. One of the people I called on was Christine Keeler, and she looked at me in a funny way, as if she recognised me – not that I've ever met her before, I might add.

Friday 1 May
I have had a tremendous number of phone calls about the suggestion I made at the Shadow Cabinet last week and at the Tribune Group on Monday about Bobby Sands being allowed to take his seat as an MP. The banner headline in the *Bristol Evening Post* was 'Benn Backs Sands – Let Him Sit as MP. Tribune Group is shocked.' I have put a perfectly sensible argument and, having let the argument get across but not pressing it, I think I have achieved all I can. I was infuriated that Don Concannon, our Front Bench spokesman on Northern Ireland, should have gone to the Maze prison to interview the hunger strikers and then said on television that the Labour Party agreed 100 per cent with the Government and endorsed everything the Secretary of State for Northern Ireland, Humphrey Atkins, had said. We are back to bipartisanship and, until that is broken, there is no hope whatever for anything to be done.

Saturday 2 May
Flew to Scotland, and stayed with Tam and Kathleen Dalyell at The Binns, which is Tam's seventeenth-century house. Kathleen's parents, Lord Wheatley and his wife, were there. He was the Lord Advocate for Scotland in the postwar Labour Government and then went on to become a judge. We had a good old talk, and I came upstairs and am dictating my diary, absolutely exhausted, but the warmth in Scotland is so tremendous and so direct, it is really very moving to come here, and I enjoy it.

Sunday 3 May
Up at 6.30 and had breakfast with the family. We left at about 7.40, and Tam drove us to the Lee Jeans factory in Greenock, where we were met by the shift who were occupying the place against closure. The factory is owned by Vanity Fair, and the occupation has been going on for about twelve weeks; the average age of the girls working there was about twenty. There were sixteen-year-olds who, when they were sacked, suddenly realised they had nothing to lose, so they took over the

factory and it was really very impressive. Helen Monahan, the chief shop steward, is most efficient, and she took us round and showed us how neatly they had kept the factory, with all the jeans carefully covered and the place spotlessly clean. They were sitting knitting in the canteen, and they keep a round-the-clock watch; local trade-unionists from the shipyards have promised to defend them if there is an attempt by the police to get in. They have got friends at the Sheriff's office who will tell them as soon as a warrant is brought out for their eviction. They have decided to be removed bodily if the police turn up (but the police are quite sympathetic).

Tuesday 5 May

I wasn't feeling very well today. I have had this tingling in my legs and now my hands, and my face has been very hot and my skin has been rough, and I did wonder whether I was getting high blood-pressure. In the Lobby at about 8, I asked Maurice Miller, who is MP for East Kilbride and a doctor, if I could consult him professionally. I went into the first-aid room with him and he took my blood-pressure, examined my heart and looked at my eyes. He said my blood-pressure was on the high side of normal, but he didn't see anything wrong and said it might be stress and I should take things easier. So, once he had told me there was nothing wrong, I felt much better.

Wednesday 6 May

Jon Lansman and Nigel Williamson came in for a couple of hours and went through all the letters I had had about the deputy leadership. Jon is about twenty-four, a Cambridge graduate in economics; he was unemployed and worked as a van driver for a while and is now employed almost entirely by the CLPD. Nigel Williamson, who is about twenty-eight, has been in a DHSS benefit office and is now doing a history course at University College, London. They are both serious, active, efficient, helpful.

Thursday 7 May

I went and voted in the Greater London Council elections. There were eight candidates – Labour, Conservative, Communist, Liberal, Workers' Revolutionary Party, Social Democrat, Save London Group and the Ecology Party

Then we heard that Labour had swept county councils throughout the country, including Avon, which is fantastic because we never thought we would win Avon. This is what all those campaigns against the cuts were about.

Friday 8 May

I am absolutely whacked out, I've still got this tingling in my arms and legs, and I am feeling exhausted. I think the very knowledge of the engagements I've taken on is beginning to worry me.

Tony Banks telephoned and asked Stephen to turn up tomorrow morning, when they are going to be co-opting members for the ILEA. Stephen didn't win his seat, but never expected to. Also Ken Livingstone was chosen as Leader of the GLC over Andrew McIntosh.

Saturday 9 May
Joshua's twenty-third birthday.

I caught the 1.20 train to Bath for a meeting of the Quaker Socialist Society: there were about fifty or sixty Quakers from all over the country. There is something dull about the Quakers: I have always been impressed by them, but they are most frightfully worthy and unresponsive.

Nobody asked any questions at all, so I said, 'Well let me ask a question. Is it possible that the Quaker idea and the dissenting idea of the priesthood of all believers – that each person has a direct contact with the Almighty – might have a negative side? Although people think for themselves, they tend to emphasis the idea of individualism and individual salvation and individual success at the expense of the general collective interests of the community and the group.'

They couldn't really answer it. Then one of them said, 'We don't really want to make our views as socialists known because it would upset other Friends.'

Another said, 'The Friends have found an easy way out; they do good works, become teachers and social workers, but they don't actually speak up.'

I came away with a slightly uneasy feeling that it had been a non-event.

Monday 11 May
Frank Chapple's attack describing me as a Stalinist was on the radio this morning, and the papers are full of the election victory of François Mitterrand as President of France, having defeated Giscard d'Estaing.

At 5.30 I chaired the Home Policy Committee and spent most of the time discussing an emergency resolution from Tony Saunois following Bobby Sands's death, condemning the Tories' stand on prison conditions in Northern Ireland. The resolution asked for prisoners in all prisons to be allowed to wear their own clothes, for access to books and writing materials and unsupervised visits.

Dennis Skinner said he had not been involved in Irish matters until he joined the National Executive, but that Ulster was our last colony. 'Long Kesh men *are* political prisoners, contrary to what Concannon said. Michael Foot conned us at the PLP by telling us he had a new initiative, and actually it was sending Concannon to support Thatcher. Sands should have been seated, and the Party wants withdrawal from Northern Ireland. We have had thirteen wasted and violent years, and I am not prepared to bury my head any more.'

Alex Kitson thought that what Dennis Skinner said was irrelevant; a working group which had been examining the issue for over a year had visited Northern Ireland and the Maze, and this emergency resolution should have gone to that working group. He moved the remission of the

Letter from 'Robert McCallum, H4 Block Long Kesh. On behalf of all Irish Republican POWs.'
Written on Government Property lavatory paper.

matter to the group and said we should certainly talk to the prison officers who were trade-unionists.

Michael Foot supported him.

Neil Kinnock said he wanted a ruling: was this an emergency?

I said it was an emergency. 'If you don't like it, you can move me out of the chair. Partition lies at the root of this problem. We have heard the Pope, the Secretary-General of the UN and Mrs Gandhi protesting, and in my opinion the United Nations might come in with a peacekeeping force.'

Joan Maynard commented, 'It is easy to condemn violence, but we have shut every door. Bipartisanship at Westminster builds up the IRA. World opinion is against us.'

Eric Heffer said that he had opposed the movement of British troops to the province in 1969. He would like to see a united Ireland and a working-class Republic. 'We cannot ignore the Sands election. There was an overwhelming vote for him.'

Kinnock went back to his point that it was not an emergency resolution. 'This will ensure a worsening of sectarianism. The repercussions in Northern Ireland will be serious. The gravity of the situation does not create an emergency. Sands would not have taken his seat anyway. There will be no peace until the British withdraw. Troops Out is popular, but this is not the issue here. The prisoners have had their conditions improved, and this resolution gives a victory to the Provos. We should wait for the working group.'

I then put the motion, and by 9 votes to 3 it was decided to remit the resolution – the three were Joan Maynard, Dennis Skinner and myself. (Saunois did not have a vote.)

Went to the campaign committee meeting at 8 with rumours circulating that Eric Heffer was going to declare his candidature tonight.

It was agreed Tony Banks would look after the trade union side with help from Francis Prideaux and Victor Schonfield, and that we should break down the constituencies by region and concentrate on trade union conferences. I will ring the National Union of Seamen. We also made arrangements about financing the campaign through the Rank and File Mobilising Committee.

Wednesday 13 May

To the House of Commons for the Shadow Cabinet. We got through next week's business in a fairly straightforward way; but, in discussing the forthcoming defence debate, I moved that the official Opposition amendment should read '. . . declines to support a defence policy based upon the threat or use of nuclear weapons by Britain, the siting of US nuclear weapons in the United Kingdom, and calls for defence spending to be brought in line with the percentage of GDP devoted to it by our allies in Europe.' I added, 'This is Conference policy and I think we should put it forward.'

Michael Foot disagreed. 'That isn't really so because our Conference resolutions were slightly contradictory between unilateral and multi-lateral disarmament; and this is only a holding operation.'

Mike Cocks said, 'Whatever you do, don't split the Party.'

'If we are going to follow Party policy, why doesn't Tony follow it on the question of retention of troops in Northern Ireland?' asked Denis Healey.

After next week's business, Michael Foot said, 'I want to talk about the situation in Northern Ireland, before I meet the Northern Ireland Study Group at 8, and I want Tony Benn to explain a broadcast he made yesterday on Northern Ireland. The Home Policy Committee discussed the matter on Monday, despite the fact that the Executive had decided that all resolutions were to be referred to the Northern Ireland Study Group, and Tony's interview is contrary to Party policy. Don Concannon visited the hunger strikers at my request; their five demands have been rejected by the Party. Saunois's resolution should never have been discussed at the Home Policy Committee. What we are discussing, Tony, is your integrity.'

'As to the question of Shadow Cabinet responsibility,' I replied, 'let me make it absolutely clear that this is not followed by other members of the Shadow Cabinet. In a public speech in Croydon, Neil Kinnock reported the proposal I made in the Shadow Cabinet that Bobby Sands be allowed to take his seat. As a matter of fact, my views on Northern Ireland are very well known; they are settled views reached over a very long time. I spoke at a fringe meeting at Conference which was very well reported. I must tell my colleagues that the present policy is a dead end, that world opinion is opposed to us, that a fresh initiative needs to be made; and that I am, in any case, a candidate for the deputy leadership of the Party, and I must have the freedom to speak on matters of political concern before the election as I did when I stood as a candidate after Harold Wilson's resignation, even though I was in the Cabinet. I do not accept for one moment that it has got anything whatever to do with my integrity, and, if that is to be raised, then what about the views of other members of the Shadow Cabinet which are totally contrary to Party policy?'

Michael Foot commented, 'It should never have come up at the Home Policy Committee. You should never have allowed it to come up.'

'I must tell you, Michael, that I think those arguments are totally unpersuasive. I have dealt with the question of integrity. It is not for the Shadow Cabinet to enforce decisions at the National Executive, and, if so, it would apply over the whole range of policy. Did you actually hear my BBC broadcast?' He said he hadn't. 'Well, you had better read it, because I never mentioned political status and I never mentioned bipartisanship but I intend to speak my mind as a member of this committee – I am not a member of the Shadow Cabinet, I am a member of the Parliamentary Committee. I know colleagues don't accept the distinction, but it is a fact that I have been offered no Front Bench position, though I was ready to undertake any responsibilities that I was asked to do.'

Michael said, 'I offered you devolution.'

I said, 'You did not, Michael; you said you would *think* about devolution. I am not able to speak in the House, I am not able to speak in the Party meeting, and now you tell me that I am not to make any further speech without checking it with you.'

Stan Orme declared, 'The NEC decision binds you.'

I said, 'Well, the NEC decisions don't appear to bind the Shadow Cabinet, and you cannot have two classes of members of the Parliamentary Committee – those who are on the Executive and are bound by Executive decisions, and those who are not and who are not bound.'

Michael Foot went on, 'Well, Don Concannon's mission was at my request. Gerry Fitt, one of the bravest men in the House, made a speech on 10 December opposing this. You should have consulted me. You are sabotaging policy, and I must ask you, Tony, not to make any more speeches on Northern Ireland.'

'Michael, I am very sorry, but I am not prepared to accept that. If that applies over the whole field to everybody dealing with Party policy, that might be one thing, but I am not prepared to accept that you or anybody else has the right to veto my speeches.'

Merlyn said, 'In December 1976 the political status of prisoners ended. There is no solution to the Northern Ireland problem – the army have got to get out of Northern Ireland, but the IRA don't really want troops out. Whatever you do, don't speak your mind.'

A most extraordinary comment, but it showed the utter dead end we have got into when people who know something about it don't say what they really think.

Then Don Concannon, who is a decent guy, spoke. He looked absolutely miserable. 'All I would say, Tony, is, all right, fight in an election as hard as you like, but don't trade votes for lives' – which was a gross distortion of what I had said. He went on to describe what an agonising mission it had been. He had gone to see Bobby Sands and talked to him for a bit, and then to see Francis Hughes (who died on hunger strike yesterday). He said, 'Francis Hughes is the hardest man I know. He probably shot 150 soldiers in his time, and when he was captured he had to have three most painful operations and he declined to have anaesthetics. As to the rest, what actually happened was that the hunger strike was ended before Christmas. A man who was dying on the hunger strike was a friend of Francis Hughes, and Hughes saw him dying and slipped him a cup of soup. When Francis Hughes went back to the compound, Bobby Sands attacked him for having done it. Francis Hughes subsequently went on hunger strike himself.'

Concannon went on to say that one of the others on hunger strike was actually cheating but he didn't want that mentioned, and he said it was the most awful job he had ever done in his life – I am sure that is true. He had done it for Michael and he had refused to go on the media. He found the whole thing terrible. It was an extremely unpleasant meeting.

As I was going through the Division Lobby, somebody told me the Pope had been shot, so I put on my little radio and heard he had been shot in the Vatican.

This evening I wasn't feeling at all well.

Thursday 14 May
I got up early and went to see Dr Stein. I only see him about every five years, and after an hour's talk with him I feel much better. But I reported the fact that I have got this tingling in my legs. At the moment, walking is like having on wellington boots full of water with a sponge in the feet. I don't have any feeling in my feet and my hands tingle. I just don't feel well at all. He examined me, and there's nothing wrong with my blood-pressure or my heart, so he thinks it might be some nerve condition.

I went to Wolverhampton by train for the People's March for Jobs.[1] There were 230 marchers, all bright and cheerful, with the mayor, who is nearly eighty, marching briskly at the front. The Bishop of Wolverhampton was there, and we marched back to St Peter's Church for a service, which I recorded. The Spinners sang 'The Family of Man' and we all sang 'Jerusalem'. Then we went out into a square where there were about 4000 people, and there was tremendous enthusiasm.

As I left the platform, Lew Gardner from Thames Television came up and asked me a few questions, and finally enquired, 'What do you think of Frank Chapple's statement that you're a little Stalin?' That was too much for me, so I said, 'Lew, you were in the Communist Party yourself, you know.' He flushed up – because indeed he was. He was in the Communist Party, worked for *Tribune*, then went to the *Express*, and now he is a real Frank Chapple himself.

Friday 15 May
Tony Banks rang to say that SOGAT had decided to come out in favour of me.

Saturday 16 May
Up at 7. The *New Statesman* supported me on Ireland.

Caught the train to Blackpool for the ASTMS conference. I read Reinhold Niebuhr's book, *The Children of Light and the Children of Darkness*, on the way.

I am being followed at the moment by two television cameras – Lew Gardner of Thames Television and Mike Cockerell of *Panorama*, who are covering the trade union conferences. It is amazing really: looked at one way, the deputy leadership of the Labour Party is, I suppose, the right of succession to Michael Foot and hence the claim to be the next Labour Prime Minister after him, if he ever becomes Prime Minister. I tramp around in the underground and talk to people in the train and have my tea and sandwiches and have no secretary, no bodyguard, nobody at all. Caught the train back.

Sunday 17 May

Hilary rang at 2 to say 'ASTMS have backed you!' And so they had, by a very narrow majority of about 650, in a vote of 28,000. So that gave me a huge boost, and it is a real kick in the teeth for Clive Jenkins, with his 'poisoned chalice'.

Monday 18 May

Tremendous press coverage of the ASTMS vote.

Tribune Group at 4.15. I had rung Ken Coates, who had spoken to Stuart Holland about getting an amendment to the debate on the defence White Paper tabled at the meeting, so Stuart had drafted it and he raised it there – 'that this House opposes any defence policy based on the use or threatened use of nuclear weapons, pledges to close down all nuclear bases, British or American, on British soil or in British waters, and calls for initiatives necessary for the establishment of a European Nuclear Free Zone.'

Jo Richardson said, 'The Party outside will expect us to do this.'

Six names were put forward of those who want to speak in the defence debate on Tuesday and Wednesday and it was agreed they should all sign it. So it will go on the order paper, but it won't be called.

Tuesday 19 May

I am really feeling weak at the moment, I can't run or jump, and I feel as if I am walking in heavy wellingtons; my throat is getting constricted, and my hands are tingling.

Wednesday 20 May

Had a meal with Caroline in the House and then I went to vote in the defence debate. As I was going into the Lobby to vote against the Government, Robin Cook said to me, 'The Lobby is buzzing with stories that you have resigned from the Shadow Cabinet.' I said, 'There's nothing in it at all.'

There was a note in my pocket from Michael Foot, but I voted before I read it, and it said there had been great concern about leaks from the Shadow Cabinet last week (which I know quite well came from Michael himself) and that 'we must have a discussion about the Tribunite motion on the order paper today.' So I wrote a note saying, 'Of course we must discuss it.'

Thursday 21 May
The papers were full of stories about my vote last night – along with seventy-five Labour MPs in the Lobby who refused to abstain.

Wednesday 27 May
I walked in to the House slowly, anxious that people shouldn't see how lame I am. I heard today that John Silkin had submitted his candidature for the deputy leadership.

Monday 1 June
Went to see Dr Stein again and he is sending me to see a neurologist at Charing Cross Hospital. I do take it seriously because it is really incapacitating me.

Joshua took me to County Hall, where there were about 1000 people from the People's March for Jobs, sitting in the bright sunshine. I spoke and paid a warm tribute to the *Morning Star* for their support.

From 3.30 to 4 I stood outside St Stephen's entrance to the House, meeting the marchers. Some of them are worried because when the march is over they will be just unemployed people again.

Wednesday 3 June
Paul Routledge of *The Times*, who had been briefed by Tony Banks, had an excellent article today on the deputy leadership, and Ian Aitken had a piece in the *Guardian* recognising that it was not going to be as easy to crush me as was thought.

I rang Dr Stein, who hadn't sent the letter to the hospital, so he gave me the name of the neurologist, Dr Clifford Rose, and I rang his secretary. She said, 'Oh, you must be Joshua's dad. How is he?' She said she would fix for me to see Dr Rose tomorrow.

At 10.30 I caught a taxi to ASLEF's offices for their annual conference. BBC and ITN were even waiting there, and one of them actually had a camera filming me getting out of the taxi. I was terrified that my unsteady gait would be noticed. Inside the ASLEF offices there was tremendous excitement. They have never had the media in a conference before and Ray Buckton was pleased. The place was crowded with journalists. Had a cup of tea downstairs and talked to four members of the NUR executive.

Went into the conference at 11.30 and got a standing ovation. I felt extremely nervous. First of all, I am a bit unsteady on my legs; secondly, the cameras were there; thirdly, it was very hot; fourthly, it was a serious conference speech and these are all middle-aged men of tremendous trade union experience, not the 'bedsitter Trotskyites' of the kind that Wilson was always talking about. They only laughed once when I made a joke about the House of Lords, but at the end they gave me a standing ovation. Ray Buckton presented me with a plaque, a cigarette lighter and a union badge. It was most moving.

Afterwards I went down into a beautiful garden – the house used to belong to Sir Thomas Beecham – and I gave an informal press conference to about twenty journalists. Was driven back by Tony Banks.

Shadow Cabinet at 5, which was sensational. I didn't make very full notes but I have got a rough idea of what happened. By 5.20 we had come to 'any other business' and Michael said, 'I want to refer to the fact that, despite the Shadow Cabinet decision to abstain on the defence debate, a Tribune amendment was tabled. Tony Benn signed it, and voted against the Government. I take this as a criticism of me, and it makes a shambles, and I would like to ask him if he has anything to say.'

I answered, 'I think it would be more sensible to recognise that there really is here a very big constitutional issue, a conflict between two concepts of collective responsibility: one is the idea that the Shadow Cabinet can have collective responsibility; the other is that the collective responsibility is to the Party and Party policy and Conference policy, and I think that that is the way it should be looked at. As far as collective responsibility itself is concerned, in the House of Commons on 16 June 1977 Mrs Thatcher asked Jim Callaghan a question about collective responsibility and he replied, "Yes, I certainly think that the doctrine should apply except in cases where I announce that it does not." That is really what it is about. It is entirely arbitrary. It is seen as the power of the Prime Minister or the Leader of the Party. It has got no constitutional foundation. It isn't any good saying that this can be left to the Shadow Cabinet to decide whether or not they will do it.'

Michael said, 'Well, I now wish to read a statement that I am going to have published. There has been a great deal of suspicion and it is Tony's fault. There have also been a lot of leaks.'

I interrupted. 'May I make one thing absolutely clear. I know people in the Shadow Cabinet don't like me writing notes but I have never described what has happened in the Shadow Cabinet; and I know that other members of the Shadow Cabinet do. I want it to be absolutely established, whether people believe it or not, that I have never given a briefing on the Shadow Cabinet.'

Well, Michael then read this twenty-five-page statement which showed he was in an absolute panic. 'In view of what he has said and done over recent weeks ... I have told Tony Benn that, in my judgement, his only course now is to stand against me ...'

He read it right through, and I won't repeat it here in full, but it was about how I was questioning his allegiance to Party policy, how the guidelines on collective responsibility were clear – he went through it all. It had obviously been drafted by Denis Healey, Peter Shore, John Silkin and Neil Kinnock. The main emphasis was that I must stand against him as Leader and let the movement decide.

When he had finished, I asked, 'May I comment briefly?'

He said I could.

'I certainly welcome the suggestion that we have a discussion with the PLP. I welcome many of the policy points that are included in the statement, but I hope you won't publish it. First of all, it was written before you heard me today, and, secondly, it is very personal and it will confuse people. Two months ago you said I shouldn't stand against Denis, and now you say I *should* stand against *you*. But of course *you* stood against Denis. I really think it would be inadvisable to publish it.'

Michael said, 'On the deputy leadership, I warned you, and I shall make proposals for collective responsibility in the future. It is a question of trust and I have been humiliated.'

There was a lot of banging on the table by Shadow Cabinet people, and John Silkin looked at me like a cat about to spring on a mouse; the hatred there was unbelievable.

Went to the Tea Room and showed Dennis Skinner the statement. He said as a joke, 'Perhaps you *should* stand against Michael, and John Silkin would beat Denis Healey.'

I staggered back to listen to the 9 o'clock News. I could hardly walk; I was pulling myself along by both arms in the corridor. It was banner headlines on the news. I rang Frances Morrell, who said, 'Don't get into a great argument with Michael, but you must let it be known you are not going to take up his offer.' So I asked her to ring the Press Association, which she did, and later I confirmed that it was authentic. Then I listened to the 10 o'clock news, which was all about it, but as a matter of fact the ASLEF speech today had established my position so clearly that I didn't really have to reply to Michael's arguments. The only thing was, I did have to say what I would be doing.

Caroline and I went and had a meal, and I drafted a statement on the following lines. 'I voted for Michael Foot when he stood for the leadership of the Party against Denis Healey last November. I continue to support him in that role, and there is no question of my standing against him for the leadership. I shall also continue to campaign for the deputy leadership in support of the policies of the Party as agreed at successive Conferences and without any references to personalities. I appeal to the whole movement to back up those policies.'

Michael was on *The World Tonight* interviewed by Anthony Howard for twenty-two minutes and it was the most muddled interview. 'Tony is in a difficulty', and 'Lenin said this' and 'Trotsky said that'. He sounded like Ramsay MacDonald in his rambling days.

I gave Chris Moncrieff of the PA my statement, having checked it with one or two people. Mik thought I should say, 'Unlike most other members of the Shadow Cabinet, I voted for Michael Foot.' But I thought that was silly.

When we got home, Hilary and Joshua turned up, and the family are rallying round like anything.

Thursday 4 June

I got up at about 4 am. I couldn't sleep, my legs were hurting, and so I worked for a couple of hours in case they keep me in hospital. Caroline has been looking in the medical dictionary and has found an illness that corresponds to all my symptoms.

Took Caroline breakfast just as a sort of final gesture, and outside the front door were a couple of camera and radio units and a lot of photographers. Hilary turned up early, went and bought all the papers, and there was a hysterical headline on every one, such as 'Fight Me Dares Foot.' Hilary put my bags in the car and then drove it round.

I walked out very slowly because I didn't want anybody to see how unsteady I was, and there were ITV and the BBC like a couple of jackals. I said I wasn't going to fight Michael Foot because I had supported him, that I was going to continue the deputy leadership campaign on the issues and not on the personalities. Then, thinking they might just use a short extract, I said in answer to four different questions, 'The policy is how to get out of the Common Market, how to get rid of American nuclear missiles, how to get back to full employment and how to abolish the House of Lords.' As I discovered later in the day, they decided to play all four answers, so it looked as if I was slightly scatty.

Hilary drove me to the Charing Cross Hospital and I was taken to see Dr Clifford Rose, who examined me. I hadn't got reflexes in my legs or arms.

He told me, 'I think I know what this is. If this was only a medical consideration, I would recommend you came into hospital at once.'

I said, 'Well, I'm perfectly happy to do that because I am simply incapacitated.'

So I was taken to the tenth floor and put in a single side-room. Hilary and I drafted a statement, which I checked with Dr Clifford Rose, saying that I had been admitted to hospital for tests for a suspected viral infection. The media then descended *en masse* on the hospital. The security people came and asked what they should do, so I said I wasn't going to see them.

I had my little television and I watched the various programmes and the discussion arising out of the Foot proposal, which was the big news story. What I need is a rest. I am not saying that it caused the viral infection, but I have been grossly overdoing it for ages, and a rest now comes at a convenient time because I am not really needed for the campaign. The issues have got across, and if I take a couple of weeks off I can come back whenever I like, provided I'm not thought to be unfit in a major way.

A Mars Bar from the Tony Benn fan club was delivered by two punks, and flowers and telegrams and letters poured in – including a letter from the Joint Shop Stewards Committee at the hospital asking if I would like to address their meeting on Wednesday, which I will do if I am still here.

Friday 5 June
I had all sorts of neurological tests today, and it may be necessary to have a lumbar puncture. Dr Rose was in yesterday morning, then Dr Kapidoo, who is the senior registrar, then Dr Clive Handler, who is the neurologist. Dr Lawrence comes and spends a lot of time getting my medical history and testing my reflexes. The nurses are extremely nice, and all the cleaners are members of NUPE. I received lots of flowers, so I put some in the day room, some in the cleaners' room, and gave some to the nurses.

Talked to the patients. One is an old lady called Mary who has had a stroke and who sang, 'Maybe it's because I'm a Londoner.' Then there's an ex-policewoman called Ann, who is now an art student, and she has got the same sort of thing as I have but she's completely paralysed and is in considerable pain. There are people with strokes and emphysema and so on.

I have visitors drifting in and out and it's really nice. The good old health service.

From 6 to 20 June, as a result of my stay in Charing Cross Hospital for what was eventually diagnosed as Guillain-Barré Syndrome, I did not keep a daily diary. The following notes of those weeks were made on 20 June and are in the form of events recalled and reflections on the hospital staff, the press and so on.

Saturday 20 June
When I first saw Dr Clifford Rose, he said, 'You must come in for treatment. That is my medical advice. It is polyneuritis, but we don't know what exactly.' I was given the most exhaustive set of tests – an ECG, brain X-rays, a brain scan, tests on my nerves and ultimately a lumbar puncture. What they discovered in the second week was that I

had Guillain-Barré Syndrome, identified by two French neurologists in the nineteenth century. The press had to be told that I wasn't going to be out after just a weekend of tests but I would be in for a fortnight and it would be a long recovery. Those tests confirmed that my general condition was excellent but that I had a disease which is very distressing, and which will take about three months to overcome. Frankly I looked forward to the holiday.

By the Tuesday or Wednesday after my going into hospital, it became quite clear that the Shadow Cabinet had been guilty of a serious overkill of vilification, and they began laying off a bit, particularly when they realised that I would not be able to attend the meetings. The elephant trap they had dug for me in the form of Michael's challenge couldn't be used, so reluctantly they had to pause.

The other political factor was that there was a tremendous sympathy vote building up, and during the fortnight I was in hospital I had about 4500 letters, only half a dozen of which were unfriendly. They were from a wide range of people expressing their encouragement, and the line of argument gave me an indication of the support for these ideas, which I would never have been able to monitor in any other way. Moreover, my absence makes no difference to the campaigning, which is well and truly under way and is known to be about the issues and not the personalities.

I was in Ward J, 10 South, in the hospital, which is in Fulham Palace Road. They gave me a room to myself, although I said I didn't want it, but, given the enormous number of visitors, it would have been difficult if I had been in the ward. The doctors were very friendly – one Adrian Wilson, turned out to be a great-nephew of Laurence Lister, who married my Aunt Hermione, Mother's sister. Then there were the nurses – Nursing Officer Frances Russell, who wore a red cape, Sister Marion Ross, Night Sister Susan Bellairs, and a whole range of others. The hospital security was under John Nichols. He had a terrible job because the camera crews and journalists were camped outside the hospital, and one of them tried to get in dressed as a doctor. Another admitted himself to casualty with a pain and when they examined him they found a camera in his trouser-leg. They were offering bribes of £400 to get photographs of me, which they never succeeded in doing. I had a very high regard for the security system. Roy Turner of the GMWU branch brought the letter from the Joint Shop Stewards Committee inviting me to address their meeting, but unfortunately I wasn't well enough. I felt sustained and supported by all the staff.

Caroline had an awful lot on her plate, with a number of education conferences coming up; but she visited me every day and was magnificent, as she always is. Mother came in on Sunday 7 June, her eighty-fourth birthday, with all the family. Chris Mullin came before the weekend was up and we had a talk. Alex Lyon, Joan Lestor, Tony and Sally Banks, Michael and Molly Meacher also paid visits, and it was nice to see them all. I was anxious that my friends should realise that I was not ill in myself.

On 17 June, our thirty-second wedding anniversary, I was discharged, and Hilary and Caroline arrived; we left to an onslaught of press, television and radio. We came out with Sister Ross, and we sat down in the sun and I gave an interview.

It was so lovely to be home, and Caroline had organised things so that the front room next to the bedroom will be my temporary office, where I can sit and work. When I got back I found Julie with Jon Lansman and Nigel Williamson who are helping with the campaign. I brought home five sacks of unanswered mail.

Wednesday 24 June

I can start working at about 11 in the morning, though I have to rest in the afternoon, and it's still painful to walk. I'm reading *Red Shelley* by Paul Foot and am enjoying it very much indeed. The only book I have read about Shelley is *Ariel* by André Maurois, and that was when I was a student. What Paul Foot has shown beyond doubt is that Shelley was a genuine romantic revolutionary who was a republican, an atheist, a leveller and a feminist, and that he was the great inspiration of the Chartists and the working-class movement until all that was forgotten by poets who managed to suppress the political Shelley and emphasise his more precious poetry. It is a brilliant book, scholarly and very readable, and Paul Foot, whom I have met only once, added a note when he sent it to me: 'Just to show that not everybody from the *Daily Mirror* or the Foot family is hostile.' Very nice of him, and I wrote and thanked him.

Wednesday 1 July

The trade union left turned up, that is to say, union general secretaries who are supporting my campaign – Walt Greendale of the T&G, Ken Gill of TASS/AUEW, Bill Maddocks of the National Union of Dyers, Bleachers and Textile Workers, Doug Grieve of the Tobacco Workers' Union, Ray Buckton and Johnnie Walker of ASLEF, also there were Tony Banks and Alan Meale. There is now a clear and friendly understanding between us as to how the campaign should be run. They are keen that I shouldn't do anything that alienates the other general secretaries because, as Ken Gill said, there are three groups in the trade unions – the ordinary members, the activists and the leaders. He said, 'You have got one of those groups, the activists, completely on your side, but the ordinary members and most general secretaries are very doubtful at the moment; you must say something official about trade-unionism and its role with the next Labour Government which will reassure people – but don't say it so near the TUC Conference that it looks crude!'

Thursday 2 July

Stuart Holland brought Ben Bella and his wife to visit me. Ben Bella, who is sixty-five, has spent twenty-three and a half of the last twenty-seven years in prison. He was one of the five Algerian leaders who, in November 1954, formed the Council for the Revolution in Algeria. Later Ben Bella was kidnapped by the French, held in the Bastille in solitary confinement, returned after the Algerian war was over, and became president of Algeria, a national hero. Then there was a military coup, Boumedienne took over, and Ben Bella was imprisoned again. With the help of some of his friends abroad, the sentence was reduced to house arrest.[2]

He thought the changes going on in Islam were very important. Caroline believes that his wife, whom he married ten years ago, may have had an effect in defusing his political faith and making him into more of an Islamic socialist. To cut a long story short, the cutting edge of the old revolutionary had been somewhat diminished. But at the same time he was thoughtful and serious. He was interested in nuclear disarmament and in agricultural development. He said the Algerian revolution had failed because it hadn't been able to rid itself of the capitalist framework within which it operated, many of the leaders of the revolution were corrupt, and so on. I thoroughly enjoyed his visit and I think he did too.

Stuart Holland came out of it very well. He is a great figure, is Stuart; he's been at Number 10 as adviser to Wilson, active with the French and Italian socialists and the Democratic Socialists Organising Committee in Washington. He'd be a good Foreign Secretary; he'd certainly be better than David Owen was.

Friday 3 July

Collected Mother for our summer break at Stansgate. It is more or less a month since I went into hospital and I hadn't walked about in London. So when we got there I walked around the garden, then found I could drive the car, so I went and picked up Melissa and her friend Tim.

Wednesday 8 July

I have not really been keeping up with news in my diary at the moment, but there have been riots in Southall, Toxteth, Manchester, Wood Green and they are dominating the news stories. This is a new factor of considerable importance in British politics with Robin Day and so on asking if the police should have riot shields, tear gas and rubber bullets, and whether the army should be brought in. Mrs Thatcher says it is just a fall in moral standards. Whitelaw maintains that parents should control children, that some eleven-year-olds are involved and *they* have never been unemployed, quite forgetting that most of their families are probably unemployed. The Labour Party is responding quite vigorously.

Tuesday 21 July

I went to the House of Commons for the first time since my illness. I drove in very nervous, but I must say everybody was warm and friendly; Tory MPs, the policemen at the House, all sorts of people. But one of the dangers of being ill is that people are a bit too benign.

I didn't make elaborate notes today because so much went on. All I can say is that I am exhausted.

Thursday 23 July

Today I worked in the office all day, dealing with my correspondence and bringing my diary up to date. Gradually the workload will melt, but I am never going back to the lifestyle I had before because it was too exhausting. I couldn't cope with the volume of meetings and it wasn't really necessary, so my illness comes at an opportune moment. Strange it should have happened in the middle of the deputy leadership election because that's the time you would have thought one would need to be frantically active. But I have learned from this how dispensable I am. Nobody is necessary at all, and I think what the Party wants now is considered and fair argument. I don't think frantically dashing round does any good.

Sunday 26 July

Today Chris Mullin and Tony Banks calculated the figures so far. Joshua has worked out a computer programme and we tested a lot of possibilities. It is clear I am going to need about 450 constituencies, 85 MPs and 2.8 million trade union votes to win, and that's not very likely.

Tuesday 28 July

Got home after 10, just as the royal wedding fireworks were beginning in Hyde Park. There were about half a million people in the park (including Joshua) and it was a splendid display.

Then on the news they showed the riots that had taken place in Toxteth again last night; there were burning objects, not fireworks but cars, with the police banging their batons on their shields and beating people up. It was a great contrast – between riches and rioting, privilege and poverty. It's terrifying.

Wednesday 29 July

Sat and watched the royal wedding on TV. There were perhaps 2 million people out in London, and this tremendous ceremonial display was watched throughout the world by 750 million people – without any doubt the biggest television audience that had ever seen anything. The image presented to the rest of the world was of a Britain about as socially advanced as France before the French revolution! We are slipping back to eighteenth-century politics. We've got to fight like anything to recover the position that we had even in 1945. I had that feeling most strongly. It was feudal propaganda, turning citizens into subjects.

As an utterly convinced republican, I believe that a monarchical system of government is fundamentally undemocratic, and that the powers of the monarchy have got to be taken away. But republicanism frequently ignores the legal and constitutional powers of the monarchy and concentrates on attacking the royal family. I think we must focus on attacking the powers of the monarchy rather than the royal family itself. Anyway, I've got my first reference to the monarchy in my book *Arguments for Democracy*.

Today the press were outside my door all day. They knocked on it once an hour from 9.30 to 4.30. I presume it was the *Sun* or the *Daily Mail*; a marvellous example of harassment.

Thursday 30 July

I'm a complete stranger in the House of Commons at the moment. I haven't been there properly for months because of my speaking engagements; my division voting record will be appalling. This whole campaign is a great risk. It may be premature, but it has involved aligning myself with the left and the rank and file outside Parliament and then making a re-entry.

I personally would like to see some kind of Labour Representation Committee set up in place of the Rank and File Mobilising Committee, a Labour Representation Committee that harnessed the Labour MPs together with the left in the unions and at grass roots in the constituencies, and that would have a powerful influence on the development of British politics.

It may be that one aspect of the forthcoming Conference – which will be excellent on policy, unilateralism, the Common Market and defence – will be a swing to the right, and I mustn't assume that the NEC will always be weighted our way. We might lose control of the Executive; in those circumstances, we might lose our majority in Conference next year and I could be displaced from the Home Policy Committee and so on. So I may be driven to being a backbench member of the National Executive, arguing the case and campaigning in the country.

I'll stick my neck out now and guess the outcome of the electoral college. I think I'll get 43 per cent and Denis 57 per cent.

Friday 31 July

Went to the hospital and saw Clifford Rose, who thought I was better, but I'm not sure I am in terms of mobility and sensation. Went and had some painful tests.

Came home and found that, in the storm, water had poured into the bedroom and soaked the bed.

Thursday 6 August
Fantastic thunder and lightning.

In the evening we had the campaign committee to dinner: Michael and Molly Meacher, Stuart and Jenny Holland, Reg Race and his partner Mandy Moore, Chris Mullin, Tony and Sally Banks. It was great fun. Copies of *Arguments for Democracy* arrived from the publishers this afternoon so I was able to give everybody a copy. Joshua put on a fantastic computer display showing the possible outcomes, and it flashed up 'Benn Wins' or 'Healey Wins', and it was very entertaining. Everybody is worried about the SDP and what they really mean, so I said I would write something about it. *The Times* and the *Daily Mirror* had a horrible picture of me with my toes turning in, looking as if my hips were out of joint. This is the new press line – that, in addition to being mad, ambitious, incompetent and communist, I am sick as well.

There are now over 200 nominations for me, but this morning's press was soured by an open letter from Janey Buchan, Labour MEP for Glasgow, and wife of Norman Buchan, which appeared in *Labour Weekly* and has been released *en bloc* to the daily papers. It was a filthy attack, saying I should repudiate those of my supporters who were criticising people, particularly herself, who were not in favour of my candidacy. She mentioned Arthur Scargill, and rebuked me for my 'wild pledges' on the House of Lords and the Common Market. She got it all wrong. George Galloway rang me up from Dundee for a chat because he and Janey Buchan were to be on the one o'clock news together to discuss it. He handled it brilliantly.

In the afternoon I.F. Stone, the famous American liberal socialist columnist and writer, came in to talk to me and Stephen. He wanted to know how he could project my views the most sympathetically to the United States. He's a little, quiet man in his seventies, very shrewd, thinks Britain is ossified, hierarchical and undemocratic, and asked what could be done. He listened, and wished me well, and said that Europe should get America off its back because America, having won all the wars since the beginning of time, had now lost three in succession – Vietnam, Iran and Cuba – and were just busting for a fight. I agreed with that view.

Sunday 9 August
Collected Mother and left for Stansgate with three clear weeks ahead for our holiday.

Wednesday 26 August
The nomination figures were released today. I have got 225 constitu-

encies, nine trade unions, three socialist societies and thirty-two MPs, so far. Healey has thirty-two constituencies, nine trade unions, one socialist society and seventy-two MPs. Silkin has eight constituencies, no trade unions, no socialist societies and thirty-two MPs. Healey launched an attack on me, but on the whole the campaign is going well. Every day I talk to Jon Lansman, to Nigel Williamson, to Frances Morrell, to Joshua and Stephen, and the campaign couldn't have started better with these nominations.

Saturday 29 August
Joshua worked out tonight that I would get a better result had there been a one-third, one-third, one-third division of the electoral college, on the basis of present indications, than I would from 40–30–30.

Sunday 30 August
Fantastic weather. The *Sunday Times* confirmed that Jim Callaghan will come out of retirement to campaign for Denis Healey. They predicted that if I won, the PLP might even elect its own leader. The *Sunday Express* had a Cummings cartoon of me dressed up as a fascist with a hammer and sickle on my sleeve and the caption 'Ein Volk, Ein Reich, Ein Führer'.

If I was asked to stick my neck out now, I would say I believe Healey will win with about 53 per cent to 47 per cent, and I would be very content with that. If I got less than 45 per cent I would be disappointed, surprised if I got more than 47 per cent, and if I won I would be astonished; but anything is possible.

Thursday 3 September
Michael Meacher had phoned to say he was going to be on *News at One*, and the Callaghan attack was featured together with an interview with Joe Gormley, who said he was sure I would be the Leader of the Labour Party. If he had a vote, he said, he would vote for Healey, but he was sure I would win – which was a tremendous boost. Then Michael Meacher was smashing. He said Callaghan was deeply respected, he'd held many offices of state, but of course he was in favour of the Common Market, in favour of the neutron bomb, in favour of Cruise missiles, in favour of a wage policy, etc., and had led us to the greatest disaster since 1931. It was devastating.

Did my first public meeting since I became ill. I was a bit nervous, actually, in case things went wrong. It was a meeting of the NUPE London branches – Gerald Kaufman representing Healey, Judith Hart representing Silkin and myself. There were about eighty people there – of whom over seventy were for me I should think. The Silkinites were odious, saying things like 'We should abolish the deputy leadership. It doesn't matter. Why have it?' – arguments which were quite incredible to the audience. Kaufman said that under free collective bargaining the miners had taken money out of the hands of the NUPE people, and were trying to split the labour movement.

Friday 4 September

Papers full of confidence that Healey would win, of Jim Callaghan's attack on 'sectarian dogmatism', and of Joe Gormley's statement that the NUM had decided that the miners would vote for Deputy Leader in a pit-head ballot, and that I would be the Leader of the Party in the end.

Left for Bristol at 8.30 and Dawn met me. She and Mike are having great difficulties there.

To a joint meeting of the Labour Co-ordinating Committee, Rank and File Mobilising Committee and Gwent Alliance at the College of Technology. Ann Clwyd, a Member of the European Parliament, was there. She told me that not a single Labour MP in Wales would appear on a platform with me, and it does confirm my view that, despite all the rhetoric, the Welsh labour establishment have lost their fire, and that's why Wales is being trampled on. I was a little nervous, but I made the speech without any difficulty.

Monday 7 September

At 10 I was collected and taken to BBC Radio London, and who should I meet there but Robert Morley, the actor, who you would think was a typical Tory but I knew was an old fan of mine, so I greeted him warmly.

Did the interview for Radio London and another one with Tony Blackburn, the disc jockey, a real Tory, the epitome of the power of radio stations and free enterprise. A real Thatcherite. But he has a reasonably large audience. Then on to Broadcasting House for an interview 'down the line' with a guy called Vincent Kane for BBC Wales, and for BBC Radio Scotland.

Tony Banks rang to say that the news from the TUC Conference at Blackpool is that we should now get the TGWU to vote for me on the first ballot – and that would be a sign of confidence. The miners' news is good.

Tuesday 8 September

Caroline and I went off early and caught the train to Blackpool for the TUC, where Jeremy Corbyn and Jon Lansman met us. We sat in the Conference and listened to Michael Foot, who made a disgraceful speech; that's the only way to describe it. It was a ritual attack on Mrs Thatcher and Heseltine, but most of it was devoted to attacking 'sectarian dogmatism' and the 'undermining' of parliamentary democracy – quoting Aneurin Bevan, of course.

To the Carlton Hotel for the ACTT party to celebrate Alan Sapper's re-election as General Secretary. Had a word with Stan Pemberton, Chairman of the T&G. He kept saying, 'The best of fucking British luck to you, comrade. Just keep your head down this month and you'll be all right.' There is a real hope that the T&G might vote for me on the first ballot of the deputy leadership contest.

Wednesday 9 September

Mass press coverage of Foot's speech; it's now just continuous headlines – 'Foot Bashes Benn', 'Healey Bashes Benn', 'Shore Blasts Benn', 'Hattersley Attacks Benn' – and it's just such a ritual that in a way it's losing its impact.

Caroline went back to London and I went into the Congress. My first appointment was with Arthur Scargill and the Durham miners. They were confident that the Durham vote would go well.

Tony Banks picked me up and with Nigel Williamson we drove to Newcastle, three hours across the Pennines, for a meeting organised by NUPE. We went into the City Hall and it was fantastic. The Red Umbrella Band were playing 'The Red Flag' as we went in. They had taken a bit of a risk booking the City Hall and didn't expect to fill the balcony, but there were 2300 people there.

Tom Sawyer, the NUPE organiser, was in the chair. I spoke and dealt with Michael Foot's infantile and trivial critique, and then I went on to give a lecture on democracy and socialism, and I got the most prolonged ovation I think I have ever had in my life. Then we had some excellent questions.

Afterwards Tony Banks drove us back to Blackpool, and I collapsed into bed.

Thursday 10 September

Up early and read all the papers. There were a few reviews of *Arguments for Democracy*, which is officially published today: Bernard Crick attacked it in the *Guardian*; the *Telegraph* said it was a charter for moles and militants; Denis Lehane in the *Express* compared it to *Mein Kampf* – such a gross distortion as to be beyond comment.

To the Clifton Hotel and met Madame Allende,* whom I had never met before, a very beautiful woman who must be in her mid-sixties. She had just arrived from somewhere and was going straight off somewhere else, and I said, 'You are travelling all the time, aren't you?'

She replied, 'That's how we keep the movement alive.'

'May I ask you a question, because everybody asks me this. If we get a radical Labour Government, how do we avoid suffering the same fate as Salvador Allende?'

She didn't understand it to begin with, so it was translated. Then she

---

* The widow of Salvador Allende, President of Chile. Allende was murdered during a military coup in September 1973, which was backed by the US Government, and led by General Pinochet.

answered, 'We never created a Marxist socialist state; we began the democratic control of our own society and our own economy, and we nationalised the copper – that was all we ever did in Chile. All the international bankers clamped down on us, the internationals, the IT&T, the American Government. It wouldn't happen to you; you are much stronger than we are. Look at France.'

I said, 'Well, I agree, look at France. But is there anything you could have done differently if you had known what was going to happen?'

'No, it was inevitable, and, whatever we could have done in Chile, it would have happened, because they were determined to crush us and we were weak.'

I told her that Chile in the 1980s was what Spain was for the 1930s, and she said, 'We are not prepared to live under fascism for as long as that.' So I asked her what we could do to help and she said, 'Stop supplying arms, particularly ships. Clamp down on credits, and you can bring real pressure on Pinochet.' I asked if the Reagan administration made it worse and she replied, 'Much worse, because they entirely support this regime; the American Ambassador to the UN was recently in Santiago and he said America would rather have dictatorships sympathetic to America than democracies that were against.' She said the murder of a Chilean former Minister, Orlando Letelier, in Washington in 1976 has now been clearly identified with American forces, but they won't publish the truth. A remarkable woman.

We went back to the flat where Tony Banks and Nigel Williamson and the others are living for the TUC conference. I worked on my speech and practised it, something I don't normally do, but it had to be less than ten minutes. Then back to the Winter Gardens and into the theatre where the debate between the three candidates was to take place. John Silkin was the first to come up and I shook his hand, then Denis came up and we had a friendly word. It was the first time we had met together since the three candidatures were announced, and all of a sudden I felt a certain warmth, because after all we know each other very well and it isn't as if you have to be unfriendly. Jim Mortimer was in the chair, Alan Sapper and Jim Curran were on the platform. There must have been about 1400 people there, and it was crammed with television cameras and photographers taking pictures. There was a buzz on the microphone, and we had had that problem last night in Newcastle, so I was damned if I was going to speak until it was cleared. They tried to deal with it.

The lots had been drawn by Tony Banks and I was first, so I went to the rostrum knowing I couldn't pause for any heckling or applause and I spoke for 9 minutes and 44 seconds. Healey spoke, followed by Silkin, then we had questions and then wound up in the same order. Healey was honest and straightforward, but he did pursue this communist and Trotskyist and élitist stuff which I think is damaging to him. Silkin sold himself like a product but did manage to establish the argument for unity. He hadn't anything like the weight required, but he did well, and it was a good meeting.

Afterwards we went to a NUPE party where there were tons of friends. One MP was apparently saying something about the 'Benn bully boys' – I thought it was a bit much that Denis writes for the *Express* and never attacks it, while it compares me with Hitler. Ken Cameron said he wasn't convinced the Fire Brigades' Union was going wrong but it was just a possibility.

Tony Banks and I were ready to leave for the station, having fifteen minutes to catch the train, but the taxi wouldn't start, so we pushed it, but it still wouldn't go, so the son of the proprietor of the hotel, a man of about twenty-eight, leapt in his Volkswagen and drove us to the station. It was pelting with rain.

Caught the sleeper at Preston and am dictating this diary on it. It is very exciting; I've had a marvellous three days in the north. Tony Banks, Nigel Williamson and Jon Lansman have been terrific.

Monday 14 September

Arthur Scargill rang to say he was sure the miners were OK. The NUPE vote will not be available until the Sunday of Conference.

Joan Lestor has written to me to say she is going to abstain, and I gather a round robin from about twenty MPs is in circulation explaining why they are going to abstain – that's the ex-Tribunites. Neil Kinnock is going to issue a pompous 3000-word statement saying he is going to abstain, and Michael Foot is encouraging it in the hope that the T&G will do the same. No doubt Kinnock is also trying to influence the T&G.

Thursday 17 September

Had a word with Arthur Scargill, who said we now had the Scottish branch, South Wales, Yorkshire, Scottish crafts and North Derbyshire. It is important that we should get the miners' support before the T&G conference because it will influence them, and it was mentioned on the 10 o'clock news that the T&G is going heavily, by six regions to three, in favour of Healey. Whether this is productive for Healey or not, I'm not sure, but it is a factor I must take into account. Clearly if I lost the T&G, I would be totally lost, and Healey would romp home. If I win the miners and the TGWU, and if NUPE stays firm, I might squeak home.

Saturday 19 September

Caroline and I went to Birmingham for the Party's national rally on unemployment, and had a hell of a job trying to find the march because of the impossible Birmingham road system. We finally found it, and walked for about three miles to Aston Park.

Casualties of the Thatcher years:
Geoffrey Howe (*with wreath*), Leon Brittan (*below*) and Nigel Lawson (*foot*)

Michael Heseltine (*above left*) came back; Douglas Hurd survived

...Alan Meale and (*right*) Jo Richardson

Into the wilderness, June 1983
(*Left*) Rethinking the future with (*left of tree*) Stuart Holland and (*below*) Tom Sawyer and Jeremy Corbyn...

... Reg Race and Jon Lansman (*above*), Ken Livingstone (*left*) and Chris Mullin (*far left*) in his Brixton garden

Comrades: With Mick McGahey, miners' leader and (*below left*) Jim Mortimer (*below*) Ralph Miliband, founder of the ILCS

Campaigning for the deputy leadership: Foot (*top*) disapproved, while Michael Meacher and Chris Mullin supported

The Gang of Four in their hey-day

A gang of six at Labour Conference

Chesterfield by-election, 1984: Roy Hattersley shares a platform

Denis Healey, the old trouper, in Chesterfield, 1984

Neil Kinnock on by-election walkabout, 1984

The rumours that NUPE have gone bad on us are too strong to be disregarded. I saw Ken Cameron, who had news that the Fire Brigades' Union were not very friendly either.

On the platform were Michael Foot, Denis Healey, David Hughes (National Agent), Ron Hayward (General Secretary), Alex Kitson in the chair, Stan Orme, Eric Heffer and others. Laurence Coates (son of Ken Coates), who is to be the new YS representative on the NEC, was there. Eric spoke first; he established the main policy points and got a good reception. Stan Orme was heard in silence. I got a tremendous cheer when I appeared and after I spoke. Michael Foot's speech was just absolute flat rhetoric. Denis Healey was heckled and booed.

We got back about 6, in time to see the television news, which showed Denis Healey being continually barracked at the meeting and prevented from speaking. Frank Allaun rang me about it – I will have to make it clear that there should be no shouting and that all the candidates should be listened to respectfully.

Sunday 20 September

Up early. All the papers full of the booing of Healey – the *Sunday Mirror* saying 'Healey Booed by Benn Mob'.

Was picked up at 11 and taken to London Weekend Television for the *Weekend World* discussion with Brian Walden, Denis Healey and John Silkin. We got stuck in a traffic jam, and the guy behind ran up and banged on the window and said, 'The press are all over the place. Go in the back way.' Then in the next traffic jam he came up again and said, 'The back way is blocked. Go through the garage.'

Brian Walden had told me the plan for the programme was to ask, 'Why are you fighting the election', and then he was going to put doubters' questions to each of us. So we went into the studio, and, after we had all spoken, Brian turned to me and raised the question of the booing and heckling yesterday. I said that I was strongly in favour of free speech, and Healey should have been allowed to speak. He pressed the point about the 'undemocratic' nature of yesterday's events.

When he turned to Denis, Denis talked about the Party being in danger of sectarianism and bitterness, and then made the astonishing allegation that 'Mr Jon Lansman' was responsible for orchestrating the booing and heckling. He claimed that at a rally in Cardiff in July Lansman was also responsible for leading the crowd. Brian Walden said, 'That is an amazing statement to make.' Denis repeated it, and it was put to me. I said, 'I wasn't present at all of the meeting, but I am in favour of free speech', and so on. But the Lansman episode dominated the questions.

Came home and had a bite to eat. At 2 the campaign committee arrived. I heard from them that Jon Lansman had not been present in Cardiff in July nor had he been at the Birmingham rally yesterday.

Well this was unbelievable. So we tried to get through to Jon on the phone, and eventually he rang back. He is putting out a statement that he was in Wales yesterday and can prove it, and he was on holiday in Italy at the time of the rally in Cardiff on 4 July. Then ITN rang me up about it. Did I have a photograph of him? And so on. I said, 'No, you have just got to report the fact that it was a complete lie.'

Arthur rang to say we had won in Nottinghamshire, so we've got the NUM vote.

It had been suggested that I ring Alf Dubs, the Battersea South MP, who had doubts about the crowd behaviour, the shouting, the 'lack of democracy', and who is not sure how to vote because of it. So he came round. I answered his doubts as best I could and he was friendly.

At the end he said, 'I want to tell you what I am going to do.'

'Don't feel that you have to, because I am not canvassing.'

'Well I would like to. I am definitely voting for you on the second ballot. The question is, do I vote for Silkin on the first?'

'There definitely will be a second ballot,' I said, 'but you must do what's right.' I gave him a copy of my new book and he went off.

I watched the ITN ten o'clock news bulletin, which had a devastating denunciation of Healey, including an interview with him saying, 'If I made a mistake, it was unwise', and so on. Then a statement from Jon that if he didn't get a proper apology he would consider legal action. It has done Healey endless damage to have said something with such certainty which was absolutely false and without foundation. John Golding is going to raise it with the NEC on Wednesday. I don't want to get muddled up with these stories; I intend to get back to the issues.

Monday 21 September

Another momentous day today. Got up and heard the 6 o'clock bulletin with a summary of today's papers, and Healey was the main headline – 'Healey Blunders', 'Healey Drops a Clanger', and so on.

To a sub-committee of the TUC-Labour Party Liaison Committee to discuss a paper prepared by David Lea and Geoff Bish. It was a real bureaucrats' paper – let's copy France and Japan. There was nothing about social justice or socialism.

After David Lea had introduced it, Norman Atkinson said, 'Well, I don't see any rejection of the market mechanism', and people looked as if he had shouted in the British Museum!

Geoff Bish said, 'Well, the Party hasn't opposed the market mechanism for a decade or more. It hasn't been rejected by the Party for years.'

So Peter Shore commented, 'I'm glad Norman has taken us back to our philosophy, but, you know, we discovered long ago that when you intervene in industry you pay the price.'

'Can I say I think this is a very important point,' I said. 'It is much more complicated than we make out, because after all the nationalised industries have been made to conform to an artificial market mechanism, and private industry doesn't even conform to the market mechanism because it has never invested against future demand. We should therefore redefine our concept of the market mechanism and make it absolutely clear that we are talking about the difference between the big companies and the 98 per cent of companies that are medium and small businesses; and it is not true that we are trying to bend some inexorable law that represents the most economic deployment of resources. In fact, it is more expensive to neglect your railway investment and your capital investment.'

Came home, and I had a phone call that the Transport and General Workers' Union had decided to support me in the second ballot. All hell broke loose. First of all, twenty journalists and cameramen camped outside the door, and I wouldn't comment. Others phoned, and I still wouldn't comment. The Healey campaign has backfired in his face. So it is possible now that I might actually win. The BBC news at 9 was a funeral oration.

Tuesday 22 September
The papers were full of attacks on the executive of the T&G for supporting me yesterday – 'Votes hijacked' and all that. It's hard to know how to react. I refused to speak to the journalists and film crews waiting outside the front door.

Joshua drove me to the station for a train to Leeds, and there was a BBC television crew trying to get a comment from me. I said I would be making a speech in Leeds and got on the train. When I arrived I had a cup of tea and a couple of eggs and chips in a little cafe. Then I went to the Town Hall, which is a most beautiful place, for a fantastic meeting – with 2100 people inside and 2000 turned away. Yorkshire audiences are very quiet when you're speaking and they cheer at the end. There were questions and a bit of heckling from a Namibian group and from the H-Blocks people.

Wednesday 23 September
Went to the National Executive, where the barracking of Healey in Birmingham was raised. Alex Kitson said it was atrocious, and he proposed we pass a motion condemning the conduct of those responsible. Michael Foot said it was right to condemn it.

John Golding supported condemnation, but said there had been co-ordinated barracking and he wanted an inquiry by the Organisation Sub-committee – and he wanted a report from the Midlands Region and the stewards. He believed we must expel from the Party those who did this sort of thing.

Denis Healey argued that, since we financed these rallies, it just encouraged anti-Labour reaction, and we should seriously consider whether it was worth having the rallies at all.

Tony Saunois said, 'We must discourage the shouting. But, when John Golding addressed the YS, they heard him in complete silence.'

At my suggestion, Jo Richardson said, 'We should add condemnation of the media handling of the campaign.'

Betty Boothroyd, who has replaced Shirley Williams, didn't want the press matter added.

I said, 'Well, I'm all for condemning, but who did it? We all know who did it. We all know it was the SWP, the WRP, the anarchists, the H-Blocks people – they heckled me for six minutes last year at a meeting. It was not orchestrated by people in the Party. As to the role of the media, I don't want to press it in this resolution if people don't want to do it, but I've been described as Oswald Mosley in the *Mirror* and as Hitler in the *Daily Express*, and nobody condemned that; and I have never made anything of it because I always thought Harold Wilson made a great mistake to complain about smears.'

Dennis Skinner made a hilarious speech and remarked, 'Don't make heavy weather of it. There's more barracking in the House of Commons, with animal noises and shouting at least as bad as at Birmingham.'

Friday 25 September
The Times had a profile of the three candidates, and under me the caption included some absurd claims about my owning a farm in Essex and having a trust in the 'tax haven' of Bermuda.

Well, Julian Haviland rang me a couple of days ago and asked me about my financial position, and I told him I had inherited shares in Benn Brothers, the publishers, had bought a house in London which cost me £4600 and had a house in Stansgate, Essex, bought by my father for £1500 before the war. I also told him that I had never bought or sold a share in my life and I had some earnings from freelance work. He said, 'Well, we're doing a bit of financial background on each candidate.' *The Times* never mentioned that Healey had earnings from the *Daily Express* or that John Silkin had declared that his average private income over the last ten years had been £15,900 per year.

I decided to write to *The Times*, drawing attention to the lie they had printed in August 1977 about my children receiving private medical treatment. I rang them later and was told my letter had been set up in type and was before the editor, Harold Evans, for approval.

Then someone from the business desk rang me back, and I said I had never heard of the trust. He asked if I had any money in Bermuda and I said 'No. I answered all Julian Haviland's questions and he never reported. You have printed two lies and you had better correct them.'

Julie rang to say she had appendicitis and was going to hospital. The phone rang continuously.

My campaign committee arrived with lots of information, which I didn't really have time to absorb. They are not confident about NUPE and think we may lose. We also had the figures from Vincent Hanna at *Newsnight* of forty MPs who might abstain, and we did a lot of calculations, but it's very hard to predict. But tonight *Newsnight* are going to predict that I will win.

It does now depend on two things: on NUPE, and on whether left MPs are prepared to abstain. If they all vote for me, it will be all right.

Labour Party Conference, Brighton
Saturday 26 September
Got up about 6.30, very tired. *The Times* printed my letter and apologised, so I've caught *The Times* out on two lies now, the 1977 story and now this.

Packed up for the Brighton Conference. What an incredible time! It is pouring with rain but I am really looking forward to it and enjoying it.

We packed up all our stuff in tons of bags – video recorder, Joshua's VDU, etc. – and we got to Brighton at 11.45 and found one of the London MEPs, Richard Balfe, and his wife Vivien and others had set up a marvellous office in the Grand Hotel with an electric typewriter, photocopier, radio, the lot!

Joshua was working on his computer and if the T&G and NUPE vote for me, then I'm home comfortably, even with forty abstentions and only 480 constituencies. If NUPE vote for Healey but the T&G vote for me, I could just win if I could scrabble together a few more MPs and a few more constituencies. If NUPE abstain, I could probably still win on forty abstentions and 480 constituencies, or it could be neck and neck. So there is clearly a sense of confidence about it which I have never had before.

Agreed to meet the campaign committee at 8.30 tomorrow morning. The word is going round now that we are going to win; I think confidence is the major factor, particularly with MPs, and that is what is going to decide the issue now. NUPE is in the balance. I don't know.

Sunday 27 September
The day of the election for the Deputy Leader. I didn't have time to read the papers. There was no word from Michael Foot, though I had expected there would be. The campaign committee had a meeting at 8.30 and we agreed on a last-minute leaflet.

There were photographers everywhere.

We went to the CLPD meeting in the Metropole Hotel at which Dennis Skinner made a brilliant speech. When we went in we heard that NUPE had decided to vote for Denis Healey – which most people thought was the finish of us, but we knew it wasn't.

Caroline drafted with me a statement for release after the result.

We went over to the conference hall at 5 pm. The press were hysterical, people were cheering and shouting, and, as I got my papers for the first ballot, we heard a rumour that the T&G, who were voting for Silkin in the first ballot, had in fact decided to abstain in the second. Well, that was a body blow! Joshua immediately worked out some computer predictions on the basis of an abstention from the TGWU on the second.

Anyway, we went in, and I was prepared for a massive defeat and was feeling pretty gloomy, but I tried to look as cheerful as I could on the platform. The Conference began with the usual address by the Mayor, the Chairman's address, the Conference Arrangements Committee report – during which some women made a terrific protest to get positive discrimination for women debated. Then the Chairman, Alex Kitson, took a show of hands on smoking, and that was banned from the conference hall.

At the end of that, the first ballot result was announced, and it showed precisely what Joshua had predicted – Healey 44.536 per cent (Joshua's figure, 45), me 36.639 per cent (Joshua's, 37.5), Silkin, with the T&G, 18 per cent. Rumours then began circulating on the platform that the T&G *had* decided to vote for me on the second ballot – which they did – and Joshua's prediction then was that Healey would get 51.3 and I would get 48.7 per cent.

The second ballot was called immediately, and while it was being counted there was a debate on South Africa. I got three separate messages that I had won, and finally, after the address by the Secretary of the Socialist International, the result was announced: Denis Healey got 50.426 and I got 49.547 per cent, which was an absolute whisker's difference.

I came off the platform, and all the press were there and I had a job saying anything. Then I picked up Caroline and we walked with a barrage of press and masses of cheering and pushing back to the hotel, where people cheered in the lobby and all the way up the stairs.

We had sandwiches and then decided to go out to the *London Labour Briefing* meeting at the Queen's Hotel, and it was packed out. I spoke briefly. Came out, and I declined to comment any further. Then Caroline and I walked to the fish and chip shop and the media followed us in there. We came back to the hotel and slowly we briefed ourselves on what had actually happened.

It has been a staggering result with all the media against us, the most violent attacks by the Shadow Cabinet, the full intervention of Michael, the abstention of a group of Tribune Group MPs who, in the end, turned out to be the people who carried the day – Stan Orme, Martin

O'Neill, Neil Kinnock, Jeff Rooker, Joe Ashton, Tom Pendry. We got within 0.8 per cent of victory, and it was the best possible result, because if I had won by 0.8 per cent people would have shouted 'cheat'. It only requires four or six Labour MPs to join the SDP* for Healey's majority to disappear, and then he will hold the post but not have the authority.

So sitting on the bathroom floor of the hotel, so as not to disturb Caroline, I bring to an end the report on the first electoral college ever held to allow the members of the Party to vote for the Deputy Leader of the Labour Party, and it has been far more successful than I could possibly have dreamed at the beginning.

Tuesday 29 September
At 9, Andrew Murray and Martin Gostwick of the *Morning Star* came to do an interview in the hotel. Then we had the results of the NEC elections, which were a disaster for us – Norman Atkinson lost the treasurership to Eric Varley, and we lost Charlie Kelly, Renée Short and Margaret Beckett. Shirley Summerskill and Gwyneth Dunwoody replaced Margaret and Renée.

Came back to my room and didn't budge until 11. Tony Banks came over with Sally and Stephen [Benn] to say that Alex Kitson and Judith Hart wanted to do a deal with me about the NEC chairmanships because they are afraid the right are going to seize the lot. I'm not disposed to talk to anybody. My main concern is what I shall say at the *Tribune* rally tomorrow night.

Wednesday 30 September
The Conference discussed defence, and we scored a great triumph on the motion moved by Larry Smith of the TGWU committing the Party to unilateral nuclear disarmament. But we lost the composite calling for withdrawal from NATO. Brynmor John, our defence spokesman, walked out on the grounds that he had not been called to speak.

Hilary walked with me over to the Dome for the *Tribune* meeting, where about a couple of thousand people were gathered. Jo Richardson was in the chair. A delegate from the French Socialist Party spoke and got a tremendous reception, then the Greek representative, then Neil Kinnock made the annual *Tribune* collection with lots of jokes that fell flat. Michael Foot spoke and left soon after. Margaret Beckett made a speech defending me and my right to stand – it was quietly and strongly delivered and was devastating. I spoke for half an hour, which was a bit long, but it was about how we proceed from here. Then Dick Clements at the end talked about tolerance and socialism – an absolutely meaningless contribution.

* Over the months that followed the Labour Party Conference of 1981, nine Labour MPs who had voted for Denis Healey joined the SDP – Dickson Mabon, David Ginsburg, Tom McNally, James Dunn, John Grant, George Cunningham, Ron C. Brown, Jeffrey Thomas, Bruce Douglas-Mann.

Thursday 1 October

Joshua and Hilary left, Stephen having gone back in the middle of the night. When I went into the Conference, lots of people came up. Alf Dubs wanted me to try to protect Neil Kinnock from recriminations because of his abstention. I said, 'I'm not in the business of going round with a first-aid kit helping people to bind up their self-inflicted wounds.'

I was interviewed by ITN, Michael Foot having told them he hadn't talked to me this week but hoped to do so, and also hoped I would stand for the Shadow Cabinet and be elected to it, take some position in it. The bribe is quite clear. He'll probably offer me Shadow Minister of Employment, and the right will vote me into the Shadow Cabinet on the assumption that I will shut up. But I won't shut up. If we go in, we go in on a proper left slate, on the principles of the deputy leadership election, and claim the right to speak on everything, to speak in the PLP meetings and not to be cramped by Shadow Cabinet decisions that are contrary to Party policy.

Dick Mabon [MP for Greenock and Port Glasgow], who voted for Healey, resigned from the Party today, and it is thought that Richard Mitchell [MP for Southampton Itchen], who abstained, and one or two others may go, so I should think that by next week Denis Healey's majority will have disappeared and morally I will be the Deputy Leader of the Labour Party.

What a week it has been. Although the right think they have won control, of course they haven't. I did talk to the lobby journalists, and I pointed out to them that we were not going through the same game again, and the deal – we'll offer you a job in the Shadow Cabinet if you'll shut up – wasn't on. I don't think we've done too badly at all, because this is a left that means to win, not a left that is prepared to make its point and lose and go along with another Wilson-type fudge; that isn't on. If Michael Foot wants to win an Election, he's got to make some move towards the Conference, not the left but the Conference, and he can't compromise all the time to keep the Dick Mabons and David Owenses and Shirley Williamses in the Party. I think Michael is going to have a bit of a shock; certainly over the last few years he has always believed a fix would solve everything, and it won't.

Tuesday 6 October

President Sadat was assassinated in Egypt tonight.

Wednesday 7 October

Sally went in to University College Hospital and at 3.42 gave birth to a boy, Michael Graham Clark Benn – my first grandson. Hilary was there, and Caroline visited the baby in the afternoon.

Went to see Mother, who is now a great-grandmother. Came home and there was Hilary and 'Uncle' Joshua, and we were all very excited.

NOTES
Chapter Two

1.   (p 131) The People's March for Jobs was an initiative, supported by the TUC, to draw attention to the serious and rising levels of unemployment in Britain: by May 1981 there were two and a half million people out of jobs and in Merseyside unemployment was 18.4 per cent. Two hundred workers started the March from Liverpool and they were joined by feeder marches from areas of high unemployment such as Consett. It culminated at the end of May with a rally in London of 200,000 people. I met the marchers at various stages of their March.

2.   (p 140) As chairman of the Algeria Committee of the Movement for Colonial Freedom I was actively involved in the 1950s in the Algerian Liberation Movement campaign against French imperialism. Algeria won its freedom in 1962, and the Algerian leader, Ben Bella, subsequently became President, but was deposed in 1965.

3
The Falklands War
October 1981–June 1982

Thursday 8 October
Arthur Scargill came to lunch and told me that he was considering the possibility of a merger between the NUM and the TGWU, in which case he would run for General Secretary. He thought the two unions should increase their affiliations to the Party in order to strengthen the left-wing vote at next year's Party Conference.

Sunday 11 October
I read the typescript of Chris Mullin's new novel, *A Very British Coup*, the story of how a Labour Government elected in 1989 is brought down by the security services.

Harry Perkins, the Prime Minister, is a steelworker who drinks tea from a mug with a tea bag and was a former Secretary of State for Energy who had rows with his civil servants about nuclear reactors. To cut a long story short, he is brought down by a scandal. It's very well done. I gave Chris a couple of hints and he's going to change a few details.

Caroline and I went for a walk.

Wednesday 14 October
At 5 I went to the old deputy leadership campaign committee, which Norman Atkinson chaired. I said I had reached the conclusion that the constituent bodies of the old Rank and File Mobilising Committee had come to the end of their mandate, which was the deputy leadership campaign, and they needed to consult and refresh their mandate.

We read a paper written by Chris Mullin. 'The Left After Brighton', discussing the future of the left organisations and whether or not the RFMC should be wound up; and suggesting priorities for next year in maintaining the impetus for reforming the Party.

Vladimir Derer said, 'Constitutional campaigns have waned and our support is weaker now.' He feared we would be accused of being divisive.

I talked to Chris privately before I left. He has got in touch with the Bank of Bermuda and they say there is no such trust, so I'm going to pursue that matter more fully with Harold Evans when I have the time.

Thursday 15 October

I went to the hospital to see Dr Clifford Rose, who told me that the electrical tests in July did show that there had been serious damage to my sensory nerves and it would be up to two years before they would know the extent of the recovery. I am beginning to realise that I may be handicapped for life. I would like to be able to run and jump about before I die but I've got to face the possibility that I never will. It was a bit of a shock, though I had guessed it.

In the evening Caroline and I went to Hilary's to visit little Michael. Hilary put him in my arms and I just looked at him for about half an hour. I am so thrilled with him.

Ken Coates rang me up and told me a couple of interesting stories. First of all, Tariq Ali and Paul Foot are thinking of joining the Labour Party, which is highly significant. Secondly, at Michael Foot's birthday party recently there was a flaming row between Jill Tweedie of the *Guardian* and Neil Kinnock about me; Neil got enraged, Ian Aitken said Jill Tweedie was stupid, and Michael Foot became extremely vitriolic. Then Neil Kinnock whispered something to Jill Tweedie and she walked out of the party, and Michael Foot sent Kinnock out to fetch her back. I really must not forget that, over and above the political arguments, Michael Foot dislikes me, and the old left, as they think of themselves, are very critical.

At 2 I went to the Commons for a meeting with the people who had supported my deputy leadership campaign, plus MPs John Tilley, John Prescott and Clive Soley. We discussed the possible formation of a left grouping other than Tribune.

Frank Allaun declared, 'I don't think we should have any recrimination between the hard left and the soft left. We should argue from inside the Tribune Group. Tony Benn should not stand for Deputy Leader in 1982 and there should be a Shadow Cabinet slate of fifteen made up of hard and soft left.'

Bob Cryer said, 'There must be a new examination of the role of the Tribune Group and there must be links with the left outside Parliament.' He didn't think the chairman of Tribune should be a Front Bench spokesman, which was a way of saying he didn't want Norman Buchan to become chairman of the Tribune Group.

I spoke last, and said that I agreed it would be a great mistake to have recriminations but a big movement had begun outside the PLP and the real significance of the deputy leadership election was that it had politicised people. The Conference had confirmed our policies, and now we had to consider how to advance them, what to do to maintain our position in the NEC. I added, 'I hope nobody is in any doubt that the Tribune abstainers, by electing Denis Healey, denied Audrey Wise a seat on the Executive. There could be further constitutional changes and we have also to look at what is going on outside Parliament in the industrial world and in local government.' It wasn't so much a question of the future of the PLP or the Shadow Cabinet, but what our work was now. We had to start with certain objectives and develop our campaign themes for 1982.

We adjourned, and are going to meet again. While we were there, I circulated my resolution calling on the Social Democrat MPs to resign their seats. It was signed by all those Labour MPs present – Dennis Skinner, Jo Richardson, Joan Maynard, Frank Allaun, Michael Meacher, Stuart Holland, Ernie Roberts, Allan Roberts, Stan Thorne, Ray Ellis, Reg Race, Bob Cryer, Willy McKelvey, Ernie Ross, James Lamond.

I wore my hearing aid at the House of Commons for the first time today. I got it in July and had been a bit self-conscious about it, though when my hair is long it isn't very noticeable. As I was standing in the lobby, Nicholas Comfort of the *Daily Telegraph* came up and asked me about the Tribune Group, and he added, 'Is it true you have a hearing aid?' 'Yes,' I replied. So he asked, 'Is it an NHS one?' I answered, 'Yes, like my spectacles and my treatment, of course it is.' I thought: What a fantastic newspaper industry we have, that in the middle of the deepest crisis whether I have an NHS hearing aid should be an issue.

Wednesday 21 October

Tariq Ali rang to confirm that he was thinking of joining the Labour Party and also to tell me about the new Socialist Society. Hilary Wainwright, Ralph Miliband and Paul Foot are interested. We discussed the possibility of a new weekly magazine for the intelligentsia to replace the *New Statesman*. I am in favour of that.

At 4 I went to see Michael Foot. I wasn't looking forward to it and I had no particular strategy. I decided to begin by saying I had seen his interview with Brian Walden and that he had been strong on nuclear policy and so on.

He looked at me rather quizzically and said, 'I thought it would be a good idea if we had a talk because I would like you to stand again in the Shadow Cabinet election next month, and I would then appoint you to an appropriate Front Bench responsibility.'

I told him, 'I haven't made up my mind about standing yet. The factors that would influence me on this would be, first of all, whether the Front Bench arguments reflect the clear decisions that have been taken at Conference on the alternative economic strategy, on defence policy and Europe. Secondly, whether the NEC, now under right-wing control, does change the chairmanship of the Home Policy, Organisation and International Committees and whether it intends to try and reverse the constitutional changes that have been made. Of course, it is perfectly entitled to put forward constitutional amendments. Because if the NEC tries to reverse the changes – then I will be very busy over the next twelve months.' I think that registered.

I made it clear to him that I linked the question of my standing for the Shadow Cabinet with whether I continued to be chairman of the Home Policy Committee, and I think, having made that point, I achieved most of what I wanted. I said I didn't want anything from him and I didn't want him to think that I was here to discuss a job.

On the question of Europe, Michael said, 'I think that there is a pretty wide measure of agreement that we will have to change our relationship, but it's a question of how, and we have got to take account of the fact that Mitterrand is friendly', and so on. 'The most difficult thing of all is defence,' he continued, 'because there are people who feel very strongly about Cruise missiles, and the defence spokesmen who attacked the policy were really only responding to your vote.' (He was referring to my support for the Tribune Group amendment and vote against the Government on nuclear weapons, against Shadow Cabinet advice, in May.) Michael thought it had been ill advised of me and other Labour MPs to sign the Tribune amendment. He said he had appointed Brynmor John as Defence spokesman last November on becoming Leader because Bill Rodgers wasn't acceptable, and he hoped he would be able to keep the two sides together.

I found it very significant indeed that he picked out defence as the most difficult issue of all. I got a clear indication of a fairly harmless fudge on the alternative economic strategy, a potentially dangerous fudge on the EEC and a serious problem on the defence issue.

I remarked, 'On Europe, there can't be many people in the PLP who are still passionately pro-Europe. You know Clem [Attlee] used to talk about a "minority mind", meaning there were some people who were so used to being in a minority that they couldn't adjust to being in a majority; there is also such a thing as a majority mind, and that seems to me to be the question that must be faced – that there has been a clear decision by Party Conference and the TUC on Europe.'

Then Michael said, 'You know, you've got to be careful about the PLP. They've got a useful job to do.'

'I agree with that, but my own opinion – and I know you and I don't agree about this – is that the reason the PLP are demoralised is because individual Members of Parliament are caught between two grindstones – the grindstone of patronage and the grindstone of reselection – and they have really abandoned their proper responsibilities. They have traded power for status.'

He suggested we should talk again before the nominations close for the Shadow Cabinet.

Came home and watched *The Borgias* on television. Although it is a second-rate movie, it is interesting to see Italian politics in the late fifteenth-century reflected in the life of the church; religion and Labour politics are identical – the lust for power in both is identical and the loyalties called for by both are identical, though one is in the name of God and the other in the name of the working class.

Thursday 22 October

Overslept. Rang Michael Foot and said I would like to speak on the oil question in the debate on the Queen's Speech, and it will be something of a test of whether Michael Foot wants to put out feelers to me. I'll make a bloody sight better speech than Merlyn Rees. It will be an opportunity to show knowledge of the industry and to use Parliament properly.

Friday 23 October

The big news today is the SDP-Liberal Alliance victory at Croydon.[1] Predictably, Foot was on the television saying that one of the factors had been the distractions over the last few months, ie the deputy leadership election.

We lost the Croydon by-election for three reasons. First, twenty members of the Party including some senior ex-Cabinet Ministers formed their own party and decided to attack us. Secondly, this attack was supplemented by Labour leaders' criticisms of Party policy on nuclear disarmament and the Common Market. Thirdly, we lost because the campaign, like all Labour campaigns at the moment, was just anti-Tory, and what we really need is something constructive.

Saturday 24 October

At about 10 Caroline and I set off by taxi for the CND march, which began near Hungerford Bridge. An enormous procession was gathering, and Canon John Collins, the Founder Chairman of CND, was at the head. I shook him rather coldly by the hand. I read the other day in *The Times* that he had voted for Mrs Thatcher in 1979. Also there were Hugh Jenkins, Chairman of CND, Canon Paul Oestreicher of Southwark Cathedral, Robin Cook and one or two others but not many MPs. We left at 11, marched through central London and got to Hyde Park at about 12. As there was a pause for entertainment, we came home and had a bite to eat, and I must say, my legs were beginning to give out. Then we went back to the park; there must have been a quarter of a million people there. I have never seen such a crowd in any one place in Britain before. I should think it was the biggest political meeting ever held in the history of British politics, unless you include the Peasants' Revolt, and even then I'm not sure as many came out at any one time.

We got through to the stand and we saw Michael and Jill Foot but we didn't speak to them. Lord Soper, old Donald Soper, the pacifist and former Methodist president, came up and said 'I'm a Bennite!' – which was very sweet of him. Talked to Mick McGahey, to Gordon

McLennan, General Secretary of the Communist Party, and to the Dean of St Paul's. There was a German general there, Gert Bastion, who was dismissed from the German army because of his opposition to nuclear weapons. I gave a number of interviews. Then I was called to speak after a woman from Greenham Common; just a few of them are left camped there now.[2] It was a tremendous experience climbing up on the platform and seeing the enormousness of the crowd. I spoke for five minutes.

Came down from the platform, and who should we see across the railings of the park but Hilary and Sally with baby Michael, seventeen days old, my first grandson. So we went over and stood with the baby and got someone to take a picture with my camera; so that little fella really started his political career early!

Sunday 25 October
Went out to get the papers, and the *Sunday Express* said, 'Anti-nuclear crowd causes chaos in London', as if nuclear weapons wouldn't cause chaos. I think the *Sunday People* said, 'Foot faces mob at ban-the-bomb demo' or some such remark.

Monday 26 October
At 9 I went to the caucus prior to the Shadow Cabinet where we discussed a draft joint statement that might be issued by the Tribune Group candidates for the Shadow Cabinet. MPs present were myself, Bob Litherland, Stuart Holland, Dennis Skinner, Ernie Roberts, Bob McTaggart, Joan Maynard, Bob Cryer, Willy McKelvey, Ernie Ross and Reg Race.

Tuesday 27 October
To the Commons in the evening, having been told last night by David Clark, MP for South Shields, that he, Derek Foster and Dale Campbell-Savours, MP for Workington, wished to see me, so I said I would see them at 7.30. They are all Healeyites, and it turned out to be an attack on me. I was told I was a hated figure, I would bring the Party to disaster, and they asked what I was going to do about it.

Campbell-Savours said he would have followed me to the end of the earth until he got into the House. He asked my why I didn't take legal advice, have better public relations, and so on.

I told him, 'It's not about that. If you argue for a certain point of view, the establishment will try and destroy you.'

The other two listened more than he did and I think it was useful; at least it was frank.

Wednesday 28 October
The NEC meeting was held at Transport House. First Russell Tuck

and Alan Hadden tried to move two emergency resolutions, one attacking Ronald Reagan for his comments on the possibility of a limited nuclear war, the other on the sale of BNOC's assets.

Michael Foot began on the membership of the NEC sub-committees by saying he would like to explain his position. 'This is a time of supreme crisis for the Party.' (It's always supreme crisis with Michael. He lives in crisis and feels he can only be listened to when there is a crisis.) 'I have talked to Ron Hayward, as the Leader always does about the membership of committees. Ron has adopted the traditional method of giving senior members of the NEC first choice as to which committees they would like. The NEC can, of course, suggest changes, but I favour no changes in the chairmanships.' So it looked as if my interview with him had had some impact.

We voted on each sub-committee, making some changes to individual committees.

Went into the House for a vote at 10. As I was sitting in the Lobby talking to Reg Race, Norman Buchan came up to me and I thought he was going to have apoplexy. He said, 'What's this about a loyalty oath? This is Stalinism and I know about Stalinism. I've never seen anything so disgusting.' This was about the statement we had drafted for candidates on the Tribune Group list for the Shadow Cabinet. 'Over twenty years, you've just been out for yourself. You are arrogant and you think Party policy belongs to you.' He was almost speechless with anger. I was just fed up, so I said, 'Oh, get stuffed.' I don't normally insult people but it was more than my patience could stand.

Tuesday 3 November

Went to the Shadow Cabinet in the evening, and I must say I do find it an absolute nightmare. Sixty members of the Manifesto Group, the group of right-wing Labour MPs, have said that unless the Militant Tendency are expelled they will leave the Party. Well, candidly, if I had to trade the YS for some of them, I wouldn't be sorry to see them go.

Wednesday 4 November

Didn't go to the state opening of Parliament but I did record it on video. I find it absolutely fascinating. I discovered that the opening of Parliament was carried out in its present form only in 1901 when Edward VII was determined to overcome the republicanism that had grown during the lifetime of Queen Victoria by having a big royal event. So it isn't all that old, although presumably there was some sort of ceremony in earlier centuries. Queen Victoria didn't attend very often after Albert's death, though apparently, 100 years ago, she did object to one phrase in the Queen's Speech (which was read out on her behalf) – namely, 'My Ministers intend to withdraw from Afghanistan.'

To the PLP meeting, where Stan Orme told me that employers at Laurence Scott Electromotors in Manchester have sacked all their workers. 650 engineers were thrown out after a break-in at night by thugs under police protection. He said a helicopter is being used today to remove the finished goods as a way of breaking through the picket line. Evidently James Anderton, the Chief Constable of Manchester, authorised the helicopter's involvement – a very dangerous operation in the middle of Manchester.

Had a bite to eat in the Tea Room with Norman Atkinson, Stan Newens and Bob Edwards, the veteran Member for Wolverhampton South-East. I told Bob that I was reading Trotsky's book *Where is Britain Going* and he said, 'I've got that. It was given to me in English by Trotsky himself and he signed it.' Here was a man of seventy-six, a former General Secretary of the Chemical Workers' Union, who actually talked to Trotsky in Moscow in 1926. Amazing!

Saturday 7 November
To Birmingham for a meeting and came back in the train with Fenner Brockway and Joan Lestor, who were also speaking there.

'As I get older I get philosophical,' Fenner said. 'There only ever was a tiny percentage of the Parliamentary Party who were socialists – thirty before the First World War, fifty in the days of the ILP and now probably fifty in the PLP. So we have to see ourselves as being a permanent minority in the sense that you never get a majority of people who convert to socialism. But that minority can offer leadership to the rest because the characteristic of the right is that they are bankrupt. Their main concern is to fight off socialism, but the middle ground will swing with the victory. So if we did get a proper left leadership, which is not inconceivable with the electoral college, then we would go from being a quarter of the PLP to more than 50 per cent.'

I found that comforting. Fenner is a shrewd old man and I can't over-emphasise my affection for him.

Monday 9 November
To the Organisation Committee,* and we had a long discussion on Croydon.

John Golding said that, wherever he went, the reason for the defeat was given as Benn and Livingstone.

Ron Hayward remarked, 'PLP morale is at a low level and the bitter attacks make it worse. The SDP are traitors, but, on the other side, when I went to a Cardiff rally and read a three-sentence message from Tony Benn who was lying ill in hospital, everyone on the platform cut me dead for doing so.'

---

* In 1981 the name of the Organisation Sub-Committee of the NEC was changed to Organisation Committee. However, to this day it is still known as 'Org Sub' and the two names for the committee are interchangeable throughout this volume.

Denis Healey said, 'Morale is very bad, the NEC has caused it, and *London Labour Briefing* calls for "no pity" on reselection.'

Neil Kinnock complained, 'Labour's internal war blanks out our policy. The next Election is lost and I will have wasted all my time on education. We are in big trouble. Unity is the only basis. Some people want us to lose the next Election, but fifty years of Callaghan is better than one year of Thatcher.' (That is really an indication that Neil Kinnock, in certain circumstances, would favour an alliance with the SDP rather than have a Thatcher Government next time round.) He said, 'I am a unilateralist. We have got alternatives but people are deaf to them because of what has happened. I abstained in the deputy leadership election to give me a platform from which to say what I want.'

Tuesday 10 November

Went into the debate on North Sea oil at 3.30, and Merlyn Rees opened. I was in the debate most of the time, and Mother and Stephen came to listen. Towards the end, at 9, I wound up. I had determined that I would clearly get into Hansard the full range of Party policy: that we would renationalise without compensation; that we would take BP into 100 per cent ownership; that we would move towards 100 per cent ownership of oil; that we would use the revenues and other money for the alternative economic strategy, industry and the public services; that we would have planned trade and public ownership; that we would withdraw from the Common Market, and so on. When I made my speech the House was packed, and it went down like a bomb. When I came to renationalisation without compensation Lawson got up and asked me to clarify it, which I did. But when I sat down Michael Foot was absolutely fuming and Peter Shore was boiling like a kettle. I said, 'Well, it's all Party policy.' Actually my side gave me quite a cheer when I sat down, but that is clearly going to be a big issue.

Wednesday 11 November

Shadow Cabinet at 5 was a long and painful meeting. Michael Foot said he wished to make a statement and he had it all typed out, exactly as on 3 June this year. He said he wanted to make further reference to the question of unity. He then read out from the statement that dissent had distracted the Party from its real work and that the Social Democratic Party was 'our own creation'. He went on, 'After Brighton, I made an appeal that Denis Healey and Tony would serve in the Shadow Cabinet. I supported Tony on the NEC chairmanships. Tony was a party to the document agreed by the Shadow Cabinet on the renationalisation of North Sea oil and gas. The NEC on 28 October used the same wording, so there is unanimity in the light of Conference decisions. This is a clear illustration of the need for collective Shadow

Cabinet responsibility which is not a fuddy-duddy old rule but necessary to guard against conflict. With his speech yesterday Tony has brilliantly succeeded in throwing the Party into a fresh internal crisis and the whole responsibility rests with him. If Tony goes on in this way, his presence in this Shadow Cabinet will make it unworkable and our conduct will be a shambles. I would not and could not vote for him for Shadow Cabinet in these circumstances though I still hope he will stand on the terms I have set out. But I must make it clear that the main responsibility rests on Tony.'

He also asked me to repudiate an article in *London Labour Briefing* called 'The Myth of Tolerance' which had a 'hit-list' of Labour MPs who had not voted for me in the deputy leadership contest.

I replied to Michael. 'First of all, may I say that I think it is unwise to say that the SDP is the creation of the Labour Party – that would be a hostage to fortune. Secondly, it would be quite wrong of me to repudiate *London Labour Briefing* because I haven't seen it. I wrote an article in it, and as far as I know there was no objection to my article, but to hold me responsible for what is in the rest of the paper is like holding members of the Shadow Cabinet responsible for what appears in Tory newspapers for which they write.' On the question of compensation, I said there was no reason why I shouldn't have quoted in Parliament a Conference resolution and, as to the Shadow Cabinet elections, I intended to stand and the only way we could get unity was round Party policy.

Michael Foot repeated, 'I insist on a condemnation of *London Labour Briefing*.'

'I haven't seen it.'

Michael then said, 'On the oil compensation issue, there has been a change of attitude now. Why didn't you support Merlyn Rees in the debate? The Tory press had a field day. Common sense and comradeship would have pointed to the need not to do what you did. The Shadow Cabinet can't be run on a system of having debates in Parliament about what the policy of the PLP should be.'

Merlyn Rees spoke next. 'All right, the policy on compensation was decided at Conference, but Sam McCluskie changed it last year. The Shadow Cabinet will have to take collective decisions. At the Shadow Cabinet, Tony said nothing against a statement we issued on oil. I did not know what Tony was going to say in the debate but he made me look very foolish. The morale of the PLP and the constituencies is very low.'

Stan Orme commented, 'I heard both Merlyn and Tony yesterday and Tony was excellent until the last five minutes of his speech. The Shadow Cabinet must stick together. Labour MPs are shattered, and it shows the danger we are in.'

Neil Kinnock said he was a unilateralist, so he had been in the minority for years. He then delivered a lecture on Party unity and said, 'Our electoral standing is not due to ourselves. Tony, you are essential', and something like 'I address your conscience. You are being used by others. You are the most important single member of the Party.'

I chipped in again at that stage. 'First of all, Sam McCluskie did not have authority from the National Executive to say what he said. We had agreed to accept the resolution which repeated that there would be no compensation. If Michael Foot says there is no infringement of the Conference resolution, then repeating it can't be an infringement of the Shadow Cabinet statement.'

Albert Booth said that he must confess he had used similar words during the debate on the bill to denationalise transport.

Peter Shore said, 'I have attacked Tony, and it is time we got round the table to discuss this. The Shadow Cabinet approved a statement on the oil business, and for Tony to say that there is no difference with Conference is untrue.'

It was agreed we would come back to it next week.

The mood of the meeting was horrible, the atmosphere icy, and Michael was angry. I am used to it now. The things they said were extreme, but of course they are frantic. After that, it was quite clear that that was the end of me.

Thursday 12 November
The press turned up outside the house.

I worked on a statement to the PLP meeting, and at 2 I took it to the left grouping of the Tribune MPs and they made some suggestions which I incorporated. I went to see Michael at 4 and I said, 'Now look, I have come in goodwill and a conciliatory spirit to try and see whether we can reach an agreement which I am sure we can. I do have my own view about how that compensation question should be dealt with.' I handed him my statement.

He read it and observed, 'Well, I think it is a move, but you ought to add a couple of other paragraphs.'

So I did add them and I said, 'May I suggest you don't comment – let things go quiet over the weekend?'

'I can't be sure. I haven't made up my mind,' he replied.

So I had it retyped and copied, and went to the PLP at 6 where I read it out. It was heard quietly, with a bit of ironic comment when I mentioned unity. There was some banging of the table by a number of our supporters.

Then Michael Foot got up and said, 'I'm wearing my best suit.' (A reference to the criticism about wearing his duffle coat at the Cenotaph.) He continued, 'This is a serious question. Ever since I was elected Leader, I have concentrated on unemployment and peace, which are the key issues. There have been dissensions and distractions which have injured us, and the deputy leadership was a distraction which had a bad effect on the result in recent by-elections. In one miserable sense, the SDP *is* our own creation. After Brighton, I tried to make a fresh start. I opposed removing Tony from the Home Policy Committee for the sake of Party unity. I hope Tony will be elected to the Shadow Cabinet. But I can't remove from my mind the *London Labour Briefing* article "The Myth of Tolerance". I still hope Tony will repudiate it. Tony's speech in the debate turned an attack on the Government into an internal crisis. The prime responsibility was Tony's. What happened was a classic case of breakdown of Shadow Cabinet collective responsibility.

'The question is, is Tony going to help us with the next Election or not? His behaviour on Tuesday would make the Shadow Cabinet unworkable. I hope Tony will stand on the inescapable terms of Shadow Cabinet membership and, if he does, he will have a contribution to make. If he chooses the course of fresh attacks or fresh dissensions, then the responsibility would be with him. My response to Tony's statement is that it has gone some way but not all the way, and I take it that he accepts what I have said and will abide by it. If he can't, I hope he will make that clear. I challenge Tony Benn to answer.'

I had taken a great deal of trouble to try to get Jack Dormand to agree that there would not be a discussion, but Alex Lyon, Phillip Whitehead and Judith Hart wanted me to respond. I said, 'Well, I'm sorry to be asked to comment, but it is a central issue. Can the Shadow Cabinet agree a policy which, in this way, has the effect of changing Party policy?'

At this there was a lot of shouting, and during Judith Hart's speech there was jeering and baying. Somebody got up and moved next business. A very unpleasant meeting. As I left, I handed copies of the statement I had made to the Press Lobby.

Friday 13 November
The media siege continues. Yesterday I actually had to fight my way out of the house with Joshua's help.

According to the press, Michael Foot had given me another twenty-four hours before he would sack me from the Shadow Cabinet, so I rang to suggest a meeting. Just as I was leaving, the phone rang; it was Michael Foot, and he snapped, 'Come and see me now.'

I said, 'I can't, I'm going to Bristol immediately for an engagement.'
He said, 'Well I can't see you in that case.'
'I'll see you over the weekend.'
He said, 'That's no good. Will you or won't you?'
'Well, Michael, I was going to make a suggestion to you that the Shadow Cabinet should actually lay down certain rules and get them agreed, and that you shouldn't endorse or not endorse anybody.'

He said, 'That's no good.'
I told him, 'I'd like to see you.'
'I can't see you after the weekend.'
'Fair enough,' I replied.
He said, 'Well, I'm putting out a statement today.'
Heard the late news; in his statement Michael denounced me up hill and down dale.

Monday 16 November

At 6.30 I had a little meeting in my room with Vladimir Derer, Joan Maynard, Willy McKelvey, Norman Atkinson, Michael Meacher, Tony Banks, Frances Morrell, Chris Mullin and Stuart Holland. I explained what had happened, and Norman Atkinson said, 'We want to say thanks to you, Tony, for standing up through all this.' He told me they were going to meet on Sunday at 2 in County Hall to discuss it.

Willy McKelvey said, 'The PLP support for Tony was enormous during the debate. The trouble began when Michael made his statement and the Shadow Cabinet discussed it. The public don't understand, but don't be disheartened; if Tony had been elected as Deputy Leader, there would have been a row afterwards anyway, and the hysteria is because Tony nearly won.'

Frances Morrell declared, 'I have real anxieties. We always think we are right, but we were wrong, and it would be better to admit it. We chose to challenge on the wrong issue. We should have chosen nuclear weapons. Compensation is not a burning issue, and great damage has been done. We will lose our traditional left-wing base. I have real fears for unity, because everybody I have met, including good colleagues in the PLP, are against Tony.'

Stuart Holland said, 'The country wants a clear alternative. We can't fudge it.'

'I think it has been damaging but we have got to go on,' said Chris Mullin.

Frances Morrell asked me, 'Well, what *was* your strategy? Did you want to get elected to the Shadow Cabinet or not?'

I told them I had wanted to get elected, that Caroline had said afterwards, 'You're too old a hand to make a mistake like that', and that Stephen had said, 'Dad, you goofed.'

Anyway, the one thing that came clearly out of it was a unanimous view that I should put on the record an account of what happened. So I rang up Richard Gott, the features editor of the *Guardian*, and he agreed to take 2000 words if I could write it by tomorrow. I came home and wrote it; it's now 2 am, and it will be ready in the morning.

Wednesday 18 November

The PLP meeting on the state of the Party began at 10.30. Jack

Dormand, chairman of the PLP, commenced by saying that everybody recognised that this was one of the most important PLP meetings that had ever been held.

Jack Straw got up. I should say about Jack that he was the radical young president of the NUS ten or twelve years ago. He then became a barrister, worked for the ILEA, was political adviser to Barbara Castle and to Peter Shore, and got himself elected for Blackburn to replace Barbara. When he came into the House he joined the Tribune Group and was made a Front Bench spokesman after eighteen months. He is a classic Neil Kinnock type. It is hard now to believe that he ever was in Tribune. He is a keen supporter of Peter Shore who is now one of the most right-wing leaders in the Party.

Jack Straw began by saying that a year ago the polls for Labour were the best ever and now they were the worst. Why had this happened? Not because of our policies, because on nuclear disarmament, monetarism and the Common Market they were popular. The reasons were as follows. First, defections to the SDP. Second, internal arguments which had helped to build up the SDP. 'The time has come to end internal strife. I think Tony Benn holds the primary responsibility for what has happened and we have to re-establish the role of the PLP. Conference resolutions should not be seen as a holy writ. I appeal to Tony to condemn the article in *London Labour Briefing* which appeared to suggest that there should be recriminations. Politics is about personalities and how we behave as personalities, and whether our actions point to comradeship.' Jack Straw is on the way to becoming a Peter Shore or an Eric Varley.

The second speaker was Bob Brown, MP for Newcastle West. 'I just want to deal with one issue – nationalisation without compensation. I will not be committed by anyone to confiscation or organised theft. The electorate will not accept it; the CP is against it and so is Walworth Road. But the Trotskyites, particularly the Militant Tendency, the SWP and the WRP, are in favour of confiscation, and Tony is prepared to embrace them all. There is no future for the Party unless we embrace parliamentary democracy, and confiscation would destroy the Party. Jimmy Reid in the *Glasgow Herald* last Friday wrote, "To confiscate property is only possible if there has been a civil war", and, if we were contemplating democratic change, it would not be possible.'

Frank Hooley referred to the constitution of the Party. 'The first part of Clause 4 states that we must maintain a PLP in the House of Commons, secondly that we should co-operate with the TUC, and thirdly that we should give effect, as far as practicable, to the policies of the Party. The NEC, the Shadow Cabinet and the TUC all agree that "no compensation" is not practicable. The Shadow Cabinet, the Executive and the TUC have got to work out their policy and get out of the damn-fool practice of writing articles for the *Guardian*.'

Joan Lestor said, 'The PLP is where the poison is coming from, and it is no good blaming the media. On the issue of "policies not people", we have the policies, but it is recrimination against abstainers which makes it about people. I must warn the party, you will destroy individualism if the CLPs decide what we do and if we have a Leader and Deputy Leader who conduct themselves differently.'

After Joan Lestor, John Morris spoke and commented on reselection. 'Some who do not believe in parliamentary democracy would like to turn MPs into puppets. When you go to the Tea Room, you find that the politics of reselection and the deputy leadership election dominate MPs' thoughts. Whoever Militant or the communists or ex-communists or the WRP are, they now appear to be applying to join the Labour Party in order to get control of the Party. On entryism, the NEC and the Shadow Cabinet must act, or workers and Labour voters will vote for the SDP. The Party is getting worse, and, short of a miracle, we cannot win; neither Michael nor Wedgie can win. And if a year from now it is worse, each one of us must consider our own position.' This was an indication to Michael that he might have to leave the Party.

Bob Cryer spoke next. He said the political message of the Party had been obscured because of attacks within the Party. 'Hattersley described the NEC as being elected by "mindless and unrepresentative extremists." As to compensation, collective responsibility within the Shadow Cabinet must be even-handed. Denis Healey rejected unilateralism, but when Party policy is advocated by Tony Benn it leads to trouble. Merlyn Rees wrote an article in the *News of the World* and Wilson wrote one saying that "the good people of Crosby would rather be dead than vote Labour", that Shirley Williams was an excellent candidate, and so on.'

Then came Joe Ashton. Four years ago, he said, he had raised the dangers of reselection and warned then what would happen. On entryism, he commented, 'The extreme left don't want a Labour victory because they want 5 million people unemployed and riots and a deadlock in the next Parliament and then a revolution. Victory for the Labour Party would wreck the prospect for the Trotskyites. Look at the Young Socialists. In the old days they ran discos, but now the YS are run by brainwashed zombies organised by Militant and *we* are paying for this. We should cut their funding and end the YS. The NEC should ask Militant Tendency what they are up to. We cannot proscribe, but the NEC can demand the facts about the Militant Tendency, where they get their money from, the names of the people who work for them.'

He continued, 'If we don't win the next Election, the Norman Tebbit Bill against the trade unions will bankrupt the unions and the Labour Party.* MPs should be out in the country campaigning on housing and

---

* As newly-appointed Employment Secretary in November 1981, Norman Tebbit had just announced the provisions of his proposed Labour Law Bill, which threatened trade unions with court injunctions and damages during industrial disputes.

jobs. The deputy leadership was irrelevant, I have respect for Benn, but he doesn't think we can win the next Election and I represent the Party as much as Conference because I have been re-elected. Michael is there until the next Election.' At this there was loud applause.

Michael Meacher spoke up for Conference policies. 'If the Conference is unilateralist, the Shadow Cabinet collective leadership cannot reject it. On the Common Market and economic strategy, the Shadow Cabinet are putting forward markedly different alternatives.' He went on, 'The SDP policies are not popular. The SDP are vulnerable, they are not new, they are yesterday's men and women. Their policies cannot work. We must emphasise that the effect of the SDP vote could be a hung Parliament and a Tory coalition.

Phillip Whitehead, who has a majority of only 214 in Derby North, despaired of the meeting. 'I spent four hours over the weekend trying to persuade members in Derby not to leave the Party. In 1974 we were seen as humane, but now the SDP appear to be more competent, more international and more in favour of decentralisation than we are. People are picking at the PLP like children tearing wings off a beetle and, when they have torn most of them off, they say that at least the beetle is accountable.' He deeply resented that at the *Tribune* rally one person (that was me) had said we had to win the PLP to socialism. 'We have to win the country to socialism and we have substituted Party for country. The entryists must not be allowed to continue.' There were more cheers for Phillip's speech.

Many other people spoke during the course of the meeting before Michael wound up. He said he had had lots of letters from Labour MPs about their constituency parties. He declared, 'I am aware of the anxieties expressed today, particularly following the by-election at Croydon. I also know my responsibilities in this matter. If we let Mrs Thatcher in again, it will be especially my responsibility, and I am not seeking excuses, alibis or scapegoats.' Then he went all over the same ground about the oil debate. 'Hordes of journalists are involved in reporting disputes in the Party. I am a fully paid-up member of the sick and tired brigade. It is almost criminal to go on in this way. I've had an argument with Tony about Shadow Cabinet responsibility, but it has nothing to do with silencing anybody. The Shadow Cabinet cannot change party policy.

'We don't want to control speeches, but people must use their judgement. I ask for six months' self-denying ordinance on examining the Party's entrails. There is anxiety about entryism and Trotskyism, but there is no chance of re-election if this goes on and I have to be cautious about expulsions. Militant is a pestilential disease, but surgery is messy. I would like to sustain our liberal principles to protect unpopular people, though I do not rule out action. I am concerned more with the tendency to form caucuses than with entryism. We have always had caucuses, but now they are more elaborate and more deeply disruptive of the democratic process.

'It is amazing that advocates of open government should favour caucuses, and I hope action will be taken to denounce *London Labour Briefing* with its hit-list of London Members. We will carry through our manifesto. The nuclear arms race, however, may not wait until we are elected. We must affect the climate of opinion now. The Shadow Cabinet have been carrying our policy forward.' That was more or less it, though Martin Flannery interrupted, to say 'Denis Healey attacks Party policy.'

At 5 I went to my last meeting of the Shadow Cabinet.

Thursday 19 November
Before I went into the House, Ernie Ross rang up to tell me I had got 66 votes in the election for the Shadow Cabinet – which was surprisingly high. So at 6 I went to the Party meeting knowing what the vote was going to be. The Shadow Cabinet has been increased from 12 to 15. Eric Heffer, Peter Archer, Gwyneth Dunwoody, Bruce Millan and some-body else were newly elected on. Denis Healey told me he thought I had got a sympathy vote because I was in such poor health! I have mixed feelings, but I'm glad I'm not to be in that Shadow Cabinet.

Sunday 22 November
To County Hall for a very important meeting that had been called to consider the future of the left. Norman Atkinson, who had organised it, took the chair, and among those present were the usual left people plus George Galloway from Dundee, Rachel Lever, Ernie Roberts, Michael Meacher and Jo Richardson.

When we came to the possibility of contesting the leadership next year, Tony Banks said, 'The decision not to oppose Michael Foot last year may not apply this year, because of Michael Foot's shift to the right. If Foot goes on, we will have to fight him. We must argue at union conferences, and the best defence of the electoral college is to use it.'

George Galloway said, 'The party would never forgive us if we fought Michael Foot next year. It would marginalise us and make us look foolish. But the right may attack him.'

Others contributed, and at 4.45 I said, 'We've only got fifteen minutes left. I think this should be the last informal meeting we have. A meeting should be convened using all the contacts we have – the Broad Left in the unions, national, regional and parliamentary – sending them a note of our objectives and asking them all the following questions: How are we going to advance these objectives? Will you tell us about your campaigns? Will you help us with campaigns that you are interested in? We should call the group Labour Representation Campaign '82, or something with '82 in it.'

In the end we asked Norman Atkinson, George Galloway, Vladimir Derer, Jon Lansman, Audrey Wise and, I think, Rachel Lever and myself to draw up a list of interested people and call it Labour Liaison Committee 1982.

Wednesday 23 November

At 2 I went to Room W4, off Westminster Hall, for the first meeting of the Campaign Group, which has been constituted from the old deputy leadership campaign committee. Last night I had drafted a note saying: 'The Campaign Group, open to any member of the PLP, meets on Monday, Tuesday and Wednesday at 2 pm and at 5 pm on Thursday with the following agenda each day: (1) Today's news; (2) Today's Commons business; (3) Liaison with the labour movement; (4) Business for the PLP; (5) Future work; (6) Media.'

We are in fact a different type of group from the Tribune Group, which is strictly parliamentary and doesn't have links outside, is closed to anyone who isn't a Member and only meets once a week.

Saturday 28 November

Up at 5.30 and caught the train to Sheffield to see David Blunkett, Leader of Sheffield City Council. Bought the *Guardian*, which is engaged in idol-worshipping of Shirley Williams and has endless editorials predicting the end of British politics as we know it.

Owen Briscoe, the General Secretary of the Yorkshire Miners, met me; he is a good, solid socialist. I was taken to David Blunkett's office, and also present were Roger Barton, the Deputy Leader of the Labour Council, Dick Caborn, the MEP for Sheffield, Bill Michie, a councillor, and Keith Jackson, the Vice-Principal of Northern College.

To cut a long story short, they told me they thought I had made a mistake to make an issue of the North Sea oil compensation and thereby get myself thrown off the Shadow Cabinet. They were anxious that the left shouldn't be blamed for disunity. They were nervous of what they thought was a sectarian London set dominating the strategy that I follow – which isn't really true – but I tried to assuage their anxieties and I'll get them invited to the Labour Liaison 1982 meetings.

Back to London. In the evening Caroline and I went to the Inn on the Park to see Andreas Papandreou. When I first met him a year ago, I had a complete rapport with him, and it was the same again today. He is not as extreme as he is made out, but he is determined not to allow the Common Market to dominate his economy and not to allow the Americans to keep their nuclear weapons in Greece.

We talked about the EEC summit, and he said that Schmidt was angry that he was removing American nuclear weapons. Of course, the German Social Democrats are under pressure from their left and I think Papandreou would in effect strengthen the left in the German SPD.

At the end, he said he would send me an official invitation to Greece through the Greek Embassy. Altogether it was a most pleasant evening.

Sunday 29 November
Up at 6 and Caroline and I drove to Bristol for the reselection conference for Bristol South East. The votes cast were 28 for me and 8 for the other candidates, Dave Parsons and Viv Bath. So it wasn't a mere formality. At the press conference afterwards I was asked what would happen if the constituency were abolished in the Boundary Commission's forthcoming report. I stressed that I would continue to fight for my constituency to the bitter end but if it was abolished I would be eligible for the short list for either of the new constituencies: the majority of my constituency may go into Bristol South, a completely new constituency.

Monday 30 November
I worked at home. I worked on the draft of my Foreign Nuclear Bases (Prohibition) Bill.[3]

Thursday 3 December
To the House, and I found the Members' Lobby buzzing because today, at PM's Questions, James Wellbeloved, the SDP Member, had asked Mrs Thatcher to comment on a statement made by Peter Tatchell, the newly-selected Labour candidate for Bermondsey,[4] about extra-parliamentary action against the Government. Michael Foot had jumped to his feet and declared 'that the individual concerned is not an endorsed member of the Labour Party and as far as I am concerned, never will be'. Foot had confused him with Tariq Ali or someone, but the one thing that is clear is that his endorsement will be opposed and an excuse for an enquiry will be cooked up. The witch-hunt has begun, and of course, when our leaders give the go-ahead for that, others will jump for joy.

To the PLP meeting, where David Winnick got up and said, 'I want to express a minority view about Peter Tatchell. I greatly regret what Michael Foot said. Local parties have the right to select the candidates they like – I'm not a Marxist but a lot of people came in as Marxists.'

Eric Heffer said it was a matter for the NEC, and Michael Foot agreed: 'It is for the NEC Organisation Committee to discuss, but let me underline that the issue of parliamentary democracy is at stake, and if I had said nothing the SDP would have made the running.'

Friday 4 December
Papers full of Foot's attack on 'extremism' in the Party. The whole machinery of vilification is being set in motion again. Michael has made a tragic mistake and constituency parties just won't go along with

it. He now has to lie on the bed that he has made. I know he's trying to clean up the Party so that the SDP will rejoin, and that is the strategy of disaster. We'll have to go through a difficult time but at the end we shall come out much stronger.

At 6 I watched the news, and Peter Tatchell was interviewed. The reporter was completely unable to fault his arguments. He wouldn't criticise Michael Foot and he said he looked forward to meeting him.

Saturday 5 December

The press today were even more hysterical about Bermondsey. The *Mail* predicted the local party there would be disbanded and a new candidate would be selected. A leader attacked Foot for his weakness in agreeing to see Tatchell. Peter Shore and Merlyn Rees attacked the left yesterday. Peter said the left was like Dracula – refusing to see the light of day.

Sunday 6 December

Caroline has persuaded me that not only should Party unity take precedence at the moment but that I am so damaged by my single-handed combat against Denis Healey and Michael Foot that I'm a bit of an embarrassment to the left. So I shall pull out a bit and see how things develop.

The Tatchell affair in Bermondsey is absorbing everyone's attention. Nobody is sure why Michael did what he did, but many, including me, think that he got confused with Tariq Ali or Peter Taaffe, editor of *Militant*. Peter Tatchell is coming out of this very well – he believes in parliamentary democracy but also in public pressure on Parliament, which Michael Foot has engaged in all his life. Michael may be such a prisoner of the right that he has no choice, but he can't win, because Tatchell has now been supported publicly by the five candidates he beat in the shortlist, and if Michael keeps Tatchell out there will be a war to the death with the CLP; if he fails, the right and the public will mock him as an extremely weak man. He has made a ghastly error.

Monday 7 December

I went to the Organisation Committee of the NEC at 2.30 and the room was absolutely packed.

On the Bermondsey item, Michael Foot read a statement which was in effect as follows:

'I fully understand the concern of the Party. It is not our normal practice to refuse endorsement of a candidate unless there are irregularities, and I am suggesting no irregularities. I want to explain why I said what I said, and I hope that this committee will not endorse Peter Tatchell's candidature in Bermondsey.

'I met Peter Tatchell this morning and I am deeply concerned about the question of parliamentary democracy. I put to him my reasons for opposing him. They are not personal but a matter of political judgement. His candidature would be a disaster for the Party. The NEC have to take account of this situation. The article he wrote in *London Labour Briefing* advocating anti-parliamentary action would be used by the SDP against the Labour Party in Bermondsey and elsewhere; it would be spread far and wide and is a gift for the Social Democrats. The article did not accord with our view of parliamentary democracy, and that is why I intervened in the House of Commons.

'I want to underline the fact that I could not have taken any other view. If he were to be endorsed it would lead to a serious electoral disaster.

'Also I want to refer to the attitude of Labour MPs to the article. Many MPs would not go to Bermondsey to campaign if Tatchell were the candidate. The SDP would gain from it, and as Leader of the Party I have a responsibility. I have therefore asked Peter Tatchell to withdraw his candidature and restore a true choice to the local party in respect of local candidates. The NEC has the right to do this.'

Eric Heffer said he regretted that a comment had been made in the Commons in response to a question put by an SDP traitor; he thought it had done great harm to the Party and therefore he moved a resolution 'that in view of the public statements made in respect of the candidature, the NEC should make a report on the situation and to that end a small committee be established to report back on 16 December.'

Frank Allaun seconded that. He said our job was to examine irregularities, and there was no evidence of any in this case. He was glad that Michael Foot had not used this argument, particularly in view of the fact that Peter Tatchell had taken a courageous stand opposing the Vietnam War and was a supporter of homosexual rights. The article did refer to extra-parliamentary activities but we were all involved in those. Michael had said that Tatchell's views would lose an election, but Tatchell was *not* a Militant. Frank Allaun concluded, 'I am a Foot man and I don't want to humiliate you, Michael, but you have made the most serious mistake of your life, and your only alternative now is to get Bob Mellish to stay on. I believe Tatchell's candidacy is worthy of support.'

Dennis Skinner moved that Peter Tatchell be endorsed. He repeated Frank Allaun's sentiments and argued that the right wing were engaged in extra-parliamentary activity too through their directorships and so on. There was no criticism of the selection procedure. Michael Foot had simply fallen for what Jim Wellbeloved had said, and had picked up the bait. It was a grave error, and we should not penalise the candidate for it.

John Golding said Tatchell had 'pin-ups of Lenin' in his flat.

Sam McCluskie thought that Michael had made a mistake. But we all made them. How many people here realised that the feelings of the people of Bermondsey were of loyalty to the Party and to the Leader? We had to support Michael.

Joan Lestor supported Eric Heffer's motion calling for an inquiry: whatever we did would put Michael in a difficulty. 'Pin-ups of Lenin mean nothing. I had pin-ups of Castro when I was young because I thought he was dishy.' We could not ignore the press and the effect this would have on our people, but we owed it to Michael to support him.

I said I accepted the helpful spirit in which Eric had made his suggestion but there was nothing to inquire into. If we did decide to reject the candidate we would certainly have to disband the local Party because they would obviously reselect him. Then the Leader would be expected to comment on all candidates in future, and every endorsement would be a vote of confidence in the Leader. We had to be more positive. We shouldn't have an inquiry but should reaffirm the resolution proposed by Attlee and passed by the National Executive in 1934: "The Labour Party, as has been repeatedly made plain in official declarations, stands for parliamentary democracy. It is firmly opposed to individual or group dictatorship whether from the left or right." Of course we believe in democracy but we also believe in conscience, in freedom of speech, in a free press; we should also believe in socialism. If we are going to have these types of interrogation then they will have to be extended more widely.' I thought that we should send Eric and the Chairman of the Party and the General Secretary to Bermondsey to satisfy themselves that Eric's resolution was acceptable to the Party in Bermondsey. We should recommend endorsement today, subject to this report.

Neil Kinnock said it was all a matter of political judgement. 'We were all extra-parliamentary – Michael was too – but the question is: are we talking of extra-parliamentary or anti-parliamentary behaviour?' It was so pompous, and I completely lost track of his argument. He went on interminably, as he always does, and got warmly cheered by Russell Tuck and Shirley Summerskill. You can't say more than that.

Eric agreed to amend his motion from 'investigate the Bermondsey Party' to 'report on the situation' and to shift it to the NEC. That suited me fine.

Kinnock droned on. He said we were really deciding the direction of the Labour Party, and we had to draw a line when candidates weakened the Party – Tatchell did weaken the Party and he did not have the welfare of the Party at heart. Russell agreed with Neil. We should endorse Michael, not Peter. Then someone added that the fact that Tatchell was a homosexual made him less inclined to support him.

Denis Healey thought the constitutional priority was that we had a right and a duty to judge whether candidates were suitable. However, no investigation was needed.

Michael Foot spoke, and more or less reiterated what he had said earlier. We must give him some leverage because the SDP would use it nationally. 'Many people within the Party on the left, right and centre were saying, "If you don't speak out we will"', and, if I hadn't, people would have said I was a coward. Tatchell will not withdraw, and therefore I shall take the matter to the NEC.'

He gave the game away when he said he was pressed by MPs – no doubt he felt that if he hadn't acted they would have joined the SDP.

In the end, the substantive motion that we didn't endorse Tatchell was carried by 12 to 7, and will go forward to NEC.

Tuesday 8 December

Tariq Ali phoned. He's so civilised and charming. He told me he had met Michael Foot at a party at Jill Tweedie's on Sunday and hadn't wanted to embarrass him so he didn't look him out, although they had spoken together on many platforms in the 1960s. But Michael had searched him out and asked Tariq if he had really left the IMG. Tariq had replied he wasn't accustomed to telling lies. Tariq reminded me that he had, of course, been in the Labour Party from 1963 to 1966.

Michael had then asked him if he was prepared to campaign for the Labour Party. Tariq said, 'You mean even if I'm not in it?' and Michael said yes. Tariq said he would. Michael suggested that we couldn't let him into the Party for the moment because it would be difficult. He told Tariq that Peter Tatchell was very impressive but that there were problems. Michael asked him what he thought would happen in the next Election and Tariq replied, 'If you capitulate to the SDP and fudge, you won't win, but if you stand up and give a principled defence of your policies you stand a reasonable chance.' Michael had apparently replied, 'You know we could win even if only 30 per cent of the electorate supported us if the vote split between the Tories and the SDP.' So that is clearly Michael's strategy.

Wednesday 9 December

Arthur Scargill's election as President of the NUM is really encouraging news.

The Organisation Committee met, and the question of Militant, which had been referred from November's NEC, was put on the agenda. John Golding proposed that there should be an inquiry into Militant and Michael said he was against proscribed lists, but he thought this action was necessary.

Eric said fine, but if we were going to look at Militant we must look at Denis Healey too, and he put forward his amendment – that we should oppose witchhunts and should conduct a political education campaign.

I said we'd already considered the Underhill Report on Militant in 1977 and 1980, and Conference had endorsed it; if we reopened this now, we'd find a large number of other people who write in other papers that are opposed to the Party, like the *Express*, which Denis Healey writes in. I said it was amazing to me that we didn't have inquiries into possible defectors. One of them had recently been appointed to the Front Bench and he had left within twenty-four hours. It wouldn't stop with Militant.

Dennis Skinner said the *Sun* was telling us what to do. 'We'll get screaming headlines if we proceed.'

Denis Healey responded. 'Tony has a persecution mania and he won't repudiate *London Labour Briefing*.'

Neil Kinnock said the left wanted a clean-up – this was a free country but in every democracy you had to take stringent measures to defend democracy. We were on a dangerous road anyway, and we should reassert our ideology.

Laurence Coates warned that an inquiry would lead to a witchhunt. Attacks on Militant were in marked contrast to the support expressed for some of the SDP defectors. Party members wouldn't accept civil war. John Golding had referred to Tony Benn as a 'mad dog', according to the *Express*. Michael was being blackmailed by would-be defectors. The fact was that the right had lost the arguments on policy and were using organisational methods to try to regain control; that would only deliver us into the hands of the Tories.

Michael said that in 1979 he appealed for unity. He was anxious to get away from discussing our internal affairs. 'Tony's idea that we are really wanting reunification with the SDP is wrong. It is to *defeat* the SDP that we must do this. We created the SDP, but if we act on Militant we'll keep people in the Party.'

Eric's motion against witchhunts was lost by 10 to 9.

The resolution to investigate Militant was carried by 10 to 9. If Judith Hart and Alex Kitson had been there to vote, it would have gone the other way.

Tariq Ali's application to join the Party was also considered. David Hughes, the National Agent, suggested we interview him to see if he accepts the 'parliamentary road to socialism' and has renounced his links with the Fourth International, but John Golding moved that he not be accepted. Syd Tierney spoke passionately against Tariq Ali and said he wouldn't believe a word he said.

Denis Healey seconded Golding's motion, and said that if Tariq Ali were accepted there would have to be a substantial probationary period. Neil Kinnock moved an amendment to that effect, saying that the communist tendency of the IMG believed that the IMG should enter the Labour Party, and Tariq was trying it out and calling our bluff. This was a test case.

I supported the National Agent's view that we interview him; we couldn't go on blackening people before we'd heard them out. Denis Healey had done it with Jon Lansman and in fact his allegations weren't true. We had done it to Tatchell and now Tariq Ali. We looked like a Star Chamber court.

My amendment to support the National Agent was defeated by 8 to 11 and the motion to refuse his membership application was carried by 11 to 6.

Thursday 10 December

Jim Callaghan has a centre-page spread in the *Mirror* arguing that Labour must expel Militant, prepare for a coalition with the SDP after the Election and consider proportional representation. So that's Roy Jenkins, Jim and Ted Heath all contemplating a coalition; this is the beginning of the National Government which was a disaster in 1931 and will be this time. At least it's out in the open now, contrary to what Foot and Healey say. I know that Healey's research assistant told someone that you couldn't attack the SDP because we will be in with them after the Election.

Friday 11 December

Talked to Dawn on the phone; she decided to cancel the surgery and the GMC tonight because Bristol is snowbound.

She told me that John Golding had been down to Bristol last month, urging trade unions to affiliate to local parties in Bristol to 'defeat the influence of the far left in local CLPs'. This is, of course, in preparation for when Mike Cocks comes up against me for the new Bristol South constituency selection. Dawn had seen a letter from Roger Godsiff of APEX to the TGWU in Bristol convening the meeting with Golding.

Saturday 12 December

Still very cold today with snow on the ground.

Tuesday 15 December

At 10 the Executive met to pick the new General Secretary from a short list of Richard Clements, editor of *Tribune*, Bryan Davies, the Secretary of the PLP, Alex Ferry, General Secretary of CSEU, Joyce Gould, David Hughes, Jim Mortimer and Bob Wright of the AUEW.

Jim Mortimer, who was ultimately chosen, was the fifth to be interviewed. He said, 'I want to make five points. I am sixty years old, and I am applying not because I am looking for a job but because I might be able to help to win the Election. I want to reaffirm the strong trade union base of the Party; trade unions are close to working people, and this Party can therefore never go off the political scene permanently. I suggest four priorities. First, full employment and growth, all worked out with the unions. Secondly, removing the anti-trade-union legislation. Thirdly, reduction in military expenditure and the removal of US military bases. Fourthly, we must negotiate our way out of the Common Market and the Treaty of Rome. Also there are staff issues, and perhaps my experience as industrial relations officer of London Transport and at ACAS might help. I want to help the Party to look outwards.'

On the first ballot Jim Mortimer got 13, and we proceeded to a second. At the second ballot Alex Ferry got 14 votes, Jim Mortimer 15 votes. That was the result Michael Foot wanted, and it was one of the few occasions when I voted with him. I think Jim's a decent guy and I shall certainly hope to get on well with him.

Dawn Primarolo has sent me the notes made by a trade-unionist on John Golding's visit to Bristol to address the local trade unions on 23 November. Golding apparently asked full-time officials to join GMCs; they needn't attend regularly, he said, but they could go to the annual general meetings and to the selection conferences and, as this matter was so confidential, it would be better if nothing was written down and all communication was by telephone.

Wednesday 16 December

I went to the Executive, having discussed with Caroline some points to make.

Under matters arising, Frank Allaun moved that Peter Tatchell, whose candidature was to be raised later in the meeting, be allowed to attend this meeting with colleagues from Bermondsey. Judith said, 'No, I can't allow that, and if you want to suggest it you will have to move me out of the chair.' There was a vote, and by 17 to 11 the Executive voted not to allow Tatchell to give evidence.

At 11 we came to Organisation Committee matters, and Eric Heffer moved the reference back to the item on Tatchell. Frank Allaun, seconding Eric, said, 'There must be a Chinese proverb saying, "Before you start out on a journey you must know where you intend to end up." A hundred more letters came in this morning in support of Tatchell, and you will end up having to disaffiliate the Bermondsey Party. It will then have to go to Conference. Anyway, we have already endorsed four *Militant* supporters as parliamentary candidates.'

Michael Foot said, 'There is strong feeling on both sides, and I should like to explain what I did. I am solely responsible for it, but if I had not taken this action there would have been a serious crisis for the Party. I know the Bermondsey background because Bob Mellish has been to see me and I had to prevent him from resigning. Right, left and centre MPs came to see me, and none of them said they would leave the Party, but they did say, "If he is adopted, we will not be able to support him and we will attack his article." It would have been a gift to the SDP.'

Dennis Skinner made a marvellous speech. 'Michael Foot doesn't like Tatchell, and all the patronage men have goaded Michael into this, living in this glasshouse in Westminster. Mellish has got a £16,000-a-year part-time job.' (This is the deputy chairmanship of the London Docklands Development Corporation.) 'Why? Because he was a member of the Labour Party. We should endorse Tatchell. The SDP and the press are dictating our policy, and we should be true to ourselves.'

I spoke next and said, 'Michael, you are a very powerful man, the Leader of a political party, and in the House of Commons, not the Organisation Committee, you denounced this man. He is a little man. Nobody had ever heard of Peter Tatchell outside Bermondsey until he was attacked, and the public may not understand the niceties of politics, but they understand questions of natural justice.

'They will see we have done something very unfair, indeed disgraceful, now we have refused to hear him. Secondly, we are denying the right of constituency parties to choose their own candidates. We would be denying the history of extra-parliamentary activity which has given us our rights – the fight for Chartism, the fight for female suffrage, against the Combination Acts, and so on. It will open up endless argument which will go on from now until Conference, occupying all our time and maybe beyond. It is absolutely wrong that we should vote on a matter of this kind as if it were a vote of confidence, because we have had enough of votes of confidence and the use of patronage to enforce them. Now we are being told that the power of patronage is to be used to enforce the removal of a parliamentary candidature. We open ourselves to threats on everything if we succumb to this – the Mellish threat, the threat from MPs who are leaving at the rate of one a week – and, if we allow these sorts of threats to decide things, next it will be on policy. We shall recover from it, but what we are doing today is disgraceful, and I think the Executive should consider very carefully whether it wants to go along this road.'

Next came Sam McCluskie, who said, 'I cannot accept Michael's argument about the NEC having a right to overturn selection. We should have an inquiry, and I'm afraid, Michael, the argument goes against you.'

'I don't know what Tony Benn means when he talks about patronage,' Joan Lestor said. 'Is he suggesting that because I have got a Front Bench job from Michael that is going to influence me? My loyalty is to Michael Foot. We should have met Tatchell, and I regret Michael's statement. But it is a leadership issue. If it is a question of confidence, I shall support Foot.'

Neil Kinnock started by defending Foot. 'Michael has been goaded in the last twelve months. He was uncharacteristic in what he said in the House; it was not thought out, as I would have done if I had had the responsibility. But if Michael had wanted to be really ruthless he would have said, "Let Tatchell be the candidate, let him be beaten." The SDP exists, and we *shall* have anti-parliamentary campaigns. Tatchell is giving the Tories a cheap asset to use against us, and Michael has been goaded by the deputy leadership election, by Tony's response to his support for the Home Policy chairmanship, by the Shadow Cabinet. There has been no loyalty from the left, and this is a loyalty vote in Michael, and we don't want it to be said of him that he copped out and was trampled on. I'm going to give critical support, and Tony may be thinking of giving the support that Trotsky speaks of. It's not bloody good enough. I'll speak of Tatchell to Conference, even if it's my valedictory. What we have thrown away is victory at the next Election and the chance to get unilateralism, the alternative economic strategy, out of the Common Market, the education policy. We have demolished the Party's prospects by vanity, and we should support our people even when they are wrong.'

Eric Heffer said, 'This is the most important discussion in the NEC for years. Michael has to take account of the position of the Party, but so does the NEC. It is amazing listening to Joan and Neil and others saying that they disagree with Michael but want to support him because he is the Leader. We have got to do what is right.'

We had a recorded vote to 'refer the item back,' ie not proceed with it, and there were 14 in favour, 15 against. That one vote is interesting, because Healey remains on the NEC as Deputy Leader as a result of the SDP defectors' votes in the deputy leadership contest. So Tatchell's candidature was disallowed.

I walked out, all the press were waiting. I told the journalists that I would make a statement, which was that I was disappointed that by one vote the NEC had decided not to hear Tatchell before disallowing his candidature, but we had expelled lots of people in the past, indeed we had just appointed as General Secretary a man, Jim Mortimer, who had been expelled from the Party. 'Speaking as Deputy Leader of the Party, because of course Denis Healey's entire majority has now defected to the SDP, I want to say to Labour Party people at home not to be discouraged but to go on campaigning for peace and social justice because that is the only policy that the British people can rely on to deal with their problems. That is all I have got to say.'

I was pursued, but refused to say anything more.

Thursday 17 December
At 5 we had the Campaign Group. We had a brief discussion about the PLP meeting tonight, and Dennis Skinner said, 'I don't want to make much of this, but Tony should not have said yesterday to the press what he did about the deputy leadership. We have got to make clear that we are concerned with policy on behalf of the people we represent, and it is not about individuals, that's not what it is about.'

It was quite clear from the atmosphere that there was considerable hostility to what I had said about being the Deputy Leader, and I felt a bit uneasy about it, but thank God at least my friends are prepared to criticise.

To the PLP meeting. I was nervous, actually, and the atmosphere was icy.

Laurie Pavitt, MP for Brent South, was the first called to speak. He said, 'I am not a member of a group, and the Tea Room is the loneliest place in the world. My Party have got a hit-list. The GMC is against me, and there is a witch-hunt against good Party members. I'm on a hit-list over the deputy leadership. I have known Tony Benn very well, and I respect him and admire him, and I am very sorry indeed that Tony should be in this position, but he has got two loyalties – one to the Party and one to these outside groups – and he has got to make up his mind which he follows.'

Well, that was the opening shot, and I spoke next. I said, 'I would like to suggest to the Party tonight that what we decide to do is to have a work programme for the PLP. I think policy is more important, and, much as I admire Laurie Pavitt, I can't believe that reminiscences about constituencies are really the key to this.'

After I had said that, and in a way criticised Laurie, who is a very popular figure, there was a lot of shouting. I went on, 'I think what will bring us together is working out in detail how we will do the manifesto to publish it this summer.'

At this there was a lot of interruption, and Jack Dormand had to call for silence. I said, 'I don't mind. I've written all this down, and if you would rather I sat down I'll circulate the written speech.'

So they were quiet and I continued, 'It seems to me that, if we are to protect the people we represent, we shall have to have the biggest intervention ever in market forces since 1945, and, if we are to meet the very modest needs of jobs, homes and schools and dignity in retirement, we shall have to have the most radical programme ready. There is a very wide area of agreement in the Party on policy, but there are some areas of difficulty, and I don't see any prospect of doing what has to be done unless we can lift the twin obstacles of the Treaty of Rome and the House of Lords from our path. And we simply won't be able to afford money on nuclear weapons. As chairman of the Home Policy Committee, I am writing to all working groups and the subject groups to focus attention on what are the priorities for the next Labour Government, what powers we would need, what costs and savings would be involved, and I hope the message that gets out of this meeting is that we have begun that task.'

In the event, strangely, the main part of the speech was listened to in silence. I think they had expected me to attack the right wing of the

Party or justify the deputy leadership remark, and somehow I got by and set the tone of the debate.

David Clark, MP for South Shields, said, 'Tony, it is not just about policy, it's about regeneration. How do you retain the support of our people? The history of this Party is that we produce great leaders and create idols – Victor Grayson, Oswald Mosley, Nye Bevan and Tony – and Tony has got to make up his mind whether he is going to work with the Party or not.'

I did resent the comparison with Oswald Mosley, but I don't think he meant it in quite that way, so I spoke to him afterwards and he was a bit shy.

Bob Mellish got up. '*I've* been a Member a long time. I've been here thirty years, and I've always argued my case. Tony, there is no one who doesn't want disarmament, but multilateralists are now called right-wing fascists. I had a superb Party once, we won every seat for fifty-five years – borough, GLC and parliamentary. The rumour that we were a moribund party is untrue. I was affronted that when Tony spoke recently in Bermondsey it was in front of a big banner that said "Keep St Olave's Hospital open", when I was actually chairman of the strike committee and Peter Tatchell did nothing at all. I have never been involved in a witch-hunt. Michael has never coerced me. I applied for the Chiltern Hundreds in the autumn, but the local Party in Bermondsey pleaded with me not to resign from Parliament. I will never join the SDP, and, if I resign, the Labour voters would be without a party *and* a candidate.'

So, in effect, Bob Mellish was telling us he wouldn't resign and force a by-election, and that there was now no pressure on Bermondsey.

Finally Michael Foot summed up. He asked me yet again to repudiate *London Labour Briefing*.

'Tatchell's speech was an attack on parliamentary democracy. This is the most critical time in the history of the Party, and if our opponents can fix a label on us it will do damage throughout the whole United Kingdom. The Party needs tolerance and compassion. Memories of Nye Bevan in Room 14 were of a suffocating discipline, discipline which denied Nye his rightful destiny, and I am against that sort of discipline. But the Tribune Group then and now is not in any way similar to Militant.'

He continued, 'Now that it's all over, we'll have a quiet Christmas, and in the New Year we must get the policy together.'

Thursday 24 December
Caroline was preparing things for Christmas but she has the most terrible cold and fever.

I went to see Mark Arnold-Forster, who is dying of cancer. Val and their five children were there, and her mother and brother. The doctor has prescribed enormous amounts of morphine. I looked in on Mark. It was such a shock: he's sixty-two, only five years older than me, but he looked eighty-five – his face pinched and yellow and two days' growth of beard. His eyes started out of his head, and his hands and feet were swollen.

He recognised me and was glad to see me, but he was a bit restive. I asked him about the situation in Poland, and he thought it was bloody awful. Val said it was the first time he'd recognised anyone for two days, since Alastair Hetherington, the former editor of the *Guardian*, had been to see him.

A very different Christmas Eve – the first time for many years that Mark and Val haven't come to visit us on Christmas Eve. The first Christmas too that we've had a grandchild. Ralph and Ann Gibson are away too, so it will be the first Boxing Day for years that we haven't been to see them.

A traumatic year in so many ways.

Friday 25 December

Christmas Day. Caroline had bronchitis and was very poorly. Josh got up, and we began with a row, because I went down to my basement and found the washing-machine was leaking and the floor was awash with water, with my papers on the floor.

Later Val rang to say that Mark had died at lunchtime.

Monday 28 December

Caroline a bit better and eating. She slept a bit. We are both very physically and mentally exhausted.

Thursday 31 December

Lovely sunny day. In the evening we set off for Stansgate, arrived just before midnight, and sat and talked as the year came to a close.

Politically it has been the most dramatic year of my life – the deputy leadership campaign. Was it right? It's still arguable, but I think it was. It was also a year in which the Party became more politically educated than ever before, and a year in which the policies were agreed.

I became very ill with the Guillain-Barré syndrome, and it still affects me in that my legs are a bit wobbly and my fingers are not perfect. It will be two years before I am completely recovered.

Both of us were active politically. Caroline continued to work with the SEA and produced the Voluntary Schools Report, was involved with the TUC Educational Alliance, with UNESCO, to which she was reappointed. She edited *Socialism and Education* and *Comprehensive Education*.

I think now – and my friends agree – that we should fight the General Election on a status quo agreement, whereby the policy is agreed, the constitutional changes are accepted, the left holds off on further constitutional change, the purges are dropped, and the leadership is not challenged.

The first significant political development of the new year came on 5–6 January 1982 at a joint meeting of representatives of the NEC/PLP and Trade Unionists for a Labour Victory (TULV). The meeting was organised by ASTMS at their country club at Bishop's Stortford. Those who attended were anxious to ensure that there would not be another deputy leadership election during the year, and I circulated unofficially a paper, 'Working for Unity', to the members of the NEC and to the trade union general secretaries, outlining the basis for a 'truce'.

In consequence there was reached a tacit understanding that we would fight the next General Election under the existing leadership (ie Michael Foot and Denis Healey), with a manifesto based upon the 1981 Conference decisions, a moratorium on constitutional changes, and a halt to any purge of left individuals or groups.

As a result of the discussions over the two days, David Basnett was able to announce that 'peace had broken out' in the Labour Party, which was much trumpeted by the political commentators.

Sunday 10 January 1982

I had the first of my home meetings for some time with Norman Atkinson, Tony Banks, Vladi Derer, Jon Lansman, Ken Livingstone, Michael Meacher, Frances Morrell, Chris Mullin, Reg Race, Nigel Williamson, Audrey Wise and Valerie Wise.

I handed them all a copy of the statement on unity which I had circulated at the Bishop's Stortford meeting, and there was a very good paper by Chris Mullin called 'The Basis for a Truce'. We had a long discussion that went on till about 10.45.

Williamson said there was a fear on the left that there had been a sell-out, and Frances agreed it was a big change.

Jon Lansman said the left was at a low ebb now and therefore we wouldn't lose by a truce – it was the best way to protect our gains.

Audrey Wise resented the idea of a deal or a truce and said we couldn't be private in any sense; we had to activate the rank and file to defend its rights.

Michael Meacher agreed with Chris Mullin's paper. He was in favour of existing policy and we should hang on to our gains, but Chris was a bit too defensive and we should raise the voting balance at Conference. PLP reform should be put forward, if only as a bargaining counter. Further, we should concentrate on policy in an early manifesto dealing specially with inequality and privatisation.

Tony Banks thought that what had been agreed wasn't a deal, it was an understanding. He said we ought to leave the deputy leadership alone, but we might actually have to fight the leadership this year.

I said that if Michael Foot did make a hash of it there might be a great demand for a strong left leadership during the year and you couldn't rule that out. All we should say was that we expected these things to happen. We had to face the fact that we wanted a Labour victory – we had to trundle those awful old duds in the Shadow Cabinet back into Whitehall offices and what we had to do was go for public campaigns: to get an Election victory; to have a vigorous defence of the trade unions and local government; to spell out the policy; to put socialism back on the agenda.

Monday 11 January
Bitterly cold. The country is under the worst conditions within living memory.

Tuesday 12 January
International Committee. A resolution on Poland was moved by Eric Heffer and Joan Lestor. I agreed with the sentiments, but I suggested we differentiate ourselves from Thatcher and Reagan, who did not truly support Solidarity at all and just used it to whip up the Cold War. We ought to add the Solidarity demands for free trade unions and access to the media in order to make a distinction between ourselves and the Tories, who just support anything that embarrasses the Russians.

Wednesday 13 January
At 2 Robin Blackburn, Fred Halliday, Perry Anderson and Anthony Barnett, all from the *New Left Review*, came to discuss a 10,000-word interview with me. It was a very interesting discussion, because the Socialist Society is being founded next week.

Friday 15 January
Michael Foot had a scholarly essay on Tom Paine in the *Guardian*.
    Lunch with David Basnett at the GMWU headquarters in Claygate, Esher – a huge country house set in eleven acres of ground with an old manor house round which had been built a Victorian castle with crenelated walls and towers. A swimming pool and a new office block have been added.
    We touched on the Bishop's Stortford accord, and we talked about wages policy and how the errors of the past might be avoided. David was one of the most senior members on the TUC General Council during the Heath, Wilson and Callaghan Governments. I told him I was in the same position on the NEC.
    David Basnett gave me the general impression that he would like to work personally with me. He said it was very important that there be a senior trade-unionist in the Cabinet – clearly *he'd* like to be in the Cabinet. I think he would be a sensible Cabinet Minister. He said we'd

need to have an extra-parliamentary dimension to economic planning –
ie somewhere between the unions and the Government. There is this
corporatism idea among many senior trade-unionists, which is
reflected by the palatial offices in which they work, and you realise that
they are an integral part of the establishment. Their resentment against
Mrs Thatcher is that she doesn't acknowledge them as such.

I had a letter from a Peter Burton today about his daughter, who has
Guillain-Barré syndrome. He was so concerned that he wanted my
advice, having read of my experience. I rang him and cheered him up.

Saturday 16 January
Ken Coates rang me in the evening and said his Institute for Workers'
Control and Peter Hain and others were hostile to the idea of Labour
Liaison 1982. He didn't want to be tied up with that group – he wanted
to broaden the influence of the left into the centre of the Party.

Sunday 17 January
Foot had an article in the *Observer* defending Callaghan and attacking
me for 'monstrous perversion.'

Monday 18 January
Travelled back from Bristol, and a message came from the drivers
asking if I'd like to travel on the footplate. So I went along to their cabin
and sat in a very comfortable chair and flew to Bath at about 90 miles
an hour in this new 125, through the Brunel tunnel. I got out at
Chippenham, went back to my compartment and worked on some
papers.

Tuesday 19 January
The Cuban Ambassador, Mr Hermes Harrara Hernandez, came to
issue us with a standing invitation to visit Cuba, and paid the most
elaborate tribute to me for the help I gave him last year during the
American threat to invade Cuba.

Josh was watching a programme about Carter's last day in office. All
Carter's people were in the Oval Office, Mondale, Muskie, Lloyd
Turner, Hamilton Jordan, Jodie Powell, Mrs Carter, and so on.

I thought what a very ordinary little group of people they were with
that great responsibility. This was the same group that would decide to
drop the bomb, and you realised that the most powerful country in the
world still has major positions held by a crowd like that; none of the
people there, with the exception of the President and Vice-President,
was elected. At least a British Cabinet is made up of elected people.
Even the Secretary of State and the White House staff are basically
cronies of the President. Stephen is writing his thesis on the White
House Staff and knows a great deal about it.

Saturday 23 January

Up late and went off to County Hall for the founding meeting of Labour Liaison 1982. Norman Atkinson had taken on the job of convening it. The LCC and the IWC didn't want to come, and there was some trouble with the Socialist Campaign for a Labour Victory, who were a bit shirty about what happened at Bishop's Stortford. Anyway, there were about seventy people there.

During the day Hilary had asked me what I was doing on 29 May and I said I hadn't got my diary, why? 'Well,' he replied 'Sally and I are thinking of getting married then!'

Caroline and I went to the Socialist Society launch party with Robin Blackburn, Tariq Ali, his partner Susan Watkins, Hilary Wainwright, Lynne Segal. Hilary and Lynne are authors of the book *Beyond the Fragments*, and Lynne told me that she has joined her local Labour Party – which is lovely, because I tried to persuade her a couple of years ago to join. Hilary Wainwright looked a bit embarrassed because she hadn't joined; still, it isn't the be-all and end-all of life.

The Socialist Society has its founding conference this weekend, and it is a great initiative to bring all the socialist groups together on a non-sectarian, comprehensive basis to publish works about socialism – it's a bit élitist and a bit too London-based, but still a very imaginative idea. A thousand people turned up at the Institute of Education in Bedford Way and many of the 'old boys' were there – Raymond Williams, Stuart Hall, Ralph Miliband, Perry Anderson and lots of others. The SWP and IMG were represented.

Sunday 24 January

To the Socialist Society conference after lunch. We talked about whether there should be individual membership, about affiliation to the Labour Party and so on.

Raymond Williams moved that 'the Socialist Society be founded'. A historic event. He was, of course, one of the organisers of the New Left in 1956, and he spoke about the many starts before but said this was a fresh one and he thought it would work.

An ASLEF worker spoke about the railway strike, and the decision by drivers at King's Cross to black Murdoch's newspapers.[5]

Thursday 28 January

To St Martin-in-the-Fields, Trafalgar Square, Mark Arnold-Forster's memorial service. The church was packed for a lovely service. The first lesson was read by John Cole in his beautiful Irish accent, and the first address was given by Commander Dreyer, who must have been Mark's commanding officer during the war. The second address was by Ian Aitken; and Mary Tuck, a neighbour of theirs, spoke about the family, the house, and so on.

I talked to Alastair Hetherington on the way out – I hadn't seen him for ten years – and he told me that *The Times* had asked him to contribute an article on Saturday about the ASLEF drivers and the *Sun*. He walked all the way back to the Commons with me and I gave him the background. Clearly ASLEF's refusing to carry the paper has brought the issue to the forefront.

Tuesday 2 February

I went to a press conference at the Commons to launch the report published today on the real cost of nuclear power. The conference was organised by the Committee for the Study of the Economics of Nuclear Electricity. It was packed with authors and scientists of nuclear power, like Colin Sweet, Professor J. Jeffrey, Edward Goldsmith and Sir Kelvin Spencer;* David Penhaligon was in the chair. I sat at the back, but Kelvin Spencer kept insisting on bringing me in; I must say the old boy was marvellous. He said he had read all my books and asked me what was happening in the Labour Party now.

The meeting raised all the fundamental democratic questions about open government and information, of chairmen of nationalised industries and the accountability problems of controlling technology.

To the Machinery of Government Study Group, which has John Silkin, Patricia Hewitt, Robert Sheldon (MP for Ashton-under-Lyne), John Garrett (MP for Norwich South) and others on it. I had put up a proposal that we use a Humble Address as a way of abolishing the Lords, by appealing to the Queen to create a thousand peers.

John Silkin lashed out at it. Silkin's authority depends on everything being too difficult, and he is infuriated by anyone who makes something appear easy. He said it was too clever by half, just an intellectual gimmick.

Bob Sheldon didn't want to abolish the Lords anyway, Patricia Hewitt, General Secretary of the National Council for Civil Liberties, said there wouldn't be any public support for it.

Wednesday 3 February

Worked at home this morning and drafted a little note to CND. I hope they will accept my Foreign Nuclear Bases Prohibition Bill at their executive on Saturday.

Dictated a seven-page memo on how to abolish the Lords, which I really enjoyed doing.

Thursday 4 February

Several people from Bristol and from CND and the Ecology Party came

---

* Sir Kelvin Spencer, Chief Scientist at the Ministry of Power, 1954–9, whose initial enthusiastic support for the civil exploitation of nuclear energy changed to active opposition.

to see me about my bill to ban foreign nuclear weapons from Britain.

They were very serious, and afraid that if it was a Labour Party effort it might affect all-party support, that it might alienate our Front Bench, and that it might be too narrow because it didn't include the banning of all bases, or chemical weapons. Also, it didn't deal with unilateral disarmament in Britain as a whole. I tried to satisfy them on all these points. I said, if they couldn't help on it, perhaps they could note it. But of course it would be much better if they could positively support it.

Friday 12 February
Caroline and I drove to Bristol for my surgery, followed by the Annual General Meeting of Bristol South East Party. We elected some very good new officers: Meg Crack as our first woman chair, Pam Tatlow as secretary, Brenda Diamond as treasurer, Jenny Smith as membership secretary, Sue Beckingham as youth officer, Dawn Primarolo as political education officer. So that's six women as officers of the Party. Very pleasing.

Wednesday 17 February
Hilary was selected by 28 to 20 to fight Ealing North for Labour in the General Election.

Thursday 18 February
Home from an exhausting three-day trip to the United States. It was worthwhile – it is good to go to the US on occasions.

Reagan has made a tremendous impact on American politics. He is not quite like Mrs Thatcher, because he presides like a monarch over American society, whereas she is a leader and a teacher of a much more formidable kind. They have both won the battle of ideas, because the old New Dealers capitulated as the Old Left did in Britain, but in the course of fighting against that old decaying corporatist, liberal, capitalist structure a great generation of really tough people was bred, and they are now taking over and carrying through a counter-revolution. They are serious people to fight. We have to breed, by discussion and struggle, a group who are equally capable of doing what we want to do; the present leadership of the Democratic Party is no use at all. Edward Kennedy is a completely empty vessel who thinks of politics as a management job without any ideology.

America is very conscious of its fall in world power, and that is what makes it so very dangerous.

Thursday 25 February
I was asked to go to Bedford Square where there is the first strike of NUJ members in the book division of the union, editors who work in publishing houses and whose real income has fallen about 12% over the

last two years. Comparable white collar and administration work in London is about £9000 a year and they're on £7000. There were about 350 people outside the Publishers' Association office in the square. I spoke through a loudspeaker. I was shown a letter from Robert Maxwell's publishing house threatening the mother of the chapel with the sack if she went on strike today. He a former Labour MP!

Tuesday 2 March

CND are anxious that I get Kinnock to sponsor my Foreign Nuclear Bases Prohibition Bill. In fact, yesterday he sent me a note saying he would be delighted to sponsor the bill, then another note saying that after consulting John Silkin he declined to sponsor it. Very interesting. The list of sponsors now is Frank Allaun, Norman Atkinson, Bob Cryer, Ioan Evans, Stuart Holland, Joan Maynard, Ian Mikardo, Jo Richardson and Stan Thorne.

Norman Atkinson told me that Rupert Murdoch had had lunch with Mrs Thatcher no less than three times last week. He had heard that from Ian Gow, Mrs Thatcher's PPS, and he had the impression that the Tories were panic-stricken that *The Times* might come out for the SDP. So they were offering Murdoch all possible help in return for support for the Tory Party.

Thursday 4 March

I went into the Commons to present my Foreign Nuclear Bases Prohibition Bill. A Tory MP jumped up and asked if it wasn't an abuse of the House that a bill should be introduced when it had no chance of enactment. The Speaker said that the Right Honourable Gentleman (me) was entirely within his rights. So the Tory MP suggested it be referred to the Procedure Committee, and the Speaker said that was not a matter for him.

I dashed upstairs for a press conference, with copies of the bill, Party Conference resolutions on which it was based, and De Gaulle's letter to President Johnson in 1966 calling for American bases to be removed from France. Bob Cryer, Ernie Ross and Norman Atkinson turned up, as did Bruce Kent with a statement supporting the bill. Very good. The key points came out. The press suggested it would embarrass the Labour Front Bench, but I didn't jump to that bait.

Friday 5 March

Worked at home. Only the *Morning Star* gave the bill any decent coverage; the *Daily Mirror* had a tiny little item. Every other paper ignored it. That is the power of the press. The *Guardian* and the *Telegraph* had referred to it in its earlier development, but the power to ignore the presentation of a bill signed by twelve Labour MPs and backed by probably a hundred MPs is formidable. The CND has three times as many members as the SDP, three times as many MPs supporting it, but, when the media come up against something they know will strike a responsive chord with the public, they have a choice between denouncing it and ignoring it.

Tuesday 9 March
Up at 7, and Josh drove us to London Airport, where we caught an Olympic Airways flight to Athens.

We arrived in Athens at about 5.15 and were greeted by three of Papandreou's advisers. Greece reminds us of Portugal in that the communists in Portugal fought hardest against the fascists, just as in Greece, where after the war 2 million members of ELAS, the National Popular Liberation Army, were crushed in a civil war in which the British supported the Greek right-wing government, restored the monarchy and got rid of the communist-led guerrillas. The Communist Party in Greece is very Moscow-oriented – there are in effect two parties, one pro-Moscow and the other Eurocommunist – but there is no need for coalition with them because PASOK has a sufficient majority. Of course, although the army are prepared to go along with Papandreou because of the national interest which leads them to suspect the Turks and hence the Americans, they are still no doubt riddled with the same sort of sentiment as at the time of the Colonels, and are not prepared to have any communists in the Government. This guarantees that PASOK will remain a radical liberal Government with socialist rhetoric (and no doubt some socialist aspirations).

They are genuinely trying to liberalise the regime. They sacked all the senior civil servants, they are changing some of the judges, they are bringing in political advisers. But they have a severe economic crisis and they haven't really got an industrial base. As with Portugal, Greece reminds me of Edwardian or late Victorian politics in Britain. I don't want to sound arrogant, because British politics at the moment are early Victorian or late eighteenth century.

Wednesday 10 March
Caroline went to lunch with Margaret Papandreou, having previously visited the Minister in charge of higher education.

I was taken by car to visit Papandreou at his house in a suburb of Athens. His father George, who was Prime Minister in the 1960s, was under house arrest there during the period of the Colonels. He had an officer in every room and had no privacy, not even when his doctor examined him. His wife died there only last summer at the age of about ninety-five; George died some years ago.

The house had a garden, and there was a police guard outside. The press corps was waiting for Andreas Papandreou to meet me but I went in instead and was met by his private secretary. Andreas showed me the house. His study was panelled with pictures and photographs of the children and a photograph of Tito. On his desk I noticed Mao's *Little Red Book* in Greek.

We talked for about an hour and then went into lunch with Mr Karalos Papoulis, the Vice-Minister of Foreign Affairs; Dimitri Koulourianas, Governor of the Hellenic Industrial Development Bank; Angela Kokkola, Papandreou's private secretary, and several other Ministers and young economic advisers.

Andreas raised the problem of the Greek black economy. He said there were 200,000–300,000 Greeks living in luxury off three sources of income: speculation, much of it in land and associated with the tourist trade; commissions, which were really corrupt payments in connection with contracts; and tax evasion. Compared to these people the industrialists were not too bad. He said they had to find a way of taxing this black economy. There really was extensive corruption in defence contracts, and what happened was that officers were pocketing the commission, the Government having paid up to 50 per cent above the real price of the equipment. He said they didn't prosecute the officers, but simply moved them into other jobs.

Of course, at the heart of the 'defence of the free world', to use the jargon of NATO, there must be enormous corruption, and I drew attention to what happened in Saudi Arabia. Anyway, he's decided to deal with it directly by going straight to the French, who are big arms suppliers, and signing a framework agreement with the French Government, to eliminate all these corrupt practices.

He went on to discuss his Civil Service. He said in order to deal with the senior permanent officials, they were going to abolish the two top grades of the service – in British terms, Permanent Secretaries and Deputy Secretaries – and retire existing officials. This allowed them to get younger people into the service who were more sympathetic to his Government.

Next they were tackling the universities, and here they had a problem, because the universities had constitutional autonomy. They'd had to reshape the power structure within the universities – by saying that professors and others in positions of power would be elected by the lecturers and the students. This self-management in the universities had not interfered with their autonomy but had totally changed their power structure. He said the professors had just taken a mass of jobs outside – on the council of this or the board of that – and they had to deal with that problem.

As to the army, he said there were a number of factors which had been favourable to PASOK. For example, the Americans who had supported the Greek Colonels also supported Turkey, which is a dictatorship, and Turkish policy in Cyprus. Papandreou was very much afraid that, if the Americans ever wanted to destabilise Greece, all they'd need to do was turn a blind eye to a Turkish invasion of a few Greek islands. This had made the Greek army more sympathetic to PASOK than you might expect.

There had been indignities imposed on the Greek army – for example, American sergeants ordering Greek generals about. The generals liked a glimpse of the big time when they went to conferences and were now paid great respect by the Americans at top level. He had to watch that.

On relations with the US, he remarked that Alexander Haig, the Secretary of State, didn't listen to anything anyone said to him. He had met Haig at the NATO meeting in Brussels and he had appeared incapable of taking on board any of his comments. Haig had asked if he could visit Athens soon after the election, but Arafat, the PLO leader, was in Athens and Papandreou did not think it suitable for Haig to come then. Caspar Weinberger, the US Defence Secretary, was, he said, a very sharp American lawyer and much more sensitive to what was going on.

The police in Greece were absolutely corrupt, but he couldn't bring the evidence before the courts because some of it had reached him through illegal telephone-tapping.

The Intelligence Services were efficient in external services, but the internal service was violently anti-left, and he had ordered them to close their files on the labour movement and put a new man in charge.

When I asked him about NATO, he told me he had refused to sign the NATO communiqué that had been put before him at the NATO summit because it made no mention of Cyprus. Secondly, he refused to support sanctions against the USSR over Poland because he thought it was hypocritical, and, thirdly, he refused to recognize the legitimacy of a Common Market peacekeeping force in Sinai following the Camp David agreement. He said the Americans did realise that the Greeks were serious about removing their nuclear bases from Greece, though, as far as he could make out, all that they had were some pretty old nuclear weapons which were held in depots.

I was most impressed by Papandreou. When I first met him in 1980 I had great sympathy with him, and here was a left-wing Labour-type Government with all the right ideas about the Common Market and NATO and industrial development. The fact that Stuart Holland is much trusted by them, and goes over there a lot, impresses me too. When I got to Greece I had a fear that Papandreou was another Mario Soares, ie that he must have been at least tolerated or even promoted by the right-wing social democrats in order to see that the communists never got into any position in Greece. However, I have come to the conclusion that there was something much more radical going on there, and I came away from the discussions very much encouraged.

Friday 12 March
Up early, and we were taken to the airport.

We had a most enjoyable time. Papandreou is a man of considerable talent and ability, and the Ministers are genuinely trying to do their best. But the Government consists mainly of intellectuals, and they are governing a rural society, with ill-developed industry and huge tourism, which is their greatest source of revenue.

Monday 15 March
Voted against the renewal of the Prevention of Terrorism Act with about forty-five MPs. In the process the Front Bench lost Clive Soley, one of the Northern Ireland spokesmen, who voted against it. That is a perfect example of the very issue raised last year over collective Shadow Cabinet responsibility. The Party Conference voted to repeal this Act, and when Clive votes against its renewal in Parliament he loses his Front Bench seat.

Sunday 21 March
To LBC for an interview, and while I was waiting in their studio I saw in the waste-paper basket the news bulletin that had just been read out by the newsreader. It included an item that stated, 'Left-winger Tony Benn MP said yesterday in Nottingham that . . .', and then another item: 'Transport Secretary, Mr David Howell, said . . .' So I straightened the paper out and added a little note to the newsroom:

> Why left-winger for me and not former Cabinet Minister, or chairman of the Home Policy Committee, or Bristol MP? Why not monetarist David Howell, member of the right-wing Conservative Cabinet, or Mrs Thatcher's hardline Transport Minister?

A woman in the newsroom apologised, saying she was from the Bermondsey Labour Party – as if that excused her, whereas it made it worse.

Came home, and Caroline and I drove to Greenham Common, the women's peace camp, for their festival. It was marvellous; thousands of people were there. Each gate into the site had been given a separate identity – the ecology gate, the music gate, the women's gate, the religious gate, and so on. There were tents, and jugglers and mummers – everyone tramping through the mud. We went to the main gate and signed our name, and I recorded some of the songs being sung by the women.

Monday 22 March
To London Airport to get the flight to Glasgow, and who should I see at the airport but David and Debbie Owen going to Hillhead to campaign in the by-election for Roy Jenkins who is standing as the SDP-Liberal

Alliance candidate. Then George Brown came in and headed for the
bar. So sitting in the airport were three people who had been Cabinet
Ministers together at different times, and two of them had defected and
were going to speak for Roy Jenkins. Brown and Jenkins – two former
Deputy Leaders of the Labour Party.

I was met at Glasgow and taken to the Hillhead Labour Party
committee rooms, where I had a cup of tea and a bun. Then I was taken
into a little room in an old Co-op funeral parlour where the candidate,
David Wiseman, and others were gathered – a panelled room where no
doubt grieving Glaswegians were handed the bill for burying their
relatives. Helen Liddell, the secretary of the Scottish Council of the
Labour Party, said they were frightened about my coming – Helen is
very right-wing. They kept bringing up 'extremism' in the Party and
said, 'Your Marx Memorial Lecture didn't help'.

I went to the meeting attended by 1500–2000 people. The SDP had
put out a little red-baiting, McCarthyite-type leaflet referring to my
lecture.

Thursday 25 March
Was picked up at 10.45pm to go to the ITN studios to comment on Roy
Jenkins's victory in the by-election.

Thursday 1 April
Met Graham Allen, Bob Cryer and Willy McKelvey, and for forty
minutes we cried in each other's beer, because after Hillhead we are
very depressed. The Party isn't doing well, the left has lost the impetus,
and the right hasn't grasped it because they haven't anything to offer,
but they are benefiting from the defeat of the Labour Party.

*On 2 April 1982 the Falkland Islands, comprising two main islands 300 miles west
of Argentina, and the dependency of South Georgia, a further 800 miles south-east,
were invaded and occupied by Argentine troops. Fewer than 2000 islanders lived on
the various parts of the territory known to Argentina as Las Malvinas.*

*British sovereignty had been established in 1833, and Margaret Thatcher adhered
from the first to 'the principle that the wishes of the islanders remain paramount'. But
Argentina also had a longstanding geographical and historical claim to this territory,
and to the South Sandwich Islands, a dependency 470 miles further south.*

*Over many years, attempts had been made to settle this question by negotiation,
without any real progress; and one important factor influencing the parties was the
knowledge that oilfields, as yet unexploited, existed around the islands.*

*Judging the signs in early 1982 to be favourable, the right-wing military
dictatorship of General Galtieri took the opportunity to secure the islands, and a
military campaign ensued, lasting two and a half months, although no actual
declaration of war was made. Six debates were held in the House of Commons
during the course of the war.*

My diary entries deal largely with the debate within the Labour Party and not with the progress of the war itself. A chronology follows of the main incidents and developments of those ten weeks, during which an estimated 258 British servicemen, civilians and islanders and 746 Argentinians died.

2 April	Falkland Islands invaded by Argentinian troops, a garrison of 70 marines surrendered and a military governor installed. Announcement of preparations for a Task Force of military and requisitioned civilian ships.
3 April	Emergency debate held, for the first time on a Saturday since the Suez crisis in 1956. UN Security Council agree Resolution 502 calling for an immediate withdrawal of all Argentinian forces from the islands.
5 April	Task Force sets sail from Portsmouth, for three-week journey to the Falkland Islands, 8000 miles away, via Ascension Island, halfway there. Resignation of Foreign Secretary Lord Carrington and Foreign Office Ministers Richard Luce and Humphrey Atkins. Defence Secretary John Nott's offer of resignation refused by Mrs Thatcher. Appointment of Francis Pym as Foreign Secretary.
7 April	Emergency debate. Maritime Exclusion Zone of 200 miles around the islands, applying to Argentinian naval and auxiliary ships, is announced, to come into force on 12 April. United States Secretary of State, General Haig, visits London and Buenos Aires in an attempt to prevent war.
10–23 April	Haig visits London with 'specific ideas for discussion' including an Argentine offer to withdraw if Britain recalled its Task Force, but with no negotiation on sovereignty.
12 April	Peruvian Government proposal for a 72-hour truce.
14 April	Emergency debate; House of Commons recalled during recess.
19 April	Argentinian peace proposals presented via General Haig.
21 April	Argentine Government asks for full sovereignty over Falkland Islands in any peace proposals.
22 April	Landing of Special Boat Squadron marines on South Georgia. Pym visits Washington with proposals; Haig and Pym agree US peace plan.
23 April	Denis Healey visits Washington to see UN Secretary General.
25 April	South Georgia bombarded by British warships and recaptured by marines.
26 April	Mrs Thatcher rejects in Commons the Argentinian claim that Britain is 'technically at war' with them.
27 April	Total Exclusion Zone, applying to all shipping and military/civilian aircraft regarded as hostile, announced by Britain, to take effect from 30 April.
26–28 April	Organisation of American States passes resolution recognising Argentinian sovereignty over Las Malvinas, calling on Britain to cease hostilities.

29 April	Emergency debate.
30 April	US peace initiative fails. US take trade measures against Argentina. Peru proposes 7-point peace plan after consultation with Galtieri. *General Belgrano* torpedoed, 30 miles south of Total Exclusion Zone. Foot rejects Mrs Thatcher's invitation to all-party talks 'on Privy Councillor terms'. David Steel and David Owen accept.
3 May	*Alferez Sobral* attacked.
4 May	HMS *Sheffield* sunk by Exocet missile.
5 May	Motion for an immediate truce signed by 65 Labour, Plaid Cymru and Scottish Nationalist MPs.
6 May	New US–Peruvian proposals rejected by Argentina.
9–14 May	Bombardment of Falklands and landing of SAS.
19 May	Proposals for UN-negotiated peace rejected by Argentina, who refuse to accept South Georgia in any interim agreement of both sides to withdraw all troops. Sea King helicopter lost.
21 May	5000 British troops land on East Falklands. HMS *Ardent* and *Antelope* attacked.
24 May	Nott announces re-establishment of a British base on Falkland Islands.
25 May	*Atlantic Conveyor*, a requisitioned container ship, hit.
27–28 May	Recapture of Darwin and Goose Green by British forces.
4 June	Britain and US veto a draft UN resolution calling for immediate ceasefire. (US try, too late, to change vote to abstention.) *Sir Tristram*, *Sir Galahad* and other targets attacked by Argentinians.
11 June	HMS *Glamorgan* attacked.
14–15 June	Formal surrender of Argentinian forces.
January 1983	Debate on the Franks Report into origins of Falklands War.

Friday 2 April

Today the Argentinian navy were sent to the Falkland Islands, thousands of troops appear to have landed and overwhelmed the British garrison of seventy marines and a population of 1800. The Government's defence policy has been completely shown up – not that I would favour sending the British forces in, because it's a colony we grabbed years ago from somebody and we have no right to it; neither has Argentina, though it is closer to South America. Some 1800 British settlers do not constitute a domestic population whose views can be taken seriously, or rather whose views can be allowed to lead us into war. But of course the real interest there is the oil. There is oil around the islands, and Caroline pointed out that we should have done a deal years ago. Take the oil, divide it into two – say Argentina can have half the oil and overall theoretical sovereignty, while we would retain the administration and the population would be given shares in our oil. But that isn't the way these things actually work.

We have the Polaris submarine and nuclear hardware but absolutely no capacity to fight a war at that range.

To Radio London at 8 to record a programme of my favourite records. I chose 'My Old Man' by Marie Lloyd; the hymn 'He Who Would Valiant Be'; 'The Road to the Isles' sung by Kenneth McKellar; 'The Kerry Dances'; the theme from the film *The Way to the Stars*; 'I Know My Love' by Burl Ives; 'Sheep May Safely Graze' sung by Kirsten Flagstad; the chorus 'For Unto Us a Child is Born' from Handel's *Messiah*; 'The Baal Chorus from *Proud Valley*, sung by Paul Robeson; 'The Ballad of Joe Hill' sung by Joan Baez; 'The World Turned Upside Down' sung by Roy Bailey; 'Slow Train' by Flanders and Swann; 'Grandad' by Clive Dunn; 'We Shall Overcome' sung by Mahalia Jackson; and finally 'Jerusalem', played by a massed band and choir.

The station staff brought me a birthday cake – which was extremely nice of them.

To Bristol, and talked to Meg, now chair of the Party, who expressed the widely shared anxiety that I'm not active enough in Bristol: a serious criticism. They are afraid that all the hostile press coverage is having an effect in the constituency. I feel a sort of fatalism about it – not much that I can do, really. I no longer believe that in Bristol views are any different from those of people in London, though I used to think they were. Every time they turn on their TV sets and see me engaged in some controversy or other they ask why they don't see me in Bristol. There is a sacrificial element about it, and the price may very well be my defeat.

Herbert Rogers and Joyce Perham have told me they think I should look elsewhere for a seat because there is no hope of winning in Bristol once the boundaries change. But I feel I must go down with the ship.

Meg dropped me back at the station and I caught the 8.10 home.

At 11.30 Martin Jacques, editor of *Marxism Today*, came to collect my corrected proofs of the Marx lecture for the May issue. I asked him in, and he ended up staying till 12.40. He's one of the new young thoughtful communists, and he certainly has made a great success of *Marxism Today* – very imaginative. I've done three minor pieces for him now, the Hobsbawm interview, the discussion on the People's March for Jobs and this lecture.

Saturday 3 April

My fifty-seventh birthday.

The Falkland Islands is the big news, and I bought the papers and went to the House. This the first time it has met on a Saturday since 1956, and we had a three-hour debate on the Falkland Islands.

The Prime Minister opened the debate, and she was really very uneasy because the invasion and the surrender of the seventy marines stationed there has been a humiliating setback for her.

Michael Foot followed and was aggressive. He attacked Argentina, blamed the Government and said the whole situation had to be put right. He got a tremendous cheer from the Tories.

The House was in a jingoistic mood. Enoch Powell said the marines who had surrendered after two hours of fighting should in effect be court-martialled, and David Owen made an even more aggressive speech.

The only person who stood out against the mood was George Foulkes, the Labour Member for South Ayrshire. 'What do you want to do? Kill thousands of Argentinians, thousands of British sailors and the Falkland Islanders?' A very courageous speech, for which I congratulated him later.

But the House was in the grip of jingoism. Silkin and Nott made very poor speeches, Nott trying to turn it into a Party attack, which didn't go down very well. I came away full of gloom because it is obvious that a huge fleet of forty or so warships will set sail for the Falklands, arrive three weeks later, probably be attacked by the Argentinians, and then there will be a major battle. The Falklanders are in effect hostages, and I don't think the US will support us, since the last thing they want is a big British fleet in the South Atlantic overturning the Argentinian dictatorship. And that's what will happen, because General Galtieri, the Argentinian President, who attacked the islands to divert attention from the fall in living standards in Argentina, could himself be deposed. The Americans don't want that, since the whole of Latin America would be set ablaze. Very difficult.

It shows our Intelligence Services are so busy finding out which trade-unionists read the *Morning Star* that they can't tell you what's happening in Argentina, where you would think intelligence agents might know something.

I found the whole atmosphere awful. I'd like to have spoken but I didn't. There will be a proper debate next week, and I'm tempted to speak then and say that before this exercise goes any further let's consider some of the consequences. Someone has to say it. If we'd wanted to keep the islands we should have had an airstrip there which would have allowed transport aircraft to land, we should have kept proper communications, with a small ship going round the islands. But the real argument is about oil. That's why we want it and that's why they want it – nothing whatever to do with 1800 sheep farmers.

Sunday 4 April
The Falklands invasion dominated the papers. The announcement that the battle fleet is to sail tomorrow overrides everything.

Monday 5 April
To the Tribune Group to discuss the Falklands. Stuart Holland said

the real interest was the £5 billion investment in Argentina, and Lord Carrington and other Ministers had resigned because they disagreed with Thatcher's policy. He said there was high drama in the Tory Party about it.

Robin Cook pointed out that the Argentine navy possessed British missiles and ships, and that nuclear weapons were useless. The Government had blundered, the position couldn't be reversed, and the Falklanders wouldn't want us back.

Mik said there was a danger of our being carried away. In the long term, was a Labour Government committed to the return of the Falklands? A show of force was no use because we wouldn't be able to hold it afterwards. We could sink the Argentine navy, raze Buenos Aires, sign a death warrant for the Falklanders and alienate the world, or we could evacuate the islands, compensate the islanders and have the fleet on standby.

I believed that it was a complex question about the remnants of empire, that we had to be realistic and recognise that the islands were indefensible. As with Suez, we would find that the Americans didn't support us in the end because they had great interests in Latin America. From their point of view the Anglo–American alliance was less important than their control over the whole of Latin America, and jingoism couldn't help us. We should take a clear and united stand condemning the Argentine Government for their invasion, holding Her Majesty's Government responsible for their failure to provide minimum military protection, believing that the prime concern of the Government should now be to secure the future of the Falklands under an administration that would safeguard their interests. We should decline to support the Government in its preparations for war against Argentina, a war which would cost many lives and threaten the life, safety and security of the Falklanders. We should urge the UN to take responsibility for seeking a settlement that would meet their needs, secured if necessary by the presence of a UN peacekeeping force while international negotiations took place.

Stan Newens disagreed. We were acting in defence of international law. British islanders had the right of self-determination and we must support them. The responsibility was ours, because of the right-wing dictatorship which had been responsible for the murder of thousands of people in Argentina. We should split the link between the US and the military dictatorship, and we were wrong to say we would not attack Argentina. He supported the blockade.

Stan Orme agreed, arguing that we must fight fascism and help the Argentine working class. A British presence may help to destabilise Argentina.

Afterwards I saw Norman St John Stevas in the corridor, and I asked him why Peter Carrington had resigned as Foreign Secretary today, together with all the Foreign Office Ministers. Did he think it was because Carrington didn't agree with Mrs Thatcher's policy? He said there could be a number of factors involved, but perhaps one of them was that he couldn't stand 'that woman' a moment longer!

Tuesday 6 April

NEC International Committee at 10, and at 10.15 we came to two resolutions on the Falklands – one from Eric Heffer and another from Denis Healey which was identical to Eric's in the first three paragraphs but then called for a position of strength in negotiating with dictatorships. The discussion was very largely around those alternatives.

Eric's resolution concluded:

> The NEC urges that the first step must be to ensure the safety and evacuation of the people of the Falklands either to Britain or to a Commonwealth country . . . and that full-scale negotiations take place on the future status of the Islands.
>
> The Labour Party wishes to avoid war, widespread destruction and bloodshed and believes it is not in the best interests of the country to allow a jingoistic, militaristic frame of mind to develop which would have disastrous consequences for the future peace of the world.

Healey's motion concluded:

> The NEC believes that when negotiations are undertaken with a military dictatorship they must be based on a position of strength and that the British forces now sailing towards the Falkland Islands must be used to lead the Argentinian Government to an honourable settlement which has the support of the Falkland Islanders.
>
> On behalf of the British Labour Movement, the NEC reiterates its full support for the right of the people of the Falkland Islands to live under the sovereignty of their own choice, which is the right of free peoples throughout the world.

We had three choices, Eric said: diplomatic action backed by force; a shooting war; or diplomacy through the UN. He thought war would endanger the Falklanders as well as the British in Argentina, and who would Britain's allies be? Chile might support Britain but the Falklanders didn't want war. The left in Latin America would support Argentina. This wasn't like Suez. We should use the navy for a diplomatic settlement. Thatcher's total reputation was at stake, and Trident and nuclear weapons had been shown to be useless.

Jo Richardson seconded Eric's motion, arguing that we couldn't retake the islands without bloodshed and that we had hitherto neglected the islands.

Healey agreed with most of Heffer's resolution but objected to the idea of evacuation – if we removed the islanders, there would be nothing to negotiate about. We must have military strength, as we learned with Hitler and Mussolini. He quoted from Michael Foot's brilliant book *Guilty Men*, attacking appeasement. He supported the fleet, and thought the fear that we would use force might compel Reagan to act. In Suez the issue was property; this time it was human rights. He thought a minimum use of force would be justified.

Michael Foot said Denis and he had drafted the resolution. He thought Eric spoke for many, but if we took his view it would look as if Labour was giving in; if we didn't resolve it now, we would play into Galtieri's hands. We had to consider other threats – for example, against Belize. Jingoism was not to be confused with protection of our people. We must be prepared to use force as we did in Borneo, otherwise Galtieri would use it.

Judith Hart said she wished she could support Denis and Michael but she couldn't. People and not property were our prime concern, and was it in the islanders' best interests that we should send the fleet? The war sentiments might be more suitable if we had the power, but Thatcher's motives were different – her brinkmanship was for her own ends. We shouldn't trust the Government, Reagan was retreating, the Organisation of American States was meeting, there were oil and mineral interests, the Falkland Islands Company was owned by Charrington, which was itself owned by Coalite in Bolsover. She couldn't go along with that. We should evacuate.

I supported the common paragraphs in the resolutions – Michael's statement on the legal position was right. But now we were faced with the fleet going to war, and when John Nott was asked whether he would exclude the possibility of an attack on the mainland he said no. The purpose of the battle fleet was to recover Mrs Thatcher's reputation, and the issue for us was the Labour Party position. The Foreign Office had been trying to negotiate some sort of condominium for years, and I was sure Carrington had resigned because he disagreed with the policy that was being pursued. I said that selling the warships to Argentina also threw a different light on the matter, and our objective should be the evacuation of the islanders and recalling the Task Force. We should try to fend it all off. Warships might have helped earlier, but we wouldn't know and we must be realistic. We should not tie the Labour Party to Thatcher's collapse. Public opinion would shift very quickly if there was a humiliation. The Labour Party should not support a war.

Frank Allaun said a war wouldn't save lives. Afterwards, the navy in the Falklands could be on patrol for ever, and it would cost practically nothing to resettle these people. The Labour Party was not giving in, but we just didn't want a bloody disaster.

Joan Lestor asked Denis if he would use force and he said yes.

In the end, Heffer and Healey agreed a common form of words:

The NEC believes that when negotiations are undertaken with a military dictatorship they must be based on a position of strength, as under the last Labour Government in 1977, and not in a spirit of Victorian jingoism. The purpose of such negotiations must be an honourable settlement which has the support of the Falkland Islanders.

The NEC recognises that the paramount consideration must be the rights and safety of the people of the Falklands and that all actions of the British Government must be directed to their protection, rather than by concern for property interests, natural resources or salvaging the pride of discredited Ministers.

So I moved an addendum: 'The NEC opposes the dispatch of the Task Force and the Government's apparent intention to use it in a war with the Argentine, believing that this will imperil the safety of the Falkland Islanders, which should be the Government's prime concern.' That was defeated by only 6 to 5, which wasn't bad. Eric Heffer didn't support it.

The composite resolution was then carried by 11 to 0. I abstained on that.

That was the first real row in the Party about the Falklands, and I think we got our foot in the door. Michael is clearly overboard on this, and my doubts about his stand have been confirmed.

In the afternoon Caroline and I took the train to Salisbury for a longstanding engagement to address officers at the UK Land Forces HQ at Wilton. Sir John Stanier, who was recently made Chief of the General Staff (to take up the post in August), told me that his function was to maintain the defences of the UK but his command did not become operational until there was a war.

The idea of a quiescent command is a strange one. I asked him (later at dinner) about the structure, and in effect the country is divided into districts, each with a major-general. The military districts, the police districts and the local authority command structures are brought together, so that there is a general, a police chief and a civil administrator running each district, and there would also be a Government Minister appointed in each military district.

I found it hard not to believe that one of the prime purposes of having the army structured like this was to deal with civil disturbance and opposition to a war. I imagine that's why his number two was none other than Lieutenant-General Sir Frank Kitson, the guerrilla warfare expert.

We had a drink with some of the officers and were taken into the lecture hall, where about 140 people had gathered – quite crowded.

I gave my regular lecture describing the position of the Labour Party, and the history of socialism, and I said there was an extremely interesting political debate in progress, but the tragedy was that many people thought it was a question of men of goodwill on one side being threatened by a clutch of revolutionaries on the other – which was nonsense.

All their questions were about the trade unions. If anyone really had any doubts about the class war, they should listen to officers in the army. They always ask about the unions – just as radical trade-unionists are interested in the scenario of an army takeover.

Over dinner Stanier said he was the one British army general who was not under NATO, and he went out of his way to tell me what bad politicians soldiers made, so he was bending over backwards to reassure me. He made an interesting remark. 'I can't say anything about the Falklands, but I can only tell you that I think the decision to dispatch the Task Force, taken before the House of Commons debate on 3 April, is a decision that we shall all live to regret.'

Whether it was that he wanted to alert me that the generals were not unanimous in their view or whether it was for some other reason I'm not sure, but it was useful information.

Tremendous courtesy from them all – like senior civil servants, all public-school, Sandhurst types. They commented to Caroline on the fact that American officers were not the same as British officers, meaning they didn't all come from the middle and upper classes. Caroline replied, 'Well, over there well-to-do people wouldn't go into the army.' I thought that was very funny. I do think they find these crude American generals with their crew-cuts, chewing their cigars, very unsettling.

At the end of the dinner I said I supposed Stanier would be made a field marshal when he finished. He told me that would be normal, and I said, 'I should jolly well think so.' He said he thought I'd be against that sort of thing. 'Not at all,' I replied. 'I am strongly in favour of field marshals; they are a cut above the others, and anyway a baton would look good on your coffin.' He was relieved and amused.

Wednesday 7 April

To the PLP meeting. Michael began to read the resolution passed at the International Committee, and Ioan Evans supported him, and the possible use of force.

Robin Cook, Stan Newens and I repeated our respective views.

Giles Radice said he didn't know whether to laugh or cry. If we did nothing, Thatcher might be in trouble and there could be a gain for us; but, as the Opposition, we couldn't order the fleet back. We must not undermine the fleet in order to benefit if things went wrong. We should keep a low profile, make no moral gestures or mock-heroics, and wait to put the boot in at the appropriate moment.

Tam Dalyell wanted us to call for the return of the fleet or for halting it at the Azores. We must keep the Commons in session. We could not pull out once the troops were used.

Pat Duffy, who is one of our defence spokesmen, supported Stan Newens. We had to have the will to use weapons. The credibility of the deterrent everywhere depended on readiness to use force. The Royal

Navy needed the support of the people, the House of Commons and the Labour Party. Half the naval personnel on those ships were under twenty-one and a quarter of them were just boys: 'They will go as boys and come back as men', and he appealed to the men in the Party not to behave like boys. Absolutely grotesque.

Bruce George [Walsall South] said that on the BBC he'd been virtually accused of treachery. 'The Government have rushed into this, and the Argentine force is formidably armed by the British. We have Harriers and they have Mirages. Could we hold the islands? We abandoned them years ago.

'I am not unpatriotic, but the Royal Navy is ill equipped, and they don't want men and ships lost. Two-thirds of our NATO fleet is now on its way down to the South Atlantic.'

Barry Sheerman [Huddersfield East] was impressed by the debate and he thought that jingoism and populism had not surfaced. We needed skilled judgement, and Michael and Denis had that. They had played it absolutely right. Their judgement must guide us – leave it to them. For God's sake, leave it to the people we trust, leave it to the leadership. That's no exaggeration of what he said because I wrote it all down. I've heard him go on like that before.

David Lambie, the Member for Ayrshire Central, opposed sending the Task Force. It was wrong then and it was wrong now, and jingoism would be worse once the fighting started.

Michael Foot wound up the debate. He said that George Foulkes had made a good speech which had been a credit to the Party. He didn't want to raise the temperature; he foresaw the dangers. 'The Party will have to take responsibility for our judgement, and our judgement here and now is that we should be wrong to oppose the dispatch of the Task Force.' We would look absurd as a Party and play into Galtieri's hands; it would be a gift to the fascists, and British opinion wouldn't have it. The Tories would exploit our view and it would be an escape route for them. If world support faded, that could be attributed to the Labour Party's attitude. Therefore he supported the UN Charter, which gave us the right to use force.

He went on, 'Tony mentioned Suez, but the origins of Suez were quite different because then the UK was in the dock. We have the moral right to use force, and public opinion is different now. The world will only be safe if little people are safe from bigger powers. Tony said he hoped I would not support a doomed Prime Minister. Well, *division* in the Labour Party might well *rescue* a doomed Prime Minister.'

I went into the Chamber later and spoke in the Falklands debate. David Owen had made an attack on me, as he had warned me earlier he was going to do. I made a passing reference to him.

The debate was a little bit quieter than it had been on Saturday.

Michael was more cautious, having heard so many doubts at the PLP meeting. Mrs Thatcher listened to the whole debate most carefully.

Afterwards John Biffen came up and congratulated me on my speech. He said he didn't agree with it but it had to be made. I just wonder whether the Tories are quite so keen on what's being done as we think.

Thursday 8 April

Chris Mullin came for a talk from 11.30 till 3.30. He's just been appointed editor of *Tribune* to replace Dick Clements. *Tribune* has now admitted that circulation is down to 7800; there are two months' unpaid print bills, and the whole paper has just been killed by a completely weak political line. I think now we are going to see some big changes. We discussed various ideas and plans. The paper will have a cutting edge, and that's important.

Saturday 10 April

I tried to get through to the Archbishop of Canterbury this morning, and spoke to his private secretary. I asked her to put to the archbishop the idea of including in his Easter sermon an appeal for a deferment of military action to give diplomacy a chance. I never had a response, but I did ring up the Press Association to tell them I had done that. Of course he sees his function on an occasion like this as chaplain to the British people, and, having been a tank commander during the Second World War, no doubt he feels a special responsibility. The concept of an international Christian brotherhood in favour of peace and against killing people would not, I suspect, have occurred to him.

Sunday 11 April

Stansgate. Easter Sunday. Lovely weather. Everyone is waiting for 5 o'clock tomorrow morning when the Maritime Exclusion Zone comes into force – after which we are free to sink any ships inside it. We probably have three or four nuclear-powered hunter-killer submarines that are no doubt perfectly capable of doing that.

Hilary and Sally and Michael arrived after lunch, and we had an Easter-egg hunt.

Monday 12 April

Easter Monday. The family watched Michael's bathtime; he was lying kicking and smiling.

I had a temperature of 102 and went to bed later. Falklands still dominant but no shooting yet.

Tuesday 13 April

Stayed in bed all day. Caroline worked on her book – full of zest at the moment. This afternoon Sydney and Anna Higgins came down to Stansgate – Sydney is writing a biography of Father.

General Alexander Haig has visited Buenos Aires and London, and Parliament is to be recalled again tomorrow for an emergency debate.

Wednesday 14 April

I drove to London and met Judith Hart in the Commons. She told me she had been to a meeting this morning of nine MPs to try to get an alternative proposal put forward for halting the Task Force half way to the Falklands, at the Ascension Isles. She said she had gone to see Michael about it but had got the brush-off from him.

I sat through most of the debate. Foot pledged his support to Thatcher and devoted some of his attention to attacking those in the Labour Party who opposed sending the Task Force. Judith called for a pause for peace. Alex Lyon made a brave speech saying that the Falklands should be returned to Argentina.

I was still a bit shaky and left for home – to bed with a temperature again of 102.

Reflecting on where we stand now – Michael has completely committed us to supporting the Task Force and to using it, and what was most revolting was David Owen congratulating him. Michael has acted very foolishly, but I think we just have to pause. The peace case has been established: about a dozen of us have come out now for peace and made our case, and it is on the record. We can't go on about it – we just have to see what happens. If there is a military confrontation and many people are killed, as I believe could happen, or if there is a tragedy involving British servicemen or Falklanders, then we will have established the right to argue how the matter should be handled.

Of course, if the Government does make a hash of it and public opinion shifts against the Tories, Michael Foot will turn on Mrs Thatcher for mishandling it. I am not interested in attacking her, I'm interested in developing an alternative view and building our credibility. She is not going to get what she wants – she knows it very well. The Americans cannot support her, and the whole political situation is going to be really interesting. I just hope people don't get killed; but I fear they will – and in vain.

Thursday 15 April

Chris Mullin rang to tell me the *Daily Star* had a heading 'Whose Side Are They On?' with pictures of the ten of us opposed to the Task Force, implying our treachery.* It is bound to happen; you couldn't expect otherwise at this early stage of jingoistic fervour.

* The *Daily Star* listed the ten Labour MPs – 'no friends of their country, of freedom or of their own party' – as: Alf Dubs, George Foulkes, Frank Allaun, Stuart Holland, Reg Freeson, Tony Benn, Ernie Roberts, Judith Hart, Tam Dalyell, Joan Maynard.

Friday 16 April
A very painful cough. My temperature was down to 94 degrees. Lay in bed all day – Falklands again dominating the news. Didn't feel at all well.

Saturday 17 April
This morning Caroline took me to the doctor, who diagnosed viral pneumonia and put me on antibiotics and cough linctus. I felt very tired, and it was horrible to be stuck in my room on such a beautiful day.

Tuesday 20 April
The press covered my visit to the hospital, saying I was seriously ill. I feel a bit lonely at the moment.

Wednesday 21 April
Beautiful day. Frances Morrell looked in. We had coffee and a talk. The news of Chris Mullin becoming editor of *Tribune*, so that the non-Trotskyite left now has a paper, is very important.

Thursday 22 April
Bristol, to the Holy Nativity Church for a meeting which was filmed by ITN. I was very nervous to be in my home patch, and wondered whether people would listen to me there, because the local papers have made so much about how unpopular I am. But I think the Falklands argument is getting across, judging by the applause.

ITN used a little bit of my speech but they didn't include pictures of the crowded meeting – just showed me speaking, with no applause, and followed it with their political correspondent saying I was in a tiny minority, and Michael Foot saying I was supporting the Argentine position.

Friday 23 April
Masses of letters pouring in about Argentina; the overwhelming majority in support of my position. There are a handful of really vulgar and abusive ones. I'm certain that a majority of the British people are against the war with Argentina but the media are preventing that view becoming apparent.

To Croydon for the funeral of Terry Parry, General Secretary of the Fire Brigades' Union, a very popular man. A fireman picked me up and took me to the entrance of the crematorium, and the fire brigade was out in force – hundreds of them – as Terry's body was carried on a fire-engine covered with flowers and a Union Jack. Bill Jones, Walt Greendale, Moss Evans, Clive Jenkins, Len Murray, Jack Jones, Hugh

Scanlon, Gordon McLennan, Mick McGahey, Jimmy Milne, Enoch
Humphreys, Ken Cameron, Jim Mortimer – the labour movement's
leaders were there in force.

The service, which was conducted by Bruce Kent, was really
moving. Bruce said he had never known Terry Parry, but Terry had
requested that he conduct the service. Jack Jones made an excellent
speech, Len Murray not such a good one. A friend sang 'The
Impossible Dream', and I'm afraid I sat there with tears rolling down
my cheeks.

Afterwards I talked to fire officers from all over the country. I was
invited to go in their coach to Crystal Palace Football Club for a little
party.

Monday 26 April

I sat in the House for about an hour so I could hear Mrs Thatcher make
her statement on the capture of South Georgia. Michael Foot
intervened and was all over the shop. I was called after David Owen. I
asked if the Prime Minister was aware that, though the House was
united in opposing the Argentinian attack on the Falklands, Britain
would not follow the Government into war with Argentina, because
people would be killed, we'd be isolated, and the war could spread.
People wanted negotiations and a UN role, and if there was any loss of
life she would be responsible. She responded in a rather snarling way. I
can't think of many reasons for being an MP, but being able to speak to
her there, in the Commons, on an issue like this does make those initials
worth having.

Tuesday 27 April

Did a radio interview for BBC Wales on the Falklands. At 10.30 four
people from *New Socialist* came to see me – James Curran (the editor),
Ann Cesek, Ann Pettifor and the business manager. We talked about
what the magazine could do, whom it should feature, and so on. It was
a very rewarding and interesting meeting. Caroline joined us, and she
talked about the role of education and the need for *New Socialist* to cover
it.

In the House, Michael Foot broke with Mrs Thatcher, saying he
could not support an escalation of the violence without the UN being
brought in. David Steel stated that he was not prepared to commit
himself to an escalation of the violence, and he wanted to be brought in
on the decisions.

I asked if it wasn't now clear, in view of the Prime Minister's
statements and TV interviews, that she never intended negotiation
anyway because she had never gone anywhere near the UN. The Task
Force was always a military expedition and intended as such, and
hadn't she grossly misled the House and the country? I didn't get

tremendous support from the Labour benches, but I did push forward, and Michael is advancing under my reconnaissance.

Wednesday 28 April
At the NEC there were two crucial motions on the Falklands – Foot's, supported by Healey and Heffer, which called for discussions with the Secretary-General of the UN; and mine, supported by Judith, calling for a ceasefire and withdrawal of the Task Force. Michael said that my resolution would detract from the first motion because withdrawal of the Task Force would involve the abandonment of South Georgia.

Denis Healey said the PLP position was set out in *Labours' Programme 1980*: he had just returned from a mission to the UN in New York, where the Commonwealth representatives were for us. Last Friday he had seen the UN Secretary-General, who could, however, only appeal to individual member countries – if it went back to the Security Council there would be the risk of a veto. Haig would give up soon, and then we could go to the UN and maintain support for Resolution 502. He said Haig was open-minded, and therefore he hoped there would be a unanimous resolution today.

Heffer supported Michael and called for unity – the polls were confusing, and we had to keep the Party together. If the Government got a quick victory we'd have to see where we should go. If there was bloodshed we'd come out of it well. The politics of this were complicated – Argentina had a fascist dictator, and you couldn't give him credence. Eric appealed to me to withdraw my resolution.

Healey suggested we unanimously agree on the first motion, and we did so.

I welcomed what Michael had said in the Commons yesterday and his resolution today, and I hoped that the Executive would give my resolution unanimous support as well. The military machine was now in control and had been since we sent the Task Force. There would be no doubt that the PM had lost control. I went over the resolution line by line and argued the position.

Judith seconded it, saying the Falklands issue had helped the junta and peace would undermine the junta. As to party politics, we must hope to present a united Party position, but when it came to peace and war you had to dissociate yourself from party politics, and the Party's credibility was at stake. She said young people had all left the Falklands, and Port Stanley was now mainly populated by retired people.

Michael said he understood the spirit of the resolution but he would vote against it. He hoped Tony wouldn't press it because he couldn't vote for it for five reasons: it would help the junta; its representation of Resolution 502 was inaccurate and it would appear to prohibit self-defence; on sovereignty, whatever we might negotiate on we shouldn't declare it now; it would have implications for the Task Force; and it might involve dismantling what we had achieved in South Georgia. We had to get Argentina to withdraw – which required the threat of force. He said he hoped there wouldn't be a vote and we'd look at it again in a month. He pleaded with me not to press my resolution.

Frank Allaun welcomed Michael's statement yesterday, and he wondered whether Judith and Tony would accept the words 'to South Georgia' after the phrase 'withdrawing the Task Force'.

We agreed, so those words were added.

Sam McCluskie said that now the Government had committed the troops we had to support them – there were thirty-six merchant ships in the Task Force, including Swedish and Norwegian ones. He hoped Tony wouldn't press his point. He said my analysis was absolutely correct, but it was too late.

Joan Lestor remarked that my resolution referred to resettlement, and that was a departure from Party policy. She hoped the resolution would be withdrawn. She stressed that she was not pacifist, and that she supported the South American liberation movements.

Eric Clarke said nobody was criticising Michael Foot. We were getting political strategy muddled up with moral issues. There was a huge armada, and it would have to be used or withdrawn. He feared escalation. 'This is a new ball-game now and not something we can settle by passing a resolution. We have to be bold and courageous and say no. The two resolutions are compatible, the Party is based on morality, and we should withdraw to Ascension Islands.'

Doug Hoyle wanted me to withdraw the motion or have it amended.

I spoke and appealed to others to support the resolution which Judith and I had amended.

Joan Maynard said she couldn't see any conflict, but anyway we had a recorded vote, and my motion was defeated by 15 to 8. Those in favour were Frank Allaun. Eric Clarke, Judith Hart, myself, Joan Maynard, Jo Richardson, Dennis Skinner and Les Huckfield. Foot's was carried *nem con*.

An exhausting day. I got another 400 letters today, making 2500 this week. Overwhelmingly supportive – I suppose coming primarily from middle-class people. Some white feathers and vulgar abuse. The mail is the biggest I've ever had.

Thursday 29 April

PLP at 11. Denis Healey reported on his visit to the UN. He told us they didn't want to intervene until the Haig mission had expired. Haig would favour a withdrawal of all troops, an interim administration and some long-term solution. Once Argentina had withdrawn, an UN administration and perhaps a trusteeship might be established. The Argentinians insisted on sovereignty.

George Robertson attacked *Labour Weekly* for giving so much space to me and George Foulkes and the anti-war lobby. In 1979 our policy was that we would not hand over the islanders to the junta, and we confirmed it in 1980. The Party view was clear – Foot and Healey were the leaders of the Party and deserved our unanimous support.

I said we had a right to self-defence but we were not discussing that. However when Ian Smith rebelled against the Crown for fifteen years, with 6 million Africans under his rule, I didn't remember the Labour Party pressing very hard for military action. We were not discussing whether or not to hand over the Falklands to the junta. I knew of no one in the Party who was going against Party policy on that. What we were discussing was whether a war with Argentina was right, and how we should define and secure our objectives.

I said we all agreed on the NEC resolution passed yesterday, we all agreed on a UN approach and no escalation, we agreed on no all-party talks. But we had to face the inexorable timetable of the Task Force once it was sent – it had to be either used or withdrawn – which was why we hadn't wanted it sent in the first place. Admirals were in charge now, and Thatcher had lost control. World opinion would isolate us. We had to define our objectives – an administration sympathetic to the islanders and negotiable sovereignty.

Frank Hooley thought it was significant that we had a Tory Government and unemployment, riots and now war. He was glad the UN was back in the picture. The sovereignty issue was not a valid one; we should amend the Nationality Act and arrange for the islanders to reside in the Falklands or in the UK, with generous compensation.

An excellent speech from Frank, who has been extremely good throughout on this matter.

Finally Michael Foot spoke. He had no complaints about the debate in the Party, and Denis and he had tried to consult people primarily on Party policy towards the UN. He had favoured sending the Task Force, and if the Party had opposed it that would have injured us and helped Galtieri. He quoted today's leader in the *Financial Times* which stated that the military operations were hard and the objectives unclear. We should use force only as a last resort, Michael said. We needed further negotiation; an invasion would undermine us; and public support would come to us. The Labour Party could stop the war.

Michael's speech caught the new mood, although later, in the Chamber, he was less clear.

Into the debate itself at 3.30. Mrs Thatcher began by trying to create the impression that she was in favour of peace and negotiation, so she had responded in mood at any rate to what Michael had said on Tuesday. Michael was less tough-minded than he had been on Tuesday.

Jim Callaghan spoke with absolutely naked support for Mrs

Thatcher. He is just an old Tory warmonger. As a former PM he carries a lot of weight, but he certainly doesn't speak for the Labour Party.

Enoch Powell delivered a speech which might have been made in Edwardian England.

I was called at about 7 and I spoke for twenty minutes – longer than I meant to – but there were thirteen interruptions from MPs. I didn't give way at all. The Tory right wing was hysterical. I went on and developed the argument, and the Party actually responded quite well – partly, of course, because I was being so violently attacked.

Tony Marlow [Conservative MP for Northampton North] asked, 'On a point of order, Mr Speaker, is it in order for the Right Honourable Gentleman to act as an apologist for the Argentinian junta?' Exactly like Bernard Braine in 1956, in one of the Suez debates, when he called me 'Nasser's little lackey'.

The debate ended with Denis Healey, who was all over the shop. Pym was tough but rather ineffective.

Sat in the Tea Room afterwards and corrected my Hansard, and a Tory MP, whom I don't know, came up to me. He said, 'I didn't agree with everything you said, but you were using building blocks of pure gold, and if only you'd given way to interruptions I think the House would have listened a bit more.'

Friday 30 April

Another 500 letters, and although the balance has altered a little bit it was still 99.5 per cent in favour of my position. Some of the programmes I have done provoked more hostile letters.

To Bristol for my surgery. I heard on the radio there that Haig had decided to support Britain. Haig's actual speech was broadcast, and he said that, although he would provide material assistance, American forces would not be involved, and a military settlement could not be permanent because it would lead to long-term instability in the South Atlantic. So really American support for us was qualified.

Their proposals for peace included withdrawal of all forces, the re-establishment of local administration with Argentinian, participation and a tripartite body (Britain, Argentina and the USA) to carry out any agreement. Those proposals, which the Argentinian Government has allegedly refused, would also be quite unacceptable to Mrs Thatcher.

My surgery in Bristol was interesting because an anxious grand-mother of someone in the Task Force came to see me; she was so overcome with emotion she could hardly speak.

Watched *News at Ten* in my hotel room, and there was no mention of the Haig proposals, nor of the fact that he said a military solution wouldn't help, nor that he wouldn't provide American military assistance. You could see the Government censorship operating directly.

Saturday 1 May

May Day in Bristol, with lots of trade union banners and the Great Western Band, whose musicians dress up as French sailors and play *The Red Flag* in ragtime. Lovely.

We marched right round the shopping centre in Bristol. Very jolly.

This morning I heard that the British had strafed airfields at Port Stanley using Vulcan bombers operating from Ascension Island 4000 miles away. They must have refuelled many times in mid-air and they made low-flying attacks. This is an escalation of the war, and I was horrified to hear Denis Healey say it was quite reasonable. I think our campaign will have to be much stronger. I put out a press release including the text of a letter from the fiancée of a marine:

Dear Mr Benn

. . . My fiancé is a Royal Marine with the Task Force and this morning I received a letter and poem from him. It was a very harrowing letter. He says that the majority of his Company do not want to fight over islands so far from home and expresses disbelief that the British Government can think of letting so many young men die for this issue.

The press and TV insist on showing the few who are itching for a fight but most of the 'men' under him are 18 years old on average. These boys come from working class families and have joined up to escape the dole queue. They wanted to see lands outside of an unemployed lad's pocket but now most of them won't even see the rest of their young lives out. This Government is sending them to their deaths for a lost cause and the poor lads know it before they even get there.

Please do anything in your power to stop this tragic thing happening.

I did not mention her name. The *Bristol Evening Post* carried her story.

Sunday 2 May

The *News of the World* and the *People* carried the marine's fiancée's letter, which I had read to them over the phone. But otherwise the censorship is unbelievable, and it's just pure jingoism.

Drove straight home after lunch, picked up a suitcase full of letters and took it with me down to Chris Mullin's flat in Brixton Road, where he had his first editorial meeting as editor of *Tribune* with Frances Morrell, Audrey Wise, Stuart Holland, Victor Schonfield, Vladimir Derer, Jon Lansman (just appointed promotions editor), Michael Meacher, Reg Race, Mandy Moore, Francis Prideaux, James Curran, Tony Banks and Valerie Wise.

Michael Meacher thought we ought to have monthly meetings, and it was left that Chris and I would convene them.

On the Falklands there were two critical points: Michael should not join the new all-party talks, and we should organise a national campaign. I referred to the *Sunday Times*, which said that 3 out of 5 people questioned thought the Falklands were not worth the life of a single serviceman or islander.

Chris Mullin was in favour of saying no war in principle and in practice. James Curran agreed. We haven't got it together yet and we'll be having a further meeting the week after next.

Heard about the attack and torpedoing of an Argentinian cruiser by a hunter-killer nuclear-powered submarine.

Monday 3 May

Heard in the House that the navy had sunk an Argentinian vessel which they said had attacked the fleet. They have also requisitioned *Queen Elizabeth II*. This whole war mood is awful. I wouldn't trust anyone with nuclear weapons.

Tuesday 4 May

To the House and heard Thatcher at Prime Minister's Questions. Tam Dalyell scored a direct hit by asking, 'Did the Prime Minister herself, personally and explicitly, authorise the firing of the torpedoes on the *General Belgrano*?' Thatcher said yes, in effect, she had the Task Force under political control.

Pym made a statement about his visit to the UN and looked uncomfortable, like Thatcher. I think they're beginning to worry in the Cabinet because of public disgust at the loss of life on the *Belgrano*.

I was called by the Speaker at the very end of Pym's interrogation, and I got in a pretty good point: 'Had the Foreign Secretary's attention been drawn to the fact that in the *Sunday Times* a public opinion poll showed that 6 out of 10 people in Britain were not prepared to see one serviceman's life, or a Falkland Islander's life, put at risk, and that such a majority in Britain will not be rejoicing with the Prime Minister at the loss of life when the ship was torpedoed without a declaration of war well outside the Exclusion Zone? Will the Foreign Secretary take account of the desire for peace in Britain by agreeing to a ceasefire and to the transfer at once to the United Nations of sovereignty of the Falkland Islands and its administration pending a settlement under UN auspices?'

The House exploded at my comment 'not be *rejoicing* with the Prime Minister' – the Tories were furious because it echoed Mrs Thatcher's own use of the word on reacting to the *Belgrano* sinking. I simply repeated the point after the noise had died down. The public really are shocked by what's happened, and it had to be reflected in some way. The Labour benches weren't enormously warm in their response to me but they are uneasy. They are pleased with Michael's refusal to go into the secret talks between Mrs Thatcher, David Steel and David Owen this morning, and now of course the SDP and the Liberals are absolutely part of the Government coalition and can't ask questions: David Steel didn't ask any while I was there.

Sunday 9 May
Left early for Bristol to discuss the boundary changes. Then came back to London for an anti-war rally with speakers including Tam Dalyell, Mick McGahey, Gordon McLennan, Donald Reeves of St James's Church, Piccadilly, Donald Soper and myself. About 3000 people.

Monday 10 May
One thing I record with regret and sadness. A woman from Portsmouth rang me up in great distress and started to abuse me. It transpired that her husband had gone down in HMS *Sheffield*, and she felt, as she was bound to, that his death had been in a good cause, and therefore she hated me for having opposed the war. I tried to tell her how sorry I was, but she rang off.

I wrote an article for *Tribune*, and sent a letter to the PM asking if the *Sheffield* had been armed with nuclear weapons when she was attacked.

Three nasty telegrams were waiting at the House. I'm sure things will get more unpleasant.

Tuesday 11 May
To the International Committee of the NEC, where we had two resolutions on the Falklands, one from Michael and Denis, and one from Judith Hart and myself calling for an immediate truce.

I spoke on ours, and said it had the support of seventy-nine MPs and twenty-four constituency Labour parties. The Labour Front Bench position – to say send the Task Force but don't use it, cripple ships but don't sink them – wasn't credible. The Government was not trying for a peaceful settlement, and, once sent, the Task Force would have to be used. They had taken no interest in the UN. The war was escalating, the pressure to go on to the Argentinian mainland would be strong, and the question of nuclear weapons arose. Support was eroding in the Common Market countries and in America, and what did temporary success prove? That we had better missiles than they had. We would have to withdraw at some point, and trusteeship would have to come eventually. Why not now? The Government was using the war to beat Labour and get five more years in office, and we shouldn't be any part of it.

Eric Heffer thought the people were not with us – the majority wanted the Task Force to go. Anyone close to the people would know that. Was Tony in favour of fascist regimes taking over? We couldn't be too simplistic about it. The Shadow Cabinet didn't like jingoism, but we would have ˙ ˙n called the Munich Party if we'd done nothing. At the peace demʊ on Sunday some banners had said 'Victory to the Argentine Junta. We would have been in an impossible position if we hadn't supported the Task Force.

Frank Allaun supported Judith. He said that the majority might be against it but we couldn't just say what was popular, we had to say what was right. This war was to save Thatcher's face, and Labour activists supported us.

Denzil Davies said the omission in Judith's resolution of the reference to the UN was a weakness. We couldn't pick and choose between the bits of Resolution 502 that we liked.

Sam McCluskie, who is Assistant General Secretary of the seamen's union, was in a socialist dilemma. Argentina were the aggressors and a thousand seamen were in danger; we had to protect them. There had been references by Healey to his time at the MoD but we'd better examine our record. Labour Governments have been selling arms to the junta and only the fascists could negotiate with fascists. The National Union of Seamen couldn't contact its people any more, and we wouldn't get a truce. We were in a terrible dilemma. He added that twice as many volunteers had offered to go on merchant ships requisitioned for the war as there was room for.

Michael Foot wound up, and especially addressed Frank Allaun. He said popularity *should* be no guide for us; we had to do what was right for a peaceful solution. But we would injure our influence with the Government if Judith's resolution was passed. He didn't believe the Task Force was in charge. We wanted to use it for a settlement. We had applied our principles, and our belief in the UN, from the outset. But the truce would not be a proper use of the UN; it would destroy peace prospects and be a gift to Galtieri. The Argentine Government would be delighted, and it would injure the Party because of the public mood. The *Belgrano* sinking was not a wise action and probably involved a breach of political control. If the Party's position *had* been damaged, it had been by xenophobia and by Tony's speeches up and down the country. He (Michael) didn't believe Thatcher wanted a war, and the people didn't believe it. We should support any settlement coming from the UN Secretary-General, and Tony's position would lead to a shambles in the war and a shambles in the Party.

Eric Heffer said something else, and got very angry and began shouting and a row broke out over Judith's right to move the resolution. Then Joan Lestor announced she was going to make the ruling that she would accept a motion by Betty Boothroyd (seconded by Gwyneth Dunwoody), who 'moved the previous question' (ie stopped the debate). That was carried by 8 to 4 – Judith, Frank, Jo Richardson and myself against.

That is the first time in twenty-three years on the NEC that I have ever known a chairman accept a motion to prevent a vote.

Thursday 20 May
About twenty-five MPs who oppose the war met at the House, under the chairmanship of Tam Dalyell – Andrew Faulds, Ray Powell, Bob

Cryer, John Tilley, Mik, Judith Hart, Frank Allaun, Dafydd Ellis Thomas (Plaid Cymru MP) and so on.

A short press statement was drawn up saying that those who intended to vote against the Government tonight after the debate on the war were pressing for an immediate ceasefire, and they would vote against for the following reasons: (1) they wished to avoid the loss of life involved in a British landing (2) they wished to continue negotiations in response to the latest appeal of the UN Secretary-General.

It was an orderly meeting, and the only reservation was from Andrew Faulds, who said that if our troops were actually fighting he might have doubts about an immediate ceasefire. Alf Dubs raised whether it would be wise to vote if there weren't many MPs in the Lobby. But it was a firm decision.

At 6 the PLP met, and Foot announced, 'I want to urge those who are thinking of voting against not to vote tonight. It would be a diversion in the Party. The Shadow Cabinet is going to abstain.'

Allan Roberts, MP for Bootle, asked 'If the Government disregards what Michael Foot said today and there is war, what will the Opposition say over the weekend?'

Joe Dean of Leeds West pointed out that a hundred MPs were away and it would not be fair to them to force a vote. But Bob Cryer said the Government had cancelled pairs, so these people shouldn't be away. Martin Flannery argued that abstaining was not seen by the Government as disagreeing and that we ought to be united in voting against.

I appealed to Michael to join us in the Lobby tonight. 'A very wide spectrum in the PLP will be voting, including Leo Abse, Andrew Faulds, Tam Dalyell. The Labour Front Bench has criticised Mrs Thatcher for withdrawing the terms of the interim agreement, as she did in the House today. If there is no vote against she will use it to say there is unanimity. We have not gone to war officially; the Task Force left without a vote; there hasn't been a vote on anything yet. Those who vote against will be voting against the Government, and it is outrageous to suggest that we would be voting against the Shadow Cabinet, and even more so to say we'd be voting against the UN.'

Stanley Clinton Davies, the MP for Hackney Central, said the junta would use our vote against the Government as support for them. 'Tony wants capitulation.'

Stan Newens argued that MPs had the right to vote but the vote would be seen in the country as a split in the Party. This had been presented wrongly as jingoism versus non-jingoism.

Judith said Thatcher had rejected Michael's appeal and we had to vote. There were boys of seventeen out there, and resolutions against the war from local parties were pouring in to Walworth Road.

Michael Foot said he understood the passions but the Party had a commitment to the UN Charter. An unconditional ceasefire was simply an argument in support of the fascists. We must sustain support for UN Resolution 502 because if we deserted it now it would wreck the Party. 'Tony's appeal for a vote would be interpreted by the press as support for Tony and Judith in the argument inside the Party. A vote against tonight would be interpreted by the jingoistic press as a stab in the back.' So there was Michael saying that we would be stabbing the troops in the back.

In the debate, Tam made a very good speech, and Denis Healey made an awful speech supporting the Government up to the hilt. When it came to the vote, Tam moved the closure at one minute to ten, and 33 Labour members went into the No Lobby; 296 voted for the Government – less than half the Commons. It wasn't a bad vote.

It's clear now that there will be some sort of British invasion of the Falkland Islands tomorrow or the day after, and then I think it will be wholesale war. If Tam Dalyell is right, Argentina is very well armed, and the whole thing looks just ghastly. The Labour leadership has absolutely failed the Party and the nation – it has not used its leadership to check the jingoistic spirit as it might have done. I can't see how Thatcher will come out of it, because even a victory would not be sustainable. Michael will jump on her bandwagon of temporary success. So we're taking a great gamble in arguing for the ceasefire – the PLP will never forgive us for having made this a parliamentary issue.

I saw Enoch Powell in the lavatory, and he was quite clear that the Government interim agreement was a sell-out, ie conceding the substance of sovereignty. As we stood side by side I said, 'Well, Enoch, we may disagree about what we should do but our analysis is the same – they are selling out.'

'Yes, of course,' he said.

'It seems to me,' I went on, 'that Parliament has absolutely failed to do its proper job.'

'I agree. The House of Commons over many years has abandoned its function; it has traded power for status.'

Friday 21 May

It's clear that Michael is going to sack the three Front Bench spokesmen who voted with us last night – Tilley, Faulds and Dalyell. He's not going to put up with any intra-parliamentary activity, let alone extra-parliamentary activity.

This evening we heard that the invasion has begun. A helicopter has gone down with 21 dead. Five British ships have been attacked and damaged, and the British claim they have shot down about fifteen Argentinian planes; we have established a landing on the Islands.

Sunday 23 May

Caught a bus to Hyde Park for the peace rally. It was pouring with rain, and I've never seen so many media people from all over the world. The Argentine press asked me for a comment, so I said, 'Free the Argentinian trade unions.' Australian Radio were very hostile.

We marched to Downing Street to hand in a letter. In Whitehall some Falkland Islanders had hung up great banners saying 'Bann Benn', 'Traitors', 'Communists', and so on. A loudspeaker was blaring out 'Land of Hope and Glory' and the National Anthem! Stuart Holland told me to be careful going home, and offered to come with me but I said I'd get the bus. So he organised three tough stewards to take me to the bus stop. There were no buses, so I hailed a taxi. The first taxi driver who saw me gave me a V-sign and passed by, and then another stopped – a Scotsman who was passionately anti-Thatcher and against the war.

Tuesday 25 May

Heard on the 10 o'clock news this evening that another warship had been sunk. Absolutely tragic loss of life. People are going to ask how long this madness will last – 26,500 men out there and a hundred ships, of which we have already lost four, for 1800 Falkland Islanders who could all be brought safely to Britain if they would only come. Absolutely crazy.

Wednesday 26 May

NEC this morning and we had a discussion on the Falklands. I moved an amendment to Michael's motion but I was defeated by 14 to 9. Michael and Denis's motion – 100 per cent pro-Mrs Thatcher, even talking about 'our country' rather than 'the British Government' – was carried by 15 to 9.

Saturday 29 May

I watched live television coverage of the Pope at Canterbury Cathedral – a very impressive piece of ceremony, and of course a historic moment because it was the first time any Pope had been to Canterbury, and the first time a Catholic bishop had been there since the Reformation. There was a great congregation of Anglicans, Free Church, Methodists and Baptists, Greek and Russian Orthodox – a symbol of a great desire for unity. The Pope gave a shrewd speech which no doubt the Vatican had worked hard on – impossible not to be enormously impressed by it.

It was good to see old wounds healed after hundreds of years, and it was a beautiful ceremony, with brightly coloured robes and medieval outfits. The Archbishop and the Pope prayed together on the site where Thomas à Becket had been murdered.

In the afternoon he held mass in Wembley Stadium; 100,000 people were gathered. He is a very attractive character – as Mother says, a good man giving bad advice.

He talked about the sanctity of life beginning with conception. He mentioned the Falklands, but the Catholic Church never takes a strong line on saving life in war, only in abortion and contraception. In the latter case, you are not killing a foetus, you are just preventing one being formed. So that's very strange. But I might add that the Pope, partly because of his large Latin-American flock, has been strongly against the war, whereas Archbishop Runcie has come out in favour of it.

Sunday 30 May

The Pope spoke most strongly against war, saying that nuclear war was completely unacceptable and conventional war should be put back into the history books – a formidable statement.

Sunday 6 June

Got ready for the CND anti-war march. There were without any doubt a quarter of a million people on it. The police estimated half that number, as they always do for left-wing gatherings but not for the Pope, etc.

CND had laid on a tent where the speakers could have a drink, and the proceedings were planned to last from 12.30 to 5.30. There was a most almighty thunderstorm and pouring rain, but eventually the sun came out.

Talked to Arthur Scargill, who told me I must stand against Michael this summer. Walt Greendale was more doubtful. Ken Livingstone was there, having just come from County Hall, where London had been declared a nuclear-free zone.

Monday 7 June

I rang Charles Douglas-Home, the editor of *The Times*, and declined the column he had offered me, explaining that I wasn't principally a journalist, but if he was interested in publishing an article by me at any time, maybe a speech, I would be happy to contribute.

The NEC met at 5.30 – a very unpleasant meeting.

Healey attacked me for putting forward an emergency resolution on the Falklands, and attacked Judith, in the chair, for accepting it. Golding said it was dishonest and sharp practice to accept a resolution when we were there to discuss other things. Gwyneth Dunwoody appealed for us not to discuss it and also violently attacked Judith's 'egotism'. The idea that we should even discuss the resolution was defeated by 11 votes to 10.

President Reagan arrives in Britain today, and we considered a letter drafted by Denis Healey to Reagan from the Party. We deleted a reference to the fact that our post-war relationship with America revolved around NATO. I moved that we should make clear that our ultimate aim was the dissolution of NATO and the Warsaw Pact, and that was carried by 10 votes to 9. I got another change – that a Labour Government would not permit the stationing of Cruise missiles, carried by 17 votes to 0. Finally I got this passage from the end of the letter removed: 'Throughout its history the people of the US have always shown themselves willing to sacrifice themselves for great causes, ignoring commercial and material advantage.' I said that wasn't true and we'd look stupid if we said it. So it was taken out.

President Reagan is having dinner at Windsor Castle. I rather think that Michael Foot is there. Caroline advises me that I am in a minority now and I should let them have it all: I can't win in the short run – I should just outflank them, raise new matters, and not let the war absorb the whole of my life. Absolutely right.

Tuesday 8 June

The streets were packed with police for Reagan's visit. He began the day riding around Windsor Great Park in a coach and four with Nancy and the Queen and the Duke of Edinburgh, followed by 350 TV cameras.

Later he flew into London by helicopter and addressed both Houses of Parliament, in the Royal Gallery – an event I did not attend – and made a violent attack on the Soviet Union. He had lunch with Mrs Thatcher and another exchange of speeches. Back to Windsor Castle in the evening for a banquet at Queen Victoria's dining-table, which seats 144. Michael Foot was there, I think, and Reagan made a speech about the Falklands, as did the Queen.

It was quite unlike the Pope's visit, which was much more human. Reagan is just a movie star acting the part of a king, and the Queen is like a movie star in a film about Britain. Mrs Thatcher is an absolutely Victorian jingoist. I find it embarrassing to live in Britain at the moment.

Wednesday 9 June

The NEC spent the whole morning going through *Labour's Programme* – our manifesto. I had one success on the foreign policy section when I got the phrase 'we shall seek to withdraw from the Common Market' removed and replaced with 'we will withdraw'.

On democracy and human rights, we had a long discussion about whether to commit ourselves to reduce the age of consent for homosexual acts from twenty-one to sixteen. As we predicted, the right – Summerskill, Dunwoody, Golding *et al.* – opposed it. Kinnock suggested a Royal Commission. Michael Foot voted against it, and it was left to Dennis Skinner, who wasn't very enthusiastic, Laurence Coates, Joan Maynard, Joan Lestor and myself, a minority, to vote the other way.

Thursday 10 June
At lunch Harold Walker, the MP for Doncaster Central, came up and handed me two photocopied pages of a pooled telex report from six war correspondents giving an account of the damage done to British forces by the Argentine air attack on 8 June, which sank the *Sir Galahad* and *Sir Tristram* and during which seventy or eighty men were badly burned. The telex had ink comments by the Ministry of Defence and square brackets around the number of people burned and the number on board the ships. Tension between the media and the MoD is growing, and I considered carefully whether I'd raise it in the House.

I decided first to listen to Nott's statement, and when he came to casualties he stopped reading from his typed statement and picked up another piece of paper. 'The military authorities are of the opinion that it would not be in the interests of the UK if the number of casualties was released at this moment.' Then he put down that paper and went on.

I left it, because I felt I couldn't establish beyond doubt what had happened; but it was clear by then that the casualties were severe.

Friday 11 June
The Times and the *Telegraph* printed extracts from the report I had seen about the casualties in the Falklands War but left out the bits that had been square-bracketed by the Ministry.

Monday 14 June
Caught the train to York, and talked to the first senior woman steward on BR. She got into an argument with a seaman from South Shields who is off tomorrow to join the Task Force in the South Atlantic.

While I was on the train, it was announced over the loudspeaker that there was a ceasefire in the Falklands, and it's obvious that the war is now over.

Tuesday 15 June
There has been an Argentinian surrender, and the reaction now is one of tremendous enthusiasm and support for Mrs Thatcher. However, this is not the moment to unbend but the time to reaffirm everything that we've said. It won't be popular, but if you take a principled position you don't withdraw from it.

I went to the House to hear the Prime Minister's statement announcing the surrender. Michael Foot congratulated her and her forces; somehow it was odious and excessive. I was called, and I asked if the PM would publish all the documents and the cost in terms of life, equipment and money of a tragic and unnecessary war. The Tories erupted in anger because this was Jingo Day. I said the world knew very well that the war would not solve the problem of the future of the Falkland Islands. 'Does she agree that in the end there must be negotiations, and will she say with whom and when she will be ready to enter into such negotiations?' She said she couldn't publish the documents, she saw no reason to negotiate with Argentina, she thought the war was tragic but not unnecessary, because the freedom of speech which the Right Honourable Gentleman made such excellent use of had been won for him by people fighting for it. Rubbish, but the Tories loved it.

Wednesday 16 June

The papers today are hysterical about the Falklands victory, though it's not quite clear that the war is over. The popular press has gone berserk – Union Jacks, 'VF' day, and the Queen smiling and Thatcher looking stern, and pictures of our troops and God knows what. I find it utterly distressing, but there you are.

NEC on the *Labour's Programme 1982* again. Michael Foot moved and carried by 9 to 8 (the vote was recorded) to remove the reference to 'swamping' the House of Lords with our own peers, on the grounds that the Crown would get involved. He is in fact saying that if we want to deal with the Lords we have to deal with the monarchy, which is the last thing he wants to do. I argued strongly that there was no reason why we shouldn't tell the electorate that we were entitled to have a majority in both Houses, and that in this way we'd abolish the Lords, leaving a democratic House of Commons. But we were committed simply to 'limiting the power' of the Lords (which Callaghan put into the 1979 manifesto), thus avoiding the responsibility for abolition.

Healey tried to remove the clause that there would be no American or British nuclear bases in this country and he was defeated. He tried to delete our opposition to Cruise, and this also was defeated. No fresh attempt was made to get us to stay in the Common Market. We got in a paragraph about trade union recognition in the armed forces, and a little bit about repealing Heseltine's housing legislation. An attempt to remove all our media proposals failed.

I came away with Joan Maynard feeling very depressed. A bloody awful day.

NOTES
Chapter Three

1. (p. 162) At the by-election in Croydon North-West in October 1981, William Pitt won the seat as the first Liberal/Alliance candidate since the Liberal Party and the SDP had agreed an electoral pact in June that year. The parties agreed that in certain constituencies either an SDP or a Liberal candidate would stand, but not both. In the case of Croydon, the by-election was created by the death of the former Conservative Member and pressure

was brought to bear on the local Liberal Party to allow Shirley Williams to stand as an SDP/Alliance candidate, she having been defeated in the 1979 General Election. However, the party had already selected Pitt as their candidate and refused to withdraw him. One month later, Shirley Williams fought and won Crosby as the SDP/Alliance candidate in another by-election caused by the death of the sitting Conservative Member. Both Pitt and Williams lost their seats in the 1983 General Election.

2.   (p. 163) When the Conservative Government announced in 1980 that stocks of American Cruise nuclear missiles would be moved into RAF Greenham Common and RAF Molesworth, which both housed US airforce establishments, groups of women started to set up little settlements – peace camps – outside the bases to protest. They lived in intolerable conditions but were resolute and determined and their activities included cutting through the fences surrounding the bases and invading the runways; some of the women underwent repeated prison sentences for their 'crime'. They were given financial and other help by CND and voluntary donations from the left.

3.   (p. 176) The 'Foreign Nuclear, Chemical and Biological Bases (Prohibition) Bill' was presented by me in the Commons, supported by Campaign Group MPs, as part of the overall argument for a non-nuclear defence strategy.

I have in my parliamentary life introduced many such bills, none of which have ever been debated, but which remain on the record and which encourage public discussion of sometimes very important themes.

Backbench Members of Parliament have little scope for putting forward views to the House, other than through Parliamentary Questions, motions which are tabled but never debated or the occasional speech during a debate. However Standing Orders of the House do allow a Member to draft and present a bill to propose a serious piece of draft legislation. The bills are drafted officially and obtain a formal first reading after which they proceed no further.

In the 1980s I drew up and presented a number of bills dealing with industrial democracy, amnesties for penalised trade unionists and councillors, land ownership; I also wrote a series of constitutional reform bills which culminated in May 1991 in a 'Commonwealth of Britain Bill', providing for a radical written constitution for Britain.

4.   (p. 176) The whole sorry story of the 'Tatchell affair' is given in Peter Tatchell's excellent book *The Battle for Bermondsey* (Heretic Books, 1983).

The inner London constituency of Bermondsey had been represented by Bob Mellish for over 30 years, but in November 1981 the local Labour Party had selected 29-year-old Peter Tatchell to succeed Mellish, who was retiring. As a result of Michael Foot's denunciation in Parliament, the issue of Tatchell's candidature became one of confidence in Michael Foot's leadership. To add to the pressure Mellish threatened to resign and force a by-election (which he eventually did), which would split the Labour vote. The fact that Tatchell was an active campaigner for gay rights was used by his opponents outside and inside the Labour Party.

As a result, Tatchell was hounded and vilified and at the notorious by-election, which fielded sixteen candidates including a Mellish-backed 'Real Bermondsey Labour' candidate (former local councillor John O'Grady), Simon Hughes, the Liberal/Alliance candidate, turned a 12,000 Labour majority into a 10,000 Liberal/SDP Alliance one.

5.   (p. 192) ASLEF train drivers in January 1982 held a series of one day strikes over a new 'flexible rostering' system which BR were trying to impose on the union, and over a 3% pay rise which had been withheld pending the other dispute. During the course of the strike the *Sun* newspaper quoted two ASLEF members who alleged impropriety on the part of some drivers. As a result, the 500 or so drivers at King's Cross Depot voted to refuse to carry any News International papers on their trains for distribution. The action forced News International after several days to give ASLEF the right of reply in the paper.

4
Goodbye to Bristol South East
June 1982–June 1983

Monday 21 June
The London Underground was completely disrupted because London Transport's Executive were having to make cuts in the services following the Law Lords' refusal to allow the GLC's Fares Fair scheme.

At this moment trade union militancy is reappearing; the health service workers have been having one-day stoppages with the support of the miners, and a rail strike is due next week. So despite mass unemployment the unions have begun to find the will again to protect services as well as their jobs and incomes.

At the NEC meeting on 23 June, the Hayward-Hughes Report on Militant, so called after its authors, General Secretary Ron Hayward and National Agent David Hughes, was presented. Its intention was to bring the issue of Militant to the forefront, in order to clear the way for disciplinary action in the future.

It found that the Militant Tendency was a 'well-organised caucus, centrally controlled . . . with its own programme and policy for separate and distinctive propaganda', and therefore was in breach of the Labour Party's constitution, Clause 2.

In place of a proscribed list, which the Party had abandoned in 1973, the report proposed a register of non-affiliated organisations, to which groups within the Party could apply, and each group would be required to meet certain criteria before being placed on the list. However, in relation to Militant itself, the report recommended that the Militant Tendency was not even eligible to join such a register.

Members of Militant persistently challenged the constitutional validity of the Register and claimed that it was an unworkable document.

The question of constitutional legitimacy was to become very important in the future when Militant members used it to challenge the Labour Party in the courts. A number of political groups, including the Campaign Group of Labour MPs, refused, on principle, to register, and no action was taken against them. The only penalty they suffered was that the official Conference diary for some years did not carry notice of their fringe meetings! In 1991, after many efforts to persuade the NEC to abandon the Register, it was finally dropped.

Wednesday 23 June

NEC, and the crucial debate on Militant. Ron Hayward was present for his last meeting – a tragedy that he should end his time as General Secretary recommending a register backed by expulsions.

Ron began the discussion by saying that he and the National Agent had received a great deal of evidence, read everything and found Militant very co-operative. 'We ended the list of proscribed organisations years ago, and there have been no expulsions, but we want openness.'

David Hughes said there was no divergence between himself and Hayward, and the NEC had given them a task to perform.

Then Michael Foot said we had a duty to protect the constitution. Militant was a distraction; it was based upon democratic centralism, which he attacked. It was a secret conspiracy.

Golding believed Militant was guilty and we wouldn't get mass working-class support if Militant remained in the Party.

After much debate, Eric Heffer moved his oath of allegiance, a 'statement of democratic socialist principles' which every member would be required to accept when joining the Party. Eric supported parliamentary democracy and said his statement would be preferable to a purge of Militant.

Frank Allaun seconded Eric's motion. He said we didn't want endless appeals from Militant supporters, and Eric's way was best.

I said I thought this had little to do with Militant and that all we were doing, as in 1960, was clarifying, amplifying and reaffirming Clause 4. There was a danger of making fools of ourselves because we were now confronted with tendencies towards democratic centralism in the Labour Party. We were highly illiberal. Peter Tatchell and Tariq Ali had been kept out without a hearing. Three Members had been thrown off the Front Bench for their conscientious position on the Falklands, and now groups were to be ruled out.

It was a thoroughly muddled report, anyway. The question that had to be faced was: what was the problem? We had ignored socialism for years and nurtured within our ranks at the highest level Tories like Reg Prentice, Liberals like Christopher Mayhew and the SDP Ministers, Rodgers, Jenkins, Owen and Williams – those 'pestilential nuisances'. The Lib-Lab pact was the beginning of the SDP. It was the exitists, not the entryists, that I worried about.

I went on, 'All that's happened in this report is that we've been given a flimsy constitutional excuse to expel a group on the grounds of secrecy and centralisation. What about TULV? They are centralised. They meet secretly. There were caucuses even in the last Cabinet. Registration is simply the proscribed list under another name. Are we to be told by Denis Healey, who doesn't even support Party policy and who is going to examine those of us who do, to decide who can stay in the

Party? I have been a member of the Labour Party for forty years and I shall die an unregistered socialist. I will not register, and CLPs will not expel.'

Joan Maynard said there was no constitutional provision for a register, and anyway the PLP leadership kept up attacks on the Party. Militant grew where the Party was in a mess; the NHS workers, railway workers and miners were now struggling. We must not now turn in on ourselves.

Joan Lestor declared that if we lost the next Election it would be because of the deputy leadership campaign last year, not because of Militant. Eric's 'oath of allegiance' was inoperable. She had voted against having an inquiry, but we had to take action. This was not an attack on political views. She said she was a republican, and Militant was free to hold and advocate its own views – no one would be thrown out because of their views. But this was a question of the *organisation* of Militant, which was aimed at gaining control for a different ideology. She believed there should be a register.

Neil Kinnock said Tony Benn was quite wrong about democratic centralism, which was based upon 'impossibilism and entryism', and the objection was not to what people think but to what they do – not to Marxism but to Militant's actions. A democratic party could not have an ideological test – all it could do was check organisations; and no Trotskyite could accept Clause 4. Militant was an organisational menace; it was not a flimsy constitutional reason for expulsion.

Jo stated that she had been in the Party all her life but she wouldn't register. It wouldn't work. There had always been groups nationally and locally. How would we force registration? What about Tribune? Could she go to Solidarity meetings? What about the Labour Abortion Reform Committee? Was the Register to be open to people who were against abortion?

Laurence Coates said he could not believe that Ron Hayward supported this – Ron having burned the MI5-type files kept by the National Agent during the 1950s.

Dennis Skinner understood Eric Heffer's proposal but thought it wouldn't work. An oath would be a register and people wouldn't sign. He said he'd looked through the telescope to see where it would end and it would end in blackness. He referred to individual Militants – a girl in a wheelchair who wouldn't live long and who wanted a revolution in all five continents by next year. Would you expel her? 'I am for fighting the Tory tendency – the CBI – and I will not travel along this road with you.'

Eric Clarke declared he wouldn't be a party to this. He didn't agree with Militant, but he defended their right to speak out, and we had opted out of any serious socialism.

Michael Foot said this had been a long debate and he fully

understood what had been said. Eric Clarke had referred to the right of Militant to speak, but that was not the constitutional issue. The charge was different against himself and Nye Bevan: Militant was a party and they were not. It was a secret conspiracy with paid organisers. Tony had raised a lot of red herrings which were absolutely laughable.

He asked us to vote against Eric's and my amendments, and to accept that people would be expelled from the Party but we would win and come out stronger.

Eric was defeated 22 against 5, and my resolution by 16 to 10 with Doug Hoyle abstaining – Kinnock and Lestor voted against. Michael's motion endorsing the report and instructing implementation forthwith was carried 16 to 10, with Hoyle abstaining again. So that was that matter disposed of.

That was the end of a horrible meeting, and when I came out I gave a very full interview to the press.

Saturday 26 June

Tony and Sally Banks picked me up and we drove to the South Bank, where, built into one of the arches forming Waterloo Bridge, the famous Polish artist Feliks Topolski has his studio.

Topolski is seventy-five, came to England between the wars, knew Bernard Shaw and is vaguely left-wing. He has painted some portraits and sketches – Nye Bevan, for example – and he wants to paint me. His study was absolutely crammed with his work. His daughter Theresa was there, and she sat and talked to me while he was painting. I did feel inhibited. He autographed the bottom of a mug for me!

He seemed to get beneath the surface and capture my character, and I think if he didn't like someone the painting would not work. I think he was a bit uncomfortable too. Still, the oil painting was interesting – he gave me a long neck and a pipe.

Tony, Sally and I had a meal at an Italian restaurant.

Tuesday 29 June

Lots more letters – encouraging by and large, some warning me not to go too far ahead of the public. The media are the main theme of most of the letters. Some Party members think I'm dividing the Party. It's like a daily criticism of what I'm doing. I must never underestimate their impact.

I'm depressed at the moment. The pressure is enormous and Caroline and I would like to be out of the firing line for a bit.

Friday 2 July

Flew to the Palais de Congrès in Brussels for the END conference. About 1000 delegates from all over western Europe were gathered, together with observers from America and eastern Europe. END was originally organised by Ken Coates and the Bertrand Russell Peace Foundation.

Ken is one of the most remarkable people in British politics, very little known outside the labour movement, although he has written numerous books, organises conferences, and has imaginative ideas and the resources to pursue them.

Dropped my stuff at a hotel and had lunch with Ken, Luciana Castellina of the Italian Socialist Party, and Rudolf Bahro, a former East German bureaucrat who wrote a critique of the DDR and of socialism in eastern Europe called *The Alternative in Eastern Europe*. He was jailed for two years and now works in Hamburg. He is about forty-eight and still apparently a Marxist, a member of the Green Party because he sees in ecology the solution to the world's problems.

To the Halles de Schaerbeek in the rue Royale, where we all spoke briefly; there was a rough translation system and then questions and answers. There was a discussion of how the American peace movement might be brought in, and there was one critical question about my proposal to reunite the world trade union movement.

Wednesday 7 July

Joined the ASLEF picket at King's Cross at lunchtime. There were about fifteen MPs there including Dafydd Ellis Thomas, and a huge gathering of media. I gave an interview and made a speech with Dennis Skinner and others. The press hostility was phenomenal. When I got home I had to lie down to recover from the strain.

Friday 9 July

To Bristol for the picket lines at a BR depot. I noticed most of the pickets were in their fifties. The reason the Western Region workers have been so solid in the strike – no trains running at all – is because they are experienced people who remember the 1955 strike and know that under flexible rostering they will be thrown on the scrapheap because of their age. They are really decent men; I like them so much.

It began to rain, and we stood together under the railway arch. Two well-dressed men came up – the regional manager and his PR man. The regional manager said he had sent me a message and asked me to study the rosters. I said I couldn't, they weren't negotiating with me; he should show them to Ray Buckton. So he said he'd tell the BBC that I wasn't interested in discussing the issue. I said that was entirely up to him, but I appealed to him to restore the old rosters and negotiate with the men.

He got involved in a huge row with men on the picket line. He was arrogant, and they shouted and waved their fists at him. I slipped away while they were talking.

Monday 12 July

The Organisation Committee met – an important meeting to consider Bermondsey and Peter Tatchell. I had tabled a resolution that Tatchell be endorsed on the spot, and Eric Heffer, who had visited Bermondsey, suggested they run another selection conference including Tatchell.

Michael Foot said Eric had done a good job in Bermondsey. Our position was based on the consequences to the Party of Tatchell's being the candidate, and he feared a disastrous by-election. But he had told Bob Mellish that he disapproved of what he did, and therefore he supported Eric's proposal that they hold a fresh selection conference with no bar on Tatchell. A total victory!

Friday 16 July

Today Hilary married Sally.

The family left for Acton Town Hall and arrived at 2.30, two weddings ahead of time. There was an Indian wedding in progress, with the women in the most beautiful colourful saris. Then another family and then us: the Benns, and Sally's parents, Aileen and Graham Clark (both architects), and their grown-up children.

At one point the registrar said, 'Now, Hilary and Salary . . .', which made us laugh. (We discovered later that he had been engaged in wage negotiations that morning!)

We took photographs and all left for Ealing Abbey, the chic Catholic Church in West London, where the priest greeted us. Mother read the lesson most beautifully and it was such a sight to see that old lady climbing up to the pulpit and reading the lesson, just as she had at Hilary's first wife Rosalind's funeral three years ago.

When I think of the tragedy of Rosalind's death and the tremendous suffering and unhappiness that Hilary has had, and indeed that Sally's older sister Caroline was killed about three years ago in a car smash, it was nice to think of this happiness coming to the family at this time.

Stephen referred in his speech at the reception to the fact that Rosalind and Caroline were in everybody's mind today.

Saturday 17 July

The big news is that the TUC have sat all night and have decided to tell ASLEF that they must end the strike and go back to work – a major defeat for the labour movement. With friends like that, what hope is there for any group of workers standing up to protect their living standards? A gloomy day.

Tuesday 20 July

To the Commons for Leo Abse's meeting to consider whether the thirty-three MPs who voted against the Government on the Falklands crisis should take a libel action against Cyril Smith, Liberal MP for

Rochdale, who had said on Radio Trent that we should be tried for treason; this was subsequently reported in the *Sun* and then other papers.

I said I'd be satisfied with an apology and asked if I could pull out of the writ.

Paired and came home.

Saturday 24 July

To Bristol with Caroline and up to Party HQ, where I talked to officers of the Party about arrangements for the next Election. There will be enormous complications with the ward boundaries changing for the district elections next year, and for the General Election when it comes. The Party has an overdraft of £1000 and can't even afford to repair the roof.

Then to a fair at Barton Hill, where there were lots of kids from the National Front who operate in the youth club nearby. I went over and talked to them and looked at their club – nothing but a TV set, a ping-pong table and a pinball machine. They were bitter because they said that in St Paul's the riots had produced better facilities for young black people than in Barton Hill. They asked me if I was a communist, said the Conservative and Labour Parties were just the same. It was the dead-end of Thatcherism – racialism among people with no future.

Monday 26 July

I fell flat on my face today. If it hadn't been for my big black bag my face would have hit the concrete. As it was my glasses frames were smashed and I grazed my knees, hurt my ankle and a finger – and I was badly shaken. Not as young as I used to be, and when you have a fall at nearly sixty it's more serious. A taxi driver was awfully kind – helped me pick up my wallet and things – and as I dragged myself up I thought I was going to have to go to hospital but after wiggling a few bones I was taken to the station and managed to walk to the train. The accident was a combination of not looking where I was going and the Guillain-Barré syndrome, which meant my brain didn't tell my feet to avoid the kerb.

Wednesday 28 July

Mother received the honorary fellowship of the Hebrew University today at a private lunch in Hampstead. I couldn't go but Melissa went. She said afterwards what a marvellous speech she had made. She was so proud of her grandmother. Mother's last twenty years have been tremendously creative and constructive.

Friday 30 July

I feel somehow that we are at a real turning-point in politics. I can't quite describe it. The military victory in the Falklands War, Thatcher's strength, the counter-attack of the right of the Labour Party on the left, the fact that unemployment has weakened the unions, and so on, make me feel more than ever before that I need to pause and think and work out a new strategy. Caroline has persuaded me that the press assassination of me was successful and that I've lived in a dream world believing it wasn't really happening. The NEC is in a bitter state, set on expulsions. ASLEF was sold down the river by the TUC, and even if they hadn't been I'm not sure how long they could have survived the Chairman of BR, Sir Peter Parker. The media are now in an absolutely hysterical state. I feel we have just come to the end of an era.

On the train back from Bristol I read Kenneth Harris's life of Attlee which I am reviewing for the *Labour Herald*. After the betrayal by MacDonald, the Party went sharply to the left for about three years – the Conferences in 1932 and 1933 were extremely radical. The ILP finally broke away and thus denied the Party the influence of the left. Then, with Ernest Bevin emerging as a major figure in favour of rearmament, and the expulsion of Stafford Cripps in 1938, the Party sustained a second loss of left-wingers. The coalition of Attlee, Bevin, Morrison and Cripps (although still expelled) in the wartime Government produced a postwar Labour Government of very experienced people who were clear in what they wanted to do: to use the wartime planning powers to plan for full employment and welfare. There was no real socialism in it, I think – it was consensus politics born during the war. The Labour Party as a party played only a marginal part. I can see that happening again now, only I don't think the left will withdraw this time.

Monday 2 August

In the evening, as it was the thirty-fourth anniversary of the day when Caroline and I met, we wandered out to a local Italian restaurant and sat in the garden and had a lovely talk. We went right over the years.

Bob Mellish resigned from the Labour Party, issuing the usual ex-Labour MP statement attacking the Party. He added that he intended to resign his seat in Parliament the day that Tatchell was endorsed, and of course that gives another lease of life to the whole saga.

Thursday 19 August

Stansgate. The big crisis of the moment is in the Lebanon, where the Israeli invasion, allegedly to get rid of the PLO terrorists' bases has turned into a siege, and parts of the country have been mercilessly pounded. The Palestinians have held out tremendously well, but in the process Israel has lost world support. Indeed, in a vote at the UN General Assembly this month only the Americans supported Israel – the rest of the world community were opposed or abstained.

Thursday 2 September

Watched the last of the TV series *The Twentieth Century Remembered* in which Harold Wilson was interviewed by Anthony King. It dealt with the years from 1970 until 1976, when Wilson retired as Prime Minister, but it was vulgar and shallow. Wilson talked about the Labour Party Conferences with a supposed quotation from Nye Bevan that Conference resolutions were just masturbation that did no harm to anyone else – a denigrating thing to say. At one stage he referred to me. He said if he had looked into those 'lunatic eyes' – then quickly corrected this to 'wide staring eyes' – and had realised what I was about, he would have reported me to the head of London Zoo.

It won't do me any damage, but it's interesting that the assessment I made of Wilson from 1968 onwards was more or less correct and that we had to put up with him for another eight years before he finally retired.

At the end he was asked by King what his greatest achievement was, what he would like to have on his tombstone, and Wilson said, 'I would like them to say about me, "He kept the Party together".'

Drove to County Hall for a press conference at 11 for *A Very British Coup* by Chris Mullin, published today. It was attended by the political journalists, plus Ken Livingstone, Chris and myself. Anthony Bevins of *The Times* suggested that the phrase in the book 'Harry Perkins regarded America as more of a threat to British democracy than Russia' was Chris's personal view. I do think that is putting it too strongly, and I said those who were in favour of democracy were really the ones most feared by the establishment.

Tuesday 21 September

The NEC today voted by 22 to 3 to adopt a resolution by Denis Healey, amended by me, on the Lebanon. We condemned the massacres in Beirut, called on a UN force to be dispatched, and called for guarantees for the security of Israel and the establishment of a Palestinian state, with the PLO involved in the negotiations. A major development of Labour policy.

Wednesday 22 September

Today was the National Health Service Day of Action called by the TUC. I spent it in Bristol. When I got to British Aerospace for a mass meeting, the chief shop steward approached me and told me I couldn't speak. He said it was a non-political meeting. I told him NUPE had invited me to come, but he said the shop stewards felt that there were a lot of Conservatives present and it would be unwise to allow me to speak – people would walk away.

Frank Huff, the regional secretary of NUPE, spoke, and another trade-unionist, and by this time, after a consultation among shop stewards, it was agreed that, since the meeting was over, I could then speak. Nobody walked away. I thought, if the TUC can actually call a day of action against the Government for trying to destroy the NHS and at the same time say it doesn't want Labour MPs to take part, that is an indication of the decline of the labour movement and the total failure of all of us to introduce some political understanding into trade-unionism.

Then to Gypsy Patch Lane for the Rolls Royce meeting. There had only been 1500 at British Aerospace, but here there were 7000 people, along both sides of the road, and the atmosphere was entirely different. Rolls Royce is much more radical, particularly in Bristol. At the end of my speech there was a hand count of those who wanted to come out on strike for the rest of the day and all but a hundred were in favour.

While I was in Bristol I heard the absolutely tragic news that Frank McElhone had died of a heart attack while on the NHS march in Glasgow; he was only fifty-three. Helen, his wife, had apparently specially asked that I be told, and I tried to ring her, but her number was engaged, so I sent a telemessage of sympathy at once.

I first met Frank when he was elected in the by-election in 1969 for the Gorbals after Alice Cullen died, and he had a most remarkable life. He came from a very poor home in Glasgow, went into the army, became a sergeant, then left and decided to buy a little greengrocer's shop. From there he just helped everyone and became a sort of local adviser, then a Labour councillor, and was adopted as candidate. He became my PPS and close friend, but he was disappointed when I didn't respond to his advice, which was 'Keep your head down'. But he was terribly kind. In the Department of Industry I think he didn't understand the political controversy, and feared it would affect his own position. He resented Frances Morrell, who was my political adviser then. In the end he resigned as my PPS and was later made Minister of State in the Scottish Office, and in Opposition became the spokesman on Third World Development. He was highly respected, and Helen was devoted to him. They had four children. His death does deprive the labour movement in Scotland of a very important figure, much trusted in the Catholic community.

Thursday 23 September
We're heading for a really tough struggle to save the health service, and it's going to intensify and get more and more bitter. The trade union leaders cannot run away from this one. Thatcher won't give way. This will be a test of solidarity, and if the labour movement lets this go by it will demoralise the movement and assure Mrs Thatcher an Election victory. That's what this is about really – whether Thatcher is going to get another five years, and whether we are going to lose our health service.

Labour Party Conference, Blackpool
Saturday 25 September
Compared to last year, when the left was riding high with successes everywhere, this year the left is very much tail-between-legs. We did unleash a violent backlash from the right supported by the media and the general secretaries, and although the Party is pretty solid on policy it doesn't want divisions, so we are caught by the constraint of unity – whereas they, being on the warpath, are not, and are demanding the expulsion of the left. It's very unpleasant but I shall just let it ride over me; at this stage we have to accept that the right have won and there isn't much we can do about it.

Sunday 26 September
NEC from 11 till 12.30 and 1.30 to 5.30.

As the NEC swings to the right and I am more and more isolated in a minority of about seven or eight, it begins to prepare me for my defeat in the Home Policy Committee chairmanship. A pity, but there you are. I shall have to spend next year still putting forward proposals on the NEC and arguing for them on the back benches. Whether the right want me in the winning team for the Election is a matter for them.

Monday 27 September
The Conference discussed the Hayward-Hughes Report into Militant today. The papers are having a field day against Militant, minimising the Conference's impact on the public. This is what I think Foot has achieved – damaged the prospect of the Conference winning support for Labour.

It was an appalling debate. Martin Flannery and Pat Wall from the Bradford North CLP made extremely good speeches. But Michael Foot was weak; I didn't look up once during his speech. The recommendation to set up a register was carried by about 5 to 1, an overwhelming victory, all the big unions having voted without consulting their members. They have just loaded a responsibility on to the new Executive which will enable it to carry out any purge it wishes.

A pretty black day, but at least the Party's political bankruptcy is being made more explicit than ever before. When they have to throw the rulebook at you, you know they haven't got any ideas. I think it's *this* note of optimism from the left that we ought to spread, because first of all the left needs a bit of a lift and secondly the right needs to be exposed for what it is. After every NEC I suppose we'll have located a couple more Militants and say, 'Unfortunately we didn't have time to discuss unemployment this month because it was taken up with this or that inquiry or expulsion.' I think the right are in very deep trouble and we should laugh at them.

Tuesday 28 September

First debate on Tebbit's employment legislation, and then we had the results of the NEC elections. Michael Meacher was absolutely trounced by Varley, for whom the T&G had voted.

Joan Maynard was beaten – which was terribly sad. The right-wing have been trying to get her off for ten years and they finally did it. Les Huckfield was beaten, as were Eric Clarke and Doug Hoyle. Some good comrades gone. It is a much harder-right Executive. Audrey Wise managed to beat Joan Lestor. Joan will say it was because she opposed me in the deputy leadership, but actually it was because she voted for the purge.

The left has really got to rethink its whole position. It can't be a liaison of all the groups because that would split on ideological grounds. We have to build an issue-oriented socialist campaign.

Back at the Conference Michael Foot made his speech – pretty rhetorical, but it got an immediate standing ovation in which I did not join. It would have been entirely hypocritical of me to stand, though I did applaud. Dennis Skinner had gone to the back, and others had moved off the platform. I felt pretty lonely.

New Socialist fringe meeting with James Curran, Jo Richardson, Hattersley and Kinnock. Kinnock spoke, followed by me and then Hattersley.

Kinnock was utterly vacuous. Hattersley made a very good speech – he came out of it with a certain degree of integrity, I thought. Lots of questions, during which Hattersley stated that he wanted to stay in the Common Market and thought no one really believed we would ever come out. He, like Kinnock and myself, came out for abolition of the Lords.

Later to a Labour Gay Rights meeting and stood at the back; the chairman asked me to speak. Joan Lestor made an extremely good contribution, and I followed her – my first time at a Gay Rights meeting at Conference.

Wednesday 29 September

In the afternoon there was a tremendous uproar in the hall when it was announced that the SOGAT nuclear disarmament resolution including the removal of American nuclear bases had been carried by more than a two-thirds majority, which means it will be in *Labour's Programme* – though with the present NEC I don't suppose it will be implemented. Still, a very significant event.

Thursday 30 September

It has been a very unusual Conference – a few fringe meetings but absolutely no social life. At the beginning of the week Militant had an apparent clobbering but the expulsions are unworkable. When it came to Party policy, everything I wanted went right through. Marvellous. Foot said he'd like to have me in the next Cabinet – an absolute re-run of last year – provided of course I accept collective responsibility in the Shadow Cabinet. My position remains the same.

Friday 1 October
The press are hailing the Conference as a great victory for Foot, but a lot of people want to know whether unilateralism will be in the manifesto and the answer of course is that it won't be. Michael Foot will fudge it because he doesn't want Denis Healey to resign from the Shadow Cabinet over it on the eve of an Election. The thing will rumble on and create terrible difficulties.

The conference was very good in that the whole of *Labour's Programme*, in particular the ban on nuclear weapons, went through on a two-thirds majority. That was a consolidation of over three years' immensely hard work. Longer. Secondly, the constitutional changes were not overturned as we had feared, so that every single gain of the last three years' campaigning was preserved. On the other hand, the big union leaders who wanted to support Michael Foot and who thought that divisions in the Party were damaging to our prospects in the next Election decided to change the composition of the NEC.

Wednesday 6 October
Five women from the Greenham Common Peace Camp came this afternoon. They are being charged with action likely to cause a breach of the peace, because they walked deliberately into the base and occupied a sentry box for a couple of hours. They are to appear at Newbury magistrates' court on 15 November, and Caroline and I made suggestions as to whom they might call as expert witnesses – peace campaigners like Philip Noel-Baker, Group Captain Cheshire, or maybe Brigadier Harbottle from CND. It was moving to hear their story. They had no socialist analysis, and they didn't understand the political background or the history of nuclear power or nuclear weapons: they were just deeply morally committed, and they felt that everyone had a duty to contribute directly and that all representative government and even CND itself tended to diminish people's sense of personal responsibility. It was a real evangelical movement of a formidable kind.

Friday 8 October
The NHS dispute has now been going on for six months, with some days of action and accident and emergency services only. In September the Government proposals were leaked, which suggested that to cut three or four billion pounds off public expenditure the NHS would have to be wound up, and private compulsory medical insurance intro-

duced. The health service unions – the rather conservative COHSE, the radical NUPE and others – have managed to hold together fairly well, but it came to light recently that Albert Spanswick, General Secretary of COHSE, had had private talks with the Minister without telling Rodney Bickerstaffe, General Secretary of NUPE. So it's all a bit tense and difficult.

Tuesday 12 October
The pamphlet Caroline helped to write, criticising the Youth Training Scheme, came back from the printers today. It is a first-rate piece of work, the first major pamphlet the Socialist Society will be publishing.

In the afternoon, Peter Hain, Nigel Stanley and John Denham (who is the Labour candidate for Southampton Itchen in place of Richard Mitchell, who joined the SDP) came to discuss the future role of the Labour Co-ordinating Committee. There was pretty fair agreement that we'd have to accept the Register. We would fight expulsions and campaign on the manifesto, but we'd need to look at the block vote at Conference.

I said I didn't think we should waste time on the Register, or highlight splits within the left over what to do about it.

I'm anxious to mend fences at the moment; you can't fight with everyone all the time.

Wednesday 13 October
Great media coverage of the big Falklands victory parade yesterday, and the interesting thing was that the Queen was away and no other member of the royal family attended. It was Mrs Thatcher's victory parade organised by and for Tory Central Office.

TUC Economic Committee – probably my last. We had a report of the last NEDC meeting, at which the Director-General said what a marvellous economy the Japanese one was, and made no reference whatever to the Japanese trade unions except to say that they were always consulted and were very constructive and there was less confrontation in Japanese companies because of a general commitment to consensus. That is basically what the TUC leadership want. They don't dispute control of the economy, they just want consensus.

I came away with my usual feeling of utter detachment.

Friday 15 October
Jeremy Corbyn, a NUPE organiser for London, took me to St Mary's Hospital at Paddington. In the canteen there were about 150 people for a meeting to prepare the ground for next week's day of action in London. They are determined not to have the NHS destroyed.

Tuesday 19 October

Lunch with Alastair Milne, the new Director-General of the BBC, his deputy, David Holmes, and Alan Protheroe, co-ordinator of news and current affairs. I was jolly and funny and used humour to hammer home a lot of points.

I knew Milne when he was on *Tonight* years ago, but I hadn't seen him for a long time. He asked what I was really saying in my attacks on the BBC.

I told him, 'Well, you don't present the full range of opinions, there is a whole range of views that is suppressed, there is hostility to the unions, to the Labour Party and to socialism, and this has made the BBC distrusted and disliked.'

He wasn't convinced, though I didn't expect him to be. He thought many of my criticisms were unfair.

I objected strongly to the BBC's thinking they had the right to label some people as 'extreme' or 'hard left' and describe others in favourable language. I said they ought to publish all the policy statements reached by the Board of Governors, including their minutes.

I was good-natured, and I managed to get under their skin. Alan Protheroe growled, 'I am going to say something now which I hoped I wouldn't have to say. It is impossible to look at the Glasgow University Media Group work without wondering what their real objective is – whether it is subversive, to destabilise our society – and I feel bound to say that.'

I replied 'What you are saying is you don't like being criticised – nobody does. But you have not given the proper opportunity for those matters to be discussed. You've answered the Group, but you haven't allowed a proper discussion.'

That was the only sharp exchange, and I sent a note afterwards thanking them.

Wednesday 20 October

The Campaign Group met this evening to consider the new situation in the light of the defeats at Conference. Afterwards I had a meal with Stuart Holland, Chris Mullin, Joan Maynard and Bob Cryer and we had a good talk.

Chris told us that he had heard that recently Ian Aitken from the *Guardian* described him as 'the editor of that poisonous paper'.

I have decided that I shall not rejoin the Tribune Group but I won't make a fuss about it. I'll probably go to next Monday's meeting and then quietly fade out.

Sunday 24 October

Melissa, Caroline and I picked up Michael and went on the march of

Babies Against the Bomb, which is associated with Pensioners for Peace. There was just a glimpse of Michael on the BBC news.

Monday 25 October
Saw St John Stevas in the Commons and asked him, 'Norman, do you want to be Speaker?'

'Shhh, Shhh.'

'Well, that answers my question,' I said.

Looking embarrassed, he indicated that of course he did.

Wednesday 27 October
The papers all week had been predicting the massacre of the left at today's meeting of the newly elected NEC, which was due to decide on the composition of all its committees.

I decided to sit in a different place, opposite the chairman, in recognition of the changes that were coming, and I had Dennis Skinner and Audrey Wise on either side of me to sustain me.

Shirley Summerskill moved that we ban smoking from the meeting – carried by 18 to 13.

After a bit of business, we came to the major question of the committees. John Golding was the prime mover in all the votes. Eric Heffer blew up. 'You buggers are trying to break the Party. For a year I haven't been on television but you just say what you like on TV; when the left had control we had the decency to vote right-wingers on.' He banged the table. But you can't shout and scream when you've lost. No one took the slightest notice.

In a nutshell, there was a clean sweep of the left on all the committees. Foot appealed to us not to reveal what had happened, that we should leave it to the General Secretary. So when the left had a majority, and Golding gave a press conference three times a day outside every committee, that was OK, but now that the right are in power we are gagged.

As I went out I was pursued down the road by the media.

I feel quite liberated, frankly.

Had a call this evening to say that Tony Banks had beaten Arthur Lewis, Ted Knight, Dave Wetzel and Mandy Moore for the Newham North West candidacy. He had an overwhelming majority, and so he is in for life in a very, very safe seat – marvellous. I rang Sally. It shows that just when you think everything's gone wrong things begin to pick up.

Thursday 28 October
Bought all the papers, which were full of headlines such as 'Benn Gets Boot' and 'Benn Routed'. I've seen these headlines so many times,

especially in 1975 after the Referendum. I'm tempted to look up the press cuttings, because I am sure they all said the same.

There was a lot of coverage in the papers about the miners' ballot, which defeated Scargill's demand for a 30 per cent wage increase and opposition to pit closures. The NUM ballot requires a majority of 55 per cent, and of course the press are rubbing their hands with glee at the thought of Arthur's humiliation, but he won't be humiliated because he knows that, since the miners have voted down industrial action, the Coal Board and the Government will be able to ride over them completely: there will be pit closures, and the whole coal expansion plan will be set back in favour of a massive expansion of nuclear power. Although Arthur may be attacked in the short run, he will be shown to be right in the long run.

Monday 1 November

I began reading a collection of articles by women, published in 1936, *Our Freedom*. There was a most interesting piece by the secretary of the Association of Moral and Social Hygiene on changes in sex morality – an extremely good résumé of the struggles of women against the Contagious Diseases Acts of the 1860s, which established brothels for the armed forces in navy ports and major garrison cities. She described how prostitutes had to be examined surgically every two weeks and could be locked up for treatment.

The role of Josephine Butler and W.T. Stead was described, and it was explained how this created a discussion about sex and provided the background against which the suffragette movement really began. It was something I knew nothing about. I saw the woman's movement in a new light, because the Labour Party has tended to see everything in terms of class, and the women's movement stresses the exploitation of women by men: so this was a pre-class-struggle campaign of a formidable kind.

Wednesday 3 November

Lots of letters expressing sympathy at my losing my place on the eight NEC committees and at the right-wing purge. Some implied that people would simply leave the Party and not bother any longer if that was the way things were going. I don't say people will leave the Party or abstain from voting Labour, but I do think that it will take the stuffing out of the active people upon whom work really depends.

Watched the opening of Parliament on TV – odious. Here is a country with 4 million out of work, just after a war, and there was all the ancient grandeur, the Queen in her crown, Hailsham in his wig and Lord Cockfield holding the Cap of Maintenance; and the obsequious, creepy David Dimbleby doing the commentary. There was Foot looking more and more moth-eaten, walking beside Mrs Thatcher, who is tough and confident. I was so ashamed of it.

Friday 5 November

Taxi to the BBC for 2.30. From there I was driven to Marlborough to do *Any Questions*, picking up David Jacobs from Knightsbridge on the way.

On the panel were a go-ahead young businessman, Norman St John Stevas and Bea Campbell. Bea is a member of the Communist Party. She used to work for the *Morning Star*; now she is working for *City Limits*.

Back in the car with Norman St John Stevas in the front and Bea Campbell and me in the back. I asked Norman how things were, and he said the wets were totally in retreat. He told me he had seen Lord Home this morning, what a charming man he was, and how ignorant was that woman Thatcher. He thinks she hates his guts.

Norman told me about the moment when he realised he was going to be sacked; at the time he was Chancellor of the Duchy of the Lancaster. Geoffrey Howe was late for the Cabinet. Norman said that 'the old hen' had come in, looked round the table and asked where the Chancellor was. Norman had said, 'I'm the Chancellor', and she given him such a dirty look that all the other Ministers, who had been laughing at the joke, froze immediately. He realised then how much she hated him and that he would go.

He also told me he had been offered the job of Minister for the Arts, without a seat in the Cabinet, and had turned it down because it was such an insult. I asked what prospect there was of his joining Ted Heath, Roy Jenkins, Shirley Williams and David Steel and challenging the right wing. He said there was too much cohesiveness in the Tory Party for that to happen.

What is so interesting about his position is that it depends so much on the concept of patronage. What the wets like is a nice patron like Home or Macmillan, not a nasty one like Mrs Thatcher. The idea of going out and mobilising opinion to defeat the people at the top hadn't occurred to him. Norman will wither on the bough, and he'll be remembered as an amusing person. He won't get to be Speaker because she would never have him. He also said Jim Prior could have stopped her if he'd refused to go to Northern Ireland. Prior had kept ringing Norman up and discussing it, and finally he rang and said, 'Norman, the die is cast.' Stevas was about to congratulate him on challenging Thatcher, but Prior meant he'd accepted the Northern Ireland job.

It was an insight into the Tory Party, and though I have known Stevas since 1946 I haven't really spoken to him at any length for about fifteen years. That Tory tradition has been extinguished. He felt Thatcher would leave a strong legacy in the Tory Party and I think he's right. Her ideas will continue to exist long after she or her legislation has gone.

Bea Campbell was most interesting. She comes from Carlisle; her mother was German, her father a Communist. She herself is a

Communist, aged thirty-five, and has written a book with Anna Coote on the early days of women's liberation. She is highly intelligent. I talked to her about my position now – how I'd like to use this period creatively and help to give people confidence but needed to understand the women's movement.

Bea chastised me for not reading what women were writing, when women had read all the male books in order to keep abreast of thinking. That was a fair point. She said it wasn't just a question of listening to what women were saying. Women constituted a different sort of movement, representing more than half the population and not a minority. The egocentric, macho, non-sharing, non-cooperative person had to change. I said it sounded like a religious challenge. She didn't know what that meant because she was brought up in a dedicated Communist household. In effect, of course, she was saying that it is harder for a man to get to heaven than it is for a camel to pass through the eye of a needle. She said in one way she'd like to bring people to see me but the whole situation would be wrong: it would just become a salon for 'the great man' to dominate, and that was the very thing women were against. She mentioned the 'feminisation of society', which I had heard of before from Melissa.

Sunday 7 November

Ken Coates rang this morning. He had seen Eric Hobsbawm at a conference in Yugoslavia, and he said how conservative Hobsbawm was now, flirting with the SDP and apoplectic about me – he thinks I've lost my marbles.

Members of the Communist Party have, like Eric, lost confidence in themselves to such an extent that they are trying to build up the centre again, to get the CP absorbed into the establishment. In Britain you have people like Sue Slipman, an ex-Communist, in the SDP.

Chris Mullin rang in the evening to tell me about the new financial crisis at *Tribune*. On leaving *Tribune*, Dick Clements had pulled the plug on the paper. There were debts of about £9000. Chris lives from day to day, but it's a nightmare keeping the paper going.

Monday 8 November

The TUC called off today's Day of Action in support of the NHS workers because there are supposed to be some talks in progress, but of course it is a capitulation and a collapse. The TUC leadership has been abysmal, and the health service workers must feel a terrible sense of gloom. But though the campaign may have failed it has been the first stage in the battle to save the NHS from the Tory Party, and a major factor in helping us to win the next Election.

Wednesday 10 November

Up early, opened my mail and went to the Commons for the Organisation Committee.

The chairmanship was discussed, and four people voted for Eric Heffer to continue – himself, Frank Allaun, myself and Jo Richardson – and thirteen voted for Russell Tuck. So Foot congratulated Tuck and said he had a difficult job. He renewed the plea that no one speak to the press after this committee except for the chair and the General Secretary. Frank paid tribute to Eric Heffer, Foot seconded.

We devoted three hours today to discipline in the Party considering the cases of Tariq Ali, Peter Tatchell and the Militant Tendency – no discussion about the Election at all, and there will have to be *another* meeting. The attempt to expel is going to be much harder now the courts are taking a greater interest in natural justice. People should be entitled to exercise their legal rights – particularly if they are about to be expelled from a Party of which they have been a member for thirty years.

But we did at least confirm that Bermondsey could hold a fresh selection conference, including Tatchell.

The first meeting of the Home Policy Committee since Conference was held today, and nominations for chairman came up.

I had been in the chair since 1974 and helped to push through *Labour's Programme* for 1976 and 1982 – the monuments to my chairmanship. It's the first time I've known a sitting chair actually be defeated. Four people voted for me – Eric Heffer, Tom Sawyer, Dennis Skinner and myself (Judith was absent) – and twelve voted for John Golding. So he took the chair. It has been a historic eight-year period. I didn't express my thanks because I thought that would be silly. It is important to get this defeat out of the way and get on with the job.

I'm reading Ralph Miliband's *Capitalist Democracy in Britain*, which he sent me this morning – a first-rate book, about how the British political system has contained and defused pressure, and I think he's absolutely correct.

Thursday 11 November

I had arranged to see Jeremy Seabrook and Trevor Blackwell, two sociologists in their early forties, this morning. They have been writing a lot of stuff, in effect saying that the Labour Party is finished, the old working-class alliance has gone and working-class consciousness has declined. It is a sort of wet sociological pessimism coming allegedly from the left. They are mesmerised by Thatcher with her messianic message, and, although they claim to be Marxists of a sort, they are really potential members of the SDP. I was suspicious of them, truthfully.

In the evening I got a phone call from Herbert Rogers, telling me that his wife Lily died about three hours ago. She was eighty-four and they had been married fifty-eight years. Lily Rogers was a modest, kind woman. She had a full and long life, but suffered terribly through a fall which put her in a wheelchair for the last few years, and that was a great strain on Herbert. He is a great old leader of the labour movement in Bristol, and I hope this will allow us to show our feelings for him.

Friday 12 November

Leonid Brezhnev died on Wednesday. He was General Secretary of the Soviet Communist Party for eighteen years, and the power struggle in the Kremlin was resolved today with the election of Andropov, former head of the KGB. It looks as if the transfer of power will be quite peaceful. Will the west use this breathing space to allow new contacts to be made? We have an opportunity now to press for a rethink in the siting of Cruise missiles, and to strengthen the peace movement generally.

To Bristol and went at the invitation of BAC shop stewards for a general talk. When one of them said, 'The real problem here is class,' I asked in what sense, and it all poured out.

They said there are five dining-rooms at BAC British Aerospace Dynamics: the directors', the executive mess, the management mess, the senior females' mess (ie secretaries to directors) and the works canteen. There are different gradations of subsidy for each one.

The personnel office door is actually locked with a computer code which is changed regularly. You have to ring the bell and they open a little window, then you have to wait for a statutory five minutes. You then go along a 40-foot corridor to Personnel and finally you are allowed to raise your point. Everything is on a computer now, so they just go to the records and say, 'You were late four times this year', or whatever, and they have you before you even start. The stewards said the computer can calculate everything except the backpay owed to you! When that subject is raised, they say the computer can't manage it. The situation had, they believed, got much worse since the Tories came to power.

At Hawker Siddeley Dynamics, a branch of BAC, they are sometimes invited to have tea with the management, and if the management want to get an agreement the workers have tea in china cups, but if the workers want something the tea is served in paper cups or not at all.

They described in detail the hierarchy in the company where the colour of the desk, the type of chair, and the presence or absence of carpet reflect the status of the individuals concerned.

We discussed mass meetings. The weekly-paid staff have to hold these outside, while the monthly-paid staff have theirs inside. If the trade union conveners make a recommendation in support of the company's proposal and the vote is in favour of the proposal, the employees are paid for the time they are at the meeting. But if the conveners recommend against the company's proposal or the vote goes the other way, pay is deducted for the time they spend at the meetings.

We talked about solutions – directors on the board, election of the board, access to information, the right to delay management decisions, etc – ideas included in the workers' plan drawn up by Ron Thomas which I supported way back in 1971.

They came back to the problem of the need for a labour newspaper, and said the men read the *Sun* from back to front starting with the sports news, then page 3, then the front page, past eight pages of Tory propaganda. There is not much we can do about a paper until the Election, but afterwards we really will have to get that off the ground. Of course, Cabinet Ministers won't care about it once Labour is elected.

Going down in the car to my surgery in Windmill Hill, the shop steward who gave me a lift said the workers at Hawker Siddeley believe I am a communist and am against all defence for the country. He said there was nothing he could do to persuade them otherwise. He emphasised the difficulty of his position, because if he was too political he would be removed as shop steward. This is the real problem. The workforce is conservative, the *Sun* both shapes and reflects it, and Terry Duffy and Frank Chapple are part of it.

At the GMC, I referred to the death of Lilian Rogers and said I hoped people would turn up at the funeral. At that moment, the door opened and there was Herbert. He didn't want to come to the meeting because he said he'd be overcome by the tributes paid. Joyce Perham, a marvellous woman, is taking care of him, and they have been friends for many years.

Saturday 13 November

To the AGM of the Avon Pre-School Playgroup. They weren't expecting me, but I think it was appreciated that I turned up. They were a mixture of Fabians, SDP and progressive Tories, middle-class women who do most of the work in voluntary organisations, and I'd guess that, if you had a poll among the eighty or so people there, Labour and Tory would have got about fifteen votes and the SDP about fifty.

A health visitor from Widnes in Cheshire, with grey hair and a blue blouse, was the main speaker, and I apologised to her for not being able to stay and hear her.

'That's a pity,' she said, 'because I am going to speak plainly to politicians about their neglect of the social services.'

I replied, 'I am responsible for many things but not for Mrs Thatcher's cuts in the social services.' I criticised her for lumping politicians together, but later I realised that she was rather sympathetic, just fed up that nothing was being done. She told me she was a supporter of Arthur Scargill! It shows you shouldn't judge by appearances.

The way the women had organised the meeting was very modest – no real speeches, just points raised. The women's movement is like that, very different from men's meetings. Back to London and worked until Caroline got home. I told her that Pam Tatlow thinks I should leave Bristol because of the difficulty of getting elected in any of the three redistributed seats. Caroline has been saying that for some time. I would have preferred to stay on and fight at least one of them, but it has become clear to me that I should leave. Whatever happens, it would be a bloody battle – Cocks is very shrewd and would probably defeat me in a selection contest in Bristol South because he has a majority and would use the attack on Militant to expel members of his GMC who he thought were sympathetic to me. At Bristol East there is Ron Thomas, whom I much admire, and who was defeated in Bristol North West last time. In Kingswood there is Terry Walker, for whom I have no time, but I couldn't try and get that because he is a local man, and lost by only 300 last Election. So the best thing all round is to give up and announce that I won't contest any of the seats.

It would be humiliating if I lost, and if I won it would create bitterness. I'd like to stay in Parliament, and I depend on my parliamentary salary and my secretarial allowance to cope with the enormous volume of work that I undertake, but the whole parliamentary scene just now seems to be closed to radical opinions. The assumptions of the 1960s about full employment and the welfare state have gone. If you articulate Macmillan consensus views, you are trounced from the right, while the Labour Party leadership just thinks they are impossible to implement.

Caroline pointed out that I have been destroyed by the media not only nationally but also locally. Therefore I would do better if I were adopted somewhere else; but every seat will be allocated by March next year. If I don't get adopted, it will be the first General Election since 1950 that I haven't fought as a candidate. I could fight a hopeless seat just to keep the flag flying but that wouldn't be sensible. The whole of my political life has become misty and I can't see my way through beyond next June.

I can't help comparing the situation with my Father's, in 1918. Then, when he was away at the war, his seat, St George's, Tower Hamlets, was redistributed under the Parliamentary Reform Act and another Liberal managed to get himself selected against Father. Though disappointed and hurt, Father did the 'high sublime' with the encouragement of his own father – he handed over his constituency organisation, committee rooms, etc., to his rival and moved on to Leith, where he was elected as a candidate opposing Lloyd George's Coalition. When I think of it in this way, a huge sense of relief comes over me, because the last thing I want is to be engaged in the kind of in-fighting necessary to get rid of Cocks or Walker or even Thomas, and I think it will be the right thing to do.

Last year Caroline felt it was unwise of me to stand for the deputy leadership. When I look back, her advice has always been right. I think in future I will actually take her advice. So on Thursday, if, as I expect, I am not elected to the Shadow Cabinet, and if I decide not to stand for any seat in Bristol, I shall be a senior Labour figure without a seat. There will then be an election for the Leader while I am out of Parliament, someone else will be elected, and I will then pass on to another phase. I just have to put all situations involving personal advancement completely out of my mind. If you don't want anything for yourself, you are less vulnerable to attack by the media. In any case, since I failed against Healey in 1981, such damage was done that I probably wouldn't succeed anyway.

Depressed at the moment – the reverses that have occurred in the last twelve months have taken a long time to penetrate into my mind and at the moment I'm feeling a bit like a burnt-out meteor. Still, it won't last for ever.

Sunday 14 November
To Bristol for the Remembrance Day commemoration. It was pelting with rain. I wanted to be there because of the Falklands War. I am not prepared to concede to the Tories and the warmongers the sole right to remember the dead of war. Also, it might be my last Remembrance Day in Bristol.

Usual crowd all in their ceremonial dress, and the Lord Mayor's coach.

I was nervous about the event because I thought this jingoism of the Falklands would have reflected itself in a much larger crowd, but it was actually very thin. Although a man from the British Legion began by saying, 'Let us remember those who died in action in the South Atlantic and in action in the United Kingdom,' (referring to Northern Ireland), the rest of the service went normally.

I had an interesting discussion with William Waldegrave (Tory MP for Bristol West) about the Conservatives' 'Think Tank' in which he has worked. He said Victor Rothschild had done a marvellous job as its first Director-General, how useful it was that there should be advice available to the whole Cabinet, and so on.

I asked him about Mrs Thatcher's decision to appoint Sir Anthony Parsons as special adviser on foreign affairs. He is currently our UN Ambassador and was previously our man in Teheran when the Shah was on the point of being removed. I drew out of Waldegrave the view that, with Parsons at Number 10, clearly he would be more important than the Permanent Secretary at the Foreign Office, and the Foreign

Office would be isolated. He said Francis Pym, the Foreign Secretary, felt really out on a limb, and this would certainly add another layer between him and the Prime Minister.

So she intends to be an anti-consensus politician, building up around her her own people – Sir Oliver Wright, Parsons, Sir Frank Cooper and others – who will be at the heart of government working with and for the PM against the rest of Whitehall (whom she distrusts as consensus civil servants) and against the wets in the Cabinet. I can understand her motives, because that is the way to push things through Whitehall.

Monday 15 November
Drove to Newbury magistrates' court for the trial of eleven women from Greenham Common, who were charged with action likely to cause a breach of the peace for standing in a sentry hut a few yards inside the perimeter fence on 27 August. They've been camping outside now for a year, first in huts, which were destroyed, and then in tents and sleeping bags. Bruce Kent was in court, and BBC, ITN and Channel 4 were present.

The court was packed, and there was applause as the women came in. Two women barristers represented them. One of the magistrates was a tough-looking man with greased hair and moustache.

The barristers asked for the proceedings to be recorded, and one tape recorder was allowed, provided that any transcript was submitted for authentication. The magistrates warned that they would remove people if there were any disturbances. Then the defendants rose and were named, and the prosecution began.

The prosecuting lawyer said, 'Eleven ladies have been brought before the court, having occupied a hut, which caused inconvenience and was likely to cause a breach of the peace.' The prosecution had been brought under the 1361 Justices of the Peace Act. He described the events of 27 August. He admitted that the demo had been non-violent, but said that whether they intended violence or not was irrelevant. The prosecution was not a criticism of the ladies demonstration against nuclear weapons but that their action violated the rights of others over private property and the rights to privacy. This campaign would not stop; it would get worse.

He went on to say that the 1361 Act as reported in the laws of England was required 'for good behaviour towards the king and his people'. Then he referred to Lord Justice Templeman, who had ruled that powers must exist to deal with passive resistance and minimum force. He quoted Gandhi, who had said that 'passive defence is only possible if it is successful'. All those who interfere with the lawful rights of others are guilty of a breach of the peace, the prosecuting counsel stated.

We had to leave at that stage. Caroline went back to London and I flew up to Scotland.

Tuesday 16 November

In the House I bumped into Tory MP Julian Amery, who said he had someone he wanted me to meet. It turned out to be Ian Smith, former Prime Minister of Rhodesia. I didn't wait for him to say anything. I just shook his hand and said that the last time I had seen him was in January 1965 at Churchill's funeral. I said I'd spent time in Rhodesia and knew it well, and we chatted a bit. Julian told me later that Smith had been very surprised because he thought I had horns and a tail. He'd been flattered that I had remembered him and that I knew about the country. I must say that seeing a traitor to the Crown and oppressor of Africans wandering round Parliament did give me pause for thought.

A group of students from St Brendan's Sixth Form College in Bristol came to visit the House of Commons, a really tough bunch. I notice now that there are Thatcherites in every audience. She has armed a lot of bright young people with powerful right-wing arguments, and, although I enjoy discussing them, I realise I am no longer dealing with the old consensus but with a new breed of right-wing concepts. It confirms me in my belief that there will be a hard inheritance which will never be forgotten, even when all Thatcher's legislation has been repealed.

Thursday 18 November

We went to Bristol for Lilian Rogers's burial. Herbert had asked me to say something in the little chapel of rest. Their son Irving and grandchildren and lots of family and old friends were there. The Reverend Peter Allen, who used to be a Labour councillor and is the retired rector of St Leonard's Church, took the service.

Home, and I heard the Shadow Cabinet results. I got 9 more votes than last year, making 75, but I was runner-up, missing by 7 votes. Now I can concentrate on trying to win the Election for Labour with as good a programme as we can get.

Friday 19 November

To Heathrow by Underground, and I got the shuttle to Glasgow for a rally in Dundee and to open the Dundee West Labour Club. I found myself sitting next to two shop stewards from the EETPU who had been on a course. They were both Frank Chapple supporters, and in their eyes I was the source of all the trouble in the Party, but after we'd talked for a while I felt the atmosphere melting. One of them, from Portobello, said he'd be writing to Chapple to tell him to reassess his attitude to me. Very funny!

There is a special warmth about Dundee, unparalleled anywhere else. Glasgow is very friendly, but Dundee is smaller and more compact, and the labour movement there is very strong. George Galloway, Secretary of the Dundee Party and the rising star of the Scottish labour movement, was there.

We went for a meal with the Lord Provost. I didn't eat the gammon steak – I should say that Caroline and I gave up eating meat about eighteen months ago – just the chips and peas and the pineapple ring.

On the platform were Ruth Seymour, a doctor whom I've met before, Charlie Bowman from ASLEF (who is the Labour candidate for Dundee East), Ernie Ross and myself.

There must have been about 800 people there – a good turnout for 6 o'clock on a Friday. After the rally, which was tremendously successful, we all went to George Galloway's house: he and Elaine have a lovely baby called Lucy, and later I opened the 'Tony Benn' lounge in the Labour Club!

Saturday 20 November
The English Collective of Prostitutes asked Caroline and me to go to their occupation of the Holy Cross Church near King's Cross. About forty women, of different nationalities and ages, some with babies, were occupying the church in protest against police harassment and racism. They told us their grievances, and I dictated a letter in their presence to the Home Secretary, to local MPs Frank Dobson and Jock Stallard and to the Metropolitan Police Commissioner. They gave us tea and were photographed with us.

Friday 26 November
To Bristol Royal Infirmary, where in Ward 61 Sue Beckingham, aged about thirty-five, lay dying of cancer. She is the mother of two children, and wife of Bryan, who is a fulltime organiser for the *Militant* newspaper.

Sue is a woman of extraordinary conviction and strength of character, and it is tragic that she has been overtaken by cancer. She has only a few days left, I think. There was no one with her when I arrived. I told her about the NEC, and talked about the last Conference, at which she had spoken so bravely, and she talked a little but her eyes were glazed. I think she was stuffed full of painkilling drugs.

Tuesday 7 December
A cold and misty day. Caroline and I went to Bristol for Sue Beckingham's funeral. After the service we went up to the Labour Club and talked to Sue's parents, who were Conservatives, and who blamed Bryan, in a way, for what happened to her – for the life of sacrifice and dedication which she had led. That was a bit rough.

Bryan's parents, old Labour sorts, were also there, and there was not a dry eye. Meg Crack spoke first about Sue's work in the constituency, then I spoke, then Peter Taaffe, editor of *Militant*.

Caroline, who is shrewd on these matter, made the point that as socialists of whatever kind we need rituals and ceremonies to use on occasions like births, deaths and marriages, and we should use the many beautiful words available to us in socialist literature to encourage and comfort people.

To an ILEA party in the evening at County Hall arranged by Frances Morrell and Bryn Davies. There was a sense that County Hall was the bastion of liberty and socialism across the river from the Commons.

Thursday 9 December

I was sitting in the Tea Room when John Biffen, Leader of the House, approached me; though a monetarist, he is a straightforward man. I asked him about the speakership; he said it would have to be filled before the end of Parliament, and no one really believed that the House would reassemble in October 1983 – which was an indication of a June Election.

I was called tonight in the debate on Ireland. I made the case for withdrawal of Britain. I did it quietly, without attacking anyone, and said the policy had failed and the only solution was to withdraw. Prior interrupted to say it was nonsense, and someone else shouted. Afterwards, while I was correcting my Hansard, Ian Paisley [Democratic Unionist MP for Antrim South] said in his strong Northern Irish accent, 'Tony, you ought to come to Belfast and talk to all the people at an open meeting.' I said I'd like to, but not of course under his auspices!

Sunday 12 December

The Greenham Common women invited a huge crowd to turn up to 'embrace' the base today. Men were allowed, although it was primarily for women, and Caroline and I arrived at 9 am. A little group of about seven women were living in a tent in the mud; they asked if we had any tea with us because they couldn't get their fire going. I emptied my thermos into their mugs and gave them two Mars Bars and a coke. They were living under appalling conditions, and it was pelting with rain. We talked to Rebecca Johnson, who told us about her experiences in prison. She was put in a cell with three other women, who had been brought in for shoplifting or prostitution or other offences, and she listened to them and asked them about their experiences of lawyers, judges and police. She taught them some peace songs and they would all sing together. On one day she refused to work and was put in a punishment cell: she was hauled before the assistant governor, who said she was just a convicted person like all the others, he wasn't interested in why she was there, and it had nothing to do with politics. She tried to tell him about the peace campaign.

Later I watched a news bulletin, and there were between 20,000 and 30,000 women there; it was tremendously moving to see those women surrounding the whole of this huge air base, arm in arm, with pictures hanging on the wire fence – everyone had been invited to bring a picture of a child, friend or loved one to hang on the fence.

Monday 20 December
George Galloway rang. When I was in Dundee last month I mentioned to him the problems in Bristol, and how I might find myself without a seat. George was ringing to suggest I try the brand-new constituency of Livingston, being created between Tam Dalyell's and Alex Eadie's seats in central Scotland. Alex will fight in his truncated constituency, which is winnable, and Tam will do the same, so this new constituency has no other MP with a claim to it.

I thanked him and said I'd talk to Tam. The sooner the invitation comes from one of the wards in the new Livingston constituency the better, and if I were adopted there before the selection conferences in Bristol I would be able to say that, since I didn't want to cause any bitterness in Bristol, and since my seat had gone, the proper thing for me to do would be to move to another seat.

To the Commons and saw Tam, and talked about it. Tam said, 'Of course the Scottish constituency would expect you to have a *pied-à-terre* in Scotland and be there a great deal.' I said I appreciated that, and it was agonising to leave Bristol, but it certainly was a possibility.

He thought about it in a very 'Tammish' way, and said he could see no difficulty in it. Robin Cook, whose Edinburgh Central constituency will be unsafe after boundary changes had no special claim, and Alex would be friendly.

Tuesday 21 December
To the House for a post-mortem on the Falklands War.

John Silkin made a speech which illustrated how terribly weak the Labour Party position is, having supported the Task Force. John Nott made a farewell speech as Minister of Defence. It was interesting, but it had nothing whatever to do with the Falklands. It was about trying to refocus our minds on to fighting the Russians, and he spoke as if that war had already begun.

The anti-Falklands campaign was well represented by Judith Hart, Michael Meacher, myself and Tam Dalyell. Tam made a devastating courtroom indictment, in effect saying that peace had been possible on the night of 2 May, when Galtieri had agreed to withdraw his troops, and this was conveyed to the Americans via their intelligence and back to London. It was because Mrs Thatcher ordered the sinking of the *Belgrano* with such a massive loss of life that the war continued. He delivered it at high speed, but it will read well in Hansard and will get a lot of attention. If this is true – and on the face of it it looks like it – the

Government itself torpedoed the prospect of a peaceful settlement by attacking the *Belgrano*.

Until we destroy the Falklands factor we are going to find it difficult to win the Election.

Wednesday 22 December
I decided that I would bring up in the Commons this afternoon the role of the Secretary of State for Trade, Lord Cockfield, in his handling of the Charter Consolidated takeover of Anderson Strathclyde. Yesterday the Prime Minister had announced that because Lord Cockfield had 5000 shares in Charter Consolidated he had asked his Minister of State, Peter Rees, to make the decision on the Monopolies Commission recommendation against the takeover of Anderson Strathclyde.

After the announcement, I looked at the 'Procedure for Ministers' issued by Callaghan in 1976. It made it absolutely clear that on assuming office, if there is any danger of a conflict of interest, a Minister should divest himself of any controlling shareholding; and in exceptional circumstances where he has a minority shareholding and it touches upon the business that concerns him as a Minister, he should divest himself of the shareholding.

So the Prime Minister had defended Lord Cockfield's transfer of responsibility to another Minister while the rules of procedure show that he should have divested himself of the shareholding.

I have for a long time wanted to get this 'Procedure for Ministers' published – it is marked 'Confidential' and I can't hand it to the press without breaching the Official Secrets Act. So I decided that this was a good opportunity to get it tabled in the Commons. I rang up the Clerk of the House, Sir Charles Gordon, and asked to table the document.

'Only a Minister can table a document,' he said.

So I suggested I would deposit it in the Members' Library.

'You'd better speak to the Librarian.'

I then spoke to Dr David Menhennet, the House of Commons Librarian, and he said the Speaker had ruled that only Ministers could deposit documents in the Library. So a document that was highly relevant to a current controversy was being prevented from perusal because the Speaker wouldn't permit it.

I spoke to the Clerk of the House three times, but he was extremely unhelpful. It reminded me very much of the peerage case (1960–3) when I used to go and see the Clerks. They play with their toy soldiers, but any suggestion that there might be a real war frightens the life out of them. It brought back to me how totally undemocratic the Commons is, how the pretence that the Speaker represents the legislature against the executive is a fraud. I gave notice to the Speaker that I would raise it and I rang Number 10, the Department of Trade and John Biffen, since he is Lord President of the Council.

I went into the Chamber armed with advice, and, when Peter Rees got up to make the statement, I asked why the rule in the 'Procedure for Ministers' had been disregarded. He was very abusive. Afterwards I raised a point of order and the Speaker wouldn't hear it. I came back two or three times and asked, 'The Prime Minister cited part of the document in March 1980 – why can't the whole document be published?'

'That was two and a half years ago.'

'Well, why can't we put it in the Library?'

'That has been the rule for a long time.'

So I was defeated, at the top. But the press began to take an interest, and I briefed individuals in the lobby.

Friday 31 December

This year began, as far as the Labour Party was concerned, with the Bishop's Stortford Conference and the truce around the existing leadership and policy, with no contest for the leadership or deputy leadership, no variation from Conference policy and no witch-hunts.

But the NEC has swung sharply to the right this year, and many good colleagues including Doug Hoyle, Joan Maynard, Les Huckfield and Eric Clarke were defeated. Then there was a complete sweep of all the existing chairmen of the NEC committees and their replacement by John Golding, Russell Tuck and Alan Hadden, the only one not challenged being Alex Kitson.

On the left, my attempt to set up Labour Liaison '82 ran into the sands because the ultra-left groups tended to dominate, which annoyed the Broad Left, and so that died a death in the spring. But we did have the great success of Chris Mullin getting the editorship of *Tribune*.

The other achievement was the foundation of the Socialist Society, with which Caroline is more deeply involved than I am. This provides a forum within which the Communist Party and various left groups can get together, produce pamphlets, hold conferences, and so on – a welcome development.

The peace movement grew in strength, with successful CND demos, the Brussels Convention of END and, of course, the women's campaign at Greenham Common. The focus of activity has moved from male trade-unionists fighting over wages and jobs to women fighting for peace.

Saturday 8 January 1983

Stansgate. Caroline and I went on a long drive south of the River Crouch and visited Canewdon, where there is an old Norman church. It was at Canewdon that King Canute, the Dane, fought a battle with Edmund Ironside, King of the Saxons.

The vicar of the church, the Reverend Kelly, appeared, and he handed us a couple of his parish newsletters. I must record what was in the November message, because it was so unbelievable. He described how teenagers on TV say, 'Here comes the law', when they see a police officer. Then he goes on to say, 'No. The monarch, the Queen, is the law and no one else. Why cannot the Queen do wrong and be prosecuted like us? Because the monarch is the source of law, just as God cannot sin because God is the source of goodness. You did not know? You have missed church for a long time. You cannot expect it all in a Parish Letter, can you?'

Monday 10 January

We had before us at the Organisation Committee the report of Peter Tatchell's successful reselection for Bermondsey.

Michael Foot said he hoped we would endorse him, and that he had written to him and intended to support him; the only reason he had opposed him a year ago was because it would have been a difficult time to have had a by-election.

Golding was alone today in opposing the endorsement. To see John Golding in a minority of one was a straw in the wind that may be the end of that sort of right domination.

Monday 17 January

George Galloway rang to say that of the thirty members of the GMC of the new Livingston constituency Labour Party a minimum of twenty would support me, and ten might go for Robin Cook. I decided to type out a statement for Bristol South East so that they would know what was going on.

Went into the House to find that a group of peace women had tried to demonstrate in the Strangers' Gallery but the police had pulled them down the stairs and into Westminster Hall. There the women had lit candles and sung peace songs, surrounded by police. Some of them had been released but others were kept. We have to be absolutely clear that we support them.

Tuesday 18 January

The Franks Report on the Falklands War was released today, and our two Members on the Franks Commission, former Ministers Harold Lever and Merlyn Rees, believe it or not, had signed a unanimous report saying that the Government could not be faulted on any of the decisions they had taken, nor could they be held responsible for the invasion. They have given the Government a clean bill of health and have removed the last opportunity for the official Opposition to criticise Mrs Thatcher. Merlyn Rees and Harold Lever have put the Party in an impossible position.

The Prime Minister was very tense at Questions, and for the first time I felt that she was losing her cool. She was totally put off by a point of privilege raised by Tam Dalyell about the leaking of a report by Bernard Ingham, the PM's press officer. She looked very worried about that. Later she got agitated about her own position. This is a test of her reputation, and this obsession has become evident in recent months.

Wednesday 19 January

We had a very good meeting of the Campaign Group, the first I have attended for some time.

We agreed to sign a letter nominating the women of Greenham Common for the Nobel Peace Prize, and that was signed by almost everybody in the PLP in the hours that followed.

We agreed that we should have a manifesto and a candidate for the speakership and press our candidate really hard. We are going to raise everything from points like 'Why is the Strangers' Gallery so called and not the Electors' Gallery?' to measures which will benefit Members themselves, such as a time limit on speeches, no privileges for Privy Councillors in speaking in the Chamber, and so on. We are also going to ask questions about, for example, the role of the Speaker in taking over the residual prerogatives of the Crown (ie the power to ask somebody to form a Government and the power to advise on the dissolution of Parliament). Although we will be soundly beaten, we will be defending the legislature's independence from Government control.

Thursday 20 January

At the PLP meeting, Tam began with a prepared speech, the gist of which was that the Prime Minister had lied to the House because she had known the invasion of the Falklands was coming and did have time to prevent it. He went on for so long that the Chairman Jack Dormand said, 'Look, Tam, we all appreciate the work you have done, but do you really want to say it all now rather than in front of the House during the debate?' So Tam curtailed it.

Michael Foot said, 'We are going to have an official Opposition motion on the Franks Report. Its conclusions are not justified by the facts. The Government did not hold a Defence and Overseas Policy Committee for eighteen months, Cabinet Government had collapsed, and they got it wrong.'

Having supported Mrs Thatcher in the decision to send the Task Force, having welcomed the victory, having attended the victory parade and having appointed Merlyn Rees to the commission, Michael Foot now declaring that the real lesson was that Cabinet Government had collapsed was incredible.

Michael turned to me. 'As far as Tony is concerned, the last Labour Government dealt with it properly. The NEC took a strong line on the rights of the Falkland Islanders and we couldn't deal with fascist dictators.'

Jim Callaghan said there was a devastating case to be made against the Government, but added, 'I appeal to Tam not to pursue the case that Mrs Thatcher knew about the impending invasion and lied to the House, because there is no proof of that, while there *are* things in the report which we can take up. It was a slipshod Government, we drifted into war, and Tam will get the headlines but will it help us politically? There is a jingoistic spirit now, in contrast to 1947, when we rationed food in order to send grain ships to India.

After that, we had a report by Jack Dormand saying that on two consecutive weeks the Shadow Cabinet had decided not to support the new People's March for Jobs. So Dennis Skinner asked why?

Michael got up and said, 'Well, in 1981 there was a lot of trouble, it's expensive, it would divert us from campaigning, it might be taken over by other people, and I am strongly of the opinion that we shouldn't support it.'

'Well, I hope Michael will think again,' I said. 'In 1981 it was a great success, and indeed I was present when Michael greeted the people at the end of their march. It was supported by the churches, it gave people hope, and I hope we are not going to be told that on principle members of the Shadow Cabinet would decline to have anything to do with it.'

So Michael got up again and said it had caused trouble in 1981, that there had to be a collective decision about it, and so on.

The reality is that the leadership of the Labour Party do not trust themselves at mass meetings.

Wednesday 26 January

At 5 we had the Campaign Group.

My paper on the speakership was discussed. It proposed that the Speaker should end established practices and introduce sweeping new measures for running the House.

Dennis Skinner said he was doubtful whether individual Speakers could improve the situation at all. A change in the environment in Parliament was needed, and, if we did contest the speakership, a low-key approach would be the best; but we would need support from the centre of the Party to make any changes.

Reg Race commented, 'I understand what Dennis is saying, but the speakership election is a vehicle for discussing and explaining the defects of this place. Parts of the PLP are not on our side because they want Parliament to be kept under the control of the Front Bench.'

Ernie Ross thought it was a tactical matter; there was a danger of people saying that 'The loonies are playing silly buggers again.' He added, 'We should therefore try to get wider support.'

Bob Litherland observed, 'In Manchester we tried to reform the office of lord mayor, and there was a hell of a row because people thought what we were doing was irrelevant.'

Jo Richardson said she had misgivings, that timing was critical and we should take the issue separately.

I was disappointed they didn't like my paper, but I agreed with them really, because it was written from a parliamentary rather than a socialist and democratic point of view. I shall rewrite it completely as a result of what was said.

Sunday 30 January

Ken Coates rang, having come back from Berlin, where END is organising a Convention on Peace from 9 to 15 May. He told me that END had approached the new General Secretary, Yuri Andropov, in Moscow and asked that Arbatov, the great Soviet expert on disarmament, should be allowed to go to it. Yuri Zhukov, chairman of the official Soviet Peace Committee, had been writing to the trade unions and all the Young Communist groups around the world, trying to discourage people from attending the convention, but had failed. Ken thought it was going to be a success. I said we ought to go more explicitly for a non-aligned position, a non-aligned Europe, free from the Russians and Americans but without being either anti-Russian or anti-American. He hopes I'll have a chance of speaking at one of the meetings – which I would like to do. Ken is such a creative guy, imaginative, liberal, decent, absolutely straightforward, and one of my closest political friends.

Admiral Sir Terence Lewin, who has just retired as Chief of Defence Staff, stated in an interview that David Owen had been wrong when he said that in 1977 orders of engagement had been issued to the fleet, giving them authority to sink Argentinian ships within fifty miles of the Falkland Islands shoreline. I dug out my diary for 21 November when the Defence and Overseas Policy Committee met. There was no evidence that rules of engagement had been discussed or issued, confirming what Lewin, then First Sea Lord, says. So David Owen's great claim that he sent an armada with instructions to open fire is intended to give the impression that he handled the affair better than Mrs Thatcher.

Tuesday 1 February

To the *Guardian* office by invitation to attend and address their staff conference. There were a lot of familiar faces there – Polly Toynbee, John Torode, David McKie, Peter Preston (the editor), Terry Coleman and others.

I began by making a short statement and then I was pursued for about an hour on a whole range of issues: what I meant by fascism, whether Mrs Thatcher was cruel, what might happen to the SDP. The

Guardian is really an SDP newspaper. We had some discussion about Labour policy – whether we could win, whether there was a parallel today with 1945. I was challenged on whether Michael Heseltine wasn't saying the same as I was about revitalising capitalism and so on. It was a bit like trying to sculpture a blancmange but I'm glad I went.

Afterwards I had lunch with the six principal people – Peter Preston, Ian Aitken, Julia Langdon, Michael White, Peter Jenkins and David McKie. They questioned me on a number of things and tried to separate me from Michael Foot and Peter Shore, but I said, 'You're not going to drive a wedge between me and my Front Bench colleagues, because we want to win.'

Then I was asked to defend the Party's constitutional changes, and Michael White gave his view that they had nothing whatever to do with policy-making. I disagreed and said, 'They are there to buttress policy.'

'Yes,' he said, 'but the policy changes went through on the nod and there was no argument about them.'

I pointed out, 'In fact, the right no longer fight policy changes, they hope to bypass them. It's what Ken Livingstone calls the blancmange principle – that you concede on policy but just don't do anything about it.'

Michael White had asked whether it would be practicable to take on the Common Market and the Americans at one and the same time. I said, 'In my opinion, it would be easy to put the Americans on notice to leave British bases and then give them plenty of time to leave. As far as the Common Market is concerned, I would be quite happy to see a status quo agreement, provided we re-negotiated the treaty and restored the powers of self-government, which is all I ever cared about.' It was a successful defence of a well-thought-out position.

Terry Coleman asked me after the lunch, 'What do you mean, Mrs Thatcher is cruel?'

I said, 'Well, she attacks weak people.' The *Guardian* staff are mesmerised by Thatcher but at the same time would like to preserve a reputation for liberalism.

Down to the Fox Hotel, Bristol, for the Windmill Hill ward meeting, which was excellent. I reported briefly, gave a short speech and was asked lots of questions on the media, on whether a Labour Government would really ban nuclear weapons, on the NEC and Militant, on the possibility that we might be toppled by the Americans and the Common Market.

Wednesday 2 February

To the Campaign Group at 5 with Bob Cryer, Martin Flannery, Joan Maynard, Jo Richardson, Willy McKelvey, Reg Race, Ernie Roberts and Ernie Ross and also Mandy Moore, Janet Pickering and Ann Pettifor. I think in thirty-two years in Parliament it was the first time I had actually heard women members of the Labour Party coming and telling Labour MPs what they wanted by way of positive discrimination.

Mandy Moore presented the basic case: that women were intellectually equal, were physically tough, were wrongly stereotyped and were entitled to equality, and socialism did not automatically solve the problem. Experience in Russia had proved that, she argued. The Labour Party had been a party of discrimination in favour of working-class people but had been weak in advancing women's rights.

Ann Pettifor said, 'Women are excluded from power by men. There are fewer women MPs than there were in 1945. Women are trying to displace men – that is why there is resistance. They are kept out by the structures of the Party, they are frustrated by men at the Labour Conference. The annual Women's Conference needs to choose its own standing orders, to elect its own executive, elect the women's section at the Annual Conference and to have a woman on every shortlist. There will be great resistance, and we know John Golding is mobilising against it. The Women's Committee of the NEC has been taken over by a right-wing bloc, and this is a serious problem.'

Dennis Skinner suggested, 'Well, I think we should try and get articles in the trade union papers. The miners have got a new paper. Organise for a new NEC.'

Martin Flannery argued, 'This is a class matter; it is not a matter separating men from women, which is divisive. I fear you are giving a wrong lead. As a Marxist, I believe in a class change, and believe that you cannot jump the gun.'

Thursday 3 February
Sent off copies of the first draft of my lecture 'The Case for the Disestablishment of the Church of England' to the Archbishop of Canterbury, Cardinal Hume, the Chief Rabbi, the Reverend Donald Reeves, Gerald Priestland at the BBC and others. I hope to get quite a bit of comment on it before I deliver it at St James's, Piccadilly, on 2 March.

Sunday 6 February
Up early and read the papers. The *Sunday Times* had a big exposé of the preparations for siting Cruise missiles, claiming that Jim Callaghan, David Owen, Denis Healey, Fred Mulley and possibly Michael Foot had known all about it before the 1979 Election.

To the Socialist Society at William Collins School behind Euston. Robin Blackburn was obviously very disappointed that the second meeting attracted only about 200 people compared to 700 last year. Pessimism has spread to the ultra-left who joined the Socialist Society a year ago and now find that the more mellow attitude of the left towards each other has not mellowed the establishment's attitude towards them, socialism, the left of the Labour Party or indeed anybody. There are extraordinary rumours going round that the Eurocommunist wing of the British Communist Party is now talking quite openly of an alliance with the SDP to keep Mrs Thatcher out. This is Eric Hobsbawm and others, and, if the Italian Communists can talk about the 'historic compromise', there is no reason why the British Communists can't, and it looks as if that's what they're about.

Wednesday 9 February

Jo Richardson brought five or six women from Greenham Common along to the Campaign Group. A woman of about thirty described the bad press coverage they had had when Heseltine visited the site and was allegedly brought to the ground by the women, but she said there had in fact been no violence and that the police, who were not local police, had walked over the women.

They told us about forthcoming court cases. On 22 February there is a High Court case at which they are being charged with much more serious offences. We considered how we could help.

Friday 11 February

To Bristol South East Party headquarters. Caroline had already arrived. This morning we heard the news that the Labour Party's legal case – in the persons of Foot, Hughes, Michael Cocks and Jim Mortimer – against some of the Boundary Commission's recommendations had failed, so we realised that the meeting tonight, which was to have been the AGM, might in fact be the very last meeting of the Bristol South East Labour Party, and it was rather moving. We went through the normal business and the annual report of the work of the Party, and I spoke a little about the local Party's history. I recorded the evening's proceedings.

After the meeting we had a drink and stood while Meg held up her glass and said, 'To socialism and to the traditions of the Bristol South East Labour Party', and everybody raised their glasses.

It was a nostalgic evening because I have been the Member there for thirty-three years this year, a third of a century, and to find the constituency going, with all the uncertainties, is very moving.

Sunday 13 February

I read a book sent to me by David Downing called *Russian Revolution 1985*, an extremely readable novel about an attempt to reform and liberalise the Soviet system which gets out of control. There are food riots in Russia, then a period of repression following which the army plan a coup, but Andropov and the KGB arrest the guilty generals. Then there is a revolution calling together representatives of workers from all over Russia, with demands for democratic reforms which are eventually conceded by the Central Committee of the Communist Party. A world banking collapse brings the west to ruin, leaving Russia pretty well free from the risk of attack and able to liberalise and develop its own form of democratic socalism. It is a very good novel.

There was an item in the *Observer* today saying that the Queen Mother made it a habit at her dinner parties to propose an anti-loyal toast and on one occasion recently had toasted 'Tony Benn, Idi Amin and President Jimmy Carter'. Caroline suggested I should write to ask her if it was true.

Tuesday 15 February

I had four letters back about my forthcoming disestablishment lecture. I had one from the House of Commons with a translation from Norman French into English of the petition of 1376 against payment of taxes to the Pope and a copy of the Blasphemy Act of 1697 under which, up until 1967, it was a criminal offence to attack the Trinity in public.

I had a letter from Lord MacLeod, former Moderator of the Church of Scotland; a letter from the Bishop of Malmesbury, who is deputising for the Bishop of Bristol, saying he thought I had over-emphasised the influence of the establishment upon episcopal appointments because his 'Uncle William often criticised the Conservatives and was made Archbishop of York and then Archbishop of Canterbury'. Out of curiosity I rang Freddie Malmesbury, and it turned out that his uncle was Archbishop Temple, so we had quite an interesting talk.

The Chief Rabbi replied, saying he didn't want to commit himself but would be happy to talk to me, so I spoke to him on the phone for about half an hour. A most interesting chat.

We were talking about the Jewish Community in Britain, and he told me that the readmission of the Jews into England had been effected by a rabbi from Amsterdam, who had gone to London to put the case to Cromwell. His argument had been theological – that it was prophesied that the redemption could not come until the Jews were dispersed to the ends of the earth, and that while the Jews were not allowed into England they couldn't be said to be dispersed to the ends of the earth. Therefore, would Cromwell please admit them, to bring the redemption nearer? It was that theological argument that had convinced Cromwell.

He went on, 'Britain is deeply rooted in tradition, and anything which undermined the cohesion and fabric of our society would be unfortunate, in the same way that the monarchy is a major cohesive factor in our society, and anything that changed it could be destabilising.'

I reminded him that that argument had been used against all reforms throughout history.

Tuesday 22 February

I am very, very depressed. This sense of overpowering tragedy in respect of Britain and the Labour Party has got me by the neck at the moment. Here is the Government doing awful things unchallenged, the media engaging in campaigns so disreputable that they defy description, good left-wingers being frightened, the Party turning on Militant and the left turning on itself. There will be no recovery by that route. I feel the pressure on me now and a sense of isolation, from which Caroline thinks I have protected myself by self-deception and optimism. I really feel gloomy and uncertain about the future. So I'll end my diary in that spirit of deep political and personal gloom.

Wednesday 23 February

Today the NEC expelled five members of the Party who were on the editorial board of *Militant*. There was a *Militant* picket outside Walworth Road, and it was sickening to see the Bermondsey Party banner there to protest against the leadership of the Party while there is a by-election going on.

An item referred from the Publicity Committee concerned the centenary of Karl Marx's death. Eric Heffer suggested perhaps Michael Foot would give a lecture.

John Golding said this was the Labour Party of the past, and we would not help ourselves by referring back to an eminent German academic who had a relationship with a Manchester industrialist.

Michael Foot suggested we leave it. 'Although we recognise the towering greatness of Karl Marx, it would not be meaningful if we republished our 1948 pamphlet. Marx had doubts whether he himself was a Marxist.' Neil Kinnock agreed.

The motion to make more of the celebration of Marx's death was defeated by 16 votes to 10.

I moved a motion that we unanimously support Peter Tatchell in Bermondsey, and this was agreed.

At 12.53 the Militant question came up. Before the editorial board of *Militant* arrived, Jim Mortimer explained that the only questions to the five that would be in order would be those that related to whether or not they were in fact members of the Militant Tendency.

I then asked why a memorandum I had submitted had not been circulated. Sam McCluskie, in the chair, said, 'I never saw the memorandum. I was simply told on the phone by Jim Mortimer that you had submitted a list of questions.'

I reminded him, 'Jim Mortimer told me you were in the room when the paper arrived and you said it wasn't to be circulated.'

John Golding moved that the General Secretary should open the questioning and that the supplementary questions be put at the discretion of the chair.

Denis Howell said, 'It is monstrous to put questions.'

Audrey Wise added, 'This is a farce. My emotional instinct is that I should walk out.'

'Militant is an organisation and therefore *Militant* must cease publication,' said Michael Foot.

After more heated discussion, the editorial board members came in. Jim Mortimer told them, 'I will address Peter Taaffe, but I am speaking to you collectively, and I want to put a question. Are you members of the editorial board of *Militant?*'

Peter Taaffe replied, 'Yes, we are members of the editorial board. We are responsible for the publication of *Militant*. We do not accept that we are members of the Militant Tendency.'

Then the second question was put: 'Are you to be regarded as members of the Militant Tendency?'

Taaffe said, 'No.'

'Will you give an undertaking that you will not now or in the future support the Militant Tendency?'

Taaffe said, 'We do not accept your assessment.'

Mortimer went on, 'As to the Militant Tendency organisation, you must have an opportunity to give an undertaking that you will not support financially or organisationally the activities of the Militant Tendency.'

Peter Taaffe replied, 'It is an alleged Militant Tendency. *Militant* is a newspaper, and the newspaper is not the Militant Tendency organisation. I want to protest on behalf of the Labour Party at the timing of this inquisition. I had suggested postponement because of the Bermondsey by-election, and it will all be grist to the mill of the Labour candidate's opponents there if the NEC chooses to expel us today. As to our record, we are not trying to get parliamentary careers, we are not careerists; we wish to serve loyally ideas on which we have been working for a long time, I myself since 1964. These ideas have made an impression on the rank and file. We have been refused sight of the evidence against us. The evidence is malicious gossip given by full-time officials, some of it tape-recorded. One piece of evidence was from a man in the south-west who was mentally unstable, and he was offered a council house in return for giving evidence. This stinks of Stalinism. This is not Moscow in 1936 or 1937, this is Merseyside in the eighties.

'There are fifty-two organisations opposed to expulsion. If you want to use organisational measures against ideas, you will fail. I agree with Michael Foot that we cannot allow the Tory press to pick the membership of the Labour Party. The NEC has no constitutional power. You think we are shaping young people, but, if you think our ideas are wrong, fight for your ideas and fight our ideas with better ideas.

'The last point is this. We are not intimidated by expulsions. We are going to work in the trade union movement, in the class from which we come. We are trying to win an Election, and we are enthusing young people who are disillusioned, demoralised and disheartened, and you are putting the Labour victory at risk.'

Lynn Walsh spoke next. 'I wish to protest. I have been a member of the Party for nineteen years. I have done my fair share of work. I have had no career in the Party. My aim is to advance the Party. There is no justification for what the NEC is doing; there is no evidence that we have broken any rule. This is a show trial, and all this legal argument is meaningless. This proceeding is fraudulent, because the Conference voted against bans and proscriptions. We applied for inclusion in the Register after the Conference, and our application to register has never been considered by the NEC. This is a revival of proscriptions, it is bureaucratic, it is repressive, and it is against the trend of opinion. It is a witch-hunt. Our crime is our success, because we have clear, coherent ideas and support. You are using your temporary majority on the NEC, but it won't last for long.'

Clare Doyle said she had been in the Party for nineteen years, she had been an officer in her local Party, organising the YS, and was a delegate on the GMC. What was happening was doing untold damage to the movement, and people would leave the Party in disgust. 'For the last two months I have been recruiting members and building up trade union membership. Do the NEC want an election victory or not? On our finances, there are no mysterious sources. We raised £150,000 for the fighting fund last year. Before the by-election, my ward said they would not accept a ban. We are just members of *Militant*'s editorial board and you are asking us to wind up that newspaper.'

Keith Dickinson said the NEC was ignorant of the movement. He asked, 'Where do you get the idea that the rank and file want to expel us? The *Militant* editorial board is only part-time. I myself am a caretaker of some Labour Party rooms where I do the sweeping and the mopping. Where is the support for the National Executive action amongst the rank and file? The press is *your* constituency.'

Last came Ted Grant, who said he had listened with amazement, and what he had heard was a lawyer's trick and had nothing to do with natural justice. 'The real issues are the problems facing the working class. In one, two or three years, things will change. We are in the eighties, and there is a real crisis of capitalism. We have had seventeen years of Labour Governments, and now the answer to criticism is to expel people. It is not the end; it is the beginning. You can't win elections just by using a television. You can't raise enthusiasm by a witch-hunt. Thatcher, Tebbit, Heseltine and the SDP want this row, but the rank and file are on our side, and we will be back when the right wing have joined the SDP and the Tories.'

I must say they were very impressive. At 3 we had questions.

Eric Varley said, '*Militant* have a distinct policy which is not always in line with Party policy. You say you have no organisation. Don't you have readers' meetings? Aren't they organised systematically?'

Peter Taaffe answered Eric's question. 'We deny that we disagree with Party policy. We favour the thirty-five-hour week, an increase in public expenditure, the implementation of Clause 4. We support the Party, in contrast to some parliamentary spokesmen who are anti-unilateralist and in favour of incomes policy, and it is hypocrisy to suggest we are different. We have readers' meetings where everyone can put their view, and we don't fear discussion. If the NEC had abided by the constitution, we would not have contemplated legal action, but the majority of the NEC have lost the battle for the hearts and minds of the Party. We will fight politically at Conference. Nye Bevan was prepared to use the Committee of Privileges, which was the highest court – which was one reason that no further action was taken. We have the right to go to the courts; after all, the trade unions go to the courts. This is the cynical use of *Militant* as a scapegoat and it won't succeed. We shall fight it every inch of the way.'

Eric Heffer moved a motion, 'That before this NEC proceeds to any vote on expulsion, it calls on the members of *Militant* editorial board to meet with the NEC or their representatives to discuss what steps can be taken to allow *Militant* to register in accordance with the decisions of the last Party Conference.' Jo seconded.

In response, John Golding moved that the members of the *Militant* editorial board (whose names he gave) be excluded from membership of the Labour Party forthwith. We had already previously decided that they would have a right to appeal to Conference.

Neville Hough of the GMWU seconded Golding's motion.

I said, 'I looked up my notes for the meeting of 12 March 1955 when Nye Bevan was expelled from the PLP, and exactly the same arguments were used then as now, including the fact that it was a vote of confidence in Clem Attlee as Leader. It can only damage the Party, because the evidence is secret. We have reversed the 1973 decision not to have bans and proscriptions. If you proceed and get rid of candidates who support *Militant*, you'll have eight Bermondseys before the election. If anyone thinks this is the way to win popularity with the Tory press, they don't really understand what is going on, because the Tory press will just demand more. If you are prepared to drop *people* in order to be popular, what about policies?'

Dennis Skinner reiterated what I had said, and added, 'As to the evidence of the polls, we're down again despite all this. You can never appease the enemy.'

Tom Sawyer said, 'I wonder if we can persuade our trade union colleagues to vote for Eric's motion. The trade unions have not complained, and we cannot prove it. Where is the evidence? The only safe thing to do is to vote for Eric Heffer.' Tom Sawyer from NUPE is a first-rate member of the Executive.

Judith Hart spoke against going back to expulsions and then Alex Kitson announced, 'I'm not having it. I'm not going to be kidded. They *are* a party within a party. They deny there is an organisation, but one of them is a member of my family and I *know* there is an organisation. If they have got money, let them give it to us.' In response to Tom Sawyer, he added, 'I am going to do what I think is right. I don't represent the Transport and General Workers' Union here, I represent the whole trade union movement.'

Neil Kinnock was against them. '*Militant* is not, as they tell us, only a newspaper. They have endorsed all the reasons for the expulsion. *Militant* never prints letters critical of itself, and somebody is organising something. Either Taaffe is not telling the truth or he is telling a lie, and this, of course, is a Trotskyite policy.'

We had the vote, and Eric's motion (on a recorded vote) was defeated by 19 to 9. Golding's was carried by 19 to 9.

Then Jo moved that, following the expulsions, no member of the Party should be expelled simply on the grounds that they read the *Militant* newspaper. But Sam McCluskie said, 'We've had enough today – we can come back to that.'

There was a huge crowd waiting outside, and I felt ashamed, but I slipped by.

I gave Dennis Skinner a lift back to the House. He said, 'I believe that could well be the last NEC that Michael Foot attends as Leader. They'll go for him now, I'm sure they'll go for him now.'

Got to the Campaign Group at about 5.15.

We discussed the Party leadership, about which there is now a great deal of speculation, and Reg Race said, 'I think we should just opt out. If we have a right-wing leadership and we lose an Election, that proves what a failure it is.'

'We must support Michael Foot,' said Stuart Holland.

I agreed. 'I think we must support Foot.'

Reg Race asked, 'Why? We'll lose Bermondsey and the General Election.'

'I think we should criticise Foot privately,' I replied.

I went to see Jack Dormand in the Members' Lobby, and I said, 'Jack, I'm not in the gossip business, but I must tell you quite frankly that I support Michael Foot and so do an awful lot of other people, and I think it would be most inadvisable for him to be removed.'

Thursday 24 February

To Bristol, and stayed up to watch the end of the Bermondsey by-election, which was terrible. The 11,000 majority that Bob Mellish had received in the last Election was converted to a 10,000 majority for Simon Hughes, the Liberal candidate. Poor old Peter Tatchell, who had been massacred by the press, only got 7,600 votes, but he came out of it with considerable courage and dignity.

I resolved there and then in that hotel room not to desert Bristol and that, when I go to Scotland on Saturday for a meeting I will make a statement saying I couldn't accept nomination for Livingston.

Saturday 26 February
To Scotland. I was met at Edinburgh by Hugh Wyper, the Regional Secretary of the T&G in Scotland, an old friend of mine, and a long-time member of the Communist Party.

George Galloway was at the T&G offices and was very disappointed when I showed him my statement, but I explained the position. Then we went to Leith Town Hall for the quarterly meeting of TGWU shop stewards; Sam McCluskie was actually in the audience. I made a strong, tough speech, which Sam appreciated, and afterwards he said, 'It was bloody marvellous.'

So I felt I had re-established my link with Sam, who up to now has seen me as a bit of troublemaker over Militant. The old left are very anti-Militant. It is important to remember throughout this whole story that the ex-Communists and Communists hate Militant because it reopens the whole Trotsky/Stalin argument.

Then I was taken to the Grosvenor Hotel, Edinburgh, where the Livingston Party people had arrived in a bus. I must confess that I was a bit worried about meeting them and letting them down. They had been organising, and had found that at the most pessimistic estimate I would have 24 votes out of 50, probably more. I had a very candid talk with them, thanked them and explained the position.

They asked, 'Well, will you come to Livingston if you don't get Bristol?'

I said, 'Well, yes, but I can't say that publicly because it fudges what has to be a clear statement. I have got to make clear that I am not running away.'

One woman finally said, 'You know I wouldn't be supporting you, Tony, if that wasn't the position I knew you would take.'

They were very nice to me.

Gave a press conference, and I think if I had announced that I was going to accept a nomination I would have been hammered. The Livingston people were sitting at the back during the press conference, and they heard me say how proud I would be to be the Member for Livingston but how my duty was to Bristol.

Monday 28 February
I did two television interviews on my decision to stay in Bristol. I was

asked if I wasn't taking a terrible risk. I said, 'My duty is in Bristol. It doesn't matter what happens to me.'

Wednesday 2 March

I went to St James's, Piccadilly, with Caroline to give my lunchtime lecture on the disestablishment of the Church of England. Donald Reeves, the vicar, is in with the peace movement and so on. Mother turned up, which was very sweet of her, and there were about 400 people in the church. I delivered my case for disestablishment, which I had worked on and thought about for well over a year. It went down very well – good questions and discussion.

Thursday 3 March

Went to the Commons in the afternoon, and Gordon McLennan, the General Secretary of the Communist Party, came to see me. We sat alone. He asked if Eric Hobsbawm had spoken to me, as he had suggested he should. Gordon thought there should be more talks between the Communist Party and the Labour Party, that the 'Eurocommunist' position (though he didn't like the term) was pluralistic, and he believed everyone should choose their own road to socialism. He said that *Marxism Today* had done some interesting analytical work on Thatcherism, on the labour movement of the future, on the trade unions and on the SDP-Liberal Alliance which they took very seriously. He emphasised the importance of internationalism.

Gordon was pretty cold, actually. He said that the composition of the working class had altered, that the change in the make-up of the TUC General Council was a great threat, and that the CP now believe there should be a progressive alliance with autonomous developments under working-class leadership but not under a solely Labour Party umbrella. He thought Militant was a real danger, and disagreed with the view of one trade union leader that, 'without Tony Benn, Militant would never have been heard of'. On proportional representation, he believed it to be a basic democratic principle that must be upheld.

Sunday 6 March

At 8.45 I was taken to Lime Grove studios for a religious programme, *Sunday Night*, on the disestablishment of the Church of England. I found myself sitting next to Archbishop Hurley, who, I discovered, is the Roman Catholic Archbishop of Johannesburg, I think, but I didn't realise who he was at first.

He said he had heard me on the radio yesterday and couldn't think of a single argument against what I had said. The Bishop of Manchester had said to me that, to get over the problem of the privilege of the established church, all Christian denominations should be represented in the House of Lords, and I had answered, 'Does anyone really think that if the twelve apostles had been made theological advisers to Herod or Pontius Pilate it would have advanced the cause of Christianity?'

I asked him whether the Dutch Reformed Church was established in South Africa, and he said, 'No, it is really just a religious expression of Afrikaner tribal nationalism.'

Looking back on the disestablishment lecture, I think it has succeeded in its purpose in that it has planted the idea of disestablishment, seen from the parliamentary angle, into the minds of the church and the public. It has also highlighted the issue, so that when the next Archbishop of York is appointed by Mrs Thatcher people may be more sensitive to its political nature. Thirdly, it is a long-term perspective which will grow and bear fruit.

Monday 7 March
To the Commons, where I had a meal with Bob Edwards. I asked him about Trotsky, and he told a fascinating story about when he visited the Soviet Union in the 1920s.

'I was present at the Bolshoi Theatre in Moscow for a debate between Trotsky and Stalin. I was one of an ILP delegation, and we were put in the Tsar's old box. We had an interpreter. Trotsky was a tremendous orator: he spoke without a note, inspired the audience, and they would call, "Trotsky, Trotsky, Trotsky!" Stalin was a quieter man, who read his speeches. Trotsky carried the day in that particular debate. However, two days later, on May Day, Trotsky was womanising in his dacha outside Moscow and didn't turn up at the rally, and that did him an awful lot of damage. He was really rather lazy. A few months later, he was expelled from the Party.'

Bob went on, 'After Trotsky was expelled, he was deported to Turkey. The ILP subsequently arranged for him to stay in Mexico as the guest of one of their contacts there.' It was there that he was murdered in 1940.

In the mid-thirties, Bob said, a number of members of the Socialist International, with which the ILP was associated, went to Russia, and fourteen of them – Germans, Austrians and others – were arrested and disappeared in Russia. Bob went over to plead with the Russians, and he said that four of them were released but ten were never heard of again. He said it wasn't safe to go back to Russia until after Stalin died.

But he went back in 1960, and an old man came up to him in Tiflis and said, 'You don't remember me, do you?' He was one of the people arrested by the Russians. He spent twenty years in Siberia, and when Khrushchev came to power he was released, stayed and married a Russian. Bob went to another city, where an Austrian told him the same. Bob was convinced that the Russian Embassy had arranged for these people to make contact with him while he was there.

I asked him about Trotsky and Stalin. He maintained that the argument wasn't only over the necessity for a world revolution. Stalin believed that the only way to safeguard the Russian revolution was to build heavy industry at tremendous cost and to be able to defend the country. Trotsky believed that a European revolution, particularly in Britain and Germany, would safeguard the Russian revolution. But he also believed that the Russian people should be allowed access to more consumer goods, and this would have been at the cost of building up heavy industry. 'Actually,' said Bob, 'Stalin was right in the event and not Trotsky.' I must persuade somebody to interview Bob Edwards before it's too late.

Friday 18 March
To Bristol, where the main news was that Mike Cocks had organised the wards so completely in the new Bristol South constituency that he would have a majority of thirteen or fourteen over me in the Bristol South selection conference. So should I go for Bristol South? Or stay with Bristol East? The Livingston people keep ringing to persuade me to accept a nomination.

Sunday 27 March
Michael Meacher had a gathering at his house, and we analysed what has happened to the left. We identified four different lefts now. First there is the fragmented left, that is to say the CLPD consisting of the Bennite and anti-Bennite left, the feminist left and Socialists for a Labour Victory (which has just been founded by Ken Livingstone, Ted Knight, John Bloxam and Reg Race). The second group comprises old Tribunites, who are now indistinguishable from the right wing – Eric Varley and Neil Kinnock are really indistinguishable. Next there are the old popular-front people who believe broadly in an anti-Thatcher alliance – Gordon McLennan, Eric Hobsbawm and Edward Thompson – and are in a sense trying to outflank and defeat the Labour left. Finally there's the left in the trade union movement which is much more serious and down to earth and includes some members of the Communist Party and some Militant people working at the union level and making something of an impact.

After some discussion about this, with Michael Meacher wringing his hands, we came to the conclusion that we should stay clear of deep involvement in this fragmentation. Frances Morrell said we were defeated; we had no troops. I tried to cheer them up and said we were paying the price for victory: we have changed the policy of the Party completely in four years; we have wheeled democratic reforms into position; we are disliked because we have exposed and outflanked the others. Our real allies now are probably the trade union left.

Wednesday 13 April
The PLP held a meeting to consider the campaign document which will be the basis for the Election manifesto as soon as an Election is called. Only about one-tenth of the Parliamentary Party had bothered to turn up, together with a few peers and Party officials.

On the defence section Lord Stewart, our former Foreign Secretary, asked if the agreement to get rid of the bases meant a multilateral agreement or a unilateral commitment, ie was it a conditional or an absolute pledge? This, he said, must be made clear.

David Winnick [MP for Walsall North] argued that there was great anxiety about getting rid of the bomb; the Party was not pacifist and we might have to spend more on conventional weapons.

Eric Deakins [Walthamstow] said we should be careful about my commitment to raise the lowest level of pay to two-thirds of the national average, because it would lead to inflation.

Ioan Evans thought it was an excellent document, but the Lords and devolution were not urgent matters and he hoped we would emphasise the EEC and agriculture.

Hugh Brown, from Glasgow Provan, said he felt totally demoralised. He commented on how few Members had turned up and suggested, 'Perhaps the reason is that everybody knows what Tony Benn is going to say. I want to say that policies don't win elections. The last three years have been very unpleasant. We have paid a heavy price for reselection and for the arguments over the manifesto and the democratic reforms.' He was ambivalent about the policy, and said, 'It's not clever to put up candidates who are vulnerable to attack', and added that he wasn't referring particularly to Tatchell but that homosexuality was a matter on which 'some of us are ahead of public opinion'. An awful speech, weak and wobbly, and nothing to offer.

George Robertson said he had reservations which were reflected in *Tribune* and the *New Statesman*, and as far as he was concerned, American nuclear bases must stay.

Michael Meacher thought it was a good document; he hoped it would not be watered down and that we could have assurances that the manifesto itself would reflect the policies contained in the campaign document. He then said, 'I hope that *both* sides of the Party will be associated with the policy.' That was a clear reference to the exclusion of the left from any role in the Party now.

Jack Straw argued that there was a credibility problem, and, when we came to unemployment, we would have to see that the incomes of those at work did not rise so sharply as to keep others out of work.

I spoke just before I left at 12.30. 'I want to make a few simple suggestions about how confidence can be built. First of all, we have got to have confidence in our programme. We should show confidence by preparing now for the implementation of policies by asking subject groups to look at how each part of the programme could be implemented within the Departments in which they were interested. The unions could prepare their side of the agreed development plans, and local authorities could prepare for the day a Labour Government is elected.'

I left the meeting and walked across to Central Hall with Stan Orme, our shadow industry spokesman, to meet 2000 Post Office Engineering Union workers who were protesting against the privatisation of telecommunications. It was very nice that they had asked me and Stan to speak. I told them I supported their strike, that I had seen the City of London put a pistol to the head of the Labour Government from time to time and I didn't see why we shouldn't do it in reverse. 'What we should now do is to plan in detail how we take the telecommunications industry back and then take the battle to the country.'

Sunday 1 May
In Liverpool for a public meeting with Eddie Loyden, the ex-MP for Garston, who has been selected to fight it again. I stayed overnight in the Liverpool Atlantic Tower Hotel.

At 1.30 in the morning I woke up coughing and choking. I was desperately trying to breathe in, and it was absolutely terrifying. I went into the bathroom and began turning blue, gasping for breath and coughing. I really thought I was going to die on May Day 1983. I won't say my whole life raced through my mind, but I did go through the likely sequence of my death – the final choking, the weakening, the extinction. But after a while the coughing began to ease and, although my throat was very sore and I was frightened, I managed to calm myself and finally went back to sleep.

Two hours later, I was woken up by the most appalling wailing noise as if a police car was in the bedroom. I leapt out of bed again, thinking it was the hotel alarm clock, which had a note on saying it did sometimes go haywire. I looked out of the window to see if it was a police car but it wasn't. So I went into the bathroom, where the noise was even louder. I tried to get out of the room to look along the corridor but I had locked the door, so I had to search for the key. By this time the noise was driving me crazy and I thought it must be some sort of fire alarm. Just as I got the door open, I saw the porter and the manager banging on all the doors, shouting, 'Evacuate the building at once.'

I was in my shirt and my underpants, but I thought I could put on my clothes, and I didn't want to lose my papers and wallet and tape recorder, so I got everything together. The manager said, 'Go down the stairs.' Well, it was *twelve* flights down! When I finally stumbled out at the bottom, somebody in the hall ushered me outside, where there were three fire-engines but no sign of a fire. I had a little folding seat which I had put in my bag for the May Day march, so I sat there with my bags, just gazing out at Liverpool at 3.30 in the morning.

Eventually they said we could go back in. I was so exhausted by this time, I fell asleep on the bed fully clothed, and woke up three hours later when they brought me breakfast.

Tuesday 3 May
Home in time to watch the television programme *People and Power*, which dealt with the Bristol South selection conference. It made it quite clear that Mike Cocks had packed the general management committee; indeed, they had quotes from John Golding saying 'What's wrong with that?' and someone else saying 'Packing the committees is the name of the game' – a pretty open confession of what had happened.

Friday 6 May
Today the whole Shadow Cabinet, the top leadership of the trade union movement and the Executive (I suppose the upper directorate of the Labour Party) met to discuss the Election. Michael Foot welcomed us, saying there were indissoluble links between the trade unions and the Labour Party and 'When the day of judgement comes, my claim to fame will be that trade union membership rose to the highest figures ever while I was Secretary for Employment.' He declared that there were bitter battles today and that the Labour Government would repeal the Tory legislation. Most of this was just guff.

Then, in a typical Michael Foot statement, he said, 'After the distractions of the policy debates and the democratic reforms and the deputy leadership election, we are doing better. We have turned extrovert again. The mood now is that people are ready to listen.' He paid a warm tribute to Denis for helping him as Leader, and added, 'We have a better range of talent than the Tories. As to the Election, we don't know the timing yet, but we can win it.'

I must say, to have a swipe at all the great changes in the Party, to pay a tribute to Healey, who was against them all, and then to say we had more talent than the Tories was amazing!

David Basnett thanked Michael Foot and said that the trade unions were helping themselves when they helped the Party. Election defeat would be catastrophic for the movement. It would detach the unions from the Party.

He went on, 'A MORI poll showed that only a minority of trade-unionists vote for the Labour Party. So we must get across the message to the rank and file of the trade unions. We have been losing the battle about the redistribution of wealth, about economic planning – where the PM's view seems to hold sway. Eighty-nine per cent of the public say unemployment is a major issue, yet they continue to support the Tories.

'The movement has its problem, there is still an appearance of disunity, but our unity is real. We need a new slogan; perhaps "Caring makes economic sense" would be best. On campaigning, we have three important platform themes, and we want a mixture of speakers on platforms – left and right.' (That was interesting, because it was the first time David Basnett had ever said publicly what he had told me privately, that he wants to be a healing influence in the Party, unlike Michael Foot, who hasn't spoken to me for eighteen months.) 'We should use our resources wisely. We must find £2.5 million. We are fighting for the labour movement.'

After tea, Denis Healey began the session. 'There is a big "don't know" element, and we have got to try and persuade the unions and council tenants. We could lose if people don't think we can win. Thatcher has dropped her programme, her record is appalling and produces anger, and her intentions produce fear. The cost per family of Tory policies is £6 per week.' Then – and this is amazing for Denis Healey – he said that civil liberties were threatened by the new Police Bill and the weakening of the Citizens' Advice Bureaux.

He went on, 'It is difficult to get unemployment down to one million. We depend on co-operation with the unions and with the employers. Consensus must be the basis of our policy. As for slogans, "Caring makes sense" or "He who cares wins" might be better than "Caring makes economic sense". We have got to freeze council house rents. We have got to make clear we are going to offer £8 child benefit. We must cut fares, rates and VAT. On the peace question, it is uncertain electorally, but we should emphasise the freeze on Trident and Cruise, and the phasing out of US bases.

'The unions must accept responsibilities that go with the rights that the Labour manifesto would give them. For example, they have got to be concerned about the unemployed, the old, children, the sick. We will need a social wage – which will mean a smaller pay packet for some.'

Here was Healey already harking back to the old pay policy of earlier years which led to such a disaster. It's significant that the right wing on the parliamentary side feel confident enough to say that.

Eric Heffer thought that 'Labour is good for you' might be a plausible slogan. He warned, 'Don't attack Mrs Thatcher's as a fascist Government – that will rebound on us. It is a Bismarckian Government, and remember we have our *own* Victorian values.'

Roy Grantham of APEX, who is very right wing, said, 'Governments lose Elections, Oppositions don't win them. We should attack the Government's credibility, attack unilateral rearmament with the Trident, draw attention to the waste of North Sea oil riches which are being used to buy out jobs and close factories. Italy now produces more manufactured goods than the United Kingdom!'

John Smith thought we should concentrate our attacks on Thatcher; we should ask, 'Would you have voted for her?' He stressed the importance of North Sea oil, from which she had received £20 billion in revenue since May 1979.

Roy Hattersley argued that ordinary voters were not all that interested in politics. People wanted us to sort out Militant. 'We should limit the issues we talk about, perhaps dealing less with data protection, fox-hunting and civil defence.'

Finally, Bill Sirs, General Secretary of the Iron and Steel Trades Confederation, said we had a vested interest in getting rid of Thatcher. On the Common Market, he said 'I would be against leaving, but we have got to be sure that, if we do leave, it doesn't mean a threat to jobs. Anyway, public opinion is shifting towards staying in the Common Market.'

Jim Mortimer, David Basnett and Michael Foot slipped off to give the first of their press conferences, where I think David Basnett said that 'optimism was breaking out'. They've always got a phrase ready.

Saturday 7 May

To Bristol for a very important decision-making meeting with the officers of my Party, before this afternoon's selection conference for the new Bristol South seat. I had worked out a timetable of decisions, and, to cut a long story short, I had drafted the case for staying and the case for running. Clearly Bristol East is not safe and will be less so as a result of the bitter press coverage, which, Ken Coates warned me, would be a 'lynching party'. I put the case for cutting and running from Bristol.

The case for staying was, however, much stronger. First, I had said I *would* stay and it was a question of integrity. Secondly, by going I would be condemning Bristol East and Kingswood to defeat by assuming that they would be lost. Thirdly, by assuming they would be lost, I would also be saying that the Labour Party would lose the Election because if they were lost we couldn't win the Election. Fourth, I did have a requirement to show leadership when things were going badly, and that carried the day. Meg Crack, Dawn Primarolo and George Micklewright, my election agent, agreed; Paul Chamberlain thought I should announce this afternoon that I was leaving Bristol.

I was left to work on my speech. At 3 Meg and Pam Tatlow came back and gave me a lovely card wishing me success. I was driven to the Labour Club, where Bristol South delegates had gathered. Then I was shown into a room no bigger than a lavatory. Mike Cocks was there looking extremely worried; I talked to two children and we played shove-ha'penny. Then I shifted the conversation to postage stamps, which I knew Mike Cocks was quite interested in. Simon, Bryan Beckingham's son, asked me and Mike Cocks quite innocently, 'Did you go to the Militant Summer School last August?' It was like asking Mrs Thatcher if she had attended the last Communist Congress! It was very funny and Mike Cocks frowned. The children said how much they had enjoyed it.

I drew the straw first and went into a huge room where they were all sitting. I could see a few friends, but there was a sea of trade-unionists who had been brought in under the Golding aegis, and women in their early sixties from the Co-op Women's Guild. I swear many of them had never been to a political meeting before in their lives. I knew I was going to lose, so I was relaxed, made a speech, answered a few questions and left. Then Mike Cocks went in.

I left the room, wandered round and had a word with a few journalists. When Mike Cocks came out I said, 'If you address the press, tell them I'll see them later if they want me to.'

He said, 'You're assuming I'm going to get the selection.'

'It's obvious you are.'

Anyway, Vic Jackson, the chairman, came out and announced 'The selection is for Michael Cocks.'

He and I went in and I looked at them all – it did change my attitude, being the defeated candidate. I remember thinking how awful it must have been in 1950 for Arthur Creech-Jones, a former Cabinet Minister, when I beat him. Anyway, Mike Cocks thanked them and said a word of thanks to me. I congratulated him and said that on my way here I had passed the Fighting Cocks pub and as it turned out he was.

I am glad I went. To be defeated does no harm unless you allow it to. He had worked like anything to fix the selection conference. Many of his supporters had never been before and will never attend again. But the left will come back to haunt him.

During my press conference, Caroline arrived; it was lovely to see her. We had a cup of tea with Meg Crack and went over it all.

That was the end of a memorable day and possibly a turning-point in my life, because, having been defeated for Bristol South, and facing the possibility of being defeated in the General Election at Bristol East, I would therefore be ineligible for the leadership of the Labour Party after the Election (if we lose it).

Sunday 8 May

Caroline and I had breakfast in our hotel room and read the papers. At 10 we went to the Bristol East selection conference in Ruskin Hall, Wick Road, the place where I had been carried shoulder-high by three lads after the count on 30 November 1950, and it looked exactly as it did then. Ron Thomas was there contesting the selection with me, and he is such a friend. There was quite a busy crèche with ten or twelve children being looked after by two men.

Ron knew I would beat him. It was a much smaller conference, and I made more or less the same speech. The vote was 46 to 3. Afterwards I paid tribute to Ron, who was very generous in defeat.

Monday 9 May

Someone from *Channel 4 News* rang up to tell me that the Election would definitely be on 9 June. Shortly afterwards a phone call came cancelling the next NEC Organisation and Home Policy Committees.

Wednesday 11 May

The 'Clause 5' meeting to draw up the manifesto was called today at 2.30. The last time we had the Clause 5 meeting was in April 1979, when Jim Callaghan had announced that in respect of the House of Lords, and by implication on other issues too, he would resign the leadership of the Party rather than accept certain policies, even though they had gone through Conference.

But the labour movement has been alerted to the significance of the Clause 5 meeting. Because we pushed so hard this time on policy and it was endorsed by the TUC, the trade union members of the NEC cannot pull back from it. The parliamentary leadership know that if they try to obstruct it there will be trouble. So we went into the meeting with a tremendously strong moral position.

Sam McCluskie took the chair and, to cut a long story short, asked Geoff Bish if a shorter version of the document before us, *New Hope for Britain*, was possible. Geoff said we could only save 1000 words, and it would hardly be worth it.

I then moved that *New Hope for Britain* be adopted as the manifesto of the Labour Party at this Election.

Sam McCluskie said, 'We can't accept motions, I'm afraid.'

'Well, that's my suggestion,' I replied.

Peter Shore said he was shocked to hear a member of the NEC, who was against this Clause 5 procedure anyway, proposing that the document be crammed through. He declared, 'The purpose of a manifesto is to win an Election.'

He then said this campaign document was a list of meaningless promises, and on this occasion we were addressing the country.

It was courageous, in a way, because he just denied the right of the Party to have any role, and put it on the record.

Foot said, 'I want to reply to Peter. It is not the case that the document is being crammed down our throats. This is a proper Clause 5 meeting, and anyone can raise anything. We are seeking a consensus and we have got to strike a balance.'

John Golding made a very strong point, arguing, 'The Shadow Cabinet has had its say. This is a joint document. You can't condense a document like this, and it has had a very good reception.'

The general consensus was that it was a good document and we should stick to it as our manifesto.

It was the product of a lot of campaigning over an awfully long period, and, although I know the Shadow Cabinet wouldn't implement it if they were elected, at least we have got that as our commitment to the British people.

I had to leave early to go to the House of Commons.

Thursday 12 May

I went to my room in the House and cleared all the pictures, the NUM banner from Arthur Scargill, the typewriter, and so on, and put them in the car. As I left, I did wonder whether I would ever be a Member of Parliament again. I am relaxed about it, because I think the situation is so serious that socialists or representatives of socialism and of working people are being driven out of Parliament. I may have to help the labour movement and socialism without necessarily being in Parliament.

Tuesday 17 May

I've made hardly any reference to the Election campaign generally – which I suppose I should do.

The *Daily Star* came up with a MORI poll today suggesting that the Tory lead had been cut to 7 per cent. I watched the Tories' party political broadcast, which was just like a presentation to a group of businessmen, with pictures of the so-called Winter of Discontent, showing the Tories reducing inflation and so on, and finishing up with pictures of Mrs Thatcher. I found it informative, skilful and practical. Michael was on television pounding the table in Lancashire somewhere, and really looking quite good. I felt the atmosphere beginning to shift towards us a bit.

I must say, watching David Owen, David Steel, Roy Jenkins, Michael Foot, Denis Healey, Peter Shore, Cecil Parkinson and Michael Heseltine on television all the time is excruciatingly boring.

Wednesday 18 May

Went to Transport House in Bristol; the organisation is fairly minimal. A very nice woman called Joan Hammond, who used to be a Labour councillor and whom I met at Greenham Common, has come in to take phone messages. George Micklewright, my agent, arrived later, and we sorted out the Election address.

My anxiety at the moment is that things in Bristol haven't started, or, if they have, there's no sign of it, and we do need all 25,000 promises of a Labour vote to win that seat.

Got back late.

Thursday 19 May

I had asked the telephone operator for two alarm calls and had set two alarm clocks, but I woke up at 5.45 before any of them rang. Packed up all my Election gear and drove to Bristol. Got to Broadcasting House,

Bristol, at about 8.15 for *Election Call* with Robin Day. This is an entirely new television technique – a phone-in, with one camera on Robin Day and one on me. I was told not to look at Robin Day but to look at the camera so that I was looking at the person putting the question. Robin Day was quiet and quiescent. The questions were almost all critical. It was fun and relatively easy to do because the questions are similar to the ones you get at public meetings.

Did a bit of canvassing. I had the old canvass records for the local elections, and I went to one street where two houses had been listed as Tory and two as doubtful; in fact every house was pro-Labour, and I found that encouraging. A *Financial Times* reporter and Mike Lord of the *Bristol Evening Post* are attached to me to cover my campaign.

Sunday 22 May
Campaign committee in Bristol. My inclination is that we should go for a low-key, local campaign, no frantic handshaking, no loudspeakers, no razzmatazz, and ·I have limited myself to the absolute minimum television. I think people want assurance that the problems are manageable; and we should draw the parallel with 1945.

I went back to the hotel and worked until 2.30 on various articles and letters. Spoke to Frances Morrell, who is obsessed with her responsibilities as the leader of ILEA, where she says Trotskyite teachers are being difficult.

Tuesday 24 May
Went to Castle Green for CND Women's Day. They had decided, on a vote, that they did not want me on the grass at their picnic, first of all because I was a man and secondly because CND is non-political. So I stood away from the Green and did an interview with BBC Wales. A few of them came over with something to eat and said they appreciated the fact that I supported their view. The whole political situation is so interesting. The idea of a candidate or a leader as a hero who can turn up and take an event over is completely dead.

It's difficult to make out how the campaign is going. If the polls mean anything, there'll be a Tory landslide and I'll be beaten, and that will be that.

Wednesday 25 May
For the Election meeting tonight in Bristol, I used a piece of extremely interesting information. On 17 August last year the Chief Executive of Sedgemoor District Council wrote to the Chief Constable of Avon about a meeting of police and chief executives to discuss civil defence. In the letter, a copy of which I had acquired, and the veracity of which I had checked, was a phrase concerning the 'shooting of looters or the gravely injured'. It was such an incredible letter that I quoted it at the

meeting, then I went on to make my normal speech, and in the middle a man from ITN, who were filming the meeting, came on to the platform and removed the microphone, so I said, 'There you are. They have all come tonight hoping I would make some reference to the nuclear question, and as I haven't said what they want me to say they have packed up their gear and gone.' We had very good speakers afterwards.

Thursday 26 May

Caught the train to Liverpool, where I was driven to the NUR club for a public meeting. On the platform were Terry Fields, the Labour candidate for Broadgreen, myself, Pat Phoenix (of *Coronation Street*) and the actor Tony Booth, the man she lives with. Derek Hatton of Liverpool Council was in the chair. There is tremendous excitement in Liverpool because of Labour's landslide victory in the district council elections, and it recharged my batteries.

Pat Pheonix and Tony Booth drove me to Manchester for *Question Time* with Sir Geoffrey Howe and David Penhaligon, the Liberal MP for Truro. Back to Bristol in a BBC car and got to bed at about 1.15.

Saturday 28 May

Went to the service in Bristol for the People's March for Jobs which the Dean of Bristol had organised. It was all very informal and extremely moving, but, when it comes to industrial relations or the class struggle, the church is all over the shop. The dean took up the theme in St Matthew about the labourers and the owner of the vineyard. He said how generous the owner had been, and how, like the labourers, we should all have the same money. There were some prayers for the unemployed and for husbands and fathers, that they might retain the respect of their families – no reference to women at all! Then we had a hymn, 'Crown him with many crowns, the lamb upon the throne', which turns Jesus the carpenter of Nazareth into a god among gods and uses the language of royalty, which I think is awful.

Afterwards, I spoke to Ernest Tinsley, the Bishop of Bristol, and I said, 'If I might make a modest suggestion, the prayers about the unemployed might have been redrafted to include some reference to women.'

He agreed. 'Yes, it stuck out like a sore thumb.'

But I didn't raise the other points and I thanked the dean for his kindness. It was the Church of England moving carefully and tentatively towards a liberation theology, working with the T&G and the People's Marchers who were held up as people you should pity.

Wednesday 1 June

The tactical-voting game is beginning, and it looks as if David Steel has now taken over the leadership of the SDP-Liberal Alliance from

Jenkins. The Alliance is beginning to grow at the expense of the Tories, and it is possible that enough Tories will vote for the Alliance to allow Labour to slip in.

Thursday 2 June
Caroline and I went to Transport House for a public meeting with all the Labour candidates in Bristol, which Michael Foot was addressing. The skies opened and it poured with rain. Michael Foot made a good speech about Labour's policy on unemployment and so on, then we all went to Broadmead for his walkabout. There were hundreds if not thousands of people there. It was the only bit of razzmatazz I've been involved in.

Had a meal and a talk with Michael, the first since the row over collective Cabinet responsibility after the deputy leadership fight. He was friendly. Then we went to his press conference, and there were all those media creeps trying to press him on whether he agreed with Denis Healey that the Prime Minister 'gloried in slaughter,' and whether he was in favour of an inquiry into the sinking of the *Belgrano*, and so on. Michael brushed the whole thing aside, and when they tried to question me about it Michael tried to prevent them. I said I was in favour of an inquiry and I did think the Prime Minister had used the sacrifices of our servicemen to advance her own political position, which is what I believe. The media are unspeakable.

It was Michael Foot's circus coming to town. Leaders shouldn't expose themselves to the media. They should say, 'If you want to watch the Election you can do so, but it's our Election and we are talking to the people. You can observe us if you wish.' Otherwise, the Election becomes focused on the polls and the media and not the issues that confront voters.

Michael went off, and Caroline and I did some leaflet folding because the machine has broken down.

Friday 3 June
I had breakfast with David Butler and his son Daniel. David is observing the Election from a political position somewhere near that of Willie Whitelaw, Ted Heath, David Steel, Roy Jenkins and Roy Hattersley. Although he was less certain about the outcome of the Election, he believed that the Labour Party would have to move to the centre if ever it was going to pick up, and that it had been marginalised by extreme policies. David is an old friend, but seeing him is really like being parachuted for half an hour into the SDP-Liberal Alliance camp.

Saturday 4 June
Watched a *Newsnight* programme on how the *Observer* was working out its editorial line on the Election. It was just typical of this Election – the

media commenting on the media, not on politics. They had filmed the editor Donald Trelford (who is SDP), Anthony Howard (who claims to be Labour) and Adam Raphael (who is SDP) in editorial session making up their minds. The *Observer*'s leader was called 'Keep the Tories Tame'. *Newsnight* had a 'candidate' wearing a pink rosette, walking down the road shaking hands with people, kissing babies, talking over a loudspeaker – just mocking the democratic process completely. Then they showed a man wearing three rosettes – Labour, Tory and SDP – singing a cynical song.

The papers point to a huge Tory landslide of seats in the House of Commons. I have to recognise that I am beaten in Bristol.

Sunday 5 June

From the canvassing returns, it looks as if we have got 19,000 promises out of a target of 30,000, and the total opposition is 11,459 Tories and 10,372 doubtfuls. If they all voted Tory, that would give them 21,000, but some of those doubtfuls are going to be Liberal, so the Liberal vote might save me.

Went to the Sikh temple to address the Indian Sikh community, and I sat with my shoes off and something around my head. The point I have made at the different religious places of worship is that the ethnic communities have enriched our society by their culture and their religion, like the Romans and the Danes and the Saxons and the French. It was important that all the laws of England respect people's particular faiths and it was also important that we repeal the Immigration Act of 1971 and the Nationality Act of 1981, which were very unfair. I told the Sikhs that I was a man who always spoke my mind and I would expect them to speak their mind with me. I have sensed great warmth and friendship from them over the years.

Monday 6 June

To the boot and shoe factory in Kingswood, where men and women were sitting in front of sewing-machines which must have been sixty years old. When the hooter blows in the morning, they have a ten-minute break for tea, then at 12.30 they have an hour's lunch, after which they work straight through to 4.45. It was sheer wage slavery. HTV and BBC were there to take a picture of me, and I was presented with a beautiful set of boots and shoes.

Tuesday 7 June

Clive Jenkins arrived in Bristol, all bouncing, to campaign for me. We went round some shopping centres. Clive hogged the mike and went along like an emperor. You would have thought he was the candidate!

Wednesday 8 June

We drove to the Brislington shopping precinct and I spoke for a moment. Caroline went to a Community Enterprise Programme, where there were a lot of young blacks who said they weren't going to vote; she converted about seventeen of them with a few sharp words.

At Asda supermarket, the security man told me, 'The manager has asked you to leave the premises.'

So I replied, 'Perhaps you'd let me have that in writing.'

Nothing happened, so we carried on, and the manager came up with a heavy-looking guy and said, 'I must ask you to leave.'

I asked, 'Why?', and was told, 'Because our customers object to canvassing here.'

So I said, 'Well, I'm walking through your shop, and if you want me to leave you'll have to put it in writing. I'm a candidate.'

He said, 'Well, I hope we don't have a silly confrontation.'

'Well, I hope we don't either,' I replied.

I went on walking through the shop and then left.

Bill Owen, who plays Compo in a very popular television series called *Last of the Summer Wine*, arrived with my old friend, Ian Flintoff, to canvass for me.

To three eve-of-poll meetings. I resolved that tonight, as the Election is nearing the end, I would rehearse suitable farewell speeches to get on the record. Saw June Gibbs, with whom we had gone round in 1979 and with a spray gun had changed 'Benn must go' slogans to 'Benn must go on.'

I dictated my diary for Election day, 9 June 1983, on 18 June, more than a week after the General Election. The reason, as I put in my diary, was that 'What happened was so momentous and involved such a change that I simply didn't get down to it, and I'm not sure I particularly wanted to.' The following entry is therefore as I recalled the day of a traumatic personal and Party defeat.

Thursday 9 June

Caroline and I arrived at Transport House at about 9, and Paul Chamberlain and Alan Beynon, who have been solid friends and helpers throughout the whole of the campaign, had planned a route round the constituency. From 9 until about 4, we drove round to each of the polling stations and committee rooms. The weather was quite good and the turnout high for the early part of the day, which usually means that the Tories are voting and everything then depends on whether the Labour turnout is good at the end of the day – which, in the event, it was not. Caroline had been more cautious about the result; she thought we might *just* win by 500 but that the most likely result would be that the Tories would win by nearly 2000. Of course, all the polls in the morning predicted an enormous Tory landslide, and also predicted that the Alliance might do better than Labour.

People were extremely friendly and there was more activity than I had seen before. All the committee rooms were fully manned and the canvassing was efficient.

We went back to the hotel at about 5 and rested, then went out to do a bit of loudspeaker work. I put a three-minute message on a repeating tape. We saw cars with Labour stickers full of people being taken to the polls, but we didn't see those queues you see at the polling stations when you know there is going to be a good Labour result.

Back to the hotel just before 10 and switched on the ITN programme. They had a computer prediction based on their 'exit poll', that is to say they ask people how they have voted after they leave the poll; this showed a huge Tory majority, and it was quite clear we would have a tremendous job holding on. I must confess that even at that stage I was a little bit hopeful. We went to the count at the Brislington Comprehensive School at about midnight. We arrived just a few moments after the Tory, Jonathan Sayeed. We had to walk past a mass of TV units and had that sense of harassment and siege, as if they had come to witness the executions. Caroline and I put on our smiles and forced our way through. I had my portable TV set, which we sat and watched.

I didn't go into the count; I just sat and watched the defeat of our best MPs, with the obvious certainty that Labour would be badly beaten. Caroline came in at one stage and told me that, from the count so far, it looked as if we might be just marginally ahead, so I had a feeling that I might have scraped home. The enormity of what was to happen was not apparent. I had prepared what to say in advance and had kept it in the back of my mind – not that it would be much different whether it was a victory or a defeat for me, because clearly it was going to be a bad day for the Labour Party as a whole. A few people gathered in the room with us. Finally Caroline came to me at about 1.30 and said, 'They are almost ready. You have lost.' She had seen the votes piling up on the table.

So we walked out of the room, and all our Party workers gave me a dazed look, and I don't think they fully appreciated what had happened either. We walked arm-in-arm into the assembly hall, and when we got there we saw Sayeed and his wife and the Liberal candidate, Peter Tyrer, and the Ecology and the National Front candidates. The whole thing seemed like a dream. The returning officer read out the result, and I had lost by about 1790 votes.

A great cheer went up among the Tories when they discovered they had won. Sayeed spoke and paid tribute to me, saying I could have fled Bristol and gone to one of the left-wing strongholds but I had stayed to fight. He said he would do his best for a better Bristol and a better Britain, or something.

I came forward, and there were film units trying to film me, and photographers and journalists jostling. I had resolved what I would say, and I paid a tribute to the Chartists and the suffragettes. I then thanked the people in Bristol for what they had done and said I didn't regret for one moment staying there to fight. The Labour Party still had things to do – to protect people, to build a mass party, or something or another. Finally, I said, 'If I may be allowed a personal word, I shall carry on with my commitment outside Parliament.' Then we all went outside the school and I had to say it all over again for the television and press waiting there. But this time I added, 'I hope nobody will shed any tears for me, because I am going to carry on my work.'

It was a warm evening, and we drove back to Transport House in Bristol. For the first time since 1950, I had been defeated. It was no longer an area which I represented but an area where I was a visitor. When we arrived, the media were all outside and one photographer from the *Observer* managed to get in, so we chased him out. I made a speech again, and the only person who marred it was a tall man who was drunk and kept leaning forward and interrupting. It is out of events like this that history is made; it was a rather moving occasion, all the Party people crying their eyes out, and here was this drunk saying, 'Why did you do it, Tony? Why didn't you leave Bristol?' But I managed to silence him, and then I went round and gave everybody a hug and thanked them.

I can't say I was surprised, but the campaign did buoy me up to the point where I thought I might have won.

NOTES
Chapter Four

1. (p. 232) Under its leader Ken Livingstone, the GLC had in 1981 embarked upon a *Fares Fair* policy for London's bus and tube transport whereby fares were cut and services and customers increased. Initially the subsidy to London Transport Executive would need to have been increased, necessitating a rise in rates, until the scheme paid for itself. But in a series of court cases initiated by Bromley Council, the scheme was eventually ruled illegal by the House of Lords on the absurd grounds that the GLC had abandoned 'business principles'.

5
Member for Chesterfield
June 1983–March 1984

Friday 10 June
We left Bristol at 9.30 followed by three cars full of photographers. We tried to shake them off but it was impossible. The funniest thing of all was that we turned into a one-way street and had to stop and reverse, so they all had to do the same. They followed us nearly all the way back to London and then overtook us so that they would be waiting for us outside the house. When we arrived, there was a camera crew and a horrible woman, the clicking of whose high heels on the pavement I shall never forget, shouting instructions from the pavement in a high-pitched voice. I must say that if there was any violence in me I would have knocked them all down, they were so awful. They rang the doorbell and knocked, but we just stayed inside. Slowly began unpacking.

Caroline's support has been phenomenal. It has not been easy for her, but her advice is always measured and careful, her judgement excellent, her support perfect, and the effort she puts in is enormous. There was no regret expressed in any of the papers that I had been beaten, but, when I look at the result, it was no worse than any other seat – which is remarkable in itself, considering the enormous press campaign.

Saturday 11 June
The full scale of the losses is enormous: Albert Booth, Neil Carmichael, Arthur Davidson, Joe Dean, David Ennals, John Garrett, Ted Graham, Frank Hooley, Alex Lyon (a great loss), Jim Marshall, Stan Newens, Ossie O'Brien, Gwilym Roberts, Chris Price, David Stoddart, Ann Taylor, Frank White, Phillip Whitehead, Roland Moyle and many others. But there are a lot of good new Members now in – Tony Banks, Richard Caborn, Bob Clay, Frank Cook, Jeremy Corbyn, Terry Fields, Bill Michie, Dave Nellist, Bob Wareing.

Sunday 12 June
Chris Mullin had a post-mortem at his flat in Brixton. Most of our friends were there – Tom Sawyer, Jeremy Corbyn, Audrey Wise, Ann Pettifor, Francis Prideaux, Les Huckfield, Michael Meacher, Tony

Banks, Mandy Moore, Frances Morrell, Reg Race, Jon Lansman, Jo Richardson, Stuart Holland, Alan Meale, Ken Livingstone. We sat in the garden at the back of Chris's flat.

I arrived early for a talk with Chris and Tony Banks. Michael Foot let it be known today, or rather it was known as a result of his refusing nomination for the Party leadership, that there would be a leadership contest, and Tony, who has just been newly elected for Newham North West, offered to stand down so that I could have his seat and be eligible to contest the leadership. I wouldn't hear of it. It would be manipulative and I wouldn't contemplate such a thing. But I have *never* known anyone make such a generous offer before. Neil Kinnock, Roy Hattersley and Peter Shore have indicated that they will stand.

Looking back on it, I suppose I should have played my cards differently. If I had not stood down from the Shadow Cabinet after 1979, had played a less active part in the campaign to change the policy and to bring about the democratic changes, and had not stood for the deputy leadership, and if I'd gone to find a safe seat this year, I would have been in the running now. I may even have won. But history didn't work out that way, and the price paid for playing it differently has been enormous in personal terms. I have lost successively my seat in the Shadow Cabinet, the deputy leadership of the Labour Party, the chairmanship of the Home Policy Committee last October after Conference and, this year, my seat in Parliament. Four major setbacks. But the reward is that the Party has, I think, been irreversibly shifted back towards socialism and is more democratic, and that is the most important thing of all.

We put Reg Race in the chair. Chris Mullin took some photographs and then we had a brief discussion on the campaign. I said I thought there should be no personal recriminations and we should look at the long-term developments we would need to bring about if we were going to secure a Labour victory next time on socialist policies.

Mandy Moore said, 'Whatever we say about that, the right wing are certainly going to lay into us and we had better be ready for it.'

Michael Meacher stressed Party unity. 'It is all-important; we don't want to reopen policy questions. Class and inequality should be raised, because poverty was excluded almost entirely from our campaign. Why was it that our policy to deal with unemployment did not bite?'

Jeremy Corbyn (who is now MP for Islington North) didn't want a binge of recrimination. The campaign had started well and then everything had been fudged. We had the support of traditional Labour in the inner cities, the ethnic vote, middle-class activists and pensioners. 'There was great incompetence in the Party machine; the leaflets put out were absolutely bland crap.'

Ann Pettifor agreed. 'The Left should be seriously concerned about

Party headquarters. It is totally incompetent and has completely wrecked our relations with the media as compared to the Tories.'

Frances Morrell asked, 'Well, how much influence do we have in the Party? Walworth Road cannot be shifted until the NEC changes. People say "no recriminations". Well, a leadership election now is a recrimination against us.'

Stuart Holland complained that the leadership would not use our policies, that Foot was a man of the old left, and he asked if we should go for an abstentionist vote on the leadership.

Tom Sawyer said, 'The unions will want unity, and we should not demand policy changes. Neil Kinnock will be the Leader; Hattersley will go for the deputy leadership. We need new faces on the NEC. Frank Allaun should not stand. We need to bring on new leaders, and Tony may not now be available for that purpose.'

We discussed candidates for the leadership. Jon Lansman believed that Kinnock could win on the first ballot, and that we should accept that and go for the deputy leadership again, rather than contest the leadership.

Audrey Wise regretted having supported Foot and did not want to go for Kinnock. 'I would rather lose with a candidate we have confidence in. If we are looking for a young alternative to Kinnock, then Michael Meacher; if an older one, then Eric Heffer.' On balance, she favoured Heffer for Leader and Michael Meacher for Deputy Leader.

Tony Banks said, 'Heffer has no chance. Dennis Skinner would be more credible. We must try and get Tony into a position whereby he can stand.'

'That would be difficult,' Ken said, 'because of the time involved. Kinnock is repellent, but Hattersley would at least have to accommodate the left.' He thought Jo Richardson would be a good candidate.

But Jo said, 'I won't stand. Personally, I like Heffer – he has been a unifying influence – but there is an alternative in Joan Maynard.'

Chris Mullin strongly supported the idea of putting up Joan.

Stuart Holland said, 'We must try and get a by-election for Tony, by getting somebody to stand down.'

'I don't want to stop you, but I couldn't possibly contemplate that,' I replied.

Les Huckfield said, 'Kinnock is the cause of our problems.'

Mandy Moore didn't like the idea of Heffer. 'He is in the old mould and is an abysmal choice for women. As for Kinnock, he seems ready to say anything to win. It will be tragic if we don't put up a candidate.'

Reg Race declared, 'I couldn't vote for Kinnock; under him, we'll have a witch-hunt, and he'll try to reverse the democratic changes in the Party. He would appease the right. We would lose if we supported him, and anyway he does not believe in the policy commitments. We can't have him as Leader. Therefore we should run Eric Heffer, Jo or Michael. Really, Jo must do it.'

Alan Meale said, 'We will get Tony into the House of Commons by next year, therefore *this* year Heffer is the best bet as leadership candidate and Jo or Joan for Deputy Leader. Benn can beat Kinnock next year.'

Frances Morrell liked Jo for the deputy leadership. 'She is a serious candidate who would appeal to women.' She suggested I stand for the treasurership, which everyone else thought would be a mistake. Chris Mullin raised the idea again later but Tony Banks said no.

In effect, we decided that we hoped to persuade Michael Meacher to stand for the leadership or deputy leadership and that, if he stood for the leadership, Jo should stand for the deputy leadership.

Having sat and listened to all this, it seems to me inappropriate that I should be involved in this sort of discussion, particularly because it may be thought that I am trying to mastermind things outside Parliament. So I will keep up a good bilateral discussion with my friends, but I don't want to be involved in the plotting and planning.

The effects of the Election come over me in waves. Many people will suffer terribly under the Tories and it is immensely distressing. It's easy for us to sit round talking about what we should do, and to overlook the fact that the inward-looking nature of the Party has done us down.

Monday 13 June
I ordered some stationery because I have been using House of Commons letter-heading for thirty-three years and I haven't even got any with my name and address. The cost of stamps is astronomical; at this present rate, assuming I get 1000 letters a week, it would cost £120 on stamps alone. I did enquire about my redundancy pay, and I think I get £14,000 tax free, and a couple of months' winding-up allowance. I'm keeping Julie on. I had a letter from Richard Gott of the *Guardian* inviting me to write a column every week, which will mean £175 a week coming in.

Tuesday 14 June
Roy Jenkins resigned as Leader of the SDP, and it is expected that David Owen will succeed him.

Michael Foot wrote to say he would like to see me, and no doubt he would like me to come out in favour of Neil Kinnock (which I have no intention of doing). I might also note that Jim Callaghan wrote in sympathy.

Mike Lord of the *Bristol Evening Post* came to interview me. If the *Post* had been sympathetic before the Election, the outcome might have been different. I'm just living to see my own political obituaries.

Wednesday 15 June
Lovely warm day. My objective at home is to clear this office

completely, because this does mark the end of an era, the end of thirty-three years in Parliament. I think I'll probably keep the Bristol correspondence, which might be of use to somebody in the future, and there's a lot of material I can put away in the attic. I am hoping I will get back into Parliament, but I mustn't assume it will be that easy. Father was defeated in 1931 in North Aberdeen and didn't get back for six years. I've got to accept that you can't go round saying the same thing over and over, you've got to take account of what's happening.

Thursday 16 June
Went to see Mother, then on to do *Question Time* with Willie Whitelaw (who was made a hereditary peer today), Michael Meadowcroft, one of those decent grassroots radical Liberals, and Donald Trelford, the editor of the *Observer*.

Some of the things Willie Whitelaw said at dinner were interesting. He's an overgrown schoolboy, but completely genuine. I told him that Alex Lyon had said, 'He's the best Home Secretary we have had since the war – not that there has been much competition!'

He laughed and said, 'The thing I am proudest of is that I managed to handle the riots in 1981 without being forced to take more repressive measures. The riots – that was the key point of my office.' He went on to say how the right wing of the Tory Party had made his life absolute hell for not being tougher, particularly in the *Daily Mail*, the *Express* and the *Sun*. He had withstood all that.

We discussed his peerage, and I joked, 'It's very convenient, it will create a by-election for me.'

Whitelaw replied, 'Well, you'd be very welcome to it, my dear boy, particularly considering who our candidate is likely to be.' I gather it may be Ian Sproat.

He kept blathering on about his 'duty to take a peerage' and how we need strong leadership. I don't suppose Mrs Thatcher has got a lot of time for him personally, but she probably finds it convenient to have a tame, wet sheep-dog at her side, to give the impression of a balanced Cabinet, even though it is made up of absolute hard-line people. He said that for the first time he felt his age during this Election, that at sixty-five he was out of touch with what young people were saying and thinking.

We discussed the 1979 Election, and he said he thought Jim Callaghan might have won if he had gone in September 1978, though Whitelaw himself had been advised that the Tories would win then. *He* had been certain his Party would win this Election. Whitelaw has always been kind to me, and always personally signs all his letters to me. He said his office ask him to sign 10,000 letters a year! That's remarkable for a Home Secretary.

Today Eric Heffer announced he would stand for the leadership.

Friday 17 June
Reading the letters of condolence has been very moving, and I am in tears much of the time. I have had two or three letters from Tory MPs, lots from Party members and Young Socialists – many of them from women. There is no question that my remark after the declaration – that nobody should shed any tears for me – encouraged people to write. But I must admit that I am enjoying the rest from the strain of Parliament at the moment. .

Saturday 18 June
Peter Blaker, the Tory MP for Blackpool South, rang to express sorrow about my defeat. He was made a Privy Councillor in the honours list and was then promptly sacked as Minister of State for the Armed Forces by Mrs Thatcher.

Norman St John Stevas also rang and I said to him, almost in fun, 'Are you still in for the Speakership, or is that all over?'

He replied, 'Oh yes, I certainly am, and if you could have a word with any of your people it would be most helpful' – which made me laugh.

Robin Day had said on the air during *Question Time* that he believed Ian Mikardo might resign to make room for me. So I raised it afterwards with Barbara Maxwell, the producer, and yesterday I rang Mary Mikardo, who was terribly upset. I wrote to Robin Day expressing my regret and asking him to write to Ian Mikardo.

Wednesday 22 June
Went to the House for the first time since the Election feeling absolutely miserable. I never want to go near the place again but there are meetings to attend. I wasn't sure that I could go in through the private entrance by Westminster Underground station, but the policeman gave me a wink and said it was OK. I saw a couple of journalists, and found it pretty painful. I was allowed into Room 8 for the Campaign Group, even though non-MPs usually have to wait for the MPs to arrive. I shouldn't really feel embarrassed; after all, I fought a battle and was outvoted, and I don't feel defeated. Probably the feeling today was rather like that of a man thrown from a horse deciding to get on the horse again immediately.

The new Campaign Group was well attended – Bob Clay, Martin Flannery, Dennis Skinner, Brian Sedgemore, Frank Cook, Dave Nellist, Mark Fisher (the son of ex-Tory MP Sir Nigel Fisher), Willy McKelvey, Stuart Holland, Joan Maynard, Jo Richardson, Kevin Barron (the miner from Rother Valley), Ron Brown from Leith, Jeremy Corbyn, Harry Cohen, Michael Meacher and so on.

Again, the discussion revolved around the leadership. When Kinnock's name came up, Jeremy Corbyn said, 'Well, Kinnock lost the deputy leadership for Tony in 1981 deliberately and specifically, and he was busy preparing himself for the leadership campaign during the General Election. There must be a left candidate. Heffer is a candidate, he is against the witch-hunt, and I think we should consider him.'

The new MP for Coventry South East, Dave Nellist, said, 'Heffer and Meacher are both pro-policy. We should have meetings which will attract new Party members; and as we can't have annual Parliaments – which is what the Chartists wanted – at least we can have annual leadership elections.'

Saturday 25 June

Had a chat with Chris Mullin. He would like to give up *Tribune*, which he has edited for eighteen months; he has a few more novels he wants to write, but he also would like to get into Parliament.

Monday 27 June

Had a talk with Caroline in the evening. We are both sort of decoupling from the old style of political work. I am disenchanted with the Labour Party, and she feels she's getting nowhere with it.

Wednesday 29 June

An editor from Faber & Faber came to see me about publishing a socialist reader of quotations from British history. I dug out all the relevant papers I had. The aim would be to publish it for next year's Conference, but I think it's worth doing in its own right.

Thursday 30 June

Caroline and I went to lunch with the Cuban Ambassador, his wife and another diplomat. It is the third time we have been to lunch with the Ambassador and on this occasion we were actually invited to visit Cuba.

Friday 1 July

Visited Bristol for a meeting at Baptist Central Hall; it gave me a very funny feeling. As I walked down the station approach, a man stopped me and said, 'Aren't you Mr Benn? I am so sorry . . .' Then at the corner of Old Market and Temple Way a disabled newspaper seller came out of his kiosk saying, 'I've followed you all through your career. I am sorry.'

I went into the Hall, a bit early, and sat down. A cleaner came in and asked, 'Don't I know you?' I said, 'You may have seen me.' She asked, 'Have you got a friend in Stoke Bishop?' I said, 'No.' She said, 'Well, who are you then?' I replied, 'I'm Tony Benn.' She said, 'Are you *sure* you haven't got a friend in Stoke Bishop?' So it was a good corrective for any superstar delusions I might have!

Monday 11 July

I had to go to the Organisation Committee of the NEC, and the policeman at the subway entrance said, 'If anyone asks you, say you went in by St Stephen's public entrance.' It's all a bit embarrassing.

At the committee we spent ages on the 'progress' of the Register. Then we came to a resolution which has been before the conference two years running, calling for the standing orders of the PLP to be integrated into the constitution of the Party as a whole 'so that the PLP's responsibility for deciding how to implement the process . . . as agreed by Conference is made clear.'

Michael Foot made a long and boring speech saying the PLP didn't like it. 'The PLP is independent, and we cannot alter the relationship between it and the Party without serious consequences. The PLP is answerable to the electorate as well as to Conference.'

That is the Edmund Burke belief, absolutely nothing whatever to do with democracy within the Labour Party.

He went on to say that if PLP proceedings were recorded it would be a disaster; the left had always been against it because they would suffer as a result. He added, 'A minority of the PLP must be protected.'

Dennis Skinner leaned over and said to me, 'Put this in your diary: "Skinner says Michael Foot is a complete and utter bore." ' So I wrote it in the margin of my notes.

Foot continued, 'It would be overriding the individual rights of MPs, and it would be opposed to parliamentary democracy.'

Eric Heffer supported the idea of a small joint working party of the PLP and the NEC.

Kinnock was in full flood, and declared, 'I am against a working party. I know that either it would be the status quo or it would open up Labour MPs to having a role in policy-making, which would mean more Labour MPs would insist on being on the National Executive – which I oppose. We all base ourselves on Clause 4. The PLP doesn't pay the salaries of MPs, and you can't impose duty and ask for co-operation under threat. To suggest the standing orders be incorporated in the constitution would be illiteracy.' He went on to say that we needed an autonomous PLP, he wasn't basing himself on Burke, he was answerable to his own GMC, and a weekly meeting with a debate and a vote would mean that Dennis Skinner would have to back the system, and that martyrdom would be sought by those who wanted to take another view. It was a question of libertarianism versus the Register.

The chairman, Russell Tuck, said, 'Welsh oratory is very impressive, but you did say "Now my final point" three times, Neil, and I think we should vote.'

Russell Tuck had to cast the chairman's vote, which he did against, so it was not carried. We adjourned at 5.22. There was quite a lot of goodwill, but none of the arguments have gone away and we are back to where we were before the Election, with most time being spent, as usual, on this ridiculous Register.

Home Policy Committee at 5.30. We had a paper from Geoff Bish on 'policy development' in the wake of the Election disaster. He introduced it briefly,

I criticised it because what it says, in effect, is that we don't listen to the public, and that our policy is too inward-looking, and therefore it comes up with a managerial solution to settle things by abandoning NEC sub-committees and groups. 'We can't have these managerial remedies. It would involve degutting the constitution of the Party and would arouse deep suspicions at the Conference. The policy will need to be more radical as the years go by. We can't underestimate the role which campaigning plays in actually winning support for our policies. After all, monetarism in 1967 was a weird Chicago cult, but Mrs Thatcher campaigned for it, and now it's the policy of the country. We have got to do the same.'

Jim Mortimer disagreed with the paper. He thought the trade union input kept our feet on the ground and there were real differences of opinion. Although Denis Healey had tried to help in the Election by playing down his personal opinion, the public knew we were disunited and we must win back some of the ground we had lost – by campaigning in support of full employment as a legitimate objective of Government, in support of the health service and of the rights of the trade union movement.

Denis Healey said, 'I agree with Geoff. I said so two years ago. All these little sub-groups are a waste of time. What Geoff is doing is suggesting that we pull back to the situation when we *won* in 1945. We have got to give leadership from the NEC, the Shadow Cabinet and the trade union leaders if we don't want to be controlled by model resolutions from CLPs or the LCC or by arbitrary groups of intellectuals and their friends on the NEC. The Conference cannot make policy unless it is totally reorganised. The big unions have got communists on their executive committees. Trade union *members* think the trade unions have too much power, the trade union leaders make policy their members don't like, so we have lost the votes of working people. Then there is all this manipulation by the left which is abhorrent to the mass of trade union members. The Conference cannot tell MPs how to vote against their consciences. The Shadow Cabinet cannot clear speeches with the NEC. We want more tolerance of the Shadow Cabinet by the Party and the NEC must accept the former's leadership role. We must be flexible and go back to the techniques we used when we *won* Elections.'

Wednesday 13 July

The temperature is in the nineties in some parts of the country. I went to record my lecture on Karl Marx for the *Opinions* series on Channel 4.

At 5 the Campaign Group met, and it was overwhelmingly the best meeting I have attended – nearly thirty people, MPs and others were present.

Ken Cameron of the Fire Brigades' Union had been invited to speak on behalf of the left union general secretaries. He said that today the TULV general secretaries had decided to co-ordinate an attack upon the policies of the Party and were in favour of talking to Tebbit, which would be dangerous. 'The pressure is on us from the TUC right. The question of the right to strike, which the Government may try to remove in essential services, is a key question for the FBU.' He had told Len Murray that the FBU simply wouldn't accept removal of the right to strike, but Murray was trying to argue in favour of such a restraint. He added, 'On civil defence, the FBU won't co-operate, and we are trying to enlist the help of Labour-controlled local authorities but they say they are not prepared to break the law. The Home Office undoubtedly will confront the FBU on this.'

Eric Clarke, the Secretary of the Scottish NUM, said he was pleased at all the new MPs who had joined. He said we did now face an industrial confrontation and that Scottish pit closures were taking place without the statutory consultation laid down. The Coal Board were crudely bribing miners with money, extra holidays and special transfer payments. This is a Coal Board closure strategy for the whole industry. He said the Scottish NUM had decided to uphold the Party's policy on unilateral nuclear disarmament against this 'trans-atlantic understanding committee' supported by Frank Chapple, David Owen and Bill Rodgers. He hoped the Campaign Group would not be the phoney left (a typical Scottish, anti-London, communist view).

I said it was important that we nip in the bud the myth that if only the Party hadn't changed its policy, if only it hadn't gone for the democratic changes, we would have romped home in the Election, because it wasn't true. This coming Conference was critical, and this group was very important because it could bring about liaison.

Jeremy Corbyn observed, 'There is some equivocation in the Party. People are saying that the job of the PLP is to go for the middle-class suburban vote, but the Campaign Group must be there on the picket lines and at the workplace level. In inner-city areas where there are no major employers except local government and some public services, there just isn't trade union experience, and school-leavers know nothing about the trade union or labour movement.

The House of Commons had six divisions tonight on capital punishment, all voted down.

Thursday 14 July

Worked on my *Guardian* column, an article on Ireland. I wanted to get the tone of it absolutely right, so I spent about five hours editing it and getting it to exactly 800 words, and then, blow me down, I failed to save it on to the floppy disc, and I went to bed in a state of utter despair! That's life for an old man coming to terms with the technological age.

Friday 15 July

I started re-dictating to Julie the *Guardian* piece, and it was probably better the second time round. I said that British army withdrawal from Northern Ireland, replacement with a UN force and termination of British jurisdiction, should now be at the centre of the debate. I took that theme because the Irish are coming to London to see Ken Livingstone on 26 July.[1]

Durham for the Miners' Gala and dinner. It was the centenary Gala, and they had decided to make a big occasion of it, with bands and banners from outside Durham – two or three from Wales, Yorkshire, Lancashire. In all they had eighty-five banners. It was a beautiful day.

Neil Kinnock was at the dinner, having had a miraculous escape from a car crash on Tuesday; also there were Michael Foot, his last Gala as Leader, Arthur Scargill and Lawrence Daly. I sat at the end of the top table with the Scargills. It was very funny, because the President of the Durham NUM announced, 'We're very glad to have Mr McKinnock here.' I suppose he was thinking of Kinnock and Mick McGahey. Then, when he came on to say something about Arthur Scargill, he remarked, 'Arthur Scargill, our President, whether we like it or not' – an incredibly candid thing to say. Then he turned to Michael: 'We're very glad to have you here, and we did hope, Tony, that you would be Prime Minister.' So he was obviously muddling Michael up with me.

Arthur said afterwards, 'We'd better have a talk.' So we went to my hotel room. He is very disappointed that I didn't get a safe seat. It is a fact that some people think that by sticking to Bristol I betrayed the wider movement because I am now ineligible for the leadership.

Sunday 17 July

I picked up little Michael and took him to St James's Park. He was so excited seeing all the ducks and geese; he chased pigeons and pushed his pram, and a little girl about his age with her grandparents gave him bits of bread to throw to the ducks. A man approached me and said how nice it was to see an MP enjoying himself with his family. Then he added, 'My wife's father was in the Middlesex Yeomanry and knew your father in Mesopotamia in the First World War.' Amazing.

Tuesday 19 July

Today Merlyn Rees had a letter in the *Guardian* saying that when he was Secretary of State for Northern Ireland, he had considered withdrawal, and that the Northern Ireland Committee of the Cabinet had considered it and rejected it with the support of the Irish Government, the then SDLP Leader Gerry Fitt, the Irish Labour Party and the TUC. That itself was interesting, because the Cabinet was never told, though everybody else obviously was.

Apparently, the letter has caused a row in Dublin.

Friday 22 July

Flew to Aberdeen for *Any Questions*. Norman St John Stevas was funny and very personal. Ann Leslie I don't like. Russell Johnston, the Liberal MP for Inverness, was serious. The questions ranged from Prince Charles's latest speech to smoking on buses and the honours list. I let myself go back to being my old funny self, before I became a Minister in 1964. It was the first time I had ever come out on a republican note in relation to the monarchy, and there was strong applause. There must be a sizeable minority of people who are absolutely fed up with the royal family, but people put up with it so long as individual members don't make political speeches. Of course, as the gap between rich and poor widens, the idea of Prince Charles saying anything about the unemployed or juvenile delinquency infuriates people.

I caught the train back with Norman St John Stevas, and I asked him if things were easier now. 'Yes,' he told me, 'there's a bigger Tory majority, so I've got a bit more freedom in the House. I have got a smaller majority in Chelmsford, which means the Chelmsford Party will rally round me.' He went on to say the Government had fallen flat on its face on a number of matters since the Election – on Nigel Lawson's handling of the economy, Leon Brittan's role in the debate on hanging, and others. So I got the impression of the Government coming a cropper.

I said, 'You ought to speak out a bit more, and re-establish the Macmillan tradition in the Party. Do you still feel pessimistic?'

He replied, 'Well, I'm fifty-three. I don't think I'll get any further.'

He borrowed a sleeping pill from the man next door and went off to his sleeper, and I slept like a log.

Sunday 24 July

Conor Cruise O'Brien attacked me in his column in the *Observer* for my proposal for withdrawal from Northern Ireland. This shows I must be on to a good point because he is the Edmund Burke of our day, one of those former progressive Irishmen who believes that anarchy, murder, robbery and rape are just around the corner.

The Kinnock-Hattersley leadership race has become more interesting. There was a violent exchange between Hattersley and Foot at the PLP meeting on Thursday night; apparently the right had tried to get the Shadow Cabinet to recommend to the PLP 'one member one vote' in reselection procedures. So, when it came up at the PLP, the Kinnockites had packed the meeting to secure its defeat, and Max Madden (the MP for Bradford South) had moved that it not be discussed. Michael Foot had abstained. Hattersley had been furious, shouting, 'Where's the bloody leadership now?', and Michael Foot had allegedly replied, 'Don't ever speak to me again like that – I'll skin you alive.'

Had a long talk to Ken Coates on the phone about the conference in Japan on the anniversary of Hiroshima; he said the forthcoming great theme will be non-alignment. He is not going, and I may be the only British representative on behalf of END. I don't know anything about the Japan Council against Atomic and Hydrogen Bombs but it is apparently a vaguely Euro communist non-aligned movement.

In the evening we had the usual group to the house – the people who have met in my home over many years and are now primarily concerned with getting Michael Meacher the deputy leadership.

We were told that Eric Heffer had about thirty MPs, Hattersley forty MPs; Kinnock had a lot of constituencies, trade unions and MPs. On the deputy leadership, we were told that Meacher had about 200 CLPs, thirty-three MPs and three or four unions. Michael had spoken to Neil Kinnock about the possibility of running with him but Neil had been pretty non-committal. Michael Meacher looked good for the deputy leadership, and Roy Hattersley's abuse of Michael Foot at the PLP meeting would be bound to help. NUPE are likely to nominate Kinnock and Meacher.

Tom Sawyer said, 'Michael Meacher is a serious candidate, and we must make it clear he's not an *ad hoc* candidate for Tony. Some want Hattersley because they want him tied into the leadership.'

Tuesday 26 July

To County Hall to meet Gerry Adams, the new MP for West Belfast, and Joe Austin of Sinn Fein. We sat in Livingstone's room while GLC councillor Steve Bundred went through their programme and told them that they would be asked, 'Are you going to take your seat in the House of Commons?' and 'Are you going to visit the Chelsea Barracks?' (where people were killed in the bomb outrage in 1981).

Then we moved to a bigger room, where Tony Banks and other GLC councillors including Valerie Wise, George Nicholson and Stephen were waiting.

Gerry Adams began the meeting by thanking Ken Livingstone for his invitation. He said there was an ongoing attempt to develop a dialogue as a basis for that peace. In 1972 he had seen Willie Whitelaw, then Secretary of State for Northern Ireland, having been released from internment for that purpose. Adams said, 'We have a lot in common with British socialists. You can't be a socialist in Britain if you support British imperialism in Ireland, or even if you ignore it. Imperialism enslaves the British as well as the Irish. Sinn Fein are antagonistic to the British Labour Party mainly because of the activities of Concannon, Rees and Mason. You know that the Irish socialists played a large part in building up the British labour movement, and Ireland belongs to it's own people. That's our attitude.'

Joe Austin talked about the problem of Sinn Fein's identity in British eyes.

Gerry Adams said that, in the early days, poverty in Northern Ireland was appalling, with the use of the Payment of Debt Act. 'Our theme is self-reliance. Sinn Fein have won the confidence of the people. Catholics have been persuaded to register on the electoral roll, and this has produced our victory in West Belfast in the last Election. We are trying to do a comprehensive job, and we do, in fact, deal with complaints against the IRA. But plastic bullets are a form of community control, because if you shoot someone it keeps other people off the streets.'

I welcomed the dialogue, and said I thought this should be seen as a mission of peace. 'People are beginning to realise that, whatever attitude they adopt towards Northern Ireland, the present policy is one of absolute bankruptcy. We are told that shooting is wrong, that talking is wrong, that standing for Parliament is wrong, that the hunger strikes are wrong, but there is a Labour tradition of support in Britain.' I referred to the Republican Clubs in Bristol in the nineteenth century and to a general anti-partition sentiment. Secondly, I said, we had a joint interest because unemployment and poor housing were common to the six counties and to Britain, that types of repression in Northern Ireland were being practised in Britain, and, perhaps for the wrong reason, because a lot of people just wanted Britain to get out altogether – a view that the *Daily Mirror* reflected.

'What is the basis of the opposition to troop withdrawal?' I asked. 'I think it is primarily defence. But there are problems here. There is ignorance and fear because of the media. There is uncertainty about *how* to withdraw and what the consequences would be; therefore, the techniques of withdrawal need to be considered. Then there is the problem of the Labour Party: there is no discussion in the Labour Party, in Cabinet, in the NEC, and trade unions don't want the border issue raised in case it divides the Northern Ireland unions. I think it would also be a good idea if you' – addressing Gerry and Joe – 'could sometimes support what the British labour movement is doing.'

Thirtieth anniversary as a
Bristol MP, November
1980

Chesterfield by-election, with
constituents outside the
House of Commons

People power:
(*above*) the Berlin
Wall defeated,
1989 and (*opposite*)
Gulf War protest-
ers in London,
1991

Speaking up for
health workers

The miners' strike, 1984–5: Arthur Scargill (*above*) with his members and Peter Heathfield (*on Scargill's left*) were the targets of violent media attacks

On the picket line with Colin Welland (wearing sticker)

Rupert Murdoch's fortress: Wapping, 1986

Addressing Falklands War rally, Trafalgar Square, 1982

'Illegal' reading from *Spycatcher*, Speakers' Corner, 1987

George Nicholson asked, 'What are your relations with the Workers' Party in Ireland?'

Gerry Adams said, 'The Workers' Party are in favour of re-unification, they are active in the Republic, but they want the unity of Protestants and Catholics first and then hope it will all come right later. The army used to break up any united action that did develop between Protestants and Catholics, and we have tried to work on small issues like road safety – but Paisley has also preached against it. The Workers' Party adopts too classical a pattern of socialist analysis, which means that national demands have to be ignored. The Loyalist unions are affiliated to the British TUC – which is ridiculous. They have no interest in breaking the British connection. The British gerry-mandering is so effective that even Derry has a Loyalist council. Therefore you should remove the prop and then we can start class politics. You can't unite the working class and then throw out the British; it must be the other way round.'

Joe Austin added, 'The Workers' Party actually support the RUC, which is rather like the blacks in South Africa supporting apartheid while waiting for a common working-class front to develop. The Protestant working class at least know our position, and the Workers' Party are not trusted.'

Gerry Adams went on, 'The Workers' Party say that revolution must be based on the industrial working class, but in the Republic most people are working in agriculture, and therefore, in a strange way, the Workers' Party are supporting multinational investment and the EEC in order to achieve industrialisation, in order to build an industrial class. Fianna Fail are bogus nationalists because they don't really want unity, while the NILP, the Workers' Party and the SDLP all ignore the national question.'

Tony Banks said, 'I've been to Belfast in connection with my trade union work, and the situation there is very different; the British people simply don't understand what's going on. I don't see how the British troops can be bombed out of Ulster because of their enormous efficiency in counter-insurgency operations, and the British establish-ment want to keep them there because lessons are being learned in the six counties that are being applied in the rest of the United Kingdom. So there won't be any withdrawal by this Government, and, if the next Government were to be elected with a popular demand for withdrawal, what would happen then? *Would* there be a bloodbath? Is that true?'

Gerry Adams replied, 'You're talking about the optimum solution, a Government withdrawal, which would be the most advantageous condition. Otherwise we shall have to go on fighting. The bloodbath argument does have to be tackled. The Loyalists would react of course, through the UDR and the RUC. We have got to get rid of the "Loyalist veto" against unification. Britain should disarm the UDR and the

RUC and negotiate a withdrawal. I don't agree with Tony's idea of UN troops, although we know why he proposed it.'

Joe Austin added, 'The IRA armed resistance is the factor that makes the British people want to withdraw, and the real Loyalist fear of being absorbed into a Catholic united Ireland must be taken seriously. That must be resolved, and we must discuss how to do it; Republicans and Loyalists have met secretly.'

I said my point about UN troops was intended to deal with the argument about a bloodbath, and anyway Dublin had suggested it in 1969. Secondly, Britain cannot physically reunite Ireland by disarming the UDR. What we can do is remove the veto and withdraw, but not much more. Therefore, it seemed to me that the strategy would be in two stages: first of all military and judicial withdrawal, which we would hope would then lead to reunification.

Gerry Adams replied, 'I accept Tony's point about the UN role being to neutralise the argument about a bloodbath, but the nature of Loyalism is very difficult to deal with. It was in a sense the first fascist movement in western Europe. The Loyalists have a wholly cynical ideology and it has got nothing to do with religion. We have talked formally with the Protestant extremists and the Loyalist leaders, and they have come to terms with the situation.

'The Loyalists have no tradition of resistance; indeed, they have a massive identity crisis. When Sinn Feiners are imprisoned they feel they are being imprisoned by the enemy, and when they are in jail they know why they are there. But when the Loyalists are imprisoned by the British and tortured they don't understand. The Loyalists come to Britain, and if they have an Irish accent they are still called Paddys; they don't understand it. The Loyalists accept the inevitability of a British withdrawal, and they accept that Sinn Fein will be a major force in the six counties once the British have gone. The identity crisis is their problem, and once they face the reality of British withdrawal they can resolve it.

'The UDR is a British force; it is controlled by the Government and must be disarmed. The veto is psychologically crucial, and we don't expect HMG to reunite Ireland. Sinn Fein want normal relationships, and we want to free the Loyalists from sectarianism.

'We accept the consequences of withdrawal and we know youngsters will fight. But there is a longing for peace in Ireland and the conditions have got to be made right.'

I had to leave at that stage.

Saturday 30 July
At 4.20 Caroline and I went to Bristol for the farewell social at Bristol Transport House, where 750 people turned up, including the BBC and HTV with lights and cameras which upset people, particularly

Caroline. Herbert Rogers and Dawn spoke, and Caroline was given a leather bag made by Arnold Smith. Pam Tatlow presented me with a beautiful illuminated address, drawn by Hazel Gower, which was decorated with pictures of Mars Bars, cups of tea and Concorde – everything that reminded the members of me; and also the text of a miners' hymn from the old days of the Bristol mines. We sang 'We'll eat pie in the sky by and by' and then the 'Internationale'. They played 'The Red Flag' as we walked out, and it was extremely moving. It's hard to believe that thirty-three years are over, but I'm glad the party was left sufficiently late for people to have recovered from the immediate shock of the defeat.

Driving back to London after what was a moving and tender and lovely evening, I did feel that the work had to begin again. At a personal level, I'll have no difficulty earning a living from media work, but talking about politics is not the same as being an active political figure; being engaged in the business of preparing to hold power is what provides you with a platform and gives greater meaning to what you're saying.

Sunday 31 July

I caught the Japan Airlines flight at 2.30 and the plane flew to Tokyo over the North Pole. I read the various briefs I had had prepared for the World Conference against Atomic and Hydrogen Bombs, including one on the General Council of Trade Unions (Sohyo), which is a sort of progressive, democratic and vaguely socialist federation, the largest in Japan, supported by the Japanese Socialist Party. I also read about Gensuikyo, the Japan Council against Atomic and Hydrogen Bombs.

Monday 1 August

To the reception, where a lot of journalists wanted to interview me, and I did speak to many people, but my deafness is a real barrier at the moment and the Japanese accent is very hard to get used to.

I am the only person at the Conference who has been within a mile of political power, in terms of ministerial office (I think there are a couple of Canadian MPs), and, to that extent, it's strange: political life usually starts with meetings like this and hopefully ends with summit meetings with world leaders. I'm back to square one – people look at your label and say, 'Tony Benn. What do you do?' After years of being a top dog, it's quite humbling. However, it does provide an entirely different perspective. The people attending are not concerned with getting power but with immediate, pressing problems and how to resolve them.

In a way, Japan is rather like Britain – they are both islands, self-contained, inward-looking, conservative and hierarchical, facing the same economic pressures which are driving politics to the right.

Tuesday 2 August
I had a fascinating talk with Robert Alvarez, an American from the Environmental Policy Institute in Washington. I asked him about the sale of British plutonium to the United States. He told me that it started in 1959 and went on until 1979, when it was probably terminated by President Carter. It was a barter agreement under which the United States supplied us with tritium and high-enriched uranium for nuclear-powered Polaris submarines in exchange for plutonium from our Magnox civil nuclear power stations for use in American nuclear weapons.

Alvarez said the Americans wanted the Magnox plutonium because it was purer than that from the PWR. He told me that in 1980 the supply resumed, partly to fend off criticisms of Carter by Reagan on the eve of the presidential election.

From 1966 to 1970 and from 1975 to 1979 I was the Minister responsible for atomic energy, and I had absolutely no knowledge of this. Encouraged by my officials, I used to give talks on the uses of civil nuclear power, while all that time our civil power stations were supplying plutonium for American nuclear weapons. Recently Ross Hesketh of the CEGB made a statement in Britain in which he revealed this story, and he was promptly sacked by Sir Walter Marshall, Chairman of the CEGB – which has led to some argument in Britain.

Wednesday 3 August
Lunch with Mr Ishibashi, the chairman-elect of the Japanese Socialist Party.

Ishibashi produced a series of notes showing defence expenditure as a percentage of GNP, from the United States (which had the highest percentage) and Britain (second), right down to Japan (the lowest). Then he compared labour productivity, with America the lowest and Japan the highest. It is an argument I have often used, but I asked him for a copy of his charts and was given some. He was most courteous and friendly.

One of the most interesting discoveries of the week is that, after Hiroshima, the American operation in Japan was mainly an experiment – to discover how many people were killed, what were the after-effects of the bomb, and so on. Even the alleged treatment they gave victims was in fact experimental: not to make them better but to see the effect of different remedies. It was a disgusting operation, rather like the German experiments in their concentration camps. The Americans suppressed what happened to these victims for a very long time. The records, I found out, are still held by the US Defense Department and are not available to the World Health Organisation. It was only quite recently – I think in the sixties – that knowledge of what happened first came to light, and later it transpired that the Americans had some films of Hiroshima (which were sold to the Japanese).

Thursday 4 August

I was driven to see the Governor of Kanagawa, through these enormous industrial areas. It must be the greatest accumulation of industrialisation to be found almost anywhere in the world. It makes my heart bleed to think of all the previously productive areas in Britain which are now just decaying and declining.

Later I caught the flight to Hiroshima.

There I went to the meeting with the 'Hibakusha', as the victims of the actual bomb raids are called. An old lady, who said she was thirty-five in 1945, now seventy-three, was terribly badly injured and couldn't stand upright. She was working near Hiroshima in August 1945, for the military, and had been 1.1 kilometres from the epicentre of the explosion. She had seen the flash. She had been trapped in wreckage, was unconscious for two days and had suffered blindness, loss of hair, bleeding gums, fever and diarrhoea, and loss of power in her fingers and toes. All her organs were affected. She said, 'I try to lead a normal life. My father died of acute leukemia in October 1945. I had breast and kidney cancer and operations for cataracts. My fingers and limbs still tremble. I can barely walk. And', she said very quietly, 'I so much resent the production of nuclear weapons. Atomic bombs have made no positive contribution to the world. I am very old now, but I am still learning what we can do to help the world and I feel keenly that I must work for peace. I want to be of service and I hope to live to see peace established.' It was very moving.

There are 370,000 Hibakusha left but there is a rapid death rate among them, particularly recently through cancer. Two-thirds of them die of cancer. In Japan the doctors don't really reveal the cause of death. The man told me, 'It is most important to record our experiences before we die. There are no social security payments for the survivors, and most are suffering from a disease known as "atomic bomb bura-bura". The Government doesn't recognise it. Of course, the American Government is really responsible, but the Japanese Government is too.'

A Russian delegate told the meeting that he had lost his family among the twenty million Russians killed in the war. The bomb, he said, was dropped by American imperialists. Fixing the responsibility for dropping the bomb is very important. I had always accepted the general explanation that it was done to hasten the end of the war, but actually the then US Secretary of Defense revealed that it was done to establish a strong position *vis-à-vis* the Soviet Union before the war ended.

I got back to the hotel at about 11.30 and dictated from my notes.

Friday 5 August

To the Peace Museum which was absolutely packed, and the exhibition moved me to tears. Children were handing out labels to the visitors saying 'No more war'.

There was a huge model of Hiroshima just after the bomb was dropped showing absolute devastation except for a few buildings that survived. From the ceiling hung a black rod at the bottom of which was a red blob showing where the epicentre was. Next was a vivid scene of a life-size model of a woman with her hair standing on end, bleeding, with the skin burned off her and another woman with a burned child. Behind them was a massive backdrop of Hiroshima burning. There were samples of the girders which had melted and children's little luncheon boxes containing food scorched by the bomb. There were some granite steps which had been outside a bank, with the permanent imprint of someone who had been sitting there when the bomb fell. It was terrifying. I wrote in the visitor's book. 'Every child in the world should see this museum.'

I had to go out to recover myself. No sane human being could possibly assent to the use of bombs 1000 times as great as that. It cannot be right. There are some views you come to in life from which you can never be shaken, and nothing will ever shake me in the view that such a weapon cannot be used and therefore should not be built and must not be threatened. If it ever happens again, it will be the greatest crime in the whole of human history, because far more people will be killed.

Outside, in front of the car park, there was a disturbance involving some fascists in blue overalls who were standing beside four vehicles displaying the old imperial Japanese flag. I took a few pictures. They were addressing us through loudspeakers, apparently saying that the future of Japan lies in nuclear energy, Japan must have nuclear weapons and communism must be contained.

We went off to the atom bomb victim's hospital where the vice-director ran through a description of the various injuries they deal with – burns, blast, radiation, cancer, leukaemia, kidney trouble, cataracts, cheloids, purple spots, lassitude. I asked about genetic effects, but he had no information on that. The hospital is run by the Red Cross and gets no Government money.

Saturday 6 August

The thirty-eighth anniversary of the dropping of the first atomic bomb on the city by the United States.

Up at 5.30, and we set off by bus for Kumamoto to attend the ceremony, where there must have been 100,000 people. The A-bomb memorial cenotaph, a sort of open archway with water and fire, was the centre of the whole affair. At 8.15 the bell, which I think had fallen from the cathedral in Hiroshima but was unbroken, began to toll, and the tears came to my eyes. At one point in the ceremony it was announced, 'We are going to put water on to the flame because the survivors at Hiroshima cried for water and there wasn't enough.'

We caught the bus back and I had breakfast with the German Peace

Union people. They had a complete contempt for the German Greens, whom they regarded as utterly opportunistic and who were always trying to find publicity. The German Peace Union is a political party but it doesn't put up candidates. I was told that the END conference in Berlin had been interpreted by the Russians as anti-communist because the organiser was known for his hostility towards communists.

Sunday 7 August
We caught the train to Nagasaki for a seminar consisting almost entirely of speeches by the European delegates.

I forgot to mention that when I was in Hiroshima I met an American from a group known as the American Hibakusha, ie American victims of nuclear weapons. He was a quiet, decent man of about fifty, and had been one of the soldiers sent to watch the hydrogen bomb explosion in Bikini in 1954. He had suffered serious injuries including cancer and cataracts and was nearly blind. He thought there were about 250,000 Americans who had sustained injuries in one way or another in the nuclear weapons programme: in the mining and development of uranium, in processing plants, in the production and testing of nuclear weapons, in the disposal of nuclear waste and the radiation from various plants, including civil ones.

Monday 8 August
Had breakfast with the Venerable Sato. Sato was pleased with the conference and said the media coverage had been excellent. I thanked him very much indeed for making it possible for me to visit Japan.

At the airport I met some Japanese correspondents, who told me that the trade unions in Japan aren't really interested in the low-paid or the unemployed, but mainly in skilled workers and maintaining the differential, very much like the old craft unions in Britain.

Only 25 per cent of Japanese workers are established employees with big firms, and their jobs are not guaranteed by law. The big firms are laying off their full-time employees and taking on part-timers who are much less well paid and actually work long hours for less money.

The United States and Japanese nuclear links are close, and the Japanese correspondents said there is considerable pressure from the US on Japan to reduce their fast-breeder reactor programme, to cut back on their coal industry and shut pits in order to open markets for American coal. Japan has an experimental coal-fired ship under construction, using fluidised burning, suitable for coastal shipping. This confirms what I was told by the National Union of Seamen.

The journalists said that Japanese Foreign Office officials have come to accept that Japan must and will rearm and that, whatever may be said by the left, this is going to happen. It was a reminder that you can run a campaign, as against German rearmament, but there is no power on earth that will stop a really major country from rearming if it so wishes.

Looking back on the week, it certainly was an interesting experience. The peace movement has a life and vitality of its own and its leading figures know each other well through having met at previous conferences. During the years that they were working on peace problems, I was a Minister in a Government that was building nuclear weapons and following international policies which the peace movement itself found anathema.

Viewed from such a distance, Britain appears as a primitive, aggressive, feudalistic colony of the United States, gradually being taken over by the EEC, the multinationals and the IMF.

Tuesday 6 September
Sally went into the West London Hospital and a second little boy, James, was born to her and Hilary early on Wednesday morning.

Kinnock was on television and made it clear he did not think I should be chairman of the NEC Home Policy Committee. With his support going to somebody else, that means I shan't be re-elected.

Monday 12 September
Went to a special meeting of the NEC, called in place of the Home Policy Committee, to discuss the result of the General Election.

Jim Mortimer said the reasons for our defeat were both organisational and political. The role of television was underestimated, the organisation had defects, but disunity had been our major handicap. He said the SDP had damaged us – the shift to the SDP at the end of the campaign as a result of public opinion polling had probably lost us 2–3 million votes.

He added, 'It was a political defeat because the majority didn't want a Labour Government despite all that has happened. The public didn't blame the Tories for the slump. The pensioners wanted price stability above everything else. We were advised that our attitude towards the sale of council houses had not been very popular. On peace, defence and nuclear weapons, the unilateralist question diverted us from other issues. Therefore in future we should concentrate on things that matter to people, like reducing the age of retirement. The trade union movement is most unpopular, yet we *must* support the trade unions.'

Dennis Skinner attacked Callaghan and Peter Shore for references to the 'witch-hunt' during the Election campaign. Denis Healey retorted that he had recently had talks with Papandreou, who had expelled 500 Trotskyites from his Party in Greece two years before his election, and that Mitterrand had won because of his rearmament programme. 'Our slide began in 1981 with the Party split, with the image of extremism and the Labour Party rallies. There was a lack of public confidence in us to run a Government. We gave too low priority to managing the economy. The policies were repugnant to many people, and those who tried to modify them were pilloried. We must change the policies.' He added, in a typical smear on Michael Meacher, 'Even the present candidate for the deputy leadership, supported by Militant, is in favour of some change in our policy towards nuclear weapons.'

Tom Sawyer was very restrained. He said the leadership had been weak; we had failed on unity, loyalty and confidence. 'The Militant question did not help. Michael can't be blamed. The tragedy of the last twelve months is that, although we may have satisfied our activists, we haven't satisfied the electorate. Callaghan's role cost us 10 per cent of our vote. The question of leadership is important, and NUPE will expect me to fight for unity under the new Leader. The unions definitely need the Labour Party.'

I raised a number of points that I thought might help bring us together, but I said there were deep-seated problems. 'The main problem is economic change. The welfare state is disappearing, the consensus has collapsed, and don't tell me that it is all due to a change in the structure of the working class. On credibility, people thought there was no alternative, that Labour couldn't solve the problem, that we didn't mean what we said. We are faced with genuine demoralisation and weakness of analysis, and what we have to do instead is to put the issue squarely before the people. History will show that what we said in our manifesto about the future under the Tories was correct, but we have to give more of an explanation and get away from "Thatcherism" and all that language. We should develop our trade union links, particularly with workplace branches of the Party. We should recognise that the Government has made good use of "fear of Russia" to influence voters, and we should discourage it.'

Michael Foot said he had a sense of shame that we had let the Tories win. 'I accept my responsibility; I was a party to the decisions.' He agreed with Jim Mortimer's analysis that on organisation there had been problems, disciplinary matters had occupied too much attention, and we had to protect the Party's constitution without taking up too much time; for this we needed an appeals tribunal. He thought the manifesto was good, and that we must stand by the themes because if we repudiated the manifesto it would ruin us in the next Election.

He went on, 'I don't agree with what Tony Benn said about the welfare state. There are deep-seated problems in the nature of the electorate. The class war is not over, but big changes are being produced by the welfare state; the trade unions are changing too. There will be no automatic majority for many years to come, but we have every chance of winning it back. The NEC and the Shadow Cabinet should have absolute power to decide the strategy of the Party in secrecy. I stand by socialism, but it has got to be put across more intelligently.'

So, in effect, Michael Foot was defending the policy. As Dennis Skinner said, it was a good statement, but he wanted to carry on the witch-hunt using an appeals tribunal and he wanted secrecy, the very opposite of accountability.

Sunday 25 September
The *Mail on Sunday* carried an interview with Neil Kinnock by Jilly Cooper, and it was worse than I had been warned to expect. He was asked about various colleagues and came out with some astonishing remarks. He said Meacher was regarded as my vicar on earth – 'He's kind, scholarly and weak as hell.' He called me a spent force who 'couldn't knock the skin off a rice pudding', and denied he had once said I was a blind-worm trying to be an adder. This clever-clever Kinnock, who has been getting away with funny remarks which endear him to the media, will find, as he approaches the leadership of the Party, that they give enormous offence. Apparently he rang Michael Meacher to apologise and said he had been misquoted. But he didn't ring me! That type of approach to personal relations, combined with his general inadequacy, is not going to be good for him.

I am feeling a bit depressed at the moment. I think the real effect of losing my seat is apparent, and no doubt being out of the leadership election has caught up with me. It is a fact that I have lost a platform and an income, and have no absolute certainty that I will get back. Indeed, if I do get back, I fear it may be on the basis of a tremendous battle with Shirley Williams or someone put up to fight me. I do understand how unemployed people lose their sense of self-worth.

Wednesday 28 September
At the NEC I passed a handwritten letter to Neil Kinnock:

Dear Neil,

I understand that you were misquoted in the interview with you that appeared in the *Mail on Sunday*. May I take it that these misquotations also covered the comments you were reported to have made about me?

I attached a photocopy of the article, in which Jilly Cooper had asked if it was true that he had once described me as a blind-worm trying to be an adder. The relevant paragraph read: 'For a second Mr Kinnock flickered between discretion and the desire to be accredited with a wise-crack, then opted for the former, saying: "Attribute that to me and I'll kill you."'

I got a response later, as follows:

Dear Tony,

Many thanks. Yes, I was most certainly misquoted – misrepresented rather. In a statement I put out on Sunday, I said that my reference to you was in the context of the charges of extremism malevolently levelled at Tony Benn. My reference was entirely intended to dismiss those daft allegations and the quote should be in that context and should have said 'wouldn't, not couldn't' [knock the skin off a rice pudding].

. . . I am, incidentally, following your lead in getting a tape recorder.

Yours, Neil.

Well, that settles the matter as far as I am concerned.

To the GMC of Kensington Labour Party, who have very kindly made me their delegate to Conference; otherwise I would be ineligible for the NEC. I was mandated to vote for Eric in the first ballot and Kinnock in the second for Leader; in the deputy leadership ballot, to vote for Meacher and to abstain on the second ballot.

Thursday 29 September
At 11 Andrew Murray of the *Morning Star* came to do an interview. He's intelligent, responsible and highly thought of. I asked him about the CP, which is in a state of complete disintegration, with the old Stalinist hardliners absolutely fed up with the more liberal Eurocommunists who, like Hobsbawm, are virtually in favour of an alliance between the Labour Party and the SDP.

Labour Party Conference, Brighton
Sunday 2 October
I confess that I am dictating this on 14 October from very accurate notes.

At the meeting of the NEC, there was an attempt to remit the T&G resolution committing the next Labour Government to scrapping all nuclear weapons systems unilaterally, but by 14 to 11 we accepted it. Kinnock abstained, made a big thing about abstaining and then tried to get the issue reopened, but Sam McCluskie wouldn't have it. I was confirmed to speak on the unemployment debate, and I reported that I would be moving the Irish resolution from the floor on behalf of Kensington GMC.

Neil Kinnock overwhelmingly won the leadership on the first ballot, and Roy Hattersley the deputy leadership on the first ballot. The TGWU went against the recommendations of their executive and voted for Hattersley instead of Michael Meacher, which was a scandal, but nobody referred to it because everybody wanted the 'dream ticket'. Meacher himself voted for Kinnock and not for Heffer, which was a disgrace, really.

Tuesday 4 October
I was elected top of the NEC constituency section again with the highest vote I have had for twenty years, the tenth year in a row I have received the most votes.

Michael Foot made his farewell speech and got tremendous applause. Caroline went back to London to take her evening class; she doesn't like Conference.

Thursday 6 October
In the afternoon Kinnock made his first speech as Leader. It was pretty vacuous, I thought, but he got a huge ovation.

In the debate on Ireland, I moved the composite resolution, which said that 'the Unionist veto on progress towards a united Ireland is itself undemocratic, represents the major stumbling block on progress towards that aim and cannot be supported by the Labour Party.' It did go down pretty well with the Irish delegates. The debate was interesting, because, although we got less than a million votes, we certainly opened the question up and it was a serious debate. The veto is an issue on which it is possible to take a very clear line, and, in the end, Labour thinking will shift.

Friday 7 October
The move to introduce 'one member one vote' into the electoral college for election of Leader and Deputy Leader was defeated.   Looking back on the Conference, I think it has achieved everything that was hoped of it in the sense that the Party has now put behind it the arguments of previous years. But I am very depressed at the way I am slipping further and further into the political wilderness, and Caroline isn't very happy. From briefings and leaks I have had, Kinnock does not wish me to be a chairman of any committee, let alone of the Home Policy Committee. His new establishment will try to build itself up by recruiting the so-called Bennites – who don't really exist – into his camp and then will court popularity by proving that he has attacked the left.

Sunday 16 October
Up at 5, and Caroline and I caught a taxi to Victoria station. As usual, old tramps were sleeping on the few seats to be found, most of the benches having been removed because they attract the homeless in London of whom there are many thousands. Caught the train to Gatwick and flew to Cuba via Madrid. The Cuban plane for Havana was just like a country bus.

One advantage of my defeat in the June Election meant that Caroline and I were able to make long-planned foreign trips, such as one to Cuba in September 1983. While there, I gave a lecture and had talks with Cuban officials. I had also hoped to meet the President, Fidel Castro, but while we were in Havana, an American invasion fleet left for the island of Grenada following the arrest of the Prime Minister, Maurice Bishop, socialist leader of the New Jewel Movement. As a result of this serious development in American intervention in the region, talks with Castro had to be cancelled at the last moment.

The hostility of the American Government towards Cuba, which has taken the form recently of a tightening of the economic blockade of the island, was a clear indication that Washington was not prepared to tolerate governments like those in Cuba, Grenada and America's 'backyard' generally. The concentration of resources on health and education there emphasised the unfavourable conditions in literacy and health and social conditions prevailing in the USA.

Saturday 22 October

Had a morning at the beach. We swam in the Caribbean and the water was beautiful; it was almost too hot. Changed and had lunch with our Cuban hosts.

When we got back, we were told to expect a summons to see Castro. We were as excited as a couple of kids would be at the prospect of Santa Claus coming down the chimney.

They gave us a further briefing on Grenada, to which the American government have sent a warship and 2000 marines.

Caroline is packing and I am bringing my diary up to date, but in effect we are waiting for the telephone call.

To cut a long story short, it didn't come off. Javier, Silva and Adolfo, our hosts, sat in the garden until the party broke up at 1.30 am and every now and then they got messages, and finally Eloy turned up and apologised very profusely, saying that a meeting with 'a certain comrade' could not take place because the situation was so serious in Grenada, and senior comrades were at meetings all day.

Monday 24 October

Flew to Prague, but the flight on to London was fully booked and we went to the International Hotel, an enormous, drab place built in the 1950s. It was shabby to a degree. After many panics we got a flight back to London.

Wednesday 26 October

Television crews were outside Walworth Road because it was Neil Kinnock's first NEC as Leader, and as he came in he leaned over to me, looking very white and strained, and said, 'Dick Clements will be getting in touch with you to have a word.'

On the agenda was Tariq Ali's membership. He had been given five minutes to address today's meeting, and he came in wearing a check shirt and a sweater.

Jim Mortimer began, 'In 1981 the NEC resolved not to accept your membership. However, your application form was accepted by your local party, Hornsey Labour Party, and we have received legal advice that you are or may be a member of the Party. Annual Conference accepted the NEC recommendation not to accept you as a member. The NEC, in considering this now, believes you do not accept the Party's constitution.'

Tariq replied, 'The five minutes you have given me to speak is sufficient. I decided to join the Labour Party because I wanted to support and help it. If I had thought it would cause all this trouble, I would have delayed my application. I was in the Party from 1963 to 1966, an active member, but I left at the end of 1966 like an awful lot of other people and, like other people, I tried to set up another party. However, after the SDP was formed, I felt it was foolish to continue working outside. I left the IMG genuinely. I am a member of no other organisation. I know individual Marxists who have been accepted in the Labour Party. Conference has made a decision and I would be reasonably happy to discuss a way out; I could reapply in two, six or twelve months' time if that would help. But how long will this bar apply, because it is rather disturbing?'

After he had left the meeting, I said, 'The Hornsey Party want Tariq Ali as a member, and we will have to face a real problem if we expel him and the Hornsey Party don't accept our decision. Therefore a compromise seems obvious. He has suggested he might apply next year, and if we thought that was right we could recommend acceptance of his membership at the 1984 Conference.' I then moved that 'Having noted the statement made by Mr Tariq Ali, this NEC would be prepared to consider a further application from him next year and make a recommendation to the 1984 Conference.' Dennis Skinner seconded it.

Jim Mortimer was strongly opposed to expulsion. 'The press are only interested in making trouble. An ideological test for excluding people would be a very dangerous precedent.'

Gwyneth Dunwoody attacked Jim Mortimer. 'If he's a member of the Labour Party, we *must* expel him and the press will go on anyway.'

Ken Cure said we should expel him.

Jim Mortimer was beginning to swing opinion when Neil Kinnock said, 'It is not plausible to expect everyone to accept the constitution, but to accept someone who is historically in contradiction to the purposes of the Party would be impossible. The constitution says that we will pursue matters by parliamentary means, collectively and in a libertarian way. We do not embrace a revolutionary philosophy, and to talk about extra-parliamentary as being revolutionary is ridiculous. Extra-parliamentary activity is all right, revolutionary activity is not. At the IMG annual meeting in 1981, there was a split between the liquidationist faction, who wished to abolish themselves and go into the Labour Party *en bloc*, and others who wished to uphold the IMG. It would be gullible of us to believe that Tariq Ali had changed. We are all tired of this internal wrangling, but, when it comes to socialist ideology, some people have a vested interest in wrangling. Tariq Ali himself has behaved very well. It would have been foolish of him to bang the table. We should respond in an adult way. Tariq Ali's views have not changed; he is simply one of many revolutionaries adopting a new tactical position. The question is, does Tariq Ali embrace the constitution of the Labour Party? Strategically the Party does more harm by accommodating Ali. Conference has made its decision, and Ali has made his position clear. He can apply again.'

It was a disgraceful speech. Nobody thinks Tariq Ali is a revolutionary except in the use of some revolutionist language, and anyway the word revolution means so many different things. But it was Kinnock throwing his full weight against Tariq. He knows perfectly well that the Hornsey Party want him.

That's what the trade union leaders expect from Kinnock; though, if they do have to reach these agreements to get elected, surely they can sometimes break them in favour of tolerance of the left.

The substantive motion to expel him was carried by 14 votes to 10.

Thursday 27 October
Michael Meacher and I had lunch with the Soviet Ambassador, Popov.

He began by telling us about Andropov's latest interview with *Pravda* correspondents in which he expressed a readiness to reduce significantly the total of Soviet missiles.

We knew that before the General Election Michael Foot had written to Andropov for his views on disarmament, and I asked why Andropov's reply had not been delivered to the Labour Party until polling day, when it would have been most useful during the Election campaign. The Ambassador replied, 'Foot's letter arrived a fortnight before the Election, and we were told by the Labour Party to hold back our reply until after the Election.'

Well, that is staggering because this issue was raised at the International Committee in September by Frank Allaun and we were told then that the letter had only been made *available* to Walworth Road on polling day.

We went on to discuss Grenada. He told us that Soviet intelligence knew that two weeks ago the United States had considered an imminent invasion of Grenada. That was a week before Maurice Bishop was murdered.

At 9.30 Arthur Scargill came along with Roger Windsor, Chief Executive Officer of the NUM, and Nell Myers, who is Arthur's assistant. We had a talk about his discussions with Ian MacGregor about the miners' wage claim.

Saturday 29 October
This evening the telephone answering machine was installed – an absolutely amazing invention.

Sunday 30 October
At 7.45 I was collected and taken to *TV-AM* for a discussion with Alan Coren, the editor of *Punch*, Peregrine Worsthorne of the *Sunday Telegraph* and Norman St John Stevas about US foreign policy. David Frost presented it, and he loves to get a good punch-up going – it's good television. Peregrine Worsthorne's arguments and thinking are extremely reactionary. Norman St John Stevas is a wet, but today he praised Mrs Thatcher to the skies (in the hope, I fear, that he might be offered another job). Alan Coren was given about thirty seconds, and agreed with me. St John Stevas said in effect, 'Save the Atlantic Alliance', while David Frost just interrupted me all the time. Peregrine Worsthorne supported the Americans entirely and said that Mrs Thatcher was having her dirty work done for her by Reagan.

Joy Hurcombe, the Secretary of Labour CND, rang to say there have been mass resignations from the Labour CND Committee on the grounds that it had been taken over by 'extremists' masterminded by Robin Cook on behalf of Neil Kinnock with the co-operation of Edward Thompson.

Monday 31 October
The telephone answering machine is a great asset but also a bit of a curse because you have to ring people back, and that increases the phone bill.

The debate on the siting of Cruise missiles in Britain took place in the House of Commons this afternoon. Although it was embarrassing in its timing, coming after the Grenada invasion, the Government had to hold it today because the first missiles are arriving this week and the Government had to get some sort of authority from the Commons.

Tuesday 8 November
International Committee at 2.30. I raised the question of Andropov's letter to the Party having not been published until after the Election and why Walworth Road had told the Soviet Ambassador to hold on to it until polling day. It caused great embarrassment.

Friday 11 November
I went to Bristol to attend a memorial meeting for Alan Mason, the South West Regional Organiser, who died recently. While I was there Mike Cocks told me privately that Eric Varley is meeting his Party's executive committee in Chesterfield tonight and intends to announce that he is resigning from Parliament to become Chief Executive of

Coalite. I must admit it took some time for this to sink in, but it became quite clear that this would mean a by-election in a seat with a 7000 Labour majority.

When I got home (on the last train) I spoke on the phone to Arthur Scargill, who had a word with Peter Heathfield, General Secretary of the Derbyshire Miners, who is also a member of the GMC of the Chesterfield Party, and Arthur rang me back and said, 'You must move quickly. We will get statements put out in the constituency to the effect that they would like you, and you must be ready to say you would be pleased to respond.'

My prospects may possibly have changed a bit.

Sunday 13 November

Peter Heathfield was interviewed on Radio 4's *The World This Weekend* about Chesterfield. He happens to be an old friend of mine, a close friend of Ken Coates, and he said he was sure I would get the support of the miners, or hoped I would. I was interviewed too, and of course I said, 'It's not for me, it's for the constituency, it's an important by-election', and so on.

If they select by Christmas and the by-election is held in the spring, I could have a very busy six months ahead of me. It would be nice to be back in Parliament in my sixtieth year.

I phoned Peter Heathfield when I came back, and he said the Chesterfield executive committee would be meeting on Wednesday to decide what to do. He is going to say, 'This is a big election; we ought to pick Tony Benn.'

David Blunkett telephoned from Sheffield, and I was nervous that he was going to tell me he would be going for it, but in fact he was ringing to give me his support. Then he told me he was going to be in Chesterfield at their annual dinner on Saturday and he'd do his best for me.

Current opinion in Chesterfield is that the GMC will be 60–40 against my candidature, and the word is spreading that if I was the candidate Labour would lose the seat. On the other hand, work is going on. The AUEW is being approached, and Chesterfield has a good left-wing district council.

Friday 18 November

Tam Dalyell came to breakfast. He told me about his campaign for an inquiry into the sinking of the *General Belgrano*. He has just been to Peru, and he saw the President and all the documents about the Peruvian peace plan, which he is convinced Mrs Thatcher knew about. But he doesn't want to cause trouble by releasing anything that might not please the Government there. So Tam is in a bit of a jam, but he is discussing it with *Panorama* and hopes they will take it up.

I decided to do a bit of research on Chesterfield.

I thought to myself: I wonder if I have got any local connections with Chesterfield. So I went to the family tree that Debrett's had produced and discovered that my grandfather, my great-grandparents and my great-great-grandparents were all born within a 45-mile radius of Chesterfield.

Saturday 19 November
I have been in touch with Tom and Margaret Vallins, who are both on the Chesterfield executive committee. Apparently the NUM are allowed only five people at the selection conference out of a total of 132 votes, so the miners haven't actually got a dominating role. They have decided to nominate a miner, and vote for me on the second ballot – which is better than nothing. The YS have nominated me, but whether that's a good start or not I don't know. The AUEW are pretty strong. Alan Tuffin of the Union of Communication Workers sent instructions to the UCW there to nominate Charles Morris, who lost his Manchester seat in the boundaries redistribution. That caused some resentment among the UCW people in Chesterfield. ASLEF have got a strong branch there. Tom Sawyer is getting on to NUPE and there are two or three wards that could nominate me, so I might end up with a few nominations. The first hurdle is to get shortlisted, the second hurdle is to get into the final ballot, and if that happened I think I would have a reasonable chance.

David Blunkett told me that when he was in Chesterfield he found that a lot of people had been influenced by the hostile press campaign. The local papers and the *Daily Mail* have been using polls to influence the selection process.

Doesn't look too good, but it's not entirely impossible.

Wednesday 23 November
This morning the *Daily Mail* had a big heading, 'Stop Benn Call in Key Election'. The article began: 'An urgent message was on the way from Labour Party chiefs last night. It was addressed to Chesterfield, where the darling of the left has thrown his hat into the by-election ring.' It added that Kinnock was involved and had made no secret of his antipathy towards me.

So I wrote to Neil in my own hand:

Dear Neil,

I attach press reports which suggest that you are working to prevent my selection for Chesterfield, for which I have been nominated, and that you have sent out instructions to that effect to the constituency. May I take it that these reports are incorrect and that you are not seeking to influence the choice that Chesterfield has to make?

Yours, Tony

I took the letter with me to the National Executive. I got stuck in the lift with five other people, which was slightly frightening, but I managed to force the door open with my penknife.

At the NEC, Jo Richardson said to Neil, 'I see in today's *Daily Mail* a report that there is a "Stop Benn" movement. I know it is not true, but could Jim perhaps intervene with the press and tell them it's not true?'

Kinnock replied, 'There have been a number of reports in the paper that I am engaged in a "Stop Benn" movement. I have resisted the temptation to make a statement, because it's a bit like the question "When did you stop beating your wife?" I did brief the lobby last Thursday, telling them that it would be folly for anyone to stop any candidature, including Tony Benn's. But it only builds up the story if I make a statement. I am obviously very concerned at Tony being portrayed as a *bête noire* or a bogeyman. I condemn it, there is no truth or foundation or substance in it, and I am glad for the chance to say so.'

I think that story is stone dead. It is absolutely manifest that Neil realises the damage it is doing.

At home, in the office Julie was struggling with the word processor trying to get it to print standard letters. Both my telephones were out of action and I discovered I hadn't paid the bill.

Thursday 8 December

To the public inquiry into the building of a PWR nuclear power station at Sizewell, Norfolk. I am giving evidence on behalf of the NUM.

Breakfast with Arthur Scargill, then we drove over to the Maltings at Snape, where the inquiry is sitting. The Inspector is Sir Frank Layfield, a distinguished planning lawyer, and representing the CEGB was Lord Silsoe, who inherited the title from his father Sir Malcolm Trustram Eve, the first Baron Silsoe. There were about fifty people in this lovely auditorium, including a lot of objectors. I sat on the platform facing Sir Frank Layfield, with the QCs and solicitors.

Arthur addressed me first to present evidence for the NUM, and I read from my brief. Then he examined me, pushing me in directions we had agreed upon. Layfield was a bit cautious and I played it very quietly; it looked as if Arthur was pushing me further than I wanted to go, but in fact Layfield knew exactly what was happening and was smiling.

Then Silsoe cross-examined me for over two hours or more, trying to catch me out and treating me like a criminal. When we came on to the plutonium question, he pressed me on my assertion that there were strong military reasons for the CEGB and the AEA wanting the PWR and suggested I should withdraw it.

I said, 'I repeat the answer.' I stuck to my guns and explained why I would not withdraw. I think, on the whole, I confused Silsoe. As far as he was concerned, he did his best and that was it.

Sunday 11 December

Caught the train to Chesterfield to meet Party members. The train didn't actually stop in Chesterfield station but went straight through, then halted, and I thought the driver had forgotten to stop in Chesterfield, so I opened the carriage door and jumped on to the line and walked back about half a mile. In fact they were having to back the train into the platform. It was a risky thing to do, but I couldn't afford to be late.

Ken Coates and Tom Vallins took me over to the old Market Hall for a pre-selection meeting between the candidates and members of all the wards. The other candidates were John Lenthall, the treasurer of the Chesterfield Party, Cliff Fox, the NUM candidate, Bill Flanagan, leader of the council Labour Group, Phillip Whitehead and Paul Vaughan, President of the Party. I had prepared my speech too much, and it was a bit offputting because it was so rigidly controlled. I was asked three questions. One was about the media attacks, another about my age and health and one, from the YS, asking if I was in favour of MPs taking the average workers' wage. I felt very discouraged.

Tuesday 13 December

To Chesterfield again to address trade union members, Tom Vallins picked me up. He's a great guy; he and Margaret are really my closest and warmest allies. We went to the old Market Hall again.

I went through the points I wanted to make about solidarity and then I got questions. One was about the NGA dispute.[2] I said I thought Len Murray was absolutely wrong, and that if Terry Duffy had been alive at the time of the Tolpuddle Martyrs he would have told them to pay the fine and go to Australia quietly. I suppose it was going a bit over the top, considering there must have been a lot of Terry Duffy's supporters there.

Then I was asked about the work of a local MP. I said my constituency work was the key, and I was not the sort of MP who got elected and the next you heard of him was that he was on the board of a big company. That was also a bit over the top because it was an obvious reference to Eric Varley, but I was also thinking of Dick Marsh, George Brown, Roy Jenkins and so on. Actually, I got a warm response, and it is a strange thing that I felt more rapport with the trade union people than I did on Sunday with the Labour Party people.

Newsnight had a programme on the Chesterfield by-election including a poll – the first pre-election polling, before even the selection conference! It is clear that they are trying to prevent Chesterfield from selecting me. The purpose of the poll, financed partly by the *Guardian* and partly by *Newsnight*, was to suggest that, although it was a safe Labour seat, if I was the candidate it would become a three-way marginal.

Wednesday 14 December

At the NEC there was an emergency motion tabled by Jo Richardson and Doug Hoyle in support of the NGA. There is also a special TUC General Council meeting today, which Charlie Turnock mentioned, adding that if the NEC supported the NGA it would embarrass Neil Kinnock.

Kinnock concurred. 'I don't want the resolution withdrawn, but why go head-on and beat your head against the wall?' Then he said the immortal words, 'Today of all days, this is uncalled for', implying that the very day the NGA needed our votes was the worst day to give our support. He added, 'It is inappropriate to endorse any resolution on any side of this matter at this moment, and this is not the time when anyone should try and jog anyone else's elbow.'

It was a classic statement of Labour Leader abstentionism when the going gets rough.

Came home briefly and then went to Chesterfield for the St Helen's Ward nomination meeting. I was absolutely certain that Paul Vaughan, who is chairman of the ward party, would get it.

When I got home, I rang Tom Vallins for the result and heard I had won the ward by 11 to 8. Then I heard that in Moor Ward, where they nominated without hearing the candidates, there was a tie between me and Paul Vaughan, and the chairman gave his casting vote in support of Paul.

Wednesday 21 December

Bea Campbell came to do an interview for *City Limits*. She pursued me on a number of points but she is obsessed with my class. She was trying to suggest that on a particular day in 1966 I met a worker at the Upper Clyde Shipbuilders and this was when the scales fell from my eyes. It isn't quite as simple as that, but it was a useful discussion, and she wants to come back and pursue Hobsbawm's argument for a popular front, she being a member of the Eurocommunist wing of the CP.

Thursday 22 December

Vincent Hanna rang last night and I had a long talk to him about the *Newsnight* poll. He said the highest levels of the BBC had been consulted because *Newsnight* had known it would annoy me. I pointed out to him that it was the first time that the BBC had ever begun intervening in by-elections even before selection of the candidate had taken place. He argued, 'We have the right to investigate', and so on. I said, 'Well, of course, but if you persuade people that, if they choose a certain candidate, Labour will lose . . .' he showed a bit too much interest in that point. I didn't intend to encourage him! But I'm sure it will be a problem.

Friday 23 December
I went out shopping for Christmas.

A programme called *The Week in Politics* has decided to devote half an hour on 6 January to the Chesterfield by-election, looking at what effect my being re-elected to Parliament would have on Kinnock's leadership. I discovered that their plan was to interview Labour MPs Brian Sedgemore, Tony Banks, John Golding and Austin Mitchell, then have a twenty-minute interview of me by Peter Jay. I felt this was a gross intervention, so I rang the IBA and then Dick Clements to see if he could stop it. He was doubtful.

Sunday 25 December
Melissa brought us Christmas breakfast, which is certainly a new ritual. Caroline cooked for sixteen.

Wednesday 4 January 1984
Arkady Maslennikov, the London correspondent of *Pravda*, came to interview me. He had said he would very much like to see how my computer worked, so, before he arrived, I prepared 'a message from the Central Committee of the CP in Moscow to the London *Pravda* correspondent'. The message stated that it was amazing that he was still using a typewriter, which was a tsarist invention, that he might even be using a medieval instrument known as a pen, that all correspondents had to equip themselves with computers in order to demonstrate the Soviet lead in technology, and 'would he please confirm the receipt of this message by sending a carrier pigeon at once to Moscow'. Maslennikov laughed heartily when I called up the message on the screen. Then I showed him how it could be printed in various typefaces, and he took four copies away with him.

Friday 6 January
In the afternoon, I went to record *The Week in Politics*. In the event they used three people who were sympathetic to me – Brian Sedgemore, Chris Mullin and Tony Banks, plus Austin Mitchell, who was very contemptuous but did say some funny things, one of which was that Neil Kinnock was a marvellous leader because 'like all Labour Leaders he talks left and walks right.' It was such an open and honest confession of what it's all about in the eyes of a cynic. Peter Jay having been a civil servant, a *Times* journalist, then Ambassador in Washington, then working on *TV-am* which went bust, is now an interviewer like Brian Walden or Alastair Burnet. Strangely, he lacked confidence. I was determined to be confident myself, because, if I am going to tell the Chesterfield Party not to be frightened of the media, I mustn't be frightened of them.

After midnight, the telephone rang, and it was Tom Vallins saying that I had not been put on the shortlist drawn up by the Chesterfield executive committee (which had been meeting tonight), although I had received thirteen nominations. Thirteen candidates had been considered, and I had been squeezed out in a way that is quite common, by delegates voting first for their own candidate and then for duds in order to keep the favourite off. It happened to Michael Foot in Ebbw Vale in 1960. But it greatly upset Tom, who said, 'I'm going to resign from the Party or move a motion of censure on the executive.' He told me that the Assistant National Agent, Walter Brown, had insisted that the list be kept absolutely secret. He didn't want any mobilisation in my support before the GMC met on Sunday to endorse the shortlist, at which meeting I could be added to the list.

So I rang Dennis Skinner, who said he would talk to people in Chesterfield. I then rang Chris Mullin, who said he would ring the BBC and the Press Association. This was the beginning of a very hectic twenty-four hours. I finally got to sleep at about 2 am.

Saturday 7 January

The BBC and ITN turned up outside my front door. Wearing a sweater and trying to look relaxed, I stood there and said, 'The decision about shortlisting and selection is entirely for the Chesterfield Party and I have every confidence that they will do what they think is right.'

Of course, the BBC's correspondent, Peter Hill, said on the bulletin that my defeat would be 'welcome to the Party leadership'. This is the continual theme – that Kinnock is opposed to me, a rumour which John Cole, the political correspondent, said had reached him through an unimpeachable source.

Eric Heffer rang in a state of great anger about Kinnock's attitude and proposed to issue a statement in support of me.

Sunday 8 January

The papers today were beginning to dance on my grave in advance of today's GMC to decide the shortlist. Caroline and I wanted to go for a walk but there were journalists at the door.

Graham Hinds, a freelance reporter, phoned at about 5 and said, 'You are on. They have put you on.' So it's 5.10 on Sunday and I'm definitely on the shortlist.

The *Daily Mirror* has just phoned, and all I said was 'I am very proud to have been included.' I do think a low-key approach is needed now.

Tuesday 10 January

At the International Committee, there were two motions on Grenada criticising the CIA and calling for the withdrawal of American forces. Jenny Little said that we shouldn't attack the CIA. Neil Kinnock declared that we had no proof the CIA were involved, and anyway we had better be clear that the American invasion was 'bloody popular' with the Grenadians. So we lost on that one.

Friday 13 January

Met Tom and Margaret Vallins and Cliff Fox at Tom's flat. Then they took me to a meeting of the Derbyshire Miners Students' Association. Outside, there was a crane with a camera perched on top so that the media could take pictures of me through the window.

Sunday 15 January

We left for Chesterfield at 8 am for the selection conference of the GMC, and arrived in snow and blizzards. Caroline dropped me off at the NUM offices in Saltergate where there was an enormous crowd of media people standing about as the snowflakes fluttered down. There was the usual checking of Party membership cards and trade union membership as delegates arrived. I drew number six in the speaking order.

The final list was Cllr Dave Wilcox of USDAW, Phillip Whitehead, Bill Flanagan, Cliff Fox, John Lenthall and me.

I finally went in just after 6 pm. I had only been speaking for two minutes when a miner in the front row had an epileptic fit and had to be carted out. He was a very heavy man and had been sick, but they managed to move him and left him at the back so officially he could hear the speeches. I had to recover after that incident. I was asked the obvious questions – 'didn't we lose the General Election because you fought against Healey?', 'how would you deal with the media?', and so on.

There were three ballots, and, to cut a long story short, I was selected. I shook hands with the others and said I hoped to see them all in Parliament in other seats after the next General Election. Phillip Whitehead and Bill Flanagan made little speeches of congratulations, then all hell broke loose. As I went out the front door, there were the media surging about with cameras. We moved slowly across their ranks to the Labour Club, where I gave a press conference. Afterwards I had a word with all my supporters and then Caroline and I drove home.

Caroline was marvellous all day. I have overcome the biggest hurdle, despite the huge press campaign designed to prevent my being selected. I did actually win with more votes than the next two candidates combined, so that was something.

Monday 16 January

In the afternoon I went to the House of Commons to see Neil Kinnock and Dick Clements about the by-election. Caroline had suggested how to play it and I took her advice. I said, 'Look, Neil, first of all, it should be as early as possible.' He agreed, and we settled on 1 March. I said,

'Next, I think Chesterfield should become a platform for the Front Bench. I gather you are going to come up. I am delighted, and I hope the others will be coming with you. When you arrive, give the press conferences and do a walkabout. I'll be canvassing all day, because that's where the work is really needed, and we'll meet in the evening, then any Front Bench people can catch the last train home, and I'll stay and deal with the questions.' He was delighted with that and it suits my book fine.

Tuesday 24 January

Chesterfield. Went to the Party headquarters for talks. Then to an old people's home with the mayor and began the procedure of previous elections of talking to old people, overwhelmingly women, who know so much about the constituency. I ask who the oldest person is, his or her first memory, and that way I hear the most fantastic accounts. One woman told me she was eighty-seven, had started work when she was twelve, at Robinson's factory, did a twelve-hour day, six and a half days a week, and was paid 4s 6d a week.

It was a marvellous day.

Thursday 26 January

I heard that the Liberals had captured a seat in New Whittington ward in a council by-election. They had not stood for twenty-five years, so from nothing they overtook the Tory and Labour Parties and won by ninety votes. I woke in the middle of the night and did actually wonder whether Chesterfield could be lost.

Saturday 28 January

Moved into Room 4 in the Westdale Hotel, a little place next to the Labour Club and the NUM headquarters, were I shall be based for the by-election. It has got two doubles and a single bed, and we have all our equipment there.

Wednesday 1 February

Went to see Neil Kinnock, and there I found assembled the team that Walworth Road had organised for the by-election campaign – Michael Cocks, Richard Clements, Monica Foot, Nita Clarke, Joyce Gould and others. It was a sort of act of conciliation. We discussed the campaign; they asked about the New Whittington by-election, and whether we should get a message of support from Varley.

From 3 February to 25 March 1984, I kept extensive notes of the by-election campaign in Chesterfield and subsequently dictated a day-by-day account, short extracts of which follow. The campaign was distinguished by an unprecedented amount of national press and broadcasting coverage, which forms a significant part

*of my recollections. Members of the family travelled to Chesterfield to help with the
canvassing, as did many friends from all over the country. My own press campaign
was undertaken by officials from Walworth Road, in particular Nita Clarke, the
GLC's Chief Press Secretary, who was seconded for the task. But, in consultation
with the Chesterfield Party officers, I refused to hold press conferences, obliging the
'media circus' to follow us around the constituency as we canvassed and addressed
public meetings.*

Friday 3 February

Went to the shopping arcade, where I found the media out in force –
which makes it impossible to do anything natural. Vincent Hanna was
asking me to go and talk to this or that person and so on, and I must say
my anger at the whole BBC *Newsnight* operation did reach a bit of a peak
this morning. I was even followed to a fish and chip shop at lunchtime.

Tuesday 7 February

Visited the Arkwright colliery, where the manager had told the media
they were not allowed to come inside. I went down the pit for the first
time since my illness in 1981, and I did wonder whether I would stand
up to it because my legs are still a bit shaky. Fortunately it was a drift
mine, and they took me down in the man-rider. I still had to walk three
and a half miles underground on a 1:4 gradient. John Burrows, the
treasurer of the Derbyshire NUM, and Cliff Fox came with me. I went
and talked to the media in my pit clothes before I had a bath.

Sunday 12 February

Laurie Flynn, who is a friend of Maxine Baker on *World in Action*, came
to discuss a programme they want to do on the media coverage. I was a
bit suspicious, truthfully.

Today Meg Crack, Chris Mullin, Ian Flintoff and Jon Lansman
arrived; my team is beginning to assemble. I visited a Labour club,
where, I think, Vincent Hanna had interviewed people and, seemingly,
only two out of 150 supported me. They began the bingo, and when
number 10 was drawn they called out, 'Number Ten, Wedgie's Den.'
Everybody laughed; it was a sort of sign of acceptance, and Dennis
Skinner who organised it, was absolutely thrilled.

It's bitterly cold at the moment, and I have to wear two pairs of socks
and two woolly jumpers.

Monday 13 February

Hattersley arrived today; the real start of the campaign. Roy felt it
necessary to say things to justify his position – that this represented a
major change in the Party, etc, etc. He was caught out by a questioner
who asked about Kinnock's finger on the nuclear button because Neil
has said he would never push the button. Instead of answering, 'Well,

who does want to press the button?' he said, 'It depends what you mean, Neil's been misinterpreted', and so on. I thought he made a bit of a fool of himself. The London press were trying to cause trouble with quotations from statements that had been made at one time or another.

We had an open meeting in the Market Hall, which holds about 600 people; it was packed, with another 1000 overflowing into the square. So Meg Crack, Roy Hattersley and I went out on the balcony overlooking the Market Square and spoke to them. There was tremendous enthusiasm.

Heard that Peter Tatchell visited Chesterfield today. I said that was fine, but the Party hierarchy are obviously agitated.

Tuesday 14 February

The Times had a report that Peter Tatchell had visited Chesterfield and had been sent back. There was another report claiming that 'one of Tony Benn's aides said, "Tony is learning fast."' I was absolutely furious, as were Caroline and Margaret Vallins.

At the Centre for the Unemployed, I said I was delighted that Tatchell had been to Chesterfield, it was quite untrue that he had been sent away, and I would be proud to have him back again. If I had let that story go unanswered, they would have played the old trick – we'll give you a good press if you repudiate your own people. Once the press realise they cannot divide you from your own Party, then they stop trying.

To the Edwin Swales School with Joan Maynard and Phillip Whitehead. It was here that I vigorously attacked Vincent for his coverage of the by-election, saying that he was the SDP candidate for Chesterfield and that he wanted a Liberal victory. It was triggered off by the *Newsnight* programme, by Hanna's behaviour at the shopping centre and also by the treatment of Peter Tatchell. It fired a warning shot across Vincent's bows and created dismay among our own Party workers.

Wednesday 15 February

The press was full of 'Benn supports Tatchell' stories.

At the daily campaign meeting Monica Foot and the people from Walworth Road were sunk in gloom at my decision to attack Hanna and support Tatchell. Joyce Gould was in a panic because there is an unspoken alliance between Vincent Hanna and the Party officials, and I was breaking it. I thought perhaps it had been a mistake to refer to Hanna, but with the benefit of hindsight I can see it did the trick. He wrote a letter and the BBC issued a statement saying Vincent Hanna had their full support.

Sunday 19 February

Seventeen candidates have been nominated – a record. I should mention a couple of the other candidates. Screaming Lord Sutch,

David Sutch, of the Monster Raving Loony Party Last Stand turned up at some of my meetings. He has become something of a friend. He's a decent guy, he is actually quite serious and liked the things we were saying, and my view of him altered completely. He appears to be making fun of the Election but he's shrewd: he's a court jester in the medieval sense.

Neil Kinnock came up today. I met him at lunchtime at the Labour Club and there was a photo-call. For the purpose of the battle, you have to be seen side by side, and he played it very well. We went on a walkabout in the market and were mobbed by the media; there must have been sixty of them walking backwards in front of us. I wonder whether it was worth doing, because hardly anyone in the market could get near us. Even when we went for a cup of tea they surrounded us.

Kinnock performed his part excellently. At the public meeting, we held up our hands together and I called it 'The Return Ticket', a comment on the so-called 'Dream Ticket'.

I did have a chance to talk to Neil about his visit to America. He had seen Reagan, who had said to him, 'Do you think the United States would ever have used nuclear weapons on Japan if Japan had had the bomb?' So Kinnock replied, 'Well, that would be Qadhafi's case for having the bomb!' Reagan couldn't think of an answer to that one.

Kinnock was quite friendly throughout, but it was a formal occasion. That part of the campaign is over, and Kinnock must want it to succeed.

Thursday 23 February
Vincent Hanna had asked to see me and we talked for about an hour in one of the rooms in the NUM headquarters. Peter Coleman, the Party's regional organiser, sat in. Hanna was absolutely white-faced. He said, 'I am shocked that you should have said that I was the SDP candidate. My mother-in-law' (who is the wife of Gerry Fitt, former socialist MP defeated by Gerry Adams in Belfast West) 'is not at all well and was made much worse by it.'

I replied, 'I am sorry about that, Vincent, but my *wife* was very upset by your programme. I think your coverage has been most unfair. It has been in support of the Liberals, talking about the importance of tactical voting. I am here to support the Labour Party, and anyone who gets in my way is going to be hammered, and you've just got to accept it.'

So he said, 'Well, I can tell you that Neil Kinnock didn't want you to be the candidate.'

'Maybe he didn't,' I answered.

I think he regretted saying it. He then tried to be friendly, and he said, 'Now, confidentially, I can give you some useful information.'

So I said, 'Well, let me be clear, Vincent, I don't want anything confidential from you. I don't want to be in your debt at all.'

Peter Coleman was pretty shocked too.

Friday 24 February
I went to the Chesterfield Royal Hospital. Patricia Moberly and Jenny Holland from Vauxhall were here canvassing. Hilary, Sally, Michael and James turned up, and it was lovely to hear Michael cry out, 'Dan-dan!', which is what he calls me.

At the NHS rally in the evening with 500 people, I did a very silly thing. To show how fit I was (I suppose), I tried to leap on to the platform, which was only about 18 inches off the ground, but I missed and fell and broke my specs. It hurt like anything, but I was determined not to show it.

Sunday 26 February
The last Sunday before polling day. Pat Phoenix, Tony Booth, Dennis Skinner, Caroline and I went out for four hours in the morning and four hours in the afternoon. It was cold and wet and exhausting, but I must say Pat Phoenix was marvellous. There were over 1000 helpers from all over the country – a great response.

Monday 27 February
Jim Mortimer, Eric Heffer and Denis Healey arrived for a public meeting. I must say Denis played it like an old trouper. He spoke before me, and just as he said, 'Tony and I are inseparable, like Torville and Dean', the Party banner behind us fell off the wall; it was hilarious, and it was impossible not to laugh uproariously. He made a great speech and got a good reception. Then we went to the Hopflower pub, where he played the piano and we sang together, 'Here we are again, happy as can be, all good pals and jolly good company!' He was extremely good, and even the press were laughing.

Wednesday 29 February
Eve of poll. Went canvassing with Colin Welland, who wrote *Chariots of Fire*, which was such a success, and Stephen Lewis, who plays an inspector in *On the Buses*; he is a committed socialist and extremely amusing, very direct and couldn't have been better. At a canteen meeting and later at the Brimington Ward eve-of-poll meetings I spoke about restoring our self-respect and getting rid of the Tories.

A series of eve-of-poll meetings with Jo Richardson, Ken Coates, Peter Heathfield and Stuart Holland. Bed at 12.

Thursday 1 March
Joshua worked all day feeding canvassing information into the computer system set up at the Westdale Hotel. I went round the constituency all day.

The *Sun* had an article, 'Benn on the Couch – a top psychiatrist's view of Britain's leading leftie', in which they said they had fed my

Ye Quaint Olde 18ᵗʰ Century Ceremony as former Lord SuperBenn takes his seat in Parliament

personal and political details to a psychiatrist in America who had concluded that I was power hungry, would do anything to satisfy my hunger, was prone to periods of fantasy and so on.*

Dozed, had a bath at the Westdale, then watched TV.

Just after midnight, we walked over to the Goldwell Rooms in the snow and the rain for the count. When we arrived, there was a huge crowd outside being held back by police. I did a few interviews, and the result was declared – Labour 24,633, Liberal 18,369, Tory 8,028. So the majority was 6,264, which was 663 higher than Varley's. There were rowdy scenes as we got on the platform, and all the young Labour people came in chanting, 'Tony Benn, Tony Benn!' I made my victory speech. Payne, the Liberal, made an angry one which was greeted with so much noise that I had to quieten people down in order to allow him to be heard. Bourne, the Tory spoke briefly.

We withdrew like boxers after a big match and went back to the Labour Club with the media around in huge numbers, the police having a job to hold them back. Outside the Labour Club I spoke to the crowd again. Then I went inside and stood on a table and addressed the members.

Got to bed at 5 exhausted, but what an extraordinarily good result it was, though *Newsnight* were able to describe it as a very poor result for

* The press coverage of the Chesterfield by-election and of my political career is analysed thoroughly in *The Press and Political Dissent* by Mark Hollingsworth (Pluto, 1986).

Labour. I must confess it was a triumph for the left and showed that socialist policies are not a deterrent.

NOTES
Chapter Five

1. (p. 305) The trip to London by Gerry Adams and Joe Austin of Sinn Fein in July 1983 for discussions with GLC councillors created a great political storm. The visit had originally been arranged for December 1982. At that time Michael Foot repudiated the invitation, in a letter to the leader of the GLC, Ken Livingstone. But in any case, a bomb explosion in County Derry, which killed sixteen people days before the visit, prompted the Home Office to issue exclusion orders under the Prevention of Terrorism Act. By July 1983, Gerry Adams had been elected MP for Belfast West and was again invited by Livingstone and Jeremy Corbyn, newly elected Labour MP for Islington North.

2. (p. 328) Newspaper proprietor Eddie Shah had become involved in a dispute with the print union NGA in 1983 when he attempted to introduce computer technology to his plants in Warrington and Stockport and replaced NGA workers on strike with non-union labour. The scenes outside the plant, the arrest of pickets and the ultimate sequestration of £175,000 from the NGA for non-payment of the fine were the precursor for the much bigger and more violent dispute at the Wapping Plant in London's Docklands belonging to News International, in 1986–7, in which Rupert Murdoch succeeded in breaking the power of the print unions with the aid of huge numbers of police and Court action.

6
War on the Miners
March 1984–March 1985

Immediately after my election to Chesterfield the Miners' Strike of 1984/5 began. It was the culmination of a long conflict between the Conservative Party and the mineworkers' union, the history of which can be traced back to the General Strike of 1926, which the Conservative Government defeated, and the strike in 1973/4 which led to the defeat of Edward Heath's Government.

This history still rankled with the Conservatives when Mrs Thatcher came to power, and the Government was determined that trade unions would never again have such influence. In order to break their power, which represented organized labour, in favour of those who owned and controlled wealth, the Conservative Government decided to take on the NUM, the strongest and most political union, and over a period of time to introduce radical restrictions on workers by a series of Acts – including four Employment Acts between 1980 and 1990, a Trade Union Act (1984) and Wages Act (1986), and Codes of Practice on picketing and industrial ballots. The net effect of this legislation has been to cripple trade unions by using injunctions to prevent 'misapplication of funds', by the levy of fines and by powers to sequestrate union funds for contempt of court.

Detailed preparations were made to renew the conflict against the NUM. Nicholas Ridley was credited with the overall strategy, produced in 1978 (before the Thatcher Government had come to power), whereby an incoming Conservative Government would provoke a strike with the coal industry and a) build up maximum coal stocks, b) make contingency plans for the import of coal, c) encourage recruitment of non-union lorry drivers by haulage firms who would cross picket lines with police protection, d) move to greater oil-firing of power stations. Ridley suggested that the strikers should have their 'money supply cut off' (ie starved) and that a large mobile squad of police should be equipped and prepared to uphold the law against violent picketing.

Ian MacGregor was appointed to the chairmanship of the NCB in 1983 to supervise the imminent battle. Some pit closures had occurred before the NUM was ready to respond to the Government's challenge, but when the decision to close Cortonwood colliery in Yorkshire was announced in March 1984, when coal stocks were high and energy demand about to fall in the summer, the miners there resolved, in the absence of any national officials, that they would take strike action and call on the NUM to support them.

The NUM had, at a series of previous delegate conferences, resolved that if a major closure programme was imposed the Union would respond with strike action.

For this reason the NUM leadership felt entitled to call for solidarity from its members in every mining area.

The fact that there was no national pit-head ballot was used by critics of the NUM – including the Labour leadership – as grounds for withholding political support. But the NUM had not forgotten that, when an incentive scheme had been rejected by a national ballot during the lifetime of the previous Labour Government, the Nottinghamshire area had successfully applied to the courts for permission to hold their own ballot; as a result of this they accepted the incentive scheme and effectively reversed the national ballot.

The issue of a national ballot was really irrelevant because had it occurred – and the NUM nationally had come out in favour of a strike – Nottinghamshire area would have won permission for its own ballot and remained at work; and if the ballot had gone the other way the Yorkshire area would have come out and other areas would have had to decide whether to give support.

The extent of the support in the NUM as a whole was evidenced by the overwhelming majority of miners who remained on strike until it ended in 1985.

The only legitimate question that may be raised about the tactics of the NUM nationally was whether the Yorkshire miners, by picketing Nottinghamshire so early and so vigorously, alienated those they were seeking to influence, and whether the NUM underestimated the degree to which the Government had stockpiled coal for a long hard fight.

In the event the Union of Democratic Miners was set up among working miners in Nottinghamshire, with the encouragement and support of the Government and sections of the media, repeating the history of the old 'Spencer' Union, which had been established after the General Strike as a company union in opposition to the Miners' Federation of Great Britain.

I was fortunate to find myself representing a mining area which was one of the centres of the strike activity right at the inception of what became a historic battle.

The assault on the miners did not cease after the miners' strike had ended. The NUM was in receivership until summer 1986 and a war of attrition against it continued throughout the Eighties, particularly against Arthur Scargill and Peter Heathfield who, under anti-trade union legislation, ran the risk of bankruptcy and imprisonment. Robert Maxwell, proprietor of the Daily Mirror, *in particular, and other journalists, made scurrilous allegations of personal corruption concerning NUM funds. The smears continued into the 1990s and it was indeed ironic that Robert Maxwell emerged, after his death, to have been the crook while the miners' leaders behaved throughout with total integrity.*

Saturday 3 March

There was a leak in the basement and I had to call a plumber in. I was so tired, I felt quite unwell and had to go to bed.

Monday 5 March

The task of unpacking from Chesterfield and opening the mail had begun in earnest. Three thousand letters came in during the by-election. Just the opening and sorting of them is terribly difficult. In the evening, Laurie Flynn's *World in Action* film on the media coverage of Chesterfield, 'The Press Gang', was a brilliant and devastating exposure, particularly of the *Sun*.

Wednesday 7 March
I feel rather as Father felt when he went to the House of Lords. I am being welcomed back to the House of Commons 'where you belong', as so many articles and letters have put it. I feel that the Commons has been incorporated into the Government.

Thursday 15 March
The miners' strike has been triggered off by the Government's decision to accelerate pit closures, and there has been a ballot in the various areas. Derbyshire voted by only 16 votes against striking, and Nottingham by 3 to 1. It has precipitated a great new crisis in the mining industry and a big political crisis in Britain. I attacked the Home Secretary, Leon Brittan, in the House when he made his statement on picketing, saying that a 'major co-ordinated police response, involving police officers throughout the country, has been deployed to ensure that any miner who wishes to work . . . may do so.'

Friday 16 March
I drove to Chesterfield for a surgery. Margaret and Tom Vallins have got it all organised, and Margaret has agreed to be my constituency secretary, part-time.

Monday 19 March
Thousands of police are being used to stop the miners from picketing; in Kent, miners were stopped from travelling through the Dartford Tunnel. I heard that Michael Foot, Merlyn Rees, Eric Heffer and Tony Banks had protested to the Press Council about the *Sun* story, 'Benn on the couch'.

Tuesday 20 March
Went to the Commons for Prime Minister's Questions, and got in one about the use of the police in the strike. The whole mining industry is now up in arms because of flying policemen coming from all over the country to try to stop picketing in Nottinghamshire.

Thursday 22 March
Caught the train to Chesterfield. Tom and Margaret met me and we went straight to the Duckmanton miners' wives meeting which had been organised by Margaret Vallins and Betty Heathfield.* One

---

* It was at this meeting that the Women's Support Groups – which became a national movement – were formed.

woman, whose five-week-old baby had died in a cot death in January, had received a bill for £206 for a headstone, to be paid by the end of March. She was getting no strike pay from her husband.

They asked if I would go on to the Bolsover colliery, in Skinner's constituency, where there were apparently hundreds of police, but by the time I arrived the police had gone. I went into the NUM office and someone said, 'All the police are now at the Creswell colliery', so we went on there. The police had obviously heard I was in the area and had all left before I got there.

The accounts I have heard of police bullying and brutality and arrests are hair-raising.

Friday 23 March

Up at 6.15 and went on the soup run to six collieries with Margaret and Tom and Betty Heathfield. At Duckmanton there were 200 police in buses and, as soon as I appeared, the buses went off in convoy. The word has got round that if Tony Benn turns up at a colliery the police go away, so the demand for me gets greater. It was a useful piece of work.

Sunday 25 March

To the Market Hall for the AGM of the local Party. The important event was the election of Johnny Burrows as president and Tom Vallins as secretary of the constituency Party, so the executive has swung from right to left. That was good news.

Monday 26 March

All hell broke loose at the TUC–Labour Party Liaison Committee. The Government's proposal to abolish the six metropolitan councils and the GLC came up, and I said, 'Don't you think the House of Lords should vote on this? I know they don't normally vote against second readings, but surely they could put down a motion saying it would be inappropriate for a hereditary and appointed chamber to remove the franchise from the people of London and other cities.'

Stan Orme said it would just be a gesture. Roy Hattersley said it would set a precedent. In the end, the discussion was terminated because Neil Kinnock, who was in the chair, said it was inappropriate for this committee to discuss tactics in the House of Lords. The fact is, the Lords simply won't vote – they just won't do it.

Wednesday 28 March

All of London Transport was on strike today in opposition to the Government's plans to remove the direct responsibility for London Transport from the GLC to the Secretary of State for Transport.

I went to the NEC, where we passed an emergency resolution in support of the miners. During the day I had a phone call asking me to ring the NUM office in Chesterfield, and I heard that the police were now blockading the roads around Chesterfield. I rang up the Speaker about putting in a Private Notice Question but it was too late, so I went into the House of Commons and raised a request for an emergency debate under standing order number 10. The speaker turned it down, but I was able to speak for five minutes on it so that the police conduct was placed on the record. There was a lot of disturbance in the House.

The Speaker is trying to be friendly to me and I don't want a row with anybody, but I think I do have to go on pushing this because it is an important question.

Thursday 29 March
I went to the PLP meeting at 6, and Joe Ashton tried to persuade the Front Bench to amend next week's business so that a debate on education on Tuesday could be replaced by a debate on the miners.

Then Don Concannon, MP for Mansfield, a former Nottingham miner, said, 'You talk about the police conduct, but I can compare atrocity with atrocity.' He was Minister for Northern Ireland – a real right-winger.

Dennis Skinner, Merlyn Rees and Kevin Barron all spoke up for the miners.

When Kinnock got up, he went over the top. If he had said that there was a bit of a difficulty at the moment, could we leave it and think about it, everybody would have understood. But he said, 'We shouldn't lead with our chins. You're asking me to jump out of the window. This would just be a gesture.' It was wholly unnecessary, and people looked mildly embarrassed.

Mike Cocks, who was in the chair because Jack Dormand is in Cuba, said, 'I'm not prepared to allow a vote. We never have a vote at PLP meetings.' So although there were a lot of people there by then, seventy or eighty I should think, there wasn't a vote.

Friday 30 March
I went to Bristol for a crowded meeting with Joan Ruddock, Ken Livingstone, Joan Maynard and others. Came back on the train with Ken and Joan Ruddock, who is thinking of becoming a parliamentary candidate. She is calm, collected and reasonable and would do extremely well as an MP. She told me that this Easter CND are going to campaign primarily on American bases, of which they have identified 102, and are trying to add a foreign policy dimension and tackle the issue of nuclear power.

Ken described the success of his GLC campaign. Even the *Evening Standard* opinion poll revealed enormous support for the GLC. I think 62 per cent want to keep the GLC and only 22 per cent want to abolish it.

Sunday 1 April

To Chesterfield with Caroline. She went to the Women's Action Group meeting at the NUM offices. During the Election, the group was a major canvassing team; then Margaret Vallins and Betty Heathfield reorganised and restructured it to cope with the miners' dispute. They have been doing the soup run. It has no officers, includes Communists, members of the Labour Party and people who have no particular alignment.

I went over to the Labour Club, where the left of the NUM's national executive was meeting, and I could hear them shouting away at one another, mainly Arthur Scargill's voice coming through the door.

Monday 30 April

I went to Eastbourne for a fringe meeting of the USDAW annual conference. Militant were prominent there and they really are giving a lead within the trade unions and are more thoughtful than before. They are not just reciting 'Nationalise the top 250 monopolies under workers' control', but are now relating directly to the needs and interests of individual industries and are building up trade-unionism as a political force. Now that they have so much influence in Liverpool and also have two MPs, they are a significant group.

If you look at the other left groups, the *Morning Star*, which is actually concerned about maintaining a cutting edge of socialism, is in conflict with the CP, which is now under Eurocommunist influence – the Eric Hobsbawm line. *Socialist Action*, the old IMG, is a good paper and is highly analytical in its approach to society, but sympathetic to the Labour Party. *Socialist Organiser* is run by a hard-left group. *London Labour Briefing* seems to have lost some of its influence. *Labour Herald*, run by Ken Livingstone, Matthew Warburton and Ted Knight, is opening its pages to the whole movement. *Tribune* is hanging on but I think it is over the hump. *Labour Weekly* has gone soft, in line with the leadership of Kinnock and Hattersley.

Wednesday 2 May

Worked in my dressing-gown all morning – shocking!

I went to Wales for the Cynon Valley by-election caused by the death of Ioan Evans, who had once been my PPS. The Labour candidate was Ann Clwyd. I was taken to a miner's house for a meal, and all the best china was brought out.

The public meeting was absolutely packed and the atmosphere electric. Terry Thomas, of the South Wales miners, made a good speech. Everyone stood and cheered, and I said, 'Let's sing "The Red Flag".' So we sang that and then 'We'll Keep a Welcome in the Hillsides'. The whole evening was great. Half the people there were miners on strike; and there is 20 per cent unemployment in the valleys.

What we are doing now is simply reawakening the socialism in people which was thought to have died and which can't be preserved in aspic with public-relations gimmicks and campaigns. It is the experience of the brutality of capitalism that makes people radical. It was a very moving meeting.

Friday 4 May
Hilary rang and told me that he knew of a policeman in Ealing who said he hoped he would be sent to Nottinghamshire because the pay was so good and it would finance his summer holiday. It is reported that the police are getting between £600 and £1000 a week. I heard later in the day that the cost of the miners' dispute to the Derbyshire Constabulary was already £3,529,000.

At my surgery in Chesterfield I had a tragic case of a family whose little child had found and eaten a chemical stolen from a local factory and had died.

Keith Harris, a miner, drove me to Nottingham for a Euro-election meeting. He told me that one miner had gone to Felixstowe port in Suffolk to join the picket against the import of coal, and in the line of policemen he had seen his own son, who is in the Welsh Guards. I have heard so many stories of this kind that I am persuaded that this is what is happening because there just aren't that many police available to move about. The authorities must be using the army.

Apparently some of the men still working in the pits are waving their £50 bonuses in the faces of the pickets. In Nottinghamshire, 10,000 tons of coal a day is being produced instead of 28,000 tons, and that means the subsidy on it would be £70–80 a ton.

Saturday 5 May
It looks as though the miners cannot beat the Government. However, with 85 per cent of the pits out, coal stocks must be shrinking like anything, and the steel industry is beginning to be affected. The miners won't budge, and it is a very long strike, already longer than the 1926 strike. The TUC has got to back them, because, to put it bluntly, if the miners are beaten, the Government will ride all over everybody and workers couldn't stand up to it again, so the miners *mustn't* be beaten.

The success or failure of the Government doesn't depend on their capacity to bring in police to beat a particular group of workers, it depends on whether they carry the public with them, and they have gone so far over the top on democracy, trade union rights and brutality against the poor that the public are beginning to see it; but what a battle it is.

Monday 7 May
May Day rally in Chesterfield, the biggest ever, with 10,000 people

marching through the town – an indication of what a powerful NUM and trade union movement and politically conscious Party can produce. There were one or two hiccups during the speeches. No woman speaker had been included, and the women demanded the right to speak, so Margaret Vallins got up. Dennis Skinner also hadn't been asked to speak, so by general demand he got up and made a tremendous, impassioned and courageous speech which brought the house (or the tent) down!

Wednesday 9 May

At the NEC we discussed the critical question of Liverpool.* A motion pledging support for the councillors, in their refusal to set a budget this year, had gone through the NEC Local Government Committee, proposed by David Blunkett and seconded by Eric Heffer; and it was a good resolution. Charlie Turnock of the NUR objected to it because he said the Liverpool councillors were acting against Conference policy. He said he would move the reference back.

Blunkett said, 'Liverpool is behaving responsibly.'

Heffer pointed out that the Liverpool Council, under its present leadership, had received over 50 per cent of the popular vote, and even the Liverpool press were now coming out in favour of Liverpool's case.

We then had a heated discussion about the whole Liverpool problem.

Kinnock said, 'It is not a question of standing back, it is a question of a form of words. The people who are in the front line are not the councillors, they are the old people in Liverpool, the workers, because an illegal budget would hit jobs. Our hearts can bleed as much as we like, but the best thing we can do is to make representations on their behalf. There is a danger of bankruptcy in Liverpool, and the choice is between a gesture which would be inoperable, with dreadful consequences, or a compromise. Our obligation is to the poor of Liverpool.'

Dennis Skinner said he was surprised that Neil had gone to the stake on this one and remarked that the Tories were longing for us to do exactly what Neil suggested, to do their job for them. 'The Tories are in a jam and they need us to protect them. Whose side are we on? That's the question. It's them or us. Kinnock is trying to help the Tories.'

Kinnock said, 'Rubbish.'

Skinner replied, 'Well, your judgement is wrong. No Labour local government can win if Liverpool is beaten. The Tory press will praise Kinnock but will demand more, just as they did with Michael Foot. We must stick together.'

Kinnock barked, 'Who are *our* people? They are the poor of Liverpool, and it's just a bloody gesture to support the council.'

It got very nasty.

* See pp. 418–19.

After much discussion, Kinnock said, 'Well, I move we suspend standing orders,' in order to amend the resolution.

'We can't,' Heffer told him. 'If the NEC does not support Liverpool, it will be treachery. I will tell Neil now that the Liberal Party put out leaflets during the municipal elections in which they quoted Neil Kinnock's own words criticising the Liverpool Labour Council for their plans to have an illegal budget. We must help.' He spoke with great feeling.

In the end I proposed a form of words, which was agreed. The reference to the councils' proposal for a 9 per cent rate increase was deleted, which somehow made the right feel they had won in opposing the illegal budget, but it meant nothing.

Afterwards, Neil Kinnock went up to Heffer and said, 'Don't you ever use the word "treachery" about me again.'

Eric blew his top and told him, 'You're not worthy of any position in the Party, Kinnock.'

Relations between the two men are now very, very bad, and it's a good thing we have got Eric in the chair this year, because it is an important year for the Party.

Stephen turned up at the House. He is the only member on both the GLC and ILEA Campaign Committees, sees Ken Livingstone and Frances Morrell every day and is tremendously respected. Stephen's work on campaigning has been outstanding. We had several cups of tea together in the course of the evening and he told me how the fight was going.

Incidentally, the editor of the *Daily Express*, Larry Lamb, has devoted the centre-page spread to Arthur Scargill, setting out what he ought to say to the miners, which was, more or less: 'Comrades, we have made a mistake. I am wrong. We have got to go back. We're beaten.' A scandalous article.

I learned from Arthur that the SOGAT workers at the *Express* had today gone to the editor and demanded the right of reply for Arthur Scargill. The editor refused, so they got together with the other chapels in Fleet Street and Bill Keys, the SOGAT General Secretary, told the *Express* that, if Arthur didn't get the right of reply, they would shut down the whole of Fleet Street. Lord Matthews, Chief Executive of Express Newspapers then agreed, so Larry Lamb said he would resign.

I rang Arthur and he was busy writing his reply. I suggested to him we have a motion of censure against the Government, which I would propose at the next PLP meeting.

Thursday 10 May

John Prescott came up to me in the House and said, 'I am worried about this Arthur Scargill business. Stan Orme claims to be in contact all the time with Peter Heathfield, but Neil Kinnock says he hasn't seen Arthur Scargill. Why won't Arthur ring Neil?'

I answered, 'Candidly, I don't know. It may be because Neil goes on and on about the ballot and hasn't come out in support of the miners. Perhaps Neil might get on to Arthur.'

John said, 'Well, it's not for Neil to chase up Arthur Scargill.'

'These things can be easily arranged,' I remarked.

Anyway, I did write a letter to Neil Kinnock:

Dear Neil,

As John Prescott may have told you, I was going to suggest at the Party meeting tonight that perhaps we might have a full-scale motion of censure against the Government which would be very opportune and would provide us with an opportunity to deal with the handling of the mining dispute. I have taken soundings, and I know that this initiative would be welcomed by the NUM.

Monday 14 May

Up at 6.30, and at 7.30 I went on the soup run with the warden of the Labour Club and Sheila and Audrey, two shop stewards from Robinson's factory who are active in the Women's Action Group. We went to about five collieries, the usual routine – in other words, when you arrive, the pickets say, 'You've just missed the police', the police having radioed ahead. It was a beautiful, cloudless, sunny day, and all the blossom was out. The soup was distributed to the pickets and was greatly welcomed.

Tom Vallins drove me to Mansfield for the NUM rally, the biggest demonstration the NUM has ever had, with 45,000 to 50,000 people. I marched with Peter Heathfield, Arthur Scargill, Dennis Skinner, Mick Welsh (the MP for Doncaster North), one or two of the other Yorkshire miners' MPs and most of the NUM executive.

A platform had been erected. Peter Heathfield took the chair and we all spoke. Mr and Mrs Jones, the parents of David who was killed in one of the early incidents, were there. The young miners are just so keen. It was a marvellous day and there were banners from every coalfield – Scotland, Kent, all over.

Tuesday 15 May

Roy Hattersley sat down next to me at tea and I had a chat with him. He told me he thought the miners would lose, and I said I thought we ought to take a stronger line because there were votes to be gained from strength and there was a sense of weakness prevailing at the moment. He agreed with that. He said he had had to protect Kinnock from getting the wrong line on Liverpool, and there was a twinkle in his eye.

I followed this up by saying, 'I suppose Neil will be the first Prime Minister at Number 10 who has never held any ministerial office.'

He said, 'No, there was Ramsay MacDonald!'

It was quite a friendly talk and I think the truth is that Roy Hattersley would like to build up alliances on the left a bit. In that situation, Hattersley would be easier to deal with than Kinnock, just as Healey would have been easier to deal with than Foot.

Wednesday 16 May

The papers this morning reported that American female personnel at Greenham Common had strip-searched some peace women who had broken into the military base.

There was also a report that Rhodes Boyson, the Minister for Social Security, had told a delegation from Scotland that when miners were given food parcels the DHSS would reduce the benefit being paid by the value of the food parcels.

Incidentally, Anne Scargill was arrested today.

I went to the House for a meeting of the PLP.

There were a number of motions asking for a censure debate on the miners' dispute and for a £5 levy on MPs towards the miners' strike. Max Madden, MP for Bradford West, made a brilliant speech, describing how miners and nurses had stood together on the hospital picket lines to try to prevent the closure of Thornton View Hospital, which was in his constituency. He said that in Chesterfield he had met a miner who said, 'For the first time we are beggars, and we never thought we would be.' He told us that huge sacrifices were being made, and at the moment a miner's wife had only £13.85 a week to live on. At his GMC, £80 had been raised, and tinned food was being collected outside supermarkets. He moved a motion for a £5 levy from all Labour MPs. He said he was disappointed at the amendment which had been put against the £5 levy and he hoped those responsible would withdraw it. He stressed, 'Money is vital, because this will be a long dispute.'

Willie Hamilton, the MP for Fife, who is a hard-line right-winger, gave his credentials: he was the longest-serving member of the PLP and he had always supported miners (the sort of statement that warns you that betrayal is coming). He said there had never been a motion for a levy of Labour MPs before, it was a dangerous precedent, and what would happen if a similar motion was put forward for the nurses, the engineers or the civil servants? The PLP would become a supplementary benefit organisation. 'This is not the way to help the miners. The Government has got its responsibility, and the Notts miners are good, sound working people. The strike is harming the Party and Thatcher is trying to say that we are responsible.'

Kinnock declared, 'I want the miners to win. I agree with Max Madden that there are massive sacrifices being made in the coalfields and the movement is trying to help. My own constituency has given £500. I accept also that £5 is not a sacrifice for MPs. The amendment has nothing to do with any objection to the money, but if we levy now we must continue to levy, and we, the Shadow Cabinet, are against it. A levy gives the impression that there is a reluctance to contribute, and if the levy fell below its official sum, there would be a propaganda point for our enemies.'

Joe Ashton was excellent. He said, 'We are now attempting to substitute a discussion about payments for a debate on policy. The Shadow Cabinet have been sitting on the fence for ten weeks and have now come up with this amendment against the miners. We have had no policy for ten weeks, and 2300 miners have been arrested. The police are now in charge of industrial relations. The Labour Party's gains in the opinion polls have levelled off because we are dithering. What are we scared of? We are just keeping our heads down, and we need leadership from the PLP. We should take the initiative. The strike is about despair. We should support the miners or we will lose.'

Michael McGuire, the MP for Makerfield, thought Willie Hamilton had made a courageous speech. 'I am a sponsored NUM MP,' he said, 'and the miners like plain speaking. I have reservations because I think the miners should have a ballot. There is intimidation by Scargill. The miners always stick to majority decisions, and the last ballot showed 61 per cent against a strike and only 31 per cent in favour. I am one of them, and, without a ballot, the strike is doomed. The PLP must win back the support of those who fear totalitarianism; therefore we should tell Arthur Scargill to have a ballot.'

Joan Maynard said McGuire's speech was unbelievable; when it came to the productivity scheme, the Notts miners had defied a national ballot against it. Eighty per cent of miners had been on strike for ten weeks, and this was a different kind of struggle. 'The NEC asked for a levy for the miners and, if it is OK for members of the Party, why not for the PLP? This is the Tories versus the NUM, the bosses versus the workers. The miners will win.'

Max Madden suggested, 'The term "levy" came from the NEC, but, if it is just accepted that we ask members of the PLP to give £5 a week through the regional whips, that's all right by me.'

In the end, the motion was carried unanimously. This is the second time within a week that I have witnessed Kinnock withdraw. He did so in the Liverpool case by accepting a meaningless amendment, and he did so in this case by accepting a meaningless concession. It does confirm my view that, if you keep the pressure up, the man will always give way.

Friday 18 May

Up at 6.30 for the soup run at 7.30. It was cold and a bit miserable, and I detected a different atmosphere. The miners were unshaven, looked unwell, were probably unfed, and the police were more aggressive. I was told that at one place the police had stood right up against the miners, staring at them and rhythmically beating their truncheons on their gloved hands. It is just very frightening and intimidating.

Whereas previously the police have melted away, this time they harassed us. The inspector came up and said, 'Come on, lads, get off this bit of grass. You've got to go back to the road. The pickets will see you more easily from there anyway' – which was an intolerable remark, given the fact that the police surround the pickets so they can't even be seen or heard by any of the lorries going through or by any of the people going into the pit to work. If any pickets shout 'Scab' they are arrested for using abusive language, and if anyone refuses to do what they are told by the police then they are arrested and charged with obstruction and given these restrictive bail conditions.

I went over to Chesterfield Labour Club; it was like a field hospital, with people crowding in to collect food parcels. There are miners' wives who are expecting babies, and the DHSS refuse to help with money for prams or cots or nappies, and this is causing great anxiety. So there was a big notice asking for baby clothes, and so on.

Today, the Coal Board, North Derbyshire area, put out a letter to miners saying that any man who didn't go to work would lose bank holiday pay, even though, as was pointed out to me, the holiday entitlement had been earned by work done last year.

I talked to Betty Heathfield about the attempt by the Electricity Board to cut off domestic supplies to the miners, and I wrote some letters to try to prevent it. She told me that the villages of Welbeck and Church Warsop had been virtually occupied by the police. They had put foot patrols on every corner, gone into the houses of striking miners, interrogated the families to find out if they were billeting pickets from Yorkshire, and were evicting those Yorkshire miners, though they had absolutely no right to do so. They were alleged to be 'investigating intimidation' by striking miners against working miners. Betty thought the police were trying to break up the Women's Action Group, because the Barnsley group had been arrested and the police were attacking women pickets.

Sunday 20 May

Heard Neil Kinnock on the one o'clock news. His interviews are like processed cheese coming out of a mincing machine – nothing meaty, just one mass of meaningless rhetoric that defuses and anaesthetises the listener. The last thing we want is a row with him because he is still on his honeymoon, but the fact is that the Labour leadership has totally failed to support the working class when in struggle.

Monday 21 May

At the end of the TUC–Labour Party Liaison Committee, I raised the miners' dispute, and proposed a motion condemning the pit closures and inviting the labour movement and the public to help the miners.

David Basnett said, 'I will not accept Tony's motion.'

I argued, 'Look, we are involved in this. It is the most important question. I am almost shy of putting forward this motion, because the NUM don't want the help of the TUC. But this simply says we condemn the mass pit closures by the Government – closures which are against our policy – and people should help to alleviate the hardship of the miners. It is very modest, it is conciliatory, and it will allow us to say something.'

Basnett said, 'I won't accept a motion. It shouldn't be on the agenda. Of course we are all involved, we have all made our position clear, and we should probably reaffirm it. The press are waiting for us to cause trouble. Therefore we should simply say we support the miners and reaffirm our position.'

Moss Evans observed, 'Tony's statement as such is OK. Don't be afraid to say what we believe. We have always fought job losses. It is simple. Don't be ungenerous to the miners.'

Len Murray said, 'I regret that Mr Benn has tabled this resolution.'

I have known Len Murray since 1942, so I thought it was a bit much that he should call me Mr Benn!

He went on, 'If we are trying to reaffirm support for the miners, I must make it clear that the policy of the General Council is not the same as that of the Party, and the NUM have asked us not to intervene, though I am in regular contact with Peter Heathfield. That is why we have done nothing. The General Council must decide before we can reaffirm anything.'

Bickerstaffe remarked, 'We have been plagued for twenty-four hours by this. Surely we can say something which puts it all together, because everyone is waiting for a row to break out over Jack Dormand's speech at the Northern Regional Conference of the Labour Party.'

Jack Dormand, who was present, had described Len Murray's attempt to prevent a Day of Action in the north as disgraceful, and the Conference had unanimously condemned Murray.

I said, 'Well, this actually unites us. What are we worried about?'

So David Basnett agreed he would 'convey this as representing the sense of the meeting'. It was a weak statement, but at least something was done, and I was pleased.

Tuesday 22 May

I went to an interesting meeting of the left trade union leaders, over in Alan Sapper's offices in Soho Square. I have been going for a few years now and am treated as one of the family. We sit round a circular table in this beautiful old house with bow windows. Present were Mick McGahey, Jimmy Knapp of the NUR, Ken Cameron, Bill Keys, Walt Greendale, Alan himself and Ray Buckton.

Bill Keys asked Mick how we could help. He added, 'I must warn you that there are members of the executive of the NUM who are traitors and are trying to do things that would undermine the position of the NUM.'

Mick McGahey, who is a very nice man, and rings as true as a bell, said, 'I think the strike is solidifying. We have got young miners now and they are most remarkable. Their average age is about thirty-seven. We have three problems to cope with. One is the Nottinghamshire miners, who are a weakness. The second problem is the steelworkers in Scotland who wouldn't help us on Ravenscraig: the Iron and Steel Trades Confederation is a "sweetheart" union, a company union, and their executive voted by 23 to 3 against taking action to help us. The third, which is a bit of a diversion, is the law and order question. But what matters is the main principle – energy policy for the future.'

Mick wanted a big lobby and demonstration in London, so Bill Keys said, 'We'll organise it, but don't ask the South Region of the TUC to help, because that will give Len Murray an opening to interfere.'

Ray Buckton argued, 'We must stop coal production urgently; we must stop Nottinghamshire. But we don't want the TUC involved.'

Jimmy Knapp said, 'Leicestershire and Derbyshire have now had all coal movements by rail stopped, and Nottinghamshire is next. We've got two power stations which we think are pretty well ready for action by us.'

Before I left, I commented, 'The industrial struggle seems to be going very well, the Northern Regional Conference condemnation of Len Murray is an indication of support. On the political side, let us be quite clear that the Tories are intervening; they are not standing back. They hate tea and sandwiches at Number 10 as much as they hate militancy. We really must connect all our issues together – the coal and energy policy, plutonium, the attack on the GLC and on the public services. We should use the media. Certainly the events at the *Daily Express* and the *Sun*' (where SOGAT members were not prepared to produce the paper) 'were tremendous because that really frightened Fleet Street. A strike in Fleet Street doesn't harm anybody but it frightens the life out of the establishment.'

I concluded, 'I do think it would be useful if a senior trade union leader would go and see Neil Kinnock.' Jimmy Knapp intervened to say he was going to see him on Friday.

Wednesday 23 May

NEC, which was nasty at times. At one stage, Dennis Skinner described it as a 'right-wing mediation committee'.

Neil Kinnock snarled, 'You're mad, you're mad!'

I've never seen Neil Kinnock lose his cool like that.

Eric Heffer said, 'Right, we'll suspend the meeting for five minutes.'

Dennis argued, 'We've been voting all night, and the Front Bench sloped off after a deal and left us to hold the fort . . .' and so on.

Neil Kinnock shouted, 'The time's coming when you'll have to put up or shut up!'

At the Campaign Group, Tam Dalyell came to talk about the *Belgrano* affair. He simply told us, 'You all know the score. The point is how you can help. Perhaps you would all table questions to the Prime Minister.'

What came out in the discussion, as you would expect, was that the Labour Front Bench were up to their eyes in collaboration with the Government during the Falklands War, and what the Front Bench are afraid of now is that, if we demand an inquiry, the Prime Minister will say, 'Well, I saw Mr Silkin three times on the day we sank the *Belgrano*', and 'I talked to Mr Foot', and so on, and this little alliance between the two Front Benches would be used to expose us. Tam made the point that there were nuclear weapons in the South Atlantic, and he thought Mrs Thatcher would have authorised the use of Polaris against Argentina if we had lost. I don't personally think they would have dared to do that and, if they had, the Americans would have punished her terribly because of the hostile public reaction.

It's now 9.50, and we've got the vote on the third reading of the Local Government (Interim Provisions) Bill, the 'paving' bill which removes the right of London and the metropolitan counties to have elections for their councils next year, in preparation for the abolition of the councils themselves – a democratic outrage. It has brought some of our new younger Members like Harry Cohen, Tony Banks, Jeremy Corbyn and Clare Short very much into the forefront, though they have had no support from the Front Bench. Stephen said that not once has Neil Kinnock really spoken out on the awfulness of what the Tories are doing.

I had a reply today from Mrs Thatcher to the fax I had sent her about the use of troops in the miners' dispute, and the wording she uses, such as 'no authorisation has been given', is very different from saying that it isn't happening – a highly unsatisfactory response. So I think I might possibly keep that alive a bit.

The third longest sitting of the House tonight since 1881 over this iniquitous Bill. But it was passed by 304 to 176.

Thursday 24 May

To a meeting in the Commons. Just as we were leaving, there was a huge noise outside, and out of the window whom should I see passing between the House of Commons and St Margaret's Church but Ken Livingstone and Stephen on board a wagon. I went out in time to see them and all the others arriving with a petition of 1,060,000 people against the abolition of the GLC. There was Simon Hughes, the Liberal MP for Bermondsey, David Steel and John Cunningham. Fifteen minutes late, Neil Kinnock arrived and made a speech.

I took Stephen and Ken and one or two others on to the Terrace.

Friday 25 May

I had resolved that while Caroline was in America I would do some repairs around the house. I started work at 4 pm and it was an absolute disaster. The first job I attempted was to replace the old lavatory seat, but I couldn't get the old fittings off, so I banged with the hammer and bust the lavatory bowl, and now the water comes out the back when you flush. The cost of that intervention will be £70 or £80. Then I tried to repair a faulty switch outside the bedroom, but I wasn't sure what to connect to what, so ended up putting the old broken switch back on. Then I replaced bulbs round the house.

This morning, Hilary had the whole centre page in *Tribune* on the Common Market; he is a great authority on Europe.

Thursday 31 May

Over the last few days there have been terrible scenes outside the Orgreave Coke Depot, where 7000 pickets have been attacked by mounted and foot police with riot shields and helmets. It looks like a civil war. You see the police charging with big staves and police dogs chasing miners across fields, then miners respond by throwing stones and trying to drag a telegraph pole across a road; there are burning buildings and road blocks. It is like looking at scenes from Northern Ireland or central Europe. Yesterday Arthur Scargill was arrested.

I was asked to go on *The World at One* to comment on the fact that the Police Federation had suggested that the Coal Board take legal action under the Employment Acts to deal with the miners' opposition to the pit closures. I agreed to go on, but I said, 'You will have to give me a couple of minutes to say what *I* think is happening.'

They replied, 'We can't do that.'

I told them, 'If you want me on, I want the opportunity to say what I think is happening in the dispute.'

They said, 'Well, you'll be interviewed.'

So I had a flaming row with the editor, who said, 'We can't make special rules for you.'

'I'm not going to be interviewed and treated as if I was on trial for my life and be prevented from saying what I want to say.' I left it at that.

Saturday 2 June

With Tom Vallins to a rally in the village of Ollerton in the North Nottinghamshire coalfield. When we arrived, there were police about every hundred yards walking in pairs up and down the village street. Some 5000–6000 people marched round the town singing 'I'd rather be a picket than a scab' to the tune of the Simon and Garfunkel song 'I'd rather be a hammer than a nail', and pointing to the houses of miners who were working. It's such a small community, everybody knows what everybody else is doing.

We marched to a field outside the Miners' Welfare Club. Tommy Thompson, vice-president of the Yorkshire miners, who was extremely clear and direct, described how he had been invited by Stan Thorne, the MP for Preston, to speak at an unemployment meeting alongside Neil Kinnock, but then Stan Thorne had taken Tommy aside and asked him not to speak: 'You will appreciate, it would be a real embarrassment to Neil Kinnock if you, as a Yorkshire miner, were to speak on the same platform as him.' Tommy said, 'My family have done more for the Labour movement than Neil Kinnock will do until the day he dies.'

I was presented with a stick carved with a miner's head, and a miner's lamp. I was also given a thick plastic file full of statements by Nottinghamshire miners about police arrests and brutality.

Two women who spoke – miners' wives – were brilliant, and they told me afterwards that it was the first time they had ever spoken from a platform.

Sunday 3 June

I forgot to report that at my last surgery, a man who had been pursuing me all over the place turned up. Some weeks ago he had approached me at the Albert Hall, then at the House of Commons, then in Chesterfield. To cut a long story short, he was a Home Office forensic scientist, and he told me the Home Office had brought improper pressure to bear on forensic scientists through the police, and the full evidence was not brought to the courts. He said he had written one forensic report which had been discussed with his superiors, who had cut it down and had submitted only half of it to the court. He was in a state of great distress and had been involved in some court case but wouldn't give his name.

At 4 I went to Chris Mullin's for our usual meeting with Tony Banks, Alan Meale, Reg Race, Tom Sawyer and Jon Lansman.

Alan Meale said, 'We have got to think about a General Secretary to replace Jim Mortimer. Larry Whitty's name is being mentioned.'

A few other names were discussed when Tony Banks and others asked, 'Why don't *you* go for it?'

I explained, 'I can't give up Chesterfield, and I would like to be able to write the job specification.'

Tony Banks said, 'I think the General Secretary should be an MP.' Reg Race disagreed.

Alan Meale told us Jim Mortimer would probably announce his retirement at Conference.

Tuesday 5 June

To County Hall to have lunch with Frances Morrell. She embraced me warmly and was in a cheerful mood, and we had a lovely talk. The ILEA has succeeded in defeating the Government's plan to abolish

London's directly elected education authority, by campaigning for support from the bishops, the Tories and the Liberals, and appealing to the educational hierarchy.

Thursday 7 June
Miners had come from all over the country for a mass demonstration in London; a very exciting occasion. It was headed by Arthur Scargill, Mick McGahey, Eric Clarke, Eric Heffer and Jim Mortimer. People were waving and cheering out of the windows as we walked along Farringdon Road. It was a beautiful day, and there must have been 10,000–20,000 people.

Outside the *Sunday Times* offices the SOGAT chapel had their banner on the pavement and were cheering and waving; that was really something for the *Sunday Times*. We turned down Fleet Street and passed the *Daily Express* building, and the miners shouted out, 'Lies, lies, lies, lies!' – that was exciting and long overdue. The miners were in a jolly mood, and some of them were drinking cans of beer and had stripped off to the waist, showing off their tattooed bodies. There were some hostile looks, as you would expect, and large numbers of police. At one stage, when the miners saw the mounted police, they shouted, 'Sieg Heil, Sieg Heil, Sieg Heil!' Relations between the miners and the police are at rock bottom.

We marched over Waterloo Bridge and then approached Jubilee Gardens, where I went on to the platform. We heard that the police had stopped the last section of the march, allegedly because one of the marchers had put a sticker on a bobby's helmet, so they had just sat down in the street.

The speakers included Eric Heffer, Stan Orme, Mick McGahey, Betty Heathfield, then me, Arthur Scargill and Dennis Skinner, who spoke last and got a stupendous reception, which only he could get.

Wandered back to the House of Commons for the debate called by us condemning the Government's handling of the strike and the job cuts and pit closures. Peter Walker launched into a violent and ill-founded attack upon me during my time as Secretary of State for Energy. Then Michael Foot made a rather tired old tea-and-sandwiches speech of the kind you would expect (Michael having been at the Department of Employment), completely missing the point that we have, for the first time, a Government determined to break the miners, and that what we need from the Labour Party is 100 per cent support, at least as strong as the Tory support for the Coal Board, whose strategy they are masterminding in every possible way.

I followed Ann Clwyd making her maiden speech. I had thought very carefully about what I would say. I decided that this was an occasion when one made a speech for the movement outside, not just one of marginal interest to the labour correspondent of the *Financial*

Times. The debate was broadcast on Radio 4, so some people would have heard it. It was a passionate and accurate speech, and I was satisfied with it.

Neil Kinnock spoke neither at the rally nor in the debate, although he was present on the Front Bench during the speeches. When I mentioned it, the reason given was that Mrs Thatcher wasn't speaking. But of course that was his opportunity. He should have spoken at the rally, spoken in the House, and put the Prime Minister on the defensive. I had a letter from him suggesting that we should use certain 'buzz' words to emphasise the Tory link with waste and incompetence and Labour's compassionate approach. It was just written by advertising agents, no hard political content. But that's all by the by, because we don't want a diversion.

Just as I was going through the lobby at 10.15, Dennis Skinner said, 'Sixty-seven miners are being held in Rochester Row police station as a result of scuffles in Parliament Square. Will you go and see them?'

So Brian Sedgemore, Tam Dalyell and I drove to the police station, where a group of miners were waiting anxiously outside. We went in and spoke to a man with two pips on his shoulder, a young officer type in his late twenties who was very courteous. He asked us to wait, and while we were waiting, we met a lawyer brought over by the NUM, a woman in her late twenties. She was a most determined woman. She said, 'These people are being held five to a cell intended for one, they have had no food, have been here six or seven hours, and the situation is really awful.' We were told that one man of sixty-seven who had a heart condition had been released from the cells because he was suffocating, and another man with migraine had had to be released. Somebody had been struck on the eye by a policeman, and a doctor had said it should be stitched, but nothing had been done.

The commander of A Division, which covers the whole area, came to see us. He was a rather decayed-looking man in his late forties or early fifties, wearing a peaked cap with a lot of encrusted silver on it.

We were all taken up to what was obviously the officers' dining-room and the commander sat there with the other officer. I kept my tape-recorder running in my bag. I did wonder whether it was entirely proper, but I thought: When you're dealing with the enemy, why not?

In the course of the discussion I said to the senior officer, 'I cannot understand, Commander, how it is you allow the police to be used in this way. You are provoking people, and you are being used by the Government for political purposes.'

He said, 'I can't comment on that.'

'Well, maybe you can't, but can you explain why it is that Metropolitan police constables in Derbyshire are waving their £600-a-week pay slips at miners who have got nothing to live on?'

'Well, obviously you can't justify that,' he replied.

Brian Sedgemore, who is a big, tall man, a barrister, made the point that there was no justification whatever for keeping the arrested men for hours without food, for treating them like this, when they were only charged with obstructing the highway, threatening behaviour or obstructing the police, which are pretty minor offences. We heard later that the ventilation in the cells had broken down, and the heat was intolerable.

Anyway, at about 11.45 we were told they had all been released. We never saw them in the cells, as we had asked, but we did insist upon seeing the cells afterwards. Each cell measured only 7 feet by 6 feet and had a recess across which was a wooden board with a mattress covered in plastic. Even with the door open, you could hardly breathe, and all the ventilation came in through a small plate, just about big enough to provide air for one person, but with a high summer temperature and a broken ventilator it was impossible to breathe. To have been shut up in there with no ventilation must have been a nightmare.

As we left, the commander said, 'Goodnight.' I couldn't shake him by the hand, and I told him, 'I shall never forget tonight.' We went out and talked to the miners outside.

Having taken all the details and listened to everything that had happened, I went home. I was so upset and angry to think that this is happening in Britain. The police are accountable to nobody. As Tam, Brian and I parted, we agreed to write a letter to the Home Secretary over the weekend, and we will probably release it to the press.

Tuesday 12 June
Went by train to Cardiff for the Wales TUC Day of Action in support of the miners.

I caught the train back with Rodney Bickerstaffe, who is anxious that Neil Kinnock should succeed. I think he has an affinity with him because they are about the same age. People feel the older politicians have failed – the Healeys and Benns – and I understand that feeling, although we had to take the Party through a different phase of its development.

Friday 15 June
The Portsmouth by-election result was terrible. The SDP-Alliance candidate, Michael Hancock, won. A massive defeat for Mrs Thatcher, but not good for Labour.

Monday 18 June
Michael Meacher did a devastating job on Norman Fowler, Secretary of State for Social Services, at Questions today. Michael is a most incisive and clear-headed person.

Hair-raising accounts of what happened at the Orgreave Coke

Depot: 5000 pickets and 5000 police clashed, the police lines opened, and the horses came charging through. The pickets threw stones in defence, then the riot squad went in with batons and just beat the living daylights out of any miners around. It was horrible. A kind of civil war is developing; there is no parallel that I remember in my lifetime.

Tuesday 19 June

After lunch I went into the Commons, and Leon Brittan made a statement about the picketing at Orgreave. He really is a most inadequate man. It was just self-satisfaction, pomposity and aggressiveness. What made me laugh was that when Gerald Kaufman, the Shadow Home Secretary, got up and asked a question in a very modest way, with no cutting edge, Leon Brittan said, 'That's the type of absurd fantasy and left-wing extremism that we have come to expect from the Right Honourable Gentleman.' So poor old Kaufman got no credit whatsoever for having been so cautious. Thatcher sat through it. I got in a question about the Home Secretary's personal responsibility but I had the feeling that the Tory Front Bench wasn't particularly happy about events.

I have been allocated a desk in 'the Cloisters' with about six other Members, so at least I have a telephone and somewhere to leave my bags now.

Friday 22 June

At Duckmanton a miner had been picked up by the police, and all he had been doing was sitting on the grass verge. What happens is that a busload of policemen turn up, they watch the pickets to see who appears to be the 'ringleader' – ie the person who walks from group to group talking – and at a suitable moment they go over and arrest him. If he resists, they charge him with obstructing an officer in the discharge of his duty. The thing is totally unjust, totally unfair, totally contrary to natural justice.

I went to the so-called Loggers' Camp near Warsop colliery in Joe Ashton's constituency of Bassetlaw. The camp is in a wood, well back from the colliery, approached over a dirt track. There, about thirty miners, who have been released on tough bail conditions, are being kept by the NUM away from the picket lines in case they are picked up again. They work there collecting deadwood from land which a sympathetic farmer has offered them. It was just like Robin Hood and his gang. While we were there, a police car came along the dirt road and a sergeant asked them what they were doing before turning round and leaving.

As we left, we were stopped at a road-block set up by the police. They asked, 'What are you doing here?'

I sat in the back (with my tape recorder running) and we said, 'We're just going home. We've been distributing soup.'

Then we saw another police vehicle with dogs and a police handler. So we decided to turn back. When we reached the camp, the dog patrol had gone beyond the point where they were cutting wood and had parked about 200 yards ahead. Then a police bus with riot wire over the windows arrived carrying about fifteen or twenty constables. For the first time in my life, I felt really threatened.

While I was waiting, I talked to the miners who were gathering. There were two black miners (I hadn't seen any black miners before) who had been charged with grievous bodily harm. The others had only been charged with obstructing the police. So there was this little group waiting with great anxiety to see what would happen to them. It was like being in the resistance in France, and I trembled physically. I thought I might need to be there if a fight began; the worrying thing was that the miners had electric saws and a couple of axes, so the police might have charged them with possessing offensive weapons.

There was a very responsible man of about forty with curly red hair who was on bail. The police had broken into his home to arrest him, and his fifteen-year-old boy had asked, 'Where are you taking my dad?' They had caught the boy by the hair, twisted his arm behind his back, thrown him against the garage and said, 'You bugger, we'll have you if you don't keep quiet.'

This sense of fear, of being under police occupation, is very strong. The fact is that in order to impose their will upon the populace the Government would have to put the fear of God into trade-unionists, jail them and ultimately, as in Chile, shoot them in order to get rid of the deeply entrenched commitment to trade-unionism. I can understand why the black leaders in South Africa behave with such dignity in the face of the police, because, when you are powerless, the only way you can assert yourself is with dignity. If you respond aggressively, they just beat the hell out of you, but if you have dignity you can, to some extent, overwhelm aggression with non-violence.

Saturday 23 June
Went to the BBC for an interview, and there I saw the Kitson family: David Kitson, who was released last month after nearly twenty years in prison in South Africa; his former wife Norma, who had been campaigning for years outside South Africa House; and his daughter, who is about nineteen, I suppose, and just sat next to her father and cuddled him. When he was asked by David Frost, in quite a sensitive interview, what he felt about his release, he said, 'What I missed most was being cuddled.' It was such a human thing to say. He is a man of immense courage. He endured the most appalling conditions in South African jails, the first year and a half in solitary confinement, which constitutes torture.

Monday 25 June

Caroline gave me a tremendous briefing on the new draft paper prepared by the TUC on the MSC and the YTS. This is a second draft, still much too sympathetic, but Caroline's criticisms were marvellous.

I took it to Congress House for the TUC–Labour Party Liaison Committee, where the first motion was from Stan Orme, absolutely hopeless, saying that the miners' strike was causing threats to the stability of British industry and calling for talks and so on.

I said, 'That's quite wrong. We should say that the Government is attacking the stability of British industry, and the Liaison Committee should say, "Taking note of the support of the Labour Party for the NUM and the position of the TUC", and then demand talks with the NUM to effect a settlement of the dispute to secure an expanding future for the mining industry.'

We went on to this YTS document, presented and commended by Bill Keys. I put all the amendments that Caroline had suggested: that the Government was not complacent but active, interventionist and aggressive; that the Government policy was not to reduce inflation but to create unemployment; that the difference between the Labour Party and the Tories was not just about economic management but about society, its values and its objectives. Those amendments were accepted. So it was a tremendous success; it shows that even in the present atmosphere, where the right are in charge of everything, if you have got a good case and you put it forward you can win. All Caroline's work.

Wednesday 27 June

At the NEC, Joan Maynard and I moved that the Shadow Cabinet consider tabling a motion in the House on the *Belgrano* affair.

Neil Kinnock opposed it. 'The Shadow Cabinet have been pursuing it by correspondence with the Prime Minister, and I object to this resolution on the ground that it would be a precedent for requests from the Executive to the Shadow Cabinet.'

Hattersley declared, 'I object, because we lost the Election over the Falklands question and we don't want to raise an issue on which Mrs Thatcher is strong.' Well, that gave the game away completely. I told Roy that saying that meant you believed Tam Dalyell was embarrassing the Party by raising it. Anyway, the resolution was carried with a small amendment, and Joan and I tabled a similar request for next Wednesday's PLP meeting.

Afterwards, I drove Joan Maynard and Dennis Skinner to the Commons, and we got a taxi to Tower Hill for the miners' demonstration organised by the South-East Region of the TUC. It was a tremendous march, the weather was beautiful, and all the young miners were bare to the waist. They won't go back.

Thursday 28 June

I went to a rather tense and difficult meeting with Ken Coates, Alan Meale, Stuart Holland and Michael Meacher. I put a proposal for a political campaign for the miners. Ken is out of sympathy with Arthur Scargill's rather militant use of strike action against the Tories' policy, and he is also anxious that the miners might lose.

I had a word with Ken on the phone later because, after goodness knows how many years, there is tension between us. Broadly speaking, the apparent disagreement is as follows. Ken believes the left is not giving proper political leadership to the miners' strike at this moment. He thinks Arthur Scargill just believes that trade union militancy is a way of beating the Government whereas Ken thinks there ought to be a political dimension. I agree that we need both. It's very difficult for the miners in this situation.

Wednesday 4 July

To the PLP for the debate on the *Belgrano* with a motion very similar to the one we had put down and carried at the NEC last Wednesday. Tom Clarke, the MP for Monklands West, opened it on behalf of the Foreign Affairs Committee and said there was a unanimous view that there should be an inquiry and a debate in the House.

Ian Mikardo said that the evidence now available, and coming out of the select committee, confirmed all the points Tam Dalyell had made; that Ministers contradicted each other, serving officers contradicted them, and so did Foreign Office officials. There was a prima-facie case for an inquiry. He said it would need to be an independent inquiry conducted by Privy Councillors, and the Shadow Cabinet would resist, but that looking to the future was quite compatible with looking back.

Donald Anderson of Swansea East, who is a former diplomat, said, 'The Government won't agree. We have made a lot of mileage out of it, and Tam Dalyell has done a fantastic job, but the question is would a debate be productive and should it be a priority? The Tories will say that lives were at stake, and we might end up with egg on our face. There would be more mileage in looking forward, and the priorities for debates on international affairs should really be the Middle East and Central America.'

Tam Dalyell observed, 'Mileage is important, but so is principle and so is truth. The Prime Minister's biographer* says she lied, and we could use that.'

Andrew Faulds agreed.

Kevin Barron said he supported Tam because we needed to know the truth.

Stuart Bell, the new right-wing MP for Middlesbrough, argued, 'An

* Dalyell is referring to Bruce Arnold's *Margaret Thatcher: A Study in Power* (Hamish Hamilton, 1984).

independent inquiry on Privy Councillor terms would be sensible, but we have got to think of our priorities. The public think Thatcher did well in the Falklands, and as a party of government we should look to the future.'

Dennis Canavan, MP for Falkirk West, supported Tam. 'He has established his case. And, after all, Neil Kinnock asked for an inquiry during the General Election last year.'

Neil Kinnock summed up. 'I ask Tom Clarke and Ian Mikardo not to press their motion. This would not be an appropriate use of Opposition time. We should wait for the select committee to report. Also, political considerations *should* influence our attitude. The conduct of the Government is well-known. I commented last year on the need for an inquiry and I repeat it. No one in the PLP supports the Government's view, and we are in favour of an inquiry. The question is how to put it. We want to get full and clear answers but we don't want a Charge of the Light Brigade.' He went on, 'An independent Privy Council inquiry might be desirable, but my political judgement is that a debate in the Commons is not the best way because we would be defeated. Timing is of the essence, and the only difference of opinion here is on the timing. The Falklands factor is running out; yesterday's *Evening Standard* poll proved we were climbing up, and, if we put the Falklands back on the agenda now, we would fall back. For a future debate, we could look at Fortress Falklands.'

Then we had a vote on whether to defer any debate, and the vote for deferring won. So we lost. I was sick as a dog, but at the moment MPs don't want anything that might cause a difficulty, and they want to support Neil.

Saturday 7 July

To Chesterfield. Went over to the club and there was Peter Heathfield, so I asked him about the talks being held between the Coal Board and the NUM, I must say Peter is marvellous; he's got a tremendous sense of humour, and he looked tanned and cheerful. He said the talks had gone well from the point of view of the NUM. Ian MacGregor the chairman was trying to be friendly, but after nine hours he had begun to get a bit knackered. He said Jim Cowan, the Deputy Chairman of the Coal Board, was taking a hard line, although that may have been their strategy. Ned Smith the industrial relations director, was probably less rigid. The three of them – Peter Heathfield, Arthur and Mick McGahey – are working extremely well together. Arthur is totally unyielding and is a field commander; Peter is a negotiator, a diplomat; and Mick McGahey is a straightforward old statesman. They are a fantastic team and totally united. The Coal Board and the NUM have agreed that there's no problem with closures of pits on the grounds of exhaustion or geological faults, but they are trying to find a new definition of 'uneconomic pits', a term which the NUM are not prepared to accept.

I said, 'What about suggesting to them that the finance for "uneconomic pits" should come from nuclear power?'

Peter said, 'MacGregor might agree, but that's a different matter.'

'Well, bring in the Government.'

'We don't want to involve the Government,' said Peter.

'Couldn't you suggest that the "uneconomic" coal be given to pensioners?' I asked.

'MacGregor would say that had nothing to do with it.'

It became absolutely clear – and this is what I wanted to hear – that the NUM are not going to give MacGregor an agreement. They are not going to let him come out of it with any credit.

Peter said MacGregor was trying to be very friendly and saying, in his Canadian accent, 'Come on, Arthur' and 'Peter, you must come fishing with me in Scotland' and 'What about a game of golf, Mick?' McGahey, in his Scottish brogue, had replied, 'I've never played golf in my life; it's a total waste of time!' It would be fascinating to be a fly on the wall. MacGregor had said to Arthur, 'Now, Arthur, I've got my audience to consider and you've got your audience to consider, but the important one is the third audience, the people not directly involved.' The fact is that the miners now think they are winning.

Peter was prepared to say a great deal in confidence. The morale of the miners is fantastic, the money is coming in and they can manage. He thought the strike wouldn't finish until the end of August or the beginning of September, another eight weeks.

Tuesday 10 July

International Committee in the afternoon, absolutely riveting. When we came to discuss a statement prepared by the NEC's Defence Sub-committee, the argument that Britain is under threat from a possible attack by the Soviet Union was implicit, so I said there was no evidence of that at all. 'It leaves out of account the fact that the United States itself has been pursuing policies that threaten world peace, and we say we will remove their bases without considering what will happen if they won't go. It also leaves out of account the democratic issues raised by military establishments which are very strong and secretive and which destroy democracy. It leaves out the internal role of the armed forces and the psychology of the Cold War. It would be better if we had a few amendments.'

Roy Hattersley moved that the document be accepted without amendments. For the first time since I have been a member of the International Committee of the NEC, we were presented with a major policy document which we were invited to accept *en bloc*; a document which had been drawn up by people who weren't even members of the NEC, weren't even members of the Parliamentary Committee. I protested most strongly, as did Eric Heffer and Jo Richardson.

Anyway, Neil Kinnock supported Roy Hattersley's motion, and it was carried by 7 votes to 6 without a discussion.

Wednesday 11 July
The Committee of Privileges met – my first since agreeing to sit on the committee in June – to consider its report on a complaint against Tony Banks. Tony had declared – in the House – that the GLC would use 'selective vindictiveness' in making cuts imposed on it by the Government in constituencies which had elected Conservative MPs who had voted for the cuts. My draft report had been submitted against the chairman's. When the chairman, John Biffen, moved that his report be read a second time paragraph by paragraph, I moved that the words 'chairman's draft report' be left out and the words 'draft report proposed by Mr Benn' be inserted. I then presented my draft. I went through the arguments for privilege: the duties and rights should protect the electorate – that was the justification for privilege. We should ask Members to accept them in a personal and voluntary declaration along with the oath; if we didn't, it would look as if MPs had no duties to their constituents. I argued that Banks's phrase 'selective vindictiveness' could well have been used to describe legislation, and the response to it. So I recommended that we dismiss the complaint against Tony Banks.

I voted for my own report, everybody else voted against it, so I was in a minority of one, but at least it will now appear in the published report.

There was this committee of allegedly senior people, Labour and Tory, huddled together to protect MPs and, in the case of Labour MPs on the committee, actually voting to condemn Tony Banks. I thought it was disgusting. But it was all good-natured; John Biffen thanked me for the way I had handled it and said he thought what I had said was interesting. The matter should never have been referred to the Committee of Privileges by Toby Jessel, the Conservative MP for Twickenham. It will arouse a great deal of interest when it is published. They hadn't had a vote in the Committee of Privileges for twenty years, so it needed some vitality.

Sunday 15 July
Alan Meale rang to tell me about the Durham Miners' Gala yesterday. Apparently 100,000 people were there; Dennis Skinner made a brilliant speech which got a standing ovation, but, when Neil Kinnock got up to speak, three bands started playing and moving off the field, and about 85,000 people with twelve banners just began moving away. All Neil did was to attack the Tories – he didn't give support for the miners.

Friday 20 July
Chesterfield. At 7 in the morning Tom, Margaret and I drove round the

picket lines. It was a beautiful day and hard to believe, driving through the countryside, that we were in the middle of a battlefield. In fact the police presence was less than in recent weeks. We didn't pass through a single road-block and we weren't stopped at all. I had independent confirmation from somebody who works in the DHSS that some of the police inspectors are getting up to £1500 a week, the constables £600–800. I was asked if school meals could be provided for the miners' children in the school holiday.

Saturday 21 July
I left at 8 for the Stanton and Staveley Pipeworks, owned by BSC, who have decided to lay off 150 of the 500 workers. That place employed 3000 a few years ago. It was immensely depressing, and British industry looks more and more like a museum, with old, rusty equipment and men in overalls looking like creatures from a past industrial era.

I've decided to introduce a 'passport' in Chesterfield, so that when the police stop people and ask what they are doing and where they are going they can show a card saying, 'The bearer of this card is —– who is one of a number of constituents helping me with my official duties as Member of Parliament for the town. Will you please assist in every way, and if there are any problems please let me know.'It has no legal validity, but then neither has the police action.

Tuesday 24 July
Meeting of the TUC left general secretaries today at 5.30 in the NUR offices. In addition to the usual trade union leaders, Arthur Scargill, Peter Heathfield and Mick McGahey were invited. I gathered from Ray Buckton that, as President of the TUC, he had been asked to talk to Scargill and Heathfield and find out what they wanted.

Arthur stated, 'What we would like the TUC to do, because we still don't want them to intervene in the dispute, is to say: first, no trade-unionist should cross a picket line; secondly, no industry should accept supplies of iron and coal or anything else delivered by scabs; thirdly, give money and food. About £3 million a week would be necessary to provide miners with £10 a week. At the moment 20 per cent of the money is from abroad, and 50p per week per member would be sufficient. We have to finance 10,000 pickets a day. We have incurred £2 million legal expenses already. We have had 5300 men arrested, 2000 injured and four killed – including two killed underground doing safety work.'

Peter Heathfield added, 'Of course we cannot afford a defeat at the TUC.'

Ken Gill warned, 'The TUC will not call for people to respect picket lines.'

It was agreed that a private approach might be made to Basnett. Ray Buckton had seen him, but Basnett had said he couldn't meet the NUM without the TUC unions being present. It was generally thought that Basnett should be seen privately.

Wednesday 25 July

The *Daily Mirror* had the most scandalous cartoon of the 'Loony Left', showing a toothless figure with spectacles and wild hair; the accompanying piece said that anyone who didn't go along with Kinnock didn't want the Labour Party to win the next Election.

At the NEC, we came to the defence document, which Syd Tierney introduced. He said that the alternative draft foreword proposed by me only intended to wreck it. Joan Maynard seconded me. Jo Richardson and Sam McCluskie wanted to discuss the document. Then I introduced my proposed foreword.

Kinnock said, 'This is the best defence policy we have ever had. It will produce cohesion within the party. It *is* a technical document, but it has to be technical, and it has got great clarity.' (I had said the document was too technical and not political enough.) He went on, 'Tony's foreword would complicate the drafting, would be counterproductive and would attract attention away from what we were saying.' He criticised my reference to the armed forces being a possible instrument of domestic repression, as well as my suggestion that the USSR was not intending to attack us; this, he said, could be seen as our turning a blind eye to Soviet strength and would be a hostage to fortune. On the US, he accepted what I had said but wanted a different form of words, otherwise it would look as if we were 'soft on the Russians and undermining the Yanks'.

It was a poor speech, but it revealed that I had put my finger on three important issues.

Joan Maynard pointed out that the Americans had walked out of the SALT-2 talks.

After a lot of discussion, I said, 'I would be prepared to accept any amendments you want to move to mine, but I am determined to put this forward.'

Tom Sawyer asked, 'Couldn't Neil and Tony go away and redraft it?' So I agreed to that.

Monday 30 July

Julie's daughter Kim had a baby yesterday, and Julie has decided that she wants to work with her husband Mike Elliott now that he is a Member of the European Parliament. She has been with me since 1976 – a most kindly, commonsense person with a marvellous temperament, who has seen this house through endless crises. She was an unending source of encouragement, and stayed right through the Chesterfield by-election. Julie always said I would get back in the House early, and so I did; then she set up the secretarial system for Chesterfield. I am extremely indebted to her.

Signed 300 posters for the NUM which they are selling at £1 each to raise money for the miners.

Met Stephen and we sat on the terrace until 4 am during an all-night sitting. I used to sit there with my dad, who used to sit there with *his* dad.

Tuesday 31 July

Up at 7.30 and worked on my speech on the miners for the debate we have called attacking the Government's economic policy. In the old days I would stay up all night and practise my speech, but now I just jot down a few words.

Went to the House. Neil Kinnock opened the debate and made a speech which, to be candid, was a great failure. He doesn't want to be identified with Arthur Scargill and militancy.

Then Thatcher got up and, since she has been under heavy attacks from the Tory wets, it was important for her to re-establish herself. Little did I expect that she would choose to highlight uneconomic pits, closures and investment during the last Labour Government, and no doubt Bernard Ingham (my old press secretary at the Department of Energy) had put her on to speeches I had made as Energy Secretary which gave the impression that I had favoured the closure of uneconomic pits. She read out these passages, then, using an old parliamentary trick, pointed out that 'They were the words of the Right Honourable Gentleman, the Member for Chesterfield.'

So I got to my feet at once – I couldn't let this go by. She immediately gave way; the Tories were cheering energetically. I didn't know what I was going to say, but like Mr Gladstone, who 'had never been on his feet more than half a second before the way ahead to him was clear', I launched forth, saying that the Prime Minister had delivered herself into our hands, because closures under us were by agreement, but closures under them were by imposition. The Labour people cheered like anything. Whether she wants to undermine my support for the miners, or whether she wanted to build me up in order to make Kinnock look unimportant, I don't know.

Michael Foot spoke and then I did. Though I say so myself, it was the first really successful speech I had made since my re-election on 1 March. I haven't found it easy to settle down in the House, and the new breed of Tory MPs, the Thatcherite merchant bankers and so on, are very rowdy. With all the shouting and attempted interventions, my speech lasted for twenty-one minutes.

At the end of the debate, Nigel Lawson, the Chancellor of the Exchequer, said that the money spent on the miners' strike was a worthwhile investment, implying it was a game, worth £400 million.

Today the NUM in South Wales was faced with the threat of sequestration of £50,000 for a fine imposed on them.

Wednesday 1 August
The press hailed Thatcher's triumph and Kinnock's failure, and said that I had been reduced to purée by Mrs Thatcher's interventions. You have to learn to live with that.

Vincent Hanna rang me up. I think he wanted to be friendly after the flaming row I had with him during the Chesterfield by-election. He was in bed with a strained back, and said he had heard my speech on Radio 4 yesterday and how brilliant it was. I thought: If you're offered an olive branch, seize it with both hands. I expressed concern about his back, and he said that David Dimbleby, who, in his capacity as a newspaper proprietor, has been in conflict with his trade unions, was not going to cover the Labour Party Conference for the BBC this year. Vincent and Peter Snow will be doing it.

Thursday 2 August
Lawson's comment that the miners' strike was a worthwhile investment was followed by the statement that if he had wanted a strike in 1981 he could have had one – which proves that he wasn't ready then and is ready now. The Prime Minister was on radio and television today saying that she thought the strike had gone on too long; I think they are worried.

I went for the discussion with Neil Kinnock, Roy Hattersley, Eric Heffer, Jim Mortimer and Jenny Little about my revised foreword to the defence document. Jenny, with typical Civil Service skill, had not even circulated my foreword but had written one herself and hoped we would discuss that. This is the oldest trick in the book. I had taken the precaution of copying my foreword, and Eric Heffer began by pointing out that we were meeting specifically to discuss it.

Hattersley said he found it naïve and unconvincing and he was not prepared to go along with it.

After a bit of a hassle, we went through Jenny Little's text first, and I got a lot of amendments from my text into it. Then we went through mine. In effect we adopted a reference to the need for the armed forces to be democratically controlled, which is what I wanted. We had a long discussion about the central question of the Soviet Union 'threat'. Jim Mortimer was entirely on my side; Eric Heffer, because of his anti-Russian feeling, was in the middle; and Neil Kinnock drew parallels with the Sudetenland before the war, which implied that he really did think of the Russians as being like the Nazis. But they did agree to a reference that there was no justification for describing the Cold War as an ideological conflict. The discussion showed Kinnock as being basically a supporter of the general Tory and American analysis,

Hattersley being passionately pro-NATO and Eric Heffer being anti-communist and anti-Russian.

Thirty-six years ago today I met Caroline. She put on the very same dress she wore that day and it fitted her perfectly. She looked lovely in it, and it is fantastic that we should have had thirty-six years together. We went out for a meal.

Sunday 5 August

To Chesterfield, and I had a talk with Peter Heathfield, who told me there is a cash crisis in the NUM; the money for staff wages and office costs would run out in about nine or ten weeks' time. Although the officials had given up their own wages – Peter and Arthur Scargill have not had one penny since the strike began and Dennis Skinner has handed over all his parliamentary income – they can't ask secretaries and typists and others to work for nothing. So the future of the union is at stake.

I tried to calculate the cost of the strike to Chesterfield alone and I came up with £60 million based on the loss and cost to the Coal Board, the loss of tax revenue, the policing bill, social security costs, rent and rate rebates, the local authority support costs, and so on. I checked and rechecked, and the figures are being prepared for a press conference tomorrow in support of the strike.

Monday 6 August

Up at 6 for the soup run to six Coal Board pits – Grassmoor, Lings, Williamthorpe, Arkwright, Shirebrook and Markham. At Arkwright we were told that one woman who works in the costs office arrived at 9 in her own car and normally seventy policemen had to escort her in. I saw her arrive, a very unhappy-looking woman. One of the policemen had told the pickets that it took £3000 a week to get her into work.

Concessionary coal, which had amounted to 1000 tons a day, has now stopped for pensioners and others, so the miners are cutting logs for them.

At Markham there were about 180 police, apparently from the Devon and Cornwall and Gloucestershire forces, and a few pickets.

At the press conference I circulated the Chesterfield figures. Johnny Burrows was in the chair, and also there were Harry Gaucher, Gordon Butler of the Derbyshire NUM, Betty Heathfield and Tom Vallins.

Sunday 12 August

The big news tonight is the shooting in Belfast. The RUC attacked a crowd listening to Martin Galvin, the head of the American organisation Noraid, who had been banned by the British Government. He was at the meeting with Gerry Adams, and as soon as he began to speak the police launched a prearranged attack on the crowd, fired plastic bullets at point-blank range and killed one, then drove a vehicle at the crowd. Twenty people were seriously injured. It gave a new relevance to the bill I am presenting.

Monday 13 August

Had a brief word with Gordon Butler at the NUM about what had happened at Warsop. Three miners in a car had been attacked quite wantonly by police with riot shields. The police had beaten the car, kicked the side panels in and broken the windows, shouting, 'Kill the bastards!' The men had come back really frightened.

Tuesday 14 August

I do get the feeling that the strike is building up to a real crisis, particularly when you get accounts of incidents like a policeman threatening to stick a man's darts up his nose, stories of the police being drunk and breaking cars. They are completely out of control. Went on to Warsop, where I heard that at 3 am the police had got out of their vans with their riot shields and walked in front of cottages, banging their batons rhythmically, frightening people.

Thursday 23 August

Chesterfield. Saw Gordon Butler, who had a group of workers with him from the Trent Motor Traction Company (in Mansfield). The firm is a subsidiary of the National Bus Company, and the Coal Board had asked the local company to buy some old buses and put grilles on them so they could be used to drive working miners through the picket lines at 50 mph. If this little subsidiary company didn't agree, the Coal Board would cancel their contract with the National Bus Company.

I decided to take this up, and I rang Ron Todd, the General Secretary-elect of the TGWU. He said, 'I'll give you 100 per cent support, and if necessary we'll have a national bus strike in support of these drivers.'

Tony Banks turned up in Chesterfield with a truck of food donated by his local party.

Friday 24 August

This evening Kathy Ludbrook looked in to discuss the possibility of becoming my secretary to replace Julie. She has exceptional political knowledge and experience. She said one thing to me: 'I am afraid I am very sensitive to smoking. Do you smoke a lot?' That really worried me, but we'll try it out.

Saturday 25 August

Heard today that there is going to be a national dock strike. That is good news, because BSC has attempted to import coking coal from abroad for the Ravenscraig steelworks, and action to stop it will greatly reinforce the miners.

Monday 27 August
The papers are full of the accidental sinking by a British cross-Channel ferry of a French ship carrying uranium hexafluoride, apparently for enrichment in Russia. The containers are 60 feet below the water. I have had enough experience of nuclear accidents to know how quickly the authorities cover up, and all the statements were, of course, reassuring. So I sent a letter by taxi to Number 10 to the Prime Minister, asking some questions. Then I rang the Press Association, the BBC, ITN and the *Guardian*. It is a peg on which to hang other nuclear incidents. *World at One* came to interview me. It's a way of keeping up a campaign during the recess, and it links in with the miners.

Wednesday 29 August
Finished packing and Caroline, Melissa and I drove to the airport and caught a flight to San Francisco, where Joshua is marrying Liz Feeney on Saturday.

Stephen and Hilary, Josh and Liz were already in the States and met us and took us straight to the Feeneys' house.

Saturday 1 September
Went to the Community Church at 12.30 where there were endless photographs taken. Liz looked beautiful in a white gown.

At the reception Stephen made a speech, as best man, and then Josh and Liz went of to their honeymoon in Monterey.

Sunday 9 September
I went to a little gathering at Chris Mullin's. He is resigning as editor of *Tribune* in November in order to finish a novel. He told me he had been in touch with the new Counsellor at the American Embassy, who told him the Americans' real anxiety is that their bases in Britain might be removed. We talked around one or two other things. It is a very black period.

We discussed the miners. Michael Meacher said that at the Shadow Cabinet meeting, held the night before Neil Kinnock made his speech at the TUC, there had been violent attacks on the miners from Gerald Kaufman, who said if it weren't for them, Labour would be well ahead in the polls. John Cunningham said it would be a disaster if Scargill won, and the one thing we had to do was to prevent any spreading of industrial action. Hattersley had said, 'We must step up our criticism of pit violence.' Generally speaking, the hostility of the Shadow Cabinet to the miners was unbelievable. But in the 1974 strike Wilson took the same view.

We went on to talk about the running of the Campaign Group. Stuart Holland complained it was a like a prayer meeting where everyone had to prove their ideological purity.

Frances thought it appeared to have no connection whatsoever with the women's movement.

I said, 'Well, Ann Pettifor came and spoke, and we support the women's demands. The miners support groups and the Greenham Common women have visited us.'

But Frances can't see friends where they exist. In a recent article in *Socialist Action* she said that I didn't even begin to understand what women were talking about. I thought, if that was the way they rewarded their friends, it was going to be very difficult.

We watched Kinnock on *Face the Press* with political commentators Bob Carvel, Tony Howard and Robert Taylor. Neil was full of smiles, but he made no reference whatsoever to police brutality, which is now a major feature of the strike. Still, he's going to be there until the next Election, and we have to see him as a key to the door of Number 10; that will give us an opportunity to do what has to be done. But there was general pessimism around the room that nothing would be done. It is hard to know whether the left should go on covering for the right of the Party, which is covering up for capitalism, particularly if, at the same time, the leadership is making attacks upon the basic tenets of the Party and throwing doubt on their relevance.

The main task of Kinnock, as far as I can make out, is to unpick any commitment to any policy.

Tuesday 11 September

We had the engineer in to fix the phone, and he said that 40,000 people were going to be laid off in the telephone service. When the Government were asked why, since British Telecom was making more than £1 billion a year profit, they declined to answer. But BT did confess that it would make the industry a more attractive package to sell off. He also said that, after it was sold, it would cost £40 to call an engineer out. At the moment it is all covered by your telephone bill.

Thursday 13 September

Took breakfast up to a Bulgarian film unit who are staying in the Westdale Hotel while they cover the strike.

At 7 we all went on the soup run. There were hundreds of pickets at Markham and a unit of police in yellow jackets. As I appeared on the site, the police marched off and were driven away.

Went over my schedule with Tom and Margaret Vallins, who are doing a fantastic job of work.

The Acting Chief Constable of Derbyshire, Mr Leonard, had written to me saying he would like to see me, and he arrived at the Labour Club accompanied by another officer. I had with me Gordon Butler and Johnny Burrows.

Leonard said at the beginning, 'I thought it would be a good idea to have a talk, because from some of the things you have been saying about police action you misunderstand that *I* have complete operational control. I have only got 1800 policemen in the whole of Derbyshire.'

I listened carefully, and said, 'Thank you very much, but remember I have a certain amount of Whitehall experience as a Minister. I was in the Cabinet during the Winter of Discontent, and I know perfectly well that the Home Secretary chairs a meeting with the police, the army and Ministers and that all the instructions are given by the Home Secretary. So please don't ask me to believe that you are in charge. I don't honestly believe you are.'

Then he made a great point about how in Derbyshire they had not closed the motorways, that the Metropolitan police officers who had been brought in were under his control and they weren't as bad as we thought. He said he briefed the police every Sunday night about the history and traditions of the Derbyshire miners. He then remarked, 'You may think me cynical and think I am scapegoating, but it suits our books to see the Met criticised because, when the strike is over, the Derbyshire Constabulary will be able to resume normal relations with the local people and say it was the Mets who caused trouble.'

I thought he was taking a bit of a risk saying that. He's an intelligent person and, personally, quite a nice guy. He certainly will be a Chief Constable; he is standing in for the Chief Constable.

Then I gave him some examples of people's fear of the police breaking into their homes in the middle of the night. Generally speaking, I indicated that the situation was explosive and there was no point in pretending otherwise. 'If I may say this to you, Chief Constable, I believe that you, as individuals, should make it clear to the Home Office that you resent the police being used for what are, in effect, political purposes, and that you are being used to cover up for a failure of Government policy.'

He said, 'Police dislike the idea of being described as "under the control of left-wing extremists in the local authorities". Well, I am equally against right-wing extremists in the Cabinet controlling us.' (A hostage to fortune.) 'I am quite independent. I am here to keep the peace and enforce the law, and, if there is a conflict between the two, I have, probably, to keep the peace.'

He was looking forward to the time when it would all be over, and I said, 'I think your problems will begin then.'

Friday 14 September
It is the 750th anniversary of St Mary's and All Saints Church, the famous church with the crooked spire in Chesterfield, and the

Archbishop of Canterbury, Dr Robert Runcie, visited today. I tried to get Tom Vallins to arrange for me to meet the archbishop briefly, but he doesn't want to meet me, so I turned up as a member of the congregation to hear his sermon. He and the Bishop of Derby arrived at 7.30 wearing purple cassocks. The archbishop spoke for fifty minutes. All the hymns were familiar, but when I read them again they were all about how splendid God was and how inadequate man was. You can see how the idea of sin creates a subtle and deferential congregation who will do what the bishop tells them.

The archbishop gave what was really the report of the managing director of a multinational company. He described his work in his own diocese of Canterbury, at Lambeth, in the House of Lords, and his attendance at royal weddings. He said that in Peking a cab driver had said to him, 'Royal wedding', so *he* had been seen on television in China! It had no spiritual content at all.

After he had spoken, he came down from the pulpit and answered questions. The last one asked whether it was necessary to believe in anything to be an official in the church, which was an obvious reference to the new Bishop of Durham, David Jenkins. He gave a long, fumbling answer in which he said that the Scriptures were the way we had experienced God's presence and it was up to everybody to decide.

The miners' talks with the Coal Board have broken down.

Saturday 15 September

Tom Vallins drove me to Barnsley for a huge demonstration with the miners and other trade unions. As we marched through the town, I thought people were a bit subdued. They were clapping, but there was none of that spirit as at the beginning of the strike. There is no doubt whatever that there is disappointment that the talks have broken down. What people really need now is not so much rhetoric as encouragement, explanation, information and reassurance. Arthur looked tired.

Sunday 16 September

A few things I forgot to mention this week. One of the miners told me that a friend of his, who is an army reservist, had had a letter from the Ministry of Defence asking if he was licensed to drive a heavy lorry. When he replied that he wasn't, he had another letter saying he had been attached to another part of the reserve – which indicates that they do expect to have to use troops.

Tariq Ali rang and told me that Mrs Thatcher had confided to someone that the only person she would trust to take over from her would be David Owen, but that he was in a little party with no future and would have done much better to have gone straight into the Tory Party, where he would have been more at home.

Tuesday 18 September

John Bloxam and Martin Thomas came to interview me for the Conference edition of their paper *Socialist Organiser*. When we had finished, I expressed privately my anxiety about Solidarity in Poland. All these left groups support Solidarity 100 per cent, but Walesa actually gave an interview in which he attacked Arthur Scargill and praised Mrs Thatcher. I said I feared that it was just a Catholic nationalist movement led by the Pope, and was the left wise to be so wildly enthusiastic about it? This stunned them.

I pointed out, 'The CIA, Mrs Thatcher and President Reagan support it, and I am not in that ball game.'

They replied, 'Ah yes, but the demands are genuine', and so on.

I said, 'I know, but to undermine socialism, the intelligence services may decide to support left critics.'

Saturday 22 September

Up at 5.30 and caught the plane to Glasgow for the miners' march. It was pretty wet weather. I talked to a lot of people. The Scots miners haven't been in the news as much as the Kent or South Wales miners but they are very solid.

There is a marvellous row over the Bishop of Durham's enthronement address in which he said the miners must not be beaten and that the Government didn't seem to care.

Tuesday 25 September

I asked Ken Cameron if it was true that the firemen would come out on strike if the troops were brought in to the mining industry and he confirmed it.

Labour Party Conference, Blackpool
Friday 28 September

Caroline and I caught the train to Blackpool and booked in to Florida Flatlets. It's the first time we haven't stayed at the Grand Hotel or the Imperial Hotel, and we feel liberated.

Tuesday 2 October

Neil Kinnock made his Conference speech, which lasted forty-five minutes. I was sitting next but one to him, so I had to listen. He got a standing ovation of a most forced kind. People rose to their feet and clapped in order to prolong it. Glenys was brought on and they held up their hands. Then he himself stopped it because it was getting to the point where people were standing like a sullen crowd clapping to try to get the pub doors open! Arthur Scargill had got a spontaneous and passionate ovation, and Neil didn't want comparisons drawn with Arthur.

Thursday 4 October

We had the morning session of Conference on privatisation.

The *Guardian* this morning had an extraordinary article by Raphael Samuel reviewing *Writings on the Wall*, my anthology of socialist and radical writings. I believe he wrote a piece in the *New Statesman* last week called 'The End of Bennism', attacking Chris Mullin. Today's review said I had invented 'ancestor worship' in my anthology. When a trade union leader like Arthur Scargill shows he has got the strength to do something the old academic left get frightened.

In the afternoon there was a debate on training and education. Frances Morrell made a good speech, and I could just see her as a Labour Minister of Education.

Yesterday the High Court decided it would summon Arthur Scargill for contempt of court, for repeating that the strike was official when the judge had ruled that the NUM might not describe it as such without a national ballot. Arthur says he won't go to court and won't apologise, so confrontation between them is now almost inevitable.

Friday 12 October

At 3 o'clock this morning a bomb exploded in the Grand Hotel in Brighton, and four people were killed. Norman Tebbit and his wife were injured, and it just missed Mrs Thatcher, who emerged unscathed. The IRA have claimed responsibility. It is a big event, like the

Gunpowder Plot or the Cato Street Conspiracy. The IRA issued a statement, which the press never printed, saying they had planted the bomb because prisoners in Northern Ireland were being tortured.

Saturday 13 October
Caught the 7.45 to Chesterfield. There were a couple of young striking miners from South Derbyshire on the train. They had no money at all and I bought them a cup of tea. We had two problems: first, how to get them to Derby without a ticket, then how to get them past the ticket collector in Derby. I spoke to the ticket collector on the train, who initially got very tough and said, 'I'll have to take their names and addresses.' Then he whispered to me, 'The man behind me is one of my gaffers from BR, a retired inspector.' So he took their details but won't act on it. I wrote a note to the ticket collector at Derby, explaining their situation and saying that, as the NUR was showing solidarity with the miners, I would be grateful if they could be allowed through and, if there was a problem, they should send the bill to me. I think everything was all right in the end. It gave me great pleasure that there was this sort of network of help.

Wednesday 17 October
Had a phone call from the office of Armand Hammer, the head of Occidental Oil, asking if I would like to meet him this afternoon at Claridge's. As he is such an interesting man, I accepted. I went up to his suite and we had an hour's talk on our own together. Candidly, although I was pleased that he had asked me to come, I did wonder what his reason was.

In the course of the discussion he said that, together with a consortium, he was building a reproduction of Shakespeare's Globe Theatre on its original site, with office buildings around it to pay for the cost of the theatre. Southwark Council had given him planning permission, but they had since been taken over by the left, who were now not ready to go ahead with it, and legal action would delay it. Could I help? He understood that I knew somebody who was the adviser to the Southwark Council, a Dr Stuart Holland.

So I said, 'Well, this is a controversial question, because Southwark is an area of old dockland which has been left derelict, and there is a big argument about the use that should be made of it – whether it should be luxury buildings and offices, or homes for the people in the area. One of the reasons why Southwark Council has moved to the left is over that very question.'

He took that on board, because he is a very shrewd man, and he said, 'Well, we would be prepared to help to see that there was proper housing in the area.'

This is the sort of thing Peter Tatchell was fighting against in the Bermondsey by-election eighteen months ago.

We talked about the miners' strike and about MacGregor, and the future of coal. I think he's the sort of man you can use, because he might have a word with Thatcher about settling with the miners, or carry the message in a very discreet way. No doubt he adjusted what he said to suit me, but I think it's possible to use him to introduce certain ideas which would then go straight to the top.

Monday 22 October
Went to the House, where Arthur Scargill, Mick McGahey and Peter Heathfield joined a little meeting of Campaign Group MPs – Alan Meale, Dennis Skinner, Kevin Barron, Mark Fisher, Stuart Holland and a few others. They had raised with Kinnock the possibility of a joint campaign between the Labour Party and the NUM on the miners' strike, including fund raising and coordination of support from constituency parties. Kinnock had said this should be raised with the NEC. Apparently, Arthur told Kinnock that the Labour Party leadership should go on to the picket lines and see for themselves what is happening.

I tried to raise a debate under standing order number 10, but the Speaker turned me down. We have had one of the biggest, longest and most important industrial disputes in our history, there is no provision for discussing it during this week or next, the Opposition Front Bench don't want a debate because being associated with the miners is embarrassing, and when the back benches demand a debate the Speaker won't allow it.

Tuesday 23 October
I went to the House and sat in on Prime Minister's Questions. For the first time since my election to Chesterfield, Kinnock really managed to do damage to Thatcher by asking straightforward factual questions about Government policy on cutbacks and closures in the coal industry. She couldn't answer and kept referring back, and the Tories sat silent. It was a good exchange.

Wednesday 24 October
At the NEC we discussed the miners' strike, and we passed Dennis's motion on the strike committing the NEC to a joint campaign. I did succeed in adding the words 'in the light of the imminent threat of the sequestration of funds'. The Front Bench regard the miners' strike as deeply damaging to the Labour Party's prospects, and they think pressing for a settlement is a way of looking reasonable, just as Michael Foot tried to press for a peaceful solution to the Falklands War while actually supporting the war itself.

Thursday 25 October

On the 3 o'clock news I heard that Mr Justice Nicholls had sequestrated the entire funds of the NUM, which are thought to have gone down to £4.5 million since the strike began. So when I got to the House I saw Dennis Skinner, Kevin Barron and Alex Eadie and then rang the Press Association. In Business Questions in the Chamber, I asked whether there would be a debate in view of the sequestration, and Biffen said no, so I talked to the Speaker and tried to raise it under standing order number 10 again. He turned me down for the second time this week.

Later, at the end of the PLP meeting, Dennis Skinner and I got up to raise the question of the sequestration, and Jack Dormand ruled it out of order. The Party hadn't met since July, yesterday's PLP meeting was cancelled because of Mitterrand's visit, and at today's meeting they wouldn't allow anything to be raised. So I came away feeling that neither the Government, the House of Commons, the Front Bench nor the PLP want to discuss the miners' strike.

There was a PLP meeting at 10, when the Shadow Cabinet results were announced. I failed by 11 votes to get in and sadly Eric Heffer was knocked off. I can't think of a single left-winger on it now except Michael Meacher.

Monday 29 October

Had a phone call from Arthur Scargill about the report yesterday that Roger Windsor, the Chief Executive Officer of the NUM, had been to Libya to discuss the possibility of help from Libyan trade unions. Neil Kinnock had immediately denounced it, and last night on the phone Jim Mortimer had told me he was absolutely incensed at what Kinnock had done. Neil hadn't bothered to find out what was happening.

Arthur also informed me that a firm in the Midlands, a National Coal Board subsidiary, has over the past five or six years continued to work with and train Libyan nationals, has or recently had contracts with the Libyan national airline, and Libyan nationals have apparently been training on site in the Midlands as recently as a few weeks ago. I later raised this in the House.

Friday 31 October

Mrs Gandhi, the Prime Minister of India, was assassinated today, allegedly by two members of her security guards who were Sikhs. It has thrown the world in turmoil.

Thursday 1 November

New coal talks broke down last night. There is a hell of a row between MacGregor and the Coal Board, and some miners have begun drifting back to work.

Went to the dentist because I was in pain, and Mr Dunn had to pull out a tooth.

Tom Vallins phoned. He said morale was very low in Derbyshire, and could I go up and do something? So I packed, went to Great Yarmouth for a miners' meeting that I was committed to do, and they drove me to Chesterfield afterwards.

Friday 2 November

Up at 5 after three hours' sleep and went to a pit-gate meeting at Arkwright organised by Johnny Burrows to cope with the general collapse of morale. It was pitch dark when we got there, and there were 2000 police in fluorescent jackets, just a foreign army. Apparently there are now ten miners working there; previously there had been only one woman in the office. They needed a bit of a boost.

Got back to the Westdale, turned off the light, lay on the bed, and four minutes later Tom Vallins banged on the window to say I was due at a meeting at 10, not at 11 as I had thought. So off we went, and there was a queue of people waiting to collect food parcels – it was a bit like the Salvation Army. One woman was very bitter, and said there ought to be a ballot.

Came back and had a short sleep. I heard from Gordon Butler today that two of the working miners in Derbyshire have succeeded in getting court injunctions which would have the effect of compelling each individual member of the NUM executive and each individual member, I think, of the area executives, to pay £8000 damages to those miners who have been working and who have been paying their union dues. As Gordon said, 'They'll come into my home, which is a Coal Board house anyway, and take my possessions and I'll be bankrupted, and then no doubt they'll go to court and say, because I am bankrupted, I am unfit to be an officer of a union.' He seemed quite calm about it, but when individual trade union officers are hunted down and harassed we should have no hesitation whatever about dealing a similar blow in reverse.

I never understood until now – and it has been an eye-opener – the true nature of class legislation, class law, class judges, class magistrates, class use of the police, class use of the media. It has completely shaken me. I knew it in theory, but I know in practice now what is happening.

The Coal Board have offered £650 to every striking miner who returns before Christmas. Assuming they all did, it would cost about £80 million, and it's a bribe, but many families will think it would be marvellous to get a cheque like that for Christmas. If the miners crack now under the pressure of legal threats or bribes or police harassment, then the labour movement in Britain is back where it started. It would be a huge task to build it up all over again, and all these great generals in the TUC or Labour Party leaders driving round in their limousines thinking they command an army would discover they don't, because they have neglected to re-equip that army with understanding and courage.

Monday 5 November

Eric Heffer was defeated for the chair of the Organisation Committee by Kinnock and Hattersley. Charlie Turnock got it by 13 to 6.

Tuesday 6 November

International Committee, where Eric Heffer completely lost his temper. It has been too much for him being defeated for the chair yesterday, and he shouted and interrupted Alex Kitson and Gwyneth Dunwoody, whom he called 'Vinegar Lil'. The whole thing was sickening, just like the Bevanite days.

Had a cup of tea with Alan Meale, Dennis Skinner and Joan Maynard and talked about what we should do in the light of Kinnock's refusal to speak at any NUM rallies. I drafted a letter, to be issued by the Campaign Group tonight, saying: 'We pledge our full support for the NUM in its historic struggle against pit closures and appeal to all members of the PLP to join us in this campaign and to give absolute priority to it until the battle is won.' It was put out in the names of forty-eight members of the Campaign Group and was a message to Kinnock that he should give absolute priority to this matter. The anger against Kinnock is phenomenal.

From 7 to 12 November 1984 I toured Canada and the United States, fund-raising for the miners. I visited Toronto, Boston, New York and Indiana, giving talks and lectures, and came back with approximately £2,500, to find the miners starting to dribble back to work from sheer financial desperation.

Thursday 15 November

Had a word with Dennis Skinner, who said I must stand against Kinnock or Hattersley this coming year. My own feeling is that it would be quite wrong to announce a candidature just like that. I think you have to get a statement of policy, a discussion and consultation within the Party as to whether it is sensible to put up any candidate. Then the Campaign Group would have to select a candidate. Caroline's advice later today was that I should keep out of it, which is my inclination, because I think it might cause great anger in the Party.

Saturday 17 November

Tony and Sally Banks, Chris Mullin, Caroline and I went up to Chesterfield Magistrates' Court for the bail hearing of two men charged by the police in connection with the strike.

We sat in the gallery, and when the stipendiary magistrate, who had no doubt been told that Tony Banks and I were there, came in he looked round at the people in the gallery. The guys were brought up from the cells underground like common criminals, and they stood with a policeman beside them. The charge was that they had obstructed the police. A sergeant read the charge; he said the men had been asked to move on, and one of them had moved slowly and stopped suddenly, so that a policeman had bumped into him. Actually the police had thumped these guys from behind. The wives and the miners laughed at the police explanation, and so did I, and the magistrate said, 'This is not a music hall. If there is any more disturbance from the gallery, I'll clear the court.'

Bertie Mathers, the NUM solicitor, made a very good speech. He said, 'Your Honour, as you can see, this case has aroused a lot of interest. There are many people here, witnesses' – and he pointed in the general direction of the gallery where we were. He continued, 'There is a video of what happened. I am asking for bail without restrictive bail conditions.'

The magistrate said, 'I take no notice of the distinguished people in the gallery. I am here to administer the law, but in the circumstances I am not going to impose any bail conditions.' So these two men were released on bail without conditions, which is almost unheard of in the miners' cases coming up before the courts. They were told to come back on 10 December. I felt it was worthwhile going.

We all came out very cheerful and I went with them to the police station to pick up their gear.

Monday 19 November
In the House of Commons a statement was made about the Animal Liberation Front, who claimed to have poisoned Mars Bars with rat poison, as a result of which the Mars Corporation had taken their chocolate out of the shops. The ALF said Mars were funding experiments on animals. Well, there was shock-horror-disgust from all sides of the House. The only person who spoke up and said the Government had been slow to deal with animal welfare was Dale Campbell-Savours of all people. Everyone else just poured contempt on the ALF and said how the RSPCA was being undermined by this sort of irresponsible behaviour.

Wednesday 21 November
I went into the House at 10pm. After a division, Mick Welsh, Labour MP for Doncaster North, a Yorkshire miner, got up, and he was so incensed at the cut of a further £1 a week from the benefit paid to the families of miners on strike that he stood shaking his finger. Quite sponta eously, Eric Heffer, Dennis Skinner, Dave Nellist and Terry

Fields went and stood in front of the mace; a number of people joined them, including myself. I remember the same thing happening over the Industrial Relations Act. On this occasion the Speaker suspended the sitting for ten minutes. There was uproar in the House, and I believe Dave Nellist tore up the statement that the Social Services Secretary, Norman Fowler, was making. The Speaker came back, saw people still standing and adjourned the House. It was a tremendous row, and gave publicity to the miners' strike and the demand for a debate. Things happen when you make a row, and if you don't make a row people don't give a damn.

Thursday 22 November
To Brussels for a meeting with the British Labour Group in the European parliament, and we collected £400 for the miners.

Friday 23 November
The Labour Club in Chesterfield was absolutely booming when I arrived. There was a huge coach outside, and Sean Geraghty of the Fleet Street electricians had come up with twenty-five electricians and brought £3600-worth of food parcels. It was like a victory celebration. Sean, whom I have met before, is very knowledgeable and politically absolutely on his toes. I thanked them for coming and said, if ever they wanted to close down Fleet Street, we'd come and help them.

Tomorrow I've got a rally in Derby in the morning, then two Sheffield meetings, back to London, then to Chesterfield again on Sunday for a meeting of my GMC.

Saturday 24 November
To Derby, where 5000 people marched through the city. We reached the City Square, and I was just greeting Arthur when there was a great noise and a tall man of about fifty jumped on to the platform and struck Arthur in the stomach with something. Arthur was badly shaken. I caught the man's arm and he kicked me in the shin, then he was removed from the platform and the policeman asked Arthur, 'What do you wish us to do, sir?' Arthur said, 'Nothing.' Arthur told me it was the fourth time he had been attacked.

Sunday 25 November
The violence is growing. One man was beaten up and another working miner's house was burned on Saturday. You can't be sure it's being done by other miners, but of course they are under great pressure and this is a civil war, the responsibility for which lies with the Tory Government, who have used a pretext to declare war on the mining community.

Monday 26 November

We had the debate in the House, which was granted as a result of last week's demonstration on the £1 cut in benefit payments to strikers. Michael Meacher made a competent speech, but apparently when he sat down on the Front Bench Hattersley said, 'You are a twerp. Your speech made my nose bleed, it was so ineffective. Why didn't you condemn the demonstration in the House last week?' Michael said he'd never had anything like that said to him before.

Saturday 1 December

I rang Frank Cousins who lives near Chesterfield for a talk. I thought with his wealth of experience as a TGWU leader his view would be valuable. He said, first of all, that he thought Arthur Scargill had not been political enough – which is a criticism a number of people have made; secondly, that Neil Kinnock was not supporting the miners strongly enough and, thirdly, that the union leaders can't deliver unless 'they get out and do something', as he himself had done in 1955 during the London bus strike.

Sunday 2 December

We heard on the news that a receiver has been appointed to take over control of the NUM's finances.

Ken Livingstone came to see me and we had a bite to eat. He thought it was unlikely that the GLC would be driven into illegality next year, because the Government wouldn't want to bankrupt it just before they take over responsibility themselves – an interesting and relevant point. He said the GLC now funded 2500 organisations in London to the tune of £25 million, but even so the support for the GLC was pretty shallow among activists, and the trade unions in London were only remotely connected to the Labour Party.

Thursday 6 December

Spent the morning writing a speech for a meeting in St Ives, advocating that the labour movement discuss the need for a general strike. I put out a press release and caught the train, where I met Betty Heathfield. I spoke in the Free Church Centre in St Ives, a constituency with a huge Tory majority.

Saturday 8 December

Drove through the Peak District to Keele, through winding lanes on a beautiful day, to see Stephen get his PhD. All the family were there, and we stopped for lunch before going on to Moberly Hall, where Stephen was all done up in his robes. He certainly deserves his PhD.

Tuesday 11 December

Went to meet Bert Ramelson, the former industrial organiser of the Communist Party, who had asked me to write an article for the *World Marxist Review*. He thought it possible that there would be a split in the CP but he is keeping his mouth shut because he doesn't believe in faction fighting. I felt I had a great deal in common with him. I told him what was happening in the Labour Party, how there might well be expulsions. He thought a contest against Kinnock should be left for eighteen months. He said the CP should affiliate to the Labour Party and that actually Martin Jacques was just melting away the policy contained in *The British Road to Socialism*, just as Kinnock is melting away the policy of *Labour's Programme*.

Wednesday 12 December

At the NEC Frances Curran moved a resolution calling for the reimbursement of fines imposed on trade unions by the Government not only under their own legislation but under common law.

Kinnock declared, 'We can't pass this because we mustn't forget that we lost the 1983 Election, and if we do this it would be to raise questions about our defeat. Secondly, it is an inoperable undertaking to give to those who break the law, and, thirdly, the action against the NUM has been taken under common law, not under Tory legislation. Therefore I oppose it. It would be an incitement, and after all we want the law enforced.'

Joan Maynard said, 'That is an amazing statement. It is against the conference decision to say it is inoperable, and it would give a bad impression.'

'I don't like to speak in opposition to the Leader of the Party, but if you move away from Conference decisions you are in a real difficulty,' Sam McCluskie said.

Eric Clarke made the point that the strike itself was illegal under the present law. 'Are we going to uphold that? It is class war, and we had better recognise it.'

Dennis Skinner commented, and then I spoke. I had a struggle to be called to speak. I asked for a recorded vote. I said it was a very serious thing to argue that the fact that we were defeated in 1983 changed our policy, particularly as in 1983 we campaigned for a fairer Britain. 'There is no objection whatever to retrospective legislation for an amnesty. All amnesties are retrospective. The only reason the common law is a never-ending struggle is because successive Labour Governments have never had the guts to deal with it. However you look at it, this refusal will be seen as a betrayal of the miners.'

Neil Kinnock responded to the comments. 'Anyone who says this is a stab in the back for the miners will have to answer to me. Retrospective legislation is not acceptable, and the common law is very different from

Tory legislation. What use would it be to tell the NUM that we are going to repay their fines?'

Frances Curran said, ' I accept an amendment from Eric to leave out a reference to working miners, but it would be stabbing the NUM in the back if we didn't pass this resolution.'

Finally, an amendment from Turnock to refer the motion to the Home Policy Committee was carried by 15 to 13, with Meacher voting for referral.

Friday 14 December
At 10.35pm, Joshua rang to say that William Graydon Feeney Benn had been born – our third grandchild. He is six weeks early, but seems to be all right.

Saturday 15 December
Drove to the airport to catch the early shuttle to Edinburgh for a rally in support of the miners. I was driven to the City Hall, which had a huge red star over it. It is the first time Edinburgh has ever had a Labour council, and the sense of excitement is tremendous. The rooms allocated to the Labour Group were full of posters from Nicaragua, Chile, Cuba and the Soviet Union. They were obviously having a whale of a time. They had tried unsuccessfully to get rid of the Lord Provost and substitute the title of 'convenor'; they believed that if they had chosen the word 'chairman' they would have got away with it. The Labour Councillors are in the first flush of victory.

On the march were Gavin Strang (MP for Edinburgh East), Alex Eadie, Mick McGahey and Augustine du Fresne (General Secretary of the French miners). The French had arrived in Britain with ten lorries and about £1 million worth of gifts – phenomenal. We marched through the streets, but there wasn't an awful lot of interest, frankly. I talked to Mick on the way, and asked what he made of Martin Jacques's charge that I am a class reductionist and a fundamentalist. Mick said, 'Rubbish.'

Thursday 20 December
Drove to Chesterfield and found an absolute mass of boxes of beautiful toys from the French CGT, worth tens of thousands of pounds, enough to give every miner's child two toys. My jumble seemed a modest contribution, but eight visiting miners were staying at the Westdale, so I paid their bill.

Went to the club and began talking to people about calling a general strike in Chesterfield. We agreed to hold an executive meeting early in January to discuss it. Maybe I have to redirect my effort to Chesterfield alone in getting this message across. Why wait for anybody else?

Talked to some of the French CGT people, who were charming.

They gave me a lovely medallion saying 'Solidarité Mineurs Britanniques', which I shall put on a red ribbon and wear on my jacket. I shall wear it in France if ever I go there.

Friday 21 December
Up at 5.45 and went out with Tom and Margaret Vallins, the Reverend David Pickering, dressed up as Santa Claus, and two women from the local Party, dressed up in red tights and women's Santa Claus outfits. We went to various collieries. I am trying to get across this idea that we should aim to bring about a day of action in Chesterfield. Morale is low because there is a general fear that people will drift back to work after Christmas as they face more hardship in the new year.

Tuesday 25 December
Caroline and I exchanged our gifts for the first time ever without the children! I collected Melissa and then the whole family came. Then our guests arrived for Christmas lunch, all twenty-one of them. Later we all went to the hospital to see our latest grandson, William, who is in an incubator.

Wednesday 2 January 1985
Stansgate. Sunny but cold. Doing my annual accounts, which I absolutely loathe. I just can't cope with financial matters. It goes back to my childhood, I think, when my father used to give me a penny a week pocket money, and I had another penny a week when I went to school, but I could get threepence a week if I submitted my 'accounts' to his secretary, Miss Triggs. So every week I had to explain how I'd spent the threepence. I remember on one occasion – when I was doing carpentry – I went to Woolworth's and bought a vice for sixpence, and when Miss Triggs saw 'vice' in my accounts she asked me what it meant.

Tuesday 8 January
Bought four rather clever attachments to put on my shoes so that I wouldn't slip on the ice. I've been afraid of falling and breaking my hip or something. With the remains of the Guillain-Barré syndrome I'm still not getting a perfect set of messages from my feet.

Friday 11 January
Up at 6. To Arkwright colliery and met the pickets. They looked a bit dispirited, standing by their glowing brazier. More than half are now back working at Arkwright. One or two of those men have been downgraded from face workers and are just doing haulage work and unskilled work, with a substantial loss in their income, so the victimisation has already begun, even among those who have gone back.

I did wonder whether the strike is crumbling in North Derbyshire.

Wednesday 16 January

Went to St Bride's Institute for a meeting organised by the National Graphical Association, the electricians and other print workers, on the subject of media coverage of the miners' strike.

A very important point I have noticed is the enormous pay that Fleet Street people get. I told the meeting that, if the miners were beaten, the Government would go for the Fleet Street unions next, and it would be hard to have much sympathy for people who'd done so little to help the miners and were so well paid; nevertheless it was necessary to sympathise with them, and therefore they depended upon the miners to win. I said if they did stop Fleet Street or insist on a better way of handling things then the Tory propaganda machine would immediately stop.

Thursday 17 January

Demonstration in the House today to demand a further debate on the mining industry. We got up one after the other, and when the Speaker told us to sit down we all stood up together. He suspended the sitting; then we went into the Members' Lobby and decided on one short statement to be made by me, saying that we intend to press for a debate in Government time next week. The Speaker was conferring with the two Front Benches during the suspension, and our Front Bench were furious because our demonstration had exposed their opposition to a debate.

At the PLP later Ernie Roberts and Gavin Strang asked for a supply-day debate. There hasn't been a whole-day debate since 31 July, and if there hadn't been a demonstration in the House in November there wouldn't have been one then.

George Robertson, a Scottish MP, said he had seen Mick McGahey, who had no complaint about the work of the PLP, and this action was just encouraged by *Socialist Organiser* and Militant.

Jack Ashley thought there may have been a case for a higher profile in support of the NUM, but today we had damaged the cause and demeaned ourselves.

Stuart Bell said the PLP was doing a lot, the CLPs were united, and we mustn't give the impression that we didn't support the Shadow Cabinet; it was for them to decide tactics.

Martin Flannery thought the issue was straightforward. The miners had their backs to the wall, with low morale and a bitter winter, and we couldn't avoid the issue. The miners needed more than they were getting, we needed a debate, and the PLP should unite and support the strike.

Neil Kinnock said it was a miracle that the miners' battle hadn't overwhelmed us already. We should minimise the damage and think about tactics. Only 75 per cent of the miners were out, and the root of

the damage was that there was no unity. That was why they had to go in
for mass picketing and why violence had occurred and obscured the
issue. We must give a higher profile to the case for coal. He said the
pickets didn't want public meetings – they wanted an end to the strike.
The demonstration had helped Thatcher: it obscured the issue, and it
was undisciplined self-indulgence. 'As to the Pharisees who fight to the
last drop of everyone else's blood, I can tell you this, this is the last
miners' strike we shall see in our lifetime. Raise the matter by all
possible means if you think it helps, but I beg you to understand that it
will not advance by half a millimetre the cause, will not help us to get
power, and is not the proper means of activity.'

A memorable day, though not very pleasant to get into direct conflict
with the Speaker.

Friday 18 January
Kinnock's speech at the PLP was all over the papers – 'Kinnock
Hammers Left', 'Kinnock Furious with the Left', and so on – exactly
the headlines that Gaitskell, Wilson, Callaghan and Foot got.

Left early for Chesterfield. David Basnett was on the train and he
was reading Cobbett's *Rural Rides*. I mentioned the general secretary-
ship of the Party, and he said with great authority, 'Larry Whitty will
get it', so obviously that is fixed.

Saturday 19 January
Had a phone call from *The World This Weekend*, asking for an interview.
So I agreed, as long as we didn't discuss Kinnock. They said that was
all right and they sent John Sergeant, whom I like. He asked a few
things, and then he read to me what Kinnock had said about
'undisciplined self-indulgence'. After I had answered that he came
back to Kinnock, and I put my hand over the mike and just didn't say
anything. So the interview came to a halt and I switched off his
machine.

'You said you wouldn't do that,' I told him.

'Well, I had indicated I would just ask one,' he said.

I lost my temper and said, 'What the hell do you think you're doing?
I'm talking about defending the miners, and you're trying to get at the
Labour Party.'

Then I got my electro-magnetic device for wiping cassettes and tried
to erase his interview. It was a flaming row, and I regret it, because you
should never be rude to anyone.

Tuesday 22 January
At 5.30 I walked up to Alan Sapper's office, Soho Square, for the left
trade union leaders' caucus on the eve of the TUC General Council
meeting.

Mick McGahey described what had happened. Yesterday Peter Heathfield and Ned Smith, industrial relations director of the Coal Board, had met informally.

The NCB said they had already conceded that Polmaise and Herrington should continue to operate, subject to review. The NUM pointed out that for forty years they had objected to closures on economic grounds; the Coal Board acknowledged this but said that the need for closure had been accepted by the union. The problem was one of *definition* of what is uneconomic.

The NUM wanted an amnesty for 700 miners who had been sacked. The Coal Board refused this, but recognised there would be certain related matters to discuss, including questions of dismissals and wages, after the settlement – a sort of parallel but separate agreement.

Peter had got out at 3 and found that the Government had briefed the press at 2 that the talks had failed.

Mick went on to say he wondered if it was a plan to raise morale and then drop it again. Apparently Ned Smith didn't know about the press briefing and was as surprised as anyone else. Incidentally, Ned is retiring from the Coal Board next week.

Mick said that there would be a meeting of the NUM executive on Thursday, and it would have to be agreed that every miner went back together and that there would be no victimisation. They would then write to the NCB positively about renewed discussions.

Ken Cameron suggested that no victimisation of the scabs should be part of the agreement. If talks could be held before the NUM special delegate conference on 30 January, then that conference could be cancelled. If we could get talks going, however flimsy, that would help us.

I said Thatcher was confident that the strike would crumble, and therefore she wanted to get the maximum advantage out of this. Would it be possible to talk about the economics of pit closure in a way which would cover the total position from the point of view of national accounts rather than the closure of uneconomic pits? I thought it would be much better to defer the 30 January NUM conference anyway. 'Why open up an internal fight in the NUM at this stage when you have it in your own power to defer that meeting? Thatcher thinks the NUM will split on 30 January, and that is what she is waiting for.'

Rodney Bickerstaffe agreed. Jim Slater, General Secretary of the National Union of Seamen, said the Notts miners wanted Scargill to be defeated (which is true, I'm afraid).

Ken Gill warned us not to underestimate the split in the Coal Board and on the Tory side, and argued that the media was now beginning to criticise Thatcher.

It was the first serious strategic and tactical discussion on the strike that I have taken part in, and I was gratified that McGahey and other experienced trade union leaders listened carefully to what I said; they do trust me, they give me all their confidential documents, and I feel part of the team.

Back to the Commons where I saw Derek Foster, Neil Kinnock's PPS, and asked for an appointment to see Neil.

At 8.45 I went into his office, and Neil, Derek Foster and Stan Orme were there.

I put the position to him as I understood it. The TUC couldn't do very much, the NUM and the NCB had had these talks which were torpedoed by the Government. The NUM executive were prepared to make a constructive response at their Thursday meeting and defer their special conference, and it seemed to me that a debate could then take place on the question of the Government's determination to destroy the talks. The Party would come together because it would be having a debate and the Government would be on the spot.

I stayed for half an hour, and Kinnock thanked me and said I ought to make a habit of it.

At 9.15 I went into a room off Westminster Hall to dictate my diary. At 10 I left, and found the lights off and the doors leading into Westminster Hall locked. I saw a fire exit and a key behind glass, so with my hand I bashed the glass, cut my hand, opened the door and found myself in the old cafeteria which is being reconstructed. I rang the custodians and finally got out at 10.30.

Got back and rang Arthur, and told him about the talks with Kinnock.

I had a very friendly letter from Jim Callaghan today. I had written to him when he went into hospital, and he replied saying, 'I cannot bear the thought of a divided NUM.' He quoted Bevin: 'Take what you can and go back for more as soon as you can.'

Wednesday 23 January
Today the House of Lords proceedings were televised for the first time. Some miners had managed to get tickets into the public gallery with the help of some Labour MPs, and just before 5pm they stood up and unrolled their banners and shouted, 'Victory to the miners! Coal not dole!' Some were held by Black Rod, pending the end of the day's sitting, and no doubt they were treated decently, but lawyers were not allowed to see them.

I was asked to comment on IRN news about the demonstration, and I said, 'Nobody in the Lords can complain if someone asks for a job for life, because the Lords all have a job for life, and so do their sons and their grandsons. They can't complain about not having ballots, because they don't want a ballot to decide on their own existence!' I said it was a historic – or prehistoric – occasion. Quite funny.

Thursday 24 January

To the Commons. At Prime Minister's Questions, Kinnock was a bit tougher about the miners, and Thatcher was almost hysterical and vicious in her response. But in Next Week's Business Questions there was no Front Bench demand for a debate, so I demanded one and pointed to the number of refusals to grant a debate. The Speaker got up and said, 'I hope you're not criticising me.' I said no, but that he had stated eighteen times that the miners' strike was neither urgent nor specific enough to take precedence over orders of the day. He looked uncomfortable.

At the PLP we discussed the miners. Kinnock said he didn't want the Tories to know but he was putting out a statement saying the Shadow Cabinet was watching urgently and would take a full and early opportunity to make the Government accountable – all rubbish. He also moved that we raise MPs' contributions to the miners' fund to £12 per week, and that was agreed unanimously.

Friday 25 January

Arthur Scargill told me that talks with the Coal Board are scheduled for Tuesday. He had got hold of a transcript (through Paul Foot) of a telephone call by David Hart, the PM's adviser at the Coal Board, violently attacking MacGregor and calling him something very offensive. So there's obviously tremendous trouble between MacGregor and the Government.

On to Manchester for two miners' meetings. It really is a killing programme at the moment. I've taken on much too much. It *won't* kill me, but I am very, very tired. I must get more rest. The miners' strike is at a critical stage.

Sunday 27 January

GMC at Chesterfield. I paid tribute to the miners and commented on the media position, which is that the miners are about to be beaten. The truth was otherwise. The NUM and the Coal Board want talks, whereas the Government wants no talks and no debate.

The newspapers are full of the collapse of the strike, as if it were a foregone conclusion. It may be there will be a complete collapse tomorrow morning. We'll just have to see.

Tuesday 29 January

I saw Leon Brittan, the Home Secretary, in the Division Lobby, and I asked him, 'Will you tell MI5 to stop sending your letters to me? I get two or three a week addressed to you in my envelopes – indeed, I had one this morning.' Would he ask them to be so kind as to direct them to the right person! He looked a bit discomfited. No doubt he'll make enquiries about it.

Thursday 31 January
To the Commons for a meeting at 12.30 about the strike, with Alan
Meale, Martin Redmond (MP for Don Valley), Joan Maynard and
Dennis Skinner. We had a message from Roger Windsor telling us to
meet Peter Heathfield at TUC headquarters, so we went off to
Congress House, where we saw Norman Willis.

'Who told you to come here?' he asked.

I said we were told to meet Peter Heathfield here. He looked furious,
and pointed to a room and told us to wait, and Dennis Skinner heard
him go by, saying, 'Bloody hell.'

Later I heard from Peter Heathfield that Norman Willis had said,
'The TUC is not a bloody adjunct of the PLP' – a typical TUC line.
They don't want anybody interfering in their patch, and the less well
they're doing the more they resent it. The tragedy for the TUC is that
they are generals with no troops, and they haven't even been invited to
'surrender talks' by the Government because they are not invited to
Number 10.

Peter was sad. He said there were pickets who simply couldn't go on
any more because their shoes had worn out, they hadn't got any warm
clothes, they had been evicted from their homes, and their gas and
electricity had been cut off. The union hadn't any money; they needed
£150,000 a week to keep the strike going.

Friday 1 February
At 9.30 Ralph Miliband came to see me by appointment. He's written a
lot of really great books – on parliamentary socialism, class power and
state power. His latest book is *Capitalist Democracy in Britain*.

We had a talk for an hour and a half, during which he said there had
never been anybody with my experience of government who had taken
such a radical position on institutional questions. 'You must use it
properly,' he told me. 'I would suggest that you keep absolutely away
from the in-fighting in the Party which does nothing to help.'

Then he asked, 'Have you got a think tank? Would you like me to
help you to get together a few academics who would be prepared to
assist?' I was very flattered, and asked him to keep in touch.

Monday 4 February
Typed my speech for the debate we have successfully called today on
the miners. I used the new word processor, which made it so simple
because you can revise your work on the screen.

There were some brilliant speeches in the House – from Stan Orme,
Alex Eadie, Roy Mason, Michael McGuire, Dick Douglas, Jack
Dormand, Martin Redmond, Mick Welsh and Dave Nellist. We
trounced the Tories because of all the experience we have on our side,
with a number of former miners. In general the Party was united by its

response to the basic questions raised by the miners' strike, and in the event it was only the Shadow Cabinet that didn't really come out of it well.

Tuesday 5 February

Didn't get up until almost 10 today. Caroline and I talked and it was lovely and quiet and relaxed. I am really very happy at the moment; I am getting more disconnected from the Labour Party hierarchy, but down the line it's marvellous.

As I was walking towards the Commons, a cab pulled up and the driver told me to jump in for nothing. He said, 'When I look at Mrs Thatcher, I keep reminding myself of what would have happened to me if we hadn't had the NHS. Two of my sons are haemophiliacs – one twenty-seven and one nineteen. They would have died, or I would have been bankrupted, or both, if we hadn't had the NHS.' He spoke with such feeling. When we got to the Commons I offered to pay him, and he told me to give it to the miners or the Ethiopian Famine Fund.

Friday 8 February

Tom picked me up from the station and took me to the Labour Club, which was packed with striking miners collecting their picket money – only £1 a day at the moment. How they survive I will never know, but they are cheerful, buoyant and don't look starved, even though they must be putting up with appalling hardship. There is no sign of them weakening.

Tom told me that MacGregor had considered sacking all those miners who were not back at work by the first anniversary of the strike – a sign of panic, of course.

Peter said the unions had offered interest-free loans to the miners, but they were all frightened off by Price Waterhouse, the receiver appointed by the Government to administer the NUM's finances.

Sunday 10 February

The judge in the Ponting case[1] apparently said that the interests of the state were the interests of the Government of the day, implying that criticism of the Government was unacceptable.

Monday 11 February

We heard on the news that Clive Ponting had been acquitted – a tremendously significant victory, particularly after the judge had given a violently anti-Labour summing up. He almost directed the jury to convict.

Wednesday 13 February

A man in Wales has left me in his will many personal papers, including letters from Keir Hardie to Emrys Hughes's sister[2] (while Emrys was in prison as a conscientious objector during the First World War), and a lovely ebony stick which Mahatma Gandhi gave to Hardie, and a small armchair.

Thursday 14 February

I tried unsuccessfully to get into Prime Minister's Questions. Neil Kinnock in effect withdrew his charge that the PM had lied about the prosecution of Ponting, but she didn't accept his apology. I did get in on Business Questions, and I asked (which was unwise really) whether the PM's decision not to take part in the debate on the *Belgrano* next Monday confirmed the impression that when British troops were sacrificing their lives for military victories in the South Atlantic she was ready to step forward to take all the credit, but when the criticism began she offloaded it on to others and tried to shield herself behind 'national security'. I suggested that behind her sedulously created image as a great war leader was the heart of a coward.

The Speaker pulled me up on the use of that word, and I withdrew the remark pretty well at once. I shouldn't have said it, but to undermine the idea that she is a great war leader was worth doing. The Commons didn't like it.

Yet the fact is that the Americans cover the whole South Atlantic with their satellite system, and she didn't want to let it be known that she had won the war with the aid of the Americans. We have to bust the Falklands myth of this invincible woman.

Monday 18 February

To the House, and got a question in to the Secretary of State for Energy; the miners' dispute is likely to be moving towards a conclusion with a meeting between the TUC and the PM tomorrow at Number 10.

In the *Belgrano* debate afterwards, which the Government arranged in the wake of the Ponting affair, Heseltine was mainly concerned to show how important he was and how vital national security was. He denounced Ponting.

Merlyn Rees made a funny speech, and Chris Smith, the MP for Islington South and Finsbury, made a good one. I was only allowed ten minutes, so I tried to emphasise the fundamental questions – that this was a discussion of the relationship between a Cabinet, the courts and the Commons – and to show how the prerogative was being used to silence the Commons, blacken civil servants and tell the courts what they could and couldn't do.

Tuesday 19 February

The press generally presented yesterday's debate on the *Belgrano* as a great Government triumph, with Heseltine having completely destroyed the reputation of Clive Ponting. The Labour attack hasn't really registered, and that is the problem that we are facing as a Party.

Thursday 21 February

To the Commons for Prime Minister's Questions. I asked about the Government's involvement in planning and continuing the miners' strike. Peter Walker gave a characteristically angry reply, attacking Scargill (as they all did), but this time naming Norman Willis and saying that the TUC, Ray Buckton, Basnett and so on had all tried to help, and Scargill had repudiated them and split his union from top to bottom. You can see that the function of the Labour and TUC leaderships is to deliver the working class into the hands of the ruling class. It does make you wonder whether the Labour leadership and the hierarchies of the labour movement aren't our ultimate prison, sad to say it.

Sunday 24 February

To Hyde Park at 11.30 for the miners' march. About 100,000 were there (the police said 15,000).

I marched with Anne Scargill, Ron Todd, Jim Mortimer and Ben Rubner, General Secretary of the Furniture, Timber and Allied Trade Unions. Anne told me that when she'd been arrested last summer for some absolutely trifling picket-line offence (of which she was acquitted) she had actually been strip-searched by a woman half her age. She was horrified by it.

When we reached Trafalgar Square, the police had moved in and stopped the end of the procession from getting near to the square; then, having provoked trouble, they had launched baton attacks and mounted police charges. Ron Todd said later that it was disgraceful. He had seen police vehicles with CS gas canisters in them. We just live in a police state at the moment.

Thursday 28 February

Terrible cough and a high fever. I was taken to Catford, South London, where I spoke for the miners. Then I was brought back to Porchester Hall, Queensway, for a meeting. Felt lousy.

Saturday 2 March

Stayed in bed all day – both of us had high temperatures. I coughed up blood, which frightened me a bit. I think probably I'd torn a blood vessel retching – nothing serious.

Sunday 3 March

Today the delayed miners' delegate conference took place at TUC headquarters. The NUM executive had been split 11:11 on the continuation of the strike, and Arthur had refused to use his casting vote. The delegate conference itself ultimately voted by 98 to 91 for an organised return to work.

I felt like weeping when I heard it on the news, after this great struggle – at the fact that the people who had been victimised were not being negotiated back, and at the Coal Board's and the Government's arrogance.

The strike has been a monumental and titanic struggle. The overwhelming majority of the miners and their families have supported it to the last, and the crude use by the Government of the apparatus of the state to crush the miners has been on an unprecedented scale. The lessons to be learned from that are enormous. The Coal Board as a nationalised industry has completely abandoned any legitimate loyalty from the miners – they are just state coal-owners.

The other unions who have supported them – the NUR, the NUS, and so on – have been marvellous. The TUC has been pathetic. The Labour hierarchy has been shown to be quite inadequate. But at grassroots level there has been a formidable development of support groups and so on. I think that is where we will see the moves coming now.

I rang Tom Vallins and said I'd go up tomorrow and be there when the men went in on Tuesday morning. It will just be a question of keeping morale up at the moment, because obviously the miners are a bit low. I don't think this is the end of the story, and the Government's problems will just be beginning.

Tuesday 5 March
Chesterfield. Still have a filthy cough. I got up at 4, and at 4.50 we gathered in the pitch dark outside the Labour Club. We decided to go with Johnny Burrows to Markham colliery, and as the sun began to rise people gathered around.

All the miners and their wives carrying banners, marched down the hill under the railway bridge towards Markham. It was an extraordinary day. Betty Heathfield was on the brink of tears and I hugged her. I felt drained by the end of it because every emotion swept through me like a gale – tragedy, wanting to weep at seeing these people who had sacrificed so much having to go back without having won; then tremendous pride that they could go back with their banners high and not give any sort of impression that they were beaten; then feelings of intense hate as a scab came forward dressed in his pit clothes and photographed them. They began shouting 'Scabby bastard!', and the level of hatred is frightening. Then I had feelings of hope and dignity as we stood there and applauded as they all marched into the colliery.

Later, on TV, we saw pictures from other collieries. At Maerdy, the last pit in the Rhondda, where not a single man had scabbed, they marched round the whole village and went in together. In Yorkshire Arthur Scargill led them back and was stopped by three Kent miners, who had come up all the way to picket that particular colliery because the Kent men are still out. So they all turned back and didn't go into work that day. The media will try to dance on the grave of the NUM, but they will make a terrible mistake.

Saturday 9 March
There is a great sense of pride among the miners, but of course the Coal Board are trumpeting their victory and the management will be really tough with the men. MacGregor has reappeared from his hiding place and said something about the sackings being for 'insurrectionary insubordination'.

If people do stand up and fight, they transform the morale of every other oppressed person; and they reveal the repressive nature of the state and also, unfortunately, the totally defective character of the Labour and trade union hierarchy.

NOTES
Chapter Six

1.   (p. 397) The trial of Clive Ponting acquired major significance for both practical and constitutional reasons.

Ponting had been an assistant secretary in the Ministry of Defence, and was the source of some confidential documents which led Tam Dalyell to pursue so effectively his campaign against the Prime Minister for her decision to sink the *General Belgrano,* during the Falklands War, while it was sailing away from the Exclusion Zone.

The prosecution – under the Official Secrets Act – also raised the question of whether a civil servant who was privy to actions by his Minister which he believed to be immoral had a duty to obey orders, if his conscience told him that those orders were wrong, and that Parliament and the public were being deceived.

Ponting made a spirited defence of his own position and was acquitted on the grounds that what he had done was in the public interest. This constituted a landmark in constitutional practice which led to changes in a Protection of Official Information Act, which marginally modified some of the absurdities of the Official Secrets Act, without making any substantial change.

2.   (p. 398) Emrys Hughes was the Labour MP for South Ayrshire. His sister married Hedley Dennis, a Labour Party member in Abercynon, South Wales. When Dennis died in 1984 I was bequeathed a large box of papers including correspondence between his wife and Keir Hardie and the Hardie family. I also received Keir Hardie's chair, photos and a collection of early Labour newspapers.

Having read through the collection, Caroline decided to write a biography of Keir Hardie, published in 1992.

7
The New Model Party
March 1985–October 1986

Tuesday 12 March
To the Commons for the NEC International Committee, where the case for withdrawal from NATO – put by myself and seconded by Eric Heffer – was at the top of the agenda. I presented it, and Charlie Turnock of the NUR attacked me. He said, 'Tony Benn never gives up. The NEC rejected these proposals some while ago. How can we start to get the Party right in turmoil like this? Kinnock is committed to NATO. Throw it out!'

Well, he got quite hysterical, and Eric turned on him, saying he was amazed at what Turnock had said, it was total intolerance, and all we wanted was an open and free discussion. There was a conflict between NATO membership and our non-nuclear strategy. He didn't understand why we couldn't discuss the matter. It was the same story with Northern Ireland, and all we really wanted was a debate.

Hattersley argued that defence was being cut anyway, and that of course the Americans would allow us to get rid of Cruise missiles if we were elected.

Sam McCluskie said the public feared that Britain might be left defenceless. At the Scottish Party Conference last weekend our commitment to NATO had been reaffirmed, and we had to speak with one voice.

Tom Sawyer thought that now was the time to promote existing Party policy, not the time for fresh debate, and he suggested we have a firm policy and be pledged to carry it out.

I ended the discussion by saying that the greatest weakness in any policy was when an element of it was so fragile that you couldn't debate it. Anyway, we were beaten.

Thursday 28 March
Brought my diary up to date. It would be so lovely if I had my own room. I'm a nomad with a desk, and I can't even make private phone calls – every word can be overheard.

I have a huge burden of work at the moment but it is enjoyable, and now that I've been squeezed out of the top of Labour politics I'm determined to do a really good job as MP for Chesterfield.

Monday 1 April
I have had five invitations to go on chat shows, because it's my sixtieth birthday on Wednesday. I suppose when you reach sixty the journalists think they can rehabilitate you as an eccentric, lovable, old character. These shows would be entirely personal, nothing to do with politics, and I would be presented as an attractive person if I was prepared to go along with it on their terms. But people at home who know me as a fighter would say, 'God, he's sold out.'

Tuesday 2 April
The Interception of Telecommunications Bill – telephone tapping – was being debated, with an amendment by Douglas Hogg, Conservative MP for Grantham. I was called, and spoke for twenty minutes. I said that this was not a liberal bill, it simply entrenched in legislation what had formerly been done using the royal prerogative.

Funnily enough, it was a Liberal and a Tory who came up and congratulated me afterwards – Clement Freud [Liberal MP for Cambridgeshire North East] and Jonathan Aitken [Tory MP for Thanet South]. I told Jonathan that *I* was a liberal – a genuine believer in liberalism. I dozed a bit, waiting for the vote, and heard Big Ben strike midnight, my sixtieth birthday.

Thursday 18 April
Dave Wetzel, Kay Knights and another member of the Labour Land Campaign met me for our second discussion on my proposed Land Bill. They had written to ask me if I'd support their campaign, so in response, in February, I drafted a bill to take land into public ownership. However, they think I've gone too far in advocating public ownership and are more interested in the taxation of land values.

I also had a note from Gerry Bermingham, Labour MP for St Helens South, who is a solicitor and an expert in land matters. He thinks homes should be explicitly exempted from national ownership and suggested that we include an exemption clause for a property standing in an area of land (to be specified).

We decided that the Land Bill would not apply to Northern Ireland. We added protection for farmers who actually lived on their farm and, since our criterion was land value not exceeding £250,000 (rather than acreage), at present values, any farmer with less than 120 acres would be perfectly safe. The ownership of all land in England not exempt under the bill would go to a community land trust; Scotland and Wales would have their own equivalent bodies.

Then we dealt with the distribution of the revenue from rents accruing from this transfer of land, estimated at about £60 billion a year – far greater than the oil revenues. The local authorities concerned would receive one-third (replacing the need for a rate support grant and providing a surplus), one-third would go to the Treasury, and one-third to the land dividend, ie £400 per man, woman and child per year, about a pound a person a day. Very attractive.

On compensation to landowners, I dropped the idea that they be paid through social security, and they dropped the idea of a lump sum payment. We compromised on an assessment of the personal needs of the claimant, the sum to be payable out of the national revenues by an annual payment. Then we added a qualifying clause (a very important development of Labour Party thinking on compensation) which said that the payment would be for the lifetime of the claimant or for fifty years to the heirs, whichever was the longer.

Sunday 21 April

Rang Alan Meale, and we talked about Ken Coates. Alan thought that after Ken's defeat as a candidate in the Euro-elections, and given his attitude to Scargill, he had moved closer to Kinnock. That explains the current tension between us. But it is also the pervading spirit of Hobsbawm – the deep pessimism on the left about what you can and can't do.

Monday 22 April

The first item at the TUC–Labour Party Liaison Committee was a paper about Sunday trading and the Shops Act, which the Government intend to deregulate to allow shops to open on Sundays. Syd Tierney, President of USDAW, pointed out all the dangers to shopworkers arising from it.

Kaufman said the law was out of date, and shopping had become a weekend family outing; we were the Party of consumers, and there had been no religious sentiment expressed against it as yet. The Labour Party should not oppose the Government.

Bill Whatley, the General Secretary of USDAW, said he would fight against deregulation, but in the end we might need to compromise.

I supported USDAW, and said I thought the opinion polls were meaningless. Had anyone asked shopworkers whether they'd be prepared to work a seven-day week? I had no doubt people liked to shop on Sundays, but we had to support the USDAW position.

Johnny Prescott was against deregulation.

Heffer said the Prime Minister would ignore the churches' opinion. She had attacked the Bishop of Durham. Deregulation of Sunday trading was anti-Christian; we should oppose it.

When we came to the joint policy statement drawn up for the forthcoming TUC and Party conferences, Prescott asked where our commitment to full employment was. Hattersley replied that we did believe in full employment ultimately but that the TUC thought it best to 'get away from numbers'. The pledge of getting unemployment down to under one million had lost us the Election in 1983.

I said the analysis in this paper was weak. It failed to identify why the Tories want unemployment – to get wages down, to get profits up, to control imports, to undermine the unions. 'It isn't that they are incompetent or unimaginative or ideologically blind; they are fighting a class battle.'

Jim Mortimer said we couldn't get the employers to agree with us about consensus. Doug Hoyle said partnership with employers was all meaningless.

There was a socialist element present at the meeting – Prescott, Doug Hoyle, Jim, Eric and I – but the wooden men at the top of the table just looked embarrassed.

Tuesday 23 April

Today was the christening of Joshua's son, William, in the Commons Crypt. Michael and little James ran around and took no notice of the service at all. When the vicar asked us to stand for a prayer, Michael could be heard saying, 'We've got to stand again.' But it went beautifully, and William didn't cry at all. Afterwards we all went up to the Members' Dining Room and had tea.

Barbara Castle, in one of *The Twentieth Century Remembered* programmes, was asked about the deputy leadership contest. She said she had hoped I would win because she thought I had great imagination and the capacity to excite people, but I had made a lot of mistakes and had thrown it away.

Wednesday 24 April

Bought the *New Socialist*, and there was the article by Patrick Seyd called 'Bennism without Benn' of which I had been warned. To find a socialist journal carrying an article as personal as this is revolting. Stuart Weir, the editor, is of the Hobsbawm school, and what the article says in effect is that Ken Coates, Michael Meacher, Tom Sawyer, Stuart Holland and Frances Morrell have all completely deserted me and joined the Kinnock camp and that I am now alone with 'Dennis Skinner and the headbangers'.

Thursday 25 April

New Left Review carried an article by Ralph Miliband in which he patiently took to pieces the arguments of the new revisionists – everyone from the Eurocommunists to the soft left of the Labour Party. He described how people had detached themselves from the left and were being drawn towards Kinnock with a view to 'saving Kinnock from the right', the old argument that I heard Crossman and Castle use in relation to Wilson time and again.

I had a letter from Stuart Weir, offering me the right of reply in *New Socialist* and saying the Seyd article did not represent the paper's view.

Saturday 27 April

Up at 5.30, made tea, and at 6.30 I was on the picket line protesting against privatisation of cleaning services at Scarsdale Hospital in Chesterfield. Stood for an hour in the rain with twelve people.

There are thirteen unions in the hospital, and it's just a pushover for the management to play one union off against the other. The old International Workers of the World idea of one big union is absolutely right, certainly for industrial unions. Failing that, strong joint shop stewards' committees and Labour Party workplace branches are what we ought to be trying for now in every factory in Chesterfield.

Sunday 28 April

Ken Coates rang. I haven't spoken to him for months, and he was obviously worried by what had been said about him in *New Socialist* and by claims that we were supposed to have had a bitter argument. He has had a blazing row with Stuart Weir. I was friendly but a bit cool.

The really exciting news is that Hilary and Sally are expecting a third baby in December.

Monday 29 April

Drove to Heathrow, and Jeremy Corbyn and I caught a flight to Belfast to sit in on some 'supergrass' trials.[1]

To the Crumlin Road court. The courtroom was huge, painted in two shades of battleship grey, with high ceilings and the royal crest above the judge's chair. Sitting at a table with a microphone was Harry Kirkpatrick, the informer or supergrass. He was brought in by two tough prison officers who stood behind him with their arms folded ready to defend him if any of the prisoners tried to attack him. Behind the barristers were the plain wooden benches where the twenty-seven prisoners were seated, interspersed with prison officers. Behind the prisoners, and separated by a glass partition, was the gallery where the relatives sat.

I counted fifty members of the Royal Ulster Constabulary, all with guns, and a number of prison officers – a most intimidating and terrifying sight. The prisoners were brought into a mass show trial, the link between them being that Harry Kirkpatrick was giving evidence against all of them, but for quite separate incidents.

Kirkpatrick, aged twenty-seven, was a member of the INLA and was serving four concurrent life sentences for five murders. He sat there and, with the help of his counsel, identified the names of the people with whom he had worked. It was a horrifying spectacle because, having received such a massive sentence, he was obviously eligible for great benefit from the police, and there he was naming people in the knowledge that, if they were found guilty, they would be put away for as long as he was. But he would get out.

The whole proceeding was conducted at a snail's pace, and I sat there for about an hour. Then a chief inspector came in and told us the second trial was beginning in another courtroom and asked if we wanted to go there, so we did. It was a mirror image of the first. Instead of a Protestant judge trying Catholics, here was a Catholic judge trying Protestants. Although Budgie Allen, the Ulster Volunteer Force supergrass, was not in the witness box, the trial was a complete reproduction of the other one, except this time it was in a green courtroom. There were about sixty-five RUC and prison officers.

In the courts I visited, the judges and barristers were all upper class and enormously well paid; then there were the middle-class solicitors and the lower-middle class police officers; and, finally, the working class defendants. It was the upper class trying the working class.

Afterwards Paddy McGrory, a solicitor who has been practising since 1957 and doing these trials since August, took Jeremy Corbyn and me into his room. He said he too was worried about the fact that the judges were devoid of any common experience with the defendants and had no idea what it was like to live as a Catholic or Protestant working-class person. McGrory also said that the social pressure on the judges to convict was strong; a judge who acquitted might find himself ostracised at the golf club.

Sunday 5 May
In the evening I had a useful meeting with the *New Left Review* people organised by Ralph Miliband: John Palmer, Perry Anderson (editor of the *NLR*), Tariq Ali, Hilary Wainwright and Robin Blackburn. Caroline sat in – which was a great tribute to them.

Ralph outlined the three elements of the left: the ultra-left (eg the Workers' Revolutionary Party and Militant) and some radical feminists, who were intransigent; the Hattersley to Hobsbawm left (including Frances Morrell and possibly Ken Livingstone), who lean towards the leadership; and the independent socialist left, the Bennites inside and outside the Labour Party, who wanted socialism without rocking the boat. Ralph wanted to see this last element strengthened.

He said Bennism could be summarised as 'the need for a democratic revolution' in Britain to tackle corporate power and the class structure. But how?

John Palmer was reminded of 1962–4 when Wilson had been able to co-opt the old left because it had not prepared its position. Kinnock was attempting to do the same thing. John's fears for the next Election were that a Labour or Labour/SDP Government might come to power and then fail, and that would produce a strong backlash of the right, currently held in check by Thatcherism itself. He didn't agree entirely with me on the EEC but did agree on the question of NATO.

He continued, 'We must arm the left with all sorts of weapons, weapons which may have to be used even against a Labour Government. The defeat of the miners' strike was a blow to the left, and helps to explain the shift towards Kinnock. The left has to utilise its resources to mount a massive and serious anti-Thatcher campaign, because there is no attack on capitalism by Labour at the moment.' He said there would be a hard fight inside Parliament of fifty to sixty new Labour MPs who must tell the next Labour Government, 'We will not support what you propose – neither the acceptance of Cruise nor any attacks on the working class.'

Robin Blackburn believed we must attack British capitalism and not Thatcherism, which was the worst form of capitalism we'd ever had but had meant great success for the City. We must examine the empowerment of workers and the democratisation of British capitalism.

We discussed the accusation of 'boat rocking'. John Palmer said that rocking the boat couldn't be avoided; there shouldn't be a leadership contest but there was a need for a clear challenge to Kinnock's position.

So from that beginning we decided to call ourselves the Independent Left Corresponding Society (ILCS) and meet monthly. It is what Ralph had in mind as a 'think tank', and I think we all enjoyed it. There has been a major political shift and we have to accept it without bitterness. The 'new realists' have been propelled towards Kinnock partly by the defeat of the miners and the local authorities, partly by the fact that if Kinnock becomes PM he will have a lot of patronage to offer and their own careers will be promoted. The media have been making it tough for the left. The so-called Bennites are trying to find a new base from which to advance, rooted in the trade union movement and the constituency parties.

Thursday 9 May
Joshua's birthday. To the dentist for a new bridge. He practises with the NHS but I think he mainly does private work now. Dentists, I have heard, earn on average £50,000 a year. I said I wouldn't go private on principle, but I still paid £110 on the NHS for the bridge.

Frances Morrell had an article in the *New Statesman* in which she attacked me for being a fundamentalist with an authoritarian bent, only interested in struggle in the workplace. I found it very offensive. I drafted a reply but I don't think I'll send it to her. Not worth it.

Friday 17 May
Went with Tom Vallins to Frank and Nance Cousins's house at Wingerworth, just outside Chesterfield. I hadn't seen Frank for a while – he didn't want to see me before the Chesterfield selection conference

in case he was seen to be intervening – and I was afraid this visit would be a strain because he'd had a stroke, but not at all. He was sitting with Nance, who is just as lovely as ever, in their beautiful bungalow surrounded with flowers and books. His left hand is slightly paralysed. I introduced him to Tom, they brought tea, and I asked if I could smoke, and we chatted. He said Dennis had cycled over the other day.

Frank was General Secretary of the T&G from 1955 to 1969 and dominated the union, shifting it to the left. I asked him how he became a socialist, and he told me he had been a miner in Yorkshire for five years before he got a job as a long-distance lorry driver. One day, during the 1930s, he was in the Midlands late at night and stopped at a café where there were lots of truck drivers sitting having tea and baked beans. In the corner was a pale young couple with a baby. Frank said, 'I saw her put the baby on the table and pick up a copy of the *Daily Mirror*, which she folded into a triangle and put on the baby as a nappy. Then she fed the baby with a bottle of water. I couldn't stand it. I went up and asked her what she was doing, and she said, "We come from Newcastle, and we heard there is work in London, so we're pushing the pram to London." It choked me, so I went round the truck drivers – we were all well paid – and I had a whip-round for them. She bought a bottle of milk to feed her baby, then I got one of the truck drivers to give them a lift to London. I never heard from them again, but what a state to be in! After that I applied for a job in the union.'

Of course he went on to become General Secretary of the TGWU and in 1964–6 was seconded as Minister of Technology in Wilson's Cabinet. He must be eighty-two now, and Nance is seventy-eight.

I asked Frank what went wrong in the 1964–70 Government and he said, 'For a start you elected Harold Wilson. He was no good, he wasn't a socialist, he knew nothing about socialism, and he tried to rise above trade-unionism, attacked the unions and tried to make them pay the price. The incomes policy was an absolute error, and that was why I resigned from the Cabinet.'

It was plain speaking. He said Arthur had made a great mistake because he should have had a ballot, and since the Notts coal field is so rich and so important he should have made a special effort to persuade them. 'Arthur forgot that there isn't really a national miners' union as such – it is the old Mineworkers' *Federation*. When I was a young miner I didn't know there were any other miners' unions besides the Yorkshire Miners' Association. He should have been more political.'

His memories went right back to hearing A. J. Cook, the miners' leader in the 1920s, and beyond.

I thanked him for the support he'd given me during the deputy leadership election, and talked about Geoffrey Goodman, his biographer. I invited him to talk to the Chesterfield Party, but Nance said no, she wouldn't let him!

Thursday 30 May

There was a terrible tragedy in Brussels when the Liverpool fans at the European Cup Final apparently moved as if to attack Italian fans and a wall collapsed on top of them. Thirty-eight Italian fans were killed. But the press handling of it has been absolutely scandalous, treating Liverpool fans as if they were animals. Mrs Thatcher now openly links what happens in Northern Ireland with picket-line violence and football hooliganism and demos and so on.

Sunday 2 June

Had a word with Eric Heffer. He was terribly distressed about the Brussels tragedy, being a Liverpool Member. He said Liverpool really had its head down at what had happened.

Tuesday 4 June

After the Committee of Privileges of which I am a member with Julian Amery, we sat and talked for half an hour. Julian has been a Tory MP for as long as I have been a Labour one. He said Britain was not a democracy, it was a monarchy – a collective monarchy. The collective Crown consisted of Permanent Secretaries and serving officers, and Ministers are allowed to come in and tilt the direction of policy 5 per cent either way, only if that is acceptable to the collective Crown.

I told him he should say that publicly, and he said he did, often. He asked me, 'Surely you knew it all along?'

'Not really,' I said, 'because I suppose I really did once believe in the parliamentary system.'

'Oh, we're not a democracy,' he replied. 'We're a constitutional monarchy.'

When his father-in-law (Harold Macmillan) said in 1959, 'You've never had it so good', it was less true then, he believed, than it is today, when 87 per cent had never had it so good and 13 per cent were very poor. Although conscience might affect some members of the middle class, he thought there was a built-in majority for the current consensus.

Wednesday 5 June

To County Hall for lunch with Frances Morrell, Tom Sawyer and Nigel Williamson, the new editor of *Tribune*. It was awful and I regret having gone. Frances had laid on a meal in her room and we chatted about events. I said there were only two issues that mattered – one was how to win the Election and the other what to do when we get there.

Nigel Williamson said he wasn't sure everyone did want to win. I asked who he meant, and he said Ted Knight and Chris Mullin. Chris had a piece in *Tribune* saying that the next Labour Government would be just like the last one – and Nigel said that looked as if he didn't want Labour to win.

Frances asked why there were all these personal attacks on me, and Tom mentioned that Dennis Skinner was saying Tom wanted to get me off the NEC. Tom denied it and said he wanted to work with me; he is a decent guy.

Frances persisted, so I said, 'Well, even you, Frances, described me in the *New Statesman* as a fundamentalist, an authoritarian, which deeply wounded me. What is happening is that Kinnock is trying to get a reputation for toughness by isolating and attacking the left.'

We came on to policy, and Tom objected to my proposal that Britain withdraw from NATO. I said I was trying to look ahead to a future Labour Government – that was why I was presenting these various bills to Parliament.

So Nigel chipped in that if you put forward things you can't succeed with then you are being divisive.

Frances remarked, 'No one consulted me about your bills.'

I said they had all been discussed by the Campaign Group and that Dave Wetzel of the GLC had asked me to support his Land Campaign with a parliamentary bill. 'I met the NEC left, the TUC left . . .'

'Oh, so I am excluded from your iron collectivity,' said Frances.

Nigel argued that I was putting forward maximalist demands, as a Trotskyite trick to 'expose' other people.

I said it could hardly be maximalist to put forward what had been the Party's policy on land for the past forty years, or the abolition of the Lords, an attempt which went back to 1892. Was he saying I was a Trotskyite?

'No,' he replied.

Frances thought I mustn't try for what I couldn't achieve. She was completely fed up, and said so were most people. Then she got ready to go, and asked me what was there that they had discussed today that I agreed with?

I said I could ask them the same question, but I thought we agreed we didn't want personal attacks, and we wanted to win. I said I was disappointed that we hadn't discussed how to win and what to do with our victory.

So Frances replied, 'Why should *you* set the agenda?'

Tom then shook my hand, Nigel nodded, Frances sort of frowned at me like a headmistress dealing with a difficult member of staff, and I left. It was embarrassing actually – quite distasteful. Nigel Williamson is now drawing towards Patricia Hewitt, Kinnock's Press Secretary, Tom is drifting to the right (like a lot of union leaders). I'm sorry I went.

Thursday 13 June
Bruce Kent came to breakfast at 8.30. I had had a bit of a disagreement with him because he had criticised me for saying we should leave

NATO. We had a useful talk. He is a very nice man but politically innocent, tied up with the Eurocommunists in the sense that he believes in a broadly based peace movement involving all parties, and he hasn't got much time for the Labour Party. What annoyed me was that he said that if I raised the NATO question it would split the Party.

But he couldn't have been more friendly. He gave me a seditious leaflet he'd written for distribution to the armed forces, saying it was illegal to handle nuclear weapons. Very brave. I shall try to table a resolution in the Commons – to cover him in case there is a sedition trial.

Monday 17 June
Our thirty-sixth wedding anniversary. Had a lovely talk and breakfast upstairs – I took up some roses. We talked, as we have done in endless discussions over the last few years, about our disenchantment with the present Labour Party and a feeling that we have to leave it behind us in a way – not turn on it, but work outside it as well. Caroline is keen that we should have an international dimension, and I shall have to think about that.

In June 1984 I had agreed to serve on the Committee of Privileges, which is regarded as the most senior of all parliamentary committees and meets to consider matters referred to it which touch upon the rights of the House of Commons to protect its own proceedings.

The privileges of free speech, of freedom from fear of court actions, and other rights in the Commons were fought for over many centuries, but the word privilege has a modern connotation that is confused with the freedom of the House from the Courts or any other source of external intimidation.

But some of the issues that have been put to the Committee since I have been a member have revealed an obsessive secrecy with which the House has tried to preserve over the proceedings of other select committees.

During 1985 and 1986 one such issue considered leaked information from select committees to journalists working in the House of Commons. The case discussed by the Committee in June 1985 concerned the disclosure by The Times *of Home Affairs Committee proceedings and how this and similar leaks should be dealt with.*

Tuesday 18 June
Sir Humphrey Atkins, former Secretary of State for Northern Ireland, who was dropped by Mrs Thatcher in 1981 and is now chairman of the Defence Select Committee, was appearing before the Committee of Privileges. This committee is proving to be not just a talking shop about parliamentary privilege but an extremely interesting investigation into the work of the select committees.

Atkins was asked about secrecy and leaks from the Defence

Committee. He said there had been no leaks of confidential information yet, but it dealt with so much classified evidence and secret commercial information that it was an unusual case. The Defence Committee had to gain the confidence of the MoD, and any relaxation of the rules would affect the willingness of the MoD to give the committee information. 'We also meet with foreign committees and NATO commanders, and leaking would damage our credibility.'

Biffen asked what sanctions there would be against an MP or member of staff who leaked to the press. Atkins said the newspapers should be pressed hard to tell and the MP should be sacked.

I said we all agreed that there were a lot of leaks from Ministers – and that nothing secret had been leaked from the Defence Committee. But was privilege the right answer? Wouldn't Atkins agree that Britain was too secretive? I wondered how he would have felt about maintaining the secret that we had been building the atom bomb or refurbishing Chevaline without the knowledge of Parliament.

Atkins thought Parliament must act, and his committee didn't have the cosy relationship with the MoD I had implied.

Charles Douglas-Home, editor of *The Times*, came in to give evidence from a wheelchair. He looked extremely ill; I think he must have cancer. He was arrogant but he did give us an extremely interesting insight. He is the most senior editor, I suppose, in Britain. Douglas-Home said the decision to publish the leak hadn't been taken lightly. He wouldn't publish unless they understood exactly what the information was about. They would always deliberate and would be subject to advice.

Biffen asked if it was ultimately a matter of value judgement, and he said yes. Did he himself make that judgement? Douglas-Home said they knew that Parliament could exercise its powers against the paper, but they would have to live with the consequences.

I asked him if, since he knew the rules governing confidentiality, he would normally respect D-notices. He said no. I asked if a decision to telephone members of the Privileges Committee would be taken at editorial level. He said no. I asked if he had ever paid an MP for information, and he said not in his time as editor.

Merlyn Rees remarked that the MoD leaked like a sieve when he was there – one department briefing against another – but what about non-classified documents? Should MPs be punished in that case? Douglas-Home replied that it wasn't his job to say.

I put it to Douglas-Home that he perceived it as his duty to assess whether a disclosure was in the public interest and, if so, to break the law and take the consequences. He said yes, he would accept the consequences of breaking the law.

'What about the principle of law-breaking?' asked John Morris. Douglas-Home replied that we all exceed the speed limit – very arrogant.

So Michael Havers asked about money – what was his paper's policy? Douglas-Home said it was the tradition of *The Times* not to pay because they couldn't afford it, but he didn't want to go into these darker waters, with possible hints of bribery and corruption. *The Times* did not have a higher sense of responsibility than the Commons.

All these senior MPs were sitting laughing like anything at what was a most cynical presentation of the argument with very little principle in it. At the same time I did get the editor of *The Times* to say he thought it was all right to break the law and take the consequences – which I have always accepted.

Peter Preston, editor of the *Guardian*, and Jim Naughtie, its political correspondent, were called, and Biffen asked what guidance they gave to journalists. Naughtie said they had expert journalists, and Preston said newspapers were in the business of publishing news – not to cock snooks at anyone.

I remarked to them that there had been no really important leaks, but only politically motivated ones. Could I ask about their rules? Was I right in saying they didn't disclose who were their own sources? They agreed with that. They also answered that they didn't breach the confidentiality of the lobby briefings, and that they didn't disclose the existence of D-notices. Either Preston or Naughtie said they hadn't looked at a D-notice for years. Finally I asked if the public interest was helped by openness: wouldn't it be better to open everything up – D-notices, sources, the lobby system and select committees? Preston said the lobby system should be opened up a bit, but select committees were one secret window which they'd like to keep closed; they saw select committees as part of the normal warp and weft of political exchange.

Sir Philip Goodhart, Conservative MP for Beckenham, wanted to know whether, if a member of the *Guardian* leaked confidential discussions concerning his newspaper, Preston would sack him. Preston said he wouldn't be too pleased.

Havers asked Preston if he thought he was used by MPs; Preston said all papers use briefings – Ministers use them against each other.

Merlyn Rees said he presumed they weren't going to publish the proceedings today, in this meeting, and Preston said no.

The Conservative MP for Hendon South, Peter Thomas, asked if they understood the rules of privilege, and Naughtie said yes, but the rules of the House were unworkable. Punishing the journalist and not the leaker wasn't the answer. Thomas said the rules were clear – and this was a clear breach of privilege. Would it help if the Commons clarified the rules? Naughtie said he couldn't imagine what a clarification would do. So Thomas asked, if the Commons reaffirmed the rules, would they abide by them? Naughtie said they would find it difficult; MPs would leak just as often if the Commons did reaffirm the rules.

A most interesting and revealing meeting.

Thursday 27 June

Collected from the Commons copies of my Miners' Amnesty (General Pardon) Bill, which calls for a general amnesty for all those fined, imprisoned or sacked during the miners' strike. I arranged to have a press conference tomorrow.

Friday 28 June

To Chesterfield after my press conference. It was reported on the radio that Neil Kinnock had attacked the Amnesty Bill, arguing that it was impossible to take it seriously, that it was only drafted to get attention, and so on. Totally predictable. He goes for anyone who does anything to protect themselves.

Tuesday 2 July

I forgot to mention that I saw Arthur Scargill in Sheffield yesterday, and he described his meeting with Billy Graham, the American evangelist, who had had one of his revival meetings there. Graham told him that, when Lyndon Johnson was US President, he (Graham) had lived in the White House for three months during the course of the Vietnam War because Johnson felt the need for spiritual advice. Also, he said, Reagan consulted him regularly, and he and Reagan had watched a video recording of the Barnsley Women's Support Groups rally. Arthur was amazed, but it was a great tribute to the women's work. No doubt Graham was given a proper CIA briefing about Scargill before they met.

Friday 5 July

The Brecon and Radnor by-election result was a Liberal-Alliance majority of 559 over Labour. There had been a Tory majority of almost 9000. Hattersley and Kinnock attacked Arthur and me publicly for Labour's failure to win the seat. Eric rang me up and he was ready to explode.

Wednesday 10 July

At the PLP meeting we discussed the Brecon result, and Dale Campbell-Savours got up to say that Tony Benn's Land Bill had done a great deal of damage. Well, the bill was published before the by-election campaign began, so I said it was completely untrue. I sat down again, but I wish I had added that we lose elections because of these continual attacks on the left.

Ray Powell, MP for Ogmore, said that Scargill was a major factor in our not winning the by-election.

Brian Sedgemore responded, and attacked the leadership for criticising Scargill and me.

I went home pretty sick. I don't think I will go to the PLP again.

Saturday 13 July

Durham for the Miners' Gala. This year there were lots of other banners because the strike had attracted support from all over the country. I saw John Stephenson, the Vicar of Eppleton, who writes to me regularly. There must have been 100,000 people marching. We reached the platform, where Scargill, Kinnock, Dennis Skinner and I were all to speak.

I wanted to pay tribute to Scargill, in Kinnock's presence, so I set out the miners' contribution to British political history, and the courage and leadership shown by their leaders. I then outlined the demands we were going to make for an amnesty for miners.

Then Kinnock spoke. He must have been pretty embarrassed; he looked strained, his voice was harsh and metallic, and he ended by saying, 'We must win power, we must win power . . .', which is his real preoccupation.

Dennis was brilliant and amusing – he is the great hero of the labour movement.

When Arthur, Dennis and I came off the platform we were mobbed.

Friday 19 July
Train to Chesterfield. As I went to get some tea a woman asked me if I was Tony Benn. She said, 'I'm Gareth Peirce.' Well, Gareth is one of the solicitors who has been defending the miners on trial for rioting at Orgreave, and we talked and talked. She told me the trial was of tremendous historical importance. At the beginning, the prosecution had said it was one of the gravest cases of riot in Britain, but the defence counsel had so successfully cross-examined the prosecution witnesses that it had gradually emerged, from the clear evidence of video recordings and photographs, that the police account was flawed.

She said that from reading the *Public Order Tactical Operations Manual* – the police training manual – detailing the use by the police of short and long shields, of mounted police and truncheons, it was clear that unarmed civilians were being exposed to paramilitary tactics unauthorised by common law. I am going to raise it in the House on Monday. It was a military operation without doubt – nothing to do with protecting law and order. She is going to get me extracts of the manual used at the trial.

Monday 22 July
The Speaker refused to allow me to raise the police training manual as an emergency, under standing order number 10, but I asked him if I could deposit the documents relating to it in the Library, a procedure only allowed to Ministers. The Speaker said it seemed reasonable, so for the first time in the history of Parliament a backbencher has been able to put a document in the Library – ie to publish it. So the revelations about violent police tactics in the strike are now public, and I put out a note to the press.

Thursday 1 August
The BBC Board of Governors, at the Government's request, have decided not to show a film, *Real Lives*, about an ultra-Loyalist and a Sinn Fein member in Northern Ireland. This has led to a call for a one-day strike of journalists and is a sudden clear reminder that the BBC is an agency of the Government.

Wednesday 7 August
BBC and ITN held a one-day strike today because of the censorship of the *Real Lives* documentary. The story has been running now for a week. Leon Brittan asked the BBC Board of Governors to intervene because he didn't want to 'give publicity to terrorists'. The Board of Governors, whose chairman is Stuart Young – who happens to be the brother of the Cabinet Minister, David Young – capitulated to the Government, so all the BBC journalists came out, and ITN and IRN joined them.

Tuesday 3 September
Today, at the TUC conference, the NUM got through their resolution for an amnesty, ie committing a future Labour Government to legislation enabling a review of miners convicted and jailed during the dispute, reinstatement of sacked miners, and reimbursement of the NUM of monies confiscated through Tory legislation.

Wednesday 4 September
Took the train to Blackpool for the TUC conference, where Kinnock made a speech yesterday, after the miners' resolution victory, saying he would take into account what was said at the TUC and Party conferences but he personally would decide what went into the manifesto. We've had Labour Leaders exercising a veto, but never before have we had one claiming a personal right to draw up the manifesto. It is probably the case that we are locked into a totally fossilised right-wing Labour Party, and a socialist emergence may have to be on a different basis, perhaps under proportional representation.

With Jack Spriggs, the fund raiser for the Merseyside Trade Union and Unemployed Resources Centre, to their fringe meeting on unemployment and social security cuts. The first speaker was John Edmonds, David Basnett's successor as General Secretary of the GMB, the left candidate. He got more votes than all the others put together in the first ballot.

I travelled back on the train with Larry Whitty and others, but they went off to have a fancy dinner in the dining car, so I had a sandwich and tea and then later the steward brought me more tea and wouldn't accept any money for it, just as the steward on the journey up wouldn't let me pay for my tea. I record this because I get this tremendous feeling of warmth, despite the press hostility.

I had a word with Larry Whitty about Kinnock and said I hoped he wouldn't come out strongly at the Party Conference against the miners' amnesty resolution because he would underestimate the feeling that the miners' struggle had evoked in the Party. Larry said Kinnock didn't like Scargill and has a thing about the law. Well, that's his problem.

In 1985, the time of the National Executive Committee became increasingly taken up with the problems besetting local government as a result of the Government's attempts to curb spending by local authorities through enactment of the Rates Act (passed in 1984).

Central Government control of local government expenditure had always been exercised by the use of the rate support grant agreed by Cabinet. But when Tony Crosland was Secretary of State for Environment, 1974–7, he expressed a growing Treasury anxiety that this expenditure had to be seen as part of the national exchequer calculations. In one famous speech he condemned council spending with the words 'the party is over', although for many, it had never really begun.

The Thatcher Government was determined to enforce the most rigorous control of local government expenditure by reducing the annual grant to 'overspending' authorities, and by using the District Auditor in a way that was never intended, to determine which expenditure was to be allowed and which disallowed.

Legal action was taken against individual elected councillors in Liverpool and Lambeth Councils who, in defence of their Party manifesto and the constituents who elected them, had delayed setting 'legal' budgets within the limits laid down by central Government. The legal penalties imposed on those councillors were severe, their determination to maintain their services being ruled by the courts as 'wilful misconduct,' and the councillors were individually surcharged, threatened with bankruptcy and disqualified from holding office.

The NEC, in actions of questionable legality and in defiance of every law of natural justice, was determined not to give the impression that it was endorsing illegal action and joined in the condemnation of these councils. In the case of the Liverpool councillors, the NEC attributed their intransigence to the influence of Militant, which was strong but never in a majority in Liverpool itself.

At the May 1985 Party Conference Neil Kinnock underlined the Labour Party's opposition to the Liverpool council in his notorious speech at the Annual Conference, denouncing the councillors in such violent language that Eric Heffer, a Liverpool MP, walked off the platform in protest.

Twelve members of the Liverpool District party actually gained a High Court ruling in March 1986 which questioned the natural justice of the NEC's proceedings against the Party and the councillors, but the 'witch-hunt' as it became known continued.

The expulsion of Liverpool councillors who supported Militant, and others, was part of a wider disciplinary campaign against socialists within the Party and ended with the grossest miscarriage of justice when MPs Dave Nellist and Terry Fields were expelled from the Party on the eve of the 1992 General Election, thus depriving the PLP of two distinguished Members who had been reselected by their local parties and endorsed by the NEC on which Neil Kinnock sat.

Monday 9 September

Tonight there were riots in Handsworth. Two people were killed, fire-bombs were thrown, and the media began its work. It was significant that it was the same day that a letter had been sent to the Lambeth and Liverpool councillors surcharging them sums of money that none of them can afford, which means that those who can't pay will be bankrupted and therefore disqualified from holding office. It is no coincidence that those who try to defend people democratically are punished, while those who riot out of desperation are identified with thugs.

Tuesday 10 September

I had a little success today at the NEC's International Committee, where I raised the issue of an MoD civil defence exercise called 'Brave

Defender', which is taking place as a rehearsal for a 'Russian invasion'. I thought it was scandalous that we should be told that 'the Russians' were attacking our key points. George Robertson, our spokesman for defence, couldn't see why we should object – we had criticised Soviet policy in our last defence policy statement.

Someone – Larry Whitty, I think – pointed out that that wasn't quite the same as dressing people up as Russians and shooting them.

Alan Hadden said we should write to the MoD for an explanation, but Syd Tierney supported me, and we carried a motion against it.

Friday 13 September
Went to see the doctor, who syringed my ears as he had done eighteen months ago. All of a sudden I could hear again! It's such a blessing, like a new birth, when that happens.

The Foreign Office have expelled twenty-five Soviet diplomats and journalists following the defection of Oleg Gordievsky, allegedly head of the KGB office in the Soviet Embassy in London, although it later appeared, according to Danish intelligence, that he had defected fifteen years ago, while he was stationed in Copenhagen.

Friday 20 September
Larry Whitty rang to say Kinnock wanted me to speak to Conference, on behalf of the NEC, on education and training. I hadn't expected it, and it is amusing, because Caroline knows more about the subject than anyone in the movement; indeed, she drafted the SEA resolution to Conference. So it will all be in the family.

Saturday 21 September
Weekend seminar of the Campaign Group, held in Chesterfield. This is an initiative to get the group to meet out of London, and Margaret and Tom Vallins have done a fantastic job in making facilities available.

In the afternoon we had an exceptionally painful session with Ann Pettifor of the Women's Action Committee, who came in pursuance of her letter asking for Campaign Group support for women-only shortlists in selecting Labour candidates between now and the Election.

She was tense and angry, and said women were being defeated all over the place; very few had been selected for parliamentary constituencies, women were turning to the SDP, and the class and Marxist analysis led to prejudice against women. It took a lot of courage on her part to say it, but at the same time she was most aggressive. I think the patience of the Women's Action Committee is exhausted.

Tam Dalyell asked how you could compel local parties to have women-only shortlists.

Ann argued that the ideology in the Labour Party was overwhelmingly male-dominated and somehow we had to break it.

Bob Clay said there were practical problems to the proposal and it really couldn't succeed.

Dave Nellist believed selection should be about policy – it couldn't be about gender alone.

Frances Curran, the Young Socialists' representative on the NEC, made the classic and impressive Militant case against this. She said the proposal came out of frustration, it was a sterile debate because we were not getting any politics from the Women's Action Committee, and, for that matter, why shouldn't we insist on working-class MPs only? Why allow middle-class women MPs?

I accepted that there was discrimination against women in the Party which men didn't understand because they weren't affected. But enforcing this measure from the centre would take away the power of local parties to choose their candidate. Secondly, the WAC's demands tended to be constitutional in character without being related to policy, and they might lead to a radical feminist position rather than a socialist feminist one.

Joan Maynard agreed that there was discrimination but that policies were what mattered and organisation came second – this is an absolutely classic Labour position.

Ann Pettifor replied that the rights of constituency parties must be considered but the Party was deeply sexist and the NEC should say to CLPs, 'You must deal with discrimination.' The policy argument, she said, was a complete red herring. She left, very angrily.

Tribune tonight had its relaunch. It now calls itself the mainstream Labour paper – ie Kinnockite – and it has abandoned any pretence of being a socialist paper. Within nine months of Chris Mullin leaving, it has severed all connection with the left, although it tries to reflect the views of Morrell, Williamson, Holland and Coates and that bunch. There is this new ingredient – let's do it all through Europe if we can't do it at home. It is fine to have European links, but they are no substitute for British political action.

Tuesday 24 September
Today the NEC appointed three new directors: Joyce Gould for organisation, Peter Mandelson for communications and Geoff Bish for policy.

Wednesday 25 September
A momentous day for the Labour Party. The NEC had before it the resolutions on an amnesty and reinstatement for jailed or sacked miners, and outside all the media were gathered hoping for a row. Both the GMB and ASTMS resolutions called for the reinstatement of sacked miners, a review of the cases of jailed miners but no retrospective reimbursement of fines. The NUM, of course, have called for all three.

After much procedural wrangling, Eric Clarke moved an amendment that we support TUC policy on the miners, which included reimbursement. That was defeated by 19 to 7.

Neil insisted on a vote on the ASTMS resolution, and it was carried by 14 to 1.

On the NEC's draft statement to Conference, calling for a repeal of the Government's anti-trade union legislation passed since 1980, I moved an amendment to add that the NEC shared the TUC's opposition 'to Government cash for trade union ballots'. That was defeated by 20 to 8.

When we came to Liverpool, Kinnock put forward his resolution explicitly distancing the NEC from the Liverpool and Lambeth councillors. Heffer moved an amendment to support the demonstration taking place today in Liverpool, to praise the courage and determination of the Liverpool and Lambeth councillors in support of Conference policy. He read out a letter in today's *Guardian* from Reg Underhill, our former National Agent, saying how impressed he was by Liverpool's achievements.

Blunkett attempted to amend the resolution by blaming the Government. He said the only question was whether this helped or hindered our prospects of victory.

Audrey Wise said we must support the councillors.

Kinnock couldn't accept Eric Heffer's motion because he said it would look as if we were accepting the strategy of the Liverpool councillors, and he couldn't support 'courage and determination' – their leadership was marching Liverpool deeper and deeper into crisis.

Heffer's main amendment supporting the demonstration was apparently defeated by 14 to 13, but it was obvious that the voting hadn't gone that way so we asked for another count, and that showed we had won by 14 to 13! Kinnock looked as white as a sheet.

Then Tom Sawyer, who had voted to support the amendment, left the room immediately, and the substantive motion was put. Without Sawyer the vote was 14 to 14. So Alan Hadden, as chairman, ruled that the motion was carried. Our amendment defeated by a trick.

I came out feeling utterly sick at the Party having repudiated the miners, Liverpool and Lambeth, and at our being told that victory was everything. How can you win if you create such a sense of distaste and contempt among leading members of the Party, let alone activists?

Labour Party Conference, Bournemouth
Sunday 29 September
We had the usual Conference NEC this morning to consider resolutions and statements, and a long discussion about composite resolution 69, the NUM resolution calling for the next Labour Government to review

miners' cases, to reinstate sacked miners and reimburse monies confiscated from the NUM and other unions.

Hattersley spoke in favour of taking a toughish line and then left.

Kitson came out against the miners with a bombastic speech about how he'd learned his politics from the old Scottish miners' Communist leader, Abe Moffat.

Audrey Wise supported the miners but wanted an agreement.

David Blunkett and Michael Meacher wanted a compromise – very significant, in view of what happened later today.

Eric Clarke said he felt the NUM would be happy to have further talks with the NEC about it, but he thought the miners would be bound to stick to their position.

Others spoke, and then Kinnock banged the table and shouted.

Anyway, it was agreed by 11 to 3, with myself voting against, that there should be further talks with the NUM today before we decided on the composite motion.

We met later to consider the discussions that had taken place between Larry Whitty, Alan Hadden and Sam McCluskie for the NEC, and Arthur Scargill, Peter Heathfield, Roger Windsor and Eric Clarke for the NUM.

Alan reported very gravely on the meeting. He said it had been agreeable, and that Arthur felt that he had consulted the Party sufficiently. Whitty said there had been a friendly atmosphere.

McCluskie said he had to choose between his class loyalties and his loyalties to Kinnock, and the more he heard Kinnock speak and realised what was at stake, the more his class loyalties emerged. So it was obvious that he was coming out for the miners.

Kinnock spoke and repeated his line.

Heffer moved that we accept the resolution from the miners, and Dennis Skinner spoke softly and quietly in favour of it.

Michael Meacher was still searching for a compromise, and Eddie Haigh of the TGWU said reluctantly he had to go for the miners.

Then I said that nobody could fault the miners on what they had done, there was a serious possibility that Heathfield and Scargill might be jailed, and I thought one reason why Thatcher's popularity had fallen was that she had put the boot into the miners and people did not understand or accept it. The NUM had gone out of its way to be helpful.

Anyway, the motion to support the miners resolution was defeated by 15 to 14, with Michael Meacher voting against. Any residual links I had with him are finished and done with.

He came up afterwards and said he knew I was angry with him; I said he had to live with his own future.

Tuesday 1 October
I dropped from first to third place in the NEC elections, which is almost

inevitable. Blunkett came first. The only people whose vote went up were Dennis Skinner and Jo Richardson. No one took much interest really, and nor did I, because as the day progressed it became more and more apparent what a misery it is to be in the Labour Party.

We had the health service debate, and Margaret Vallins spoke. She stood for the women's section of the NEC and got 59,000 votes – about 10 per cent of the whole – which was amazing.

Kinnock's Conference speech, and I sat through an hour and a quarter of it. The first part was very clever – hard, harsh Kinnock mocking the Government, stressing the importance of winning. But he ended with a violent attack upon Militant in Liverpool saying, 'Implausible promises don't win victories . . . you end in the grotesque chaos of a Labour council hiring taxis to scuttle around a city handing out redundancy notices to its own workers. You can't play politics with people's jobs . . . or their homes.' He spoke as if the Liverpool councillors wanted to fire people, when actually they are themselves victims of Government policy. It was all part of his strategy, going back to 1983, to kill off any left-wing challenge by appealing for unity and on that basis to get a right-wing NEC and accuse the left of being divisive. As a result of this strategy, power over policy-making has been passed to the Shadow Cabinet, a lot of charters (which have no policy status) have been issued, and the policy and the work of the International Department have been wound up.

Kinnock's speech led to a walkout by Eric Heffer and shouting from Derek Hatton and Tony Mulhearn. Kinnock has released the hatred of the Tory press against his own people in the middle of a struggle, in the hope that he can pick up the ex-Labour voters who supported Owen, knowing that real socialists and the rump of the working class have no alternative but to vote for him. He is pioneering a presidential style of government which is quite foreign to our own traditions.

I left because I couldn't bring myself to stay after that. I saw a woman delegate crying, and I put my hand on her shoulder and she said, 'I can't understand what they've done to our Party.' I told her not to worry, and I began to cry – not at what was happening, which I've seen before, but at this poor woman's distress. It absolutely shattered her.

It has been a historic day in the Party. What Gaitskell attempted in 1960 has been done again – an attempt to destroy the left, the Conference and the unions. Some people will want a candidature against Kinnock next year, but he would smash his critics and crush the left, probably even expel it. On the other hand, we don't have any obligation any more to go along with what is said, and I think it is perhaps the restoration of the freedom to speak out that is more important.

Wednesday 2 October
Debate on the miners' amnesty resolution. Arthur Scargill made an exceptionally good speech to the Conference.

Alan Hadden, who was chairing the Conference, managed to dredge up two delegates who were against the miners, and he also called Basnett, Gavin Laird and Eric Hammond against. He didn't call a single pro-NUM union leader such as Ray Buckton, Jimmy Knapp or Ron Todd.

It was an extraordinary debate – memorable for the fact that Eric Hammond described the striking miners as 'lions led by donkeys'. It caused an uproar in the hall, and, just before Kinnock was due to wind up the debate, delegates were so angry that they stood up and just pointed at Ron Todd – like iron filings aligning themselves around a magnet – shouting, 'Todd! Ron Todd! Todd! Ron Todd!' so Hadden had to call him.

Ron made a very powerful speech. He was extremely angry. In response to Hammond he said, 'I am an animal lover. I prefer donkeys to jackals.' A good response, but it might have been better to have left it without reciprocal abuse.

Kinnock ended the debate. He spoke much more softly than yesterday, but his speech was really a denunciation of the whole strike, not just the resolution. He attacked the miners' leaders for the whole way in which they had conducted the campaign. A horrible speech.

I was told later that miners in the gallery were crying. However, the resolution was carried by 3,542,000 to 2,930,000, but it did not get a two-thirds majority, and that is the comfort Kinnock will cling on to.

We came later to the local government debate, and David Blunkett was to move the NEC statement calling for reimbursement of councillors who had suffered financially through rate-capping legislation. There he was, this Christ-like bearded blind man, standing on the rostrum appealing to Derek Hatton to withdraw his Liverpool resolution asking for industrial action in support of councillors 'not prepared to carry out Tory cuts'.

'Will you do that? Will you do that, Derek?' He stood there waving his hands into the darkness.

So Hatton, who is a bit of a smart alec, ran towards the rostrum in his neat suit, got up on to the rostrum and said, 'Yes, in the interests of unity, Liverpool will withdraw its resolution.'

There was an explosion of applause. I believe the right wing were angry with Blunkett for having done that.

Thursday 3 October
The press are torn between saying Kinnock was beaten by the miners – which he was – and that his was a brave speech.

Conference this afternoon debated peace and security. The resolution to withdraw from NATO was overwhelmingly defeated, which we expected, but the resolution that we should review our membership of NATO, though defeated, received 2.5 million votes – which is enormous when you think that it was only in February that Eric and I first presented our paper. I think the reasonableness of Gorbachev and the horrible militancy and arrogance of that man President Reagan have contributed to a new perception.

Monday 7 October

The big news at the moment is the riots in Tottenham. The coverage is scandalous: the reason for the riots is ignored, and the injuries done to the police are highlighted. Bernie Grant, Leader of Haringey Council, has attacked the police because a woman, Cynthia Jarrett, died while the police were searching her house on Broadwater Farm council estate for stolen goods. She had a heart attack and died, and the police apparently just left her body on the floor while they searched. They found nothing and they didn't send her to hospital. This is what triggered the trouble off. Forty-six cars were burned, five policemen were seriously injured, and one was killed with knives. The build-up in the media is fantastic. The newsreader said that Trotskyites and anarchists were thought to be responsible (no evidence was quoted).

Thursday 10 October

Anne McDermid, my literary agent, came to see me at 9. She is a director of Curtis Brown, and she has been urging me for a long time to have my diaries published.

Kinnock today distanced himself from Bernie Grant over his attack on the police for the death of Mrs Jarrett. He distances himself from everyone. Margaret Vallins said last night that the Labour Party isn't going to be a working-class party any more and working-class people won't vote for it. I think a lot of people won't vote Labour next time; they will just abstain. Maybe someone will set up a new party.

Wednesday 23 October

Saw Tony Banks today. He told me that various friends of Kinnock had come up to him and informed him he'd never make any progress in the Parliamentary Party while he remained close to Tony Benn. Of course, that sort of pressure was put on Kevin Barron, which was why he left the Campaign Group. It is typical of Tony to tell me.

PLP at 8.15. Jack Dormand was re-elected to the chair unopposed. Kinnock welcomed Derek Foster as new Chief Whip, paid a tribute to Mike Cocks for his years of work, especially during the Lib–Lab Pact, and said how frustrating the diversions of the years in opposition had been (that was an attack on democratisation of the Party). He said the tide was ebbing away from the Government and moving towards us, summer had been a watershed, and we were now in a stronger position than we had been at any time since the Falklands War.

Monday 28 October
Tonight there was the *World in Action* programme, on which Chris Mullin has been working, about the Birmingham pub bombings of 1974, as a result of which Chris believes six innocent Irishmen were imprisoned.

Tuesday 29 October
I had a call from Anne McDermid following our talk. She said she had been to see Hutchinson about the diary project, and they had held a board meeting and had decided to treat it as a major project.

Chris Mullin came to the House, and we sat in the Cafeteria and had a talk. I congratulated him on his programme. He is just off to Laos and Vietnam for three weeks; he has a lot of knowledge and interest in South East Asia. His book *A Very British Coup* is being turned into a script for a possible film. He told me about his problems in Sunderland South, where he was adopted in June as the candidate.

I talked to him about the diary project. To publish a diary in your own lifetime and indeed while you're still active is difficult. I have always taken the view that you can't do it while you are active politically, but I wouldn't mind having it typed ready to publish in perhaps ten year's time. I would like to see my diaries published before I die, and I would really enjoy doing them.

In a way it is a decision about my own political future. In a couple of years there may be a swing away from the right. If there is a hung parliament, then there would have to be a left opposition. If we were actually defeated in an Election again, there would be a reversal towards more radical solutions.

Monday 4 November
At 10 on the dot, with diplomatic precision, the Minister at the Yugoslav Embassy, Milutin Stojanovic, came for a couple of hours' political talk.

Stojanovic thought the problem really was of the new society replacing the old; he believed the Star Wars initiative represented American determination to take over the domination of the new technology from the Japanese. He thought the American's military objective might be in part to bankrupt the Soviet Union – a shrewd view.

Saturday 16 November
Today the Anglo–Irish Agreement[2] was signed by Garrett Fitzgerald, Prime Minister of Ireland, and Mrs Thatcher in Hillsborough Castle,

Belfast. It has infuriated Ian Paisley. It will solve no problems, will be rejected by the IRA and has very dangerous implications, because the people in the North have simply not been consulted on it. I shall certainly oppose it in Parliament.

To Chesterfield for a meeting of our own international committee. There was a report on the visit of some power workers from El Salvador to Chesterfield, and we agreed to have a joint CND/El Salvador stall in the market. Our funds at the moment stand at about £50, and we sent a donation to El Salvador where there is this terrible civil war going on.

I raised the possibility of holding a debate between the American and Soviet Ambassadors in Chesterfield, and that was agreed in principle.

Tuesday 19 November

Had lunch with Ken Livingstone at County Hall. He is now a leading member of the realigned left. I asked him how he was getting on with the fight against the abolition of the GLC, and he said they were drafting a new Act which would provide for the restoration of London government under Labour, and whereby the City of London would be combined with Hackney and Tower Hamlets, the two poorest boroughs. He didn't really want to take over the City in its present form because a lot of potential Labour leaders would be attracted by the Lord Mayoralty and all the flummery, and he thought it would be better just to absorb it. Ken believed that after the Election the new intake of Labour MPs would push him and David Blunkett to the forefront. If we lose the Election, I can't think that Labour MPs would turn immediately to him to take over, but he did topple Andrew McIntosh from the leadership of the Labour Group and he took over in London, so he may have the same idea. He was pessimistic about Kinnock.

Tuesday 3 December

A young woman called Ruth Winstone came and began typing my diary from the cassettes. Chris Mullin put her in touch with me – she had worked on his book on the Birmingham bombings. She is a member of the Labour Party, and Chris has known her for twelve years. She seems competent and reliable and knows something about politics. She worked in the basement kitchen – the only spare space – on the word processor.

Sunday 15 December

To Chesterfield for the GMC, called to discuss the document 'Aims and Objectives of the Chesterfield Labour Party'. It was a tremendously interesting and successful meeting.

I had been working on the idea for some time, and the draft document had been circulated by Tom Vallins to all the wards for amendments.

Bob Pont, a member from Newbold Ward, announced that he was concerned at the overall contents. He said the Chesterfield Party's objectives had been set out in our standing orders, and this proposal went well beyond that position. He suggested the whole document be deleted after the first sentence. If we approved the document, how did we achieve those objectives? He said it would be wrong to declare different objectives from the Party as a whole; it sounded like a unilateral declaration of independence by the Chesterfield Party. Another Newbold member agreed.

Margaret Vallins said it was a good initiative – it brought Party policy to the local level, and it would help with canvassing.

I defended it, and then Johnny Burrows said all the amendments would now be taken.

Bob Pont's amendment to delete everything after the first sentence was defeated by 50 to 26.

An amendment from Moor Ward was interesting. It said that, instead of stating that people had 'inalienable human rights', the wording should be that particular rights 'should be won and maintained', on the grounds that people didn't have inalienable rights, that rights had to be fought for. That was agreed.

There was a long debate on the clause concerning conscience being above the law. Two wards moved to delete it on the grounds that it looked as if we were in favour of anarchy, but Roy Davies argued that the law was not neutral – the law was a class law. Johnny Burrows said that, in the light of the miners' strike, for him there was absolutely no question that conscience was above the law. As far as I was concerned, this was the most important paragraph in the whole document; it went to the very heart of my faith – that in the end I am responsible to myself for what I do and say.

Eventually the motion to delete the clause was defeated; only sixteen people wanted deletion.

We adjourned the meeting until 5 January.

It was the most interesting political discussion I have attended in Chesterfield because it was about ideas and not policies. The debate was excellent and there was no ill will, but both sides spoke with strength. The vitality and independence of the Party, though, was lacking in that many members felt that whatever the NEC did we should support it.

Friday 20 December
Jeremy Corbyn and I went by train to visit Terry French in Maidstone prison. He is a Kent miner and was given a five-year sentence on a jumped-up charge of GBH; during some fisticuffs in the strike I think he broke a policeman's nose, though I also suspect that some of the

police may have lied. But to get five years for that when people get two year suspended sentences for rape and murder is unbelievable.

They opened a little gate and let us in; it was like an Oxford college, except that every window had bars.

Actually Terry is a political prisoner; he is not a criminal at all. He looked very well and was wearing his own clothes, blue jeans and sneakers and an 'Amnesty for the Miners' T-shirt.

He said you had to be careful who you spoke to in prison, and no one would speak to you until they had sized you up. Some of the inmates' view of life was 'thrills, chicks and champagne', Terry said. He smoked three of the cigarettes we took him, and the governor said he may be allowed to keep the rest. In prison, of course, cigarettes are a kind of currency.

Terry said Wandsworth, where he was before, was a terrible prison. He had written a diary in a notebook in Wandsworth, and that was removed because he had been guilty of some minor offence – smuggling letters in and out through a teacher in the prison. That had cost him ten days' remission.

His new date of parole is April 1986, and the earliest date of release is August 1988. If he served his full term (ie lost all his remission), it would run to 1989. He hoped he would get parole, but it was unlikely because the authorities wouldn't want to be soft on the miners; they were determined to crush them. When I said a Labour Government would be elected, he told me he expected nothing from Kinnock. I said I thought he was right, but a lot of Labour MPs would insist that the miners had to be released. He was sceptical about that.

He was an impressive man, and I told him to write his experiences down because his impressions of the real criminals will be interesting. We said goodbye at the front gates.

Back to London. I was so angry about his situation that I thought I'd telephone the Archbishop of Canterbury, so I rang Lambeth Palace and was put through to his chaplain. I said I had a rather medieval request to make but, as the archbishop had a diocese in Kent and there was a Kent miner in jail, would the archbishop like to make an appeal to the Government for a Christmas clemency? The chaplain was most enthusiastic, and said he'd get on to it straight away. I suspect that since the Archbishop of Canterbury sponsored an inner-city report which was critical of the Government, and made a mild criticism of the Falklands War, he is unlikely to carry any weight.

Tuesday 31 December
This year has been a happy and creative one for Caroline with her comprehensive education campaigns and her teaching of access night classes, which she loves. Her joint book with John Fairley about the YTS will be out in the spring.

Stephen is an active member at County Hall, has become a part-time research assistant and it is the first year he's been Dr Benn.

Hilary is busy as always as deputy leader of Ealing Borough Council. He has been nominated for Bradford North consituency, but he is up against Pat Wall, and there is fierce constituency loyalty to Pat.

Melissa, after much determination has established herself as a journalist and writes in *Tribune, New Statesman, New Socialist, Spare Rib* and other magazines. With Ken Worpole she wrote a book, *Death in the City*, which is to be published by Canary Press. A tremendous achievement.

Josh has set up a consultancy called Communitec in which he hopes to establish himself as an adviser on the installation and operation of computers.

The really major political event was the miners' strike – the most remarkable and important event in my lifetime. The effect of the defeat, politically, was and will be profound.

By the end of this year, socialism was being written off. Kinnock has so successfully distanced himself from the left that the pundits are able to say with confidence that there isn't a socialist ingredient remaining in the Party – or, as Peregrine Worsthorne said, socialism is now a minority cult.

The Cold War is a great threat, but I think people are beginning to see through American warmongering and to detect in the Russians a genuine desire for peace, which is going to have a huge effect on international politics. The world debt crisis hangs over us.

After her brutal treatment of the miners, Mrs Thatcher has lost the sympathy of a lot of decent people. The Tory wets are getting stronger, and undoubtedly the media would support a consensus Government made up of Heath, Pym, Steel, Owen, Hattersley and Kinnock if they could get it set up. But Kinnock cannot come out in favour of that because he knows that it would finish him with the Labour Party. Alternatively, Thatcher might retire or be removed.

Some serious political developments in 1986 pinpointed the growing abuse of executive power by the Cabinet at the expense of Parliament and the people.

The first was the 'Westland affair', a crisis for Mrs Thatcher which led to the resignation first of Secretary of State for Defence Michael Heseltine, and later of Leon Brittan, Secretary of State for Trade and Industry. Heseltine disagreed with the Prime Minister over the disposal of Westland Helicopters – a relatively small Yeovil firm which had got into financial difficulties – to the American Sikorsky Company, Heseltine favouring a European industrial consortium rescue.

A complicated exchange of letters in early January, including between the Solicitor General, Sir Patrick Mayhew and Heseltine led to an 'inquiry' into the leak and a debate in Parliament, after which Leon Brittan himself resigned.

Regardless of the merits of the industrial decision itself, for a Prime Minister to use the press in such a way severely damaged the principle of ministerial responsibility and indicated the power of press officers to undermine Cabinet Ministers within the convention of lobby briefings, protected by newspaper proprietors and other lobby sources.

Following the end of the miners' strike in 1985 another industrial conflict arose, this time in the heart of London, in which the employment of state power similar to that used in the miners' strike was again in evidence. This time, the might of the print unions, SOGAT 82 and the NGA, was taken on by Rupert Murdoch, the chairman of News International group. 5500 printers from the print unions NGA and SOGAT had been dismissed by Murdoch, once he had taken the decision to move his production process to a new computer-technology plant in Wapping, East London. It is now known, moreover, as a result of the memoirs of the General Secretary of the EETPU, Eric Hammond, that the EETPU was secretly negotiating with Rupert Murdoch during 1985 for its members to set up and print his papers – the Sun, News of the World, The Times *and* Sunday Times *– a deal which involved accepting rigid working practices and a no-strike agreement. Over the next months Wapping, surrounded by barbed wire, and bathed in Klieg lights, was the scene of violent confrontation comparable in significance to the campaign against the miners, as the plant printed and distributed its four titles, protected by large numbers of police, while pickets and demonstrators gathered to prevent them leaving the plant. The printers held ballots, which overwhelmingly supported their action, but these were not considered relevant. Once again, High Court injunctions to prevent picketing, and to threaten sequestration of funds, were employed to try to defeat the unions.*

The Spycatcher *fiasco emerged in 1986 when the Government attempted to suppress a book by a former MI5 officer, from 1955–76, Peter Wright. His motive in publishing the book appeared to be discontent with the British Government over his pension entitlement, but the main theme of the book was that Sir Roger Hollis, a former Director General of MI5, was a double-agent. Revelations of attempts by officers in MI5 to remove the then Prime Minister, Harold Wilson, were among the more serious contents.*

His book was published all over the world but the Government went to determined efforts to prevent its publication in Australia (where Wright lived), Hong Kong and in Britain itself, with injunctions against newspapers which attempted to publish extracts from it. The unhappy task of defending this action fell to Sir Robert Armstrong, Cabinet Secretary, who was sent to Australia to give evidence for the British Government, and found himself up against a skilful lawyer, Malcolm Turnbull.

The basis of the Government's case was that the material in the book was covered by the Official Secrets Act and that all those who had ever worked in Intelligence owed a 'lifelong obligation of confidentiality to the Crown'; this obligation superseded any other, including that of identifying treasonable activities against an elected Government. The attempt to silence the revelations, instead of punishing the culprits, created an uproar that made the Government look ridiculous as well as oppressive.

A fourth misuse of executive power arose out of President Reagan's decision to bomb Tripoli and Benghazi in Libya. America suspected Libya of involvement in terrorists incidents, so on 15 April 1986 American planes flew from Lakenheath and Upper Heyford in Britain, on a mission to punish President Qadhafi for a supposed Libyan terrorist attack on a West Berlin nightclub (which killed one American soldier and a Turkish civilian). In the raid, President Qadhafi's adopted daughter was killed.

It was always assumed that the American base would not be used without the consent of the British Government, and when the bombing occured, the Prime Minister informed the Commons that she had agreed to the action. Whether she was consulted or merely told has never been clear. But the fact that the US could use British bases in a conflict with a third country without seeking Parliament's approval gravely worried many people. The act of terrorism for which Libya was allegedly guilty was never proved. This incident foreshadowed the subsequent use of British bases by US B-52 bombers to fly to Iraq during the Gulf War, in which Britain was again involved in a war without specific parliamentary consent.

These episodes, though desperate in their motivation and execution, offered a vivid reminder of the extent to which modern British Governments have ridden roughshod over the House of Commons to which, in theory, they are accountable.

Sunday 5 January 1986

We had the second part of the adjourned meeting on the 'Aims and Objectives of the Chesterfield Labour Party'.

There were a number of amendments to consider, including one from Hasland Ward to delete the phrase 'that nobody can demand blind obedience from us in the name of loyalty or unity'. Someone argued that we needed loyalty to Conference decisions, that without it we were just a rabble.

To illustrate how volatile political loyalty can be, I told them about how the Party membership cards in Bristol in 1932 had little holes in them where the photograph of Ramsay MacDonald had been cut out.

Johnny Burrows wanted the phrase kept to reserve our right to speak up against policy. Anyway, the meeting was overwhelmingly against deleting the phrase.

In the section on improving democracy within the Labour Party, including the election of the Cabinet by the electoral college, Henry Challands said we didn't want to reopen the constitutional argument.

I thought that, although we might not want to press it before the next General Election, it did touch on the central question of patronage by the Opposition Leader and the Prime Minister. The PM is able to appoint Ministers, archbishops, judges and ambassadors, and we have got to face that. The clause was left in.

An amendment was agreed that women should have 'equal rights' rather than 'greater rights' and that 'ethnic communities' should replace 'blacks'.

On blood sports, there was an addendum to include 'the banning of all blood sports on land owned by Derbyshire County and Chesterfield Borough Councils and, wherever possible, to seek to abolish blood sports altogether'.

Then we came to a major proposed change – to delete the reference to 'common ownership under democratic control and management of the commanding heights of the economy'. In effect Henry Challands wanted to remove all socialist ingredients because we couldn't get majority support for them from the electorate. Arthur Soloman said that you can't nationalise the banks in two minutes, and people would be frightened about their investments.

Arthur Webber supported the amendment. But eventually the meeting voted to retain the phrase.

There was some further discussion about NATO and foreign troops on British soil, but no changes were made. Johnny Burrows thanked everybody for the hard work they had put into it, and I left absolutely thrilled by the exercise.

Thursday 9 January

Michael Heseltine resigned from the Cabinet today over the Westland affair, giving as his reasons that the Prime Minister had refused to allow the matter to be discussed and had told Ministers to clear any statements with the Cabinet Secretary, Robert Armstrong. No doubt Armstrong himself suggested that in order to protect the PM from this continuing public row.

I remember that in 1974 I wanted to bring Westland Helicopters into British Aerospace, but Westland were making a lot of profits and didn't want to have anything to do with it. Then when Westland got into difficulties the Government wouldn't help them, and they were forced to look to the Sikorsky company in America, with whom they had links, and who put in a rescue package. This frightened the Europeans, and Heseltine, who is very pro-Common Market, supported the Europeans.

That disturbed Mrs Thatcher, who is pro-American, so she said that it should be left to the shareholders to decide, but it seemed she and Leon Brittan, the Trade and Industry Secretary, were indicating to Westland that it would be against the national interest for them to accept the European bid.

It has come at an interesting time, because there is this intense US domination of Britain, intense European hostility to America and a growing feeling that Mrs Thatcher is too overbearing. Heseltine, with his he-man image, has also spoken up for men against a woman's dictatorship in Cabinet.

Tuesday 14 January

Went into Prime Minister's Questions to see how she did on the

Westland affair, and she was in complete control. Kinnock was quite ineffective.

I saw Jim Callaghan, and told him that I had put in his 'Procedure for Ministers'* as evidence to the sub-committee of the Treasury and Civil Service Select Committee which is considering the duties and responsibilities of civil servants and Ministers.

He said, 'So I see. I've looked at it and I see no reason why it shouldn't be published'.

Friday 17 January

The Westland shareholders are meeting at the Albert Hall – rich and powerful people deciding the future of the whole company and its workers. It is disgraceful.

Sunday 19 January

Melissa and her friend Tim came for tea. Then I went with them to see *Letter to Brezhnev*, a film made in Liverpool about a girl who meets a Russian sailor on shore leave. The trouble is that even with my deaf aid in I couldn't hear much. Got home and heard the great news that Dawn Primarolo had beaten Mike Cocks in the final ballot for the Bristol South candidature. Cocks apparently stormed out, saying they had never forgiven him for defeating me in the 1983 selection conference. Dawn is a very able woman, and it is an indication of the strength of the left in the Bristol South Party.

Monday 20 January

I received a letter from Terence Higgins, chairman of the Treasury and Civil Service Select Committee, saying that, if I referred to the 'Procedure for Ministers' at Wednesday's meeting of the sub-committee, it would immediately go into private session. I wrote back, saying that his decision appeared to challenge the rights of privilege and that I had no alternative but to put this matter to the Speaker and to enlist his support in defence of my use of privilege.

Tuesday 21 January

Went into the House at 10.45 to see the Speaker in his flat. Jack Weatherill is extremely friendly. I put my point to him, and said that this afternoon in the House I would be raising with him the question of my own position if I were to publish this document.

He showed me some of his prints of India, including one of Father at the Round Table Conference in 1931. He loves India, and had served in

* This confidential Government paper 'Questions of Procedure for Ministers' was issued by Jim Callaghan on becoming Prime Minister in 1976. The idea was initiated by Clem Attlee in 1945, and lays down 'guidance' to Ministers on everything from collective Cabinet responsibility to 'travelling expenses of wives'. One of John Major's first acts after winning the 1992 Election was to publish this document.

the Indian Army. I told him how pleased Mother would be, so he asked me to invite her to lunch with him.

Later I received a note from Jim Callaghan stating that he saw no objection to the minute being published and that he had written to the PM and to Terence Higgins to say the same thing.

So at 3.30 I got up in the Chamber and made my submission to the Speaker, and he said in effect, 'The only question of substance is whether you can put the document in the Library of the House, and I will let you know tomorrow.'

I talked later to Terence Higgins, who said, 'I hope you do decide to give your evidence in private, and we can consider later whether we are going to publish it.'

'I'm sorry,' I replied, 'but I can't.'

Dominating everything at the moment is Westland, with statements being made, and Leon Brittan in difficulties.

Wednesday 22 January

I worked on my statement for this afternoon when I will tell the Speaker that I intended to make the document available to MPs, and to nobody else. Caroline advised me that I shouldn't get into trouble, because I had thought of putting it in the Members' Lobby where any journalist could pick it up. This way I am within my rights of parliamentary privilege.

Dashed into the House, where the place is still buzzing with the Westland story. The Speaker had sent me a letter saying he was not prepared to permit me to put the document in the Library. So I got up and made my point about giving it only to MPs. Frankly there isn't an awful lot of interest in it.

At 5 I went into the sub-committee of the Treasury and Civil Service Select Committee. Ted Heath was sitting there, giving evidence in a very relaxed way, saying he was against any leaks and that he was in favour of the Official Secrets Act. He was followed by Patrick Jenkin, an unimpressive Minister, who said how marvellous the civil servants had been, and so on.

I was called to give my evidence, and I put my tape recorder on the table. (It hasn't come out very well, but the BBC were also recording the proceedings.) I got quite a lot across, and the last person to cross-examine me was Brian Sedgemore, who said, 'I would like to quote from this document.'

At this point one of the Tories moved that the committee go into secret session.

Austin Mitchell said, 'All that was decided was that, *if Mr Benn* referred to the document, we would go into secret session.'

We all withdrew while there was a vote. The Committee Room was packed, with the heavy journalists there. Then we were called in and told they had voted for a secret session.

So I said, 'I don't want to be discourteous to the committee, but I want to make it absolutely clear that I don't feel I could accept another oath of silence, because that would compound the problem of 1976 when the document was given to me confidentially.' So I withdrew.

I was interviewed about it by Sally Hardcastle for *The World Tonight*, then went to the Campaign Group, where Sean Geraghty, a Fleet Street electrician who is a left-wing member of the EETPU, was describing what Rupert Murdoch was doing at News International's new production plant at Wapping in Docklands.

Murdoch wants all his workforce to go onto individual contracts with unlimited liability for individual employees – that is, if they got into conflict with the company, they would be liable right up to the point of losing their homes and their possessions. Sean also said Murdoch wanted a single-union agreement and a no-strike agreement, and that Eric Hammond, General Secretary of the EETPU, had committed his people to it. Sean said they did accept a no-strike agreement because with arbitration and other things it was possible to get round it.

Eddie Shah in Warrington is operating a similar agreement with his new paper, which is going to be called *Today* and is due to be published on 5 March.

Sean described the new plant at Wapping. Last weekend there were five busloads of police and a helicopter overhead. It was an extraordinary building, silent, with everybody in radio contact. There was an internal road, and paper storage capacity on the scale of an airport. The lowest guaranteed wage was something like £18,000. He pointed out that there was no longer a *printer's* job at all. Everyone who worked in the plant – and many had been brought in from America and Australia to act as strike-breakers – had to wear a colour-coding on their overalls, and the building itself was colour-coded; if you were found in a part of the building with a different colour from the one on your overalls, you were instantly sacked.

Dave Nellist asked if we should picket it.

Sean said, 'Well, the distribution scheme is very elaborate, but if we could stop the *Sun* we would really impose financial difficulties on him. The employers have put up a £50 million slush fund to beat a strike. We don't want any picket violence.'

Eddie Loyden pointed out that it was more than an industrial matter, it was a major political issue.

Monday 27 January

The Westland debate, and it was one of those 'great parliamentary occasions'. It was opened by Kinnock, who waffled, talked for too long and didn't put the crucial questions. Thatcher brazened it out and didn't look at all worried. The only people whose faces were like thunder were the two law officers – Sir Patrick Mayhew, the Solicitor-

General, and Sir Michael Havers, the Attorney-General – who appear to have been used by Thatcher to try to destroy Heseltine. When Heseltine spoke he attempted to recover his role as a Tory leader. Leon Brittan, who had resigned last week, made a cringing little speech. Michael Foot made a good one.

My speech was listened to in silence by the Labour Members. The Tories didn't like it and there were a lot of interruptions. I said that Mrs Thatcher had asked, 'Who will rid me of this turbulent priest?', and that her civil servants had done the rest and got Heseltine out. I also attacked the lobby briefing system.

Wednesday 29 January

At the NEC we discussed News International and whether we, as Labour politicians, should talk to News International journalists. It was agreed that they wouldn't be allowed to the normal press conference after the NEC meeting. I said, 'I take it that the refusal also applies in the Press Lobby', and Kinnock replied, 'That's not on our property.' I said, 'It's nothing to do with property, it's the principle.' In the end, it was agreed unanimously that the Party wouldn't under any circumstances, anywhere, talk to News International journalists.

Later in the day, having been informed of this, Chris Moncrieff, the chairman of the lobby, promptly withdrew the standing invitation to Kinnock to attend the lobby to brief journalists. So the lobby journalists stick together to support each other but are quite happy to see 5000 printworkers sacked. Kinnock will now get a disgusting press for having 'capitulated to the hard left'.

Friday 7 February

Bill Flanagan, Leader of Chesterfield Borough Council, is thrilled at the 'Chesterfield summit', to which representatives from the American and Soviet Embassies are coming to debate east-west relations. He said, 'The borough council will entertain them and take care of their hotels and organise everything.' That would suit me well.

Sunday 9 February

Watched Neil Kinnock on the Brian Walden interview on television. He is now advocating a Franklin D. Roosevelt approach. He declared that individual freedom must come above equality, that production must come above redistribution, and that taxes would not be raised except on the very rich, ie the top 3 or 4 per cent of earners. These statements, combined with his praise of the Japanese industrial system, put Kinnock and Hattersley squarely in the SDP camp.

I thought once again we must put up a candidate against Kinnock to challenge this consensus, but, as Caroline said, 'Nobody would understand what it would be about if you did it. You sacrificed yourself in 1981, when I advised you not to do it. You used up your goodwill at that moment and it isn't available to you now.'

Friday 14 February
The Turkish authorities have banned my proposed trip to Istanbul. Turgut Ozal, the Prime Minister, is coming to Britain on Monday.

Sunday 23 February
There was a small piece in the *Guardian* yesterday saying that Peter Mandelson had rung up the BBC to try to get me taken off the panel for *Question Time*, which I am doing on Thursday. This is a reaction to the fact that yesterday the NEC voted to start proceedings against Militant supporters in Liverpool District Labour Party. So I decided to write to Larry Whitty. To be banned from Turkey and *Question Time* is quite something!

Thursday 27 February
Went to Number 10 with others to hand in the petition organised by the Justice for Mineworkers Campaign, and in the afternoon in the House I presented my Justice for Mineworkers Bill which refines the provisions of the General Amnesty Bill.

In the evening I went to the BBC for *Question Time*. Michael Heseltine, Roy Jenkins and Joe Haines were on the panel. Haines writes nasty articles about me in his column in the *Daily Mirror*, but I tried to be friendly to him because I do respect him for turning down a peerage. He also wrote a very good book called *Inside Number 10*. Heseltine I have no time for; he's an absolute media figure.

Of course, I knew quite well that I had been asked on because of the Militant issue, which is always good news for media, and when I put it to the producer, Barbara Maxwell, she was a bit embarrassed.

Predictably, the first question was about Militant. Roy Jenkins was going on about Militant being a 'cancer in the Labour Party', so when it came to me I turned on him and the SDP. 'You talk about cancer! Everything you have achieved in your life has been on the backs of the working class. Your father was a miner; he was imprisoned in 1926; and every office you have ever held was because of the Labour Party, and then you kick away the ladder.'

I thought he was going to have a stroke. His face went absolutely scarlet. He is used to being buttered up as a man of principle.

Of course, then they all turned on me because of my social origins, and I just sat and listened.

Saturday 22 March
I decided to go to Wapping for the printworkers' march on Murdoch's empire. The police are behaving in an appalling way.

Last Sunday the pickets did succeed in delaying the distribution of the papers by five hours, and late newspapers are just waste paper, so it's worth going.

I went with the president of the Greater London Association of Trades Councils, who lives in Cable Street, where Grandpa Benn and Father had their Liberal headquarters in Gladstone House at the turn of the century.

We went first to the NGA first-aid caravan where people who had been injured on previous nights were tended – one man had had his collar-bone broken, another had a leg broken, and a girl had been kicked by a police horse.

Had a cup of tea and then set off on my own to walk to Tower Hill to the start of the march. There were a lot of police around. When I got there, I fell in behind the SOGAT banner and in front of the band from the Maerdy colliery, one of the most radical pits in South Wales. As we marched, we received messages through walkie-talkies that the police had removed the barriers in readiness for a horse charge, because apparently people had been seizing them, and the horses will not charge into people holding up barriers to protect themselves.

At Wapping we saw the searchlights of Murdoch's fortress, the barbed wire, the high metal fences, and lines of police with the mounted police behind them. Buses and coaches loaded with police were everywhere. When we reached the gates of the plant, a commander came up and said to Mike Hicks, the SOGAT chief marshal, 'I just want to thank you very much for keeping your crowd so orderly and not allowing it to get out of control.'

So Mike Hicks replied, 'Well, let me say something to you. We outnumber you now, but, when people go home to bed and we are smaller in number, I hope you don't do what you did last night and the night before when you sent the horses in and injured our people.'

The policeman said, 'I can't discuss that.'

Jeremy Corbyn and I made short speeches from the platform, and Diane Abbott, prospective Labour candidate for Hackney North and Stoke Newington, also turned up and made a speech.

It was an incredible night. A few years ago you would never have believed it could happen in the middle of London. Passing the Tower of London, grey-stoned and illuminated, you just felt as if you were back in the Middle Ages and it was only one step between the police charging you and hauling you away for execution in the Tower. We saw one of the huge lorries loaded with papers, coming out of the plant. But the spirit was good, just as good as during the miners' strike. I haven't as yet had to face a police horse or been struck by a truncheon, but tonight was a night to remember.

Monday 24 March

My Representation of the Workpeople Bill had been distributed at the TUC–Labour Party Liaison Committee. The bill provides for workers to have the right to elect their board of directors and to ballot before a decision was made to close plants or invest abroad or whatever. It would also give employees the right to a ballot before political donations were paid out by their companies.

I introduced it, and said, 'I am not seeking endorsement for my bill, it is intended as an educational bill, but it does turn Tory propaganda about ballots to our advantage. It would be a major counter-attack that would put them on the defensive – if you have to have ballots to elect union leaders, why not directors? It is also about the enfranchisement of labour against the enfranchisement of capital. What the Tories do is to use the statute book to transfer real power back to capital by selling off our assets. This focuses on the real question, which is whether the way forward – the answer to privatisation – should be democratisation. Having said all that, we've got to remember that the real power of working people lies in the return to full employment and in the strength of the trade unions.'

Prescott asked, 'What I want to know is will this bill ever be voted on? Because there are certain problems with it.'

I said, 'It is being presented to the House, but it will probably never be debated. I will circulate it around the movement.'

David Basnett didn't think the TUC would support it, because the provisions of the bill would bypass the trade unions.

John Evans, the MP for St Helens North, said, 'Only the unions can represent workers, and Tony's bill would stir up a hornet's nest.'

Roy Grantham, the General Secretary of APEX, asked if it would give working people the right to get rid of their *unions* if they wanted. The principle that all workers have the same rights is an important one.

I said it was a well-established principle that everyone, whether or not trade-unionist, elects the local MP and the Government and then the trade unions negotiate. 'It would be exactly the same in my bill. Every worker would elect the directors, then the trade unions would be able to negotiate with them.' I thanked them for the opportunity to put it forward. I must say I was surprised it wasn't more widely attacked.

At 5 I went to the Party's Campaign Strategy Committee, where four men and a woman from something called the Shadow Agency made a presentation entitled 'Society and Self'. They said it was a qualitative survey in which thirty groups of eight people, 240 people in all, had been interviewed for an hour and a half. We were told that the purpose was to understand the nature of the target vote. Primarily, they were non-committed Labour voters.

They flashed up on to a screen quotes which were supposed to be typical of Labour voters, for example: 'IT'S NICE TO HAVE A SOCIAL CONSCIENCE BUT IT'S YOUR FAMILY THAT COUNTS.'

What we were being told, quite frankly, was what you can read every day in the *Sun*, the *Mail*, the *Daily Express*, the *Telegraph*, and so on. It was an absolute waste of money.

They went on to talk about images and how the Party image was made up of current issues, leadership and historical ideas. They said the public were more interested in people than ideas, and figures like Livingstone and Hatton did us great damage.

Why should we pay them to tell us that our own people are damaging?

Labour was associated with the poor, the unemployed, the old, the sick, the disabled, pacifists, immigrants, minorities and the unions, and this was deeply worrying. The Tories were seen to have the interests of everyone at heart including the rich. Labour was seen as yesterday's party. The SDP gave hope but had no ideology or history.

The Labour Party was seen as disunited, squabbling, with Militants or infiltrators, and lacking in Government experience. 'The Party of my father' was one of the quotes; 'If I had a brick, I would throw it into Arthur Scargill's face' was another.

What was required in the Party leadership was decisiveness, toughness and direction: people wanted a tough person at the helm. Leadership was what it was about. Who was the Leader and what did he look like?

It was a Thatcherite argument presented to us: 'You had better be more like Thatcher if you want to win.'

I came out feeling physically sick; I'm not kidding, I really felt unwell, because if this is what the Labour Party is about I've got nothing whatever in common with it.

Wednesday 26 March

Went to the National Executive for the special meeting to hear Liverpool District Party members on 'charges' of breach of Party rules and membership of Militant. There was a huge crowd of people outside, some selling *Militant*, with the Liverpool Labour Party banner. The Executive had been reorganised into a sort of courtroom, with the chairs in two wings and a chair in the middle for the accused to sit on. The whole thing had a sinister aspect to it.

We had a report from Whitty on the court judgement yesterday and the procedure today. The original Inquiry Committee could not participate in the NEC proceedings, and there were questions raised by the judgement about the use of witnesses and legal representation by members charged.

Eric Heffer moved straight away that the proceedings should be deferred until we had had the full transcript from the court. Skinner seconded, and warned that the proceedings were fraught with legal dangers.

I warned that it was contrary to natural justice, a view the judge had taken in part. 'The people who come in today won't know what the charges are because we have got to modify them in the light of the judgement. I even heard Robin Cook on the radio this morning talk about the "bourgeois courts". If we are told we have got to obey law and order, then are we now to argue that when anybody else uses that law the courts are bourgeois?'

Frances Curran argued that we should not proceed. 'The judge said the action we are taking was dangerous and unprecedented, and should be deferred.'

Then we had Kinnock. 'The positions have been taken up by everybody and there is no justification for deferring the case. You can't pick and choose the law. A Militant lawyer yesterday said –'

I stopped him. 'On a point of order, we as an Executive are meeting to decide whether people are members of Militant or not, and before we have heard any of the people involved the Leader of the Party is saying they *are* Militant.'

'Well, I withdraw that,' he agreed. He went on to say that the Party had a right to defend itself.

Blunkett declared, 'We have only two choices: to proceed or to drop the whole thing. We must proceed, because otherwise we cease to operate as a Party.' He was very angry.

Eric Clarke said, 'What we are discussing is the credibility of the Party. How do we even know whether they are going to have witnesses or representation? We should delay for three weeks.'

We adjourned at 10 to give us a chance to read the documents before us, including ballot papers on which we had to vote 'Proven' or 'Not proven' in relation to the charges.

When we came back, Audrey Wise said, 'I want it minuted that I oppose this procedure.'

Heffer's motion was read again and defeated by 20 to 9.

Then I moved that the charges be withdrawn and reconsidered in the light of the judges' verdict, and Blunkett moved an amendment to say that we should proceed at once. I was defeated by 20 votes to 9.

The procedure was outlined, and at that stage the eight members of the Inquiry Committee – including Margaret Beckett and Audrey Wise from our side – all withdrew, thus reducing the Executive to twenty-one.

At 10.59 Eric Heffer asked, 'What is the quorum of the Executive?', and was told it was fifteen. Last night we had considered the possibility of leaving the meeting if this situation arose, to make it inquorate, but Jo Richardson and Dennis Skinner were doubtful. So there was frantic discussion amongst us as to what should be done. We knew from Meacher's voting that he wouldn't walk out.

At 11 Felicity Dowling, secretary of the Liverpool District Labour

Party and a Liverpool councillor, was brought in with her lawyer, appearing as her 'friend'.

Whitty told her, in line with the court judgement, 'All the evidence we received in confidence will be excluded from the questioning.'

Felicity Dowling said, 'I have had read out to me a number of charges that stand, and some that have been dropped. I didn't know this would happen until this very moment. Since I have witnesses I want to call, perhaps you would allow us to withdraw so that we know exactly where we stand in the light of what we have been told, and we know what witnesses we can bring in.'

Felicity Dowling is a woman of about thirty-five, who might have been a nun, or a schoolteacher. She was behaving with absolute responsibility. Anyone in that position would have been in terrible confusion. She wasn't at all rhetorical and didn't shout at the Executive. It was obvious that there was no alternative but to let her leave to consult.

At that stage, Eric Heffer, Frances Curran and I got up and walked out, and to our pleasure Eric Clarke, Joan Maynard, Jo Richardson and Dennis Skinner joined us. As we stood in the corridor, Dennis was listening at the door and heard: 'Perhaps if we made Larry Whitty into a member of the Executive that would raise the quorum.' But that was clearly impossible.

We agreed not to circulate a typed statement, because that would look as if it had all been prepared in advance. Eric Heffer sat down and wrote in his own hand the occasion for our leaving, namely the treatment of Felicity Dowling, in the interests of natural justice.

Derek Hatton looked in, all bright and cheerful, and said, 'Well done. Can I sit with you?' We said, 'No, it's got nothing whatever to do with you.' His attitude is extremely unhelpful.

We had thought we would give a press conference at the House of Commons, but decided we didn't have a choice, with the media and the crowds of Liverpool Militant supporters outside. So we stood together, and Eric read out the statement. David Rose of ITN immediately asked us if the action was designed to remove the quorum and suggested we had planned it all last night. I tapped Eric on the shoulder after he had given one answer, and we walked away and came back to the Commons.

Kinnock appeared on the news at 1 o'clock violently attacking us and saying the movement would treat us with contempt and derision. The movement will understand exactly what it is about, identifying Meacher and Blunkett with the other side.

Thursday 27 March
Tony Banks had generously asked me to attend as an honoured guest at the last meeting of the GLC before it is abolished on 31 March. I went

to his office, and behind his desk was an oil painting of John Williams Benn, my grandfather, while chairman of the LCC, and on another wall was a painting of Tony himself as the last chairman, standing very characteristically in a smart suit, with County Hall and figures from the GLC behind him including Stephen.

Kinnock arrived as a guest and I stayed clear of him.

I went into the council chamber and found a place next to Stephen. There was a formal agenda which lasted for an hour.

Afterwards I went into Tony Banks's office and had a word with one or two people, and came home feeling sad. But that's the end of an era, and now it is forward to the next thing.

Thursday 3 April
My sixty-first birthday. I asked Ruth Winstone whether she would be prepared to do the job of supervising the diary project on a full-time basis. She agreed, which is very pleasing because I think she is entirely reliable. Her typing isn't all that rapid, but she can supervise typists who come in and she can concentrate on the editing.

Back to the Commons. The new Shops Bill was being debated. The trade unions, churches, small shopkeepers and the women's movement have all been campaigning against Sunday opening, and, to cut a long story short, its deregulation was defeated. It was the first time the supremacy of market forces had been thwarted, and it sort of indicated that the Tories can't be certain of getting away with the rest of their policies, after the *Belgrano*, Westland, and now of course the Libyan crisis.

Wednesday 16 April
Commons debate on Libya. Thatcher began with her usual strident gramophone recording about fighting terrorism. Kinnock spent half the time distancing himself from terrorism – which was a bit overdone –and then criticising the bombing of Libya; he sounded a bit like Michael Foot during the Falklands. Heath made an effective speech comparing the situation to the Suez crisis. Callaghan said he would have refused permission to the Americans. Norman St John Stevas pointed out that the Crown prerogative governed such matters and Parliament was only allowed to advise *after* the event. I made a long speech, a bit longer than I prefer, but I used the opportunity to argue that the time had come to close all American bases, not just nuclear bases.

Thursday 17 April
Caught the train to Chesterfield. A nasty incident occurred; most people who come up to me are so friendly. But a woman in her mid-thirties spotted me while I was having a cup of tea and asked, 'Why are you travelling first class?'

I said, 'Well, I'm working.'

'You're not working now. You believe in a classless society, so why don't you travel second class?'

I answered, 'Because I've got a table where I can work. I travel a great deal and I have a lot of work to do and this is very convenient; I get a warrant from Parliament for a first-class seat.'

She went away, but then came back and stood aggressively over me and asked, 'Did your children go to public school?'

I said, 'No, they went to a comprehensive.'

She became really abusive and said, 'As to unemployment, my mother had four vacancies in her office and nobody applied.'

I'm afraid I was pretty rude back. 'I'm sorry, I'm working,' I said.

'You might want my vote.'

'I don't want your vote. You're a natural Thatcherite. Now would you excuse me?'

She said, 'It's a public place.'

It's the only time I can remember when somebody has been personally offensive to my face.

Tom met me at the station, and there is tremendous excitement about the 'Chesterfield summit' tomorrow.

Friday 18 April

Had a word on the phone with my brother Dave, who gave me some simple Russian phrases to use today to welcome the Soviet diplomat to our 'Summit' on east-west relations.

Tom and Caroline and I stood at Chesterfield station waiting for the London train to arrive. Off came Alexander Vershbow, from the American Embassy, and his wife Lisa, and Guennadi Shabannikov, from the Russian Embassy. Then the mayor's limousine drove us all to the Town Hall, where there were a lot of photographers – and about six demonstrators from the Sheffield Revolutionary Communist Party shouting, 'Down with the United States', and carrying little placards saying 'In favour of Libya and Ireland'.

The mayor, Tom Whyatt, greeted the guests and they were each presented with a picture of the Spire Church and history of Chesterfield. Lunch, and then on to a 'walkabout' round the Market Square. They saw the municipal horse and cart that collects the rubbish from the market, then went to the Spire Church and back to their hotel.

At 4 we had a press conference. There were reporters from the *Guardian*, *Daily Telegraph*, *Daily Mirror* and *Morning Star*.

Down to the Chesterfield College of Technology, where the debate was being held, and a splendid dinner was laid on by the students.

The hall in the college held 500 people. I couldn't hear very clearly, but during his thirty-minute speech Shabannikov gave an account of all the Soviet initiatives for peace. He got warm applause. Vershbow gave a statement of the American position, and there was a lot of anti-Russian stuff in it which didn't go down well with the audience.

We had a whole range of questions about human rights. Someone made a great attack on American policy in Nicaragua, the Philippines, Haiti, and so on. I put the last question: why should British families feel that the Russians were their enemies, and why was there so much anti-communism in the United States? I must say the American, who was only about thirty-three, did acquit himself well, though he didn't answer all the questions. Shabannikov was a bit older and had been a construction worker, whereas the American had been at Yale and Columbia.

The success of the whole day exceeded our wildest dreams. Instead of organising on the far left as a fringe, this was quite different – organising within a town, with the Labour Party, the Trades Council and the College of Technology. It absolutely delighted the local Labour Party.

Wednesday 24 April

Caroline was on Breakfast Television about her book, *Challenging the MSC*, which is published this week.

Later I went to Whitechapel Technology Centre for her launch party, and all her mates were there, including John Eversley, who had lost his leg in a bicycle accident recently.

Monday 28 April

Larry Whitty asked me to have tea with him; I guessed he wanted to see me about the witch-hunt. He looked pretty unwell and worried, and said, 'I'm absolutely sick; what shall I do?'

'First of all, don't forget you are the only senior figure in the Labour Party who isn't in Parliament, and you have enormous authority,' I told him. 'At a certain stage, you might find it necessary to say publicly, "It is my job to uphold the constitution of the Party, but any suggestion that there is to be a general attack upon socialists within the Party would be deeply destabilising, and we should all pull together and win the Election." It will be difficult. It's like being the first cuckoo of spring, but if you do decide to say "cuckoo", you've got to be sure it is spring.'

He laughed. He said he had no influence on Neil, who had told him after the Bournemouth Conference that he would be perfectly content for Hatton and Mulhearn never again to hold high office in the Labour Party. Neil saw it personally in terms of machismo: he didn't take much notice even of Blunkett, and thought the attack on Militant was popular.

I told Larry that if I was Leader of the Party I would see Healey and Hattersley regularly, but Kinnock cannot do that with the left – it would be embarrassing.

He asked, 'Why can't we have a proper appeals procedure so the NEC isn't fully occupied for two days, as it will be again on 21 and 22 May?'

'It's all very well saying that, but remember that expulsions in a political party are not really breaches of the law, they are about political opinions. People don't like other, conflicting opinions, and that is the problem. The question whether the NEC or another body should be carrying out the expulsions is like discussing whether you should electrocute or hang people. Actually the question is do we want to have capital punishment at all?'

He said he was worried that twenty or thirty constituencies were busy expelling people now, and he thought the courts would conclude it was wrong.

Thursday 1 May

On the way to the Committee of Privileges I met Fred Mulley, former Defence Secretary in Callaghan's Government, whom I like very much. I said casually, 'Did you ever see the agreement between Britain and the United States about the use of bases here?'

He replied, 'I don't know that there was an agreement; there was a sort of understanding. There may have been a letter.'

I asked him if he thought such a letter ought to be published.

'I don't think the Americans want it to be published,' he said, 'because the fact is that we have got a better deal on the veto on their bases in Britain than they have ever conceded to the other European countries with bases. If the continental countries in NATO wanted similar arrangements, the Americans would be reluctant to grant them.' Now that is a very interesting point.

He also told me that in Germany there is a genuine 'dual key'; that is, the Germans have the missiles and the Americans the warheads, and two colonels – an American and a German – do have to turn keys to activate them. In Britain, he said, in order to save money we let the Americans control the missiles *and* the warheads, in exchange for the right to be consulted. *We* have no technical veto or 'key'.

Saturday 3 May

Went to Tower Hill for the printworkers' march to Wapping. They were expecting about 10,000 people. I reached the main gates of Murdoch's fortress at about 9.30 pm, and there was a happy atmosphere, with families, older printworkers and a lot of youngsters. Across the road I could see a huge body of police, and horses; at the moment the two lines of marchers met, I saw a puff of smoke, which was a signal, and the mounted police came out and charged in all directions and cleared the road. They were followed by riot police with round shields and batons and later by the long-shield men.

From about 9.30 until I left at 12.30, there were just continual police charges on the crowd – mounted and riot police moving at speed in all directions, waving their truncheons and shields. Unlike the young miners, who pushed against the police – an old picket game – the crowd showed no defiance when the police ran up the street waving their truncheons; there were just a few people standing on the pavement – not reacting, just frightened. As soon as the speakers on the platform began, the crowd were surrounded by the riot police. I could see quite clearly below me, and nothing whatever untoward in the crowd was happening. People were jumping on to the platform to escape the police, and I thought it would collapse.

We heard that a young printworker of thirty who had marched all the way from Glasgow had had a heart attack, so I appealed for the police to let an ambulance come through, but they refused. He was put on a trestle table, and people tried to carry him through the police lines to an ambulance. I believe he was actually jostled by a policeman on a horse. Meanwhile the casualties were building up. I went over to the first-aid caravan and there were seventy casualties, of whom thirty-five were serious. I saw one man semi-conscious, with blood pouring from his head and neck. Fortunately there were two doctors there. I saw a young boy outside the caravan trembling with fear because he had been attacked by the police while he was simply standing with his dad. There was a woman in a terrible state because she had got separated from her son. It was clear that not only would the police not allow an ambulance to come near the first-aid caravan to pick up the casualties but that they were running around the caravan and the bus, chasing people and creating casualties. I was observing all this out of the caravan window, watching a succession of helmets and shields and terrified people.

Funnily enough, I wasn't frightened, because I was so busy making a note. I had my tape recorder running some of the time. One of the things I was able to do was to give interviews to IRN and BBC television, and talk to reporters.

I heard that the police had smashed some television camera lights. At one stage, having appealed several times from the platform for the police to withdraw, I went with the chief marshal, Mike Hicks, and a SOGAT solicitor and spoke to the senior police officer present. I had my tape recorder running.

The senior officer said, 'I will speak to you privately, sir.'

I told him, 'No, I can't do that. I am here with these people and I am going to raise this in the House of Commons. I don't want an argument about what was said between us.'

Then one of his officers said, 'He's got a tape recorder running.'

I replied, 'Yes, of course I have got a tape recorder, because I don't want any difference of opinion about what is said.'

I appealed to him to withdraw his men, and he said he was protecting them, and I said I didn't believe it, and in the end he walked off.

I think the fact that MPs were there – Tony Banks, Ron Leighton, Clive Soley and myself – was reassuring to the crowd and inhibited the police. I just walked through the police lines looking to neither left nor right and got through. It was horrific. I couldn't believe it – the absolute horror of standing in the middle of the night in the middle of London, seeing the police flailing about with their truncheons at people who a moment earlier had been standing talking, and to know that it was authorised, planned. Everyone was involved, from people in their sixties to young children. After midnight, of course, we saw the beginning of a convoy of huge trucks leaving the plant and people shouting 'Scab!' They actually drove out of a side gate well away from us, and there was absolutely no justification for the police to mount an attack in the streets where our people were attending the meeting.

When we finally left, we had to go through four sets of police lines. After we had walked for half an hour a man stopped his car and picked us up just by Mansion House. He worked for the *Sunday Mirror* and had just finished his shift. He had been a SOGAT official and he was a complete cynic, but what he told us has to be recorded.

'I am not a completely honest man,' he said. 'I do a lot of things I probably shouldn't, but the whole printing scene is corrupt. I will not go along any more with what has been happening, which is that people were being paid £100 a night to work and would then sit and play cards. The decision as to who was taken on for the shift would be made by the union officials. When Bill Keys tried to clean all this up, four heavies attacked him one night while he was getting into his car. It's riddled with gangsters and mobsters.'

I think that side of it needs to be given, because the whole of Fleet Street is rotten – they make millions by poisoning people's minds, at the editorial end where they sell out, cover up and corrupt the news and at the bottom where they are out for as much money as they can get. But the question still is: whose side are you on? I think what we are witnessing is the end of a rotten Fleet Street system, and something better will have to be substituted, but there will be a lot of vested interest at different levels.

Sunday 4 May

To Chesterfield. Went over to the Labour Club, and there were six women who had been at Wapping, and all had the same horrific accounts of the night.

Tuesday 6 May

The phone rang all morning about Wapping. Went into the House and intervened on a couple of issues during Prime Minister's Questions. John Biffen, who was standing in for the Prime Minister, was most aggressive; I think he feels he has to be tough at the moment because he has got to hold the fort. Also I think he has got his eye on Number 10.

I managed to get in a strong comment on Wapping, and of course Kinnock just dissociated himself completely from any violence of any kind, as if to say, 'Please don't blame me for what happens. You can do what you like but we'll never respond.' Pathetic really; he's a weak man.

Ron Leighton, Labour MP for Newham North East, tried to get an emergency debate on Wapping, but that was turned down. Clive Soley (Labour MP for Hammersmith), who was behind the police lines most of the night, said he was going to see the Home Secretary.

Thursday 8 May
Received seventy letters from people who had been at Wapping, and their accounts confirmed my experience; what they described was horrific, but all absolutely consistent in their detail.

Stayed up to watch the local election results. In Liverpool and Lambeth, where the socialist commitment had been strongest, Labour won, so that's completely overturned the judgement of the District Auditor. In Ealing, Hilary's majority went from 54 to 751, and Labour have seized power in Ealing Council. That means that Hilary, the Labour candidate for Ealing North, could be an MP after the next General Election if this carries on. In Hackney, Stephen came top of the poll for the ILEA.

Sunday 18 May
To Chesterfield General Committee, where among other resolutions there was one critical of my walkout from the NEC. It supported the NEC's investigation into Militant and censured those members of the NEC who had left the meeting on 26 March.

Somebody proposed an amendment that I be asked to make a report, but nobody seconded it, so when I got up to speak the mover of the resolution objected.

I said, 'I think I am bound to respond, since it is a criticism of my action.' I went through the recent history of the inquiry, and explained how the Executive had nearly been in contempt of court. 'Next week, on Wednesday and Thursday, we have got two all-day meetings and we are going to have these people up again; meanwhile the councillors have won their seats again in Liverpool, despite leaflets issued by the Liberals and the Tories quoting Kinnock and Hattersley attacking Militant.

'By contrast, Malcolm Withers, an editor on the *Sun*, who crosses the picket line at Wapping every day, is the Labour parliamentary candidate in Stevenage. I tell you, candidly, that Larry Whitty is very worried. My assessment is that the Party wants to win the Election, wants to support the Leader, but regards this as a diversion. I must ask quite clearly for support from this committee, because we are going back to the issue on Wednesday.' There was thunderous applause when I sat down.

Several members believed I should have stayed at the meeting – that was the greatest criticism. However, of members present, six out of 105 voted for the motion and six abstained, so it was a good response. But in some constituencies where they will not have heard the case put they may well be opposed to what we did.

Monday 19 May
Went over to the House of Commons for the Campaign Strategy Committee in Neil Kinnock's office. This is the holy of holies.

For the second half of the meeting we had another presentation from this Shadow Agency, which is made up of people from different advertising agencies who have offered to help the Party prepare for the Election.

It was a real management presentation with words and phrases being flashed up on a screen, like 'qualitative research', 'hypothetical solution', 'targeted'. This went on for ages, and Blunkett asked, 'What about democracy?'

'We haven't got round to that.' They continued, 'We must be credible, our promises must be backed by machinery. We must have sympathetic values. We must be able to answer the question "Where will we get the money from?"'

After the presentation was over, Robin Cook reflected my view. He said it didn't excite him because it wasn't rooted in experience.

During 1986 the Committee of Privileges considered another case of breach of privilege by The Times, *which in December 1985 had published information about radioactive waste material. The Times journalist concerned, Richard Evans, had received his information from a member of the Environment Select Committee, and on 20 May 1986 the House of Commons debated the Committee of Privileges' report on the affair. The report 'found' Richard Evans guilty of contempt of the House and recommended he be suspended from the lobby for six months and that* The Times *be punished by restricting its access to the House of Commons. The source of the leak – MP or staff – was not identified in the report. In the event, the House did not uphold the report's recommendations.*

Tuesday 20 May
Went in at 10 pm for the late-night debate on the report from the Committee of Privileges concerning the *Times* leak. The House was packed, because the press lobby are up in arms and have whipped it up. I was the only one in committee who had opposed the recommend-

ations of the report, ie to suspend Richard Evans from the lobby for six months and reduce the press passes issued by the House to *The Times*.

Interestingly, the recommendations were defeated. What happened in effect was that MPs, faced with the unpopularity that would result from punishing a journalist without punishing the MP who leaked the story to him, took note of the report, which was full of the most hideous ideas, but rejected the punishment. The report contained the worst of both worlds: it didn't address its mind in any way to the real issue, which is whether the electors have the right to know the proceedings of select committees. It simply dealt with privileges of the House, the lobby system and the potential punishment of a journalist.

I got a very poor hearing, and I could have made a better speech, but I concentrated on the right of the electors to know.

Mrs Thatcher voted with those rejecting the punishment.

As with many great historical events, the right decision was arrived at by accident for the wrong reason.

On 21 and 22 May my time was entirely taken up by the NEC, again dealing with alleged Militant infiltration into the Liverpool District Labour Party. The charges were, as before, breach of Labour Party rules and/or membership of Militant Tendency. On this occasion, we heard Tony Mulhearn, Derek Hatton, Ian Lowes, Felicity Dowling, Harry Smith and Terry Harrison. Four other cases, those of Carol Darton, Cheryl Varley, Roger Bannister and Richard Knights, were deferred. One, Tony Aitman's, was heard in his absence.

I made seventy pages of manuscript notes and dictated my diary on the Thursday night. The account given here has had to be heavily cut because of its sheer length, and similar proceedings were to be repeated many times with members of different parties over the following months and years, carried out by the NEC and subsequently the specially convened National Constitutional Committee.

Wednesday 21 May

There was a very big demonstration outside Walworth Road. The meeting went on from 9.30 am to 1.15 the next morning, and then from 9.30 am to 9.30 pm on Thursday. Those people who had served on the Inquiry Committee were again excluded from the meeting. The layout of the room was again like a court martial.

At 10.31 the proceedings began, and Tony Mulhearn came in, took his jacket off and sat down. Syd Tierney, who was chairing the meeting, read out the procedure and said that Mulhearn was charged with being a member of the Militant Tendency in breach of the Party rules. The General Secretary would put the full charges. Whitty then began.

Mulhearn straight away asked for clarification on some point. So Kinnock responded, 'We have had a discussion about procedure.'

Mulhearn said, 'I must understand the procedure, because it will decide whether or not I want legal representation.'

After some discussion, Mulhearn asked to withdraw, to consider his position. We sat about for about twenty minutes until he returned.

Tierney complained, 'You said you'd be away for five minutes, not twenty minutes.'

'Time passes quickly when you're enjoying yourself,' Mulhearn replied.

We then proceeded, but there was a further wrangle, and Mulhearn decided, 'I am asking for more time to get professional advice.'

Tierney said, 'We'll adjourn for lunch.'

I wandered round during the lunch hour, and there was a totally unhealthy atmosphere of camaraderie, people laughing and joking, which I found extremely unattractive. It is a very serious matter to be expelled from the Party. I had a word with Larry Whitty, and asked if they intended to proceed beyond the Liverpool case. He said, 'I hope this is the end of the matter, but I have no bankable assurances on it.' I think that one of the advantages of its being so extremely time-consuming and difficult is that it does actually discourage them from wanting to do it again.

At 1.50 we resumed, and Tony Mulhearn came in with Eddie Loyden, the MP for Liverpool Garston. Eddie looked unwell. Mulhearn explained that he had brought Loyden along because he couldn't contact his solicitor but that the solicitor could be at Walworth Road by 3.30. He requested an adjournment until his solicitor arrived, but this was refused.

Tierney asked, 'Do you accept the jurisdiction of the NEC?'

Mulhearn replied, 'The NEC have declined my request and I am in an impossible position. I shall take steps to defend my position.'

Tierney asked if he wanted to make a statement and he said he didn't. So Tierney said we would proceed to hear the case, and Mulhearn warned he would seek an injunction.

During a break, while all this was happening, Frances Curran let it be known that it was her birthday, and therefore, in a most hypocritical and falsely jocular way, the whole Executive sang 'Happy birthday' to her. It reminded me of the night of 2–3 April 1979, when the Cabinet and the NEC were meeting at Number 10 to discuss the General Election manifesto, and they all sang 'Happy birthday' to me and then proceeded to produce an awful manifesto. This occasion was particularly dreadful, as Frances is a supporter of *Militant*!

In the afternoon Mulhearn agreed to make a statement. He rejected the charges of membership of the Militant Tendency and said he had spoken at meetings, but that was proof of nothing, he was a guarantor of the building used by it in Liverpool, and he had signed all sorts of leaflets, but he categorically rejected the idea that he was or had ever been a member of Militant. He said that unlike many people in

Liverpool, he was in full-time employment, and that was why he had been asked to be a guarantor.

Kinnock asked, 'Is Militant an organisation?'

'All newspapers need organisation, but there is no difference between us and Labour Left or Campaign for Labour Victory. I don't believe that Militant is more than a newspaper.'

'Which ideas of Militant do you disagree with?' Kinnock went on.

'What do you have in mind?'

So Kinnock changed tack. 'What contributions have you made to Militant financially?'

Mulhearn said, 'I've made the odd contributions, like you yourself.'

Kinnock continued the interrogation. 'You have spoken on public platforms, and that might indicate association with Militant.'

'Many people have spoken on *Morning Star* platforms, on *Tribune* platforms, on Clause 4 platforms.'

'Have you ever attended any private Militant meetings?'

'No, only public meetings.'

'Can you differentiate between membership and association?'

'Well, I support Militant while it supports socialism.'

Kinnock said, 'Can you please answer the question about the difference between association and membership?'

And so it went on. Eric and I asked him a few questions, and then Hattersley asked about the Militant rally.

Mulhearn said, 'What's the difference between that and the Tribune rally?'

Skinner asked, 'Have you ever had any differences with Eddie Loyden?'

'The only difference was at the time of the argument in 1980 over the leadership electoral system. Eddie Loyden wanted the Conference to elect the Leader, but I went for the electoral college because I thought that was the only practical chance.'

Skinner asked, 'Is there a list of Militant members?'

'I've never seen one.'

Later Skinner said, 'There are groups who don't publish their names – like Solidarity, which has sixty to seventy Labour MPs and of which Hattersley is a member.'

Mulhearn said, 'I am aware of that, and I understand their reluctance to publish.'

Skinner added, 'There is also the St Ermine's Group of right-wingers known as the Millionaire's Tendency, and they are secret . . .'

I must say, I found Mulhearn as straight as a die, 100 per cent competent and very credible.

Eddie Loyden had to leave at this stage because his wife was seriously ill and he had to catch the last train home.

Kinnock wanted to get the Mulhearn case over and finished, and deal with Hatton tonight as well.

But Blunkett said, 'I really do think we should adjourn at 9.45 tonight and meet again at 9 tomorrow.'

To my amazement, that motion was carried by 11 to 10. But it had been planned that Mulhearn and Hatton would be expelled today and Kinnock was in an absolute panic that he wouldn't be able to carry it out. So during the next break, which lasted for ten minutes, Kinnock did a lot of canvassing, and when we met again at 6.50 he proposed that we go on after 10. So there was another motion, which was carried, that we return at 10.30 after the vote in the House.

We had sandwiches, and started again at 7.25.

I said to Mulhearn, 'Four questions. First of all, do you agree that if you are expelled the NEC will be deciding you are a liar?'

'Yes.'

'Do you also agree that all the decisions taken by the District Labour Party were taken collectively, and therefore you were no more responsible than anybody else?'

'Yes.'

'Did you have any complaints from the Party at regional or national level or from trade unions at regional or national level before the inquiry?'

'No.'

'Do you attribute your electoral success in Liverpool, after the years of delay and the Liberal majority, to the way you organised?'

Mulhearn said, 'Yes. We have the third largest Labour vote in the post-war period and we are building the Party in the city.'

Then he said something significant: 'We did make a tactical error in handing out the redundancy notices, though at the time it was supported by the shop stewards. We did upset some union leaders.'

At 9.15 there was a slight interruption, and Whitty reported that Derek Hatton's barrister had made an application for an injunction and that Hatton had gone home.

Then we adjourned, and I took a taxi to the Commons for the vote at 10. I might add that today there was a Cabinet reshuffle, and Keith Joseph resigned as Education Secretary and was replaced by Kenneth Baker. The Environment Department was taken over by Nicholas Ridley, Transport by John Moore.

When we got back at 10.30, fish and chips were served, and everyone was laughing and joking as if they were on an outing.

The NEC resumed at 11 pm and there was some discussion on the Mulhearn case.

Skinner argued, 'He made a brilliant exposition of his job and, on the Militant question, he said he respected Conference decisions and said he never attended closed meetings.'

Kinnock understood that the situation was different in Liverpool, but he thought that the frequency of sharing a platform with Militant indicated support.

I said, 'We are very much divided, but the one thing we have in common is that we want to protect the Labour Party. As far as the public is concerned, Mulhearn is blackened, abused, insulted in the press, treated as a wrecker, an extremist, a thug, an encourager of moles who want to destroy the Party and parliamentary democracy. But we saw him as an honest, competent and decent man committed to the movement. The thing about Mulhearn is that he enjoys the confidence of his people at the moment of their greatest crisis in Liverpool.

'He is certainly not an entryist, because he has been in the Party since before Militant began. Then we come to the practical question. If we expel Mulhearn, there are hundreds like him, and where does it stop? What about Dave Nellist and Terry Fields? If this goes on, it will become the major business of the Party up and down the country.'

On the charge of membership of Militant, the vote was 'proven' 13, 'not proven' 7; on breaking the rules and constitution of the Liverpool District Labour Party and the national Labour Party, the vote was the same.

The vote on membership of Militant automatically carried expulsion. Voting against the charge were me, Clarke, Curran, Heffer, Maynard, Richardson and Skinner.

Looking back on the day, this is a major event in the history of the Labour Party. No Leader in the past – neither Gaitskell, Wilson nor Callaghan – has ever had the determination to remove a complete section of the Party: because it isn't just Militant, it's the people who support Militant in their advocacy of socialism at the height of the present crisis. Kinnock is a ruthless man who thinks this will benefit him politically with the media. It is the bicycle theory of expulsions – if you stop expelling, you fall off. I think it will go much further than this.

There is a most important choice for the socialists in the Party to make – are you going to go along in silence on the grounds that you don't want to rock the boat, or are you going to alert people to what is actually happening?

I find it personally very unpleasant and the camaraderie utterly revolting.

Thursday 22 May
The NEC met all morning to consider the case of Ian Lowes of the GMB, chairman of Liverpool Council joint shop stewards' committee. He too was expelled.

At 4.30 in the afternoon, Councillor Harry Smith from Liverpool Council was brought in – a short, round-faced man with curly hair and twinkling eyes – and with him was a sallow-faced man with dark hair who kept whispering in his ear.

Smith said, 'I should introduce the man I have brought with me. His name is George Nibbs – of course, that's only his pen-name.'

Everybody burst out laughing, he was a very amusing man, though deadly earnest in what he said. He was only being charged with membership of the Militant Tendency, not with malpractice.

They asked for a deferment and withdrew, and Kinnock moved that we did not let him consult with his solicitor. Blunkett said he thought we should wait. Hattersley moved that we proceed, and that was carried by 12 to 7. When they came back in, Harry Smith protested. 'What would happen if I walked out? I am very nervous. Ian Lowes has been done in and I'm afraid you are going to do me in too. It's like two murderers before a court. The judge says, "we've hanged one now, we'd better hang the other." I'm going.'

So he left, but at 5.30 he returned and said, 'I want to make a political statement. You don't know who I am, and I want to tell you who I am.' Then he gave the most riveting account of his life.

'My mum and dad were married, and I was born six months later, so it doesn't take a very clever man to realise what they were up to. They were High Church. I was racist as a young man, and I lived in the Edge Hill constituency. At fifteen I joined the electricians' union, which was when my political education started. My family are still Tories, and I come from a reactionary, working-class Protestant family. I worked all my life on building sites and in maintenance jobs, and I got married at eighteen. My son was born when we had been married six months, so you can see at least my son has got something in common with me.' Everybody laughed.

He continued, 'I joined the Labour Party in Wavertree Ward, which only had one or two working-class members. I helped in the ward, canvassed for new members and converted it into a political ward. I got appointed eleven months later as the election agent. I later became treasurer for Wavertree, and I ran the tote –'

Tierney interrupted, 'I am not trying to stop you, but can you please come to the point?'

I said, 'Half a minute. This man is giving the reasons why he holds the views he does, and I want to know at what stage he may have heard about the ideas of Militant.'

Harry Smith went on, 'I stood as a council candidate, and gave an undertaking that I would carry out the policies. I was very nervous about speaking, but I wanted better services in the city. I had never been in any other political organisation – only the church, boy scouts and youth clubs. I have never joined any other political organisation, I have never been a member of Militant. I read the paper. I've been thrown into a high prominence by my activity for a minimum wage and a thirty-five-hour week, but I can't say I won't do it again because I haven't "done it" in the first place.'

I just note that at this stage it was clear that Sam McCluskie and Alex Kitson were going to vote in support of Harry Smith because he was creating such a good impression.

Smith carried on, 'All I can really do is speak. I did get invited to two meetings in Coventry and Llandudno' (which Hattersley had raised) 'but they were given to me to represent the Party.'

Frances Curran asked, 'Who booked you for these meetings? Wasn't it the City Council?'

'Yes, and all the speeches I did were through the Campaign Unit. I have never spoken other than for the council or for the Education Committee, or on the thirty-five-hour week or the minimum wage.'

Kinnock asked him, 'When you discovered that Militant had taken you for granted, were you angry?'

'I'm easy-going. My wife says people take advantage of me, and perhaps they do. My school report says that if I had given more attention to my work I might have been a brain surgeon.' He was hilarious.

At 6.42, by which time he had completely charmed the meeting, we had the final statement. He said, 'I apologise for leaving when I did. It has been a comradely meeting. I hope you believe me. I hope I have satisfied you, and I would like to thank you for the comradely treatment I have received.'

It was quite clear that, with McCluskie, Kitson, Blunkett and Meacher voting in favour, Kinnock would lose. So Kinnock said, 'We've heard the explanation, a very candid reply. Not being disingenuous, I think we should withdraw the charges to prove that we listened carefully.' This was the point – he was anxious to let one person off so he could argue that he had been fair. He knew he would lose, and I think he was quite happy to let Smith off to ensure there was no vote.

By 9.30 pm we had expelled two more members, and acquitted Harry Smith.

Monday 16 June

Went with Tom to Chesterfield Crematorium for Frank Cousins's funeral. Many figures from the labour movement were there – Arthur Scargill, Peter Heathfield, Henry Richardson from the Nottinghamshire area NUM, Michael Foot, Geoffrey Goodman and his wife, Bill Howden from the GMB, Dennis Skinner, and Malc Gee from the AUEW.

But the chapel wasn't full, and the vicar, who knew nothing about Frank Cousins, gave a totally inadequate tribute, another of these sausage-machine funerals that I have attended for so many members of the labour movement. Caroline has always wanted a book of socialist writings from which you could quote – Keir Hardie, Tom Paine, and so on – and then you could sing socialist anthems and hymns.

Nance was absolutely magnificent.

Tuesday 17 June

Campaign Group meeting, and Walter Greendale reported on what had happened in the TGWU, he himself having lost his seat on their executive council in January. Now that the right wing are making Ron Todd's life difficult, he couldn't even get Bill Morris, the Assistant General Secretary, nominated for the TUC General Council. I think we have to accept that the right will probably throw off Margaret Beckett, Eric Clarke and Joan Maynard (who got back in 1983) from the NEC at this year's Party Conference. We have got to face the fact that Kinnock's victory will reach its peak at the Conference and the left on the NEC may be reduced to five.

Tuesday 24 June

Worked at home until 4, when I went to Alan Sapper's office for the monthly left trade union leaders' meeting, with Ken Gill (TASS), Doug Greave of the tobacco workers, Noel Harris in place of Sapper, Ray Alderson (CPSA), Walter Greendale and Rodney Bickerstaffe.

We had a discussion about the Wapping printers, and the general view expressed was that the TUC ought to issue a statement asking unions to respect the picket lines. But Norman Willis has apparently been advised by his lawyers that this would not be possible. So the TUC is just not prepared to take the necessary action to settle the dispute. Ken Gill made the point – which is generally believed – that Murdoch is losing millions of pounds as a result of the action; it's not like the miners' strike, where the Government were prepared to pour in billions to beat the strike.

We also talked about the proposal for a national minimum wage. The TGWU are opposed to it because they think it will open the door to an incomes policy. Rodney argued that they ought to find a way round their misgivings.

Thursday 3 July

At 10, Joe Slovo, Chairman of the South African Communist Party, came to see me. He must be in his mid-fifties and is the first white member of the Executive Committee of the African National Congress. I liked and trusted him immediately.

Slovo went through the history of the Communist Party in South Africa, explaining how it had begun as a Party set up by white Communist immigrants but had become a black party, had adopted black consciousness as early as 1929 and saw itself not as a pressure group trying to capture power in the ANC but as a group trying to work with the churches, the trade unions, and so on.

I asked him about Russia, and he said he thought Stalin and Mao Tse Tung had seriously set back the cause of socialism – a rather harsh judgement.

Slovo told me that Nelson Mandela, who had been a contemporary of his at college, had argued with him strongly that change had to be brought by blacks, but that now the ANC did recognise a role for the whites.

Edward Miliband, Ralph's son, turned up for the first time and was very helpful in the office. He had just taken his O levels and is at a loose end.

New carpet was fitted in the office, and it does look nice.

To the house of Cardinal Hume, Archbishop of Westminster, to collect a letter of introduction to Cardinal Glemp, for my visit to Poland on Monday. I arranged it through Cardinal Hume's chaplain, Father Brown. I had been invited by the Polish Institute of International Affairs to give a lecture and to meet parliamentarians and trade-unionists.

Someone from Polish Solidarity in London came to give me a bit of a briefing. I don't actually want to get involved in the Polish internal situation. I have had a lot of suspicions about Solidarity. Some of its leaders really believe in market forces, the IMF, privatisation, international capital, a free market economy and industrial discipline. There is no question whatever that the Labour Party and the TUC, in supporting Solidarity, are actually supporting Polish Thatcherism. On the other hand, he said there was an element within it that is more social democratic in character, sort of SDP; and the ultra-left here have supported Solidarity because they saw workers' power and the breaking up of the Stalinist state as a benefit of it. I saw an article in *Workers' Hammer*, an American Trotskyite paper, denouncing Solidarity by saying that Lech Walesa wanted Wall Street to run Poland. I must say the two views of Solidarity – from the ultra- left and from Solidarity itself – confirm my view.

The events in Poland during the 1980s were dramatic and followed earlier eruptions of popular opposition to the Communist regime that had occured in the 1950s.

In February 1981 strikes and demonstrations led to the appointment of General Jaruzelski as Prime Minister; later that year the Soviet Communist Party severely denounced Solidarity and in December 1981, after thousands of Solidarity trade unionists had been arrested, Jaruzelski introduced martial law and arrested Lech Walesa, the Catholic leader of Solidarity, and announced the formation of a military council of national salvation.

The following year Solidarity was banned by the Polish Parliament, and it was widely thought that a Soviet invasion might occur comparable to the invasions of Hungary and Czechoslovakia in 1956 and 1968. But it never took place, and Jaruzelski believed he was due the credit for averting that catastrophe by introducing martial law. Walesa was subsequently released and met Pope John Paul II in Poland in June 1983.

The role of the Roman Catholic Church, Polish nationalists and the Solidarity movement, in conflict with the Polish Government, was one of the aspects I wished to explore when I visited Poland.

Monday 7 July
At Warsaw I was met by two officials from the Scientific Secretariat of

the Institute of International Affairs and an interpreter. They took me to a Government hotel, in a batch of buildings where there are a lot of embassies.

Unpacked, and went down to dinner with members of the institute, a charming crowd. I asked what they thought the prospects of a Soviet invasion had been, and they said it was inconceivable that after the experience of Hungary and Czechoslovakia the Soviet Union would have invaded Poland – unless Poland had actually changed sides in the Cold War.

They were keen to stress that democracy was the key question everybody was discussing. They have tribunals to identify 'failures of socialist legitimacy' and so on. I said I thought tribunals were all right but actually democracy was a way of life; it was controversial and it took power away from people at the top, who didn't like it.

My impression is that Poland is much more open now (but probably the economic problems are making them cautious and conservative and managerial), that communism in eastern Europe is moving towards social democracy and there is a sort of convergence – although at the same time, alas, social democracy is moving towards monetarism.

Wednesday 9 July
To the Council of Ministers' office to meet an extremely interesting man, Professor Zdzislaw Sadowski, an Under-Secretary of State, who is an economist. I was shown into his office in this huge building, with long corridors and soldiers downstairs. I spent two hours with him.

Sadowski said, 'The new logic for the system is not meant to be a market economy. We are attempting to construct a new system with a strategic role for central planning and a market system at the lower end, but without any privatisation. The strategic role would be concerned with central decisions, confined primarily to financial matters. As for the market, it would apply to individual firms and in the banking system on a commercial basis. Opening market forces to the pricing system and allowing some element of supply and demand would be advantageous. There would be some direct control – for example, in the field of energy conservation. At the bottom we might have to contemplate the idea of bankruptcy, but we have such clear social objectives that we absolutely prohibit the idea of unemployment at a way of disciplining workers. Our answers to labour discipline must not include the whip of unemployment.

'There might be a change of management in companies – the banks might insist on that or they might insist on a change of workers' management, and new management would be installed from a pool of sort of "company doctors". There are forty cases where that has been done.

'I would like to move more quickly, but we have to take account of social realities and the catastrophic fall in living standards from 1979 to 1982, where total output fell by 25–30 per cent.

'The prices and incomes policy is now the core of the problem. As prices rise, incomes rise, and there is inflation. The question is how to get it down. The trade unions want prices held down, but that would mean subsidies on essentials.'

He analysed what had gone wrong with the Polish economy. 'It worked all right at first, just after the war, but it decayed with what I think of as the "British disease". We had too much social justice at the expense of efficiency.' It was funny to hear a socialist Polish economist talking like Sir Keith Joseph.

I said that it seemed to me that this was a political and not just an economic problem. 'Bourgeois democracy has to discipline workers by means of democratic responsibility: surely that would be a better way.'

'I doubt if democracy is an industrial discipline,' he said. 'The Yugoslav experiment failed. You have to limit the rights of workers under democracy. The workers do have the ability to fire managers, but some workers have used those powers to sack managers who refuse wage increases, and that is quite wrong.'

I left him at 10.40 and went to do some shopping. The shops were a real mess.

I had a message to say that Cardinal Glemp would see me this afternoon. He was due to be away on holiday but had agreed to stay in Warsaw to see me. I was told that priests in Poland were the social aristocrats, with a powerful position in the villages (whereas in Italy, for example, they are poor).

I went with my translator to meet Professor Adam Lopatka, the Minister of Denominational Affairs, who is a lawyer and an expert on the theory of the law and the state. In his office was a high table, laid out with whisky, soft drinks and beautiful china, and low, overstuffed couches – when you were sitting on them only your head appeared above the table!

I told him I was glad to meet him because faith – his territory – was the foundation of all societies.

'Well, we are now discussing in Poland the very survival of the socialist system,' he replied. 'Socialism has survived, and people look to us with hope, but there are very difficult problems. We are not as efficient as we would like to be, but our ideology is too strong for us to see the need for change. We must search for new solutions – in the past we have looked to the Soviet Union to give us a guide, but now I have the impression that the Soviet Union is looking to us to point the way. We must also take account of the bad side of human nature if we are going to make progress.'

This began to sound alarm bells in my mind.

He continued, 'Some of our policies are designed for angels, but people aren't angels, and some people take advantage of the system. In the past we have had no unemployment, but we can't force people to work – there is no industrial discipline, there are no bankruptcies, inefficient firms are subsidised, and social justice has meant too much equality.'

He suggested that the Catholic Church encouraged this attitude. 'The church says that everyone has an equal soul and everyone has the same stomach, and therefore the teaching of the Catholic Church is actually in favour of "equality".'

I was surprised to hear this, but he said, 'Don't forget the parable of the talents. The man who worked all day got the same reward as the man who started in the afternoon and the man who only worked at the end of the day.'

Lopatka continued, 'I have good relations with the church, and funnily enough, when you talk to the bishops privately, they will agree on the need for change, but publicly they will oppose our reforms because they think they are unpopular. We are against privatisation. Don't misunderstand what we are doing.'

I wanted to ask about the attitude of the church towards martial law, so I said, 'Would I be right in supposing that, when the Pope met General Jaruzelski, they spoke to each other as Polish patriots? Jaruzelski said, "You may not like what I have done but I have kept the Russians out", and the Pope answered, "My son, I fully understand that, and I am reasonably happy with what you have done", then Jaruzelski said, "You could help me by quietening down Walesa a bit", and the Pope replied, "Leave it to me." '

He laughed. 'Well, you have used your imagination a bit, but I think that's roughly what must have happened.'

As I left he said, 'You should be doing my job.' I told him it was the most interesting job in Poland.

I came back to the hotel, shaved, and put on a white shirt and a smart suit to see Cardinal Glemp. We arrived at the Primate's Palace and walked through a long garden. The door was opened by an immensely tall and handsome young priest who was obviously the Primate's chaplain. He looked at Bozena, my interpreter, held out his hand and pointed with his finger at his watch – because we were one minute and a few seconds late, and I suppose you don't keep cardinals waiting, but he did it in a jovial sort of 'naughty-naughty' way.

We were shown into a room which had a throne at one end and oil paintings of all the previous primates of Poland hanging on the walls. Through another door came Cardinal Josef Glemp, a short man of about fifty-five, not a grey hair on his head, wearing a red cardinal's cap and a black cassock with a pectoral cross over it; he was rather expressionless. He beckoned us to sit at the table, and then sat at the other end, facing the throne. He had big ears that stuck out and a rather cunning expression. I got to like him more as the discussion progressed, but to begin with I was apprehensive of him because the Primate of Poland is a powerful man, and to establish a relationship of equality for the purpose of discussion was going to be difficult.

I thanked him very much indeed for seeing me. Then I said that Basil Hume was very popular in Britain, a modest man who had great influence. I mentioned the Pope's visit to Britain and his meeting with Archbishop Runcie at Canterbury Cathedral.

Glemp said, 'Basil Hume is a good man. I have asked Archbishop Runcie to come to Poland, but he can't come, so he is sending one of his senior officials or bishops.'

I told him I would be grateful if he could give me his assessment of the situation in Poland.

'Well,' said Glemp, with a slight glint in his eye, 'of course, I can only comment on church matters, but there is a very serious conflict between Christianity and communism. The church is concerned with morality, and a serious demoralisation has occurred in Poland. When the communists took over private property and made it collective, it was simply a utilitarian policy, and I am afraid there is no feeling of conscience by the public about common property. The church must be able to help the community decide what is good and what is evil.'

That was what Lopatka had said about policies designed for angels.

'I am afraid there are deep-rooted evils in Polish society caused in part by partition, in part by the occupation, and the most serious evil is alcoholism. The alcohol industry produces the greatest profits, and this is one reason why it continues to exist. We need to produce less alcohol in Poland.

'Then we come to the question of family morality. The communist philosophy and western values are undermining young people. Women are working as men do, but at lower wages. The divorce rate is rising and there is lower morality in Poland. Those are the church's concerns in the area of public affairs.'

I mentioned that, as he would be well aware, the standard of morality in the west was pretty low; there was drunkenness and drugs and pornography and vice and competitiveness.

'That is true,' he said, 'but the Communist Party defends collective values, and we also have to have regard for individual rights. Actually, the Communist Party is only against drugs because it wants people to be subservient, and if people are on drugs they can't be made subservient.'

So I told him I thought that because drugs removed people from situations of conflict, and neutralised them, some regimes actually encouraged drugs because they produced a quiescent population.

He said, 'I think the Communist Party is afraid that drugs will mean that young people won't listen to what the Ministers say.'

I turned the subject to liberation theology. In Latin America, for example, it appeared that there was a unity between socialists and Christians on the basis of social justice. What did he think about that?

'Of course, we have liberation theology in Poland too but it is different. In Latin America, the basis of it is social injustice, and the Communist Party wants to take advantage of social injustice to manipulate it for its own ends. This is designed to separate the faithful from the bishops. The theology of liberation in Poland is quite different because the church does not want the priests to be active in Solidarity.'

I asked, 'Have you possibly been using Solidarity to undermine the faith of the people of Poland in their Government, in the same way as you say the guerrilla leaders in Latin America have used liberation theology to undermine the faith of the people in their bishops?'

He misunderstood me, and said, 'Oh no, nothing could undermine the faith of the Polish people in their bishops,'

I said, 'No, no, have you used Solidarity to undermine the people's faith in their *Government*?'

He said, 'Oh no, there is no intention of using Solidarity to undermine confidence in the Government. We have only supported it as a trade union. That is the only circumstance under which the church would support Solidarity. We never supported it as a political party, and we have not used it to defeat the Government. But I must admit that the impact of Solidarity has brought some changes and some better prospects which the Party appreciates and which have led it to change many of its policies and personalities. The ideas of Solidarity have won support from the people, but Solidarity itself is political and anti-communist.'

This is exactly what people have been saying to me over the last few days.

I asked him, 'How many political prisoners are there now?'

He replied, 'About 220, and the church cares for them. Many of them have not been involved in anything really. They might distribute a leaflet and find themselves in prison.'

I said, 'Can I now turn the subject to the bomb, because there are formidable moral questions in the use of nuclear weapons, and I would like to ask you whether you think Gorbachev is sincere, what future for Europe you see, and what the church's role is in dealing with the threat of nuclear war?'

He answered, 'Rearmament is a political game. It is a crime against humanity to build nuclear weapons. I think Gorbachev is perfectly sincere in wanting peace, because the Soviet Union needs to divert resources from weapons of war, which are very expensive, and use skilled labour. But what can the church do? I know the French and the German bishops have issued a statement, and the bishops have presented papers, but I don't think we know what to do.'

So I commented, 'I suppose, Your Eminence, you could say publicly what you have said to me, which I think is very important, particularly in your assessment of Gorbachev.'

Then he made the most important remark of the whole interview. 'If I did this, it would create difficulties for the church, because Radio Free Europe and Voice of America and the BBC are violently anti-Soviet, and the Polish people listen to these broadcasts. They shape Polish opinion, and if I were to say publicly what I have said to you it would create tension in Poland. Poles would say to me, "You are pro-communist", and so, perhaps, would Radio Free Europe, the BBC and the Voice of America. I am accused of being pro-communist anyway.'

'Well, that indicates the power of the media.'

He sort of nodded rather wryly, and it was amazing that the Catholic Church recognises that the media are more powerful than it is in getting the message across.

'At least you could argue that through martial law Jaruzelski had preserved Polish independence from the Russians, because I presume that if things had gone wrong the Russians might have intervened.'

'Ah,' said Glemp, 'on 13 December 1981 the church remained absolutely quiet on the question of martial law, and if I had spoken, and had called the people out against it, the Soviet troops, who were on the border, would have come in.'

Then I asked him, 'Can I explore with you the question of your dialogue with the Government?'

He said, 'Communist Governments treat the church differently in each country – Hungary, Czechoslovakia and Yugoslavia. I have no illusions: communism wants the church to become subservient.'

I said, 'Are you saying that there is a permanent holy war between Catholicism and communism?'

'Well, there is a conflict between the idea of collectivism and individualism, and we may find some form of reconciliation.'

I put it to him that, just as Marx was entirely innocent of what happened under Stalin, you could not blame Jesus for what happened at the time of the Spanish Inquisition. You could also argue that socialism was a faith but that communist parties were institutions, like the church, in relation to belief. 'These are factors that you might take into account.'

He agreed with me on a number of things but not on this one. 'Is socialism a religion? No, it isn't because the Soviet bloc leaders do not actually believe in socialism, they just use ideology as a way to achieve personal power.'

Of course, that is an argument that Marxists have used against the churches for years! They have said the church leaders don't believe in God but they use their faith and the faith of the faithful to get themselves power.

I said, 'There have been occasions, I suppose, in the long history of the church, over the past 2000 years, when the church has been concerned with power. I suppose you could compare Martin Luther with Solidarity – Martin Luther identified certain weaknesses in the church and challenged it, and as a result, the church modified its position.'

He thought it was an interesting argument.

I had been there for about an hour and a half, so I thought it was my duty to bring the discussion to a conclusion. I thanked him very much, and said, 'I must tell you that the people I have met in Poland, the Ministers and the officials, seem to me to be good people. You may disagree with what they are trying to do, but they seem to me to be sincere people who are trying to do their best.'

He gave me rather a warm smile.

Lopatka and he were much of a muchness in a way – sincere, thoughtful people who were interested in power, were Polish patriots, had the same view of Poland and wanted to develop society.

I thanked him again and I bowed, and Bozena bowed, and as we left we could see the tall chaplain in the side chamber. We walked back through the gardens to the main gates.

Went back to the Embassy for dinner at 8. The Ambassador, Brian Barder, and his wife were the hosts, and there were a number of Polish guests including the Minister of Foreign Affairs, Mr Olechowski, and his wife. There was a slight moment of embarrassment when I had to tell Mrs Barder that I was a vegetarian, but I said I would just have the vegetables, which was fine.

After dinner the Ambassador got up and made a little speech, and said, 'We are happy to have with us a distinguished parliamentarian who has had many years of service, a very interesting figure in British politics', and so on – which was very flattering of him.

The Ambassador had asked me if I would reply, so I did, and ended by saying, 'The great thing about being beyond ministerial office is that you are free to think, speak and say what you believe. I have had the most marvellous discussions in Poland, and I believe that out of Poland will come something important. Indeed, if I am not breaking a confidence, I saw Minister Lopatka today, and he said that in the old days the Poles looked to the Russians for advice, and now the Russians were looking to Poland for advice. I am sure they will get good advice, and I wish you success in the work you are doing.' I must say it did go down very well.

Olechowski took me aside later and said, 'Minister,' (as a courtesy) 'what do you really think the prospect is for relations between the regime and the Catholic Church? One of my political tasks is to improve relations with the Vatican.'

So I told him about my talk with Glemp, and I asked him a question, as a friend. 'Why do you find it necessary to jail the members of Solidarity? It does you enormous damage worldwide, quite out of all proportion to the good that it can do you at home. If Solidarity are no longer a threat, what is the purpose of doing it?'

'I agree with you, and in a week there will be an amnesty. But we fear that they might exploit difficulties, of which there are many in Poland – for example, when meat prices go up.'

I said, 'Prison is a very high price to pay.'

'I agree.'

The guests all left at about 11, and I sat down with the Ambassador and his staff for a while; it's always rather fun to talk to the diplomats and get a debrief on the evening.

Thursday 10 July

This morning at 7.30, Janus Onyszkiewicz, the Solidarity spokesman in Warsaw, came to see me. He is in his early forties, a professor of mathematics at Warsaw University. I asked him first how many people were in prison.

'There are 300, and most are in prison for publishing illegal journals or for offences that have been created by the state to suppress the opposition. There are 700 underground papers in Poland, and a number of books are published – some with a circulation of 20,000. At the end of June, just before the Party Congress, there was a flurry of activity against Solidarity, with the Ministry of the Interior saying that Solidarity people were traitors and saboteurs. Solidarity is a trade union and is a movement. The question it asks is "Can this system be reformed from the inside?", and the answer is no, it must be challenged.'

He was a nice, decent, innocent man, a Fabian type who, I think, had probably been drawn into Solidarity after years of bureaucratic inactivity.

To the Institute of International Affairs at 10.30 – a funny little sixties building in a side street, with red-plush carpets and seats, but rather rundown and seedy.

The lecture room was packed, with eighty people sitting at tables, including the Ambassador and his wife. I did wonder whether my lecture would be out of date, because I had written it before I arrived.

Afterwards I was asked what was the British Labour Party's attitude to German reunification and the Oder-Neisse Line. I said I didn't think it was going to be much of an issue, because nobody thought you could interfere with the frontier. The questions were respectful but direct, and I felt entirely free to answer them.

It was an interesting morning, but when you are talking to people whose English is not that good it takes a long time for any little jokes to filter through.

At 7 in the evening there was a farewell dinner in a private room of the hotel, with the Deputy Speaker, the Director of the Polish Institute and a couple of other Poles. It was an extremely jolly evening, with some political discussion but mainly endless jokes.

They told one funny story about a German dog that came over the border to Poland one night, and said, 'Oh, the bones in Germany are delicious. They are the best dog bones in the world!' The dog came back the next night and said to the Polish dogs, 'You sleep in the garden, but in Germany we have blankets – luxury!' The dog came night after night, so eventually the Polish dogs asked him, 'Why don't you stay in Germany?' 'Ah,' he replied, 'you are not allowed to bark in Germany.' They did make fun of the Germans.

Friday 11 July
Up at 5 and left for the airport.

Wednesday 23 July
Kevin Morgan, who is working on a book on Post Office policy in the sixties, came in today. He is the first person to have read all of my diary for 1964–6 the period when I was Postmaster-General.

He has also interviewed Sir Peter Carey, who was Second Permanent Secretary of the Department of Industry in 1974. Peter Carey had told him that when Harold Wilson became Prime Minister in 1974 he decided to split the Department of Trade and Industry, Trade going to Peter Shore and Industry to me, to prevent me from being the head of one powerful industrial department. Peter Carey himself thought it was a mistake to divide the DTI. Kevin Morgan had expressed his surprise to Carey, who said, 'There is no question about it – Wilson gave instructions that the Department was to be split in order to prevent Mr Benn taking over.'

That is interesting, because when I had a telephone call, just after the Government was announced, I was told in effect to go back to my old office in the Ministry of Technology on Millbank. I refused to do that, because I know very well that where a Minister sits is important, so I turned up at the DTI building in Victoria Street and took over the office of the former Secretary of State, Peter Walker, and Peter Shore was moved next door.

Today was a royal wedding, and the media have gone mad about it. You've got to have one symbolic family, I suppose, but the thought of people coming up and camping on the pavements for two days and wearing paper Union Jack hats in order to get a glimpse of Prince Andrew and Sarah Ferguson I found quite incredible.

Friday 29 August
Said goodbye to Edward Miliband, who has been working here for six

weeks. He's a very bright young man who got eight A grades in his O levels.

Saturday 6 September

To the Wapping picket line – the first time since 3 May, when there was all the trouble. Frances Morrell was there, and it was rather embarrassing after the unhappy lunch at County Hall in June last year.

A march had been organised by the NUJ, and we walked slowly with the chief marshal, Mike Hicks, who had been expelled from the CP by the *Marxism Today* clique. The event had a slightly folk festival atmosphere about it. Over the loudspeaker he was making jokes about the 'boys in blue' and so on – which I can't say I liked much. There were a lot of police about, blocking off all the side roads, and behind the entrance were the mounted police, a most threatening sight. The marchers sang songs like 'If you think Murdoch's a shitbag, raise your hand' or something, which I didn't particularly care for. The thing seemed to lack any anger, and marching slowly is a sign of hesitancy and weakness. The negotiations begin tomorrow, and I was told there would probably be a settlement, a few people would be taken back by Murdoch, but he would insist on a no-arbitration agreement. If there was a ballot, they would probably accept it, and it would be presented as a victory for Murdoch.

When we got to Wapping, to my surprise we were allowed to gather right outside the works. I was the first to address the crowd and was presented with a 'Wapping Veteran' badge – a great honour. Frances Morrell spoke, and said that the ILEA had decided to stop advertising ILEA posts in *The Times Education Supplement*.

The evening wasn't at all frightening compared to 3 May, but it was impossible not to think that if only Kinnock and Willis were there every night, and if the PLP came out in force, it would make a real difference.

Labour Party Conference, Blackpool
Sunday 28 September

Very little in the press about the Conference. Apparently Caspar Weinberger, US Secretary of Defense, is expected to say that if a Kinnock Government removed American bases then America would withdraw from NATO – which greatly helps us with our Campaign Group pamphlet *Peace Through Non-Alignment*, being launched today.

NEC at 9 at the Imperial Hotel. There was a proposal for the creation of a ministry for women, with a Cabinet post in the next Labour Government. We had discussed this at last Wednesday's NEC, and Kinnock had refused. He wouldn't budge. Audrey and Jo were weak, but I pushed very hard: ' "Women's rights but not now" is what the Church of England has been saying since the 1920s.' Meacher and Blunkett voted against, and it was defeated by 19 to 8.

At 10.30 Eric, Jeremy, Ben Lowe and I went to the launching of *Peace Through Non-Alignment: The Case for British Withdrawal from NATO*. Only Nigel Williamson and Phil Kelly from *Tribune*, Mike Ambrose from the *Morning Star*, Robert Taylor from the *Observer* and Chris Moncrieff of the Press Association turned up.

Caroline and I went to the conference centre, where the security was unbelievable. We were body-searched, and the stewards wouldn't allow you through a particular door if you hadn't got the right sort of card. Then there were all the exhibitors in the reception area – BNFL, British Airways, and so on. The whole thing was awful, and com-mercialised.

Monday 29 September
Went to the Conference for the private session at which the seven members of Liverpool District Labour Party who have been expelled by the NEC were to be allowed to address the delegates before a vote was taken to endorse the NEC. But none of the Militant people turned up to take the rostrum. It is a terrible tactical error on their part; it shows contempt for the Conference and isolates them from the delegates.

During the day a broadcasting unit came up, and someone asked me to comment on the decision by the Party to adopt the red rose. But on the nuclear power debate, which I know more about than a great many people here and in the Soviet Union, I haven't been asked to comment once.

Dashed to the Labour Action for Peace meeting, at which Joan Ruddock declared she was in favour of all US bases being withdrawn – which is good.

In effect the Conference is an eve-of-poll rally: everybody wants to win the Election, and everything else must take second place. The Leader can do what he likes, say what he likes. That is the spirit of this year's Conference.

Tuesday 30 September
The National Executive election results were announced, and Eric Heffer and Margaret Beckett were knocked off. I was 9000 votes below David Blunkett, who was top. Eric was extremely upset and said he was thinking of leaving the Party, but he does take things personally; I daresay I do too.

I got called to wind up the debate on legal reform, the resolution being moved by the Society of Labour Lawyers. It did go down very well, and I got a long ovation from the whole Conference. I was a bit embarrassed in a way.

After lunch I went back in for Neil Kinnock's speech, which lasted interminably, and I had my usual annual agonies on whether to join in the standing ovation at the end. But I came to the conclusion that it was part of the eve-of-election game you had to play. The high point was when he said, 'I would be prepared to die for my country but I don't want my country to die for me' – the most crude demagoguery, which will satisfy people that he is in favour of defence, but I thought it poor stuff. The standing ovation lasted for six minutes; Glenys was brought down from the balcony and he kissed her and waved, and then she went back. The whole thing was like a Nuremberg rally, phoney to a degree.

Looking back on today, I feel that, since Militant have evacuated the field and the cuddly left have abandoned the fight because they have had no influence whatever on Kinnock, he himself now only wants us as a fan club.

Thursday 2 October
Arkardy Maslennikov, the *Pravda* correspondent, asked for an interview, and in the course of it, on to his tape recording, I said, 'I hope Mr Gorbachev is aware of the fact that he could accidentally be promoting Mrs Thatcher's Election chances by being too friendly to her in Moscow.' He said, 'I won't use that in the interview, but I guarantee that it gets through to Mr Gorbachev.'

In the defence debate about 1.5 million voted for the resolution to get rid of the US bases, 1.3 million for leaving NATO. Neither resolution was carried, but it was not a bad vote.

Friday 3 October
Eric Heffer made his farewell speech from the platform and got a tremendous reception. Poor Eric has taken it all very personally. You can see in others what happens to yourself.

Dennis Skinner made a speech on behalf of the NEC on shipbuilding. We had gone over the ground together, and I had suggested he mention the red duster, the ensign of the British merchant marine fleet, which has now shrunk to practically nothing – that is, the red duster is disappearing from the world's shipping lanes as the red flag is from the Labour Party. I stood away from the platform, watching Dennis, and he was superb. Everyone was standing around the television sets applauding and laughing, because Dennis is very, very bright and funny.

The finale of Conference is always a bit of an anticlimax. Eric had heard from the organist that she had been told the Conference was not singing 'The Red Flag', but there had been such a row about it that it was agreed that she would play it after all. As the pale pink rose is now the symbol of the Labour Party, I wrote an alternative version of 'The Red Flag' to take account of it:

The people's rose in shades of pinks
Gets up my nostrils and it stinks,
But ere our limbs grow stiff and cold
Our old Red Flag we shall unfold.
With heads uncovered swear we all
To let rose petals fade and fall.
Though moderates flinch and media sneer
We'll keep the Red Flag flying here.

At the end, believe it or not, Neil and Glenys threw a whole mass of red roses at the delegates from the platform. It was a disgusting spectacle, and I simply couldn't stand it, so I rushed out before the crowd left and caught the train to London.

NOTES
Chapter Seven

1. (p. 406) The so-called supergrass trials in Northern Ireland were held without juries, the verdict being given by a single judge sitting alone in 'Diplock' courts. Informers from both nationalist and loyalist organisations would give uncorroborated evidence against individuals supposedly involved in paramilitary activity, in return for police protection and immunity from prosecution and sometimes cash.

Many defendants charged as a result of supergrass evidence were subsequently acquitted.

2. (p. 427) The Anglo-Irish Agreement of 1985 reaffirmed the Protestant veto on a united Ireland but also set up an Intergovernmental Conference at which the two Governments would consider 'on a regular basis' Northern Ireland issues.

The Agreement was opposed by the Unionist parties in Northern Ireland, by Sinn Fein, Fianna Fail and by the left of the Labour Party. But it was also opposed by some Conservative MPs on the right, including Margaret Thatcher's former PPS, Ian Gow, who resigned as a Minister in protest. Gow was killed five years later in 1990 by an IRA bomb.

8
The State within a State
October 1986–June 1987

Friday 10 October
Kinnock is now a charismatic figure, but the Labour lead is still sagging and the whole defence argument is going by default. Labour is not asking the real questions, ie is there a Soviet threat, and can we help to reduce the burden of arms? The Party is simply saying it would be better if Britain had conventional weapons only. This is just not credible, whereas the prospects for a summit meeting beginning with the talks between Reagan and Gorbachev in Iceland this weekend could actually provide the Government and Mrs Thatcher with the role of peace-makers.

Did a tragic surgery, almost entirely about housing – young homeless who are unable to get board and lodging allowances and are sleeping rough; a woman whose house is full of mice and rats; an elderly couple who couldn't get proper accommodation and who burst into tears.

'But we won't fire him until after we're safely parked in Downing Street . . .'

Today the Trustee Savings Bank was put on the market and £1 billion was made in speculative profit. We live in an absolutely brutal society.

Monday 13 October
Caroline's sixtieth birthday.

The Reykjavik summit has broken down because Reagan would not give up Star Wars in return for the Soviet Union's proposals for the most comprehensive disarmament ever. Reagan couldn't give it up because he has put his own reputation at stake. The Republicans would eat him alive if he abandoned Star Wars before the mid-term elections so it is now explicit that Reagan is the obstacle to world disarmament. The non-aligned movement should really begin to get under way now.

Thursday 16 October
Went to the Home Office with a group for a meeting with Lord Caithness, the new Parliamentary Under-Secretary of State. We were hoping to persuade him to grant parole for the jailed miner, Terry French. Dennis Skinner, Terry's wife Liz, Malcolm Pitt (the acting president of the Kent NUM) and I went up to the Minister's office. He had four civil servants with him.

Dennis began with a tough statement which I thought was a bit provocative. He said this was a political case, the strike had been politically stimulated, the miners had been fighting for their jobs, and it was time the Tory Government faced the fact that these people were being unfairly punished compared to the police.

Caithness sat there with his mouth open, looking pained and puzzled, which is the way these young aristocrats respond to a reality that they don't like.

Malcolm Pitt took a much softer approach, saying there was a need for reconciliation and he thought this was the right time to start it.

I made the point that there were different perceptions of what happened during the strike. The Police Complaints Board recognised that in Mansfield the police had acted improperly in attacking miners but said they couldn't identify individuals. The strike was over, there was no necessity to keep Terry in prison, and there were no grounds for the refusal of parole. I asked him to consider the fact that when he was first charged there was a hung jury, and later, months after the charge, thirteen policemen who had claimed to have heard Terry French shout on the picket line were brought in. I went through a number of other grounds for acting leniently.

Then Liz spoke. 'Terry is studying and hopes to go on to university. He has shingles and arthritis. He was at Ford open prison, was given home leave, and then was sent to Wandsworth on his return and locked up for twenty-three hours a day. His health is poor, and he has been unfairly treated.'

Lord Caithness replied, 'This is not a political case; it is not about the strike. He was sentenced by the court. The reason he was moved was because there was disquiet in Ford prison.'

He admitted that French had originally been made category B, the second most dangerous category, and that prison officers had changed his designation to category D, the least dangerous category, but that after his home leave he had been shifted back to category C. So he had actually been punished for no apparent reason. There were no disciplinary charges.

Caithness said, 'The chemistry was wrong at Ford open prison, and there had been some talk of intimidation and threats.' He went on and on with all these arguments, so I asked when it had been decided to remove him from Ford, and he said, 'It was just overcrowded.' So I asked again when it was decided and he said, 'The day he moved.'

I argued that it must have been a political decision. There was a long debate about what 'political' meant, so I asked, 'Does the Home Secretary have the right to prevent parole?' Caithness said he did, and I asked, 'In the spring, when we had reason to believe that he had been recommended for parole, why was he denied it?'

Caithness replied, 'I can't tell you that.'

I said, 'If a Ministry takes a decision, it is political – that is what politics is about. You're responsible to Parliament for the decisions you take. If you decide not to tell us why you take them, that's a matter for you, but don't tell us the decisions aren't political.'

At the end, Dennis, having started tough, tried a softer approach, saying, 'Look, you've got a chance to appear liberal and good, and the Election is coming.'

I added, 'We know it will be difficult for you because the *Sun* will attack you for letting this "thug" out.'

Caithness said, 'That won't be a factor in any way.'

The interesting thing was, his officials didn't help him but let him flounder, while they listened carefully to our argument. It is so embarrassing and humiliating for miners who dig the coal to have to plead with an inherited peer. But it was worthwhile; they wrote down everything we said, so these arguments will be before him when he takes a view, though the decision will be taken by the Home Secretary and probably by the Prime Minister.

In Chesterfield, Peter Heathfield showed me an extract from Hansard for February 1972 in which Neil Kinnock, answering Conservative accusations of picket-line violence during the 1972 miners' strike, had said, 'What would be the instinct of any red-blooded man in this House, having put his family to all that inconvenience and near misery, if he saw someone riding roughshod over his picket line? I know what my attitude would be. In fact, I should be worried if it were not the case.'

Monday 27 October

Another horrible all-day meeting of the NEC to consider again the charges against Felicity Dowling.

Tam Dalyell was there, having been elected on to the NEC this year because of his campaigns on the Falklands and the Westland affair. Tam is very courageous and principled. He is fair-minded in a public-school sort of way.

At 11.30, I moved that the charges against Felicity be dropped. I said that we were meeting on the day the Japanese and American banks had taken over the City of London in the so-called 'Big Bang', and here we were meeting to expel one individual. I thought it was the most destructive and divisive NEC in my lifetime, and it could cost us the Election.

Kinnock said, 'Why are we doing it? We are doing it because Conference decided we should, and it is our fundamental duty.'

Anyway, my motion was defeated by 12 to 5; Tam Dalyell, Michael Meacher and Blunkett voted against.

At 12.15 Felicity Dowling came in, and Whitty read out the charge of membership of the Militant Tendency, which was based on three things – her name on a *Militant* leaflet, an article by her in the *Mersey Militant* and her attendance at a *Militant* readers' meeting.

Felicity must have spoken for two hours about her work in the Labour Party, and a very impressive woman she is – about thirty-six, competent, tough and determined.

We adjourned for lunch, after which the questioning began.

At 4.30 Felicity made her final statement and said, 'I have worked to the best of my ability. I shall not go away if you expel me. I shall use my campaigning talents to get rid of the Tories.'

She left, and she could not have given a better defence. I thought the NEC came out of it disgracefully.

Neil said she was obviously a hard-working person with little money, but that wasn't relevant. 'It is a secret organisation. She is a member of Militant, she is a vanguardist, and this is not a vote of confidence in the Leader but support for the constitution.'

Listening to the argument and reflecting on it, I think that Felicity Dowling's telephone must have been regularly tapped by Special Branch or MI5, which then informed the Party as to whom she telephoned; that is why Walworth Road is absolutely confident that she is a member of Militant.

On a recorded vote, 11 were for expulsion and 7 against, with Dalyell and Meacher voting with us. It was horrible; the judgement of history will be that these little pygmies expelled people of real substance.

Saturday 1 November

Chesterfield. Peter Heathfield drove me over to the NUM offices in

Sheffield for a meeting with Arthur Scargill. Peter is an old friend, a really nice guy, and he's been extremely supportive to me. He said the court case against him, Mick McGahey and Arthur, which is coming up in the spring, could cost £7 million; whatever the verdict the NUM will have to pay court costs, and this will bankrupt them. Peter thinks that is the intention. He has little to lose personally, just his furniture because the house belongs to the NUM, but he thinks the Tories might pass legislation that a bankrupt is not suitable to be the general secretary or president of a trade union. In that case they would all lose their positions in the NUM.

Arthur was in his office and he made me a cup of tea. I had gone to persuade him to put his name forward for the candidature of the Barnsley Central seat. He said he had considered it seriously but he felt it wasn't right.

I argued with him. 'I know that to be an MP compared to being president of a union is demotion, but don't forget that we may be reaching a period when we have got to think in terms of big political change and the rebuilding of the Party from the inside. Your presence in the House of Commons, particularly if you remain President of the NUM, would be highly significant.' But he's not keen.

Caught the train back. I went out to collect a suit from the dry cleaner's and locked myself out of the house in the pouring rain. So I went to the movies in Notting Hill and saw *Mona Lisa*.

When you're out in the streets in London you see so many tramps and down-and-outs now, men and women; it's really grim. That's urban life in London in 1986.

Tuesday 4 November
Caught the train to Chesterfield, and a ticket collector came up, a man of about thirty-four, and asked if I was Tony Benn. When I said yes, he asked if I had been involved in the miners' strike.

I said I used to go on the picket line, and he said, 'Did you know the army was used, dressed in police uniform?'

I told him we suspected it but were never able to prove it.

He said, 'I know, because I was in the army until last year, and during the miners' strike I was at Catterick Camp and we were regularly put into police uniforms and sent on to the picket lines. We didn't like it particularly.'

I asked him how many men.

He replied, 'At Nottingham, of the sixty-four policemen in our group, sixty-one were soldiers and only three were regular policemen – an inspector, a sergeant and one bobby. We didn't wear any numbers, didn't get paid overtime as the police did, and were told not to make any arrests because the police would do all that.' He said the soldiers used were from the Military Police, the SAS and the Green Jackets. He himself had been a military policeman. 'I shouldn't really be saying all this because of the Official Secrets Act.'

Then he added, 'Surely you could tell us because of the way we marched, and we had short hair. We were obviously the army. The police knew we were soldiers. Of course, you realise the army are now being used for civil defence.'

I told him he should write it all down before he forgot it.

He said, 'There's the Official Secrets Act, and I would deny I ever said it if you told anyone. But we must get rid of Thatcher.'

Wednesday 19 November

In the *Financial Times* this morning Mrs Thatcher was reported as saying that two more terms of office would exterminate socialism. I saw Clare Short, who asked if I had seen it, and I replied, 'Yes, but I think she'll have a job to outdo Kinnock.'

'Don't be so depressed,' she said.

'I'm not, I'm just being realistic.'

Thursday 20 November

Duncan Chalmers from the Public Record Office came to see the archives at my invitation. He is a grey-haired man in his fifties, and of course his main interest is in the preservation of Government records. He asked about papers in connection with my Government posts, and asked to look into one of my private boxes for 1976 which was crammed with Government papers of one kind or another – nothing secret, but quite a number of important documents. I thought: He's just going to report us and we'll have MI5 coming to clear out my papers.

Then Chalmers said, 'I hope you are not going to let anyone have access to this while the Thirty-Year Rule applies.'

So I said, 'No, the only things I am allowing access to, under strict control, are purely personal or political papers.'

But it was an error, and we have got to be careful. On the other hand, the fact that I had contacted the Public Record Office and in effect offered them my archives is in my favour.

One tiny point that gave me great pleasure was that he noticed that in one box I had some old recordings on wire and asked if I had a wire recorder. He explained, 'We have one wire recording in the Public Record Office, which is the interrogation of the German Field Marshal Erich von Manstein in 1945 by Allied intelligence officers, but we can't play it back.'

So I showed him my machine, which probably hadn't been out of its box for twenty years, and plugged it in. It churned and ground and the light flashed, and, blow me down, I was able to play something. He was staggered. I hoped that would soften his heart towards my papers.

Monday 24 November

TUC-Labour Party Liaison Committee, and I arrived so early that I found myself having a chat with Gerald Kaufman. I said, 'Gerald, I have been looking at some old home movies I took of you at Chequers in 1966 or 1967 with Judith Hart, Harold Wilson and Marcia Williams.'

I reminded him of the time Harold had first offered him a job at Number 10 and he asked my advice as to whether to take it.

During the committee meeting, Norman Willis raised the issue of preparations for the General Election and beyond, and Brenda Dean, the General Secretary of SOGAT 82, said, 'We have got to change the climate of public opinion. Although I am not a feminist in any way, the male dominance in the new Party image is most unattractive. Thatcher is taking a lot of decisions and holding meetings intended to help women, but the recent party political broadcast showing Neil Kinnock and all the men and the red rose was most unsatisfactory.'

John Edmonds of the GMB supported her. 'I can only say that, when our women's committee met, their hostility towards the Party publicity material really had to be heard to be believed. They must be taken seriously.'

Ron Todd confirmed that view.

I argued that the Liaison Committee ought to be used as a platform to get across views wider than the purely economic and political.

Neil answered the criticism, saying, 'We must exercise patience. Future promotions will take account of the points. We do need to set up an anticipatory assessment on the legacy and the hidden agenda and pull it together. Secondly, I agree with Tony, and we ought to have seminars – perhaps led by trade union leaders – on education, investment, science, women, working life, the trade position, social and public services and local government.' I could hardly believe my ears.

Gerald Kaufman then said, 'Tony is right. This committee can be a platform, and we should use it to make preparations. We have only two women on this committee, and the only black person who attends is the woman who brings in the coffee. It is a serious problem; there is a black employment crisis, and the black community, particularly the un-employed black youth, constitutes an unexploded time-bomb in our society. The unions are crucial: if black quotas were introduced into work in the public sector, you would find they were held back by reactionary members of the trade unions. So I hope we can use this committee.'

Later we came on to 'A Modern Britain in a Modern World', this absolutely crummy defence campaign document which we are launching on 10 December, when Neil returns from a trip to America.

John Evans suggested Neil send a note to MPs telling them not to knock our defence policies. 'I think the view of people like Austin Mitchell, who has recently written an article on defence, is quite outdated. In CND, Bruce Kent, Dan Smith and Joan Ruddock see that the main objective is to rid us of nuclear weapons and to recognise that we must remain in NATO. Other views on nuclear weapons are not really significant. We want a strong consensus around an anti-nuclear policy.'

Tuesday 25 November
The *Spycatcher* trial goes on, and it turns out that Victor Rothschild, whom I knew very well and who ran the Think Tank under Heath and Wilson, was a former MI5 man who brought Peter Wright to Britain at his own expense in 1980. Victor Rothschild was thereby supporting Peter Wright's argument that Sir Roger Hollis, the former head of MI5, was a Soviet spy.

Thursday 27 November
Sat through Prime Minister's Questions, listening to the Prime Minister trying to cope with the rising crisis in Australia; Sir Robert Armstrong has been sent there to stop the publication of *Spycatcher* but he will fail.

Went to the PLP meeting, and next week's business was announced; it included Wednesday's debate on the security services, called by the SDP. I chipped in to say I thought it was all very well making Thatcher look a fool, and having a lot of fun over Lord Rothschild and the 'fifth man', but the really important issue was that the security services were out of control. People thought Harold Wilson was paranoid when he claimed he was bugged, but he *was* bugged, and burgled; of course, Wilson himself had tapped trade-unionists' phones during the National Union of Seamen's strike in 1966. I said we really did have to establish some principle of accountability through Parliament, a proper statute governing the security services' conduct. It was the first time I've spoken at a PLP meeting for some time.

Friday 28 November
Two people from the British Library came to look at the archives – Sarah Tyacke, who is the Director of Special Collections, and Michael Borrie, who is in charge of manuscripts. The British Library is one of the three great libraries in the world, the others being the Vatican Library and the Bibliothèque Nationale in France; they have manuscripts dating back 1300 years, and their collection includes most Prime Ministers' papers.

They were thrilled by what they saw. Michael Borrie was bubbling over, and he quoted Professor Namier, that 'you can't understand history unless you know what was on the politician's breakfast table'.

Sarah said, 'If you want a job as an archivist, get in touch with us.'

It was such a pleasure, and I just felt like someone who had a precious painting and was showing it to another collector. They seem the best library for my archives because they are in central London, are committed to access and, being a British national institution, are more likely to survive for ever.

Wednesday 3 December

Went in for the Supply Day debate on the security services, opened most inadequately by David Owen, who proposed that a commission on the security services be appointed.

Douglas Hurd argued that you have got to trust the Prime Minister and the Home Secretary of the day.

I asked, 'What national interest is served by concealing from Parliament and the public knowledge that the Prime Minister of the day, then Harold Wilson, had his office and telephones intercepted and his homes burgled by the security services, which were supposed to be accountable to him?'

Hurd replied that the matter had been dealt with by the Prime Minister at the time the story first broke (Jim Callaghan).

What was extremely interesting was that it was the first absolutely open admission by Hurd and by David Owen that these affairs are dealt with on a bipartisan basis, that the state within a state which really governs Britain is beyond political controversy, beyond the control of the electors. The protection of that secret fortress of the security services is central to the government of Britain. It is as if both the dissidents and the Communist Party in the Soviet Union agreed that the role of the KGB should never be discussed.

Then Roy Jenkins dealt with the Wilson burglary, which had taken place while he was Home Secretary. He made fun of it, and said he thought it was impossible that Wilson could have been a traitor, that anyone who thought so must have had a diseased mind. But the reality is that people with a diseased mind did, while he was Home Secretary, and neither he nor Wilson knew.

Friday 12 December

I had some mail today which gave me tremendous pleasure – a long, friendly, indeed ecstatic letter from Duncan Chalmers of the Public Record Office. He said my collection of archives was marvellous and probably unique, but it wasn't appropriate for the Public Record Office because I didn't have enough Government papers. He added, 'I hope you will take care of the Government papers you do have', and played it down. So that was a relief. Then at the end he said he might consider the offer of the loan of my wire recorder.

Saturday 13 December

I was invited to speak at Wapping tonight. Mike Hicks has been jailed for four months for allegedly hitting a policeman with a loudspeaker. There were the mounted police and barbed wire and the bright lights, and in the middle of Rupert Murdoch's fortress was a Christmas tree!

A march of women protesters was routed through a street which was blocked by police, so I walked right through the police lines and joined the women, who were carrying lighted candles inside white polystyrene cups and singing Christmas carols. I looked at the policemen and wondered how many times they had heard the protests and whether these influenced them at all.

Monday 15 December

The Ambassador of the German Democratic Republic, Dr Gerhard Lindner, came to see me. I thought him rather wooden; I have always found the East Germans a bit difficult to cope with.

At the end of our conversation, I asked him, 'What would happen if you took the Berlin Wall down?'

Obviously he had had that question a thousand times. He said, 'First of all, people would come into East Berlin and cause incidents.'

I said, 'Nobody is suggesting you wouldn't have border control, but people wonder why you won't let anyone come out.'

'Well, of course, thousands and thousands of people come out on visits every year, but, if we did take down the wall, lots of professional people like doctors and dentists who have been educated at the expense of the state would be tempted away by the higher salaries in West Germany.'

So it was clear that they saw it as a check on the brain drain. I told him, 'We've had that problem too, and as a matter of fact a lot of people in Britain who are unemployed might like to come to East Germany to work.'

Lindner said, 'We get lots of requests for that, but we don't want to recruit foreign labour.'

Tuesday 16 December

Saw Tony Banks at the Commons, and he told me, 'People think you are sulking in your tent. We don't see you, you're not doing anything or saying anything, and you are being marginalised and isolated.'

I said, 'Well, honestly, I can't do anything about that. I am working very hard for the Party, going round the country.'

He said, 'But nobody hears about it.'

'Because the press don't report my press releases.'

He told me that actually people in his local Party were fed up with Militant, and if we failed again in the polls the Party would just expel a few more people and climb up again – it was getting very boring. He also thought the Party would drop the anti-nuclear defence policy before the Election, and I agreed with him about that.

Wednesday 17 December

Had lunch with Tam Dalyell. I have admired him over a long period; he has joined the Campaign Group, but since he got elected to the Executive he has voted with the right on everything.

I raised the question of the Harold Wilson plot, and he gave me the names of three people he had been consulting on security matters – two retired Permanent Secretaries in the Home Office, and a former Permanent Secretary at the Foreign Office. Now they are three of the most conservative establishment figures you could imagine, and Tam was getting the information for his campaign from them. All of a sudden it became clear; Tam, an old Etonian, is using retired, wet civil servants to beat this Government with.

To the Campaign Group at 5.30. Four tough young black men in their late twenties or early thirties wearing leather jackets and leather bonnets came in – Stafford Scott, a youth worker and three others who were from the Broadwater Farm estate in Tottenham. Stafford Scott addressed us, most powerfully, about the problems there and the police activity.

He said, 'We want you to win the Election, but it's not worth forsaking principles or people or justice for victory. The blacks in Broadwater Farm are not anti-police but anti-bad policing. Some of our young people have been given seven or eight year sentences for affray, whereas in Birmingham, when an Asian family was killed by a petrol bomb, the people who were convicted only got three and a half years.

'We believe that a lot of wrongs have been done on both sides, but what has happened has not given us justice. The police have raided 450 homes. I myself was arrested for murder, and the police said to me, "We saw you on television. You spoke very well – too good for a bloody nigger. You must be a ringleader." They charged me with murder but, thank God, I was acquitted. Labour is taking the middle road and saying nothing.

'If you believe that injustices have occurred, we want your assistance. We will provide draft parliamentary questions. We have already spoken to other Labour MPs, and we have met Lord Gifford.[1] We came here in a rush and we need more time to present our case.

'We don't gloat over the death of the police constable, but we want to remind Kinnock of the black vote. We are black youth, born here, and votes must be earned. The Labour Party must be interested in us and help us, because there is a wealth of talent and ability in the black community which the Labour Party is going to need to make this into a better society.'

It was a marvellous speech, tough and clear.

Had a chat to Geoffrey Rippon, a right-wing old Tory. He was a year older than me at Oxford, and when you've known somebody for forty years it establishes some sort of rapport.

We talked about MI5 for a moment, and I told him I thought Wilson had been toppled by the security services.

'Well, I'm not one of those – though there are many – who believe that you are a closet communist,' he said.

Then I saw Merlyn Rees, who came up to me from across the Lobby and said, 'You know, I never knew what MI5 were doing when I was Home Secretary.'

I said, 'Merlyn, that's what I told you at the time. Do you remember, I wrote to you to ask whether my phone was being tapped, and you replied that you couldn't tell me.'

He mumbled, 'Well, Jim was in charge of all that.'

This had happened in 1978, and I had also told Jim about my fears. Having protested for years that none of these things ever happened, Merlyn has now admitted that they do.

Thursday 25 December
Stephen, Hilary and Sally, Melissa and Tim, Joshua and Liz and all the grandchildren came for a huge present exchange. Another lovely Christmas, and we have been spending it at Holland Park Avenue since 1957.

Wednesday 31 December
Looking back over 1986, I think the most important event on the world scene was probably the Reykjavik summit. Gorbachev offered total nuclear disarmament and Reagan accepted but insisted on Star Wars, which wrecked the summit but left on the table something that could officially be picked up if Star Wars were dropped – the total nuclear disarmament of Europe. This caused flutters of alarm through the European NATO members including Thatcher, Kohl and Mitterrand. What it did was to confirm the seriousness and purpose of the Russians, the Americans' lack of seriousness and purpose and the Europeans' utter commitment to nuclear weapons.

In Britain, Mrs Thatcher got into trouble over the Westland affair and lost Michael Heseltine, the Defence Secretary, and Leon Brittan, the Home Secretary, early in the year. She was in further difficulties about Leyland, and was unpopular also for authorising the use of British bases for the American raid on Libya. Later in the year, *Spycatcher* led Sir Robert Armstrong to face an arrogant, young, up-and-coming Australian barrister called Malcolm Turnbull; the humiliation should have put the Government into an appalling position; but there was no credible opposition on the part of the Labour Party.

The Labour Party is a story of continuing tragedy. At the end of the year, despite everything that was done to boost Kinnock against the left, the Tories had a lead of 8 per cent – which is quite unheard of on the eve of an Election after a party has been in government for seven years. It is a tragedy for the Party, but it is no exaggeration to say that 90 per cent of NEC time this year has been spent in trying and expelling people in Liverpool and hounding Militant in a general witch-hunt. It has led to great bitterness, though nobody speaks up for fear of 'rocking the boat'.

A National Constitutional Committee is being elected; it was established after the Party Conference, in order to take some of the load of expulsions and discipline off the shoulders of the NEC.

The policy of the Party is now vaguer and more muddled than ever before. The 'Jobs and Industry' campaign was followed by the 'Freedom and Fairness' campaign; and now 'A Modern Britain in a Modern World' has been launched to put forward our defence arguments. But actually it is the biggest fall-back from our position there could be, because although we are going to decommission the Polaris it doesn't say when; the Americans will be asked to leave their nuclear bases in Britain by agreement; and the money spent on nuclear weapons is to go into conventional defence. So I don't think that will help us much.

I do find the House of Commons an extremely unpleasant place at the moment. Talking in the Chamber itself is like being in a zoo where the animals bray at you. The PLP is like an ice-box; they are terrified anything you say might lose them their seats. Being on the NEC is like being a member of the Inquisition.

I should think David Owen will try to merge the SDP with the Tory Party and leave the Liberals in the lurch, having used them as a launching pad in the interim – because that man is not going to be content to go through life as just a sort of independent media commentator.

Nevertheless, I look forward immensely to 1987. There will almost certainly be a General Election, and my guess is that, with a completely gutless and right-wing Labour leadership, the Tories could win outright.

Thursday 1 January 1987

The papers relating to the Suez War are now available, since thirty years have elapsed, and what has emerged quite clearly is that there was collusion between Britain and Israel; the grounds for British intervention – to keep the combatants apart – were completely false, and the attack on Egypt was a breach of the UN Charter and international law. When I thought about it, I realised that the one member of that Government still in office is Lord Hailsham, the Lord Chancellor, and that his life-span as a Minister has lasted long enough to see the beginning and end of the Thirty-Year Rule on Suez papers. So I wrote my weekly column for the *Chesterfield Star* on the subject, and

I also sent a telegram to Number 10 asking for the immediate suspension of the Lord Chancellor, and for a debate to establish a select committee to investigate Lord Hailsham's personal complicity in the affair. I also asked about the consequential deception of Parliament by Hailsham.

The release of the papers raises important questions: they prove there was aggression, and they show that the Thirty-Year Rule is a complete fraud, used to cover up. I contrasted this system with American law, whereby such things come to light immediately.

Saturday 3 January

To my surprise and delight, in the *Independent*, *The Times*, the *Guardian* and the *Daily Telegraph* there was really good coverage of my message to the Prime Minister. Later I wrote to Hailsham putting five questions to him which he will find difficult to evade.

Monday 12 January

At 5 we had the NEC Home Policy Committee and a long paper by Norman Buchan, who recommended an Arts and Media Minister in the Cabinet with responsibility for broadcasting, which would be moved from the Home Office to the new Ministry.

There was opposition to the idea of the Minister being in the Cabinet; Blunkett didn't want to write in Cabinet status.

Skinner said, 'Look, we're all grey men concentrating on the PSBR figures, and here's a bit of imagination. Wilson aroused excitement with his Open University in 1964, and we would catch the imagination with this on the agenda.'

Norman Buchan defended his proposal. 'Every union in the business wants it, and I can't go on if this is thwarted.'

It became clear that Buchan and Kinnock were locked in combat.

Neil said he resented the threat of resignation; he had consulted everyone from Bragg to Bragg (Melvyn and Billy), and he thought Norman's arguments were unconvincing. He added ominously, 'I'll be in charge anyway, and the Home Office must be in control of broadcasting.'

Finally Kinnock came up with an amendment that wiped out four pages of Buchan's paper, completely degutting it, and that was carried by 7 to 6. So it was clear Buchan will resign. It was a miserable meeting, and the fact is that Kinnock is against anything positive.

Wednesday 14 January

In the course of the day, Chris Moncrieff of the Press Association told me he had rung up Hailsham, who said, 'I am not going to reply to his lunatic letter.'

Thursday 15 January

To the LSE to deliver the Dalton Lecture. Had a cup of tea first with Ben Pimlott, Hugh Dalton's biographer and editor of his diaries, and Lord Gladwyn, who was Private Secretary to Dalton in 1929–31 and is now eighty-seven. It was attended by many former politicians.

Wednesday 21 January

At the PLP this morning there was a motion by Brian Sedgemore on the replacement of Norman Buchan as our arts spokesman by Mark Fisher. Norman was sacked last Tuesday, and Brian said this was bizarre, it had never been discussed by the Shadow Cabinet or the full NEC, and he thought it was in marked contrast to the way John Cunningham was allowed to advocate nuclear power against Party policy. Norman had wanted a unified Arts Ministry which included broadcasting, but Gerald Kaufman had responded violently to this idea and Neil had sided with Kaufman. Brian declared, 'This is not the way to make policy. Sacking Norman has upset a significant section of the electorate, and Neil has made a mistake.'

Tam Dalyell interrupted and said, 'I hope there will be no more speeches. An Election is imminent, and an acrimonious debate should be brought to an end at once.'

It was Tam at his most obscurantist. When I think of the *Belgrano* and MI5 and all the things that the Shadow Cabinet wished he would shut up about, I was annoyed.

Dennis Skinner supported Norman because he had an exciting policy and it was undemocratic to sack anybody.

I was sorry to see Norman dismissed. I said the issue was a simple one – who should be the sponsor of broadcasting? I hoped to persuade the Party that it should not be the Home Office. 'The history of relations between the Government and the BBC is disgraceful, and it is all because the BBC is directly controlled by the same department that deals with security and other sensitive matters.'

Norman then made a very passionate, pleading speech. He said, 'It is important which Ministry controls broadcasting. The BBC are now so frightened they are censoring themselves. All the unions, including the NUJ, ACTT and the Writers' Guild, support a separation, and so do the Liberals and the SDP.' He repudiated Kaufman.

Kinnock responded, 'I appointed and reappointed Norman Buchan, and therefore I have no criticism of him, but he said he would campaign on a policy incompatible with the Front Bench. That is how I will act.' (I took that as a warning that he will sack anyone who stands in his way.) 'It is functionally necessary for a leadership to conduct affairs in this fashion.' He said Party policy was contained in the 1983 manifesto, and to go back to the policy in 1976 and 1977 was to go back to the Old Testament. 'I shall decide who is in the Cabinet, and we will have an inquiry into broadcasting. As for Tony Benn, he gave a list of Home Office interventions against the BBC, but what would an Arts Minister do to change it?'

Of those who voted, thirty-seven were for Kinnock and fourteen against (out of 280 Labour MPs).

Saturday 24 January
Caroline and I went off to Wapping. The platform was full of distinguished labour leaders – Ron Todd, Ken Cameron, Ken Gill, Peter Shore, Arthur Scargill. I would have expected the police to behave more cautiously, but from the platform you could see them rushing out and attacking the crowd. John Bowden, a solicitor, who had a huge sign 'Legal Observer' on his jacket, was attacked by the police and his face was covered in blood. Soviet television crews had their lights broken by the police. We saw a man with a cut head being treated. What an incredible world we live in at the moment. This is going on in the heart of London, yet it gets no comparable coverage to demonstrations in the rest of the world.

Monday 26 January
This afternoon the Home Secretary made a statement on Wapping and said he thought a 'former senior Minister and Privy Councillor' should not have gone there – an outrageous statement. I objected to that.

The Speaker ruled last week that the BBC film about the defence satellite Zircon, which the BBC has decided not to broadcast, cannot be shown in the House of Commons.[2] There is a Government motion tomorrow to support the Speaker, so I went to the Library and began to do some work on it.

Tuesday 27 January
Worked all morning on my House of Commons speech, seeking out references in *Erskine May's Parliamentary Practice* and elsewhere.

Before the debate began, I saw Jim Callaghan talking anxiously to the Speaker at his chair, and then Jim got up on a point of order and said he was anxious about the Speaker's ruling on the showing of the Zircon film. So I supported him and Michael Foot, Jim and I all came in on points of order, and it was clear the Speaker was as uneasy as the rest of us, so I hastily drafted an amendment that the matter be referred to the Committee of Privileges. I took it to the Speaker, who was very friendly, and he gave it to the Clerk who redrafted it as a formal manuscript amendment. The Speaker indicated he would accept it. When I passed the wording of my amendment to our Front Bench and also to John Biffen, it was clear that I was beginning to make progress and that the Opposition would withdraw their amendment upholding the Speaker's ruling.

The debate was opened by Biffen as Leader of the House. Peter Shore spoke, then Terence Higgins, then I was called.

When we came to the end of the debate, Patrick Mayhew, the Solicitor-General, made a violent attack on Duncan Campbell and the *New Statesman*, but at the end he stated that the motion as amended would be accepted.

To my surprise and delight, the Speaker nodded to me and moved on my behalf the manuscript amendment – over and above ten amendments on the order paper – and it was passed unanimously. So this little initiative, on which I had worked the night before, had all of a sudden been sufficiently strong in argument to be accepted first by the Opposition, then by the Government and the Prime Minister.

Looking back on it three or four days later, I think it was the most important debate about parliamentary democracy that I have ever taken part in, and for that reason probably the most historic constitutional debate in the thirty-six years I have been in Parliament. My speech wasn't a great piece of oratory but it did make a profound impact. I got support from Enoch Powell, Eric Heffer and Liberal MPs, and Patrick Cormack, the Conservative MP for Staffordshire South, even offered to be a teller with us.

It also performed other functions. It got the Opposition off the hook of an absurd amendment which would have confirmed the Speaker's ruling. It also defeated the Government without a vote, by speaking directly to Tory backbenchers and particularly chairmen of select committees and others. It raised the debate to a proper constitutional level. Also it pleased the Labour Party in Parliament.

Wednesday 28 January

A bit in the press about the debate and I had a note from the Speaker congratulating me on what he considered to be a debate of 'historic importance'. It was the sort of letter a Member of Parliament does not normally receive from the Speaker in the course of three parliamentary lifetimes, and I was greatly honoured.

He suggested I bring Mother to tea. I replied thanking him warmly.

Went to the House, and a number of people congratulated me on last night's speech. Nicholas Scott, a former Tory Minister, came up and said, 'That really will have annoyed Mrs Thatcher.' Even Roy Jenkins said, 'Not only a great speech but one I much enjoyed'. I was quite overwhelmed. I recalled Father's saying that what was so intolerable about the House of Lords was the amount of goodwill there.

Friday 30 January

Went with Margaret Vallins to Ashgate House, the first privately owned and operated old people's home in Chesterfield. They had taken over an old National Health Service hospital. There is no doubt they have put a lot of money into it. They charge from £178 to £220 a week, and 70 per cent of the residents are paid for by the local authority. They are making an enormous profit.

Tuesday 3 February
In the House, Mrs Thatcher made fun of Neil Kinnock for having come out in support of the Government ban on the Zircon film; it made him look ridiculous. Then during the debate Norman Buchan got up and said this proved how right he was that the Home Secretary shouldn't be in charge of broadcasting.

When there is a major attack on parliamentary democracy by the executive – that is when the Prime Minister uses the powers of the Crown – Kinnock is totally paralysed, having spent the last three and a half years telling people that the attack on parliamentary democracy is coming from a handful of Liverpool councillors.

Friday 6 February
The big news is that SOGAT has decided to withdraw its support from the strikers against News International. The SOGAT national committee, headed by Brenda Dean, the General Secretary, never really wanted it to continue, and they have done nothing to mobilise the full strength of the print unions; the turning-point was the court order which ruled that if SOGAT did not discontinue their support they would be held responsible and all their funds would be sequestrated.

Went to the Soviet Embassy for a lunch arranged by Lev Parshin, a counsellor at the Embassy. When I arrived I found that the Ambassador had organised a lunch anyway for the Foreign Affairs Committee of the Supreme Soviet. The British guests were led by Willie Whitelaw, who is Lord President of the Council, Sir Anthony Kershaw, who is chairman of the Commons Foreign Affairs Committee, and Peter Thomas, MP for Hendon South – three very wooden, traditional, aristocratic Tories. On the Labour side, the only other person was Ian Mikardo.

Leonid Zemyatin, the Ambassador, a distinguished, white-haired man who spoke perfect English, came up and greeted me. I gave him a copy of the pamphlet *Comrades in Arms* (published in 1941 by the Government under Churchill), depicting on the cover the Union Jack and the hammer and sickle fluttering side by side flanking pictures of Churchill and Stalin. I said to Zemyatin, 'You had better hide this or the Special Branch will break in and seize it.'

Willie Whitelaw was somewhat taken aback and said, 'Oh come on! I say!'

'It's not far from the facts,' I remarked.

You get Tory MPs and the Russians at occasions like this being very friendly, and the Ambassador stood up and announced, 'There'll be no speeches, but I would like to say how proud I am to have our British guests here.' Then Sir Anthony Kershaw responded, saying what a pleasure it was to meet the Russians, how this lunch was in response to a visit to Russia by Whitelaw and Healey, and so on. It did just occur to me how embarrassed the Tories would be if television were to record one of those little lunches, because they make out they are strongly against the Russians, yet privately they are cordial and are asking themselves, 'How can we make a bit of money out of the Russians?', while they denounce them publicly. It is that difference between the public and the private attitude which ultimately catches up with them. It is a case of double standards.

I leaned across and asked Willie Whitelaw, 'Is Geoffrey Howe going to Moscow with Mrs Thatcher?' He said they hadn't decided, so I asked, 'Am I wrong in supposing that she will come back and say, "I can do business with Gorbachev because he's got the bomb, we've got the bomb and we'll be working for peace"?'

He gave me a sort of watery look. He is the one aristocratic Tory wet who supports Mrs Thatcher wholeheartedly, a cunning old man really. I teased him about being made a hereditary peer; he and George Thomas have both been made viscounts.

Saturday 7 February

Today we heard that now the NGA has pulled out of supporting the strike against Rupert Murdoch. The printers, like the miners, are strong, and that is why the Government has gone for them. Until there is a really big change of attitude by the trade unions, the labour movement will continue to be entirely subservient to Thatcher.

Sunday 8 February

We went to see Sally and Hilary's new baby, who hasn't got a name yet. He has webs about a third of the length of his toes, and when I looked at mine I found I have the same!

Tuesday 10 February

Committee of Privileges at 5.30 for the first meeting to discuss the Speaker's ruling on the ban on the Zircon film. The Tories have had their fingers burned, not being able to get the ban through the House. They know the Speaker doesn't want these responsibilities and they would like to dispose of the matter in the narrowest way possible. As usual when you get these people together, there's a great huddling around constitutional questions, and the passion for secrecy and precedent and all the rest of it makes it a very boring committee, but I'm glad I am on it because I can observe the British constitution at close hand.

Had a phone call from the *Daily Mail*, telling me that the Freedom

Association had issued a writ against me and seven others, presumably for attending a meeting last night in Conway Hall, where the Zircon film was shown. This evening it was reported that Norris McWhirter of the Freedom Association had been granted an injunction for a prosecution under the Official Secrets Act. So I went to Biffen's office, to Peter Archer, our former Solicitor-General, and to Charles Clarke (who is chief adviser to Kinnock). Then I saw the Speaker, who told me, 'There's not much I can do, you know.'

I said, 'Well, I understand that, but there are one or two points I would like to raise at 10 to get it in Hansard.'

So at 10.15 I got up, and a lot of Tories cheered. One is torn between thinking it's all very funny and treating it as absolutely serious. I put three questions. Had the Attorney-General authorised the writ? What would happen if the writ was issued in the House? What was my position as a member of the Committee of Privileges who had seen the film outside the House?

The Speaker said he couldn't give an answer, but I was content with getting it on the record.

Later, Allan Rogers told me that two or three days before the Speaker's ban on the Zircon film he and others had actually seen it in the House of Commons but had never made it known.

Monday 16 February

Today we had a meeting of the NEC and the Shadow Cabinet – the first, I think, since Neil Kinnock became Leader.

Kinnock introduced the meeting and spoke for about twenty minutes on how we were geared for Election victory. 'Tory strengths were expectations of higher standards of living, tax cuts and a successful tackling of inflation. We must tell the truth. The counter-attacks on us would be that we would introduce higher taxation, weaken defence, pursue policies that would lead to higher inflation and increase the national debt. But unemployment is the key, and we must turn anxiety into support for us. We must get rid of the surrender mentality, because submissiveness among the electorate is our greatest threat. It is a time of choice.' Then he began reciting a series of slogans.

My general impression was of a very insecure chairman of a company addressing shareholders, or rather sales representatives in the field – we were told what to do, and there was no sense of being genuinely consulted at all.

We went on to the polling presentation, and Peter Mandelson said a few words. I find Mandelson a threatening figure for the future of the Party. He came in from the media eighteen months ago and has taken over, and he and Kinnock now work closely together. Whitty is just a figurehead, and Geoff Bish has been pushed into the background.

Then the Shadow Agency, or Shadow Communications Agency as it is called, analysed their findings. They said that there had been a shift from the collective to the individual, and that people were afraid of the loony left, afraid of the future, afraid of inexperience. It was totally defensive; but on the positive side we had 'a Leader in control' and so on.

There was a discussion, in which Denis Healey said, 'Not for the first time, I agree with 95 per cent of what Tony Benn has said. The psychosis of the Cold War has had to be revived to justify the Trident. There are important changes in the Soviet Union, and it would be a historic crime to miss the opportunity that Gorbachev is opening up. The Trident depends on American targeting. Britain is not in the first division any more, it is in decline, and because of the Falklands War and our attitude to South Africa we are not taken seriously in the UN Security Council.' He quoted the scientist Sir Henry Tizard, who had said at the end of the Second World War, 'If Britain tries to be a great power, it will cease to be a great nation.'

Healey went on to say that if Thatcher had a third term it would undermine all the institutions on which parliamentary democracy rests – the trade unions, the Civil Service, civil liberties, local government, the Commonwealth and the monarch. He said Worsthorne had praised South Africa last week and this week had argued that we should restore the authority of the state – which is a fascist suggestion.

We had another twenty-five minutes of Neil Kinnock summing up. He declared, 'Thatcher won because we ran away from the idea of enlightened self-interest. We must deal with change by collectivism. We want a fair and united country with a strong pulse. We must appeal across the nation. Thatcher is the biggest weakness. She is hateful, but she is thought to be strong; therefore we must attack Thatcherism as weak and wrong. She has a personality defect, especially *vis-à-vis* America. She has used the power of the state, and the best slogan for the Election is "Get her out!"'

Thursday 19 February
Took Mother to tea with the Speaker, in his house in the Palace of Westminster. Mother charmed him and his wife, and her recollections of the House were vivid. She was born while Gladstone was still alive, remembered the 1906 Election results and heard parliamentary prayers from the Ladies' Gallery. She recalled having dinner with Sir Courtenay Ilbert, a former Clerk of the House. On the walls there were pictures of all the people who had attended the 1931 Indian Round Table Conference, and she began talking about them. 'That was the Aga Khan. I remember meeting his third wife, who had been a chocolate seller in a Paris theatre, and I remember asking him the following year where she was, and he said she was so engrossed in golf that she couldn't look after him, and he introduced his new wife. Then I

asked how as a Muslim he could drink alcohol, and he said, "When the alcohol passes my lips, it turns into orange juice!"' The Speaker was overwhelmed. Her memory for detail is amazing.

Wednesday 4 March

Terry and Liz French and a printworker turned up to see me, and Terry said the Kent coalfield is totally demoralised after the defeat. Six police stations in Kent were burned, but that never appeared in the papers because they didn't want people to know how much damage had been done and how much hostility there was to the police. That was news to me. I knew there had been some excesses but I had no idea that six police stations had been burned.

Terry said he became the 'shop steward' in the prison, and went to see the governor regularly on behalf of other prisoners. When the governor asked him to recite his number, he would say, 'My name is Terry French, you gave me the number, you remember the number, it's nothing to do with me.' He preserved his self-respect that way, though I think he put himself at risk.

He has been offered the possibility of a course at the University of Kent at Canterbury and I think he should take it, but he is afraid that if he goes to university it will take the fight out of him. I said nothing in the world would do that.

Friday 6 March

Patricia Hewitt has attacked the London Labour Party for what she calls the 'London effect', saying that the policy for the support of gays and lesbians was costing us heavily with the pensioners' vote, as were high rates. Eric Heffer rang me about it and *Newsnight* phoned, but I refused to respond.

Saturday 7 March

I remembered that Patricia Hewitt was once General Secretary of the National Campaign for Civil Liberties, and my mind turned to a foreword I had written to their pamphlet *Gay Workers, Trade Unions*. I found the cassette recording of the press conference at which they launched the pamphlet on 27 January 1981, and, as I had remembered, Patricia Hewitt was asked to speak and supported the rights of gay people. So I typed it and rang Richard Gott of the *Guardian*.

Tuesday 10 March

This morning the *Guardian* 'Diary' mentioned the Hewitt business.

Wednesday 11 March

Jim Callaghan's speech in the House on Monday in support of Trident during a debate on INF, has exploded all over the place. It is being said that because Jim never won an Election when he was Prime Minister he doesn't see why any other Labour Leader should, or that he is really a member of the SDP, or that he has nothing to lose because he is leaving Parliament and retiring. But it has done great damage; it is always the right wing of the Party that does the damage.

At the PLP meeting this morning (which I didn't attend) apparently Kinnock said that if this went on, if people wouldn't exercise self-discipline, he wouldn't go on leading the Party.

Saw Merlyn Rees in the Smoking Room, which I haven't been into for ages. We had a chat and he tried to defend Jim. 'You know, Jim made a terrible mistake, and I'm sure he didn't mean it. He didn't have any notes. He spoke for five minutes, and he knows he's made a mistake.' He was covering up as best he could for Jim, who is his friend.

Thursday 12 March
Today the five Law Lords in the House of Lords upheld the lower court in disqualifying, surcharging and bankrupting the forty-seven Liverpool councillors. There was a great crowd outside.

One woman councillor came running up to me and burst into tears. 'I'm forty-seven, and I've just been bankrupted and disqualified. We came down from Liverpool to hear the judgement and heard it from the press. We weren't even allowed to hear it in the House of Lords. You Members of Parliament have done nothing to help us.' There was real bitterness there.

Saturday 14 March
Hilary arrived with his three lovely little boys. Michael is so sweet and tender with his new baby brother, and James is all over the shop, sucking at a little deflated balloon as if it was the teat of a baby's bottle.

In the evening, Caroline and I went to have dinner in the Middle Temple at the invitation of our friends Ralph and Ann Gibson. We were dreading the thought of all those Tory judges but we are very fond of Ralph and Ann.

At dinner we sat next to one very senior judge well-known for some famous cases. I said, 'You must find it very difficult, when you look somebody up and down, to decide whether you trust them or not, and that may influence your judgement of the evidence.'

'Yes, yes, that's perfectly true. Mind you, I suppose there are *some* Irishmen who tell the truth, and I find it very difficult when I listen to a Scotsman to think that he is telling a lie.'

That was the most open admission of prejudice I'd ever come across! The remark was made in humour, and everybody laughed, but it still told you a lot.

Later on I raised with him the question of the Birmingham Six, and he said, 'Oh well, there are some people who make a profession of writing books criticising judgements, and they claim to produce evidence which could bear on it.' He dismissed it out of hand.

After dinner, with all the ritual and prayers, we went in to have dessert and port. A young judge of fifty-one came up and said he had sat in on my peerage case in 1961 when he was a law student. That really did make me feel like an old man!

Sunday 15 March

At the ILCS tonight, we agreed that a conference on the future of socialism might be organised by the Socialist Society. To be perfectly candid, I suppose what I should be doing now is preparing for a leadership campaign, but the allies are not there and it wouldn't seem appropriate.

Monday 16 March

Went into the House to meet two parties of children from Abercrombie primary school in my constituency. One of the little boys asked me to take a photograph of him in front of Big Ben, but he was so tiny that I had to lie flat on the ground before I could get him in the shot with Big Ben behind him. Of course, everyone else with cameras then took pictures of me on the ground.

Tuesday 17 March

My first visitors at 9 am were Alan Plater, the playwright, Mick Jackson and Sally Hibbin, who are turning Chris Mullin's book *A Very British Coup* into a three-part television series. They wanted to ask me what situation would face an incoming radical Prime Minister, what his relations would be with the security services, the Americans, the Governor of the Bank of England, and so on.

In a way, Chris's book has been a bit overtaken by events in a number of respects. First of all, the likelihood of a left-wing Labour Leader is absolutely minimal. Secondly, there won't be a Labour Government. Thirdly, when Chris wrote about 'dirty tricks' in 1982 they were considered a bit way out but are now sort of taken for granted. However, the general idea is interesting, and I thoroughly enjoyed meeting them.

Wednesday 25 March

At the NEC John Evans suggested that the Labour Party should discuss the Gorbachev offer to the US – that both countries should eliminate all intermediate-range nuclear weapons. He said the time had come to re-examine our policies. 'If we don't, it will make the Thatcher Government a near certainty and Kinnock will have a hard time in Washington. There should be a special NEC to discuss defence.'

Neil said he was opposed to a special NEC; Conference policies were clear. 'Everybody must know that we established our policy on US bases in 1980–1 and détente overtook us when the multilateralists controlled the Party. The Gorbachev move is significant. We shall have to make adjustments, and Reagan will be obliged to reciprocate. The Prime Minister is only interested in posturing in Moscow, and we have to take advantage of our opportunities. My view has been shaped by Gorbachev, not by Reagan, but it would be sensible to defer our policy pending the talks on intermediate nuclear forces.'

All this verbiage was just a smokescreen. He went on, 'Thatcher could wreck it all, because if we buy Trident that is an 800 per cent increase in our nuclear weaponry. It is OK so long as we are not putting forward a theological viewpoint on Polaris and Trident. Cruise would have to remain during negotiations. If the talks fail, we go back to square one.'

The old argument: we'll renegotiate and, if we don't get our way, then we pull out. That's what was said about the Common Market.

On the American F-111 planes at airbases here, he said, 'We'll get the warheads removed; but how do we know whether they have *got* warheads?' Then he added something very interesting. 'What do you expect me to do, send the Welsh Guards or the SAS into American airbases to check if nuclear weapons are there?'

He said we would continue to urge no first use for NATO. 'People would like us to keep the bomb. We need effective defence policies to win.' He was afraid we would look like a defenceless party, but he thought he could get rid of the nuclear weapons. 'We are closer to success, but we would blow it if we gave the impression of being defenceless, if we were anti-NATO or if there was any division in the movement.' And this was on the eve of his visit to Reagan.

An interview I had with a Russian journalist has appeared in the Moscow *New Times* on the eve of Mrs Thatcher's visit, attacking her record on human rights in Britain.

Thursday 26 March
The *Sun* had a page with a picture of me saying 'Benn – Twisted, Evil and Treacherous', taking up this human rights issue. It's a long time since I have had that degree of abuse.

Mrs Thatcher was asked at Prime Minister's Questions about my article, and she replied that she would be happy to ask Mr Gorbachev to give me a permanent residence permit there; I thought it was quite a funny answer.

Saturday 28 March
Kinnock and Healey returned from America today, Reagan having given them less than half an hour. It was a disaster, whereas Thatcher's

visit to Moscow has been trumpeted everywhere. It's sad for the Party, because all Kinnock did was to reassure Reagan that Britain would remain in NATO and never put Labour policy forward at all, as far as I can make out. Healey is angry about it.

Tuesday 31 March

Went to the Commons, and Chris Mullin persuaded me to go to Dublin in June for a meeting about the Birmingham Six. He said Charles Haughey, the new Irish leader, was potentially interested in raising this issue, though he thinks Haughey is an absolutely cynical, opportunistic politician. The capital punishment debate is coming up this week, and he is keen for the Birmingham case to be used in the argument against hanging.

Thursday 9 April

Melissa was at home when I arrived back from the Commons, because yesterday one of her friends, Sarah Bayliss, a young writer was knocked off her bike and killed on her way home from visiting Melissa. Melissa is absolutely shattered. Stephen and Joshua came over to comfort her.

Monday 13 April

I watched on video two programmes recorded during the 1981 deputy leadership contest, and they depressed me enormously. They reminded me of a time when I wasn't well and was being violently attacked by the media. The violence of the attacks had shaken and intimidated me, and I thought: I cannot go through that again.

One of them was the Brian Walden interview of May 1981, one of the best television interviews I have ever done. It was all about Party democracy. There was not a word I would change, but I realised that to people watching that programme in 1981 it was all about the Labour Party and wouldn't register with most of them in terms of their own interests. It came to me that the trouble with the 1981 deputy leadership campaign was that it was directed at members of the Party, whereas it should have been directed at the public, with the Party witnessing an appeal for jobs and peace. Once I had realised that, it cleared my mind, and a second campaign will have to be conducted quite differently.

Friday 17 April

This afternoon I watched Jim Callaghan on television in the second of three interviews with Brian Walden. Jim must be seventy-two now and is a very conservative, old-fashioned Labour politician. He was friendly and natural and didn't try to pull any fast ones. Walden was trying to get him to say all sorts of reactionary things about education, crime, homosexuality and abortion, but Jim wouldn't have it and avoided the

(*Top*) Voices for peace at RAF
Fairford, a young protester with an
old message (*right*) and President
George Bush: 'watch my hips' (*above*)

ACTION FOR THE THIRD TERM

An invincible Margaret Thatcher celebrates her third Election success...

... leaving
home,
November,
1990

John Major, the
new tenant of
Number 10

Nelson Mandela, free at last, 1990

Against the Gulf War with MPs Ken Livingstone (*left*) and Bernie Grant

Yeltsin, triumphant after his fall from grace, 1987, while (*below*) a dishevelled Gorbachev survives the coup of 1991

The last of the Gandhis – on the campaign trail

Yasser Arafat, caught in the Gulf War cross-fire

Emily Benn at her first (and last) ILEA meeting

The family in Cincinnati, May 1990: (*back*) Joshua, Hilary, Stephen (*front*) Tony, Caroline, Melissa, Nita, Sally

Three generations: Mother is holding Father's campaign poster for 1910

Seven grandchildren on a bed

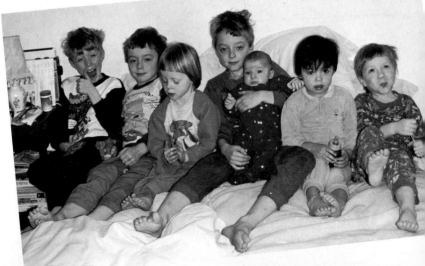

trap completely. Indeed, he said some rather sensible things, and in the light of the Thatcher years he appeared progressive, liberal, straight and reassuring. It gave a new perspective, and it was comforting to feel that this old man was on our side. It wasn't socialist in any analytical sense, but it was friendly and comfortable, and I think that's what people want.

Wednesday 22 April

Went to lunch with Leonid Zemyatin, the Soviet Ambassador. I put to him my idea that the changes in the Soviet Union opened up a completely new perspective for the left in Britain. I suggested that Gorbachev might propose to the Secretary-General of the UN a three-man disarmament and development team to visit Europe and America – perhaps Fidel Castro, Robert Mugabe of Zimbabwe and Rajiv Gandhi. This would step up the pressure for disarmament. Next I thought the UN Economic Commission for Europe might be reconvened at ministerial level to try to break down the blockage between east and west. I also suggested a series of television interviews with Gorbachev on the significance of the reforms in the Soviet Union, and possibly an exchange of TV bulletins, whereby Soviet news would be shown in Britain and British news in the Soviet Union.

Zemyatin is a thoughtful man and was extremely open to all this. On Mrs Thatcher's visit to the USSR, he said she had had long talks with Gorbachev. My points to Gorbachev about human rights in Britain had registered, because Gorbachev had asked Mrs Thatcher, 'Why don't you give autonomy to Northern Ireland, as we've given it to so many of our republics?' Of course she said she wouldn't do that.

Zemyatin thought that by calling for unilateral nuclear disarmament the Labour Party might have made a mistake; it might be better to be more active in the negotiations for disarmament. Then he said something very interesting – that Gorbachev couldn't understand why the negotiations were only with the US at the top and that the USSR wanted to make contact bilaterally with Germany, France and Britain.

Then I asked how he thought Stalin would be regarded by history, and he replied, 'He was a very competent man, and undoubtedly collectivisation and industrialisation enabled us to win the war, but 2 million people were killed by Stalin before and after the war. He became totally mentally deranged; after his post-mortem, doctors said he had a serious mental illness. When I was a boy in the Young Communist League, we thought Stalin wasn't aware of what was happening, that he couldn't be responsible and it must have been the people under him. But when I joined the Central Committee of the Party and read the Government records, I realised Stalin knew who had been killed, indeed had given the instructions himself.' A cool, clinical confirmation of what happened.

He went on, 'There is no human rights problem in the Soviet Union any more. There are Jews in Russia who want to go to Israel, but there are a lot of Jews in Israel who want to go back to Russia.'

Sunday 26 April
A beautiful day, the blossom is out, and London looks lovely.

It is clear the Election will be in June, and the Tories have an 11 per cent lead.

Monday 27 April
The *Independent's* front page was entirely devoted to key points of Peter Wright's book *Spycatcher*. I rang up the Speaker and asked for an emergency debate about the security services. In the afternoon, I rose and put the argument for having a debate, quoting liberally from the *Independent*, but the Speaker turned it down. Then Tam Dalyell, Eric Heffer and Dennis Skinner all got up on points of order.

Tuesday 28 April
I went to the BBC for an interview with Robin Day about what I had said in the House yesterday.

Afterwards, Robin told me a fascinating story about MI6. He said that James Mossman, a well-known correspondent for the BBC and others, had worked for MI6; in 1956 the BBC sent him to Egypt, where he was approached by somebody from the British Intelligence Services who said they had a job for him to do. He said he had finished with MI6, but was told, 'You must do this because we are just about to go to war with Egypt.' He asked what they wanted him to do, and the British Intelligence officer gave him a package to be dropped at the twelfth mile post outside Cairo. He was told to ring a number afterwards and ask, 'Have you read the book?', then he was to report back with the answer. James Mossman dropped off the package, and when he dialled the number a voice said, 'What book are you referring to?' It was obvious he had got on to the wrong man, but he later heard that the package had contained £20,000 in English banknotes which was intended as a bribe to Nasser's doctor to poison Nasser.

Went to see the Speaker in another attempt to get an emergency debate. He told me to see the Clerks, so I went to see Clifford Boulton, the Deputy Clerk of the House, who was very difficult. I got angry with him and said, 'Look, if Parliament can't discuss this, something is wrong. Perhaps the Prime Minister could be asked to make a statement on the matter at Question Time?'

He indicated that that would be a way of raising it, so I went back to the Speaker just as he was putting on his wig, and I said, 'I have cleared a new draft with the Clerk. If the Prime Minister refuses to make a statement, then I shall ask for a debate.' Just like a footballer, he made a mock tackle at me with his feet and laughed.

Sure enough, when the Prime Minister was asked by David Steel to make a frank statement to the House, she refused. So I got up. I didn't succeed in getting a debate, but I did register one or two new points, one of which was that in effect the Prime Minister in her answers to questions had declared that, if a crime was committed before she was Prime Minister, her law officers wouldn't prosecute the criminals.

After that, I had a word with Merlyn Rees and asked him why Jim didn't make a statement today. He got very agitated and said, 'You know, we don't know what would happen. We might be implicated if there was an inquiry. I may have done something twenty years ago that would emerge.'

I might add that I bumped into Enoch Powell, who said, 'Well, now we all know what it's about.'

I asked, 'What's that?'

He replied, 'Well, who wanted Labour to be defeated in 1974?'

'Who?'

He said, 'The Americans. The Americans are behind this.' So we had a bit of a chat. He remarked, 'Successive Parliaments took away rights we had fought for from under our very noses.'

Although Enoch is a nationalist and I am an internationalist, there is a sort of commonality of interest between us.

Wednesday 29 April

I was driven early to the BBC for a television interview about *Spycatcher* and MI5. Just before I went on the air, the producer leaned over to my seat and said, 'You cannot mention any of the allegations in the Wright book.' Since I was there to *discuss* the allegations in the Wright book, it seemed to me incredible, so I asked why, and she said, 'Our lawyers have advised us.' I was expected to sit there and discuss *Spycatcher* without saying what it was about. I said, 'I'm very sorry, but I'm not prepared to do that.'

So when we came to the broadcast I not only spelled out the allegations with absolute clarity but mentioned the attempted assassination of Nasser. I also stated that I had been approached just before we went on air not to talk about the allegations.

Monday 4 May

Caught the train to Chesterfield, and Michael Meacher was on it. We also talked on the journey back, so the two conversations are reported together.

I asked how things were going. He was concerned with the fact that Neil didn't seem too interested in policy, left it to Hattersley, was more keen on public relations. Kinnock had an authoritarian strain in him which Meacher found difficult, and Charles Clarke and Patricia Hewitt seemed to be the key figures in his office; he had a little inner cabinet made up of Hattersley, Healey, Kaufman and, I think, John Smith. There was a 'Leader's Committee' which took decisions, but Michael didn't know who was on that. He said Kinnock never consulted members of the Shadow Cabinet. Michael had only seen him three times in the last few years. There was no discussion of politics in the Shadow Cabinet, Healey took practically no interest in it and would come in for a moment and go away again. Michael feels he should leave the Campaign Group.

Monday 11 May
Spent most of the morning waiting for news of the Election date, and it was announced at about 2.15 – 11 June, as we'd expected.

Tuesday 12 May
Went into the Commons, then to the Clause 5 meeting which was being held in Transport House to discuss the manifesto. There was a huge crowd outside with red balloons, and television cameras filming it. Neil was standing on the steps waving – it had all been stage-managed. The members of the Shadow Cabinet and the NEC filed in.

Not having seen the manifesto in advance, I didn't know what would be in it, but I had typed out a whole range of 'amendments', which I called a checklist, and gave copies to Larry Whitty, Audrey Wise, Geoff Bish, Jo Richardson, Joan Maynard, Dennis Skinner, and Linda Douglas, the NEC Young Socialist. Looking round the meeting, I was reminded of Brezhnev's Central Committee; the same thing which brought the Stalin era to an end in Russia will bring the Labour Party domination of British politics to an end – an authoritarian, right-wing, passionately anti-democratic streak.

One important innovation was that there were votes taken, for the first time ever at a Clause 5 meeting. Once you introduce the idea of a vote, the Leader's veto doesn't apply to manifesto commitments, but of course on the eve of an Election a Leader has enormous power anyway.

Whitty stressed the confidentiality of the draft manifesto and wanted everyone to return their copies, but I didn't give my copy back. Here is an elected body responsible for making the policy for a General Election not being shown anything in advance and not being allowed to keep papers. That is the centralisation and authoritarianism that has crept into the Labour Party.

Larry said the draft had been drawn up by the Leader and the chairmen of the policy committees.

We went through it, and Dennis Skinner said he objected to the phrase 'Britain is crying out for a change'.

Gerald Kaufman said, 'Well, this is our slogan for the General Election.'

I didn't like it either, and I put forward my amendments for page 1 of the document.

Neil argued, ' "Crying out for a change" isn't our Election slogan, but it is true, because the public are fed up with the Government.' On my comments, he agreed that the word 'hope' should be included, and he said, 'The transfer of wealth' – which I had wanted to be included – 'is implicit in our whole policy.'

Dennis Skinner moved that there should be no incomes policy, and Kaufman said, 'Well, a minimum wage is an incomes policy.'

Audrey Wise wanted to include full employment as an objective, which was one of my amendments, and that was accepted.

Skinner moved that pensions should be raised progressively towards two-thirds of the average national income and that we should also pledge ourselves not just to 'move towards' free television for pensioners but actually to carry it out, and he wanted standing charges on fuel bills to be abolished.

Kinnock said, 'The standing charge is a problem, because it would involve increasing the standing charges for others.'

Skinner also thought there should be a reference to a wealth tax. Hattersley agreed with that, but Kaufman said it was impracticable in the first two years.

Audrey Wise wanted to phase out nuclear power and thought the phrase 'we shall gradually diminish our dependence on nuclear power' was not adequate.

Joan Maynard wanted to remove the word 'gradually'.

We lost that one.

Dennis Skinner said trade union rights should be included (which was a reference to reinstatement of sacked miners and was one of my amendments).

'It is not in doubt that we'll do something,' John Prescott said. But we were defeated.

On accountability for the police, Blunkett queried the phrase 'the Queen's Peace' and said, 'Why do we have to raise the question of the Queen's Peace? It is medieval.'

So Kaufman replied, 'Well, we are a party that believes in the monarchy, and the Queen's Peace is the proper way to describe it. We are not a republican party.'

Then I moved a number of amendments to the item on democracy, lifting the disqualification on the surcharged councillors, and restoring and strengthening civil liberties.

Kinnock said, 'I'll take a bet that if we include it the Tories will attack us on it, and we can do it without putting it up in neon lights.'

This was the argument he used throughout. If he didn't like anything, he said, 'I'll mention it in my speeches.'

I pointed out at one stage that the one group of people who *did* read the manifesto were civil servants, and if a commitment wasn't in the manifesto they didn't feel under any obligation to carry it out.

Kaufman wanted the reference to a 'Palestinian state' removed because we wouldn't know its frontiers.

I said, 'Well, the Labour Party supported a Jewish state long before we knew its frontiers, and anyway Israel's frontiers have been continually expanding.'

But the removal of the phrase was carried, and all we were left with was 'self-determination for Palestinians', which, as I pointed out, could simply mean local autonomy.

Peter Shore objected to the words 'decommissioning Polaris' and said we should only decommission it when it became obsolete.

On removal of US weapons and bases, the phrase was: 'if the negotiations failed, we would consult with the Americans and then inform them that we wished them to remove their missiles' – terribly weak.

Joan Maynard asked, '*Why* are we consulting with the Americans?'

Kinnock replied 'The remaining weapons and bases will go, but we must have consultation – that is necessary. How do you enforce it anyway if they won't go? Do you send in the SAS? They are a NATO ally. We're a sovereign state, but we don't want to smash up NATO.'

Then I moved another amendment proposing that we transfer resources from the savings on defence to peaceful purposes. That was clearly passed at last year's Conference. We were spending 20 per cent more on defence in real terms than in 1979, and nobody believed that Gorbachev was more of a threat than Brezhnev. Polls showed that 56 per cent of people thought Reagan was likely to cause nuclear war and only 12 per cent thought the Russians were.

Kinnock said, 'We must meet the argument that, if Labour were to move money from defence to civil development, we would be left defenceless. Anyway, defence expenditure creates jobs.'

We had a vote on it, and were defeated by 29 votes to 6 – myself, Audrey Wise, Jo Richardson, Linda Douglas, Dennis Skinner and Joan Maynard.

At the end, Kinnock said, 'We've discussed this for two hours, and the meeting has been held in goodwill; nobody should go away with animosity. It is not only policy we're talking about but our presentation.' He stressed our unity.

By 30 to 6, which is a ratio of 5 to 1, that meeting overturned Conference policy which itself had been carried by 5 to 1. I couldn't find anyone sympathetic except our little gang.

Wednesday 13 May

The press today had all the headlines Kinnock would have wanted – 'Kinnock Beats the Left' and so on. He wants to begin the Election with a victory over the left to show he is in charge. The *Evening Standard* said that, if he wins, he'll be able to disregard the left and the Conference. But, if he loses, nobody will be able to say that the left lost him the Election, because it will be his personal victory or his personal defeat.

Typed my Election address, including a warm tribute to myself, and left it on the photocopier at the Commons. When I returned to retrieve it, Ivan Lawrence and another Tory MP were sitting there with it.

Ivan said, 'Not bad. If I were a Labour man in Chesterfield, I think I'd vote for you. I've never thought of describing myself in such glowing terms; I've always left that to my admirers.'

'I suppose, if you wrote it yourself, you could say it was written by an admirer!'

They laughed.

Friday 15 May

A poll published today gives the Tories an 18 per cent lead. Mrs Thatcher was so confident and clear on the television news, and Kinnock was so boastful and wordy and weak. His popularity is falling rapidly.

Thursday 21 May

I watched the party political broadcast, which opened with the title 'Kinnock'. It began with a bomber flying, then a bird flying, then Neil and Glenys on a mountain top, then Kinnock talking straight to camera about his inspiration, a woman from Wales saying, 'We always knew he would make it'; he talked about his parents and Glenys was brought in again. They showed speeches by Kinnock, with tremendous applause. The centre point was his attack on Militant at the Bournemouth Conference, and the camera flashed to Derek Hatton. The high peak of his strength is that he attacked the Militant Tendency. It made my blood run cold.

Friday 22 May

Spent most of the day out in Duckmanton and Poolsbrook, mining villages on the outskirts of Chesterfield. Visited a few old people's homes. Quite a few people said they thought the Kinnock broadcast was brilliant and would have a tremendous impact.

Wednesday 27 May

Got the papers, and the slanging match between the leaders goes on.

Reagan has said how much he admires Mrs Thatcher and how he thinks he would be able to live with a Labour Government. His intervention must make people hopping mad, I would imagine.

David Steel has produced a list of '101 hard-left' MPs, and of course I was on it. So was Tam Dalyell! It was astonishing. Even Harry Barnes in Derbyshire North East is listed as a dangerous red!

Thursday 4 June

I went to the market and made two little speeches, and people did listen carefully. There was a round of applause at the second meeting – like a village cricket match when somebody scores a run.

Returned to the NUM offices in the afternoon, and Jack Dash, the old dockers' leader, had arrived for an Election meeting. He is nearly eighty-one, led many of the dock strikes, is a long-term member of the CP, and a man whom I deeply respect. He had written such a nice letter saying he would like to help, so Johnny Burrows paid his fare up from London and Bas Barker, a Chesterfield trade-unionist and CP member, had organised a meeting of about thirty or forty pensioners. He made a marvellous, reflective speech.

Saturday 6 June

Went to the Market Square for the hustings with the other two candidates. There were 400–500 people listening, and it was enormously worthwhile. There was some friendly heckling. Several old characters turned up – Tommy Tatters with his cap and his placard saying 'Mrs Thatcher's worse than Attila the Hun', and Gloria Havenhand, who used to be leader of the Tory Group on the council, all dolled up. She kept shouting, 'That! From a man who went to a public school!' – at which Johnny Burrows replied, 'That! From a woman with no education!' Then there was a weird local doctor who asked whether the Americans would press the nuclear button if Labour was elected.

During the day I had a good talk with Edward Barber, the headteacher from Norwich who runs the Common Market Safeguards Committee, and to Tom and Johnny about the post-Election scene. Looking at what is happening in the Election campaign, there is a shift away from the right, not particularly to the left, but the Tory Party will lose some seats and the balance between the Thatcherites and the anti-Thatcherites will tilt against the Prime Minister. The SDP-Liberal Alliance will pretty well collapse as a political force, and Owen might even be defeated himself.

Thursday 11 June

In the car to all the committee rooms and to some polling stations. It appeared from the first results that it was going to be a Tory landslide. Caroline and I walked over to the Winding Wheel centre where the count was, and I did actually worry about my own position.

The media were already beginning their usual chorus about why we had done badly – the hard left, the loony left, and so on, although the results weren't suggesting that at all. Eric Heffer, for example, had a huge increase in his majority from 15,000 to 23,000. Terry Fields and Dave Nellist doubled their majorities in Liverpool Broadgreen and Coventry South East. Chris Mullin won in Sunderland South, increasing the Labour vote, and my majority over the Liberal Alliance candidate was 8,500. It was in the south of England that things went badly for Labour.

NOTES
Chapter Eight

1. (p. 485) Tony Gifford, QC, a radical lawyer, chaired an inquiry into the disturbances on Broadwater Farm Estate during which a police constable was knifed to death. A subsequent campaign, led by journalist Charles Wheeler, Bernie Grant MP, and others led at the end of 1991 to the quashing of the convictions of Engin Raghip, Mark Braithwaite and Winston Silcott for the murder of PC Keith Blakelock.

2. (p. 490) The BBC in preparing six programmes in the series *Secret Society* included an investigation into a Defence project called Zircon. There was nothing very secret about developing a surveillance system of this kind, which already existed in the US and the USSR. But the Government was determined to keep it a secret and a court injunction was granted forbidding the researcher and presenter, Duncan Campbell, from revealing the information. Also, Campbell's home was raided for documents. Copies of the video had however become available and the film was indeed shown within the precincts of the Palace of Westminster. When the Speaker banned further showings of the film, an almighty parliamentary row followed. The Government skilfully decided to embroil the opposition in this by revealing to Neil Kinnock, 'on Privy Councillor terms', their reasons for opposition to the film, which he was then obliged to support.

In the resulting debate, which was forced on the Government, it became apparent that if the Speaker's ruling were endorsed it would create a precedent under which the Speaker could, permanently or temporarily, restrict the right of MPs to receive information in the course of their parliamentary duties.

My last-minute manuscript amendment was successful in referring the matter to the Committee of Privileges. The Speaker accepted this motion, I think, in part because he was uneasy at his action and feared that the two Front Benches might surrender rights belonging to the House.

In the event the Committee of Privileges upheld the Speaker's right to have acted as he did!

9
Back to Grassroots
June 1987–December 1989

Sunday 14 June
At 6.30 the ILCS gathered at home – the biggest meeting for two years –
for a post-mortem on the Election.

Jim Mortimer asked, 'What evidence is there that the campaign
altered the outcome? It was perfectly clear that 60 per cent of the people
had decided before the Election date was announced. Kinnock was
praised by the media because he was seen by them as a good
investment. There was no socialist content in the programme, no
economic content in terms of challenging the multinationals, and we
were recommitted by the leadership in stronger support of NATO.'

Jim thought Kinnock had not shifted a single vote. Compared to
1983, when there had been all the attacks on the defence policy by the
leadership, it was really a most disappointing result.

Tariq Ali said, 'Kinnock's campaign was to strengthen his hold over
the Labour Party. It pleased many members and gave them a lift, but it
was an apolitical campaign. The bourgeois media want Kinnock to
stay in charge, but right-wing careerists may be as dissatisfied as others
with Kinnock's position, and there may be a right-wing candidate for
the leadership, perhaps John Smith. We'll have to keep an eye on that.
Also, the question of proportional representation will arise again.'

One of the things that had struck Tariq was the highly non-political
nature of the campaign, which had demobilised CND, for example.
However, as CND were under the *Marxism Today* wing of the labour
movement, they had wanted to be demobilised.

It was a marvellous meeting.

Wednesday 17 June
Our thirty-eighth wedding anniversary.

Went to the Commons for the first PLP meeting, and my instinct was
to sit and listen and get the feel of it. Derek Foster, the Chief Whip, took
the chair. He congratulated the winners, welcomed people back, and
said, 'The campaign to win the next Election will start today. We must
remember the comrades who lost their seats.' He said the Parliamentary Committee had decided to back the re-election of Mr Speaker
Weatherill.

At 12.10 Neil Kinnock spoke. He said, 'This is the most successful campaign in the history of the Party. It has been recognised as such by our opponents and the pundits. It was well organised, the performances were good, and, comparing speech for speech, interview for interview and press confererence for press conference, we beat them all along the line. We fought as a team together and we have achieved a great deal. We made gains – for the first time the number of Labour women MPs is up to twenty-one, and for the first time we are a multiracial party, which I hope will affect the self-image of black voters.' He congratulated the four black and Asian Members, Diane Abbott, Paul Boateng, Bernie Grant and Keith Vaz, (the new MPs for Hackney North and Stoke Newington, Brent South, Tottenham, and Leicester East).

Kinnock went on, 'I must mention some failures. One is that we failed to win the Election, and there is no consolation for defeat in any form. Millions will suffer, the young will be isolated, the old will be frightened, the sick and the unemployed will have no prizes, but the result provides a better basis for building up.'

Then, with a lot of rhetorical flourishes, he said, 'We must show we are in charge of events. We must emphasise freedom. We must seek a refreshment of the values which we inspire. There must be a strategy for dealing with change or we will lose again. There is a great deal to play for.' He continued in this vein, and became hectoring. 'With every word, every action and every deed we must support the idea of victory. We must convince people. There is a demand for unity from the movement to disappoint the commentators, to deny them the splits. The SDP and the Liberals are divided but they are treated with kid gloves. There must be energy and commitment, the characteristic of the future. We must ensure that none of us has to dismiss this group or that group in any interview or be distracted or diverted. We must accept the light burden of self-discipline.'

Dave Nellist observed, 'We couldn't win the Election in three and a half weeks. Sixty per cent decided how to vote before the campaign, and there was a lot of time wasted on expulsions. The best swings to Labour were in Liverpool.' He said he hoped the PLP would fight outside Parliament.

There was a lot of shouting at this.

Clive Soley said, 'We want to avoid internecine war. The London situation is not the responsibility of the Party or of individuals but of the inherent situation in London.' That was quite a sensible point.

At 9 Lev Parshin from the Soviet Embassy came to see me at home. I'm sure the security services think it is some deep plot, but all he wanted was a briefing on the Election, what I thought of Kinnock's and Thatcher's positions, and so on.

He said that Zemyatin had raised with Geoffrey Howe the question of human rights in the case of Mike Hicks's imprisonment. Geoffrey Howe had never heard of Mike Hicks – which made Parshin laugh. He told me that, partly as a result of my interview in the Moscow papers about human rights in Northern Ireland, Gorbachev raised the issue of Northern Ireland with Mrs Thatcher (although he probably would have done it anyway). Parshin thought it was the first time Thatcher had ever come up against these arguments. She was in favour of capitalism and individualism and Gorbachev was in favour of peace and collectivism. She had been impressed by him.

Parshin said he would like the television programme *Spitting Image* to be available in the Soviet Union, because it makes fun of Soviet leaders. Altogether, the whole thing was so relaxed. When I look at my diary for the mid-Sixties, I realise the Soviet people I met then were not all that different but they wouldn't accept criticism.

Friday 19 June
Up at 5 and flew to Dublin with Chris Mullin for a meeting organised by the Birmingham Six Committee. First we were taken to see the Irish Foreign Minister, Brian Lenihan, in a stately home which houses the Irish Foreign Ministry. He is fifty-seven, with curly greased hair, and I formed an instant distrust of him. He shook me by the hand and said, 'Chesterfield is lucky to have such a good MP, Tony.' Then he turned to Chris; 'And you did well in Sunderland, and so did your football team in the recent game.'

We sat and talked for about an hour. Just before Christmas, he was in the Opposition and he spoke on a Birmingham Six platform, but now he is Foreign Minister it will be almost impossible to get him to do anything about the case.

Chris, who is a persistent guy, said, 'What we want you to do is to raise the case at the Anglo-Irish Agreement talks, make a public statement that you are concerned and will delay the ratification of the Extradition Treaty* until you have got these people released.'

Lenihan looked cautious, and I realised that he did not want to endanger his reputation with the British Government, since his office covers a wide range of things.

I supported Chris as best I could, and I said, 'Look, you can do it very skilfully. You could let it be known that you are concerned and have raised it. Secondly, express your confidence publicly that when the case comes to the Court of Appeal in the autumn the Government in Britain will not dare to have the appeal turned down. Keep the pressure up. Go to the United Nations, talk to the Americans – see that Britain is put under pressure. You can do it perfectly well.'

* On 1 December 1987 the Irish Government signed a treaty ratifying the Extradition (European Convention on the Suppression of Terrorism) Act 1987, under the terms of which terrorist suspects could be extradited to Britain from the Republic of Ireland.

He said, 'I see you are a pragmatic man.'

'I'm just putting my ministerial experience at your disposal for this particular purpose,' I replied.

There were three typical civil servants there, twittering nervously. I think we registered the point, and Chris has made it clear he doesn't think the Irish Government has done enough.

As we left, I said, 'I very much envy you your opportunity as Foreign Minister at this particular moment in history when the Gorbachev offers have given us an opportunity of making peace.' He was flattered by that.

We went to the Shelbourne Hotel to address 400–500 people. Other speakers were Bishop Kavanagh (the acting Bishop of Dublin), Mary McAleese, Chris Mullin and myself, and Tim Pat Coogan, the editor of the *Irish Press*, who is a very amusing fifty-two-year-old media man with white hair. The meeting was quite electric. I quoted from Father's amendment to the Queen's Speech in 1920 denouncing the Black and Tans, and I said, 'I'm a hereditary home-ruler.' This produced a tremendous effect. I went on to develop the arguments about Britain's presence in Ireland and how the Americans wanted a defence base in the Atlantic.

Saturday 20 June

Up at 5, and with Chris Mullin and Joe Colgan, a successful Dublin businessman who is one of the organisers of the Birmingham Six campaign, drove to Dublin airport through Phoenix Park, where Lord Frederick Cavendish was murdered in 1882. I got this feeling that nothing changes – 105 years ago the British Chief Secretary for Ireland was murdered in Dublin, and the violence is still continuing.

Got back to London in the afternoon, and went to the Socialist Society meeting to consider the possibility of having a conference on socialism later in the year. There were a lot of people there, including Phil Kelly, Hilary Wainwright, Kevin Davey, Anthony Arblaster, Richard Kuyper, John Palmer, Ralph Miliband, Sarah Spain and others I didn't know – young academics, socialists and Marxists associated with the Socialist Society.

To cut a long story short, it was agreed to invite everyone we know on the left in Britain – in the trade unions and the Labour Party, MPs and people outside the Party – and to hold the conference in Chesterfield. Our themes would be those we have brought forward since 1985: a million jobs a year, non-alignment and democracy – ie peace, jobs and freedom.

It was pretty well agreed, and I was tremendously pleased about this because Ralph has been urging it for some time, and we have all been a bit cautious. Some of the London intellectuals were reluctant about the Chesterfield venue!

Monday 22 June
Worked on the Chesterfield conference idea and found we could get the Winding Wheel, which is the new municipal leisure centre in Chesterfield with an auditorium and ballroom, all for £250, and then we heard that would be covered in some way by the local authority, so that's marvellous.

Tuesday 23 June
At 3 the editor and researcher on *Panorama* came to see me for a couple of hours about a programme they are doing on security, including a profile of Peter Wright, an account of the Government's attempts to suppress *Spycatcher*, and the origins and the full nature of the smears against Harold Wilson. I had said I wasn't terribly interested but they could come and have a talk if they wanted. The conversation was riveting. What they really wanted was for me to confirm rumours about myself related to security.

I said, 'Well, there are a lot of examples, but I don't want to talk about them.'

They asked, 'Why ever not?'

I said, 'Well, quite simply because I have taken a close interest in security from a constitutional point of view over many years, and personal examples will just make me look absurd. I am prepared to discuss what it is really about.'

'Well, what is it really about?'

I said, 'Well, it is about the Americans controlling British security in return for our getting nuclear weapons.'

They insisted, 'But surely you want to help us to prove that Mrs Thatcher didn't speak the truth when she said that the allegations of bugging and smears against Wilson had turned out to be untrue.'

I said, 'No, I don't want to prove that she is a liar.'

They asked, 'What do you mean?'

I told them, 'I'm sorry, but I think all you are doing is muck-raking and creating another shock-horror story, which makes people disillusioned and frightened.' I described the umbilical cord which links us to the United States through intelligence and their satellite system, and how they controlled our nuclear and intelligence policy. 'Anyway, Callaghan and Wilson were both the same, every Prime Minister has been the same. The problem is that no Labour Leaders have ever dared to touch the centre of power because, as a matter of fact, they enjoy it and use it for their own purposes.'

They said, 'Will you let us put questions to you about smears against you? Then you could dismiss all those smears.'

I replied, 'No, because it would look as if I was being evasive in my answers. I am not interested in that. The awful truth is that I don't trust the BBC – they are vetted by MI5, and they wouldn't be allowed to make a programme if it got on to the real issue, which is that the security services bug the left.'

Thursday 25 June
Lev Parshin called me to confirm that Moscow want me to go to the USSR as a guest of the Institute of International Relations and World Economy.

Wednesday 1 July
To the Commons for a PLP meeting, where there was a motion by Graham Allen: 'the Parliamentary Party, aware that the media will seek to exploit any perceived differences of view between Labour Members, requests that all future offers of interviews on television, on internal Party matters, are notified to an agreed Party authority. This will in no way inhibit members appearing, but will assist the Party and the PLP in putting over a positive and coherent strategy in the continuing battle against the Tories.'

Graham Allen has just been elected for Nottingham North. Although this looked an interesting idea, it has tremendous dangers.

I was doubtful about whether to speak, but decided I would, and I said, 'Everybody shares the concern about the use of the radio, television and the press to damage us. The resolution has three fatal flaws. First of all, it is completely impracticable, because, if you are interviewed when you are away from home by a unit that comes up in the street, you don't know what questions they are going to ask. Secondly, you get unexpected trick questions. Thirdly, it is bureaucratic, because it implies that you have got to get permission, and, if you don't notify or don't get permission, it becomes conduct prejudicial to the interests of the Party, which is now an expellable offence. You can't legislate for goodwill and incorporate it in standing orders. Therefore I hope that this is not moved.'

Well, to my amazement (my influence in the PLP being pretty minimal), Dick Douglas and Doug Hoyle supported me and everything was withdrawn, so that was a little coup. Many people afterwards said they agreed with me. I can see there's one function for me in damping down the bitter hostility there is in the PLP towards certain people. This was directed against Ken Livingstone and Members who have been a bit too free in television interviews.

Sunday 12 July
Chunks of Peter Wright's book were published in the *Sunday Times*. I must say, reading his words did make my blood run cold. Here was the American CIA trying to destroy an elected Prime Minister, and Peter Wright himself said that half the MI5 officers were trying to get rid of the Labour Government and that they 'bugged and burgled' their way

across London'. He also referred to the assassination attempt on President Nasser.

Monday 13 July

Two graduate students arrived at the office this morning to work for a while – Alice Moberly and Hywel Jarman, a nice lad who has been at Queen Mary College.

Today I wrote to the American Ambassador asking him to confirm reports in Peter Wright's book *Spycatcher* about Jim Angleton, then head of counter-espionage in the CIA, having penetrated MI5. The 10 o'clock news tonight reported it and it will greatly embarrass the Ambassador. I don't know what the hell he will say in reply, but at least it will warn the intelligence community.

Thursday 16 July

When I arrived back at Euston from a trip to Coventry I found the whole station crowded, with all the emergency services there, and discovered that there had been a burst in a 42-inch water main and the whole car park and much of the station was under water. My car may well be totally submerged.

Wednesday 22 July

Got to Walworth Road at about 9, and stood for a while with the members of the Labour Party staff who were protesting against the proposals coming before the NEC to close *Labour Weekly*, *New Socialist* and *Socialist Youth*.

At the NEC the redundancy proposal was accepted by 22 votes to 6.

Tam Dalyell said it would be a political blow to close *Labour Weekly*. He thought MPs were very committed to it, and he was opposed to all the money spent on polling.

Michael Meacher said, 'It's not the time to do this', and then promptly voted for the closure.

I wrote a little note and passed it round. It said: 'Labour's policy for the media: (1) Put ads in the Tory press at a cost of £2 million. (2) Close *Labour Weekly* and the *New Socialist*. (3) Expel anyone who sells *Militant*.'

As I listened to all these people talking, I did wonder yet again whether the Labour Party at this level isn't in a state of terminal decline, because here we are pouring money out on personality stuff during the Election, thanking the staff at Walworth Road, saying it was a brilliant campaign and then, as soon as it's over, sacking the people who had done all the work.

I don't know why I serve on the NEC, but that's the story, and when anyone comes to ask why the Labour Party died I've described it in my diary today.

Saturday 1 August
Spent the whole day working on a speech about *Spycatcher*, having been invited to read from the book at Speakers' Corner tomorrow in defiance of the ban. I rang Tony Gifford, who said it sounded all right and that they couldn't prosecute me for making a speech in a public place. So I asked if a press release about it was a publication and he said, 'No, but it is if the press release is published. That's for the publishers to decide.' I asked what criminal liability there would be if I was arrested, and he said it would be criminal contempt of the judges. There wouldn't be a jury, I would just go before the judges themselves in a divisional court, and I could be fined. They could sequestrate me if I didn't pay the fine. So I am taking a risk tomorrow, but I feel it's very important and, to be candid, I am not by any means alone in this. Lord Denning has said that the ban is ridiculous, everyone is denouncing it, and it's one of the few occasions when the media will be sympathetic.

Sunday 2 August
Turned up in Hyde Park at Speakers' Corner early and met someone from the Campaign for Press and Broadcasting Freedom.

I had prepared my speech with enormous care. I read it out and included long passages from *Spycatcher*. There was a bit of heckling from a man wearing a T-shirt with the words 'Colonel North for President' and 'Help the Russians Join CND', and shouting silly slogans.

There was a mass of journalists from all the papers and television stations, and I did several interviews. As I broke through the crowd, there was Caroline with Hilary's dog, so we walked back through the park.

Monday 3 August
Tremendous press coverage of Hyde Park, with pictures in all the papers except the *Daily Mail*. It is probably the best press I have had for twenty years because I happened to be on the side of the newspaper proprietors. But I have got to be clear about it, the newspaper proprietors just resent being told what they are allowed to publish. They have no interest in the lessons of the Wright book, because for years the left have said that the security services were out of control, that they bugged and burgled and committed acts of assassination, and the press censored it themselves. Their interest in the Peter Wright book is simply to give publicity to his argument that Sir Roger Hollis and Harold Wilson were Soviet agents.

Thursday 13 August
Stansgate. Lovely day with a little rain. Caroline is working on the Keir Hardie correspondence. He was obviously a difficult man, a loner who quarrelled with everybody. Various biographies have been written to

suggest that he wasn't a socialist but just an old Christian radical. Every generation of historians rewrites history to bring it into line with the current philosophy.

Joshua phoned from the United States to say the Hyde Park reading of *Spycatcher* was front-page news there.

The House of Lords announced their judgement on *Spycatcher*, and by 3 to 2 they voted to uphold the injunction. The lessons of *Spycatcher* are getting broader and broader – not only that there is secret material that Mrs Thatcher doesn't want publicised but that the judges are tools of the Government. The BBC World Service can't broadcast material that is broadcast by every other world broadcasting organisation.

Friday 14 August
Worked on letters. Listened to Danish radio, which had a programme, in Danish, on *Spycatcher* in which the extracts from it were in English, mostly the ones I had read in Hyde Park. I felt rather like someone in the French Resistance sitting in an attic with a radio.

Saturday 29 August
Chris Mullin's wife Ngoc, whom he met two years ago in Vietnam, arrived from Saigon a few days ago, so I drove to his flat in Brixton Road to meet her. There had been television cameras at the airport when she arrived.

Friday 4 September
Went to the press launch of the Socialist Conference held in the Commons. The questioning was much less sharp than I had expected. They picked up the fact that Dafydd Ellis Thomas, the Welsh Nationalist MP, was one of the sponsors, and tried to make something of that, suggesting it would be divisive. I dealt with it all blandly. The first thing is to get out the information that there is a conference and what it is going to do.

Saturday 5 September
There was mass coverage of yesterday's press conference. *The Times* on page 1 said, 'Benn seeks soul of Labour Party', the *Guardian* 'Benn sets a new vision for the Labour Party'.

Thursday 10 September
I had an envelope from the Indian High Commissioner, inside which was an envelope with a big seal, and inside that was a cardboard folder, and inside that was a letter from Rajiv Gandhi, in response to my letter about disarmament and development. In July I had written to Gandhi, Robert Mugabe of Zimbabwe and Castro suggesting that they form a

commission which would link disarmament with aid for growth in 'developing' countries.

I must say I was surprised to get a reply from Gandhi, and it was very friendly. He said my proposal would be considered and he awaited with interest the response from the UN Secretary-General, to whom I had sent a copy. I also this week received an enthusiastic response from the Zimbabwean Foreign Affairs Secretary. I have had no response whatever from Castro.

Thursday 17 September

The Liberal Assembly in Harrogate voted overwhelmingly to merge with that part of the SDP that wants to, and set up a new party. It is a historic moment, because the Liberal Party has been in existence for about 150 years, had a fine tradition of its own and is now throwing in its lot with people who don't share its principles, approach or anything else. It is bound to fail. David Owen's achievement is amazing. First of all, he tries to split the Labour Party and fails, then he splits the SDP, and now he has split the Liberal Party and persuaded them to go out of existence.

Labour Party Conference, Brighton
Saturday 26 September

Drove to Brighton for the Conference.

In the evening we went to the Dome Theatre for the Campaign Group rally. It was a disaster, because the hall would have held 2000 and there were only 200, so it looked desolate. We are very much in the margins now; it isn't just the leadership that is running away, there is a total collapse of confidence among the active Party members. I don't rule out the possibility that there will be a major change in the composition of the NEC, with Bryan Gould knocking off one of us. These are very thin years for the left, but you have to think ahead.

Sunday 27 September

The arguments used by the leadership at today's pre-Conference NEC were more right-wing that I can remember for years. Geoff Bish has swung to the right, recommending us against accepting any development of Party policy in a progressive direction. We hung on to support for our non-nuclear defence policy officially and our opposition to nuclear power – just.

I think the truth is that the Labour Party isn't believed any more because people suspect it will say anything to get votes. The rebuilding of some radical alternative to Thatcherism – and by that I mean all-party Thatcherism –will require us to do some very difficult things.

The weather is beautiful. The Grand Hotel, where Mrs Thatcher and her Cabinet were bombed, has now been completely rebuilt and stands there like a white wedding cake on the sea-front.

Monday 28 September
NEC elections. Margaret Beckett and Joan Maynard, who came back on in 1983, were defeated for the women's section and replaced by Anne Davis and Joan Lestor. Tam Dalyell fell off the constituency section, which is his own fault, because he voted with the right all the time. The sad thing was that Audrey Wise was also knocked off the constituency section. Ken Livingstone and Bryan Gould came on. I was second and Blunkett was top.

Tuesday 29 September
We had the Leader's speech, which I watched from the gallery because I knew the TV cameras would pick me out on the platform if Kinnock made any references that might apply to me in any way. I found the speech deeply intimidating. At the end he made a threat of disciplinary action against anyone who did anything which in his view put defeating the Tories second to 'the purity of powerlessness'.

Dennis and I talked about the deputy leadership, and he told me a lot of people would like to put up a candidate next year. He said he thought Roy Hattersley would probably want to withdraw, that it would all be set for Bryan Gould, that John Prescott would stand and there would have to be a left candidate. I said perhaps Ken Livingstone might stand. I can't say I am interested in it, but it may be right to have a candidature.

Dennis said, 'You're the only credible candidate.'

Wednesday 30 September
Went to hear Hilary speak in the education debate, and it went down extremely well, so I'm awfully pleased for him. In the *Guardian* today there was a piece mentioning that Stephen had 100 people at his fringe meeting, while I only had thirty at mine!

In the afternoon we had a vote on the renationalisation of privatised assets. There was an overwhelming majority for it in the Conference, but, after a card vote had been called, it was defeated by half a million. Peter Heathfield made a passionate speech. Ray Buckton made his farewell speech and got a standing ovation.

At 5.15 I went to the meeting of the NEC, where Neil said how good Hilary had been, and I said how good Glenys had been on television this morning. It's the first friendly exchange we've had for about four years.

Thursday 1 October
This Conference leaves me with a strange feeling. Kinnock got his franchise changes accepted, got his 'Moving Ahead' statement through, which was well received by the media, and he made his speech. But somehow things began to go wrong. Not only did he lose a

few votes but, having flexed his muscles and having cashed in on his personal election 'victory', he found that Ken Livingstone decided to make an issue of the non-nuclear defence policy. Ken said there would be civil war if any attempt was made to change it, so Kinnock, in order to avoid trouble, declared that Ken's speech was very good, and we reaffirmed the policy. Then yesterday, when Bryan Gould made a speech in favour of wider share ownership, he was booed out of existence. So all in all it wasn't too bad. People are depressed and want to put up a candidate against Kinnock, but the more I think about it the more I believe it's a bad idea.

Friday 2 October

Heard Dennis Skinner deliver a brilliant speech on legal reform which brought everybody to their feet as always. He is an inspired man, extremely funny, very serious and absolutely to the point.

Michael Meacher and I were asked to do a recorded interview for *Newsnight*, presented by Peter Snow who is the media leader of the SDP. For years *Newsnight* has done nothing but show the Labour Party as unelectable, boost the Alliance and give David Owen lots of time. They had set up in one of the lobbies of the conference centre, and it turned out they had got together a film in which the editor of *Marxism Today* appeared. The last sentence in the little film was Martin Jacques saying that I personally was a spent force.

So Peter Snow turned to me and asked, 'Are you a spent force, as Martin Jacques says?'

I said, 'Martin Jacques is a Eurocommunist who believes in an alliance with the SDP.'

'Will you answer the question?' he demanded.

I turned on him and said, 'Look, let me be clear. You've been running an anti-Labour campaign . . .' Then I used some of the arguments I've just listed, and added, 'If democracy ever dies in Britain, it will be because of you.'

Around the studio set, with Michael Meacher sitting behind me, was a crowd of about fifty people – delegates, officials, security people and so on – and my attack on the BBC led to a great round of applause.

So then Peter Snow turned to Michael Meacher, who said the left was actually in charge of the Party (which was a load of old rubbish) and the policy reviews would be undertaken with balanced views, and so on.

Then Snow came back to me. 'Now, Mr Kinnock says that he is not going to let the tail wag the dog.'

I said, 'I'm not going to discuss Mr Kinnock. His own position is clear.'

Then he asked, 'What new ideas have come from the left?'

I replied, 'All the ideas about non-alignment; that the Russian military threat is not true, that the Americans don't speak for freedom and democracy, that Chernobyl shows that nuclear weapons don't make you safe.'

This threw him completely, and he went back to Michael Meacher. At one point I said to him, 'Don't act the part of God', and everybody round burst into cheers. He had never had to do his interview in a public meeting before. It has always been in the safety of his own constituency, which is Lime Grove North!

It was a marvellous little incident. Needless to say, they didn't use the interview at all.

Went back to the Conference and stood between Joan Maynard and Audrey Wise, both of whom had lost their seats on the NEC and were in tears. Audrey is an MP, so she is all right, but Joan has retired from Parliament and she is such a strong woman that it was very sad to see her upset.

My thoughts on leaving the Conference are that the whole thing was a media show. Socialism was mentioned in every sentence, and then by nudges and winks from the platform the media were told, 'Don't worry, we don't mean what we appear to mean.' They were using that to imply that the left were a ridiculous tiny minority against a socialist majority led by Kinnock.

There was a clear denial of class in everything that was said. What the Labour Party has done is to accept the Tory description of class – that there are the employed affluent workers on the one hand and the unemployed no-goods on the other – and to say the latter are an 'underclass' which just has to be catered for in some way.

Actually, the class distinction is between the very, very rich who live on dividends and who can afford to buy their house from their dividends, can afford to pay for their children's education, can afford to pay the full cost of medical care and can afford pensions from their own resources – all without working. But the docker from Bermondsey to whom Kinnock referred, earning £500 a week, with a car and a 'small place' in Marbella and a colour television, would be lost completely if he lost his job. So we represent people who depend for their living upon what they earn, and that is a distinction which puts the rich in a minority and labour in a majority.

I don't think we should contest the leadership, but John Prescott may put up against Hattersley and Michael Meacher may then throw his hat into the ring. I'm not getting mixed up in that.

Thursday 8 October

There was a fascinating story in the press about the Duke of Windsor having given the *Daily Herald* an interview in 1937, declaring that if the Labour Party wanted to turn Britain into a republic he would be prepared to be the first president. He also said that in the event of Hitler invading Britain he would be pressed to resume the throne.

Friday 9 October

The Tory Party Conference ended with an eleven-minute standing ovation for Mrs Thatcher, the singing of 'Rule Britannia', waving of flags, and so on; yet, although they sound on the up and up, I think the base is not very secure, what with the poll tax, the attacks on the NHS and local government, and nuclear rearmament.

Tuesday 13 October

Had a long talk with Ken Coates, who said he was trying to organise a seminar on disarmament and development. I told him about the letters I had sent Gorbachev and other leaders. He thought it might be too way out and wondered whether we shouldn't start campaigning for a directly elected assembly for the UN, a sort of world assembly, one MP for every 5 million people. I think that's a marvellous idea.

Friday 16 October

In the middle of the night we had the worst storm since 1703, with the wind speed in London reaching 94 mph. Trees were torn up all over the place. In Kew Gardens it will take 200 years for the trees that were lost to be replaced to maturity. The weather men never predicted it, though it was actually a hurricane. There are trees lying all over the streets. Caroline has been staying at Stansgate, where there was a power cut. Enormous damage has been done. The whole thing was unreal; it was like a day that didn't exist, one of those days that has a special character of its own.

Wednesday 21 October
Heard that the Welsh Regional Executive of the Labour Party had condemned the Chesterfield Socialist Conference this weekend, calling on members of the Party to boycott it and calling on the NEC to consider the conduct of those members of the NEC who had participated. I did think that was funny!

Friday 23 October
The stock market is falling and there is a great panic.

Saturday 24 October
In Chesterfield for the Socialist Conference. Caroline and I went over to the conference centre at the Winding Wheel. It was a beautiful day, and people were queuing all the way down the street. I walked up and down talking to people. The *Socialist Worker* and *Workers' Power* paper sellers were there, but I don't think *Militant* is taking much notice.

Johnny Burrows was in the chair for the plenary sessions, and a Spartacist or SWP or RCP member got up and said the whole conference should be cancelled in order to force those on the platform to explain why they hadn't mobilised against the Tories. So he had to be dealt with. The Russian delegation was introduced, and the SWP objected to that. I must say, by then people were getting a bit fed up and so was I.

I made my speech, then went and repeated it in the ballroom, where there was an overflow meeting.

In the afternoon we had the theme sessions – 'Democracy' led by John Griffiths and Paul Foot; 'Economic Policy' with Jim Mortimer and Robin Murray; and 'Foreign Affairs' which Jeremy Corbyn looked after.

There were workshops in the afternoon, and Caroline conducted one on education, but there were 200 people there and it was too big to have an informal discussion.

In the evening we had a concert and speeches from Ken Livingstone and Arthur Scargill.

The mood and the excitement are great, but the Conference isn't all that well structured. There are differences that need to be sorted out. The sectarian left are a nuisance, but the feeling that something is being done dominates, and with a couple of thousand people here there is no doubt that we have launched something big.

Sunday 25 October
Up at 4.50 and went to buy the papers, looking in at the Goldwell Rooms – a great big, draughty, dirty old drill-hall of a place – where some of the comrades attending the Conference were staying. There were lots of people up having coffee. They had been sleeping on

mattresses provided by the fire brigade, and the council had provided heaters they have for use after floods. There was a woman with four children who said it was a bit better than Greenham Common!

Caroline and I went to the three sessions. It seemed the SWP had all gone home in buses, so it was much better. The Greens were dissatisfied at the lack of general participation in discussions. A Danish woman MP wanted a Chesterfield conference in Copenhagen. There was a Canadian woman, a black headmaster from Zimbabwe who was on holiday and had heard about the conference, and some Nicaraguans and representatives from the ANC, so it had a good international flavour.

Food had been laid on by the church, and the stewarding was good. There were no police or security checks of any kind. The police had wanted supervision, but the organisers had said it wasn't needed. The police argued that a conference of this kind would be 'likely to lead to drug abuse', treating us like they would a hippy convoy.

The final plenary went well, and the conference ended with a lot of goodwill.

Afterwards I gave various interviews and attended the press conference. The press corps treated us seriously. We were asked about the Trotskyites, and I said when Trotsky was advancing on the Winter Palace in 1917 I didn't think he had been planning how to disrupt the Chesterfield Conference seventy years later.

Monday 26 October
Newsnight's coverage of the Chesterfield Conference was a vicious piece of distortion. They began by showing shots of a dinner held by *Marxism Today* last Thursday night and finished up with Hobsbawm commenting on the Chesterfield Conference before it had even taken place. The Eurocommunists were being used as a stick to beat us with.

Wednesday 28 October
NEC. Neil Kinnock, being Chairman of the Party this year, took the chair. The first proposal was a change in the standing orders to say that, as from next year, the Party Conference would not be chaired by the Chairman of the Party but by a panel of people chosen by the NEC. This was designed to prevent Dennis Skinner from chairing the Conference the year after next and to remove any threat to Kinnock of an alternative power centre. It was cleverly argued so that the Chairman of the Party would still make the address to Conference and the first and last speeches.

Then we went on to the 'Labour Listens' campaign, with a mass of papers from Larry Whitty.

I said I had a strange feeling about it. 'I can't fault the ideas, but this is like planning the Duchess of Richmond's ball on the eve of the Battle of Waterloo. What would you say when there was a Wall Street crash, a war in the Gulf, rising unemployment, riots because of the poll tax, an explosion at a nuclear power station or a breakdown of the NHS leading to a major crisis? Policy comes out of struggles.'

Tuesday 3 November
Had a word with Mother on the phone. As I was talking, Norman Tebbit went by, and I shouted out, 'Norman! I have had three letters from you asking me to contribute to the Tory Party. Please go on writing – the postage will eventually bankrupt you.'

So he said, 'Let me have a copy of the letter and I'll find out why it was sent to you.'

'No, I want to go on getting them. My mother has had two letters from you too. I've also had two from Neil Kinnock saying, "I don't know what your politics are but I am sure you will agree we need a strong opposition, and would you like to help the Labour Party?" So you're one up on Neil now.'

Wednesday 4 November
At the PLP we had a long address from Neil Kinnock to give us an update on the policy review and 'Labour Listens'. He went on about how we must relate to the realities within the capacity of a Labour Government, how we must be practical and realistic; that we must not only be reactive, and that our message must be capable of being relayed to all the electorate.

He continued, 'There must be a common critique of our opponents. We must have conviction based on our values, and we must assess the trends over the next decade. The NEC, the Shadow Cabinet, the trade unions will be looking at policy. Some policies in the past have been moulded by those who have no political experience. This is not a vacuum or a post-Election limbo, it is a process of review, essential after three defeats. Two thousand flowers must bloom, even if they are not roses.' He said something about high standards and new members.

It lasted for twenty-six minutes and he got very short applause.

Saturday 21 November
Began packing for Russia. When you go to America you just take a toothbrush and know you can get anything you need there, but when you go to the Soviet Union you have to be self-contained. So I packed a kettle, batteries, cassettes, medicines, and so on. The bag was so heavy that I couldn't carry it, so I'll have to unpack some of it.

Monday 23 November
Caught the 9.50 am flight to Moscow, where the temperature was −18°C.

I waited two and a half hours for my bag, amidst people coming and going in fur hats. I could see a thin layer of snow outside, and as the snow fell it was quite romantic really, reminding me of some of the scenes from the film *Reds*. We discovered that my bag had been mistaken for that of the Kampuchean Ambassador, so we drove to the Kampuchean Embassy, where there were two officers standing in the court yard. The officers accompanied us to the door, and one of them, wearing a blue overcoat and fur cap and belt and pistol, banged on the front door, which finally opened, and there inside was my bag. By this time it was four hours since I had landed.

I was taken to the hotel and waited for one hour to register! There were twenty people waiting and only one woman, absolutely at her wits' end, authorised to check people in. There were people arguing and shouting at her. It was clear they didn't have enough rooms and they were offering middle-aged businessmen rooms to share, which they didn't want. There was one plump blonde woman with a Swiss passport who spoke fluent Russian, and two men laughing because she was saying she didn't want to share a room with them and two Germans. I tried to persuade the receptionist to take an interest in me by leaning over to point at my name on the computer printout, and she sort of smacked my hand! At nearly 9 o'clock I was given a bit of paper which I had to take to another desk to get the key for my room, which turned out to be a beautiful one overlooking the city.

Had dinner downstairs in a fancy restaurant with several people from the Institute of International Relations and World Economy. What is so nice is that one can now talk absolutely openly to the Russians about anything – Stalin, Trotsky, the Cold War, the Labour Party – and there is no restraint. They couldn't have been more friendly, though the Russian intellectuals are a bit heavy.

Tuesday 24 November
Had breakfast with Sacha Ivankhanik, my guide and interpreter. This hotel houses the Hammer Centre and has exhibition rooms, bars and restaurants. It is where business travellers stay and work. I remember in the sixties Armand Hammer played a leading part in getting it established, and it is of American design, with American equipment.

Then we went to the Kremlin for the meeting with Vladimir Karpov, who is a member of the Supreme Soviet and first secretary of the Writers' Union. The Supreme Soviet, as in all the communist countries, is a great big building with empty corridors and no women about.

Karpov is sixty-five, a charming man, short, grey-haired, a typical official; he might have been David Basnett or Norman Willis, though he was more serious and substantial than the latter. It confirmed the view I have always held that, if we had had a revolution in 1917 in

Britain, the revolutionary council would have looked like the TUC General Council – grey, late-middle-aged men.

I asked Karpov in which direction the consensus would move.

Karpov replied, 'The economic reforms are important, and we want a socialism of quality in the Soviet Union. That's what it is about – raising the quality of our socialism.'

'You have had some successes and some failures, as we have, and we must learn from our mistakes. What about a world socialist forum, a new International?'

He said that was very interesting, and I put my desire for a mission of the leaders of the non-aligned countries to Europe, to reinforce the disarmament process.

Back in the hotel I rewrote my lecture for this afternoon, and then went downstairs to have lunch with Sacha, my translator. After lunch a young man approached me and asked, 'Are you Tony Benn?' I said I was, and he turned out to be Hewlett Johnson's grandson. Johnson was known as the Red Dean of Canterbury. I asked what he was doing in Moscow, and he is studying music. Hewlett died when his grandson was three, but, he said, 'I remember looking up and seeing him washing up after dinner at home.' I thought that was a lovely image.

Went to the Institute and gave my lecture. I had a lot of questions, such as what changes have occurred in the nature of the working class, and how do you deal with the problems of technological unemployment? If Mrs Thatcher claims to have helped capitalism, why has industrial production declined to the point at which Britain has now dropped below Italy from fifth to sixth place in the world production table? How would you define the difference between left and right? Even, what was the reaction to the Chesterfield Conference?

At the end Professor Bolodyn, who is a great expert on perestroika and the economic situation, said, 'Contrary to what you have suggested in your lecture, there is no danger of any breakdown of central planning. The danger is that Gosplan is trying to hold on to its real power. It still has powers to develop the five-year plan and decide economic rates of growth, and factories simply have to comply. Next year 60 per cent of the profits will come back in taxation.' He added, 'Socialist ownership will not be changed, of that I assure you.'

After that, I talked to Igor Guriev, a deputy director of the Institute, and Professor Efim Khesin. Guriev said they were in a revolutionary situation in the Soviet Union. 'If we do not succeed in changing our society soon, there will be a real and characteristically vigorous Russian response and opposition to the Government.'

I asked if it would be violent, and he said, 'I don't know, but we are stagnating.'

I put the point that bourgeois democracy allows you to change your management by elections without changing your system, and that could be applied to communism.

He said, 'We are attempting that by allowing rival candidates to stand for office, but our situation is really urgent. Perestroika has produced nothing yet; we have only talked about it.'

Listening to him, I thought the Soviet Communist Party seemed really frightened at the enormity of the crisis, with stagnation, shortages and poor quality leading to public anger and inertia. They are determined not to move towards capitalism, but they recognise that bureaucratic command communism has not worked either. I think probably for them this is more important than disarmament. They want to reduce the burden of defence, but that is nothing like as important as getting their own economy going.

When I asked if the changes in the Soviet Union would be like those in Poland, they thought probably not, because the opposition to the Government in Poland was highly organised. In the USSR it would be sporadic and unorganised. The nature of the USSR's problems were to do with inefficiency and lack of democracy. They emphasised that there is no repression now and criticism is tolerated.

Wednesday 25 November
Went shopping, and I saw some cassettes of Russian music displayed in a shop. So I went in and asked for one, and was told they did sell them but they didn't have any in. Went to buy some food, and the shop had no bread or butter.

Met Sacha to go back to the Institute to meet Alexander Kislov, a deputy director. The taxi we had ordered didn't turn up, so we rang the Municipal Transport Service, which runs the transport for Moscow, and they said the taxi was there, but it wasn't. So we caught an ordinary taxi, which broke down, and we hailed another one, which also broke down. I didn't get a very favourable impression of Moscow transport.

I was terribly depressed, and I thought to myself: How on earth can the Soviet Union get itself out of this mess? It is like an elephant with multiple sclerosis, huge but it can't move. The Russians are a patient people, though slightly sad and resigned, and some of the young ones are cynical.

I wondered whether there was any possibility of rival political groups being set up within the socialist system, but it was pointed out to me that there was no experience of bourgeois democracy before the revolution. There would be resistance from the Communist Party itself because the bureaucrats do not like being challenged. Then there is a danger of foreign interference; political groups would inevitably be financed and supported from outside with a view to destabilisation. Lastly, there might be nationalist pressure from the republics against the Soviet Union itself. They are absolutely right to talk about it openly, and Gorbachev's speeches about perestroika and glasnost have encouraged discussion. But the remedy is really political rather than economic.

When we arrived at the Institute I was taken to see Alexander Kislov whom I had met at the Japan Peace Conference in 1983, and I had a long talk with him and two doctors. I came straight to the point. 'I have some proposals. The first is a treaty of friendship.'

Kislov said, 'That is not realistic with the Thatcher Government.'

I replied, 'I know that very well. I don't want to promote it if it wouldn't be acceptable to the Soviet Government. I don't want to be repudiated in Moscow.'

Kislov said, 'It's very constructive, very positive, a good idea.' Then he asked about the Chesterfield Conference – the third time it has been raised with me here.

I came to my next point, the possible heads of state mission, which I said I hoped Gorbachev could encourage; it couldn't be suggested publicly by him but he could send ambassadors to Delhi, Harare and Havana. They thought it was in line with what Gorbachev had been saying.

We discussed non-alignment, and they quoted the Prime Minister of Sri Lanka (before Mrs Bandaranaike), who had apparently once said, 'There are only two non-aligned countries in the world, the Soviet Union and the United States, because neither of them is in anybody else's camp.' I showed them the proposal for non-alignment that we had been working on.

They said there was a major factor which might be used to promote the idea. Greece, together with Sweden, Argentina, Mexico, Tanzania and India, was part of a committee for the promotion of non-alignment in Europe, and Greece was not only a member of NATO but also active in the Non-Aligned Movement[1] (I didn't know that). Greece stresses that membership of NATO does not interfere with its role in the Movement. Also Spain, Portugal and Greece were guests at the meetings of the Non-Aligned Movement, so being in NATO is no obstacle to being a guest. This is tremendously important.

I said I saw the UN as a sort of world parliament and the Non-Aligned Movement as a world party, and I put forward the idea of one member for every 5 million people in a chamber of elected world representatives.

'World government,' he said, and smiled.

I asked about the speech by Boris Yeltsin which had led to his removal as Secretary of the Moscow Communist Party just before I arrived there, and they said it had not been published, but he had undoubtedly offended the bureaucracy.

Later in the day I talked to Martin Walker, the *Guardian* correspondent, who told me that people he knew believed that Boris

Yeltsin had not mentioned Raisa Gorbachev (as some had said), but he had made a reference to the personality cult and had gone right over the top, accusing Ministries of inflated size. So he had been removed by the Moscow District Committee. Martin Walker said the hearings against him sounded like a witch-hunt or a denunciation.

Thursday 26 November
Went to the Central Committee of the Communist Party and met Mr Zuyev, the deputy head of the International Department of the Central Committee. With him was Mr Lagutyn, who is responsible for relations with Britain.

On the question of closer links with the European left and the recent meeting in Moscow of European parties, the first of its kind, he said, 'In fact, 120 parties came – Communist, Socialist, Democratic, Progressive, Greens, the Indian National Congress – and the only party that was not represented there was the British Labour Party. Gerald Kaufman arrived after it was all over.'

I said I was absolutely staggered that Kaufman had missed it.

After lunch I was taken to see Academician Yevgeny Primakov, Director of the Institute of International Relations and World Economy, who is one of the leading figures now in the Soviet Union, a member of the Politburo, and regarded as one of the great socialist intellectuals. I spent forty-five minutes with him.

Primakov stressed the role of the UN in Soviet foreign policy. 'We have changed our attitude to the UN. We have paid up all the outstanding debts. UN forces should play a peacekeeping role in the Gulf, and there should be a security scheme.'

I mentioned my proposal for a UN peacekeeping force in Ireland. I have been pushing the idea that the old International is wrong and that what we need now is a new forum for discussion. To be candid, most of the suggestions I have made have already been thought of in the Soviet Union.

At 3.15 I went to the Institute of Economics of the Academy of Sciences and was greeted by a man of about fifty, Leonid S. Yagodovsky. We were joined later by a specialist on East Germany.

Yagadovsky repeated what I had heard elsewhere, that they must make greater use of the credit system. He said they have got to reduce state financing, and the state must earn its keep and use credit. 'We need a flexible system of prices and incentives for workers. There will inevitably be greater inequality of incomes, and we need some form of market mechanism.'

He went on, 'Planning, decentralisation and self-management are the key to the new laws of state enterprise and industrial democracy which will come into force on 1 January 1988. There will be an Enterprise Council with the workers, the managers, the Party, the trade unions and the youth movements and *they* will adopt a plan of enterprise, not the Ministry.'

I commented, 'I find what you say about self-management very exciting, but when I say this in Britain they call me a Trotskyite.'

'Oh,' said Yagadovsky, 'Trotsky's concept was quite different. He believed the trade unions should be an instrument of state power, and actually Trotsky's view was implemented by Stalin. Stalin was Trotsky in practice.'

So I said, 'You had better send us a lecturer on Trotsky to argue with Trotskyite parties!'

He told me, 'Trotsky claimed he was expelled because his ideas were rejected, but actually his ideas were implemented. But Trotsky said that the USSR could not build socialism in one country, whereas Stalin thought it could, and it was.'

Friday 27 November

Spent twelve hours in bed tossing and turning, and obviously had a fever. I woke feeling very unwell.

Went out with a guide for sightseeing, but I had already seen Red Square and the various cathedrals. It was terribly cold, and I could feel this freezing air going into my chest. Walked to the cemetery, and it was so icy that it was like walking on glass: I was terrified I was going to fall, so altogether I wasn't in the happiest of moods. In the graveyard were statues of Pushkin and Khrushchev. Between coughing and walking and slipping on the ice, I managed to get a glimpse of them and other interesting ones.

But the greatest point of interest was my conversation with my guide, Yuri, who said he wasn't a member of the Party and didn't have any interest in being a member of the Party: he was really a budding Russian entrepreneur.

I asked about Boris Yeltsin, and he said there was certainly no glasnost about his dismissal. 'It was the old-style removal of somebody who threatened the bureaucracy. In fact, Yeltsin and Gorbachev were old friends, and Yeltsin was very go-ahead, but he had been frustrated and had previously offered to resign his job because he couldn't make any progress. He did not attack Gorbachev or his wife, but he did make some reference to avoiding the cult of personality. Actually, the bureaucracy removed Yeltsin, but the public outcry at his removal was so great because he was a popular figure that he was reinstated as Deputy Construction Minister with the rank of Minister.'

Had a farewell dinner with Alexander Kislov, Igor Guriev, Sacha, Professor Khesin and Sergei Peregudov, who is studying the Labour left and asked me to send him some material.

I asked them lots of questions, including the one often put to me: 'Do the people of Russia really want perestroika?'

Kislov replied, 'I remember talking to a Saudi Arabian slave who had been liberated, and he said he was happier when he was a slave because people looked after him, and now he was on his own.'

I drew a comparison between the Vatican and the Kremlin and said I thought they were similar in their structure.

Guriev laughed. 'You said it; I didn't.'

I asked about Khrushchev, and they said he lost a lot of support from the people and from the bureaucracy because he attacked Stalin, and the bureaucracy had worked with Stalin.

I was told the other day that on the occasion in 1960, when Khrushchev hammered the UN rostrum with a shoe, somebody took a photograph of him and he was wearing both his shoes, so he had obviously brought a spare one in his bag.

They told me that in 1985 Gorbachev had been elected as General Secretary of the Party by only a one-vote majority, and one of the anti-Gorbachev members of the Politburo had been detained in America because of a problem with the plane; if he had got back in time, Gorbachev would not have won.

They asked who the people were to watch on the Labour left, apart from myself, Ken Livingstone and Joan Ruddock. I said, 'Jeremy Corbyn, Dennis Skinner, Brian Sedgemore, Dawn Primarolo, Tony Banks, Harry Cohen and Bob Cryer.'

They were very critical of the *Morning Star*, and thought it was simplistic. I defended it by saying, 'When you're on the defensive, which we are, you repeat old slogans – that may be what your criticism is.'

Saturday 28 November

Up at 5 and packed. Sacha arrived with some gifts – a beautiful book of Russian still-life pictures and a guide to Kiev. We went to the airport together and I watched my bag like a hawk!

Friday 4 December

The Government has taken out an injunction against the BBC to prevent it from broadcasting a series of three radio programmes about the security services called *My Country Right or Wrong*, to which I contributed. I would have thought it was dangerous to alienate the BBC, but they are such craven toadies, they will go along with anything the Government says (after making a lot of noise).

Sunday 6 December

I realised this morning that I had taped my interview for this BBC series on the security services. So I copied it, then rang up the *Daily Telegraph* and invited them to print the transcript. Although there is an injunction against the BBC on the grounds that it includes interviews with former members of the security services, I am not in that category. The *Telegraph* sent a journalist and a photographer.

Monday 7 December

Into the Commons to meet Sarah Hipperson, who had been at Greenham Common since 1983. She was a Scot in her late fifties, had white hair, and had been a magistrate. She told me she had had five children, and had decided the only hope for the future was to organise at Greenham Common. She had been in prison fourteen times, most recently for cutting down the perimeter fence.

The particular reason she had come to see me was that many of the officials who worked at Newbury – the acting clerk of the Court, the chief Crown prosecutor, etc. – had been invited by the US Air Force to take a holiday in America as a reward for all they had done to make life possible for the American forces based at Greenham Common. She said, 'It's corrupt!'

She spoke with tremendous force, and as I listened I found the tears welling up in my eyes. I told her I was deeply moved by what she had to say. 'If ever we have peace in the world, it will be because of people like you and not people like me.' I promised to take the matter up.

It was all the more moving because today Gorbachev landed at RAF Brize Norton on his way to Washington to sign the Intermediate-Range Nuclear Forces Treaty (INF) which will end the siting of Cruise missiles at Greenham Common.

Friday 8 January 1988

To Chesterfield for a seven-hour surgery. There was a delegation of twenty-five people from Donkin's, the engineering factory, who had been sacked with twenty minutes' notice just before Christmas. They had been called in and told, 'You're redundant', and that they had to be off the plant within twenty minutes. Some of the workers had been there for twenty-two years.

Monday 11 January

This afternoon John Hughes, Labour MP for Coventry North East, a very devout Catholic and a member of the Campaign Group, was so incensed at the death of a constituent's child, denied a heart operation because of the NHS cuts, that he interrupted prayers and made a protest. It will not be included in Hansard because Hansard does not record prayers. It was a highly principled thing to do. He was subsequently suspended, and twenty-one Labour MPs including Kinnock and Hattersley voted for his suspension.

Wednesday 13 January

Ralph Miliband came to dinner in the Strangers' Dining Room. He was anxious about whether I might stand for the leadership, and said, 'Don't do anything that would endanger your position.'

I should add that this morning I also talked to Jim Mortimer on the matter, and he said, 'Don't do it if you think you will only get a derisory vote.'

All my friends are saying 'Don't stand', and yet there is an instinct in me that says 'Do': I will have to wait.

Friday 22 January

I do feel absolutely lousy. I've got this awful cough and I'm a bit worried about the leadership question. The *Independent* had a picture of Eric Heffer and me with the heading 'Benn to challenge Kinnock in this year's electoral college'. I think it must have come from Eric, because he is letting it be known that in the event of a contest he would like to be my running mate, but he's sixty-six, and I think two old men in their sixties would be fatal. We would have to choose a woman.

Wednesday 27 January

I had drafted a motion for the NEC in support of the possible nurses' strike, backed by Dennis Skinner and Ken Livingstone. The motion was that the NEC 'pledges its full support for any strike action . . . decided upon by the nurses if they conclude that this represents the only practicable way of bringing pressure to bear on this Government . . . and calls upon the Labour and trade union movement to give all possible financial, industrial and moral backing.'

Tom Sawyer and Colm O'Kane had their own resolution and, since they were representing NUPE and COHSE, they did have priority.

Tom said he hoped I would withdraw mine. 'This whole NHS situation is quite different and quite new, and I would greatly regret a Labour split. The configuration of solidarity would be absolutely wrong, and it would be wrong for MPs to go on the picket line. This is not a traditional industrial dispute.'

Blunkett added, 'We don't want to take the strike over. Tony Benn and Dennis Skinner sound like the Politburo.'

Ted O'Brien, of SOGAT 82, argued that calls for industrial action were quite inappropriate, and that there should be a ballot. There was a risk of sequestration of union funds.

Kinnock said, 'This motion is just a gesture in coat holding. Tony, I wish you wouldn't punch with your chin. The question is, do you want to fight or do you want to win? Coat holding is not authentic, and there is a political mileage in letting the Government take the rap, but the task we will face is millions of investment for the health service.'

I resented the attacks on the resolution. 'This is a political strike,' I said, 'and we need political action to save the health service.'

I was defeated by 20 to 4, and the main motion was carried by 23 to 4.

Then there was an item about discipline in Bradford North. I left sickened. What came out of today was the detestation (led by Kinnock) of the left, as well as the enormous fear of political support for industrial action. If the movement could see what was happening on the NEC, I think they would turn against it, particularly on matters like this.

Vladimir Derer came to the Campaign Group. He took me aside beforehand and showed me papers he'd been given from the head office of the London Labour Party. They included a list of the officers of the Bermondsey Party which was annotated with notes on the political affiliations of all the delegates to the Bermondsey general committee. There were four headings: NA (non-attender), OK (all right politically), MT (Militant) and FT (fellow traveller). The really sinister thing was that Jim Mortimer was listed as FT. When you get to a situation where the last General Secretary of the Labour Party is treated as a fellow traveller, you really are in deep trouble.

The Campaign Group was crowded because we had decided to consider our attitude towards a candidature.

I said I thought we should agree our position in principle and ask the local parties to give us their view.

We went round the meeting.

Dennis Skinner wanted a contest. 'No names now but I am in favour of the principle.'

Eric Heffer agreed. 'No names yet but we should say we are in favour of a contest this year because the Party is drifting.'

Clare Short was against. 'We should not challenge the Leader or the Deputy Leader, because if we lost badly it would damage Tony.'

Gavin Strang agreed. 'It would be disastrous and it would damage us. We should have a campaign on policies instead.'

Paul Boateng, the new MP for Brent South, said, 'We are here to win the Election. A contest would damage Labour. It would be an own goal. It would be seen as hopeless. You wouldn't beat Kinnock and you would be humiliated.'

Ron Brown, Bob Cryer, Bill Michie and Dave Nellist were in favour.

Margaret Beckett thought we should take soundings on the deputy leadership only.

Harry Barnes and Diane Abbott were doubtful.

Jo Richardson was worried about the Party, but thought there was no demand for a contest.

Bernie Grant and Jeremy Corbyn were in favour.

Audrey Wise, Bob Wareing and Dawn Primarolo were cautious.

The decision we reached was that 'the Campaign Group have agreed that a concerted campaign for socialism should be developed within the Party. We are circulating two documents entitled "Aims and Objectives of the Labour Party" and "Agenda for Labour" to form the basis of that campaign. A clear majority of CG members felt that the time *may* be right for a leadership election to form part of that campaign and are continuing to discuss this within the Party. We will make the decision as soon as practical.'

There were people who were doubtful, but a majority had spoken in favour of a contest. I was quite happy to leave the decision until a bit later, because at the moment I am getting contradictory advice.

Wednesday 3 February
Went to St Mary's Hospital, Paddington, to show solidarity with the nurses' strike. The public opinion polls today showed that 66 per cent of Tory voters supported the strike. From there to St Charles's Hospital.

At the PLP later Robin Cook made a most pompous speech about how he understood what the nurses were doing but he couldn't support their strike.

Friday 5 February
Went to Transport House for a joint meeting of the NEC and Shadow Cabinet to discuss policy.

The last item was a series of papers. Blunkett and Bernard Crick introduced one called 'The Labour Party's Values and Aims', which I'm afraid I didn't read because it was so long.

Then I was asked to introduce the Campaign Group's 'Aims and Objectives' and 'Agenda for Labour'. I said we must have a policy and values that were rooted in history, based on experience, going back to the old radical dissenting tradition and identifying conscience and tolerance.

Kinnock presented his paper 'A Statement of Democratic Socialist Aims and Values', which is really insubstantial.

Frank Dobson welcomed all the papers and said, 'The alternative to living in a jungle must not be living in a zoo. Neil and Roy have addressed that problem, but we must emphasise the means; co-operation is the key.'

Hattersley then said that Thatcher had a clear intellectual position, he thought we were in error to criticise market forces, and we must avoid the libel that we wanted a command economy.

Robin Cook was unhappy about what Kinnock had said in one paragraph about socialism being the gospel of individual rights.

Cunningham didn't believe experience *was* the basis of socialism. 'Socialism has come from an intellectual expression.' But he was unhappy about market forces and said, 'Neil doesn't address the intellectual side of the argument.' He went on, 'Every society needs an élite, and we are a political élite. We must recognise the contribution of successful people.'

Jack Straw said his grandfather was a peasant, his father was a worker, and they had produced a family of intellectuals – at which I asked, 'Who are they?', which caused people to laugh.

As we adjourned, I said, 'Well, Neil, if the press describe your statement as the Ten Commandments, remember the man who said, "Like an examination paper, only three should be attempted."'

Wednesday 10 February

Campaign Group in the evening. Ken Livingstone told me that in Brent East the Party had voted 29 to 6 for a contest. Diane Abbott said that in Hackney North demand was overwhelming. Dennis Canavan remarked that people wanted a firmer lead, that a contest now would be a beacon to millions of people.

Thursday 18 February

I had real fun this morning. I had a message to ring Tariq Ali, and when I did he told me that Robin Blackburn had been at Labour Party Headquarters, had taken a piece of notepaper and written to Tariq, ostensibly from the NEC, asking Tariq to address the NEC as part of the 'Labour Listens' campaign.

So I decided to play a joke on Robin, and I rang him up at Verso publishers and in my best Scots accent asked, 'Is that Mr Blackburn?'

Robin replied, 'It is indeed.'

I said, 'This is Alistair McAlistair from the BBC Third Programme Talks Unit. You don't know me personally, but I've been asked to take soundings about the possibility of you delivering the Reith Lectures in 1989. We felt that, twenty years after the 1968 business and with the perestroika and the changes in the Soviet Union, a distinguished socialist intellectual might look at the prospect for world socialism. I'm really only taking a sounding, and you'd get a proper letter from the Director-General.'

Robin said, 'Well, it's tremendously good of you to think of me, but I think Tony Benn would do this far better than I would.'

I tape-recorded the exchange and sent it to Tariq.

Wednesday 2 March

Went to the Commons for a meeting of the Policy Review Group under Jo Richardson and Roy Hattersley. We were discussing the royal prerogative and there were several papers presented.

Lord Irvine, who is the Party's legal adviser was present, together with Professor Pat McAuslan, who had written a good article in the *Independent* about the royal prerogative, Paul Boateng (who is a lawyer) and Roy Hattersley's researcher, David Hill. Irvine and McAuslan presented their papers after mine.

Irvine said that when Lord Donaldson stated that bugging and burgling were not against the law he had been misquoted. So I pointed out that the royal prerogative *is* the law, and that when soldiers kill in war they are killing under the prerogative because war is made under the prerogative. It gives me enormous pleasure, I must confess, to use my knowledge of a subject that I have studied for years.

Roy Hattersley said, 'We have got to be careful we don't alienate the public, who love the royal family.'

We left it that there will be a paragraph about it, which is not really good enough.

Monday 14 March

I had a talk with Mark Schreiber of the *Economist*. He told me that there was a serious possibility of Mrs Thatcher being opposed by a Tory MP in the new session. If they did put someone up as a 'stalking horse', as he called it, they would be able to get some indication of Mrs Thatcher's popularity and they could then repeat the process next year to pave the way for her removal. I can imagine quite a lot of Tory MPs saying to themselves, 'Thatcher's safe but there's no harm in giving her a bit of a shock.'

Tuesday 15 March

Took a party of business studies students from Chesterfield College of Technology and Arts around the House. Their lecturer told me with some embarrassment that politics and economics had now been transformed into business studies. He said they had businessmen in to talk about businesses.

I asked, 'What about the trade unions?'

'We have to tell the students that trade unions are about human resources, and their relationship with employers is discussed in that context.'

I asked about socialism, and he said, 'We never mention that.'

Nine years after Thatcher came to power, we have a new wave of people coming through the system for whom capitalism is not only absolutely normal but the only thing they are taught about.

Sunday 20 March

Went to the AGM of the Chesterfield Party's general committee; it had been agreed last week that we would decide whether I should put up as a candidate in the leadership election.

At the end Johnny Burrows summed up. 'I think the balance of opinion expressed today has been pretty fair. John Prescott's attempt to be considered for the deputy leadership* was described by Kinnock as an "unforgivable diversion". I wonder if in the next Election Mrs Thatcher will say an Election is an "unforgivable diversion". I will not accept that we should shut up for anyone. We have a right to a General

* In January 1988 John Prescott abandoned, under pressure from Neil Kinnock, his attempt to stand against the Deputy Leader, Roy Hattersley, but announced in March that he would be standing after all.

Election every five years, and it is right to contest the leadership and deputy leadership of the Party.'

Then Peter Heathfield said, 'I nominate Tony Benn for the leadership if he is chosen by the Campaign Group.'

Of the ninety-six delegates there, eight voted against. I think probably about eighty people voted. Peter Coleman said he thought it was about three-quarters for and a quarter against and some hadn't voted. There was a slightly nasty flavour, but you can't expect constituency parties to be unanimous on these things, and the old right wing of the Party would be opposed to it.

Wednesday 23 March
I had a message to ring Jim Mortimer, who has always been cautious and thought it would be inadvisable of me to stand, but today he said, 'I've been thinking about it and I think you should stand.'

That played a big part in my mind, so at 5.30 I went to the Campaign Group much more evenly balanced. I addressed the group, while Jeremy Corbyn took the chair.

I said, 'I am going to make a short statement and then withdraw from the meeting. This is a big decision. It may be a new start for socialism or a setback, and there may be recriminations either way, but the electoral college will decide. There have been some nominations coming in – some CLPs, the Durham NUM, some wards, some individuals. Others are strongly opposed, including good friends who fear we might be defeated and humiliated and who say we are not ready to make the challenge. In Scotland, Ann Henderson, who organises the Campaign Group there, told me she didn't think we could get a single Scottish CLP. Ken Gill and Alan Sapper are opposed. The T&G's new executive may be doubtful, and the CLPD won't support a public campaign if it is carried through the media. The case for standing is that the leadership is killing the Party, diluting policy, centralising power, capitulating. There is a general air of demoralisation. There is Mrs Thatcher's TINA – There Is No Alternative – and there is Kinnock's TINA. Even if the vote doesn't reflect our support, it is there.

'My own position has always been that I am not seeking nomination and never have done. My family will suffer, it is a high risk strategy, but I will accept and defend the decision you take and accept a nomination for two reasons: first of all, because it must be a collective decision and I am a member of the group and its chairman; secondly, because I trust my comrades. None of you ran away after 1981; you are my foul-weather friends. I hope the vote is decisive either way, and, if there is a tie, please don't proceed. If at the end you decide not to support it, leave an option open, because I don't think we want to say no definitely now.

'I shall withdraw now. I think a woman would carry weight as a deputy to run against Hattersley.'

I went up to my room and had a cup of tea. Then I had a call saying they'd decided to nominate me and Eric for Leader and Deputy Leader. So I went downstairs, fighting my way through a huge mass of journalists who had got wind of the fact that a decision was being taken. Margaret Beckett, Dawn Primarolo, Gavin Strang, Audrey Wise, Chris Mullin, Joan Walley were against a contest. Gerry Bermingham abstained. That was 21 in favour.

The vote for Eric as Deputy Leader was carried by 25 and only 4 against – Diane Abbott, Margaret Beckett, Gavin Strang and Chris Mullin.

I gather a great deal of pressure was put on Audrey Wise to stand for the deputy leadership but she just wouldn't do it.

Having been doubtful, I felt more peaceful in my own mind about it. It was a collective decision, I had given the best advice I could, I had reflected the arguments for and against, and there is an excitement about doing it.

Thursday 24 March

The press was packed with reports of the decision, all beginning with 'Labour was launched last night into another bitter row . . .' and so on. The phones rang continuously.

Tuesday 29 March

This evening at the Campaign Group we heard that Clare Short, Margaret Beckett, Joan Ruddock and Jo Richardson had withdrawn from the group. I got angry and I said to Audrey, 'If only you had agreed to stand, they wouldn't have gone.' She got quite upset; she is under considerable pressure, and of course some of the women think this is just a macho male contest and don't like doing it this way. On the other hand, having demanded a proper say in the affairs of the Party, why shouldn't they play their part? That's the way I see it. The people who have withdrawn all have Front Bench responsibilities – apart from Joan Ruddock, and she's a close friend of Neil's, so it would be difficult for her.

Wednesday 4 May

Went into the House for the PLP meeting. We stood for a moment for Fenner Brockway's death, then discussed the sequestration of the National Union of Seamen's assets by the courts.[2]

Michael Meacher had been at Dover today and said the Shadow Cabinet had been in touch with the seamen from the beginning of the strike. He attacked the restrictions on secondary action and referred to the BBC television *Brass Tacks* programme, which had pointed out how unsafe the ferries were. He supported ACAS in their arbitration and said there might be a debate in the House next week. He came out in favour of a weekly levy for MPs, which we didn't do in the miners' strike until almost a year had gone by.

Heffer got up and said, 'If the NUS goes down, it will be more serious than the miners. There are 2000 Liverpool seamen out. I hope there will be no hesitation on the part of the Party. We must give full support. The unions had no money in the bank at the beginning of trade-unionism and they have no money in the bank now. We should fight harder than we did for the miners.'

John Prescott, who has decided after all to stand for the deputy leadership and is an NUS-sponsored MP, made a strong speech. He said, 'I hope more MPs will go to Dover. The Shadow Cabinet all support the seamen with no reservations.'

At this stage, I thought Kinnock looked pale, because he was being nailed to the wall by Prescott.

Went to a party to celebrate the publication of Robin Blackburn's book *The Overthrow of Colonial Slavery*. One of the great puzzles to me at the moment is why so many intellectuals with a Marxist background have gone so soft. I think there is the simple fact that most of these intellectuals are doing well under the present Government, so that, while they claim to be horrified by what they call Thatcherism, it is quite agreeable personally. Also they receive public accord. Finally, I think many intellectuals are fascinated by Thatcher and would really prefer to be active in politics; they greatly envy anyone who is, and they are attracted like moths to the candle of power. But it is depressing. They look down on the working class and think of them as yobbos who read the *Sun* and go to football matches and cause trouble. They have none of that confidence in the working class which is what we need if we are going to mobilise sufficient strength to defeat the system.

Friday 6 May

Had a word with Peter Heathfield, who is crestfallen because the Yorkshire NUM have decided to support Kinnock as leader. I think an enormous amount of effort was put in by Kevin Barron to convert them to Kinnock.

Wednesday 11 May

Went over to the House of Commons for the debate on the seamen's strike. The Opposition was entirely on the side of the trade union, and the Government opposed to it. At the very end, Paul Channon, the Transport Secretary replying for the Government, accused the Opposition of entirely failing in its responsibilities. What it told you was that the Tory Party expect the Labour Party to discipline the trade unions and make them comply with Tory laws and Tory policy. We didn't do it today, and that was very good.

Sunday 15 May
Went to a little cinema in Haverstock Hill to watch a private showing of *A Very British Coup*. It was brilliant, and it was the first political film I have ever seen where the Cabinet, the media, the security services and the Americans were given equal weight in the question of how Britain is governed, which, in a funny way, is what my diaries are about.

The security services brought down the Foreign Secretary through one scandal and then threatened the Prime Minister himself with a scandal that never existed. It was tremendously moving to see a Labour Prime Minister announcing on television that British nuclear weapons were going to be dismantled.

Thursday 19 May
At the PLP was a motion from the Shadow Cabinet to suspend Ron Brown from the PLP for three months for seizing the mace.

Derek Foster began by talking about the need for discipline and went over Ron Brown's conduct, saying he had undermined the strength of the Party. He said, 'Do we want power? The working class wants us to have power. Sloppy intentions are dangerous.' He kept mentioning the working class, and argued, '*We care*, but they wonder if we are *competent.*'

I said, 'Everyone understands the Chief Whip's problems. The outcome today is certain because I gather that all Front Bench spokesmen have been told to vote for the Shadow Cabinet motion' – at which there were cries of dissent. 'Ron did a silly thing, and I hope he apologises, but how do you assess his crime compared to Frank Field, who called for tactical voting at the last General Election? Ron was severely reprimanded by Frank Dobson in the House, punished by the House, the union have withdrawn his sponsorship and now the PLP is taking action. If it is carried, it will be reported to the NEC; he might be referred to the NCC and be expelled or declared ineligible for reselection. It is too severe, and the Speaker is quite relaxed about it.' I reminded them that Nye had had the Whip withdrawn as had Michael Foot in 1961 and Emrys Hughes in 1968.

Eric Heffer and Harry Barnes supported me, and Eric referred to John Beckett, who had seized the mace in 1930 in an argument about India.

Ron Brown then got up and said, 'Comrades and friends, with hindsight I could have done things differently, but I don't apologise for being angry. The Tory establishment were the people to be angry with. I am deeply involved in the working-class struggle. It was no offence against Party policy. I am not that sort of a person. I am not trying to organise a party within a party. If you condemn me, you are playing the Tory game.'

Michael Foot agreed with me that the House should not expel MPs, but said the PLP had its rights. He argued that it was a political issue contrary to the spirit of the NEC; the Chief Whip had no choice, and if we defeated the Chief Whip we were giving up being a PLP. Therefore he supported the motion.

Here was the ghost of an old left-winger coming back and desecrating his own grave. It was pathetic and sad, as I remember Michael the rebel so well.

The votes were 119 for the Shadow Cabinet, 36 against. Most of the Front Bench voted with the Shadow Cabinet; David Blunkett, Jo Richardson and Allan Roberts voted all the way down the line with the Shadow Cabinet. There is no doubt that patronage in the PLP is a great curse.

Wednesday 25 May
NEC to consider the seven policy statements by the Policy Review Groups, and a historic meeting it was.

The first of the statements, 'The Productive and Competitive Economy', was presented by Bryan Gould. It was weak in analysis and vague in prescription, very backward-looking.

I said, if you worked in a profit-based society you couldn't do much about the centralisation of power. Intervening in markets wasn't any good, and I had spent a lot of my time in Government trying to bribe and bully businessmen, entirely without success.

Livingstone remarked that it was 'pure Wilson'.

Skinner said it was fudge and mudge and that unemployment would rise, particularly after the American elections. We as a party were moving towards Thatcherism.

John Smith presented the next paper, 'Economic Equality'.

I said the trouble about this paper was that it did not recognise that there was a conflict of interest between those who created the wealth and those who controlled it. The paper declined to write off the debt that is owed by the poor to the Social Fund and pledged not to increase the highest levels of taxation above the level in Europe.

Skinner said, 'I could be taxed higher. The papers must be clear on higher taxation.'

Blunkett argued, 'We have got to re-establish the idea of the social wage.'

Eric Clarke agreed with Dennis Skinner.

Smith said he also agreed with Skinner. 'But we must persuade the rich of the need for fairness, and we are going to hit the rich on the capital side.'

That paper was carried by 20 to 3, with Livingstone abstaining.

Eddie Haigh then presented 'People at Work'.

Skinner didn't like it because it accepted the regulation of the trade unions.

I said that Thatcher had actually identified the obstacles to her policy, which were trade unions, local government and the public sector, and she had set out to destroy them. 'Are we going to repeal her Acts? What about using democracy, the votes of workers, to remove the boards of companies? This is a great missed opportunity.'

Kinnock said, 'As far as Tony is concerned, Thatcher didn't disclose her policy in advance, so why should we? The public don't perceive themselves as being dominated by employers, and anyway industrial democracy was an anarchist idea used in the Spanish Civil War.'

The paper was carried by 11 to 4.

Next was 'The Physical and Social Environment', which John Cunningham described as radical, interventionist, evolutionary and international.

I criticised it because it left out the issue of nuclear power, which was central to the environment. Secondly, it didn't mention the ownership of land, which was crucial.

The paper was carried by 20 votes to 1 (Dennis Skinner). I abstained.

Kaufman presented 'Britain and the World', saying, 'It accepts the Common Market and leaves disarmament open.'

Livingstone wanted the repeal of Section 2 of the European Communities Act, which would have the effect of restoring sovereignty over legislation and statute and he moved it be included.

Evans said, 'That would take 80 per cent of House of Commons legislation time.'

Skinner remarked, 'We can deal with that by withdrawal!'

I said, 'Accepting the European Community is a great mistake. We could deal with Section 2 by saying Common Market legislation would not apply if the Government asked the Commons to vote it down. As to the Cold War, we have said nothing about that. We have said nothing on defence spending, and we are utterly stuck on NATO.'

'Repeal of section 2 equals withdrawal,' Kinnock argued. 'The electorate rejected that in the 1983 Election, and it would wreck the economy if we withdrew.' So he has come out as a full Marketeer.

On defence, Ken Livingstone moved an amendment that we should agree to the mutual dissolution of the NATO and Warsaw pacts.

On withdrawal from the EEC, 8 were for and 13 against, with Gould abstaining.

On repeal of section 2 of the European Communities Act, Livingstone moved the amendment, and I added: 'and to restore full powers to the British Parliament'. That was defeated by 16 to 7. Ken's amendment on mutual dissolution of the two pacts was carried by 19 to 2, with Kinnock abstaining. A motion to reduce defence expenditure to the level of that of European members of NATO was defeated by 13 to 7. The question of debt was not discussed. The whole document 'Britain and the World' was carried by 17 to 4.

The consumer document was carried without much discussion. Hattersley then moved 'Democracy and the Individual'.

I said, 'In order to be constructive, I will move two amendments: that the House of Lords be abolished; and that the security services be made subject to the same ministerial and parliamentary control as the defence forces.'

Hattersley agreed.

On a vote, my amendment on security accountability and control was defeated by 12 to 8, with Kinnock against: my amendment on abolition of the House of Lords was defeated by 18 to 4.

To cut a long story short, this is the Thatcherisation of the Labour Party. We have moved now into the penumbra of her policy area, and our main argument is that we will administer it better than she will. Kinnock has won because the trade union leaders don't like the left, but also because they haven't any idea of what to do, they have lost confidence in themselves and think this is the best way of winning an Election. So they went along with it. But I think the arguments we put forward were strong.

Sunday 29 May
Although I am not depressed, I have got to face the fact that the leadership election will be an absolute disaster. The question is how to use it to get across issues that are interesting and relevant.

Saturday 4 June
I woke up this morning, and out of the corner of my eye I saw a flash. There was a sheet of flame about 2 feet high stretching across the end of the bed – the electric blanket had caught fire. I leapt out and poured a cup of water over the mattress, which was beginning to burn, and threw the electric blanket out into the garden. Half an hour later it was still burning.

Tuesday 14 June
On the news I heard that Denzil Davies has resigned as our defence spokesman. Apparently he had rung up Chris Moncrieff at the Press Association at 1 am and said, 'I have resigned as defence spokesman. I am fed up being humiliated by Neil Kinnock. He never consults me on anything. He goes on television and attacks unilateralism but he never consults his defence spokesman, so frankly I do not think I have got a job to do any more; so I have resigned as from now.' It is sensational news.

Tuesday 21 June

There was an astonishing report in the *Independent* this morning. Neil Kinnock had had lunch with its editorial board yesterday and had said, 'Turn the tape recorder on, it's all on the record', and what he said was so muddled that, in effect, he said that his recent television broadcast attacking unilateralism as 'something for nothing' had not been a repudiation of unilateralist policy. Peter Shore described it as 'the Grand Old Duke of York, who marched his men to the top of the hill and marched them down again'.

Wednesday 22 June

The papers today are full of adverse comment on Kinnock's volte-face. Nobody knows where he stands at all now.

The Executive was awful as usual. We were told about phase 2 of the Policy Review, and how they would handle the reviews at this year's Conference. Neil said there was going to be a positive policy of consulting the constituencies and the unions, having 'open hearing' days, one-day regional policy conferences, and so on.

Sunday 26 June

Caught the 10.30 to Norwich for a leadership campaign meeting.

Heard at the Labour Club that the *Moby Dick*, one of the Greenpeace ships, was in Yarmouth harbour, so someone drove me there and I met the captain and the crew.

Saturday 2 July

Tariq Ali rang this evening, having just returned from Moscow. He told me a couple of stories about Boris Yeltsin, the disgraced Secretary of the Moscow Communist Party. Tariq said that, before his sacking, Yeltsin had gone to a butcher's and queued, and when he got to the counter he had asked for a pound of veal. Everybody said, 'You must be joking. There is never any veal in this shop.' So he asked to see the manager, and produced his Party card and said, 'A ton and a half of veal was delivered to this shop at 6.30 this morning, it is now 9 am, so where has it all gone?' Of course, it had all gone on the black market.

On another occasion, Tariq told me, Yeltsin had pulled up at a shop where people were queuing and said, 'I can take you to a shop a short distance from here where you can get anything – but you have to be an official of the CP to get it. We have got to put this right.' This had obviously caused chaos and confusion and anger among the hierarchy, and he got the boot.

Saturday 9 July

I had the provisional list of nominations for the leadership, and I have got twenty-nine MPs, one trade union and 101 constituencies. Kinnock has 130 MPs, a number of trade unions and about 104 constituencies. He is going to romp home, but the balance on the constituency side is better than I had reasonably expected.

Wednesday 13 July

Drafted a notice to put in the broom cupboard in the Crypt of the Commons about the suffragette who hid there on the night of the census of 1911.[3]

When I got to the Crypt I was told it was locked until after the Glorious Revolution celebrations, and I couldn't get the key, so I went to see Miss Frampton in the Serjeant at Arms office. Miss Frampton is a most terrifying creature, a woman in her fifties, plump, determined, like the headmistress of a girls' school. So I said, 'Miss Frampton, I want your help.'

'What?' she said, with a frosty look.

I showed her my little notice, and to my amazement she was tickled pink. She laughed, and said, 'I'll take you down to the Crypt.'

We went down a secret staircase I didn't know existed and we arrived in the Crypt chapel. I showed her the broom cupboard, and we closed the door, stood there surrounded by mops and brushes and hoovers and wires. I had brought six strong brass thumb-tacks and a hammer, and we hammered this notice to the back of the door. It was like a sort of midnight feast with the headmistress, and as we left I gave her a wink and said, 'We mustn't go on having assignations like this.' She giggled. Anything Miss Frampton approves is OK.

I knew she was a descendant of Squire Frampton from Dorchester, and I told her that the secretary of my local Party when I was first elected to Bristol in 1950 was Edna Loveless, who was a descendant of George Loveless, one of the Tolpuddle Martyrs whom her great-great-great-grandfather had sent to Australia. She said she knew there were Lovelesses still in Dorchester. I also told her about the Reverend William Benn, who had been ejected in 1662 from his Dorchester parish.

Monday 25 July

Our grandsons Michael, James and William, who had been out for the day with Caroline, came back for tea, and we set up three committees. The 'London Wildlife Committee' was chaired by Michael; James and William were deputy chairmen. We voted by 4 to 0 for more parks and by 4 to 0 for more nesting boxes for birds, and I pretended to ring Mrs Thatcher to give her their views. We had a 'Bus Committee', voting for more buses by 2 to 2, and for cheaper buses by 4 to 0. Michael put up a big poster and called himself 'the Socialist Wildlife candidate'.

Saturday 30 July

Jack Spriggs picked me up at Liverpool and took me to the Merseyside

Unemployment and Trade Union Resources Centre, which is housed in an old police station in Liverpool.

I have known Jack for fourteen years since he came to see me in 1974 at the Department of Industry representing the workforce at IPD (the old Fisher-Bendix plant). We had set up the Kirkby co-operative in the wake of the IPD collapse. He's a fine man, in his late fifties now, and he runs this centre, which has a bar, a cafeteria, a library, a technology unit, a recording studio, a reprographic department, a gym, a sauna, crèches, a playground and offices. It was just a rabbit warren of resource development, and I was enormously moved and impressed by it. I think the only way we are going to make progress is to pull away from the system and build our own structures.

Sunday 4 September

I must confess I am a bit low at the moment. The coverage of the campaign is poor and, despite enormous effort, no progress seems to have been made.

Wednesday 10 September

A guy called Andrew Hood, who is just about to start an MA, has offered to help in the office – a nice person, whom I like very much. I am always a bit suspicious when people offer to help for nothing but you just have to trust your judgement.

We had a farewell party for Sheila Hubacher, who is going to study homoeopathy. She has worked like a beaver for two years transcribing the diary. An awfully nice Liverpool woman.

Saturday 17 September

Came back to London and went with Caroline to see Hilary and Sally's new baby, Caroline Rosalind Clark Benn, our first granddaughter. Then we went for a meal in a little Chinese restaurant in Westbourne Grove.

Saturday 24 September

To Chesterfield, where the Campaign Group met for its annual weekend seminar.

Jon Lansman forecast that I would get between 16.5 and 17 per cent of the electoral college and said the real benefit of the campaign had been the discussion of the Policy Review. Jon has been an absolutely first-rate organiser; everything hinges on him, and he is cheerful and competent.

The difficulty of selling *Campaign Group News* was raised. We were told, 'People are fed up defending socialism, we want some sort of a vision.'

Jon Lansman said, 'The left is weak but not marginalised.'

I made quite a long speech, and said we had to be clear that the strategy of the leadership was to destroy the Party as we know it.

Labour Party Conference, Blackpool
Friday 30 September
Caroline and I caught the train to Blackpool and unpacked at the
Florida Apartments, a nice place between the Imperial Hotel and the
Winter Gardens.

I set up the fax machine, the answering machine, the video, the
typewriter, and so on.

Saturday 1 October
A beautiful sunny day. Caroline went shopping for provisions for the
week and also found some beautiful nineteenth-century books for 20p.
We both love Blackpool.

I went to the Pembroke Hotel for a well-attended press conference,
the hacks all having turned up for the public execution.

The BBC are here simply to say Labour can never win. The line now
is that Labour can't win, therefore it has got to kill the left and join with
the centre, and then it might replace Thatcher, administering
Thatcherite policies. The people who run the BBC and ITN are like
Foreign Office officials with their own line, and everything has to be
made to fit in with it. They just say Benn and Heffer are going to be
humiliated and don't address any of the arguments. The main thing is
to sustain the morale of the delegates who come here.

Sunday 2 October
We walked over to the Conference, and Caroline advised me on what I
should say after the result was announced. When the result came, it was
appalling. My total of the electoral college came to 11 per cent. I did my
best to look impassive and cheerful on the platform. I just touched Neil
Kinnock on the shoulder and smiled.

I said to the press exactly what Caroline had suggested, and they all
asked if I would stand again, a question I fended off. The only people I
wouldn't talk to were BBC Radio 4, because they had boycotted the
campaign; Jim Naughtie wanted to interview me and I refused. They
said, 'You'll have a chance of saying what you want.' They were livid,
and couldn't believe anyone would refuse the chance to go on the air.

Caroline and I went to the T&G party because I thought it wouldn't
be a bad idea to show ourselves. There were a few embarrassed faces on
the so-called left on the T&G executive who had urged me to stand and
then voted for Kinnock and Hattersley. The T&G had decided not to
ballot its members. I went right up to Ron Todd's table, shook his
hand, and thanked him for inviting us to the party.

Monday 3 October
The actual results showed that I got thirty-seven MPs, 111 constituency parties and two trade unions – FTAT and BETA. If you aggregate

the popular vote in all these constituencies and elsewhere, it was much bigger than that, about one-third of the vote.

I was a bit gloomy last night, but today people have been so friendly, and I don't think the campaign has done any harm.

Tuesday 4 October

Back to the Conference and heard Kinnock's speech. I had decided to stand during the standing ovation. He had beaten me, and that was the end of that. The first half of his speech was an attack on Thatcher and the second half was a vigorous defence of market forces. It just prepared the way for running the market economy better and for dropping our defence policy in the interest of 'electability'.

Later tonight, at the *Tribune* rally, it turned out that Ron Todd had attacked people with Filofaxes, cordless telephones and sharp suits, and said the last dregs of socialism were being drained out of the Labour Party. Ron Todd elects Kinnock on Saturday and is the villain on Tuesday.

Wednesday 5 October

I had been asked to reply for the NEC to the debate on safety in the North Sea Oil industry. I had worked extremely carefully on my speech and decided to make it an occasion for criticising market forces, the market economy and the multinationals, and to use the industry and its safety record as an argument for socialism and trade-unionism. I got a tremendous response from the delegates. Dennis Skinner, who is slow to comment on these things, thought it was the best Conference speech I had made for many years. He was in the chair for the afternoon.

Got back to the flat utterly exhausted.

Thursday 6 October

Ron Todd is in the news as the man who is challenging Kinnock's modernisation. He's the bogeyman this year. There is a lot of resentment within the T&G, and the Party doesn't work unless the T&G supports the leadership, so in that sense it's a bit like 1960, when Frank Cousins opposed Gaitskell.

Friday 7 October

All the newspapers this morning gave previews to the *Benn Diaries* programme tonight, which will be a fair way of recovering from the effect of the Conference.

Saturday 8 October

The wedding of Stephen to Nita Clarke. The family arrived and we all went to the Chelsea Register Office. Stephen was dressed up in a frock-coat, and Nita was in a cream wedding-dress with a train.

Then we went to the House of Commons, where a few more people had gathered. Richard Moberly, the industrial chaplain at the *Daily Mirror*, conducted the service in the crypt. It was a beautiful occasion. Pratima Bowes, Nita's mother, read something in Hindi from Rabindranath Tagore. Mother, who had come in on crutches and was slumped behind the reading desk causing great concern to Richard Moberly, stood up at the appropriate moment and delivered a marvellous sermon about the Corinthians. She was splendid.

At the reception held in the Strangers' Dining Room over 600 people turned up. Caroline and I stood in the receiving line as these people piled in. I had been nervous and thought it might be over the top, to be candid, but it was very successful. Caroline pointed out that the Labour right had also come, and they obviously had a whale of a time.

Thursday 13 October

The injunctions against the *Guardian* and the *Sunday Times* on *Spycatcher* were lifted. The Government must have spent millions pursuing Peter Wright around the world. It is incredible that a man can confess to crimes against an elected government, yet all the British Government want to do is prevent him publishing it rather than investigate the charges.

The Law Lords compared Wright to Philby and stated that he owed 'a lifelong obligation of confidentiality to the Crown', a most extraordinary judgement. I think this ought to be the subject of some parliamentary action.

The Thatcher years are coming to an end, and it wouldn't surprise me if this time next year she was on her way out and some Baldwin-like figure was brought in (John Biffen or Sir Geoffrey Howe) to lower the temperature of debate.

Monday 24 October

Ralph Miliband rang to say he had just come back from the international socialist gathering at Cavtat, Yugoslavia, and the atmosphere had been awful. All the communist representatives had gone overboard for market forces, and the Hungarians had declared that market forces equalled freedom. The President of the Yugoslav Assembly had said market forces were what they needed, and when someone pointed out the 2 million unemployed in Britain he had just pushed it aside.

Ann Clwyd has been sacked from the Front Bench for voting against the Government in the defence estimates debate in defiance of the whips.

Saturday 5 November

Mrs Thatcher appeared on television last night in Poland, at Gdansk shipyard with Lech Walesa in a piece of breathtaking hypocrisy. Although she is crushing the trade unions in Britain, she called for a dialogue between all sections of society in Poland. What an old right-winger Walesa is, pretending to support trade unions but supporting Mrs Thatcher. I think we are moving to a period of tyranny organised by a coalition of top people in the capitalist world, the communist world and the Christian world. The task for socialists in the nineties and beyond will be to demand greater democracy, to be internationalist in character and, at the same time, to base policies on moral principles.

Sunday 6 November
Walesa described Mrs Thatcher as 'wonderful.' He is the Eric Hammond of Poland, and she is posing as the friend of trade-unionism. The only reason the Polish Government put up with it is because they desperately want British support for an easement of their debt crisis.

Friday 11 November
Jim Sillars, the SNP candidate in the Govan by-election, formerly of the Scottish Labour Party, formerly of the Labour Party, beat our candidate Bob Gillespie last night. There had been no socialist politics in our campaign – just the idea that if you keep your head down you'll win. A 19,000 Labour majority, the seventeenth safest seat in Britain, was transformed into a 3000 SNP majority. The fact is, it was an unnecessary by-election, caused by making the Labour MP Bruce Millan a European Commissioner. It revealed that if you don't offer people analysis they go for separatism, and it was also a reflection of our failure to discuss constitutional questions, which are at the core of the devolution argument.

Caught the train to Oxford for David Butler's annual Nuffield seminar, and for the first time he was absolutely candid in his criticism of me. He said I was responsible for the destruction of the Labour Party by advocating the Referendum, by lifting the proscribed list, by encouraging entryism, and by instigating constitutional change which split the Party. David's hard-right, Callaghanite views came out, and I responded openly. It was jovial and I enjoyed it.

Saturday 19 November
To Salford University for a couple of fringe meetings at the conference organised by the Campaign for Non-Alignment.

There was a debate between myself and Peter Tatchell on the future of Europe. His argument is that the Common Market is there, it is international, there are a lot of good Greens, trade-unionists, socialists and peace workers in Europe, and we have got to get rid of the American connection and build a non-provocative, non-nuclear defence policy around the EEC. I think it is a fatal idea. Peter is a decent guy, but he and Frances Morrell and others have come out with an anti-American, pro-European, regional nationalism which I think is absolutely wrong.

Sunday 20 November
The ILCS met at my house at 7.30. We discussed the trade unions. With four or five trade union leaders – Ron Todd, Gavin Laird, John Edmonds, Ken Gill and Rodney Bickerstaffe – holding 92 per cent of the vote, it is very difficult to see how you can democratise the Party through the Conference. That was the old way of doing it, capturing the Party through the Conference.

Next we came to Charter 88, the movement launched by the *New Statesman* which among other things calls for proportional represent-ation and a bill of rights. Hilary Wainwright, Ralph Miliband and others are signing it. The problem is that, if PR is made the centrepiece, support becomes difficult for those in the Labour Party who, for one reason or another, don't want PR. If you lose your local roots you are in difficulties, although Perry Anderson rebuked me as an old Burkean for saying that. The question arose: would PR be a condition of support, and would Charter 88 people only support the candidates endorsing PR? Wasn't it a recipe for coalition politics?

I feel a bit left behind somehow. A new generation is coming up for whom normality is to be in the Common Market and so on. I don't want to get locked into combat, and I ought to try to restore my relations with people and not be so opposed to what they are doing.

Thursday 24 November
Went for the first sitting for a bust of me which is being modelled by Ian Walters, a very talented sculptor. In his studio in Battersea he had a beautiful head of Nelson Mandela, a statue of Fenner Brockway and one of Phil Noel-Baker, and a bas-relief of the Wapping dispute.

I went into the House to meet some Chesterfield students who are taking part in a large demonstration against student loans. As I was driving in, I saw a mass of police buses, mounted police and police in riot gear. Reports kept coming into the House about the police who had blockaded Westminster Bridge with a great line of men and when it opened up the horses advanced relentlessly in a line to force the students back. Dennis Skinner wasn't allowed across the bridge, but Eric got across at some stage. I went to St Thomas's Hospital, where twenty people had been admitted to casualty; another seven had been admitted at Westminster Hospital. So I went back and raised it in the House of Commons. There was some question of a ministerial statement, but it never came.

Went to see Mother. The traffic was more chaotic than I have known it in London. I think the police lay on traffic chaos to make motorists angry at the students. London was literally at a standstill for hours.

Friday 25 November
Caught the train to Chesterfield for a surgery. Some of the students from the Technical College who had been at the demonstration yesterday came and described what had happened. It was exactly the same tactics as at Wapping, though less severe. I was confirmed in my view that the police had deliberately closed four bridges across the Thames, allegedly to 'contain' the students. The gutter press had hyped it up in a most disgraceful way.

Monday 28 November
Worked for a while at home. At 6.30 I went to the Fabian Lecture in one of the committee rooms of the Commons at which I launched my proposal for a Government of Britain Bill[4]. Quite a few MPs turned up, and the room was packed.

Tuesday 6 December
Voted at 10 on the Prevention of Terrorism Act. Forty-five of us voted against its renewal, so that was a pretty successful endorsement of the Party's policy – the 1984 Conference having voted to oppose the Act. Last Thursday Neil Kinnock had said that anyone who voted against would get the 'Ann Clwyd treatment'.

Thursday 8 December
Following the horrific news of the earthquake in Armenia, the response of sympathy and understanding is amazing, with the Soviet Embassy open for gifts and messages.

Gorbachev's unilateral announcement of cuts of half a million troops has put Russian diplomacy right at the top, has ended the Cold War at a stroke and may bring hope to millions. What is so absurd is that the British defence policy is based on building bombs which would create a tragedy ten times as great as the earthquake and we are pouring money in to help Armenia. It is totally contradictory. The Labour Party has absolutely failed to think anything out.

Caroline said disarmament will lead capitalism to collapse and could lead socialism to prosper, and I think she's right.

Wednesday 21 December
Overslept. To the NEC, where we talked about the anti-poll tax campaign. David Blunkett wanted to organise a Day of Action, and there was obvious hostility to that. Peter Mandelson, who is only publicity director, chipped in and said there were many other ways of opposing the poll tax. In the end the vote was deferred.

The main discussion was on Govan. We had a report describing Bob Gillespie as 'the wrong candidate at the right time', which is an outrageous thing to say. Bob Gillespie was not the wrong candidate, because he was chosen locally and we endorsed him.

Thursday 22 December

There has been an awful air crash. A Pan-Am jumbo aircraft crashed at Lockerbie, near Dumfries in Scotland, killing everybody on board and about twenty-seven people on the ground. The plane came down on a petrol station and burst into flames. A most terrible tragedy, and of course people are worried about whether it was caused by a bomb.

Sunday 25 December

Caroline and I exchanged presents. Then the kids arrived for the huge present-giving. The whole family were there and we had the biggest Christmas dinner we've ever given. We cleared up and went to bed at 11 very tired, particularly Caroline.

The year was one of enormous change in many respects. I suppose the biggest changes were the reforms instituted by Mikhail Gorbachev in the Soviet Union, reforms which have really marked a turning-point in Soviet politics, in Marxism and in world politics too.

As far as domestic politics is concerned, Thatcher is riding high. Having been re-elected in 1987, she has introduced the most comprehensive programme of right-wing changes, including more privatisation and the poll tax.

The Labour Party is totally inadequate in the House of Commons. Neil Kinnock yaps like a little dog at Thatcher's heels and she kicks him aside. At the 1988 Conference the Party pushed through the NEC policy statements, including 'Democratic Aims and Values', which dilutes to the point of harmlessness the basic socialist critique of capitalism. It has been an extremely bad year for the Labour Party.

In Chesterfield there is a noticeable decline, because the mood reflects what's happening nationally, and membership has fallen to about 700 – about half of what it was after the miner's strike.

The leadership challenge to Neil Kinnock was opposed by many significant people in my life. Caroline thought it was a mistake, as did Ralph Miliband and John Ross of Socialist Action.

I must have done about 200 public meetings all over England, Wales and Scotland, and it was terribly tiring. In Edinburgh 1000 people attended, and 2000 in Liverpool. It was a way of putting the socialist case in its purest form back on the agenda and re-enforcing the Chesterfield Conference.

Caroline has been researching for the Keir Hardie book, work which has taken her to Scotland and will take her to Amsterdam next year researching the Sylvia Pankhurst papers.

I'm spending the last few days of the year at Stansgate with the family.

Friday 6 January 1989

Today the UN Security Council discussed the bombing of Libya. The

Americans were on the defensive because the Third World has joined almost unanimously in supporting President Qadhafi of Libya. The Americans now behave like cowboys fighting Indians: if you're a Third World country, the Americans can just do what they like – they can invade you, shoot you, bomb you.

Wednesday 11 January

I went to Broadcasting House to record *Desert Island Discs* with Sue Lawley. I'd picked the records carefully, including a madrigal by Stephen. I was looking forward to it in a way, but when I arrived I found that she had just gone through the press cuttings and picked out all the usual stories. 'Why did you change your name from Wedgwood Benn? Do you drink tea in a workman's mug? Why did you wreck the Labour Party?' I spent most of the time repudiating media myths. I rang up afterwards and suggested that, when they edit it, they cut out the media stories, which are so boring.

Incidentally, Sue Lawley handed me my BBC obituary, prepared for my untimely death! It was slightly eerie to read it. But it represented the same media view in death as in life – 'wrecked the Labour Party', and so on.

Friday 20 January

I went to the House, and several MPs had listened to *Desert Island Discs* – including Robert Rhodes James, the Tory MP for Cambridge, who asked for a cassette of Stephen's music because a relative of his at King's College, Cambridge, was always looking for new music. I immediately rang Stephen and told him. I have had some really lovely letters about *Desert Island Discs*.

Sunday 29 January

In the evening Caroline and I went to a Socialist Conference fund-raising party in Highgate. About 150 people turned up, including Salman Rushdie, who made a little speech about the burning of his new book, *Satanic Verses*, which he autographed and auctioned at the party.*

Thursday 9 February

I had a meal in the House with Eric and Doris Heffer, and afterwards we went into the television room and watched Neil Kinnock on a Thames Television programme. Harry Cohen, the Labour MP for Leyton, had warned us that Neil was going to ditch unilateralism.

Kevin Barron came in to keep an eye on what was going on. It was really everything you needed to know about Kinnock. He was

* Days after this event, an edict was issued by the President of Iran, the Ayatollah Khomeini, calling for the execution of Salman Rushdie for his supposed offence against Islam. It forced Rushdie into a life of hiding.

interviewed by an ingratiating Irishwoman called Olivia O'Leary, who was smarming and smooching over him but trying to trip him up, while Neil was at his most macho and self-confident. Among the many things he said was 'I changed the policy on the Common Market after 1983' and, on nuclear weapons, 'The whole situation has changed'.

She asked, 'Would it be right to say that, to the ordinary Labour voter, unilateralism is over?'

'Oh yes,' he said. 'Nobody will be surprised about that – I said it last year.' So he ditched the policy publicly.

Then, when he was asked about David Owen, he said, 'The trouble with David Owen was he bottled out, he didn't stay and fight in the Labour Party' – implying that, if he had, he would have been an ally of Kinnock's now.

Sunday 12 February

In the papers I read that Barbara Harris has been consecrated a bishop in America – a woman of fifty-eight who has been ordained for only eight years, was previously an oil company executive, has no formal theological training, and is divorced and black. Tomorrow in the House of Commons, coincidentally, there is to be a debate on the relationship between church and state. It is an appropriate moment to speak in favour of ordination for women.

Wednesday 15 February

At the Campaign Group we discussed Salman Rushdie and his *Satanic Verses*. Earlier this week Ayatollah Khomeini called for his execution and another mullah put a million pounds on his head. This has sent shock-waves through the British Muslim community.

Bernie Grant put forward a motion with Max Madden which proposed extending the blasphemy laws and called for a meeting with the Islamic Council. Bernie said that Rushdie knew what he was doing and that they'd cut off people's hands for years in the Muslim world. He appeared to be criticising Rushdie.

Diane Abbott said this was a matter of principle. The Muslims were being misled, and she was opposed to censorship because minorities would suffer.

Alice Mahon [MP for Halifax] said the zealots of Islam had persecuted women, and they went as far as stoning women who'd been raped. She had no sympathy for their case.

Audrey Wise said she hadn't read the book but Rushdie was simply looking at the world with questioning eyes. Khomeini's death threat encouraged racism. She had 6000 Muslims in the constituency in Preston, and many had written to her asking for the book to be banned, but she had refused, and she had had no criticism of her response.

Mildred Gordon [MP for Bow and Poplar] said all fundamentalists and all established churches were enemies of the workers and the people. All religions were reactionary forces keeping the people down and denying the aspirations of working people. She opposed all blasphemy laws.

Bernie Grant kept interrupting, saying that the whites wanted to impose their values on the world. The House of Commons should not attack other cultures. He didn't agree with the Muslims in Iran, but he supported their right to live their own lives. Burning books was not a big issue for blacks, he maintained.

Pat Wall said his constituency, Bradford North, had the second largest Muslim population but he couldn't sign Max Madden's motion. He read us a letter he was sending out, refusing to support the banning of the book. The real question was the power of the imams and the mullahs and the fundamentalists, and no socialist could support Khomeini. Class was the issue.

Bernie Grant asked why the Muslims should be insulted. They had nothing to live for but their faith, he said.

Eric Heffer thought the history of our own country and the banning of books should be warning enough. Tom Paine's *Rights of Man* had been banned. Many Muslims hadn't even read the book. He couldn't agree to the burning of books, because that led to the burning of people.

We left it there, and it raised all sorts of questions.

Wednesday 22 February

Campaign Group special meeting on the poll tax. Gary Kent, Harry Barnes's researcher, introduced the arguments for a broad popular movement involving opposition mainly within the law, though some people would take illegal action.

Eddie Loyden thought there had to be an element of illegality for the campaign to be effective.

Harry Cohen said the poll tax was a vote loser for us; there would be a lot of payment arrears in Labour constituencies, and the electoral register would be affected detrimentally to Labour. We should be looking towards the possibility of a general strike.

Pat Wall said the leadership had failed us and the Labour authorities would get the blame.

Mildred Gordon thought that appealing to people not to pay would not work.

Audrey Wise agreed. 'Can't pay, won't pay' wouldn't work because of the enforcement through earnings, but if the unions wouldn't co-operate with payment we must support them. The Labour alternative of a combination of rates and a property tax was absurd.

Dawn Primarolo said the non-payment question had polarised the issue and it was a real crisis for local government.

Jeremy Corbyn didn't think the Labour Party was serious about opposing the poll tax.

I summed up. I said that we should inform people about the effect, the danger and the divisive nature of the poll tax. We shouldn't denounce people who did pay, and those who refused to pay as a matter of principle should be treated as conscientious objectors. We should link this with other campaigns such as land ownership.

Saturday 25 February

To an anti-poll tax public meeting in Sheffield, the first meeting at which I had spoken specifically on the poll tax, and it was clear that mobilisation against it had begun. There was a great deal of anger there, and the ultra-left attacked people who said they would pay the poll tax and asked me if I intended to pay. I said it was easier for me because my poll tax was much less than my rates, but I wasn't going to tell anyone else to pay the poll tax, since I thought that would just divide us.

Thursday 2 March

To Paris for Concorde's twentieth birthday celebrations, in a plane which had been specially laid on for the many guests from Britain. The whole atmosphere was like a school outing, with a lot of nostalgia and old faces.

We arrived at Toulouse, and went in a bus to this huge hangar where about a thousand people had gathered. We began with 'God Save the Queen' and the 'Marseillaise', and then enormous screens showed lovely pictures of Concorde in flight. Then spotlights went on to shop-floor workers on Concorde and highlighted Brian Trubshaw and André Turcat, the British and French test pilots in 1969, and others. The British Ambassador, Ewan Ferguson, made a speech in French and English and paid tribute to my contribution as Minister of Technology, saying I had added the 'e' to Concorde and so on. An orchestra played, there was a great laser display and then a splendid reception. There was no class distinction – the VIPs were not taken away to be given a five-course lunch. Everyone was together – workers and ambassadors – and it made me think the French Revolution *had* made an impact.

Thursday 9 March

William Cash, a young, right-wing Tory MP who is a constitutional lawyer, came up to me and told me the Tory Party was on the point of splitting over the federalisation of the Common Market, which would leave the British Parliament without power – something I've been saying would happen ever since the whole Europe debate began. He said that in his opinion this issue would realign British politics in a way comparable to the alliance of John Bright, the Radical MP, and Disraeli at the time of the 1867 Reform Bill. What was at stake was the democratic self-government of Britain.

This was music to my ears. I told him, however, that I had never stood on a platform with Conservatives because I did not take the view that the argument with Brussels was a nationalist one – it was about democracy. I also said that if the right-wing attack on Brussels was because of the Common Market's social legislation then the Labour Party would obviously be on the other side with regard to the merits of the legislation, even though we share the constitutional argument.

I am signally ignorant about nineteenth-century politics, but fortunately had been reading an essay by Ruth Winstone for her MA in Victorian Studies on Trollope's *Phineas Finn*. She dealt with the very subject of the 1867 Reform Act. So I was not quite as blank in my expression as I might have been.

Friday 7 April
Gorbachev had lunch today with the Queen at Windsor Castle, where she gave him some jewellery and an oil painting of a Tsar. Gorbachev is going flat out to endear himself to the establishment in the west, and I suppose he's gaining a worldwide reputation which he can use for domestic purposes in the Soviet Union. Meanwhile Boris Yeltsin is quoted as saying he is a tremendous fan of Mrs Thatcher; the praise heaped on Yeltsin is obviously being given because he is thought to be the man who might dismantle socialism.

Saturday 15 April
Caught the train to Chesterfield. At 2 I went to the Chesterfield Football Club ground to receive a petition signed by 2000 fans against the Football Spectators Bill, which proposes the introduction of identity cards. I don't think I've ever been to a professional football match in my life before, an extraordinary confession! There were all these directors in their fifties and sixties wearing white shirts, grey slacks and blue blazers.

To Stansgate for the rest of the weekend, and when we got there we heard about this horrific tragedy at Hillsborough football ground in Sheffield in which ninety-four people were suffocated and crushed to death against the fences which had been put up to keep spectators off the pitch. The police had let extra people in at the back of the terraces, and they had been pushed forward, crushing all these people at the front, who couldn't be rescued. The herding of the fans, the way the people who are the source of revenue for football are treated, is unspeakable.

Saturday 29 April
I am thinking about how to handle the Policy Reviews which we are considering again in two special NEC meetings on Monday and Tuesday in Transport House. I don't want to spend the next six months

attacking them, because I think that would simply internalise the conflict, but of course they are going to be wholly inadequate – shallow and superficial. I've got to think of a few amendments that would clarify the matter, and probably I will abstain on the reviews themselves, though I am bound to vote against those on the economy and defence. If the right don't listen to us, they can't expect us to queue up to jump for joy about them.

Monday 8 May

I worked this morning on an alternative paper to 'The Productive and Competitive Economy', which we are discussing today, together with 'Economic Equality' and 'Consumers and the Community'.

The TV cameras were at Transport House, and I complained to Larry Whitty about Mandelson, who was telling them who and who not to film.

Ken Livingstone, Hannah Sell, the Young Socialist on the NEC, Dennis Skinner and I voted pretty well together.

Gould introduced 'The Productive and Competitive Economy'. When he finished, I said it reminded me of 1931, when Ramsay MacDonald had said that what he recommended went against everything the Party stood for but it was necessary. The trouble with the document was that it contained no analysis, no history, nothing about the power of capital or the impact of the EEC, nothing about the fact that technology gave you a choice, nothing about post-Fordism, nothing about public assets, nothing about the problems that would face an incoming Labour Government. I submitted my alternative draft.

Ken Livingstone agreed about the weakness of analysis. He talked about the balance of payments and moved two amendments, one to cut the defence burden and the second to control the export of capital.

Kinnock said there was no need for a historical analysis; it would daunt us. We lived in a capitalist world and we must accept the limitations of capitalism and control technology; unless we could win we couldn't tackle these problems. He said that my proposals were a detachment from reality because there was no easy way. The British public did believe in the market and we had to face that fact.

On cost, he said Ken had helped our enemies by drawing attention to the fact that we couldn't afford our policies. We must build the basis for sustainable growth and we must not promise to spend what we hadn't got. We must create growth and distribute it more fairly – shopping-list socialism was dreaming, and we should leave dreams to others.

I supported Ken's two amendments, which were defeated, with four people voting for the first one and five for the second one – Jo Richardson voted in favour of defence cuts.

Livingstone moved his third amendment about exchange controls.

Gould said exchange controls were impossible because of our treaty obligations to the Common Market; we had to make Britain attractive to investors.

We then went through it paragraph by paragraph. I raised many queries and tried out my amendments.

On takeovers, Gould said we were bringing ourselves in line with the EEC. Livingstone and I said that workers should vote on takeovers. Diana Jeuda of USDAW opposed that on the grounds that workers didn't want to know.

McCluskie thought it looked as if we were moving towards a pay policy. I drew attention to what had happened in 1978 over the Ford settlement and said a pay policy was a hostage to fortune.

Livingstone quoted Neil, who had apparently said in the *Observer* yesterday that we didn't want a pay policy. Neil fudged.

Tom Sawyer said this was not a manifesto and we could spell it out later.

We came to the reacquisition of public utilities. Ken Livingstone moved two amendments relating to reacquisition and compensation. I thought it was absurd to say that if we reacquired privatised services the cost would come into the PSBR; British nuclear fuel and British oil had never been included in the PSBR when they had been nationalised.

Gould said we must fully compensate any privatised services we reacquired, otherwise it would be electorally disastrous.

On old-fashioned nationalisation, there was a statement that 'we don't believe in it', which was deleted at my suggestion.

On nuclear energy, I pointed out that we knew it was 40 per cent more expensive than was claimed and three times the cost of coal; we couldn't afford it and we should phase it out.

Neil said we couldn't afford the cost of decommissioning the nuclear power stations.

Cook moved that we didn't commission the Sizewell nuclear station, and that was carried by 11 to 10 – the only victory of the day.

At the end of the first document, I moved my alternative draft, which was defeated by 14 to 4.

Then 'Economic Equality' was introduced by John Smith and Diana Jeuda. I moved that we remove the 50 per cent upper-limit tax pledge. That was defeated.

We adjourned and had a quick meal, then came back to the NEC at 7 for 'Consumers and the Community'. I suggested we change it to '*Citizens* and the Community' – that wasn't accepted.

The atmosphere at the meeting was quite friendly. Four of us, Ken Dennis, Hannah Sell and I, stuck firm. It is a major change, and by far the most right-wing policy during my time in the Party. Kinnock is openly arguing for capitalism, and the rest are accepting that Thatcher has won the argument but her Government might be replaced. I was as cheerful as I could be, and there was no hostility because the majority against was so enormous. As Peter Jenkins said on the news, Kinnock needs a fight to show there has been a change.

Looking back on it, I must recognise that the Labour Party has never been a socialist party, it has never wanted social transformation, it has always had a right-wing Leader, it has always wanted to pursue these policies, and it is only when circumstances require a change that the pressure comes from underneath for a transformation. When we win the Election, there will be high expectations and enormous pressure on us, and it is an inadequate economic policy for that situation.

Tuesday 9 May
To Transport House early in order to be able to give a long press interview before I went into the Executive.

At 10.07 we began work on 'Democracy, the Individual and the Community'. I had put in an alternative paper, and I moved the two amendments at the beginning of my paper – that we remove US bases and take back control from the EEC. They were both defeated by 19 to 3.

Hattersley had put in a proposal about the entrenchment of rights which would mean that a Labour Government couldn't repeal those rights without the consent of both Houses of Parliament and without having another General Election. I opposed that strongly, and quoted Tom Paine's remark that it would be the dead controlling the living. I was defeated by 20 to 3.

On the abolition of the Lords, I argued that the only way it could be done would be by swamping the Lords with Labour peers. That had been a potential weapon historically, as in 1713 and 1911. I moved that we include a proposal to create sufficient peers, but that was defeated by 20 to 4.

I also moved the disestablishment of the Church of England; that was defeated by 11 to 10. I opposed the state funding of political parties on the grounds that it would turn MPs into civil servants, would strengthen the PLP at the expense of the Party as a whole, and would weaken our links with the unions. That was defeated, with five in favour.

On the Northern Ireland section of the Democracy paper which stated the long-term solution of a united Ireland, Clare expressed doubts over parts of the paper, and I moved to amend the whole section by substituting 'termination of jurisdiction' in place of 'devolved power-sharing' using the Anglo-Irish Agreement.

Livingstone said we had failed; Catholics were forced to emigrate because there was no work, and that kept their population down.

Colm O'Kane said he was opposed to my proposal; the majority in Northern Ireland didn't want us to go, and there would be a blood-bath.

Ken's amendment to delete references to working through the Anglo-Irish Agreement was defeated with only five in favour.

The paper stated that we would make the security services more accountable. I proposed a complete and fundamental reform which would place them under the control of the police. That was defeated 17 to 5. Later I moved that Chief Constables be appointed by and be accountable to elected police authorities; that was defeated with only four in favour.

Went on to the section on the press, and Ken proposed that we encourage co-operatives. Ted O'Brien said the *News on Sunday* and the *Scottish Daily News* cost the trade union movement a lot of money, and democracy didn't work in the running of a newspaper. Ken then moved that the IBA supervise the press, and that was defeated by 15 to 6.

I moved that magistrates be elected, that before appointment judges should be examined by a judicial committee of the House of Commons, that judges retire at sixty and that the blasphemy laws be repealed. On some amendments, I received a fair degree of support.

Ken Livingstone moved that there be a common age of consent of sixteen for lesbians and gays. That was defeated by 17 to 11.

I moved that the voting franchise age be reduced to sixteen; that was defeated by 15 to 4.

Finally we voted on the whole paper 'Democracy, the Individual and the Community' which was carried by 22 to 4.

The next paper was 'Britain in the World'. The EEC was first, and I moved that the Council of Ministers meet in public. That got five votes. We moved on to the Middle East and I was defeated by 18 to 5 on my motion to favour the acceptance of a Palestinian state. Ken Livingstone moved that Palestinian refugees be able to return to Israel; that was defeated by 20 to 3.

We came to the main debate on this paper – a defence policy for Britain, presented by Gerald Kaufman. I argued that this really was reiterating Gaitskell's speech in 1960 – fight, fight and fight again. After Chernobyl it was clear that nuclear weapons were unusable. But the PLP had never put forward Conference policy on unilateralism and, if you looked at the history, Labour Governments had in fact been associated with unilateral nuclear rearmament. Attlee built the bomb, Chevaline was endorsed by Callaghan, and now we were coming along with Trident, which would multiply our nuclear capacity nine-fold.

Kinnock said we were not interested in the history of Attlee, Bevin or Gaitskell. This document was put forward in the interests of the British people. He declared, 'I have been to the White House, I have been to the Kremlin and to the Elysée arguing for unilateral disarmament. They couldn't comprehend the idea of giving up weapons with nothing in return – they couldn't understand "something for nothing". We cannot sustain the argument for unilateralism. Tony says the debate is unrealistic, but patriotism and common sense tell us that there is nothing incompatible between unilateralism and multilateralism. Realism is the greatest weapon in my argument. I have ambitions for a non-nuclear world, and we can get public support for Labour and win the Election; the choice is disarming under Labour or having a Tory Government that rearms. We want partners in negotiation and we must get to power.'

The right clapped him, and that was the first and only applause of the whole two days.

Ken Livingstone said this was a flawed analysis, and it was about US hegemony. Labour leaders had worked for the US in the past, and our interest was in a pan-European system. The question was whether we would press the button, and, if we went ahead with this, whether Labour voters would abstain or vote Green.

Sam McCluskie said he admired Neil and wanted to give him the benefit of the doubt; we had a new young leadership with new ideas, and Foot, who was the greatest Leader the Party had ever had, supported this policy.

Gould supported the document. He argued that we would inherit these weapons and we should use them to help to achieve negotiation; uilateralism was not necessary or logical, and some people just wanted theological purity.

Gerald Kaufman said that the Policy Review Groups had been to Bonn and Moscow, to Norway and Sweden, to consult. The Russians had said they wanted Britain in the disarmament talks and they wanted a Labour Government.

I moved my five specific proposals: that we decommission Polaris and Trident; that we remove the US bases in the lifetime of a Parliament; that we withdraw from NATO; that we switch from military to civil development; and that we adopt a non-aligned foreign policy. Except for the NATO point, this was broadly Party policy as stated at Conference.

Martin O'Neill said that 75 per cent of the money for Trident would have been spent by 1992, the cancellation costs would be high, Polaris and Trident were negotiating cards and we needed time. We couldn't have a deadline.

My five points were defeated by 21 to 4. Robin Cook moved an amendment for bilateral negotiations if we didn't make progress, I supported him on that, and it was carried.

Livingstone asked for a recorded vote to reaffirm Conference policy; that was defeated by 18 to 8.

So 'Britain and the World' was carried by 17 to 8 with three abstentions.

I didn't make notes on 'The Physical and Social Environment' – it was full of detailed stuff.

At 7.45 we came to the final document, 'People at Work'. In line with my own paper, I moved that all the anti-trade union legislation passed by Conservative Governments since 1979 be repealed in its entirety, and that a new charter of trade union rights should be drafted, published and discussed by all those concerned, with a view to establishing a new framework of law. The right to withdraw labour without the risk of legal or financial penalties should be reinstated.

I must say, all hell broke loose when I asked for a recorded vote on my proposal. I had put my finger on a sore point, because John Evans said, 'What are Tony's motives? What is he trying to do?' Eddy Haigh was against my proposal, and Sam said there was common law to consider.

I replied, 'If you want to know why I have done it, it's because a press briefing has been put out saying that we are going to retain the laws. I have only stated "*anti*-trade union legislation"; you can have ballots, you don't have to change your rule-books. The motive is to get the Conference decision either upheld or reversed on a recorded vote.'

By God, they were angry. Gordon Colling of the NGA said, 'We don't need consultation with the unions, there is a consensus.' Richard Rosser of TASS was furious. Sam McCluskie was against it.

Gordon Colling moved that we suspended standing orders for this amendment so that there could not be a recorded vote. So Ken Livingstone and I moved that there be a recorded vote on the suspension of standing orders. The suspension of standing orders was carried by 22 to 5, but at least we ended up getting the names on record.

Richard Rosser declared that my motion was designed to defeat the Labour Party in the next Election.

I resented that, and I said I thought Richard on reflection wouldn't want to say that. The Taff Vale judgement against the railway union was repealed by the Liberals in 1906–7. The Labour Party repealed the Trades Disputes Act of 1937 in 1946. We repealed the 1972 Industrial Relations Act in 1974. Repeal was an absolutely legitimate process.

Meacher said the unions didn't want the repeal.

In the end, my motion was defeated by 23 to 4, not on a recorded vote.

We went on to 'Safety at Work', and I proposed that the Health and Safety Executive legislation be applied to the offshore oil installations, and that was agreed.

I moved that there be an amnesty for trade unions who had been penalised by Tory laws. A number of very complex trade union points were then raised by trade-unionists, but at least I fought my corner. I haven't tried to record the drift of the argument because it went backwards and forwards so much.

So that was the day.

I suppose I ought to put my reflections down. It was a remarkable two days. The NEC *has* abandoned socialist aspirations and any idea of transforming society; it has accepted the main principles not only of capitalism but of Thatcherism, and it thinks that now the Party has a chance of winning office.

On peace, we have abandoned unilateralism and, however we dress it up, we are going to keep the bomb. That is catastrophic, because lots of people are just not going to support Labour – they'll vote Green or something. I think the Labour Party may be in a state of terminal decline.

That doesn't mean I want to join another Party or set one up. I don't want the Labour Party to lose, but I want people to understand clearly what is really happening, otherwise they are going to waste their time, they'll be cynical, frustrated, and so on.

That's my work from now until the end of my life.

Saturday 13 May
In the evening I went to take part in this live television programme *After Dark* with John Underwood in the chair. It was an open-ended discussion which started at about midnight and went on till the early hours. The other participants were the historian Lord Dacre, Eddie Chapman, who had been a double agent during the war, Anthony Cavendish, who is a former MI6 and MI5 officer, Miles Copeland (an ex-CIA man), James Rusbridger, who had worked with MI5 at one stage, and Adela Gooch, a defence journalist from the *Daily Telegraph*. Every one of them made admissions or came out with most helpful information. I was terribly pleased with it.

Saturday 27 May
I was driven to York to give a lecture on Christian socialism. It was quite well attended. A man in the audience asked, 'How can Labour win? My daughter, who is seventeen and will vote in the next Election, has never even heard of Harold Wilson.'

I said, 'I think that's why we have got a chance of winning', and everybody laughed.

Then I went to an anti-poll tax demonstration in the streets, crowded with people – a really festive atmosphere.

Monday 29 May
Went with Hilary and Sally and the kids, who are holidaying in Chesterfield, to the Spire Church. I was afraid Jonathan might be a bit noisy, so I said, 'Be very, very quiet.' So he came into the church, looked round very respectfully, smelled the incense and looked at the stained glass. When we came to the table where the candles in memory of the dead were flickering, he said, 'Birthday cake', and blew them all out!

We went to the market, the park and the fair, and to the Peak District in the evening. It was lovely having them.

Wednesday 31 May

I went to Chesterfield Royal Hospital with Tom and Margaret, and we were taken round by the unit manager, who, of course, is a chartered accountant. It is a beautiful hospital. When we came to the premature baby unit, she dropped her voice and said, 'Mr Benn, this is the most expensive end of the business.' I thought, 'God! If premature babies are uneconomic units, where the hell are we?'

Sunday 4 June

Apparently 2000–3000 students have been murdered in Beijing. The students had turned out to celebrate and to see Gorbachev, who was visiting, and the Government got worried and sent in soldiers from the local army, who were then won over by the students. So the Government then ordered army units from distant parts of China to Beijing, and these attacked and killed the students.

I was asked to speak at a Chinese solidarity rally in Soho in London. It was the first time I had ever spoken in public against a communist Government. The Chinese people were just weeping – tremendously moving. I made the best speech I could in the circumstances.

Wednesday 14 June

Kathy Ludbrook and I went by Underground to attend Jack Dash's funeral at Plaistow Crematorium. I had been to say goodbye to him when he was dying in the London Hospital. Afterwards I wandered round; it was the old working class, the people whom *Marxism Today* and the socialist intellectuals hate – old men, white men, trade union men, militant men. There were a *few* women about, but it was a tribe burying its tribal chief.

Saturday 17 June

Our fortieth wedding anniversary. It is typical of our life that we should be celebrating our anniversary at the Socialist Conference in Chesterfield, but then our honeymoon in 1949 was fairly brief because we went to a socialist conference in Boston. Caroline was running the education seminar and had written the education policy paper, so at least we were both in Chesterfield together.

A very busy day. There were about 1200 people attending, not quite as many as last year. People on the left are extremely demoralised after the Policy Reviews, of that there is no doubt whatever. The SWP have decided to co-operate, and there were some of the other fringe groups – Workers' Power, the Spartacists, etc. – but they weren't significant and they didn't try to wreck it.

Sunday 18 June

Gerry Adams is to be at the Conference today, so I devoted my press conference to Ireland, because that would dominate this afternoon's plenary.

I emphasised the civil liberties issues and answered questions. The television crews were filming Gerry Adams speaking, knowing it would be illegal for them to play the sound recording, because of the broadcasting ban on any direct speech by Sinn Fein members. The journalists would all be in trouble, might be sacked, might even be punished more severely, and I felt a cold hand round my heart as I sat there watching this censorship process taking place.

I had a talk with Adams, whom I like very much personally. We sat alone in a room together, and I said, 'Look, it is not for me to advise you what to do, but would it be possible to integrate the Irish question with other questions, such as disarmament, peace, civil liberties, the future of Europe, and social security?'

He replied, 'Well, we try to do a bit of that.'

I said, 'I think the more Ireland appears in discussions of other issues the better. Secondly, would you be able to get anybody to intercede to encourage a dialogue? What about friendly Governments? Perhaps you could raise it with them. I'm not suggesting you do anything elaborate, but you could just write letters to a few ambassadors in London, saying you would be glad if any of them were prepared to assist to get a dialogue going. Why don't you write to the Archbishop of Canterbury? After all, he made a statement last week saying that the concept of a "just war" meant that violence could be justified – not that he would agree about that in an Irish context, but he might be ready to assist in some way.'

Joan Maynard chaired the afternoon session. I made a speech in which I concentrated on the Irish question, and I don't say it was marvellous, but it did provide a clear focus and lead, which I think was useful.

Friday 23 June

To the GMC of the Chesterfield Party and gave my parliamentary report. I am beginning to detect that they are not just cheering on radical statements, they all want to win, and I want to win; therefore anything that looks as if it is likely to reduce Labour's chances of winning is frowned on, even by quite radically minded people.

I had the feeling during the evening that even the Chesterfield Party was affected by the idea that we mustn't do anything to rock the boat.

Tuesday 27 June

Caught the train to the TUC Congress in Brighton. Joan Ruddock was on the train, so we shared a taxi, arriving just for the end of the debate on defence. Of course, enormous pressure had been brought to bear on the T&G to change its unilateralist policy. I must say, the anti-unilateralist speeches were vulgar to a degree. Ron Todd made one of the best speeches I have ever heard him make. It was clear, principled and strong, and we won, so it was a huge shot in the arm.

Saturday 1 July

Little Caroline's christening at the House of Commons Crypt. There were lots of children and much screaming and shouting, and poor Father Jennings, the priest from Sally's parish, had difficulty making his voice heard. He said something about Jonathan's christening last year and added, 'I don't know that I need repeat it.' Jonathan, who is two and a half, took his thumb out of his mouth and said, 'Repeat it!' So he said, 'I see I have got a little echo', and Jonathan said, 'Echo!'

After the christening I took the children and others up to the Commons Chamber and asked if we could take photographs. The Custodian said, 'I don't see why not.' So I took pictures of Caroline at the Government dispatch box, then Hilary and Stephen at the Opposition dispatch box, then four children in the Speaker's Chair making silly faces. By this stage it was really necessary to call them to order, because the Custodian said, 'Be careful or I'll get into trouble.'

It was a lovely event and everyone enjoyed it. Stephen took Mother home in her wheelchair.

Tuesday 11 July

The bulletins today were full of tributes to Sir Laurence Olivier, who died aged eighty-two.

Wednesday 12 July

Walked over to the Lyttelton Theatre on the South Bank for a debate with Professor Scruton about republicanism, with Anthony Howard in the chair. There were only fifty or sixty people in a theatre that would hold 800, because of a public transport strike in London at the moment. It was the first time I had spoken about republicanism at any length publicly, and you can't say much in seven minutes. Roger Scruton based his argument on this mystical idea of continuity, from the past, through the present and to the future. The idea of a community between the dead, the living and the unborn was interesting coming from him, because his philosophy excludes the possibility of a community between the living across the board. It is this mysterious idea which I am sure Enoch Powell shares and, frankly, if you are going to defend the monarchy, it is the best way to do it.

Friday 14 July

The 200th anniversary of the French Revolution.

To Durham for the Miner's Gala, and after dinner I watched coverage of the bicentenary celebrations in Paris – an absolutely fabulous display. In Britain we have royal weddings and coronations which people just watch. But in Paris it was a truly popular occasion, and no monarchs had been invited. Mrs Thatcher has thoroughly annoyed the French by saying that Magna Carta was far ahead of *The Rights of Man*. She has caused a lot of ill-will – Madame Thatcher is loathed in France. She has no imagination at all, and her nationalism is really unpleasant to everybody.

Wednesday 19 July
To the PLP in Room 14 to discuss a series of motions, each of which was designed to give women greater representation in the Shadow Cabinet. I sat behind Audrey Wise, Dawn Primarolo and Ann Clwyd, and I said to Audrey, 'I will follow you on the voting.'

There were six motions. The one moved by Audrey was quite straightforward – that there should be fourteen men and seven women in the Shadow Cabinet. Marvellous.

Neil Kinnock spoke immediately and said three women in the Shadow Cabinet was enough. He made a very poor speech and shouldn't have intervened at that stage.

I said, 'The issue we are discussing is women's representation, not electoral reform. If you leave out all the motions which are designed to change the electoral system, there are only two viable ones. There is Audrey Wise's, and there is Neil Kinnock's, and Neil wants eighteen men, three of whom should be women.' It was a slip of the tongue, and everybody giggled. I said, 'Audrey's has the right proportion, indeed it is pretty modest. It doesn't threaten the existing members of the Shadow Cabinet because there would still be fourteen men. It would increase the influence of all Labour MPs by extending the electoral principle, it would get us away from patronage, and it would send a message to the electorate that we are discussing things that were of concern to women.'

Friday 28 July
Up at 5 and caught the 7 o'clock train to Chesterfield.

Held a surgery from 12 to 3 in the NUM offices. While I was there, miners were being tested for compensation for loss of hearing, so when there was a gap I went in, and found my hearing is appalling. The man who tested me said, 'I could get compensation for you without the other side even contesting the claim.' I was pleased to learn that, because my hearing is poor but people laugh at you and think you are not listening. This caused a lot of amusement in the office.

Tuesday 15 August
Went to St Thomas's Hospital, where Mother had been taken by

ambulance after a fall. She was in a poor way. Her face was vacant, her skin was white and her wig was at an angle. I talked to Dr Norman Jones, the consultant, who said she had a touch of pneumonia, and it is a high-risk situation for the next four or five days.

Wednesday 16 August

I went off to the hospital at 11 and Mother was still looking very poorly. She cried and said, 'My time has come. What is there to live for? I've lived long enough. I am ninety-two. There is no point in going on. I have nothing to look forward to.' It made me cry too.

I decided I must try to cheer her up, so I said, 'You've got a new great grandchild due next month, Stephen and Nita's baby. You've got your eye operation on 11 September and then you've got your book to finish.'

She slowly came round. We talked about the old days and about her parents, and how her father, D. T. Holmes, had been one of three survivors out of eight children. Then Joshua arrived, and she had lunch and began to perk up. She looked out of the window at Big Ben across the river.

In summer 1989, I visited India at the invitation of Dr Sisir Bose, a former member of the Lok Sabha, the Indian Parliament. While in Calcutta I gave a lecture in honour of Dr Bose's father Sarat Chandra Bose, one of the great Indian national leaders in the struggle for independence. The Netaji Bureau in Calcutta, at which I delivered the lecture, is dedicated to Sarat Chandra and his brother Subas Chandra, who raised an Indian National Army to challenge British rule in India during the Second World War.

I also visited the Prime Minister, Rajiv Gandhi, in New Delhi, who was about to attend a summit meeting of the Non-Aligned Movement (NAM) hosted by Yugoslavia in Belgrade. The Campaign for Non-Alignment in Britain, had been formed in June 1986 at a meeting in the House of Commons summoned by Jeremy Corbyn, Fenner Brockway, myself and others after the American bombing of Tripoli. I was keen to discuss the issues of non-alignment with Gandhi.

Thursday 31 August

Arrived in Calcutta, having dozed for a few hours on the plane. Calcutta was packed with people on bikes, in rickshaws, in shanty towns. Its population is 8 million, and the city simply can't cope.

Sisir and Mrs Bose met me and took me to the Bengal Club, which is an absolutely unreconstructed inheritance of the British Raj, rundown and shabby. My room was spacious and bare, and had the old round-pin plug fittings, so I had a job making tea. I had terrible toothache and felt lousy.

Driving through Calcutta took my mind back to Rhodesia and Egypt after the war. Ninety per cent of the cars are Morris Oxfords, the type my parents bought in 1954, heavy, sturdy little vehicles. There are one or two little Suzuki cars being made under licence – one of the projects Sanjay Gandhi set up before his death.

Later I caught the shuttle to Delhi, and I slept all the way, with this toothache gnawing at me and producing most unpleasant dreams.

I was met in Delhi by a journalist friend who took me to the Taj Mahal Hotel, an international-standard hotel. I might have been in New York or Washington, and it couldn't have been more different from Calcutta.

Friday 1 September

Lots of phoning to and from the Prime Minister's Private Secretary to confirm the interview at 5.30 tonight.

I also rang the acting British High Commissioner to get a briefing, and went there for an hour. I was met by one of these drab, dowdy secretaries they have at the Foreign Office. The High Commissioner never offered me a cup of tea or coffee, and was absolutely cold. I must say, I thought it was discourteous to a senior British MP. I gathered later that he had written articles in the Indian press in support of Mrs Thatcher.

Went to see a dentist, who gave me masses of penicillin and painkillers.

I kept receiving contradictory messages about when and whether Gandhi could see me, and I had given up hope when I was told he would see me at 7. So I packed up, because I had to leave straight afterwards to get the plane back to Calcutta, and was driven to the Prime Minister's house. It was a fortress, with three metal security gates surrounded by soldiers. They wouldn't allow the driver beyond the first gate because he was a Sikh and Mrs Gandhi had been assassinated by her Sikh bodyguards. It was like crossing the Berlin Wall!

I finally went into what was a modest building and was put into a waiting-room, by which time it was 6.40, and I had to leave at 7.15.

At 7 o'clock precisely the door opened, and I was ushered along a corridor with a huge photo of Indira Gandhi and into a room where Rajiv Gandhi was standing, in a white cotton shirt and trousers. My first impression was of a slightly flabby young man with a somewhat vacant face. But he certainly showed great warmth to me.

I told him how kind it was of him to see me, and he apologised. 'I'm sorry to have messed you around, but there were floods which delayed me. You knew my mother.' I think that was why he wanted to see me.

I produced a little gift – a photograph of Nehru at lunch in the Ashoka Hotel in 1961 sitting with Kenneth Kaunda, then president of the United National Independence Party, and myself. I also gave him a copy of *Fighting Back*.

I briefly reminded him that I had met Gandhi when I was a child, and added, 'I knew your grandfather and your mother, and now I have the pleasure of meeting you. I have a granchild due in three weeks whose mother is half-Indian, so I have a warm and strong connection with India.'

A photographer took a picture of us and then some coffee was brought in. I was under this terrible pressure of time. I said, 'Prime Minister, there is one point I would like to make.'

'Go on.'

'I heard Nehru speak in 1955 in London when I was a young MP about the "temper of peace" and the Bandung Conference, which became the Non-Aligned Movement. That seems to me a very important movement, and I know that you are going to Belgrade on Monday to the summit.' (The President of Yugoslavia had just succeeded Robert Mugabe as president of the NAM.)

He said, 'Well, the Non-Aligned Movement is about worldwide democracy, to end the hegemony of the power blocks.' As if somebody had to persuade me!

I went on, 'It seems to me that India has been right for a long time on this question. The Cold War is over, which is what the Non-Aligned Movement and Nehru wanted. The argument for democracy is now spreading in the Soviet Union, and the pressure for development is spreading all over the world. It seems to me that the nineties belong to the Indian argument. This is something that we should be pushing and explaining more fully.' He beamed at this. I added, 'Talking of hegemony, in Britain we have got 30,000 American troops in 130 bases. I am a member of the "Quit Britain" movement!'

He asked, 'How many bases?'

'Yes, 130. Some of them are installations and intelligence centres, but there are 30,000 troops, and a British air base was used to bomb Libya.'

Then I said, 'I wrote to you two years ago, and you very kindly replied, about the possibility of a high-level delegation of leaders from perhaps India, Zimbabwe and Cuba, to Europe and America, under the auspices of the United Nations, to argue for disarmament coupled with development.'

He said he thought it was an interesting idea.

'Also,' I added, 'the Campaign for Non-Alignment would like observer status at the Non-Aligned Movement conferences.'

He asked what the Campaign for Non-Alignment was.

'It was founded two years ago by myself, Fenner Brockway, Jeremy Corbyn and others in the peace movement, the environment movement, the radical movements of America. We would like observer status.'

He replied, 'I will think about it. The PLO and the ANC are full members. As a matter of fact, we are trying to extend the role and give new life to the Non-Aligned Movement, and one issue is the environment.'

I reminded him, 'Don't forget that there are many progressive people who support the movement, and you could use us in the west to bring pressure to ensure that campaigns of the Non-Aligned Movement were understood in the west.'

'Well, we did actually use the American media to pressure the people to force Reagan on the question of South Africa, and in the end he had to take some action.'

'The Non-Aligned Movement ought to do what Gorbachev is doing – making a direct impact on world opinion.'

He looked at his Private Secretary, who was writing all this down, and said, 'I will consider it.'

He has got to say something in Belgrade, and it was obvious that he hadn't had time to think anything out yet. I felt he was attracted by my ideas.

I said, 'You could use us as the Indian independence movement used its friends in Britain – like Annie Besant and Fenner Brockway – to advance your cause.'

'I'll consider it carefully,' he replied.

'It seems to me that if we are going to develop the movement we have got to give to the United Nations the responsibility for planetary protection, that is chemical and nuclear weapons and the environment. If you are looking for something to say in Belgrade about the environment, how about a new world order for planetary protection?'

He said, 'I like that phrase, "planetary protection".'

We went on to talk about the Indian community in Britain. He asked if they were active in politics, and I told him we had four black and Asian MPs.

At 7.15 I looked at my watch and, because I didn't want to miss the plane, I got up and said, 'You have been very generous with your time. Thank you very much.' So I left when he might have been happy to see me stay for a few more minutes.

A car drove me out of the compound, and then I was driven to the airport. Back to Calcutta and the Bengal Club, and got to bed at 2 am.

Saturday 2 September
Woke at 7 and had a bath, then had to lie on the bed to rest. While I lay there, three Indian servants came in barefoot. One took away my laundry, another went to the bathroom and I could hear him scrubbing the bath, and another brushed softly round the bed. Not a word was exchanged. I felt as if I had been thrown back fifty years.

I opened the window and looked out, and there was a beggar with no legs.

I went to the Netaji Bureau for a seminar on Sri Lanka, where I met a professor, who confirmed that there were only 10,000 troops in British India compared to 30,000 Americans in Britain now. I'm afraid I dozed off during the seminar, it was so hot.

My overwhelming impression, as somebody at the seminar said, is that India is run by anglophile civil servants, that Britain bequeathed to India the post-war British consensus of Gaitskell and Butler, and Attlee and Eden. And yet, when you look at the poverty, the case for radical reform is so strong, you can't help feeling despair that such an important country should have so little real political impetus for social transformation.

Tuesday 5 September

Up at 4 am, made two mugs of tea and went down to wait for a car to take me to the airport. Outside the door, crows were picking at a dead rat.

At the airport a little girl came right up to me and looked into my eyes and held her hand out, and I recognised her as the same girl who was standing in exactly the same spot of the airport when I arrived.

Wednesday 6 September

To my delight the *Times of India* had a report that Rajiv Gandhi in Belgrade had called for the UN to take reponsibility for 'planetary protection'. So it was worth going for that.

I slept on the plane and had terrible dreams about water overflowing in the bathroom.

Wednesday 13 September

In the evening I went to Chesterfield for a meeting with the British Medical Association branch at the Royal Hospital. I had such a terrible cough that I was sick on the train; I really did think my last day was coming. There were only twenty doctors there, and they must have thought I was the one needing advice rather than they. I was dropped back at the station, and shivered and had a fever on the train all the way home.

Labour Party Conference, Brighton
Sunday 1 October

To the Conference NEC, where we spent about an hour organising our responses to the Conference resolutions.

What was clear to me was that Kinnock apparently did not want us to be committed to anything, even to the rundown of nuclear power within fifteen years. He was just convinced that we have got to get power first. Still, we've got a 10 per cent lead, and the press is giving him smashing support.

One of the most interesting discussions was on proportional

representation, which is supported by Robin Cook, Ken Livingstone, John Evans and Clare Short. Hattersley, Kinnock, Gould, Beckett and I spoke against it. In the end there was a vote, with 23 to 4 against even having an NEC inquiry into it.

Monday 2 October
Bruce Kent, who is the delegate from Tottenham, moved the motion at Conference to cut defence expenditure to the average level of western Europe, and Barbara Switzer moved the composite motion on unconditional unilateral nuclear disarmament. I was called to speak from the floor and supported both motions, which infuriated Stan Orme and George Foulkes, who said I was bound collectively by the NEC decision. But lots of people came up afterwards to congratulate me.

Anyway, we lost the unilateralist motion overwhelmingly, but we carried the motion on cuts in defence by 4 million to 2 million.

In the NEC election results I was fifth in the constituency section. Ken Livingstone was replaced by John Prescott, which I was sad about, and Ken was shaken by it. But there is no doubt that Ken will be the left candidate against Neil if we lose the next Election.

Wednesday 4 October
Stephen and Nita had their first baby – Emily, born by Caesarian section at 2.59 pm.

Friday 6 October
Geoffrey Parkhouse from the *Glasgow Herald* gave the traditional vote of thanks on behalf of the press, and referred to the fact that during the debate on labour relations Emily Benn had been born, and he looked forward to hearing her views on her grandfather in years to come. There was a lot of laughter at that.

At the end we sang 'The Red Flag', 'Auld Lang Syne' and this new song 'Meet the Challenge, Make the Change'. Neil and Glenys stood with a little baby, and members of the staff of Walworth Road threw roses at the audience. It was just like an American convention. The Conference has been disastrous for the left.

Cleared up and drove to May Day Hospital, Croydon, where I saw Emily.

Thursday 26 October
It was announced on the 6 o'clock news that Nigel Lawson, the Chancellor of the Exchequer, had resigned because he was not prepared to work with Thatcher's economic adviser, Professor Alan Walters. Well, earlier this afternoon the Prime Minister had announced that she had full confidence in Lawson, although it became

clear that she knew of his decision to resign before she made that declaration. So when Geoffrey Howe, standing in for her, made a statement later I got in a Question, saying that, in view of the fact that the Prime Minister knew that the Chancellor had resigned before she made her statement, she had misled the House. As she is first Lord of the Treasury, she ought to take responsibility for her actions.

For the first time for a long time, our people cheered at my question. It is an enormous political event, and everyone was gossiping in the Lobbies. Then we heard that Professor Alan Walters had himself resigned – not that that makes much difference, because he can still feed his advice through to her privately. But it was seen as another massive blunder by Thatcher. She lost Heseltine and Brittan over Westland. I think the fact is that the economy is in a real mess, and Nigel Lawson is happy to get out in good time. Secondly, the British establishment want to get Britain into the European Monetary System, and therefore they want to discredit the Prime Minister, who is opposed.

Thursday 2 November
Went to the House and spoke in the debate on British membership of the EMS. I drew out political lessons from the proposals for economic and monetary union. John Major made a good speech, his first as Chancellor, followed by John Smith, who said nothing of any substance. When I spoke, Major came back and listened – which was flattering.

Afterwards I spoke to him, and he said 'I think Mrs Thatcher would have agreed with most of what you said.'

'Well, I don't agree with her! You will be in the EMS soon.'

He said, 'Yes, but it doesn't make any difference at all.'

So I think that's the way it's all going to shape up. Thatcher will be forced to bend by the Cabinet and by pressure from the City of London.

Friday 10 November
Out of the blue, and quite amazingly, the Berlin Wall is being removed. The Brandenburg Gate was opened yesterday, and today bulldozers and cranes went in and began hammering holes in the wall and thousands of East Germans are coming over into the west. But in reality it is causing enormous anxiety in NATO because the whole defence argument has changed, while the Labour Party continues to call for three Trident Submarines as a first priority. So it is an extremely important event, and very moving.

Tuesday 14 November
Caroline and I went to the banquet given by the Indian High Commissioner at the Intercontinental Hotel to celebrate the centenary of Nehru's birth. On my right, believe it or not, was Lord Armstrong, who was Cabinet Secretary during the Peter Wright affair. Our careers

have overlapped because he joined the Civil Service the same year I got into Parliament. I had a very candid discussion with him.

We began by talking about Peter Hennessy, whose book *Whitehall* had a silhouette of Armstrong on the cover. He spoke about his career at the Civil Service, and I asked him, 'What is a secret?'

He thought for a moment and said, 'I think it is only a question of security.'

'What is the effect of this obligation of lifelong confidentiality to the Crown which was raised by the House of Lords' judgement on *Spycatcher*? Am *I* bound by it? Because, after all, I dealt with international relations and security and so on as a Minister.'

He said, 'In the light of the Lords' judgement, I think you certainly are.'

We talked about the Radcliffe report of 1976, which recommended that ministerial memoirs should be submitted for vetting by the Cabinet Secretary. I said, 'I don't see why I should be denied the right to record my experiences. I wouldn't print anything contrary to the national interest, but why should I submit my stuff to the Cabinet Secretary to be scrutinised?'

Armstrong said, 'Well, all that the Cabinet Secretary would do would be to advise you what was a matter of national security and what was a matter of breach of confidence.'

I don't find that very persuasive.

We talked about Harold Wilson and Jim Callaghan, and he said, 'Callaghan wasn't as nice as he looked', which is exactly what Callaghan said to me about himself.

He said he was very interested in collective Cabinet responsibility, so I told him, 'If you are interested, I have seventy pages of correspondence with Callaghan and Wilson about it.' I added that I didn't see why discussions in Cabinet committees shouldn't be revealed.

He replied, 'Well, as an example, there was a ministerial committee set up by the present Prime Minister on Aids, and it didn't include the Minister of Health. If that had been known, people would have asked why.'

I said, 'Well, if you don't like the heat, get out of the kitchen, but that's a case for not allowing *anything* to be known.'

We talked about diaries, and Armstrong said, 'I must tell you this. I am reading your diaries, and they correspond precisely with my recollection of the Cabinet meetings at which I was present.' So that was a marvellous recommendation.

I asked what happened to the notes written by the Secretary at the Cabinet, and he said they were destroyed. I have heard this before but don't believe it. He told me, 'When Macmillan saw the official Cabinet Minutes' (which are totally uninformative) 'he said, "You are falsifying history." ' That is just what Cabinet Secretaries do!

He did say, 'If you don't write things down, you can't remember them. For example, when I took over as Cabinet Secretary, I had responsibility for looking at the background to the Anthony Blunt affair, which had just been revealed, and I wrote to Sir Michael Adeane, who had been Private Secretary to the Queen, and to Sir Charles Cunningham, who had been Permanent Secretary at the Home Office. Cunningham and Adeane both had totally different recollections from the account that was in our official files.'

Wednesday 15 November

I was picked up by car and taken to a studio for a programme called *Head On*, done 'down the line' from Glasgow. Richard Shepherd, the Tory MP for Aldridge-Brownhills, also took part at my suggestion. He is such a sensible person, and we were able to have a serious discussion.

After it was over, Richard and I fell to talking. He thinks there could well be a 'stalking horse' against Thatcher this winter. He said, 'It would be better to have a centre-right figure than a wet.' He thought a lot of people would abstain and, if there was a poor result, Norman Tebbit would go to Mrs Thatcher and tap her on the shoulder and say, 'Time to go.'

I mentioned Geoffrey Howe as a possible alternative, and he said he thought Douglas Hurd might be better. That's a matter for them but it would certainly change the political situation if there was a post-Thatcherite Tory Prime Minister.

Richard told me that Lawson left because he had failed, and Thatcher was out of touch. He thought Heseltine was popular with the activists but not trusted by MPs. He preferred Hurd. It was too soon for John Major and Chris Patten. Thatcher had a lust for power, and would join the ERM if she thought it would help. He reckoned the Labour Front Bench were more competent than the Tory Front Bench. He didn't think much of Kinnock, but he said, 'It doesn't particularly matter, because Number 10 will take charge of him.'

Tuesday 5 December

In the House, I heard that the Tory MP Sir Anthony Meyer, who decided to stand against Mrs Thatcher for the Tory leadership, received 33 votes. It has obviously shaken the Prime Minister a bit more than she would like.

Gavin Strang asked me to have a cup of tea with him this evening, and told me he was leaving the Campaign Group. He didn't give any reason, but the truth is that he was sacked from the Front Bench because he was in the Campaign Group, so he is just reading the logic of it. If you join the Campaign Group, either you don't get on the Front Bench or, if you are already on the Front Bench, you get sacked. But I was *very* depressed in a way, and he was embarrassed.

Friday 15 December
I have got a hacking cough.

Today Neil Hamilton, the Tory MP for Tatton, who had won the Private Members' ballot, put down a debate on 'the future of socialism'. Hamilton's motion was a sort of triumphalist celebration of the death of socialism.

Before the debate, there was a petition of 4.5 million names in support of the ambulance workers strike, and six of the messengers carried them in boxes into the Chamber. The Speaker tried to limit the number of boxes brought in so we had a lot of points of order. I got up and said the restriction was an affront to parliamentary democracy. It was a marvellous start for the debate, because here were 4.5 million people demanding a socialist health service.

Eric Heffer made a brilliant, historic speech. Tony Banks made a powerful one. To cut a long story short, we trounced the Tories intellectually and morally, and it was immensely worthwhile.

Sunday 31 December
A tumultuous decade and a dramatic year have ended.

World politics in 1989 were earth-shattering. In Poland, Lech Walesa came to power and emerged as a real right-wing, Thatcherite, Catholic nationalist for whom I have very little sympathy. He came to Britain saying he was going to offer cheap Polish labour to British investors, and told the CBI he wanted profit to play a larger part. Then there were demonstrations in Prague, which were put down by force and led to the total overthrow of the Czech regime and a new Government. Hungary developed in a similar way. Then the Berlin Wall came down after tremendous outpourings of public feeling, the East and West German Governments came together, and there was talk of German reunification. All this was accepted by Gorbachev, who is still desperately trying to make a go of his reforms in Russia, but there are problems in Armenia and the Baltic States, and the economic situation is terribly difficult. The Tories argued that this had all come about due to the fact that we had nuclear weapons, but people didn't really believe it any more.

The Policy Review was a complete capitulation in which we were told that, in the interests of realism, we had to accept three Trident submarines. This was just before the Berlin Wall came down. We were told that the nuclear power stations at Sizewell and Hinkley would have to be commissioned by a Labour Government, just before the Government itself announced that they couldn't privatise nuclear power because it was so uneconomic. At the very end of the year, Tony Blair, our Employment spokesman, announced that the Labour Party had dropped the closed shop because of the EC's Social Charter, without any consultation with the Shadow Cabinet, the PLP, the NEC or the Conference. Some trade union leaders went along with it, but it was totally undemocratic.

Everyone in the Labour Party wants to win the next Election, and therefore they are going along with what is happening at the top. We had a lead in the opinion polls early in the year because of the Government's unpopularity on the poll tax, the health service and various privatisation measures. Kinnock looked as if he was winning, but by the end of the year the Labour lead was beginning to shrink, and I'm not sure that 1990 won't see some recovery of the Tory Party.

Mrs Thatcher went through a tremendous crisis. I think the real reason is that her opposition to European federalism, including economic and monetary union, has angered the establishment, and they are not prepared to tolerate anyone who is against the EEC. However, being a clever woman, she will amend her position in order to bring herself back into line with what the establishment want.

NOTES
Chapter Nine

1. (p. 530) The Non-Aligned Movement was founded in September 1961 as a result of discussions between President Tito of Yugoslavia and President Nasser of the United Arab Republic (Egypt and Syria), and was originally set up as a coalition of former colonies and 'developing' countries to provide an alternative centre of world opinion at a time of Cold War polarisation between Washington and Moscow. It was supportive of the UN and especially its work in decolonisation. As the liberation movements grew the membership of the NAM rose to 102 states including Algeria, Argentina, Egypt, India, Indonesia, Nigeria, Peru, Senegal, Venezuela and Zimbabwe. Other countries and organisations, such as the PLO, have observer status. In February 1989, the NAM stated their central goal to be the establishment of 'a new international economic order'.

2. (p. 541) A prolonged strike of the National Union of Seamen began in January 1988 with the dismissal of 162 men on an Isle of Man ferry but soon involved the wider question of safety on British ferries, following the *Herald of Free Enterprise* tragedy a year earlier in which hundreds of people died and also of possible derecognition by P & O of the union. Sealink and P & O took action against the union to seize their funds and the High Court sequestrated £2.8 million of NUS's assets which eventually caused the strike to collapse.

3. (p. 548) During the Commons debate to celebrate the 300th anniversary of the Glorious revolution I referred to Emily Wilding Davison, the Suffragette who had hidden in the broom cupboard of the House of Commons crypt on the night of the 1911 Census so that as an unenfranchised woman she could describe her address on the day of the Census as 'House of Commons'. In the debate I announced that I had celebrated this event with a notice in the broom

cupboard and subsequently prepared a typed sheet which I tacked to the door. Later I had a brass plaque engraved, and screwed this, plus a photograph of her, on to the door.

In spite of an attempt by the Lord Chancellor to get me to remove it, the plaque still remains and is polished daily by the cleaners.

4. (p. 555) My interest in major constitutional reform started early with the Wedgwood Benn (Renunciation) Bill of 1955, the Peerage Act of 1963 which allowed all peers to renounce their titles, and the Referendum Act of 1975, which I initiated. My proposed Government of Britain Bill eventually became the Commonwealth of Britain Bill and was presented to the House in 1991. It provided for the establishment of a democratic, federal, secular Commonwealth of England, Scotland and Wales. It disestablished the Church of England and set out a radical overhaul of the judicial and electoral system, giving equal representation to women in the House of Commons and a new House of the People.

10
The End of an Era
January–December 1990

Sunday 21 January 1990
I have been thinking a lot lately about the role of conscience. I realise that I have got built into me, through my upbringing or whatever, a tremendously strong inner voice saying what I should do at any one moment. It says: You should get up and get the breakfast. You should ring the children. You should not smoke. You should get on with your work. You should go to bed earlier. If I disregard it – as I regularly do over a whole range of issues – then it builds up an unhappiness in me which comes out in other forms. People say I'm a workaholic, but if an inner voice is telling you all the time to do something or another, you can't avoid it. It is the 'still small voice', though sometimes it becomes quite loud.

Wednesday 24 January
To the Party's Campaign Strategy Committee, where we had a long talk about the poll tax. Neil Kinnock argued that we should oppose it on the basis that it was unfair, that it was costly, that it was not related to the ability to pay, and that we would change it.

Other people spoke, and I said we should exploit the discontent. We should have a rally in Trafalgar Square, and we should demand that the Government give enough grants to ensure that nobody pays more in poll tax than they do in rates. I was going to go further, but Dennis Skinner said, 'Leave it.' In effect, the Party don't *want* a policy for the poll tax.

Clare Short raised her unease about the statement made by Martin O'Neill, our defence spokesman, that we couldn't reduce defence expenditure. I quoted Hurd's article in the *Observer* last Sunday, saying that Britain has got to turn tanks into tractors.

Neil Kinnock said, 'It is all very complicated, and we will have to have a defence review when we get elected. I have always wished I was Prime Minister, and I wish it more now than ever before, but we must be judicious.'

Tom Sawyer argued, 'We have got to be cautious. NUPE will ask for a reduction in defence expenditure, but the Policy Review Group will have to look at it.'

Later we had a meeting of the Campaign Group, and Tommy Sheridan, who has been expelled from the Party for his work in the anti-poll tax campaign in Scotland, came to talk to us. Twenty-eight MPs have said they are not going to pay their poll tax. I am being careful – not telling people not to pay, but pledging to support anyone who doesn't. Of course the Labour Party is more frightened of the anti-poll tax campaign than they are of the poll tax itself.

Sunday 4 February

To the Hackney Empire for a meeting organised jointly by the Black Caucus, Bernie Grant and Anti-Apartheid, at which the Reverend Jesse Jackson, the American civil rights activist, was to speak. The ANC was represented, and it looks as if Mandela will soon be released from prison, though he is refusing to come out until the state-of-emergency regulations in South Africa are lifted.

There was a huge crowd, many of whom couldn't get into the hall. I was honoured to be asked to speak, and Jackson came on stage and we shook hands. He gave me a watery look and made a speech with some charisma, beginning with the slogan 'Keep Hope Alive'. Jackie, his wife, came on to the platform – which I didn't care for.

To the NEC Home Policy Committee, followed by the Local Government Committee for a long consideration of whether we wanted to come out with an alternative policy to the poll tax.

Dennis Skinner, myself and one or two others were advising: keep quiet; why divert attention away from an unpopular poll tax to proposals which we haven't even really worked out? I said we should attack the Tories, and say we will repeal the Community Charge Act, but say we want to consult widely, because it would be ludicrous to get crucified for policies we haven't yet agreed on.

Friday 9 February

To Chesterfield, from where I was driven to Rotherham for an anti-poll tax meeting. I have always been nervous that I would be pushed into saying 'Don't pay the poll tax'. I told the meeting, 'I can't say that, but I am going to support the people who don't, and I am not going to pay myself'.

Sunday 11 February

Had a phone call telling me that Mandela would be released today and asking me to go to Trafalgar Square at 12.30. There were hundreds of people gathered there and the organisers were, of course, the City of London Anti-Apartheid Group, who have been picketing outside South Africa House in Trafalgar Square non-stop for 1395 days. There was a tremendous sense of excitement. People were singing and waving their arms and kissing and hugging. Somebody had draped on Nelson's column a banner with the words 'Nelson Mandela's Column', and I was pushed on to a platform.

I'm afraid my speech wasn't very clear. I simply said, 'This is a great day. Free Mandela. Free South Africa. Free Britain. Free working people from exploitation.' There was a cheer, but I don't think people could hear much, and I could hardly hear myself.

It was a marvellous event; people were dancing and shouting, and an ANC choir were singing. It was fantastic. I don't think there has been anything like it since 1945 when the war ended.

A really great day. On television live from Cape Town was Mandela, this tall, slim, distinguished man with a strong voice, walking out of prison and reaffirming the need for the armed struggle.

Wednesday 14 February

To Senate House for a seminar organised by the Institute of Contemporary British History on the role of the old Ministry of Technology of 1966–70. I had been asked to take part in it, and it was enormous fun. Also there were Ken Binning, a civil servant from the AEA, Jeremy Bray, Parliamentary Secretary at Mintech, Tam Dalyell, Dennis Fakley, deputy chief scientist at the MoD during those years, Peter Jones, a scientist from the Atomic Weapons Research Establishment (Aldermaston), Sir Bruce Williams, my old economic adviser, and Lord (Solly) Zuckerman, the then chief scientist at the MoD.

I suggested that we use this seminar to get to the bottom of the Chevaline story. The background to Chevaline was that it had been announced by Thatcher in 1979 that this project, which included the 'refurbishing', or hardening of Polaris missiles, had been commissioned.

Peter Jones, who was head of electronics at Aldermaston, declared that they were working on the Chevaline project long before, in 1967.

Well, that was a year after I became Minister of Technology, and I reminded them that Victor Rothschild (then head of the Government Think Tank) had brought out a report recommending against the hardening of the Polaris missiles.

So Solly said, 'Well, it was American blackmail' (which forced us to continue). 'The Americans said, "You are not putting enough original work into our nuclear weapons programme." Heath was very much against it and only agreed to fund it three months at a time.'

So what was confirmed was that in fact the House of Commons and the Cabinet were kept in the dark from 1967 to 1979. Wilson had referred to it in Cabinet in 1974, and during that twelve-year period the Chevaline was being built, so in a way you can't blame Callaghan. Indeed, he said not long ago that it had been approved by two Prime Ministers before him – which would take you back to Wilson, Heath, and Wilson again.

Monday 26 February
Heard that Kate Mosse, who is publishing the diaries at Hutchinson, had her baby – Martha – last night, so I drove to Lewisham Hospital with Ruth Winstone to congratulate her and her partner Greg.

Monday 5 March
Last night I had a word with Arthur Scargill on the phone. He cannot go home because of the press siege of his house following vicious attacks on him in the *Daily Mirror* today.

In the *Guardian* there was an interview with Robert Maxwell by Hugo Young in which Maxwell said he regarded himself as a major factor in defeating the miners' strike and how much he admired Mrs Thatcher. He is a very powerful man.

The news at midnight has been all about Arthur Scargill's categorical denial of all the charges. He is consulting his lawyers. If you have to choose between Maxwell and Scargill, there is no doubt who to believe. Arthur is a person of enormous integrity.

Thursday 8 March
Went into the House for an interview with Michael Brunson of ITN on the poll tax. I said that I believed we had to go for non-violent disobedience though I wouldn't tell anyone not to pay the poll tax. It is difficult to launch this argument into the arena because Thatcher says it is all about violence, and Kinnock agrees with her, says you must pay and denounces the left. At the other end you have got Militant, who see it as a way of building their own movement; the SWP, who don't say no to a punch-up; and, at the far left, Class War with their 'anarchistic' views.

Tuesday 27 March
To County Hall for the last meeting of ILEA. It was really rather moving to think that there had been a London education authority for over 100 years, that my grandfather had been a founder member in 1889 and that my son, Stephen, was a member as it ended. Nita and little Emily were present, and Emily sat on my lap in the council chamber and listened to her dad speaking.

Saturday 31 March
To the anti-poll tax demonstration, which started from Kennington Park and marched to Trafalgar Square.

We came up Whitehall and on into Trafalgar Square, which was absolutely crammed. There must have been 150,000 people. I was pleased to see George Galloway there. Jeremy Corbyn was there, but before he was due to speak the rally was stopped because of the trouble which occurred.*

I got off the platform and began walking back down Whitehall, but found the police had thrown a barrier across the road, so that people couldn't get up or down, though they let me through. In the crowd I found myself being pressed from behind by riot police and mounted police. People were terribly frightened. I forced my way through until I came to the line of police, who didn't look like police at all. I wondered if they were soldiers in police uniform. I asked where the senior officer was and finally was introduced to a man with a crown on his shoulder.

I had a tape recorder running part of the time, and I asked, 'Why don't you let them go by?'

He said, 'They won't move.'

Well, that wasn't true. He claimed there had been a lot of violence. I think that what they had done was to break the march up, squeeze the people in the middle and frighten them, and then no doubt some bottles and things were thrown. It reminded me a bit of Wapping.

I said to the commander, 'Don't forget what the Northamptonshire police said about the behaviour of the police at Wapping.'

He got a bit angry and said, 'A few mistakes were made then.'

Sunday 1 April
The papers were full of the riots. A man rang me and left a message on my answerphone: 'You fucking cunt. Now you've lost the next Election for us.' That was the only unfriendly one.

Wednesday 11 April
Most of the letters are pretty supportive. Three Anglican bishops, a Catholic bishop and five free churchmen came out today in favour of non-violent protest against the poll tax.

Wednesday 25 April
Usual nightmare going to the NEC.

There was a paper on the production of policy statements by the Party, and we were told that Peter Mandelson would decide the timing and the content. I argued that Larry Whitty, who is the General Secretary and is elected by the Conference, should have a say. Larry Whitty said he didn't want to decide this – he had to trust his officers and so on. The fact is that Larry lets Kinnock, Mandelson and Charles Clarke run the Party. But, blow me down, I got it agreed that Larry should have responsibility.

Then we came on to a major paper on the reform of Conference

* Between 150,000 and 300,000 protestors joined the rally against the poll tax, organised by the Anti-Poll Tax Federation. Following scuffles and the use of mounted police and riot gear, buildings and cars were set alight and shops were looted.

which, in effect, deguts it, because in future delegates will not be allowed to move policy resolutions at Conference; they will have to send them to a newly elected Policy Commission, to be set up with 170 people on it – so big it will be utterly powerless.

Larry introduced it as a great reform. I said there were some interesting points but it entirely ignored the role of the PLP, it didn't touch on the fact that, even if the policies came out of the Policy Commission, the Leader had a personal veto on policy, and the commitment of the PLP and a Labour Government to Conference policy was still unclear. I said sub-contracting policy away from the Conference and the NEC meant that actually Conference would just rubber-stamp. This was a centralisation of power which would lead to a powerless NEC. It was designed to neutralise the Party before it got back into power, and it would make us into a sort of Democratic Convention.

At the end of the discussion Kinnock made a long speech in which he attacked my description of the reform as 'sub-contracting policy' and said, 'We should energise, enfranchise and mobilise.' It was obviously a prepared speech.

Friday 4 May

This morning we heard on the 7 o'clock news that Ealing Council has been lost by Labour in the local elections. Hilary himself was safe and regained his ward, but otherwise it was very depressing.

Tuesday 8 May

Jeremy Corbyn and I had a bite to eat, and then went down to the Commons Crypt with a Black & Decker drill and brass plaque commemorating Emily Wilding Davison. We screwed it on the door, in place of the temporary notice I had put up with Miss Frampton's help.

Tuesday 15 May

What a day – the day the NEC and the Shadow Cabinet looked at the latest Policy Review document which had been sent to us all over the weekend. It now has five sections: 'Creating a Dynamic Economy', 'Bringing Quality to Life', 'Creating Opportunities to Succeed', 'Freedom and Fairness' and 'Britain in the World'.

To cut a long story short, it was the most deeply, ideologically, anti-socialist and anti-Labour document that I had ever seen. It endorsed market forces to the point of saying, for example, that the policy of the next Labour Government would be 'business if possible, government where necessary'; then stating that economic growth would have to determine public expenditure (ie there would be no redistribution of wealth).

It claimed that economic development depended upon maintaining the confidence of business. There was a passage saying we would be even-handed between employers and unions, but providing for the sequestration of some trade union funds and for ballots.

There was nothing about multilateral nuclear disarmament after the great battle last year to destroy unilateralism.

What one was witnessing was a document intended to give absolutely clear signals to the City of London that we would not interfere with them, to Brussels that we would go wholeheartedly into the EMS and ultimately the EMU, and to the Americans that they could keep their bases here for ever.

Dennis and I moved one amendment after another – forty-eight in all. The others were surprised, I think; I don't know what they thought we would do – just sit in a corner and sulk I suppose.

I am not sure there *is* a Labour Party any more in the accepted meaning of that term. It was the explicit, ideological rejection of socialism. When I looked round the table and saw all the trade union representatives on the NEC voting for the sequestration of trade union funds, for ballots and, in effect, for pay policy (because that is involved in it as well), I realised what a total betrayal was occurring.

Monday 21 May
The Organisation Committee was another absolutely revolting meeting. I didn't make detailed notes, but we lost by 13 to 2 in our attempt to stop deselection of John Hughes, the MP for Coventry North East; the NEC refused a re-run of the selection procedure there which was suspect.

We had an emergency resolution condemning the All-Britain Anti-Poll Tax Federation and warning Party members not to support the Federation. It was moved by Gordon Colling for Tony Clarke of the UCW, who wasn't present. It was a typical example of an attempt to distance the Party from anybody who does anything brave – gutless and unprincipled. I drafted a modest amendment 'that the NEC recognised that millions of people simply cannot afford to pay the poll tax, respects those who regard this issue as raising matters of conscience, and invites the Party to understand and assist those who find themselves in this position.'

I added, 'This is one of the biggest popular movements there has been. I spoke at Trafalgar Square and I am glad I did.'

Neil said, 'The Federation say "Don't pay", and it is dishonest to suggest we can assist.'

'The whole campaign is to promote Militant, who are behind the Federation,' John Evans said.

I asked if Gordon Colling would consider withdrawing the motion but he wouldn't.

My fortieth wedding anniversary fell in 1989 and plans to take our children and grandchildren back to Caroline's home town of Cincinnati for an extended family reunion finally came to fruition in the spring of 1990. Fourteen of us stayed in a small hutted church conference centre in the woods outside the city.

Apart from many family events in which we took part, I gave a lecture at Cincinnati University at the same time as Archbishop Tutu of South Africa happened to be visiting.

Saturday 26 May

To the Free Store for a gathering to receive Archbishop Tutu of South Africa, who is on a visit here. The Free Store is a warehouse where poor blacks get food and materials that are handed out free. It is basically a relief operation.

Tutu arrived, a funny, jolly little man, a bit like Santa Claus really. He and his wife and son and daughter were greeted with presents and flowers. In his speech he didn't mention apartheid once – nothing other than God's wonders. Then he said God must often be despairing when he saw brutality and injustice. But when he, Tutu, saw people giving in the Free Store, then he wanted to thank them for making it possible for God's work to be done.

You couldn't but like the man; he was very human, and talked about God as if he was a friend. He said, 'There is a story that, when Archbishop Tutu went to the pearly gates, he was sent down to the warmer place, to hell. Two weeks later, the devil went and asked for political asylum in heaven because the archbishop was causing so much trouble in hell.' It was all very jolly, and people absolutely loved it. There was a charismatic element.

Friday 29 June

Caroline had her 'Return to Learning' course validated by the CNAA; she has been teaching the course now for fifteen years. What she has done is to build up people's confidence and encourage them to write, to think and find out for themselves.

Tuesday 3 July

Nelson Mandela was due to speak in the Grand Committee Room of the Commons at the invitation of the British–South Africa All-Party Group. I went in early to get a seat, but no one was there, people were very blasé and turned up later. Ivor Stanbrook, Conservative MP for Orpington, was in the chair.

Nelson and Winnie arrived; he looked very distinguished, but tired and drained of energy. He is doing a killing world tour, but it is of enormous advantage to the African cause in South Africa. It has made him the unofficial president of that country without his ever even having had the vote.

In Dublin he had mentioned the need for talks between all parties in Northern Ireland (which the press immediately said made him an IRA supporter), and Stanbrook launched into a criticism of this speech. It was most insulting to a man who had been in prison for twenty-seven years, to be rebuked by a right-wing conservative who had fully supported the South African President P.W. Botha.

But Mandela was strong and clear. He made a reference to Edmund Burke and the 'home of parliamentary democracy', as people do when they are on foreign trips, though it is a bit misleading! He reiterated his belief that there should be talks on Northern Ireland.

Only two questions were allowed, and afterwards I jumped on to the platform and said, 'Thank you for what you said about Ireland.' We shook hands, and I was delighted to have met him.

Monday 23 July

I saw Heseltine in the post office of the Commons today, and said to him, 'I noticed when you were interviewed not long ago on television that one of my books was on the shelf behind you. I presume it was there to impress people!'

'I'll remove it at once,' he replied.

Wednesday 1 August

On holiday at Stansgate. Absolutely perfect weather, temperature in the nineties – higher than in Athens or North Africa. In the evenings the sunsets are beautiful, and we saw two swans with their cygnets on the river, just heavenly. Caroline is so happy working on her biography of Keir Hardie.

Friday 3 August

Serious news today of the Iraqi invasion of Kuwait. Alliances are being built up; the Americans and Russians issued a statement, Thatcher is going to America, Bush warned that Saudi Arabia mustn't be attacked because Baghdad can't be allowed to control two-thirds of the world's oil supplies. We could be hovering on the edge of a Third World War, and the only comforting thing you can say about it is that the Cold War is over and the superpowers are not fighting this war by proxy. King Hussain of Jordan, who is a great friend of Britain but is also a friend of the Baghdad Government, has been to Iraq.

When the Iraqi Army invaded Kuwait, the Iraq Government claimed a list of grievances against Kuwait – some of which originated in the historical settlement of the borders in the region by the victorious powers after the First World War.

In 1922, the British High Commissioner, Sir Percy Cox, had delineated the borders of Iraq, Kuwait and Saudi Arabia, giving Kuwait a coastline of 310 miles, and Iraq one of only 36 miles, at the top of the Gulf. The kingdom of Iraq had comprised the former provinces of Mosul, Baghdad and Basra (which had included Kuwait).

In 1990, therefore, Iraq tried to argue that it had old territorial claims to Kuwait. But the two countries had more recent differences, including the ownership of the Rumaila oilfield, lying under the Iraq-Kuwait border, which Iraq accused Kuwait of 'slant-drilling' into. Also, Iraq was angry at Kuwait's refusal to lease two islands in the Gulf to Iraq to give her a deep-water port; and Iraq was in very serious debt to Saudi Arabia, Kuwait, and the United Arab Emirates after the Iraq-Iran War of the early Eighties, a war fought by Iraq against Khomeini's revolution and for which Saddam Hussein felt some gratitude was owed to him. Iraq also accused Kuwait of overproducing oil in order to damage Iraq's financial position.

By the time I made my visit to Iraq in November, UN Resolutions 660 and 661 calling for the immediate and unconditional withdrawal of Iraqi troops and imposing total trade sanctions on Iraq, had been augmented by 678, enabling Kuwait's allies to use force against Iraq to secure withdrawal. The go-ahead had been given for a war that was to cost tens of thousands of Iraqi lives, cause ecological devastation and leave unresolved the other regional conflict which impinged so much on the Iraq/Kuwait conflict – including the Israel/Palestine question.

Sunday 5 August

Read the papers, and it was just like Suez, with the dire warnings of war, so I decided to send a message from Stansgate (where I had taken my little fax machine) to Neil Kinnock, asking him to consider the recall of Parliament. Certainly if British troops are to be deployed it should be done. I rang the *Guardian*, the Press Association and the *Independent* news desks about it.

Tuesday 7 August

The situation is very serious indeed. The UN Security Council, by 13 to 0, with abstentions from Cuba and Yemen, decided to implement immediate, comprehensive and total economic and trade sanctions against Iraq. Switzerland, which is neutral, has agreed to go along with it, Turkey has agreed to close its pipeline from Iraq, and the Saudis are the weak link. Libya and Jordan are really standing outside the situation, and the Saudis are nervous, so the Arab world is not united. But it would be better to leave the Arab countries to deal with it if they can. The Americans have announced they are sending two huge task forces by plane to the Middle East, and I have no doubt they are flying via Britain and the RAF base in Cyprus. So we are up to our neck in it, without any consultation in Parliament.

I decided that I would formally request the recall of Parliament, so I typed a letter to the PM, with copies to the Speaker and Neil Kinnock, warning that we could be involved in decisions in which we had played no part. I also stated that a pre-emptive strike by the United States could have the opposite effect to that intended and destroy the unity that had been built up and which I welcomed in the resolution of the Security Council. I pointed out that in former years Parliament was recalled during the recess – in the case of the Suez crisis and the Soviet invasion of Czechoslovakia; MPs had the right to hear the Government's views and ask questions and express their own opinions.

The hostility to Saddam Hussein is so great, as he is being built up as a new Hitler, that any cautious voice even calling for discussion is going to be disregarded and silenced.

Kinnock is on holiday in Italy. Kaufman appears on the television every now and again demanding more urgent action. Israel says that if Iraqi troops enter Jordan it will be an act of war, even though Jordan might agree to have them there. It could be catastrophic.

Benazir Bhutto has been removed as Prime Minister by the President of Pakistan, on the grounds of personal horse-trading, and she has gone without much of a protest.

Wednesday 8 August
Today Bush did a broadcast with tremendous hyping up – American wives weeping as sailors left in aircraft carriers and all that. The British are sending forces to help King Fahd of Saudi Arabia, apparently because he requested them. In the end, it's an Anglo-American force that is in the Gulf. Saddam Hussein soon afterwards announced that Kuwait was to be permanently annexed to Iraq.

In the afternoon I was quite desperate, and rang the BBC. I asked them, 'Why won't you broadcast the fact that a request has been made to recall Parliament?' But they won't do it.

I rang the *Guardian* and spoke to Patrick Wintour, but all I was told was that the Opposition have said the situation is being considered on a day-to-day basis.

Thursday 9 August
The *Independent* and the *Guardian* finally mentioned, albeit in passing, my request for the recall of Parliament – a minor breakthrough.

Friday 10 August
The news coming in now is that it's getting more and more dangerous. The Americans started by arguing that the reason they were sending troops was to defend Saudi Arabia, then it was to get Iraq out of Kuwait, and now it is to topple Saddam Hussein. I heard that the Australians, the Canadians and some European countries are sending warships, and the Germans are sending minesweepers into the Mediterranean to replace American warships. The whole function of

NATO as a worldwide rapid deployment force to control the world on behalf of the rich industrialised north is re-emerging.

In the wake of the end of the Cold War, the Russians are distancing themselves a bit.

Monday 13 August
The Prime Minister turned down my request for the recall of Parliament.

Wednesday 15 August
Began serious work on my Government of Britain Bill. It's extremely difficult writing a completely new constitution from scratch, on your own. On the other hand, having a blank piece of paper and knowing how power works and is abused is helpful as a starting point.

The problem will be devising a constitution for Scotland and Wales. I think I shall make provision for national parliaments for Scotland and Wales, and they must decide on their own constitutions. So I am left with the English Assembly and how it should work. There is a difficulty about proportional representation and a second chamber. I've been talking about this for two years, and now everyone else is moving on it, and I shall be left behind if I don't make some progress soon.

Thursday 16 August
I worked on a letter to the Secretary-General of the UN, Perez de Cuellar, suggesting that the UN Security Council should summon a Middle East peace conference. I set out the objectives: (1) the withdrawal of all foreign forces to internationally accepted frontiers in line with UN resolutions, and the introduction of peace keeping forces into disputed areas; (2) the restoration of the independence of Kuwait; (3) the establishment of a Palestinian state and security for the state of Israel, and the negotiation of permanent peace treaties between all nations in the area to be underwritten by the UN; (4) the establishment of a UN development fund to promote the diversion of money now spent on weapons to the needs of the people, and an agreement to limit and monitor international arms trade; (5) the negotiation of a UN oil convention to guarantee a fair return to the oil producers, security of supply to the consumers, an international energy conservation programme and control over the international oil companies.

I faxed it to the UN in New York, and also to the Foreign Secretary and Prime Minister here, and released it to the press.

Then I thought I might get a bit of backing from the non-aligned countries, so I rang the Zambian High Commissioner, who will send a copy to Kenneth Kaunda, and I also phoned the Indian High Commissioner.

I also sent a copy to the Archbishop of Canterbury, asking if he would support the proposal.

This is not going to be another Falklands, more like a Vietnam War. King Hussain saw President Bush today for a couple of hours. The escalation goes on daily. The American troops have chemical weapons; the Iraqis have rounded up American and British citizens and told them to report to a particular hotel, and it is getting very dangerous.

It is interesting that it should happen within a year of the collapse of communism in eastern Europe, and it is about time the west ran into some problems, to see that market forces plus military expeditions are not the beginning and the end of everything.

Friday 24 August
Bernie Grant wants to see me tomorrow, and meetings and demonstrations are being fixed up. I am in touch by phone with CND and other people organising a strategy meeting for next Tuesday.

Tuesday 28 August
To the Quaker Peace Centre for the first meeting on the Gulf crisis. It was attended by about twenty people, including Bruce Kent (in the chair), Carol Turner, Bernie Grant, Diane Abbott, Jeremy Corbyn, Marjorie Thompson of CND, Ron Huzzard and Frank Allaun from Labour Action for Peace, Hugh Jenkins (Lord Jenkins of Putney) and several others.

We had a long talk about whether we should have detailed objectives in stopping the war build-up or not. Carol Turner had thought it should just be a campaign against the war. There was concern about the UN being used, as it was in the Korean War, to legalise an American attack on Iraq. There was a bit of tension, but I left with the feeling that agreement would be reached. We agreed on a press conference on Friday to launch the 'Stop the War in the Gulf' campaign proper.

Thursday 30 August
I rang Andreas Whittam Smith, editor of the *Independent*, and said, 'Don't you think it would be a good idea if your readers had a chance of hearing what the peace case is?' He was terribly polite and asked me to write something, which I did immediately and faxed to him. They are going to print it tomorrow.

Later today I heard Parliament had been recalled for Thursday and Friday next week, and so there will be a Commons debate.

There is going to be a demonstration in Hyde Park or Trafalgar Square.

Friday 31 August
Up at 3.50 am, and got from Stansgate to London in an hour and

twenty minutes. Worked in the office, and then to the Commons for the first press conference of the Stop the War in the Gulf campaign, packed with journalists.

Sunday 2 September

Bought the papers, and there is no doubt that the peace party – to which the *Sunday Times* devoted a leading article attacking it – has begun to register its existence. Ben Pimlott wrote in the *Sunday Times* that it was just 'two maverick toffs' (Tam Dalyell and myself) who were putting forward this view, but even he raised questions about what the Labour leadership should do.

Mrs Thatcher was interviewed by David Frost and talked about bringing Saddam Hussein to an international war crimes tribunal. Well, that really ups the ante no end.

Carol Turner phoned. She told me that Bruce Kent wanted to distance himself from the left and was uneasy about the way the anti-war campaign was going. The Greens, I believe, are also unhappy because they are not getting the coverage and publicity they would like, but that's a matter for them.

Wednesday 5 September

At 9, the Indian High Commissioner came to see me. He is a lawyer by training, born in Pakistan.

He said that the Indian Foreign Minister, who had been to Washington, was in no doubt the Americans were preparing for war. The Foreign Minister had also seen Saddam Hussein, who was quite relaxed about Kuwait and had told him he would inflict terrible damage on the west if they went for him. The Indian High Commissioner said, 'The west will rue the day it invades Iraq.'

Thursday 6 September

To the Commons for what turned out to be a difficult meeting of the Campaign Group. I circulated a motion which had the broad agreement of the Stop the War campaign – that we condemn the aggression, support the sanctions, say there is a prospect of a peaceful settlement and then demand that the Government give an assurance that they won't authorise offensive British military action without a special resolution by the UN. We should decline to support the Government in the absence of such a declaration.

Perhaps not to my surprise, there was a lot of argument about my resolution.

Dave Nellist said he didn't believe in the UN at all. He insisted that there had to be an overthrow of the Iraqi regime from within – I don't disagree with that.

Dennis Skinner said we should raise the question of the oil companies and their exploitation, otherwise it looked a bit academic.

Diane Abbott was doubtful about signing it, because she th ught the UN could be the instrument of oppression of the Third Worl 1 by the rich white countries.

Jeremy Corbyn was doubtful because of the UN, and thought we should say simply, 'Get out of the Gulf.' I should have cleared it with Jeremy first, because we are both officers of the Campaign Group.

To cut a long story short, most of them signed it, but Terry Fields and Dave Nellist wouldn't.

The debate in the House was opened by Thatcher. I put a question to her about the use of force. Kinnock made a more militant speech than Thatcher, and he called for the destruction of the Iraqi war machine, which is nothing whatever to do with Kuwait.

Ted Heath and Denis Healey spoke urging caution. The debate went back and forth, and I was called by the Speaker shortly after 5.40 and spoke for twenty-two minutes. The Chamber filled up with Members, because it was known by then that I was going to divide the House. Looking back on it, I wasn't terribly pleased with the speech – I don't know why. I felt very flat afterwards. Sir John Stokes, who is a right-wing old Tory, said he thought I had been flippant. I don't think I quite got it right, although the argument was correct.

Friday 7 September

Second day of the debate, opened by Tom King, and we had a speech from Martin O'Neill, our defence spokesman, which was very militant.

Then we had a series of speeches of which infinitely the most moving was from Eric Heffer, who is very thin and white. Everybody knows he is dying, and he spoke against war with great passion. David Winnick got up to interrupt him, but Eric said, 'I am not giving way. This may be my last speech in the House.' When he sat down he was exhausted, his head fell forward on to his hands and he crossed himself. It was deeply, deeply moving.

Douglas Hurd spoke last, and I intervened to ask whether the Saudi Government had a veto on our use of military force, a question he didn't answer. But towards the end he did say that we couldn't give a pledge not to act without further recourse to the UN because the UN might frustrate us by its veto, so he was saying we may operate outside the law too. On the basis of that, no Labour MP should have voted in the Government Lobby.

Hurd added something about the possibility of a post-Cold-War 'new world order', which is what everybody has been talking about. 'Opposition Members talk . . . in terms of great aspirations and the brotherhood of man. I see it in more traditional Tory terms as an increasingly effective concert of nations.'

This summed it up: a return to a pre-1914 situation in which the great powers – Washington, Moscow, and no doubt Tokyo and Berlin – will get together and run the world. With the disappearance of socialism from the international agenda, we are getting back to great-power politics, to nationalism, to racism, to imperialism, and to all sorts of other unattractive xenophobic characteristics.

The division was 437 to 35. But, taking the Labour backbenchers, 49 per cent voted for the Government, 25 per cent against and 26 per cent abstained. In other words, 51 per cent of Labour backbenchers didn't vote with the Government.

Monday 10 September

The NEC was meeting today to consider the crisis in the Gulf, among other items, and I decided to submit an emergency motion which was the same as the Early Day Motion we put before the House, ie asking that the Government would not commit Britain to military action before an explicit resolution was passed by the UN Security Council. It also called for a peace conference to consider *all* the issues in the Middle East.

Tony Clarke tried to prevent my motion being considered, so I said, 'Half a minute. This is the first time the Party representatives have had any opportunity of discussing the crisis.' I said that, to be helpful, I would take out the key passage from my resolution – that troops wouldn't be committed to offensive action without a positive resolution from the UN – and insert it into the statement circulated by the Party which mentioned sanctions and rehearsed the background to the crisis.

To cut a long story short, the Labour Party statement was introduced briefly by Neil, then I moved the amendment and said, 'There is a wide measure of agreement. But there is an area of uncertainty. The UN Charter, article 51, provides that a country can resort to self-defence until the UN Security Council reaches a decision on the use of armed force. The British Government, basing their actions on article 51, believe they already have a legal right to attack Iraq if the exiled Kuwaiti Government ask for help. They don't want to go back to the UN in case a member vetoes action. People have been much more cautious in the EEC. In addition, the Government have made it clear through Douglas Hurd that they don't believe that the UN represents the brotherhood of man and the aspirations of humanity but is a concert of powers.' I went on, 'We haven't got any influence anyway, because Bush will decide. Thatcher will have no influence. We will have no influence on Thatcher, and the NEC have no influence if we go along with it. We had better take a stand.'

Robin Cook said, 'I thought Neil's speech in the House on Thursday was brilliant. Of course, this question about the use of troops is important, but Neil dealt with it brilliantly. Couldn't we use a bit of his speech in the statement?'

David Blunkett agreed, 'Yes, Neil was marvellous. I suggest we bring a bit of that in.'

Clare Short said the same.

Bryan Gould said, 'We had better stick with the Government at the moment.'

After a bit of an argument in which Tony Clarke got angry, my amendment was voted down by 16 to 2: Dennis and I.

Saturday 15 September

At noon 150 aircraft flew over London to celebrate the fiftieth anniversary of the Battle of Britain. Normally I would have gone to watch the Spitfires and the Hurricanes and so on, but somehow, with the celebrations coming at a time when war is being considered again, it seemed inappropriate. People are treating it rather as if this is Britain showing our strength in war, in order to prepare us psychologically for the war against Iraq.

To Paddington for the start of the march to Hyde Park organised by the Stop the War committee. There were many banners, the SWP dominating of course. Nicholas Jones of the BBC was there with a film unit, wanting me to do a short tribute to Eric Heffer. A bit ghoulish, I thought, since he is still alive. But it had to be done.

One man came up to me, his face contorted, and said, 'Why do you believe in the UN? It's corrupt. The UN fought the Korean War. Did you support the Korean War?'

There is a lot of hostility to the UN on the left. We have got to make advances in the democratisation of the UN, otherwise nobody will have any confidence in it. Then everything will be settled by bloodshed.

There were a few shouts at the platform from the crowd, and Diane Abbott retorted, 'I'm not going to be interrupted by a few white men. It happens to me all the time in the House of Commons.' She got a good response to that.

It was a big crowd, very sympathetic. Gordon McLennan, the former General Secretary of the CP, was there, as well as Ralph and Marion Miliband, and some women from the King's Cross Collective of Prostitutes, who had sent me a card from 'Whores Against War'!

The Liberal Democrats at their annual Assembly voted to disestablish the Church of England. That gave me enormous pleasure, because I've been arguing for it for ten years.

Monday 17 September

To Friends' Meeting House, Euston Road, for the Committee to Stop the War. The left is marvellous! When I arrived I walked into a flaming row, because Mark Osborn of *Socialist Organiser* had issued a leaflet to which CND and the *Marxism Today* lot took exception. He asked on behalf of his committee to affiliate to Stop the War, but that was turned down, and he was requested to leave the meeting.

I said, 'I don't think we have any authority to do that. It's Stalinist.' So that upset the CND people.

The row went on and on, and Ann Pettifor said Mark Osborn should be told to leave. I nearly walked out myself!

Anyway it subsided, and I mentioned Ted Heath's interview with Brian Walden on Sunday and an excellent statement he has made, which I circulated round the table. He said that there should be behind-the-scenes diplomatic initiatives, and that Saddam Hussein could be offered some concessions, possibly access to disputed oil or territory. He likened the situation to the Cuban crisis, and predicted a 'ghastly' conflict if war broke out. There was general agreement that it was a good intervention.

Tuesday 18 September

A few days ago in the House of Commons I saw Lord Longford, who is getting on a bit, and he blinked at me, so I said, 'I'm Tony Benn.'

He said, 'I know that very well. I reviewed a volume of your diaries.'

So we got to talking, and I asked if he had read Hailsham's book *A Sparrow's Flight*. He had, and he said, 'I was at Eton with Quintin Hogg and he was brilliant. Everybody thought he was going to be Prime Minister – and so did he. The book is full of bitterness that he didn't make it. He puts it down to the fact that Lord Home went hunting with some well-known Tory leader just before the choice of new leader was made in 1963. Well, he was quite wrong about that – that happened the year before – but he's never understood why he didn't become Prime Minister.'

Heard that the CND council had met over the weekend and decided to come out on the pacifist side against UN action and against a war under any circumstances – ie the *Socialist Organiser* position they were so bitterly attacking!

Monday 24 September

I had asked to see Ted Heath, and at 5.45 I arrived at his house. I expected a police guard, but the door was open and his chauffeur was carrying in a box of apples, which he told me Mr Heath had picked from his garden in Salisbury. Out came a Spanish lady in her sixties, who said, 'Mr Benn, what a pleasure to see you in the flesh. Do come in. Mr Heath will be here in a few minutes.'

She took me up to his sitting-room on the first floor of quite a small house, beautifully furnished, with pictures of yachting scenes, and his piano, and two couches facing each other. As I walked up the stairs I could see him working in his office in his pullover.

He came in and shook hands, and I thanked him for sparing the time.

He offered me a drink, and I said I was a teetotaller – which he didn't know. I had a ginger ale.

I said I thought his broadcast had been very wise and reflected a widely held opinion in Britain. I wondered whether he might consider joining with other senior political figures, many of whom, like himself, had been 'through the chair', to issue an appeal for peace along the lines of his broadcast. He sat there, impassive, looking at me.

I went on, 'I was thinking, for example, of your old friend Willy Brandt. I am sure Olof Palme would have done it if he was alive. It occurred to me that Pierre Trudeau might be sympathetic. John Galbraith, Rajiv Gandhi, perhaps Julius Nyerere. You know all these people.'

He asked, 'What about Bob McNamara?' (former US Defense Secretary).

I said, 'I did think of him, as a matter of fact, because he has been in London this week. But if you were all able to say something together, it would possibly have some influence on American opinion, which I think is shifting.'

'Yes, I think it is shifting now. People are asking difficult questions.'

'Of course', I said, 'the US military are saying, "Either we've got to go in or we've got to come out." That's the pressure on the US Government.' I asked him what he thought of my idea.

'Well, it's worth a try,' he replied.

So I felt I had discharged my mission by saying that. I was very content.

I went on, 'It looks to me as if Douglas Hurd is a bit of a dove.'

'I think so.'

'I suppose there is some discussion going on in the Cabinet.'

'No, it will all be decided from the top.'

I said, 'It's just the same in the Labour Party. We couldn't even get a meeting of Labour MPs before the debate, or a meeting of the NEC.'

Ted nodded in a wise sort of way. I asked about the Tory backbenchers, and he said, 'A lot of people have doubts.'

'I think that must be so, because one or two Tory MPs came up to me after the debate and told me, "We're not as gung-ho as you may think." I gather you had a lot of friendly letters.'

His private secretary had told me that after his broadcast he had received eighty-five letters, most of them sympathetic.

I told him, 'I have had over a thousand now, from all over the world, and only thirty-one of them were critical.'

'All since the debate?' he asked.

'No, I wrote to Perez de Cuellar in August, suggesting a peace conference, and some of them stemmed from that initiative.' He was interested in that. I told him I didn't think there was the bellicose consensus in Britain that was supposed.

He said, 'I think you are right. Of course, the Government base themselves on article 51 of the UN Charter.'

'If I understand it correctly, article 51 says a country can resort to self-defence until the UN takes action. Of course, they have taken action since the invasion of Kuwait. The US don't want to go back to the UN because of the fear that they might be vetoed.'

Heath remarked, 'I think China might abstain.'

'My recollection is that the UN Charter says action has to be authorised by the positive votes of the five permanent members.'

I got the feeling that he hadn't looked at the UN aspect very much.

I said, 'People don't want another Korean War.'

'I agree with that.'

It wasn't a cold meeting exactly, but it was formal, and I suppose he must be suspicious of me because I fought him very hard when he was Prime Minister, opposed him on the Common Market, and criticised him sharply on a number of occasions.

Just before I left, I said, 'My wife sends her kind regards. We have never forgotten the time we came to dinner at Number 10 when you were Prime Minister and you were dining a West African president, I forget who it was. After the dinner we had some lovely music played by African musicians, sitting on the floor and playing their instruments.' All of a sudden he was transformed. His body began shaking with the old Ted Heath laugh, and he said, 'We always had music at Number 10 dinners.'

I got up and left. It was a memorable little event. Perhaps he will do something about it, but, if he doesn't, there you are.

Wednesday 26 September

At the NEC we had a statement on Iraq which Neil introduced. Kaufman, who is not a member of the Executive, was called in – which I thought was quite wrong. I said straight away that I was against the statement as it stood. It gave the Government a blank cheque. I pointed out that in 1958 the Tory Government themselves were thinking of occupying Kuwait and had the consent of Foster Dulles, the US Secretary of State. And the statement didn't mention oil, which was the crucial point.

Robin Cook criticised me, and it was voted on – 15 to 2, with only Dennis and me against.

Labour Party Conference, Blackpool
Sunday 30 September

Two well-dressed men came up to me at the Conference and said, 'Excuse me, sir, we are from the police. We have to advise you that somebody with a northern accent rang the *Daily Mirror* this morning saying that a contract had been put out to kill you and Ken Livingstone. Do you know where Mr Livingstone is?'

I said, 'I'll see him later, and I'll tell him. Thanks.'

I daresay we are back in the old routine of death threats, with the Gulf crisis.

The layout of the Conference is fantastic – lots of photographs and the slogan 'Looking to the Future'. The rostrum is quite separate from the platform, and everybody had been pushed up on to the second row, except for 'leading figures'. It is now all stage-managed for the telly. It is symbolic of the separation between the leadership and the membership.

Monday 1 October

I was disappointed that the Conference rejected by 3 million-odd to 2,788,000 a motion to phase out nuclear power over fifteen years.

Looking at the platform in the afternoon, I thought that all these impressive Front Bench people - Tony Blair, Michael Meacher, Jack Straw, Frank Dobson, John Cunningham – made a much better team man for man, or woman for woman, than the Tories. I think people have had enough of the Thatcher philosophy, and they want a change.

Tuesday 2 October

Watched Neil on television; his Leader's speech made no attacks on the left. Instead he talked about education and training, and about Saddam Hussein, and then said we must destroy Saddam's nuclear and chemical capability, which goes far beyond anything the Government have stated.

Wednesday 3 October

Up at 6.45, and I practised and timed my speech on the emergency resolution on the Gulf, on which I intended to speak from the floor.

Went into Conference and had a word with Jo Richardson, who was chairing the session, and said I would be standing in the front row waving a red folder.

She said, 'We are calling the Gulf debate early.' What I didn't know then, but learned later, was that it had been brought forward to ensure that Kaufman's speech on the Gulf appeared on the television, while the rest of the debate, which would be critical, was obliterated by *Playschool*. Jo said she would try to call me.

I sat near the front among the MPs, and Kaufman made a cunning speech in which he took the view that there could be no possible war without the support of the international community, and listed ways in which that might happen.

Then Ken Cameron moved the emergency resolution very well, seconded by somebody from Bolsover who sounded just like Dennis Skinner and was brilliantly funny. Then Denis Healey spoke, and John

Edmonds made an outrageous speech* in which he asked about the commanders of British troops in Saudi Arabia, 'Are they not to be allowed to make a pre-emptive strike?'

I got up after every speech, expecting to be called, and finally Jo said, 'That's where we must leave it. The Conference Arrangements Committee have allowed us five speeches from the floor.' So people on the floor shouted, 'Call Tony Benn!' Jo said, 'I've called two MPs, and nobody has a special right to speak.'

I didn't complain, but, as a result of all the fuss being made about my being excluded, the media gathered round, and in fact I did masses of interviews on what I would have said anyway. I was very sharp at Edmonds: 'For a general secretary sitting in his comfortable armchair to call for a pre-emptive strike against Baghdad when he is not going to be killed himself is disgraceful.'

Paid a flying visit to Arthur Scargill, who is in hospital with pneumonia.

At the NEC Dennis and I persuaded them to send a get-well message to Arthur – the only motion we've won!

A lovely evening, but I will be glad to get home. The Party is just a machine for putting Kinnock into Number 10, and I would like to see him there rather than Thatcher, but there is no excitement, no sense of vision, no moral commitment. Perhaps I was just a part of that vote-getting machine in the past. I hope not, and I'm certainly not like that now.

Sunday 21 October
Up at 5 and collected a large transit van on hire, to take some of my boxes of archives and filing cabinets down to Stansgate.

Lots of the young people who have helped in the office over the past few years came along – Simon Fletcher, his girlfriend Jenny Walsh, Hugh Scott and Andrew Hood.

There was a story in the papers that the American Ambassador to Iraq had talked to Saddam Hussein last January and had suggested that Iraq raise the price of oil in order to sort out their own economic situation; of course that carried with it the clear implication that there would be a dispute with Kuwait.

In fifteen American cities there were demonstrations against a war in the Gulf.

Ted Heath saw Saddam Hussein today and is hoping to come out with some of the British hostages. Bit by bit, one could see the whole of the Gulf War enterprise grinding to a halt, with the American President in deep trouble domestically over his budget.

---

* Since 1990 the Labour Party has ceased to issue a full Conference Report and therefore the exact quotation cannot be given.

Wednesday 24 October
At the NEC we had presented to us the terms of reference of a working party on alternat: e electoral systems. I thought it was too big a decision to give to a group, some of whom we did not know. But Neil made two important comments in connection with Scottish devolution. He said, 'I can hardly bear the words "Scottish Parliament" to pass my lips!' Later, during a bit of noisy interruption, he said, 'Let the victor of the Welsh referendum speak,' meaning, I suppose, that he had opposed devolution in the Welsh referendum in March 1979.

Monday 29 October
It looks as if Bush is building up for war.

It is clear that world opinion is growing in favour of a peaceful settlement, and that America is getting more militant, with the possibility of a war next weekend when the Congressmen are busy campaigning and Congress is adjourned – and, coincidentally, during the prorogation of Parliament.

The Labour Party is 16 per cent in the lead in the polls, and it looks as if Thatcher might be on the way out.

Thursday 1 November
A bombshell today: Geoffrey Howe, the Deputy Prime Minister and Leader of the House, has resigned from the Government – the last surviving member of the original 1979 Cabinet. He is a very nice man; I like him personally.

Willy Brandt is going to Baghdad. I feel a certain pride in this because Ralph Miliband had suggested I approach Ted Heath, and then I suggested to Heath that Willy Brandt might be brought in. It may have come from that. Brandt is going to Baghdad with the goodwill of the UN Secretary-General, although Douglas Hurd has complained to the German Government about it.

Howe's resignation has put the Tories into a panic, and there may be a leadership election; if Heseltine became Leader, there's not much difference between him and Kinnock, except that he has had a lot more experience.

Tuesday 6 November
The Iraqi Embassy rang, saying the Ambassador would like to see me. I wasn't prepared to go to the Embassy, so they said the Ambassador would come to my home at 1.30. I informed the Foreign Office, so that it was all above board.

The Ambassador, Dr Shafiq al-Salihi, came with his Third Secretary, and Ruth Winstone greeted them in Arabic – which I think created a favourable impression.

He said straight away, 'We have been following your statements on the Gulf crisis and I have been instructed by my Government to invite you to visit Baghdad.' He then asked if I had any advice as to how the matter might be resolved.

I said, 'Yes, I have. I think you should release all the hostages, because they are not worth anything to you in terms of bargaining. They won't protect you from a war and, if they were all released, the whole thing would look quite different. After that, I think, you would have to be prepared to put Kuwait under the control of the UN and then sit down without preconditions to consider the implementation of all the resolutions.'

'I hadn't thought of the hostage point,' he said, and added, 'If the President's programme permits, he will see you in Baghdad.' He also told me that I 'wouldn't come back empty-handed', which implied that some hostages would return.

I told him, 'My prime interest would not be in the humanitarian appeal for some being allowed out but in the political case for *all* of them coming out.'

He looked very uncomfortable. Then he asked me to dinner, and I thanked him.

When they left I rang Ralph Miliband, who was responsible for the whole idea of my approaching Heath. I also rang Heath's Private Secretary, who told me that Heath had put that very point about the hostages and had also spoken to Bob McNamara in California.

I told the UN Secretary-General's office about the approach, and faxed them my account of the meeting.

Later in the day, I spoke to Heath (who got thirty-three hostages released) and said, 'I haven't seen you for a while. Congratulations. I have had an invitation. Shall I go?'

'Yes, of course,' he replied.

So everyone I have asked thinks I should go. I'll have to work out carefully what to say, and I will make it an explicitly political mission, not one about humanitarian issues. The air tickets will cost £825.

Took part in the Frank Bough interview on Sky TV. Somebody called Colonel Mike Dewar, a smooth, so-called intellectual army officer was also on. I had a word with him afterwards and asked whether the operational control by the Americans would mean that they could command the British forces to drop or fire nuclear weapons from our planes and ships.

'Oh no, no, no,' he replied. 'There is a nuclear release document which has to go to Number 10 Downing Street and which takes about five days to come through.'

I said, 'That might be true in peacetime, but I think it would be different in a war situation.'

Truthfully, he didn't know, but it is a point to ask the Prime Minister if I get a chance.

Wednesday 7 November

Opening of Parliament today. Worked at home and gave a great deal of thought to the Gulf crisis and the invitation.

Went into the House, and at the end of her speech in the Debate on the Address Margaret Thatcher brought up the Gulf crisis and finished by saying, 'Time is running out for Saddam Hussein. The implacable message from the House must be this: either he gets out of Kuwait soon, or we and our allies will remove him by force.'

So, without having written anything, I got up later and spoke for twenty-six minutes, setting out my views.

John Biffen made a good speech.

Friday 9 November

I made it clear to the Iraqis that if I went to Baghdad I would want to see Saddam Hussein, I would want some hostages released, and I wanted to see King Hussain in Jordan.

Yesterday in the Commons Douglas Hurd had urged me not to go to Baghdad. On the other hand, letters and telephone calls of support are pouring in. Two people offered to act as interpreter. Richard Branson's office rang to say he would be happy to send one of his Virgin Airline planes to Baghdad to bring any hostages back.

To Chesterfield. Johnny Burrows had been a bit upset that he hadn't been told I was going, and he felt I wasn't consulting the local Party. But after a talk he supported me 100 per cent.

Saturday 10 November

Looked in to see Melissa, and found Joshua and some of the grandchildren there. They were very concerned about my safety in Baghdad, so I rang an Irish PhD student, Paul Lalor, who is a brilliant Arabist and who had offered his services as an interpreter, and said I might be able to take him. There is such a lot to do, and the hostages' relatives keep ringing the office with requests.

Michael asked, 'Are you going to be killed in Baghdad, Dan-Dan?'

I said no, and he looked relieved and went on watching the telly.

Sunday 11 November

I spoke to Paul Lalor, the Arabic speaker, an Irishman of thirty-two who is at St Antony's College, Oxford. He has agreed to come if I pay his airfare and expenses.

Monday 12 November

Wrote to Mitterrand, Gorbachev and Yang Shangkun, President of China, appealing to them to support peace, warning of war, and asking them to use their veto in the UN Security Council if necessary.

I also signed personal letters to Kenneth Kaunda, Willy Brandt,

Robert Mugabe, Nelson Mandela, Julius Nyerere, Pierre Trudeau, Rajiv Gandhi, Andreas Papandreou and Ben Bella, asking for support for my visit. They were sent out by fax.

Had a message confirming that King Hussain would be delighted to meet me in Jordan.

Tuesday 13 November
Geoffrey Howe made his formal resignation speech, which was devastating; he savaged Mrs Thatcher, was amusing and committed. It was all about Europe and the maintenance of the free market and so on. It has certainly transformed everything. We have really come to the end of the Thatcher era, I think.

Friday 16 November
I rang a former Jordanian Ambassador, who was most courteous and friendly and advised me how to approach Saddam Hussein and King Hussain of Jordon.

Later in the day, the Leader of the Democratic Opposition in Kuwait rang me and described the atrocities in Kuwait – the torture and rape and looting – and said he thought war was inevitable. I said, 'I suppose you don't think I should go.' He said, 'No, I don't.'

Someone from the ANC came round with a letter faxed from Johannesburg from Nelson Mandela. It said:

Dear Mr Benn,

The ANC supports any efforts which will avert a war situation in the Gulf. We encourage your efforts to explore a peaceful solution.

Yours sincerely,
N.R. Mandela
Deputy President ANC

Heseltine and Hurd appear to be competing for the pleasure of removing Mrs Thatcher.

Lots of help in the office under Kathy's guidance, and it's a pleasure to have them all here. Paul Lalor reminds me of a Civil Service private secretary and treats me with a mixture of exaggerated obeisance and a degree of studied disregard!

Tuesday 20 November

To the House, and went to the Committee Corridor because I wanted to see what was happening in the first ballot for the Tory leadership – Michael Heseltine versus Margaret Thatcher.

It is quite a historic event. By secret ballot, Tory MPs have the power to remove as Leader of their party a Prime Minister who has been elected three times by the British people.

When I got there, the whole corridor was packed from the upper waiting-hall right down to the far end, with hundreds of people. I had my radio with an earpiece and the aerial sticking up, and I must have looked like a man from outer space. I stood on a bench so that I could see everyone – Tory, Labour and Liberal MPs, clerks, secretaries, journalists – a sea of faces.

There was a bit of scuffling further up, and then all of a sudden, through the crowd, came a number of journalists, who ran by so quickly I could hardly recognise any of them. The crowd opened like the Red Sea. One of the journalists said to me, 'Second ballot. Can you comment?'

So I said, 'It is appropriate that it should have happened to her when she was in Versailles' – a point Caroline had made to me.

He said, 'Brilliant', and rushed off.

It wasn't for some time that I heard the results. Margaret Thatcher had got 204 and Heseltine 152. It was four short of an outright victory for her on the first ballot. Almost immediately I heard her on my radio from Paris, where she is attending the Conference on Security and Cooperation in Europe, announcing she was going to fight in the second ballot.

Heseltine said he had let his name go forward to the next ballot, so the crisis continues for another week.

The Labour Party is of course keen to keep Thatcher, and Kinnock has put down a motion of censure against her, for Thursday, to try to consolidate Tory support around her. It is a disgrace that in eight years this is the first motion of censure.

At 10, when a statement was made that there would be a censure debate on Thursday, Jim Sillars made exactly that point.

Wednesday 21 November
Mr Ibrahim, the Iraqi Minister at the Embassy, came to see me. He is about fifty-five, and looked exactly like an Israeli or American or French diplomat, immensely smooth and experienced.

He confirmed that Saddam would see me. I told him there were a lot of points I wanted to raise – the Britons in Kuwait, the release of the hostages, possible compliance in principle with the UN resolutions. I said, 'You must know my position on the Kurds and on human rights. I am very concerned.'

He tried to defend his Government. 'The Kurds are treated better in Iraq than in Syria or Turkey or any other country with a Kurdish population. It was the Kurdish guerrillas who joined with the Iranians in invading Iraq, and it is presumably they who were attacked when the chemical weapons were used.'

I listened carefully; it's important to hear their argument. He said nothing about human rights in Iraq itself.

He told me Gerald Kaufman had been in Iraq a year ago, had looked round, and had especially asked to meet the Jewish community and visited a synagogue. He said Kaufman was immensely impressed by the rights of the Jews there.

Mrs Thatcher arrived back from France. The rumour going round at the moment is that the men in grey suits went to see her to say, 'Time to go.' Indeed, I think Willie Whitelaw went to see her. But according to rumours she just absolutely refused to have anything to do with that advice, so then the Cabinet was polled privately and, whatever they thought individually, they took a common line to support her. So Hurd has nominated her again, and Major has signed her nomination. Actually, if you look round, there isn't a dominant alternative figure. Hurd and Major aren't really up to it, but Heseltine is flamboyant and experienced and is getting a marvellous press.

In terms of stamina and persistence, you have to admit Margaret Thatcher is an extraordinary woman. She came out of Number 10, saying 'I fight on. I fight to win.' Then she went to the House and made a statement on the Paris CSCE talks. You would think she would be downcast after that setback, but not at all. When Paddy Ashdown said that the Paris Treaty was one of the great moments of the twilight of her premiership, she replied, 'As for the twilight, people should remember that there is a 24-hour clock', which was a smashing answer.

Kinnock tried to be statesman-like but couldn't manage it.

I then went upstairs to see Douglas Hurd about my Iraq trip, and there were three officials in his room. It was the very same room in which George Brown had tried to summon Harold Wilson in 1968 on the night George resigned as Foreign Secretary, and I told the civil servants the story. They asked how I thought history would see Margaret Thatcher.

I said, 'Everyone drops into the darkest of all worlds between the headlines and the history books. Not many live long enough to come back again, but it is too soon to say.' I didn't want to be offensive. I asked, 'Who do you think will win?'

One of them said he thought Heseltine would.

Hurd came in. He is a weakling and hasn't got any stuffing.

After the pleasantries he said, 'What I am afraid of is that you might give Saddam Hussein the impression he wouldn't have to leave Kuwait.'

I replied, 'Quite the opposite. As a matter of fact, I am going to tell him that there is going to be a war.'

'Nobody wants a war,' he said.

'Well, in my opinion, that's what it is all building up to.'

Hurd was slightly thrown.

I told him, 'I am going to try and bring out some hostages, obviously, but my main argument is that he should release them all and explore the possibility for negotiations.'

He said, 'He gave Ted Heath a very rough time, talked about chemical warfare and made his flesh creep.'

'I'm too old for that! You are a diplomat and are experienced at diplomacy, and it must be frustrating that you can't do anything about it, using your diplomatic skill.'

I got the feeling he was uneasy. I think he is really a dove in this situation.

He said, 'It's very easy for him. He has only got to withdraw from Kuwait.'

'It's not quite like that. The Prime Minister talks about a war crimes tribunal, about destroying his military capacity and about compensation, and I am not sure that withdrawal from Kuwait would necessarily do the trick.'

At the end, I was given the latest list of hostages compiled by the FO. But I could feel the awful pressure from all these reasonable civil servants and Tory Ministers.

Thursday 22 November
At 9.30 some people from the Campaign for Democratic Rights in Iraq came to see me. They are primarily concerned with the internal situation there but say the war will make the prospect of domestic easement much more difficult.

I was in the middle of an interview about the war in the Gulf for *Dispatches* on Channel 4 when my secretary Kathy burst in to say Margaret Thatcher had resigned. Absolutely dazzling news, and it was quite impossible to keep my mind on the interview after that. So evidently people have been to her and told her that she can't win. She called the Cabinet together this morning and told them. The motion of censure is taking place this afternoon.

To the House, which was in turmoil. We had the censure debate, and Kinnock's speech was flamboyant and insubstantial. When he was cross-examined about the European currency he simply couldn't answer. Thatcher was brilliant. She always has her ideology to fall back on; she rolled off statistics, looked happy and joked.

Sunday 25 November

At Heathrow airport Mr Ibrahim met Paul Lalor and me at Terminal 3, and we were put in first class, although we only had tourist-class tickets.

At Amman airport in Jordan, the Deputy Chief of Protocol greeted us with the news that the king couldn't see us today, which was very disappointing. Had invitations to dinner from the Chief of Protocol and the British Embassy which I refused.

Bush is going to seek a UN Security Council meeting on Thursday with a view to getting through a resolution that might authorise the use of force. It gives a certain urgency to my visit.

A journalist from Sky TV on his way back to London from Baghdad came up and spoke to us.

Although I have no official position, the visit is being treated as important by the various Governments. I think in the Third World there is an understanding of what I am trying to do. Even if I just meet the hostages and hand over some medicines and bring a few people home, it will be worthwhile – but I hope it will be the exploration of something much more important. The Iraqi Government want to get off the hook, and I want to help them to get off the hook and help Bush get off the escalator moving towards war.

Monday 26 November

To Amman airport, where I was put in a first-class seat and Paul in economy, but I couldn't smoke where I was sitting so I joined Paul.

We were met at Baghdad by three MPs from the International Relations Committee of the Iraqi Parliament, and we sat in this beautiful, glamorous new airport which was absolutely deserted because there are no flights other than internal ones. Gave a press conference.

We were driven to the Al-Rasheed Hotel; in the car we were given the Government line about how the Iraqis were prepared to make any sacrifices and die for their people, and so on. Who should be at the hotel but Svend Robinson MP, of the Canadian New Democratic Party, whom I had met two years ago. He has been here for a week with an all-party Canadian delegation but has not yet succeeded in seeing Saddam.

We went down to dinner with the Iraqi MPs, who said Saddam would see me. I asked if they could give me an indication of how many hostages were likely to be released; they said the number would be on the same sort of scale as Willy Brandt was allowed.

Tuesday 27 November
At 7.45 am I was taken in pouring rain to the tented encampment in the garden of the British Embassy, which looked like a refugee camp. There are about fifty-seven people in the tents, and they eat in a place they call the Oasis Club, a sort of hut with some basic cooking facilities. They are all British, work for Bechtel, and have been living there since the beginning of the crisis. They are in engineering, construction, procurement and information technology, all working on contracts for the Iraqi Ministries. They are all being paid and buy food from the streets with company money. A doctor visits once a week and a nurse twice a week. One of them said that on the streets they had encountered growing public hostility to Saddam Hussein.

Afterwards I had a word with the Ambassador, who was very lanky and detached. He gave me lists of compassionate cases, and was helpful personally, within limits, but I heard from the men how unhelpful the British Embassy generally had been. He said there was some diplomatic activity with respect to hostages, but none on the crisis itself.

We were told that we were on standby for the President, so had to defer a meeting with the Indian Ambassador.

Pat Arrowsmith phoned my hotel; she is a peace campaigner of many years, and was at a village just outside Baghdad, trying to set up the 'peace camp' on the Kuwaiti–Saudi border being sponsored by Yusuf Islam, the former pop singer Cat Stevens.

Nothing came of the standby, so we went to the Ministry of Planning to meet Sa'doon Hammadi, the Deputy Prime Minister. He was dressed in an immaculate Ba'athist uniform which made him look like a general, and talking to him was exactly like talking to a general in any country.

I made a point about Kuwait, and he said, 'If we were to say we were ready to comply with the UN resolution, then the morale of our troops in Kuwait would be adversely affected.'

It was a point that had been made to me in Amman, and I said, 'I understand that, but then there is a parallel situation in the United States', and explained that the pressure that Bush was under arose from the same consideration.

He was most friendly to me personally, and said as we left, 'This is a cherished opportunity to meet you.'

At 4.20, we went to another hotel, where we met sixty-four British people who had been in Kuwait and were brought by bus to Baghdad last night quite unexpectedly. They obviously hoped there was some connection with my visit and that they would be allowed to come home. They were under severe emotional strain. Last night they had had a painful meeting with the British Ambassador in which they had brought out all their agonies and complaints and he had told them, 'Be British!' It had infuriated them, so I was prepared for a tortured meeting, but in fact they were supportive and sympathetic, and told me I was their only hope.

I said I didn't want to raise their expectations. I am so glad I did, because shortly afterwards they were collected in buses and sent off to Iraqi military installations as 'human shields'. *TV-am* had a camera crew in Baghdad, and as they were put on to the buses they shouted and struggled, and this was filmed. I'm afraid that if that is shown at home it will inflame the situation. Whatever the reason, it was an absolute hammer-blow to the trip, and I felt the whole thing had gone wrong.

To the Novotel to meet the twenty-seven construction workers staying there. Their story was quite incredible. They were receiving no pay from their companies, were getting no help whatever from the Embassy, their wives were living on supplementary benefit at home, they were being taxed while they were away and had been told to carry on working hard. They were good-natured, amusing working-class men, but there was a strong sense of anger. They should be treated like POWs, which they are, and their wives should be treated like the wives of servicemen.

Got back at about midnight, and Paul and I went over everything. Paul has kept careful notes.

Heard on the news that John Major has won the leadership of the Tory Party with 185 votes against 56 for Hurd and 131 for Heseltine; as he was only two votes short of an overall majority, Hurd and Heseltine had immediately withdrawn. So he becomes the youngest Prime Minister this century; a competent person, from a simple background, like the Archbishop of Canterbury, George Carey. He is a new type of Thatcherite really; not strident, probably slightly less ideological, more sympathetic to Europe, a hard man in terms of financial policy, but confident.

Wednesday 28 November
The *Spectator* has voted me Backbencher of the Year. Fat lot of good that does! Tony Banks is accepting on my behalf at the Savoy Hotel today.

Up at 6.30 and had breakfast with four members of the 'Committee of the British Community', and their description of British Embassy treatment was awful. They were not welcomed at the Embassy, had had absolutely no help from it, and had even been told they had to put stamps on their letters home. Because they are not British taxpayers, they were told they couldn't expect any concessions. One man's mother-in-law had died, somebody's sister was dying of cancer, and their anger at the British Embassy was great. But they have organised themselves well.

Went downstairs after breakfast with a view to meeting the Deputy Prime Minister, when I recognised the President's interpreter, Dr Sa'doon Zubaydi, and all of a sudden I realised that this was the big meeting. I said I would be taking Paul with me as my adviser, and they said, 'You can't; we haven't permission.' If I had put my foot down, I may have been able to insist, I don't know. However, not only did they refuse Paul, they took my bag off my shoulder and said I would have to leave that behind. So I put my hand in my bag to pull out some papers, and I thought that I had pulled out the full list of hostages which we had been advised should be handed in at the Presidential Office. But owing to the hurry – I wasn't even in my best suit, which I had brought for the meeting – I failed to take the list and also the box of medicines which I brought to give Saddam.

Anyway, we got into the car and had a candid talk. Dr Zubaydi asked if there were many matters I would like to discuss. So I took my opportunity and said, 'There is great anxiety in Britain about the Kurds. I know you have given them a lot of autonomy, but this is a problem. There is great anxiety about human rights.' He looked a bit uncomfortable, but at least I did raise these matters. I added, 'But I don't want to raise this now, because the central question is peace.'

We drove through Baghdad, on a circuitous route, and finally we came to a line of ordinary-looking little villas and drove into the front garden of one. This was where I was to meet the President. It reminded me of the villa at which I had met Rajiv Gandhi last year but without the three encampments and barbed wire.

There was a gathering of people in the waiting-room – Tariq Aziz, the Foreign Minister; Dr Sa'doon Hammadi, whom I had met yesterday; Mr Latif Jassim, the Minister of Culture and Information; Hamid Yousif Hammadi, the President's Private Secretary, who apparently has Cabinet rank; Muhsin Khalil, the press secretary; Sa'doon Zubaydi, the chief interpreter; and two other aides.

The Foreign Minister asked about John Major and said, 'I met him a couple of years ago in Geneva and I found him a good listener. I knew Carrington before and I didn't find him very helpful' – which didn't surprise me. I thought that was an indication that they would like better relations with the British Government.

At about 10.15 we were ushered into a room furnished with blue curtains and seats, with flowers on the table, and two television cameras and photographers. There was Saddam Hussein dressed in uniform, and I said, 'Salaam Alaikum', and he said, 'Wa Alaikum a Salaam'; at least I remembered that. We sat down, and when the cameras were on us I didn't know whether we were supposed to start speaking, so it was a bit awkward for a moment. Anyway, I thanked him for inviting me.

I began by saying that I was very conscious that between the Tigris and the Euphrates was the cradle of world civilisation, so that I was coming to the source of my own civilisation.

Then I said, 'I bring you messages of peace', and I placed the papers I had brought with me on the table – the replies I had received from Nelson Mandela, Willy Brandt, Ron Dellums, Papandreou, and so on. 'I have also brought some letters, Mr President, that were sent to me in London with the request to give them to you.' (These were personal pleas from relatives of hostages to Saddam.)

'May I say a personal word,' I continued. 'I come from a family that for a long time has supported the Arab nation. My father was a Secretary of State in 1945 and worked to bring about the evacuation of the British base in Tel El-Kebir. I opposed the Suez War and participated in big demonstrations, like now.

'My little grandson, James, who is six, asked me the other day, "Dan-Dan" (which is what he calls me), "are you in favour of a war?" I said, "No, James, I am not." "Does Saddam Hussein want a war?" I said, "No, he does not." So James said, "I understand now why he invited you to Baghdad."'

They all smiled.

I went on, 'But you know my position. May I speak frankly?'

'Yes.'

'It seems to me to be a time of great danger. There is a Security Council resolution tabled on Thursday which will begin the countdown to war. I think Bush is under pressure from the military imperative "use us or withdraw us". It is convenient, anyway, for a weak president to have a foreign enemy. It is easy to have a sense of hopelessness, but I don't want that to prevail.

'The objectives of the United States – which are to have a permanent base, to control the oil, to overthrow your Government and to demilitarise Iraq – are nowhere to be found in the UN resolution 660, and it is very important that we should recognise that those countries which have agreed to this approach have done so on the basis of resolution 660 and not of this hidden agenda.

'But Mrs Thatcher has gone, and I think this represents an opportunity.'

Saddam interrupted me to say, 'Tell me what her real motivation was. I am trying to understand what really moved her.'

'Maybe you would need a Viennese psychologist to answer that.'

The others laughed. I said, 'I think she is probably a nationalist. She thinks the world is full of foreigners, and it is. She wants the bomb, and she depends on America for that. She thinks, however strange it may be, that the President of the European Commission in Brussels, Jacques Delors, is going to try to introduce socialism by the back door.'

He asked, 'What about Mr Major?'

'I don't know him well; he is a young man but already there has been a great change on a tax proposal.' That was a reference to Major having announced that the poll tax will, in effect, be dropped. 'Thatcher was pro-Washington. But there is another view – that we should be moving towards Europe, a view represented by Mr Heath. As you know, the French and the Germans are not so enthusiastic about American policy in the Middle East.'

Saddam said, 'Why do you think the French and the Germans went along with this resolution?'

'Well, they see it as a matter of legality, and the Americans see it in strategic terms of advantage to themselves, but there is tension between Brussels and Washington.'

Then I said, 'My task is a very modest one, I must tell you, It is to campaign for peace at home and abroad.' I told him of the letters I had written to François Mitterrand, Mikhail Gorbachev and Yang Shangkun. I said, 'I asked each of them to veto any proposal for the use of force.'

He was struck by that, and remarked, 'That is not a modest contribution at all.'

Then I said, 'I think the time has come for a major new Iraqi peace initiative.

'I would like to turn to the case for restoring free movement to the foreign residents now in Iraq. The holding of these residents is no protection against war, and indeed the American and British Governments are using the fact that you are holding them as arguments for their policy, which is one reason why the British Government have refused to give me help on my visit. There is a special problem of the foreign residents in Kuwait who do want to see Kuwait liberated and want to protect their Kuwaiti friends.

'What is needed is a historic statement by the Iraqi Government that all residents can come and go freely. They would all be ambassadors for peace – which would transform the political situation, reaffirm the traditional reputation of the Arabs for hospitality, and open the way to peace talks. And I hope I may take our people home with me.'

He asked, 'What guarantee is there of a response if I do what you say? What guarantee is there that the Americans won't attack me?'

I said, 'I can't guarantee you anything. How can I? I am not a head of state. But I am sure that there will be a great public response in Britain and America. It would be very, very helpful.'

Saddam repeated his view that there was a military plan to defeat Iraq. This was a major factor in his thinking.

I replied that we must get away from the war process and on to the peace process, and that Iraq should be a spokesman for Arab rights in the world through the United Nations. The Palestinian state required the implementation of resolution 242, and it was reasonable to ask for respect for *all* UN resolutions. I suggested that it would be a good idea to invite the UN Secretary-General to Baghdad and indicate to him Iraq's readiness to comply with the UN resolutions, while reaffirming the rights of the Arabs to regional security. Iraq should offer a perspective for world peace and indicate the future beyond this crisis.

Saddam pursued me on the question why so many countries were supporting America. 'If there is a war,' he said, 'you must not assume it would be limited, and it would certainly spread' – a clear indication that he had in mind a possible attack on Israel. He went on, 'The UN has taken no notice of the resolutions in respect of Israel or in respect of the Lebanon. It has been taken over by the United States.'

I said, 'I know that very well. But the end of the Cold War gives us an opportunity, perhaps, to change that, and there is tremendous commitment to change. We mustn't let it slip through our fingers. Anyway, there is a problem of legality in the world.'

I think it registered with him, though we came back to the question of legality later.

Then he said, 'Let me say something to you which would be difficult for me to say publicly. I want to take you through the stages of our own approach to the Kuwait question. They increased their oil production, cut the price, undermined our economy, encroached on the frontier, and we had a problem of access to the sea. In the first place we thought we could just deal with the problem of access to the sea, but that didn't work. The next option was to take the disputed territory which they had encroached on. But, if we did that, the Americans would be invited by the Al-Sabah family to come into Kuwait and we would have a confrontation, so we went in and tried to establish a government which would be friendly to us. But the Government would crumble without Iraqi troops, so then we took the final decision to go into the whole of Kuwait.'

I understood that, and said they had responded to a military imperative, but observed, 'Maybe the United States did too.'

I should add that he had said he thought there was a complex conspiracy between the Americans, the Kuwaitis, the Israelis and the Saudis, and that actually the Americans had been paid money by the Saudis to come in and protect the Saudi royal family. He asked if I thought the Americans would be there if the costs weren't being paid by Kuwait and Saudi Arabia.

I said, 'We must get off the war machine and on to the peace process, and I think it would be very, very helpful if there was anything you could say, Mr President, that indicated your long-term perspective for peace. Today is the crisis, tomorrow the war, but there is a day after.'

'Well,' he said, 'we have the Arab Charter, which we got agreed. It was not a federal solution, it was a question of individual nations co-operating, and that is our perspective.'

I said, 'I think that is an interesting idea. It is not for Europeans to criticise you, because we haven't made much of a success of European unity either. But there are certain legality problems. I am a former Oil Minister, and I know very well what problems there are when a country breaks the OPEC price and production agreements. I know the difficulties of negotiating frontiers. Indeed, the Falklands War was really triggered because we thought there was oil in the area. You will remember, of course, that Britain was contemplating occupying Kuwait in 1958. But the legality problems that arise are these, even for your friends. We have been asked over the last three months to accept three different legal situations. First, Kuwait was accepted internationally and by yourself as a nation state with its own legal status. After 2 August, we were asked to accept that there were two states still, Iraq and Kuwait, Kuwait now having a new friendly Government which had been installed. The third situation which we are now asked to accept is that there is a long historical association between Iraq and Kuwait and that Kuwait, as such, has disappeared. *You* speak of the Arab Charter under which the family of Arab nations would have independence.'

I did emphasise the importance of the UN in all this. 'After all, you yourself, Mr President, are keen on a solution for the Palestinian problem, but that must be based on UN resolution 242. The Americans, if they run the world, will never let Palestine be established, but resolution 242 may very well do that if we work at it. There is a problem, to which you rightly refer, of double standards here.'

We pursued that matter for some time. But undoubtedly he made it clear that there would be a problem on the point of compliance with the resolution, because, he said, 'We have our troops in Kuwait.'

I said, 'The Americans have a problem too. If President Bush says he thinks there can be a negotiated settlement, the troops will say, "What about us? Why are we here? Why are we in the desert? Why can't we go home for Christmas?" '

He said, 'If we could have a summit, we could have all these talks in private, and when we have reached an agreement, we could both announce it, and then everybody would feel that honour had been satisfied.'

I suggested to him, 'It may be that you have a duty to try and save President Bush's face.' The idea that Iraq might save the American President's face took him slightly by surprise, I think, because people are saying it is Saddam Hussein's face that has to be saved.

He said, 'The responsibility for this belongs to the larger power, not the smaller. If we appear to make concessions, we demoralise our troops in Kuwait.'

I said, 'If Bush said something, he might demoralise his troops in Saudi Arabia.'

'That is the point. If we could have a dialogue or summit or something, we could each test out the other on proposals, and, when we have both agreed, we could announce it, and everybody would succeed.'

I think that is right, and that is what I shall work for.

He said, 'You know, we are a nation of builders. When I came to Baghdad as a young man, it was a village with one hotel. Now look at it. Have you seen Baghdad? It is beautiful. Would anyone who built as hard as we have want war?'

I replied, 'No, I am sure that is right. You have a sense of history. That is why it is so important you should be able to speak of the future.' I did add – and I thought it was a fair point – that the buildings spoken of with such pride had partly been made possible by the labour of the foreign residents, which is one reason why he might consider my request concerning their future.

I then told the story (a dangerous story to tell because emotion overcomes me) about the old lady of seventy-seven from Arbroath who sent me £5 to wish me good luck in my mission for peace and wrote, 'My father was killed in Iraq in 1921, shot through the head while defending a British pipeline. I have sent the money in case you could find his grave, put some flowers on it, take a photograph and send it to me.'

As I told this, my lip quivered, and it had a quite electric effect on the meeting and they all paused for a second. I said, 'It may seem rather an emotional point, but politics *is* about emotion and not just about statistics.'

Then we went on to the question of Palestine, and I said, 'I support you 100 per cent on Palestine and the right to a Palestinian state, but, if there is a war, think of the consequences. You can't have a Palestine without Palestinians, and they may all be killed.'

After three hours he said, 'I have detained you too long.' That was a clear sign, so we stood up and shook hands.

This was where I made my big mistake, because I had been so high-minded about not pleading for hostages and talking about politics that I had forgotten to do what Paul would have done if he had been allowed to come – that is, to ask how many hostages would be allowed out, when they could come out, and so on. I missed the boat, and, when I got back with Sa'doon Zubaydi, Paul was obviously extremely disappointed that I had failed to do the fundamental thing. I felt I had let him down most terribly.

But you must have faith, and I tried to keep it up during a pretty gloomy afternoon press conference, with the journalists all clamouring around and asking, 'How many have you got, Mr Benn?' as if it was a cricket match.

I described the meeting in a way that didn't betray Saddam Hussein's confidence, and the press were quite generous to me. I said, 'Well, I can't tell you. There are a lot of ends to be tied up. I was very bold and asked for the lot.'

By the evening, the full impact of my failure was beginning to dawn on me.

Sa'doon Zubaydi, incidentally, asked me to send him the particulars of the grave the Scottish woman had written to me about. Late in the day, a message came through that the Iraqi Government would provide me with a private jet to Amman, which means I might be able to see King Hussain on my way back.

Paul and I were in a state of gloom, but in fact a very amusing, kind Member of Parliament came to see us, and I told him I had forgotten to ask the critical question. He laughed, and he is going to try to talk to the Speaker. Later I heard that fifteen hostages had been identified to be released. It's not bad, but not as many as I had hoped.

Just as I settled down to do the diary, the phone rang, and I was told that Daniel Ortega, who lost the presidency of Nicaragua earlier this year, was in Baghdad and would like to see me.

Out of the lift came a group of what could only be called a political posse: the leader, an interpreter, a private secretary and a television crew. They came out with flashing lights and cameras rolling.

We gave them Pepsi Cola, having ordered some rolls. I had never met Daniel, though I have long been a supporter of the Nicaraguan cause. He was, sadly, defeated in the elections and agreed to serve under the US-sponsored Government, which the Nicaraguans voted in as a way of getting peace and a bit of American support.

He told me that the immediate problem was that the Vice-President had objected to a coalition between the new Government and the Sandinistas on the grounds that it had softened the necessarily harsh medicine of the economic reform programme which the Americans had made the basis of their financial support. So the Americans have now stopped giving financial support to the new Government, in order to force the Sandinistas out of the coalition and get back to the harsh Friedmanite economic doctrine.

We exchanged opinions on how we could help Saddam in his difficulties and bring pressure to bear on the Americans. Daniel said one very interesting thing. He had approached the American Embassy in the capital, Managua, saying he was coming to Baghdad, and the American Ambassador had had a special envoy flown down from Washington to brief him on the situation. He thought this might possibly mean a slight change in the American attitude towards negotiation, because Bush must be worried, and there must be some doves in the White House. The fact that he had agreed that Daniel Ortega should be his channel of communication was exceptionally interesting.

Now I have only one remaining task, which is to get to see King Hussain tomorrow.

Secretly I am amazed that my name is so widely known, and Daniel told me that when he saw Rajiv Gandhi recently they had agreed I would be high on their list of international leaders for peace.

Incidentally, I heard that, when Willy Brandt met Saddam Hussein, at one point he had looked down at his knees and said very quietly, 'Mr President, you won't like what I am going to tell you, but . . .' Then he had told him that he should withdraw from Kuwait. Afterwards Saddam had said he thought Willy Brandt was 'sweet'!

Just after midnight, Sa'doon rang to check the final list of fifteen names. He commented on some of the people who have been to see Saddam Hussein, and told me, 'Jesse Jackson is a complete fake.'

I asked, 'What do you mean?'

'He came over with a television crew; Saddam Hussein wanted to talk to him about the crisis, and he said, "I'm just here doing television programmes." He created a very poor impression.'

Thursday 29 November

We were taken to the old airport in Baghdad and took off in this comfortable little jet – just Paul, myself and the Iraqi Ambassador to Jordan, who had been for talks in Baghdad. We flew for an hour across nothing but desert except the Euphrates, and landed in Amman at about 10.

We were hoping to see King Hussain before our flight to London, which was due to leave at 12. We contacted the Department of Royal Protocol to tell them, but they were a bit angry at a demand of this kind. Anyway, we were collected at 10.30 by the royal car and driven to the palace. At 11 o'clock King Hussain came in, neatly dressed and terribly friendly. Orange juice and tea were brought in, and he called me 'sir' repeatedly, as I believe he is in the habit of doing with everybody. He speaks perfect English.

I thanked him for his hospitality and congratulated him on his leadership in warning of the disastrous environmental aspects of the war, a leadership which has had a profound effect on the Greens all over the world.

He said, 'We *must* stop the war. Immense damage would be done to the people and the planet.'

I asked him about his mission to the United States in August, which had been a failure.

He said, 'I have known Bush for years, and he treated me very badly when I went to see him. He made an announcement before I came as to what he expected – that I would simply implement the sanctions.'

I remarked, 'Well, Mrs Thatcher wasn't much better.'

'She certainly didn't listen to anything I had to say, and when the question of Sudan (which has been sending vegetables to Iraq) came up she said she had no sympathy for Sudan for selling them the food.'

I said, 'Well, we have only got six weeks to put all this right before a war is likely to break out. There is, of course, a major difference between the objectives of the UN and the objectives of the USA.'

'Of course. There is Palestine as well, and that question must be resolved. I have been trying for years to get people to realise that.'

I told him that I'd seen Saddam Hussein yesterday and that he wants a way out.

'What is needed is a dialogue,' he said.

'Do you think the United States would agree to a dialogue?'

'We are trying.'

I suggested that, if he was not making much progress with the Governments, he would certainly get an audience with the people. 'If you did a public meeting in London, half a million people would come to hear you.'

He said the trouble with this part of the world was that there was enormous wealth, and extremely poor people. The gap between rich and poor had to be solved. There had got to be democracy. He told me the Saudis were nervous because American soldiers were defending their holy places, though there was never any risk of an attack on Saudi Arabia. 'King Fahd is finished, with or without a war.'

It occurred to me that I might possibly persuade him to do a video that could be shown in Britain.

Then he said, 'You'll miss your plane if you are not careful. I have put my helicopter at your disposal.'

He came to the steps and saw us off, and we waved. Paul had been sitting in and had taken video film of our discussions. We were taken by helicopter right to the Jordanian airline plane which was about to leave.

We landed at London airport at about 4 and came through quickly, and there was Caroline waiting for me. I felt totally at home again. There were forty journalists, and I felt as if I were in front of a firing squad. They asked some hostile questions.

Saturday 1 December

This week saw the removal of Mrs Thatcher from Number 10, and apparently, as she left the building, people detected a tear in her eye. But she turned up in the House the following day, sitting in the seat Geoffrey Howe had occupied when he had made his resignation speech, and she listened to John Major. According to the opinion poll, Labour is slipping and the Tories are rising, and I think the media have at last found a candidate they can openly and uncritically support.

Yesterday I actually had a handwritten letter from Kinnock in which he congratulated me on the success of my 'humanitarian efforts'. I thought I had better take it as a peace gesture, so I rang and thanked him, and arranged to go and give him a briefing.

Monday 3 December

Saw Neil Kinnock, the first time I have been in his room in the Commons since the miners' strike.

I told him I was going to see the American Ambassador, and Neil said, 'Leave it to me. I'll ring him up. Henry's a very nice guy.' Well, I don't need Neil to get me to see the American Ambassador!

To the Stop the War Committee, where they spent a whole hour discussing whether the next demonstration should be national or regional and whether it would be on 12 or 19 January. It was ridiculous! I gave a brief report.

Thursday 6 December

By taxi to see Henry Cato, the American Ambassador. A misty day, rather like the old London fog.

I had looked him up in *Who's Who* and discovered he was sixty today, so I wished him a happy sixtieth birthday.

He said, 'Shhhhh!'

So I said, 'You're a *young* diplomat in my book!'

He took me into his office, where there were a lot of people working on word processors; his desk was at one end, and at the other end we talked. He offered me a cup of tea, and he went to the kettle and made it himself. A British Ambassador would have rung the bell and a butler would have brought it in.

Cato himself was immaculately dressed, with his teeth all fixed and crowned, and his hair slicked down.

I said, 'I've come to tell you about my talk to Saddam Hussein.'

He was surprised that I had spent three hours with Saddam, and observed, 'You must know more of his thinking than anybody else.'

'I don't know about that,' I said, 'but the main point is that he thinks you are going to attack him whatever he does, and that is the problem. With the US Secretary of State talking this morning about the "massive, decisive use of force" and with the Chief of Staff, General Powell, talking about his weapons, I am not surprised he does. I think he probably would get out if he thought he wasn't going to be attacked.' I hope that point did register with him.

I gave my assessment of Saddam – that he was a clever man, a lawyer, that he didn't feed me with propaganda, that it was a genuine discussion, and that the Iraqi Government knew my position on the invasion, on sanctions, on the Kurds and on civil rights.

Cato asked, 'Did you raise with him the atrocities that had been committed in Kuwait?'

'I did in the sense that I asked for an amnesty for everybody in Kuwait, but it seemed to me my function was to explore the possibilities of a peaceful settlement, not to go there and put him on charge. That was not what it was about. You know my view, Ambassador, I am not very supportive of the way in which it has been handled in Washington and London.'

He replied, 'Well, I know you lay about yourself with great vigour against the American and British Governments!'

'I just happen to be a member of another tradition. I don't feel that I am anti-British or anti-American, I just have a different view. In 1950, the day I was elected, President Truman said he might drop an atom bomb on China, so nothing much has changed.'

I thought him rather weak, and it was so easy to charm him.

He said, 'Reagan is here, and I had dinner with him and Thatcher last night. We were bathed in nostalgia. The thing about Reagan is that he just tells a succession of corny jokes, one after another. They are so corny, it makes you want to crawl away.'

'It's interesting you should say that – I have never heard Mrs Thatcher tell a joke,' I remarked.

'You know, you're right. She's never told a joke, and she's never told a story. Politics is absolutely lubricated by anecdotes, but she's *never* told one.'

I went into my theory about how she is really a teacher, she analyses and acts, and drives the lesson home so that her values will always be remembered. He pulled out a little notebook from his pocket and said, 'Listen to this, it's from Isaiah Berlin' (who was my tutor at Oxford). He went on, 'There are two types of people, the fox and the hedgehog.' He read a list of people who were either foxes or hedgehogs and said, 'The fox is sly but the hedgehog is committed.' Thatcher, obviously, he saw as a hedgehog and Reagan as a fox.

Later in the day we heard that Saddam Hussein had announced that he is granting freedom of movement to all foreign residents – the very thing I had asked him to do last week. I could hardly believe it.

At 8 Caroline and I went to a lovely dinner at the Commons that had been arranged to celebrate my fortieth year in Parliament. Ruth Winstone had decorated a cake with the Commons portcullis symbol on it. Tony and Sally Banks gave me a Gladstone plate from their own collection, which was extremely generous. Also invited were Chris Mullin, Ralph and Marion Miliband and their friend John Saville, the historian, who was riveted by Caroline's work on Hardie, Richard and Patricia Moberly, Jeremy and Claudia Corbyn and Maxine Baker.

At one point, the lights went out in the Harcourt Room, which is where a lot of Tory MPs have dinner, and in came the cake, and the Tory MPs sang 'Happy Birthday', not knowing what was going on.

Saturday 8 December

Caroline and I were in Chesterfield, where the Labour Club also held a party for me despite terrible snow storms. Tom Vallins, with great emotion, presented me with a beautiful illustrated manuscript with extracts from my two 'maiden' speeches – February 1951 and March 1984. The club was packed, and I got a feeling of real affection.

Within a few weeks of the ending of this diary, the bombing of Iraq – and the bloodshed – began, leaving thousands dead and the underlying problems of the Middle East unresolved. This, we were told by President Bush, was the first stage of a New World Order.

Principal Persons

(I) Political and Official

Each person is named according to his or her status as the Diaries open (June 1980). A list of Conservative Cabinets as at 1981 and 1987 is given in Appendix I; Shadow Cabinet and National Executive Committee members are given in Appendices II and III.

ALI, Tariq. Novelist and film maker. Editor of *Black Dwarf* and *Red Mole* in the 1960s and 1970s. Producer of Channel 4's *Rear Window* since 1990.

ALLAUN, Frank. Chairman of the Labour Party, 1978/9, and Labour MP for Salford East, 1955–83. Vice-President of CND and President of Labour Action for Peace.

ASHTON, Joe. Principal Private Secretary to Tony Benn, 1975–6. Labour MP for Bassetlaw since 1968.

ATKINSON, Norman. Treasurer of the Labour Party, 1976–81. Labour MP for Tottenham, 1964–87.

BANKS, Tony. Assistant General Secretary, Association of Broadcasting and Allied Staffs, 1976–83 and Head of Research, Amalgamated Union of Engineering Workers, 1968–75. Last Chairman of Greater London Council, 1985–6. Labour MP for Newham North West since 1983.

BARNETT, Joel. Chief Secretary to the Treasury, 1974–9. Labour MP for Heywood and Royton, 1964–83. Created a life peer in 1983.

BASNETT, David (1924–1989). General Secretary of General and Municipal Workers' Union (later General, Municipal, Boilermakers and Allied Trades Union), 1973–86. Chairman, TUC General Council, 1977–8, and of Trade Unionists for a Labour Victory, 1979–85. Created a life peer in 1987.

BECKETT, Margaret. Labour MP for Lincoln, Oct 1974–9, and for Derby South since 1983.

BIFFEN, John. Chief Secretary to the Treasury, 1979–81, Secretary of State for Trade, 1981–2, and Lord President of the Council, 1982–3.

Leader of the House of Commons, 1982–7. Conservative MP for Oswestry, subsequently Shropshire North, since 1961.

BISH, Geoff. Head of Research, subsequently Policy Director, of the Labour Party since 1974.

BUTLER, David. Political scientist and broadcaster, whose special subject is the study of elections; the first person to coin the term 'psephology'. Co-author of *British Political Facts 1900–83*. Life-long friend.

CALLAGHAN, James (Jim). Prime Minister, 1976–9, and Leader of the Labour Party 1976–80. Held junior posts in the 1945–51 Labour Government, was Chancellor of the Exchequer, 1964–7, and Home Secretary, 1967–70. Foreign Secretary, 1974–6. Chairman of the Labour Party 1973/4 and Labour MP for South, South-East and again South Cardiff, 1945–87. Father of the House, 1983–7. Made a Knight of the Garter and a life peer in 1987. Married to Audrey Callaghan.

CARRINGTON, Lord (Peter Carrington). Foreign Secretary 1979–82, (resigned April 1982 over the Falklands War). Defence Secretary then Energy Secretary, 1970–74. Chairman of the Conservative Party, 1972–4. Secretary-General of NATO, 1984–8. As 6th Baron Carrington held Government office while in House of Lords.

CASTLE, Barbara. Leader of the British Labour Group in the European Parliament, 1979–85. Secretary of State for Social Services, 1974–6, dismissed by James Callaghan when he formed his Government in 1976. Minister of Overseas Development, 1964–5. Minister of Transport, 1965–8, First Secretary of State at the Department of Employment and Productivity, 1968–70. Chairman of the Labour Party, 1958/9. Labour MP for Blackburn, 1945–79. Created a life peer in 1990.

CHAPPLE, Frank. General Secretary of the Electrical, Electronic Telecommunications and Plumbing Trade Union, 1966–84. Member of the National Economic Development Council, 1979–83. Created a life peer in 1985.

CLARKE, Eric. General Secretary, NUM Scottish Area, 1977–89. Labour MP for Midlothian since 1992.

CLEMENTS-ELLIOTT, Julie. Private secretary to Tony Benn, 1976–84. Labour councillor since 1971. Chair of Southall College of Technology Governing Body since 1986. Married Michael Elliott, MEP, in 1979.

COATES, Ken. One of the founders of the Institute for Workers' Control, director of the Bertrand Russell Foundation. Author of numerous works on socialism and industrial democracy. MEP since 1989.

COCKS, Michael. Opposition Chief Whip, 1979–85. Government Chief Whip, 1976–9. Labour MP for Bristol South, 1970–87. Created a life peer in 1987.

COOK, Robin. Labour MP for Edinburgh Central, February 1974–83, for Livingston since 1983. Labour Party Campaigns Co-ordinator, 1984–6.

CORBYN, Jeremy. Official of National Union of Public Employees, 1975–83. Labour MP for Islington North since 1983.

CRAIGIE, Jill. Author and journalist, married to Michael Foot.

CUNNINGHAM, John (Jack). Labour MP for Whitehaven, 1970–83, Copeland since 1983. Parliamentary Under-Secretary of State, Department of Energy, 1976–9. PPS to Jim Callaghan, 1972–6.

DALYELL, Tam. Labour MP for West Lothian, 1962–83, and Linlithgow since 1983. PPS to Richard Crossman, 1964–70. Sacked from the Front Bench during the Falklands War

DERER, Vladimir. Secretary, Campaign for Labour Party Democracy.

DUFFY, Terry. 1922–85 President Amalgamated Union of Engineering Workers.

EVANS, Moss. General Secretary of the Transport and General Workers' Union, 1978–85. National Officer of the TGWU, 1969–78. Member of the NEDC, 1978–84. Member of the General Council of the TUC, 1977–85.

FALKENDER, Lady (Marcia Williams). Personal and Political Secretary to Harold Wilson since 1956. Created a life peer, Lady Falkender, in 1976.

FLANNERY, Martin. Labour MP for Sheffield Hillsborough, February 1974–92.

FOOT, Michael. Deputy Leader of the Labour Party, 1979–80, and Leader, 1980–83. Lord President of the Council and Leader of the House of Commons, 1976–9. Backbencher during the 1964–70 Labour Government. Secretary of State for Employment, 1974–6. Member of the National Executive, 1971–83. Labour MP for Devonport, 1945–55. Ebbw Vale, 1960–83, and Blaenau Gwent, 1983–92. Biographer of Aneurin Bevan. Married to Jill Craigie.

FOSTER, Derek. Labour MP for Bishop Auckland since 1979. Labour Chief Whip since 1985.

GILL, Ken. General Secretary, Technical and Supervisory Section of Amalgamated Union of Engineering Workers, 1974–88. Joint Secretary of Manufacturing, Science and Finance since 1988, General Secretary since 1989. Chairman of TUC General Council, 1985/6.

GOLDING, John. Labour MP for Newcastle-under-Lyme, 1969–86. Political Officer to the Post Office Union, 1969–86, General Secretary of National Communications Union, 1986–88. Member of the National Executive, 1978–83.

GOODMAN, Geoffrey. Industrial Editor of the *Daily Mirror*, 1969–86, and Head of the Counter-Inflation Publicity Unit, 1975–6. Former journalist on the *Daily Herald* and the *Sun* and member of the Labour Party Committee on Industrial Democracy, 1966–7. Biographer of Frank Cousins.

GORMLEY, Joe. President of the National Union of Mineworkers, 1971–82. Member of the National Executive, 1963–73. Created a life peer in 1982.

GOULD, Bryan. Labour MP for Southampton Test, October 1974–79, and for Dagenham since 1983. Served in the Diplomatic Service, 1964–8.

GOULD, Joyce. Assistant National Agent and Chief Women's Officer of the Labour Party, 1975–85. Director of Organisation since 1985.

HAINES, Joe. From 1977–84 senior journalist on the *Daily Mirror*, Political Editor of the Mirror Group since 1984. Chief Press Secretary to Harold Wilson, 1969–76, previously political correspondent of the *Sun*.

HART, Judith (1924–91). Chairman of the Labour Party, 1981/2. Minister for Overseas Development 1974–5, sacked by Harold Wilson after the Referendum, and reinstated 1977–9. In the 1964–70 Government she was successively Joint Under-Secretary for Scotland, Minister of State for Commonwealth Affairs, Minister of Social Security, Paymaster-General and Minister for Overseas Development. Labour MP for Lanark, 1959–83. Clydesdale, 1983–7. Married to Tony Hart, a scientist and leading anti-nuclear campaigner.

HATTERSLEY, Roy. Shadow Home Secretary since 1981 and Deputy Leader of the Labour Party, 1983–92. Secretary of State for Prices and Consumer Protection, 1976–9. Joint Parliamentary Secretary at the Department of Employment and Productivity, 1967–9, and Minister of Defence for Administration, 1969–70. Minister of State at the Foreign and Commonwealth Office, 1974–6. Labour MP for Birmingham Sparkbrook since 1964.

HEALEY, Denis. Deputy Leader of the Labour Party, 1980–83. Chancellor of the Exchequer, 1974–9, Secretary of State for Defence, 1964–70. Labour MP for Leeds South East, 1952–5, and Leeds East 1955–92.

HEATH, Edward. Conservative MP for Bexley, subsequently Old Bexley and Sidcup since 1950. Leader of the Conservative Party, 1965–75. Prime Minister, 1970–74. Minister of Labour, 1959–60, Lord Privy Seal, 1960–63, and Secretary of State for Industry and Trade and President of the Board of Trade, 1963–4.

HEATHFIELD, Peter. General Secretary of the National Union of Mineworkers since 1984. Previously Secretary of the Derbyshire Area, NUM.

HEFFER, Eric (1922–91). Labour MP for Walton, Liverpool, 1964–91. Minister of State at the Department of Industry, 1974–5, sacked by Harold Wilson over the Common Market. Chairman of the Labour Party, 1983/4. Married to Doris Heffer.

HESELTINE, Michael. Secretary of State for Environment since 1990. Parliamentary Under-Secretary at Department of Environment, 1970–72, Minister for Aerospace and Shipping at Department of Trade and Industry, 1972–4. Secretary of State for Environment, 1979–83, and for Defence until his resignation in 1986. Conservative MP for Tavistock, 1966–74, and Henley since 1974. Contested party leadership, 1990.

HILL, Sir John. Chairman of the UK Atomic Energy Authority, 1967–81, and of British Nuclear Fuels, 1971–83. Member of the Advisory Council on Technology, 1968–70. President of the British Nuclear Forum since 1984.

HOLLAND, Stuart. Labour MP for Vauxhall, 1979–89. Formerly Economic Assistant, Cabinet Office, 1966–7 and Personal Assistant to Prime Minister, 1967–8.

HOWE, Sir Geoffrey. Chancellor of the Exchequer, 1979–83. Foreign Secretary, 1983–9. Solicitor-General, 1970–72 and Minister for Trade and Consumer Affairs, 1972–4. Conservative MP for Reigate, 1970–74, Surrey East, 1974–92.

HURD, Douglas. Minister of State, in Foreign and Home offices, 1979–84. Home Secretary 1985–9 and Foreign Secretary since 1989. Conservative MP for Witney since 1983, for Mid-Oxon 1974–83. Contested party leadership, 1990.

INGHAM, Bernard. Chief Press Secretary to the Prime Minister, 1979–90. Director of Information at the Department of Energy, 1974–8, Chief Information Officer at the Department of Employment and Productivity, 1968–73. Reporter on the *Yorkshire Post* and the *Guardian*, 1952–67.

JENKINS, Clive. General Secretary of the Association of Scientific Technical and Managerial Staffs, 1970–88. Member of the General Council of the TUC, 1974–8.

JENKINS, Roy. President of the European Commission, 1977–81. Minister of Aviation, 1964–5, Home Secretary, 1965–7. Chancellor of the Exchequer, 1967–70. Home Secretary, 1974–6. Deputy Leader of the Labour Party, 1970–72, in which capacity he sat on the National Executive. Labour MP for Central Southwark, 1948–50, for Stechford, 1950–76. Leader of the SDP, 1981–3, and SDP MP for Glasgow Hillhead, 1982–7. Created a life peer, Lord Jenkins of Hillhead, in 1987.

JOSEPH, Sir Keith. Secretary of State for Social Services, 1970–74, for Industry, 1979–81, and Education and Science, 1981–6. Junior Minister from 1959–64. Conservative MP for Leeds North East, 1956–87. Created a life peer in 1987.

KAUFMAN, Gerald. Shadow Foreign Secretary since 1987. Minister of State, Department of Industry, 1975–9. Labour Party press officer, 1965–70. Previously journalist on *Daily Mirror* and *New Statesman*. Labour MP for Manchester Ardwick, 1970–83, and Manchester Gorton since 1983.

KENT, Bruce. General Secretary, CND, 1980–85.

KEYS, Bill. General Secretary, Society of Graphic and Allied Trades, 1974–82, General Secretary SOGAT 82, 1982–5.

KINNOCK, Neil. Leader of the Labour Party, 1983–92, Chair, 1987/8. Labour MP for Bedwelty, 1970–83, Islwyn since 1983.

KITSON, Alex. Executive Officer of the Transport and General Workers' Union, 1971–80, and Deputy General Secretary, 1980–86. Chairman of the Labour Party, 1980/81.

LANSMAN, Jon. Coordinator of Benn's deputy leadership campaign, 1981.

LESTOR, Joan. Under-Secretary at the Foreign and Commonwealth Office, 1974–5, and at the Department of Education and Science, 1975–6, resigning her post over public expenditure cuts. Under-Secretary at the Department of Education and Science, 1969–70. Chairman of the Labour Party, 1977/8. Labour MP for Eton and Slough, 1966–83, and Eccles since 1987.

LIVINGSTONE, Ken. Leader of Greater London Council, 1981–6. Labour MP for Brent East since 1987.

McGAHEY, Mick. Vice-President, National Union of Mineworkers, 1973–87. President, Scottish Area of the NUM, 1967–87. Chairman of the Communist Party of Great Britain, 1974–8.

McCLUSKIE, Sam. General Secretary, National Union of Seamen, 1986–90. Executive Officer, National Union of Rail, Maritime and Transport Workers (RMT), 1990–91. Assistant General Secretary of NUS, 1976–86. Chairman of the Labour Party, 1983/4.

McNALLY, Tom. Political Adviser to Jim Callaghan, 1974–9. International Secretary of the Labour Party, 1969–74. Elected Labour MP for Stockport, 1979; joined SDP in 1981 and sat as SDP Member, 1981–3.

MANDELSON, Peter. Labour Party's Director of Campaigns and Communications, 1985–90. Labour MP for Hartlepool since 1992.

MAYNARD, Joan. Labour MP for Sheffield Brightside, Oct 1974–87. Vice-Chairman of the Labour Party, 1980/81.

MEACHER, Michael. Labour MP for Oldham West since 1970. Parliamentary Under-Secretary of State for Industry, 1974–5, Health and Social Security, 1975–6, and Trade 1976–9.

MEALE, Alan. Advisor to Michael Meacher, MP, 1983–7. Labour MP for Mansfield since 1987.

MELLISH, Robert. Labour MP for Bermondsey from 1946 to 1982, when he resigned from the Labour Party and sat as an Independent. Deputy Chairman of the London Docklands Development Corporation since 1981. Government Chief Whip, 1969–70 and 1974–6. Opposition Chief Whip, 1970–74. Created a life peer in 1985.

MIKARDO, Ian. Labour MP for Poplar, 1964–74, and for Bethnal Green and Bow, 1974–87. MP for Reading, and South Reading, 1945–59. Chairman of the Labour Party, 1970/71. A close associate of Aneurin Bevan and sometime chairman of the Tribune Group of Labour MPs.

MILIBAND, Ralph. Professor of Politics, Leeds University, 1972–7, and currently visiting Professor of the Graduate School, City University of New York.

MORRELL, Frances. Leader of Inner London Education Authority, 1983–7. Political adviser to Tony Benn, 1974–9. Press officer for the National Union of Students and the Fabian Society, 1970–72. Previously a schoolteacher, 1960–69.

MORTIMER, Jim. Chairman, Advisory, Conciliation and Arbitration Service, 1974–81. General Secretary of the Labour Party, 1982–5.

MULLIN, Chris. Editor of *Arguments for Socialism* and *Arguments for Democracy* by Tony Benn; *Tribune*, 1982–4. Author of *A Very British Coup*, and other political novels, and *Error of Judgement*. Labour MP for Sunderland South since 1987.

MURRAY, Len. General Secretary of the TUC, 1973–84. Member of the TUC staff from 1947. Created a life peer, Lord Murray of Epping Forest, in 1985.

ORME, Stan. Labour MP for Salford West, 1964–83 and for Salford East since 1983. Minister of State for Social Security, 1976–7 and Minister for Social Security, 1977–9. Minister of State, Northern Ireland Office, 1974–6. Chairman of the PLP since 1987.

OWEN, David. Labour MP for Plymouth Sutton, 1966–74, and Plymouth Devonport, 1974–81. Founder member of the SDP, 1981, and sat as SDP Member, 1981–3; SDP MP for Devonport, 1983–92. Minister of State at the Foreign and Commonwealth Office, 1976–7, then Foreign Secretary, following Tony Crosland's death, 1977–9. Parliamentary Under-Secretary of State for the Royal Navy, 1968–70. Parliamentary Under-Secretary of State, then Minister of State, at the Department of Health and Social Security, 1974–6.

POWELL, Enoch. Minister of Health, 1960–63. Resigned as Financial Secretary to the Treasury in protest at the Budget. Conservative MP for Wolverhampton South-West, 1950–74. Stood down as Conservative candidate in February 1974 in disagreement over the Conservative policy on the EEC. United Ulster Unionist MP for Down South, October 1974–9, Official Unionist Party, 1979–87.

PRENTICE, Reg. Labour MP for East Ham North, 1951–74, Newham North East, 1974–9. In October 1977 Reg Prentice crossed the floor and sat on the Conservative benches until 1979. In 1979 he was elected Conservative MP for Daventry and sat for Daventry until 1987; he was Minister for Social Security, 1979–81, in the Conservative Government.

PRESCOTT, John. Labour MP for Hull East since 1970. Member of European Parliament, 1975–9. Contested Party deputy leadership in 1988.

PRIMAROLO, Dawn. Secretary of Bristol South East Labour Party, 1979–83. Labour MP for Bristol South since 1987.

PRIOR, James (Jim). Secretary of State for Employment, 1979–81, Secretary of State for Northern Ireland, 1981–4. Lord President of the Council and Leader of the House of Commons, 1972–4. Conservative MP for Lowestoft, 1959–83 and Waveney, 1983–7.

RACE, Reg. Labour MP for Wood Green, 1979–83. Head of Programme Office, Greater London Council, 1983–6.

REES, Merlyn. Labour MP for South Leeds, 1963–83, and for Morley and Leeds South, 1983–92. Home Secretary, 1976–9. Parliamentary Under-Secretary of State at the Ministry of Defence, 1965–8, and Home Office, 1968–70. Secretary of State for Northern Ireland, 1974–6.

RICHARDSON, Jo. Labour MP for Barking since Feb 1974. Opposition spokesperson on Women since 1983. Member of National Executive since 1979. Chair of Labour Party, 1989/90.

RODGERS, William (Bill). Labour MP for Stockton-on-Tees (Teesside Stockton from 1974), 1962–81. Founder member of the SDP in 1981 and sat as SDP MP for same seat, 1981–3. Secretary of State for Transport, 1976–79. Parliamentary Under-Secretary of State at the Department of Economic Affairs then Foreign Commonwealth Office, 1964–8. Minister of State at the Board of Trade, 1968–9, and the Treasury, 1969–70. Minister of State at the Ministry of Defence, 1974–6.

SAWYER, Tom. National Union of Public Employees' member of National Executive since 1982. Chair of Labour Party, 1990/91.

SCARGILL, Arthur. President of the Yorkshire Area of the National Union of Mineworkers, 1973–81. President of the NUM since 1981, and member of the TUC General Council, 1987/8.

SEDGEMORE, Brian. Labour MP for Luton West, 1974–9, and for Hackney South and Shoreditch since 1983. PPS to Tony Benn, 1977–8. Granada TV researcher, 1980–83.

SHORE, Peter. Secretary of State for the Environment, 1976–9. Head of Research Department of the Labour Party, 1959–64. PPS to Harold Wilson, 1965–6. Joint Parliamentary Secretary at the Ministry of Technology, 1966–7. Secretary of State for Economic Affairs, 1967–9. Minister without Portfolio, 1969–70. Secretary of State for Trade, 1974–6. Labour MP for Stepney, subsequently Stepney and Poplar, and then Bethnal Green and Stepney, since 1964. Married to Liz Shore.

SHORT, Clare. Civil Servant in the Home Office, 1970–75. Labour MP for Birmingham Ladywood since 1983.

SILKIN, John (1923–1987). Labour MP for Deptford, 1963–87. Minister for Agriculture, Fisheries and Food, 1976–9. Government Whip, 1964–6 and Chief Whip, 1966–9. Minister of Public Building and Works, 1969–70. Minister for Planning and Local Government, 1974–6.

SKINNER, Dennis. Labour MP for Bolsover since 1970. Chair of the Labour Party, 1988/9. President of the Derbyshire NUM, 1966–70.

SMITH, John. Shadow Chancellor since 1987. Minister of State in the Privy Council Office, with responsibility for Devolution, 1976–8. Secretary of State for Trade, 1978–9. Parliamentary Under-Secretary of State, then Minister of State, at the Department of Energy, 1974–6. Labour MP for Lanarkshire North, 1970–83, and Monklands East since 1983.

STEEL, David. Leader of the Liberal Party, 1976–88, and the joint Leader of the Liberal and Social Democratic Alliance during 1987. Liberal MP for Roxburgh, Selkirk and Peebles, 1965–83, and Tweeddale, Ettrick and Lauderdale since 1983.

STRAW, Jack. Labour MP for Blackburn since 1979. Advisor to Secretaries of State for Social Services and the Environment, 1974–7.

STODDART, David. Labour MP for Swindon, 1970–83. Created a life peer, 1983.

TATLOW, Pam. Secretary of Bristol South East Labour Party, 1982.

THATCHER, Margaret. Leader of the Conservative Party, 1975–90. Prime Minister, 1979–90. Secretary of State for Education and Science, 1970–74, previously a junior Minister in the Ministry of Pensions and National Insurance, 1961–4. Conservative MP for Finchley, 1959–92.

THOMAS, George. Speaker of the House of Commons, 1976–83, (Deputy Speaker 1974–6). Minister of State at the Welsh Office, 1966–7, and Commonwealth Office, 1967–8. Secretary of State for Wales, 1968–70. Since 1983, Chairman of the National Children's Home. A former Vice-President of the Methodist Conference. Labour MP for Cardiff Central, 1945–50, Cardiff West, 1950–83 (sat as Speaker from 1976). Created a hereditary peer, Viscount Tonypandy, in 1983.

TODD, Ron. National Organiser of the Transport and General Workers' Union, 1978–85. General Secretary, 1985–91. Full time officer of the TGWU since 1962.

VALLINS, Margaret. Member of Chesterfield Labour Party. District Councillor, 1987–91. Constituency Secretary to Tony Benn since 1984.

VALLINS, Tom. Secretary of Chesterfield Labour Party since 1984. Election agent to Tony Benn since 1987.

VARLEY, Eric. Labour MP for Chesterfield, 1964–84. Secretary of State for Energy, 1974–5, exchanging Cabinet jobs with Tony Benn to become Secretary of State for Industry, 1975–9, PPS to Harold Wilson, 1968–9. Minister of State at the Ministry of Technology, 1969–70. Retired in 1984 to become Chairman of Coalite Group. Created a life peer in 1990.

WALKER, Peter. Minister for Agriculture, Fisheries and Food, 1979–83, Secretary of State for Wales, 1987–90. Secretary of State for the Environment, 1970–72, and for Trade and Industry, 1972–4. Deputy Chairman of Slater, Walker Securities, 1964–70. Conservative MP for Worcester since 1961.

WEATHERILL, Bernard (Jack). Conservative MP for Croydon North East, 1964–83. Speaker of the House of Commons and MP for Croydon North East, 1983–92.

WHITELAW, William (Willie). Home Secretary, 1979–83. Secretary of State for Employment, 1973–4, previously Leader of the House of Commons, and Secretary of State for Northern Ireland, 1972–3. Chairman of the Conservative Party, 1974–5. Created a hereditary viscount in 1983.

WHITTY, Larry. Official of the General and Municipal Workers' Union, 1973–85. General Secretary of the Labour Party since 1985.

WILLIAMS, Shirley. Founder member of the SDP in 1981, President in 1982 and SDP MP for Crosby, 1981–3. Secretary of State for Education and Science and Paymaster-General, 1976–9. Member of the National Executive, 1970–81. Parliamentary Secretary at the Ministry of Labour, 1966–7, Minister of State, Education and Science, 1967–9, and the Home Office, 1969–70. Secretary of State for Prices and Consumer Protection, 1974–6. Labour MP for Hitchin, 1964–74, for Hertford and Stevenage, 1974–9.

WILLIS, Norman. General Secretary of the Trades Union Congress since 1984. Assistant and Deputy General Secretary, 1974–84.

WILSON, Harold. Leader of the Labour Party, 1963–76. Prime Minister, 1964–70, and 1974–6. Resigned in 1976 and did not hold office again. President of the Board of Trade, 1947–51, when he resigned with Aneurin Bevan. Chairman of the Labour Party, 1961/2. Labour MP for Ormskirk, 1945–50 and Huyton, 1950–83. Created a life peer, Lord Wilson of Rievaulx, in 1983. Married to Mary Wilson, poet and writer.

WISE, Audrey. Labour MP for Coventry South West, 1974–9, and for Preston since 1987.

(II) Personal

ARNOLD-FORSTER, Mark (1920–81). Political commentator, worked on *Guardian, Observer* and ITN, 1946–81. Married to Val Arnold-Forster, journalist. Family friends.

BENN, Caroline. Born in the USA. Postgraduate degrees from the Universities of Cincinnati and London. Founder member of the comprehensive education campaign in Britain and editor of *Comprehensive Education* since 1967. Author of educational publications including *Half Way There* with Professor Brian Simon (1970) and *Challenging the MSC* with John Fairley (1986). President, Socialist Educational Association since 1970. Member, Inner London Education Authority, 1970–77. Member, Education Section, UNESCO Commission, 1976–83. Governor of several schools and colleges, including Imperial College, London University and Holland Park School, from 1967. Lecturer, adult education service, 1965-present. Married Tony Benn, 1949. Four children (see below).

BENN, David Wedgwood. Younger brother of Tony Benn; a barrister, worked for the Socialist International and later for the External Service of the BBC. Head of the BBC Yugoslav Section, 1974–84. A writer specialising in Soviet affairs.

BENN, Hilary. Born 1953. Educated at Holland Park School and Sussex University. Research Officer with the trade union MSF (formerly ASTMS). A past president of Acton Labour Party, elected to Ealing Council, 1979. Deputy Leader of the Council and Chair of the Education Committee, 1986–90. Chair of the Association of London Authorities' Education Committee, 1988–90. Contested Ealing North in 1983 and 1987 Elections. In 1973 married Rosalind Retey who died of cancer in 1979. Married Sally Clark in 1982. Four children.

BENN, Joshua. Born 1958. Educated at Holland Park School. Founder of COMMUNITEC Computer Training Consultancy, 1984–8. Director of Westway Music Publishing, 1980–82. Former contributor to *Sound International, Beat Instrumental* and computer and electronics magazines. Co-author of *Rock Hardware* (1981). Executive member of Computing for Labour. Employed by the Housing Corporation since 1988. Married Elizabeth Feeney in 1984. One son.

BENN, June. Former lecturer; novelist writing under the name of June Barraclough. Married David Benn in 1959. Two children, Piers, born in 1962, and Frances, born 1964.

BENN, Melissa. Born 1957. Educated at Holland Park School and the London School of Economics. Socialist feminist writer and journalist. Joint author with Ken Worpole of *Death in the City*

(1986). Contributor to several essay collections on feminism, the media, the police and crime; her work has also appeared in *Feminist Review*, *Women's Studies International Forum* and several international publications. Contributes to the *Guardian*, *New Statesman*, *Marxism Today*, *Spare Rib*. On the staff of *City Limits*, 1988–90.

BENN, Stephen. Born 1951. Educated at Holland Park School and Keele University. PhD for 'The White House Staff' (1984). Former assistant to Senator Thomas F. Eagleton. Secretary and Agent, Kensington Labour Party. Labour candidate GLC, 1981. Member GLC Special Committee, 1983–6. Chair, Brent South CLP. Member of ILEA 1981–90 and Chair of General Purposes Committee. School and College Governor. Court of Governors, Central London Polytechnic. Vice Chair, Association of London Authorities' Education Committee, 1987–90. Parliamentary Affairs Office for Royal Society of Chemistry since 1988. Composer. Married Nita Clarke in 1988. One daughter, one son.

CLARKE, Nita. Chief press officer, GLC 1980–86. Married to Stephen Benn since 1988.

STANSGATE, Lady (1897–1991). Margaret Holmes. Daughter of Liberal MP, D.T. Holmes. Married William Wedgwood Benn in 1920. They had three children (the eldest son, Michael, was killed while serving as an RAF pilot during World War II). A long-standing member of the Movement for the Ordination of Women, the first President of the Congregational Federation, served on the Council of Christians and Jews, and of the Friends of the Hebrew University. Fellow of the Hebrew University. Joint author of *Beckoning Horizon*, 1934.

STANSGATE, Lord (1877–1960). William Wedgwood Benn. Son of John Williams Benn, who was Liberal MP for Tower Hamlets and later for Devonport, and Chairman, 1904/5, of the London County Council of which he was a founder member. William Wedgwood Benn was himself elected Liberal MP for St George's, Tower Hamlets, in 1906. Became a Whip in the Liberal Government in 1910. Served in the First World War and was decorated with the DSO and DFC, returning in 1918 to be elected Liberal MP for Leith. Joined the Labour Party in 1926, resigned his seat the same day, and was subsequently elected Labour MP for North Aberdeen (1928–31) in a by-election. Secretary of State for India in the 1929–31 Labour Cabinet. Re-elected as Labour MP for Gorton in 1937. He rejoined the RAF in 1940 at the age of sixty-three, was made a peer, Viscount Stansgate, in 1941, and was Secretary of State for Air, 1945–6, in the postwar Labour Government. World President of the Inter-Parliamentary Union, 1947–57.

APPENDIX I
Her Majesty's Government
Complete List of Ministers and Offices

The Cabinet, September 1981

Prime Minister and First Lord of the Treasury	Mrs Margaret Thatcher
Secretary of State for the Home Office	Mr William Whitelaw
Lord Chancellor	Lord Hailsham
Secretary of State for Foreign and Commonwealth Affairs	Lord Carrington
Chancellor of the Exchequer	Sir Geoffrey Howe
Secretary of State for Education and Science	Sir Keith Joseph
Lord President of the Council and Leader of the House of Commons	Mr Frances Pym
Secretary of State for Northern Ireland	Mr James Prior
Secretary of State for Defence	Mr John Nott
Minister of Agriculture, Fisheries and Food	Mr Peter Walker
Secretary of State for the Environment	Mr Michael Heseltine
Secretary of State for Scotland	Mr George Younger
Secretary of State for Wales	Mr Nicholas Edwards
Lord Privy Seal	Mr Humphrey Atkins
Secretary of State for Industry	Mr Patrick Jenkin
Secretary of State for Trade	Mr John Biffen
Secretary of State for Transport	Mr David Howell
Secretary of State for Social Services	Mr Norman Fowler
Chief Secretary to the Treasury	Mr Leon Brittan

Secretary of State for Energy — Mr Nigel Lawson
Secretary of State for Employment — Mr Norman Tebbit
Chancellor of the Duchy of Lancaster and Leader of the House of Lords — Baroness Young

---

The Cabinet, June 1987

Prime Minister and First Lord of the Treasury	Mrs Margaret Thatcher
Secretary of State for the Home Office	Mr Douglas Hurd
Lord Chancellor	Lord Havers*
Secretary of State for Foreign and Commonwealth Affairs	Sir Geoffrey Howe
Chancellor of the Exchequer	Mr Nigel Lawson
Secretary of State for Education and Science	Mr Kenneth Baker
Lord President of the Council and Leader of the House of Commons	Lord Whitelaw
Secretary of State for Northern Ireland	Mr Tom King
Secretary of State for Defence	Mr George Younger
Minister of Agriculture, Fisheries and Food	Mr John MacGregor
Secretary of State for the Environment	Mr Nicholas Ridley
Secretary of State for Scotland	Mr Malcolm Rifkind
Secretary of State for Wales	Mr Peter Walker
Lord Privy Seal and Leader of the House of Commons	Mr John Wakeham
Secretary of State for Trade and Industry	Lord Young of Graffham
Secretary of State for Transport	Mr Paul Channon
Secretary of State for Social Services	Mr John Moore
Chief Secretary to the Treasury	Mr John Major
Secretary of State for Energy	Mr Cecil Parkinson
Secretary of State for Employment	Mr Norman Fowler
Chancellor of the Duchy of Lancaster	Mr Kenneth Clarke

---

* Retired due to ill-health, replaced by Lord Mackay of Clashfern, October 1987.

The Cabinet, July 1990

Prime Minister, First Lord of the Treasury and Civil Service Minister	Mrs Margaret Thatcher
Lord President of the Council and Leader of the House of Commons	Sir Geoffrey Howe
Secretary of State for Foreign and Commonwealth Affairs	Mr Douglas Hurd
Lord Chancellor	Lord Mackay of Clashfern
Chancellor of the Exchequer	Mr John Major*
Secretary of State for the Home Department	Mr David Waddington
Secretary of State for Education and Science	Mr John MacGregor
Secretary of State for Defence	Mr Tom King
Chancellor of the Duchy of Lancaster	Mr Kenneth Baker
Secretary of State for Health	Mr Kenneth Clarke
Secretary of State for Scotland	Mr Malcolm Rifkind
Secretary of State for Wales	Mr David Hunt
Secretary of State for Transport	Mr Cecil Parkinson
Secretary of State for Energy	Mr John Wakeham
Lord Privy Seal and Leader of the House of Lords	Lord Belstead
Secretary of State for Social Services	Mr Antony Newton
Secretary of State for the Environment	Mr Chris Patten
Secretary of State for Northern Ireland	Mr Peter Brooke
Minister of Agriculture, Fisheries and Food	Mr John Gummer
Chief Secretary to the Treasury	Mr Norman Lamont
Secretary of State for Employment	Mr Michael Howard
Secretary of State for Trade and Industry	Mr Peter Lilley
Attorney-General	Sir Patrick Mayhew
Lord Advocate	Lord Fraser of Carmyllie
Solicitor-General	Sir Nicholas Lyell
Solicitor-General for Scotland	Mr Alan Rodger

* John Major became Prime Minister in November; his job was filled by Norman Lamont.

APPENDIX II
Labour Shadow Cabinet and Front Bench

January, 1980

Mr Michael Foot	Leader of the Opposition
Mr Denis Healey	Foreign and Commonwealth Affairs
Mr Peter Shore	Treasury and Economic Affairs
Mr John Silkin	Leader of the House of Commons
Mr Roy Hattersley	Home Affairs
Mr Stanley Orme	Industry
Mr Eric Varley	Employment
Mr Gerald Kaufman	Environment
Mr Merlyn Rees	Energy
Mr John Smith	Trade, Prices and Consumer Protection
Mr Albert Booth	Transport
Mr Neil Kinnock	Education
Mr Roy Mason	Agriculture
Mr Brynmor John	Defence
Mr Norman Buchan	Social Security
Mrs Gwyneth Dunwoody	Health Service
Mr Bruce Millan	Scotland
Mr Eric Jones	Wales
Mr Don Concannon	Northern Ireland
Mr Frank McElhone	Overseas Development
Mr John Morris	Legal Affairs
Mr Tam Dalyell	Science
Mr Alan Williams	Civil Service
Mr Andrew Faulds	Arts
Mr Alfred Morris	Disabled People

July, 1987

Mr Neil Kinnock	Leader of the Opposition
Mr Roy Hattersley	Home Affairs
Mr Bryan Gould	Trade and Industry
Mr John Prescott	Energy
Mr Michael Meacher	Employment
Mr Gerald Kaufman	Foreign and Commonwealth Affairs
Mr John Smith	Treasury and Economic Affairs
Mr Denzil Davies	Defence and Disarmament and Arms Control
Mr Robert Hughes	Transport
Mr Robin Cook	Health and Social Security
Mr Donald Dewar	Scotland
Mr Frank Dobson	Leader of the House of Commons and Campaigns Co-ordinator
Mr Gordon Brown	Chief Secretary to the Treasury
Dr John Cunningham	Environment
Miss Jo Richardson	Women
Dr David Clark	Agriculture and Rural Affairs
Mr Jack Straw	Education
Mr Alan Williams	Wales
Mr Kevin McNamara	Northern Ireland
Mr Mark Fisher	Arts
Miss Joan Lestor	Development and Co-operation
Mr Alfred Morris	Disabled People
Mr John Morris	Legal Affairs
Dr Jeremy Bray	Science and Technology

November, 1989

Mr Neil Kinnock	Leader of the Opposition
Mr Roy Hattersley	Home Affairs
Mr Derek Foster	Chief Whip
Mr Stan Orme	Chair Parliamentary Party
Dr John Cunningham	Leader of the House
Mr John Smith	Treasury
Mrs Margaret Beckett	Treasury

Mr Gerald Kaufman	Foreign and Commonwealth Affairs
Mr Martin O'Neill	Defence
Mr Tony Blair	Employment
Mr Gordon Brown	Trade and Industry
Mr Robin Cook	Health
Mr Frank Dobson	Energy
Mr Bryan Gould	Environment
Mr Michael Meacher	Social Security
Mr John Morris	Legal Affairs
Mr Kevin McNamara	Northern Ireland
Mr John Prescott	Transport
Miss Joan Lestor	Children
Miss Jo Richardson	Women's Rights
Mr Jack Straw	Education
Mr Barry Jones	Wales
Mr Donald Dewar	Scotland
Mr Alf Morris	Disabled People's Rights
Ms Ann Clwyd	Development
Mr David Clark	Food, Agricultural and Rural Affairs
Mr Mark Fisher	Arts

APPENDIX III
Labour Party National Executive Committee

1980/1

Mr Alex Kitson	Chairman
Dame Judith Hart, MP	Vice-Chairman
Mr Norman Atkinson, MP	Treasurer
Mr Michael Foot, MP	Leader of the Labour Party
Mr Denis Healey, MP	Deputy Leader of the Labour Party
Mr Ron Hayward	General Secretary

Trade Unions

Mr Tom Bradley, MP (Transport Salaried Staffs' Association)

Mr Eric Clarke (National Union of Mineworkers)

Mr Alan Hadden (Amalgamated Society of Boilermakers, Shipwrights, Blacksmiths and Structural Workers)

Mr Neville Hough (General and Municipal Workers' Union)

Mr Doug Hoyle (Association of Scientific, Technical and Managerial Staffs)

Mr Charles Kelly (Union of Construction, Allied Trades and Technicians)

Mr Alex Kitson (Transport and General Workers' Union)

Mr Sam McCluskie (National Union of Seamen)

Mr Gerry Russell (Amalgamated Union of Engineering Workers)

Mr Syd Tierney (Union of Shop, Distributive and Allied Workers)

Mr Russell Tuck (National Union of Railwaymen)

Mr Emlyn Williams (National Union of Mineworkers)

Socialist, Co-operative and other organisations

Mr Les Huckfield (National Union of Labour and Socialist Clubs)

Constituency Labour Parties
Mr Frank Allaun, MP
Mr Tony Benn, MP
Mr Eric Heffer, MP
Mr Neil Kinnock, MP
Miss Joan Lestor, MP
Miss Jo Richardson, MP
Mr Dennis Skinner, MP

Women Members
Mrs Margaret Beckett
Dame Judith Hart, MP
Miss Joan Maynard, MP
Mrs Renée Short, MP
Mrs Shirley Williams

Labour Party Young Socialists' Representative
Mr Tony Saunois

1987/8

Mr Neil Kinnock, MP	Chair and Leader of the Labour Party
Mr Dennis Skinner, MP	Vice-Chair
Mr Sam McCluskie	Treasurer
Mr Roy Hattersley	Deputy Leader of the Labour Party
Mr Larry Whitty	General Secretary

Trade Unions' Section
Mr Eric Clarke (National Union of Mineworkers)
Mr Tony Clarke (Union of Communication Workers)
Mr Gordon Colling (National Graphical Association)
Mr Ken Cure (Amalgamated Engineering Union)
Mr Andy Dodds (National Union of Railwaymen)
Mr Eddie Hough (National Union of General Municipal Boilermakers and Allied Trade Unions GMB Section)
Mr Edward O'Brien (Society of Graphical and Allied Trades '82)
Mr Colm O'Kane (Confederation of Health Service Employees)
Mr Jack Rogers (Union of Construction, Allied Trades and Technicians)
Mr Tom Sawyer (National Union of Public Employees)
Mr Syd Tierney (Union of Shop, Distributive and Allied Workers)

Socialist, Co-operative and other organisations' section
Mr John Evans (National Union of Labour and Socialist Clubs)

Constituency Labour Parties
Mr Tony Benn, MP
Mr David Blunkett, MP
Mr Bryan Gould, MP
Mr Ken Livingstone, MP
Mr Michael Meacher, MP
Miss Jo Richardson, MP
Mr Dennis Skinner, MP

Women Members
Ms Anne Davis
Mrs Gwyneth Dunwoody, MP
Ms Diana Jeuda
Miss Joan Lestor, MP
Mrs Renée Short

Young Socialists' Representative
Ms Linda Douglas

APPENDIX IV
Abbreviations

ACAS	Advisory Conciliation and Arbitration Service
ACTT	Association of Cinematograph, Television and Allied Technicians
AEA	Atomic Energy Authority
AFL/CIO	American Federation of Labour/Congress of Industrial Organisations
ALF	Animal Liberation Front
ANC	African National Congress
APEX	Association of Professional, Executive, Clerical and Computer Staff
ASLEF	Amalgamated Society of Locomotive Engineers and Firemen
ASTMS	Association of Scientific, Technical and Managerial Staffs
AUEW	Amalgamated Union of Engineering Workers
BAC	British Aircraft Corporation
BBC	British Broadcasting Corporation
BETA	Broadcasting and Entertainment Trades Alliance British Nuclear Fuels Limited
BNOC	British National Oil Corporation
BOSS	Bureau of State Security, South Africa
BP	British Petroleum
BSC	British Steel Corporation
BT	British Telecommunications
CAP	Common Agricultural Policy
CBI	Confederation of British Industry
CEGB	Central Electricity Generating Board
CIA	Central Intelligence Agency, USA
CLP	Constituency Labour Party
CLPD	Campaign for Labour Party Democracy
CLV	Campaign for a Labour Victory
CND	Campaign for Nuclear Disarmament
COHSE	Confederation of Health Service Employees
COI	Central Office of Information

CP	Communist Party
CPRS	Central Policy Review Staff
CPSA	Civil and Public Services Association
CSD	Council for Social Democracy
CSEU	Confederation of Shipbuilding and Engineering Unions
DHSS	Department of Health and Social Security
EC	European Community
EDM	Early Day Motion
EEC	European Economic Community
EETPU	Electrical, Electronic, Telecommunications and Plumbing Union
EMS	European Monetary System
EMU	Economic and Monetary Union
END	European Nuclear Disarmament
FBU	Fire Brigades' Union
FO	Foreign Office
FT	*Financial Times*
FTAT	Furniture, Timber and Allied Trades' Union
GATT	General Agreement on Tariffs and Trade
GCHQ	Government Communications Headquarters
GPD	Gross Domestic Product
GDR	German Democratic Republic (East Germany)
GLC	Greater London Council
GMB	General, Municipal and Boilermakers' Union
GMC	General Management Committee
GMWU	General and Municipal Workers' Union
GUMG	Glasgow University Media Group
IBA	Independent Broadcasting Authority
ILCS	Independent Left Corresponding Society
ILEA	Inner London Education Authority
ILP	Independent Labour Party
IMF	International Monetary Fund
IMG	International Marxist Group
INF	Inter-range Nuclear Forces
INLA	Irish National Liberation Army
IRA	Irish Republican Army
IRN	Independent Radio News
ITN	Independent Television News
IWC	Institute for Workers' Control
KGB	Kontora Glabokogo Buresiye, Soviet Security Service
KME	Kirkby Manufacturing and Engineering Company (formerly IPD-Fisher Bendix)
LBC	London Broadcasting Company

LCC	Labour Co-ordinating Committee
LPYS	Labour Party Young Socialists
MEP	Member of European Parliament
MI5	British Security Service (internal security), formerly Section 5 of Military Intelligence
MI6	British Secret Intelligence Service (overseas intelligence), formerly Section 6 of Military Intelligence
MSC	Manpower Services Commission
MoD	Ministry of Defence
NACODS	National Association of Colliery Overmen, Deputies and Shotfirers
NALGO	National and Local Government Officers' Association
NATO	North Atlantic Treaty Organisation
NCB	National Coal Board
NCCL	National Council for Civil Liberties
NEB	National Enterprise Board
NEC	National Executive Committee
NF	National Front
NGA	National Graphical Association
NHS	National Health Service
NILP	Northern Ireland Labour Party
Noraid	North American And Organisation for Irish Republicans
NUJ	National Union of Journalists
NULO	National Union of Labour Organisations
NUM	National Union of Mineworkers
NUPE	National Union of Public Employees
NUR	National Union of Railwaymen
NUS	National Union of Seafarers (or Students)
OAS	Organisation of American States
OECD	Organisation for Economic Co-operation and Development
OPEC	Organisation of Petroleum Exporting Countries
PASOK	Greek Labour Party
PCI	Communist Party of Italy
PLO	Palestine Liberation Organisation
PLP	Parliamentary Labour Party
POEU	Post Office Engineering Union
PPS	Parliamentary Private Secretary
PR	Proportional Representation
PWR	Pressurised Water Reactor
RAF	Royal Air Force
SALT	Strategic Arms Limitation Treaty
SAS	Special Air Services

SDA	Social Democratic Alliance
SDLP	Social Democratic and Labour Party (Northern Ireland)
SDP	Social Democratic Party
SEA	Socialist Educational Association
SNP	Scottish National Party
SOGAT SOGAT 82 }	Society of Graphical and Allied Trades
SPD	Social Democratic Party (Sozialdemokratische Partei Deutschlands)
SS 20	Multiple-Warhead Soviet Nuclear Missile
STUC	Scottish Trades Union Congress
SWP	Socialist Workers' Party
TASS	Technical and Supervisory Section (of AUEW)
TD	Teachta Dala (member of the Irish Parliament)
TGWU	Transport and General Workers' Union (T&G)
TUC	Trades Union Congress
TULV	Trade Unionists for a Labour Victory
UCATT	Union of Construction, Allied Trades and Technicians
UCW	Union of Communication Workers
UDA	Ulster Defence Association
UDR	Ulster Defence Regiment
UN	United Nations
UNESCO	United Nations Educational, Scientific and Cultural Organisation
USDAW	Union of Shop, Distributive and Allied Workers
USSR	Union of Soviet Socialist Republics
UVF	Ulster Volunteer Force
VAT	Value Added Tax
WAC	Women's Action Committee
WRP	Workers' Revolutionary Party
YS	Young Socialists
YTS	Youth Training Scheme

Index